Perspective Warps and Distorts with Adobe Tools: Volume 1

Putting a New Twist on Photoshop

Jennifer Harder

Apress®

Perspective Warps and Distorts with Adobe Tools: Volume 1: Putting a New Twist on Photoshop

Jennifer Harder
Delta, BC, Canada

ISBN-13 (pbk): 978-1-4842-8709-5   ISBN-13 (electronic): 978-1-4842-8710-1
https://doi.org/10.1007/978-1-4842-8710-1

Managing Director, Apress Media LLC: Welmoed Spahr
Acquisitions Editor: Spandana Chatterjee
Development Editor: Spandana Chatterjee
Coordinating Editor: Mark Powers
Copy Editor: Mary Behr

Cover designed by eStudioCalamar

Cover image by Aditya Chinchure on Unsplash (www.unsplash.com)

Distributed to the book trade worldwide by Apress Media, LLC, 1 New York Plaza, New York, NY 10004, U.S.A. Phone 1-800-SPRINGER, fax (201) 348-4505, e-mail orders-ny@springer-sbm.com, or visit www.springeronline.com. Apress Media, LLC is a California LLC and the sole member (owner) is Springer Science + Business Media Finance Inc (SSBM Finance Inc). SSBM Finance Inc is a **Delaware** corporation.

For information on translations, please e-mail booktranslations@springernature.com; for reprint, paperback, or audio rights, please e-mail bookpermissions@springernature.com.

Apress titles may be purchased in bulk for academic, corporate, or promotional use. eBook versions and licenses are also available for most titles. For more information, reference our Print and eBook Bulk Sales web page at www.apress.com/bulk-sales.

Any source code or other supplementary material referenced by the author in this book is available to readers on GitHub (https://github.com/Apress). For more detailed information, please visit http://www.apress.com/source-code.

Printed on acid-free paper

Table of Contents

About the Author

Jennifer Harder has worked in the graphic design industry for more than fifteen years. She has a degree in graphic communications and is currently teaching Adobe Acrobat and Adobe Creative Cloud courses at Langara College in Vancouver, British Columbia.

As a freelancer, Jennifer frequently works with Adobe PDFs to help enhance websites and other instructional documents.

She enjoys talking about Adobe software, and her interests include writing, illustration, and working on her websites.

About the Technical Reviewer

PK Kaushal is an experienced professional visual artist with working experience in ad agencies, print media houses, and educational institutions. He is skilled in photo editing, photo restoration, portraits, documentaries, advertising films, logo design, and vector illustration. He is an arts and design professional with a Master's degree in Applied/Commercial Art from Kurukshetra University, Haryana, India. At present, he runs a photo/video production company, Wedding Moment Pictures.

Acknowledgments

For assistance with writing this book there are some people I'd like to thank. This includes my parents, from whom I inherited my drawing skills. They encouraged me to continue to find new ways to use Adobe applications. I am grateful for the assistance in selecting the final artwork for this book and doing some of the proofreading of my notes before I sent them to my editors. Thanks go to my Program Coordinator at Langara College, Raymond Chow, for his suggestions and advice on what art and drawing in Photoshop and Illustrator should be about for students. I also thank my Editors and Technical Reviewers at Apress. A special thank you goes to Spandana Chatterjee and Mark Powers for giving me the opportunity to continue writing on topics that I enjoy. I hope you, the reader, enjoy this book too.

Introduction

Welcome to my book *Perspective Warps and Distorts with Adobe Tools: Volume 1*.

In this book, you will be exploring how to work with various warping tools and filters in Photoshop, although at points throughout the book you will also be using graphics acquired from Adobe Illustrator. Knowing how to work between these two applications is a crucial part of understanding how to successfully manipulate your designs. In Photoshop, you will alter both raster images and vector graphics and learn how to do this with layers in various non-destructive ways.

The following chapters will deal with such things as

1. Introducing warps and distorts in Photoshop and an overview of Photoshop workspace tools and panels that you will be using throughout the book

2. Working with the basic warping tools found in the Tools panel, building custom brushes, working with various brush tools, and understanding color blending modes as well as correcting basic distorts

3. Creating patterns using various tools such as Brush Symmetry Paint, Shape tools, Pen tools, capturing patterns in the Libraries panel, Fill dialog box custom script patterns, and editing patterns further with the Layers panel and Offset filter. Later these patterns will be used for other projects and as textures.

4. Learning about Free Transform layers to create unusual warps and distorts using smart object layers

5. Learning about warp type layers, placing type on a path, and warping text within a label

6. Working with the Puppet Warp smart object filter

7. Working with the Perspective Warp smart object filter and looking at various content-aware commands and related tools, including Content-Aware Scale and the Sky Replacement command

8. Using basic filters and smart filters within and outside the Filter Gallery workspace and creating GIF animations using filters

9. Using advanced filters and smart filter workspaces found in the Filter menu for correcting as well as creating distortion. This includes a brief look at Camera Raw and the Liquify Filter.

10. Using some of the advanced filters when working with perspective and a few of the new neural filters and discovering how to acquire additional filters as well

Additional supplemental books that I have written that can assist you in this book include

- *Graphics and Multimedia for the Web with Adobe Creative Cloud*
- *Accurate Layer Selections Using Photoshop's Selection Tools*

Source Code

Source code or other supplementary material can be found at the following link: `github.com/apress/perspective-warps-distorts-vol1`.

Additional resources and information regarding Photoshop will be found in Chapter 1. Furthermore, Volume 2 of this book will be available soon, and it focuses on the Illustrator application and its related tools for warping and distortion.

CHAPTER 1

■ ■ ■

Introduction to Warps

Chapter goals: Set up a workspace in Photoshop. Learn about true warps and distorts versus just touching up pixels in a photo. Knowing how to warp images can be useful when working on various Photoshop projects to either distort an object or correct a distortion.

■ **Note**   This chapter does not contain any projects files. However, you can find links for other projects in this book at github.com/apress/perspective-warps-distorts.

Welcome to *Perspective Warps and Distorts with Adobe Tools: Volume 1* in which we will be looking primarily at Adobe's most popular application, Photoshop. (I will explore Illustrator more closely in a separate volume, although we will be using Illustrator a bit in this book as well.) In the chapters that follow, we will be exploring how to create various warps and distorts using tools found within these applications. If you have been working with Adobe applications for a few years, some of these tools will be familiar to you, as you use them every day. Refer to Figure 1-1.

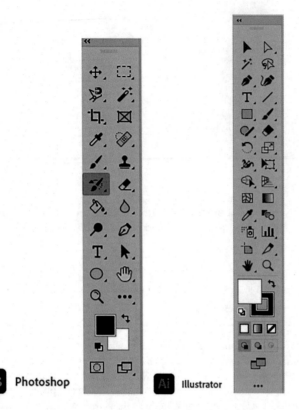

Figure 1-1. *Photoshop and Illustrator icons and tools*

However, if you haven't kept up with the upgrades and changes, you may have missed some of the new features and improvements that are made to certain tools or panels within the program every year. Hidden features in various panels are glossed over. Refer to Figure 1-2.

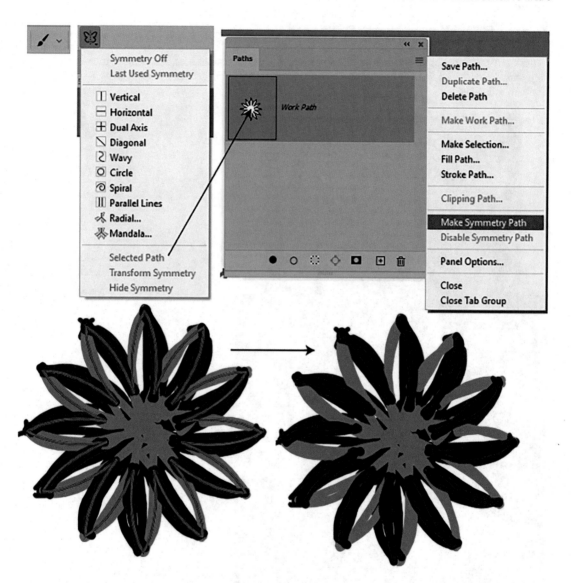

Figure 1-2. *In Photoshop, the Hidden Symmetry Paint Brush option in the Paint Brush options panel can later be used with the Paths panel to make a custom path*

I enjoy creating new projects every now and then, as it helps me to get out of a creative rut. It's great working with some of my favorite tools, like the Pen or Brush. However, sometimes I stop and think, "How can I use this tool in a new creative way? Or what tools have I neglected to try over the years?" In these books, we'll look at the numerous tools that have been added to Photoshop in Volume 1 and Illustrator in Volume 2 to warp or distort a shape or an image. I placed these tools collectively into two books so that they could be compared. As you design your project, you can easily find the right tool, command, or filter for your next distort.

So regardless of whether you're a beginner just learning these applications or have been using these applications for many years but want to learn the latest updates, these books will assist you in expanding your creative options when it comes to working with warps and distorts.

Photoshop Warps and Distorts

I generally use Photoshop for color correction or color alteration to all or part of an image. In addition, Photoshop is good at correcting or touching up cosmetic issues on models' bodies and faces. Refer to Figures 1-3 and 1-4.

Figure 1-3. *Images of a sunflower and an old statue of a pirate with damage to the exterior*

Figure 1-4. *Images of a sunflower with its color altered and an old statue of a pirate now repaired with hair and skin tone improved using Photoshop's adjustment layers and healing tools*

While these are great topics to learn, they are not the focus of this book, although we will look at some of these kinds of touch-ups and healing tools briefly throughout the book. However, it will be in the context of how they can enhance a warp or distort.

A warp or distort is defined by the Merriam-Webster Dictionary as a twist or curve that has developed in something originally flat or straight, or to twist out of a natural, normal, or original shape or condition (`www.merriam-webster.com/dictionary/warp`, `www.merriam-webster.com/dictionary/distort`).

So basically our purpose in this book is to somehow twist an image so that it no longer looks normal or does not resemble what it originally looked like. In essence, it becomes something unrecognizable. Patterns or blurs often fall into that category. Refer to Figure 1-5.

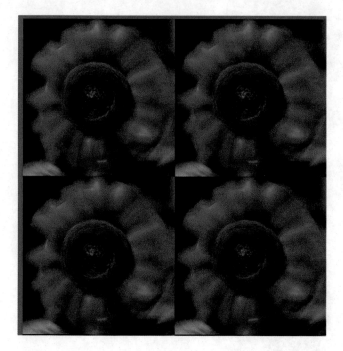

Figure 1-5. *Sunflower pattern with a spin blur*

Sometimes, if you just glance at an image, some distortion is imperceptible. If you master your distortion techniques, then you can make part of an image, text, or logo conform or blend into the rest of the picture and the viewer won't notice the distort at all. It appears as if it was always part of the original photograph. Refer to Figure 1-6.

Figure 1-6. *Some text was added to the old barrel after the photo was taken. The text was then altered and warped to make it look aged by weather*

In other situations, you might find that your photo is already distorted due to your smart phone camera lens, and you want to correct that lens distortion or angle. We'll look at that option in Chapter 9. Refer to Figure 1-7.

Figure 1-7. *After taking a photo outdoors I noticed the building was slanted. I used filters to straighten the building*

Before you get started, however, let's make sure that you have your Photoshop workspace set up. We'll also be working with Illustrator at times while working with Photoshop when we create smart objects layers, which I will talk about in Chapter 4. If you need to review in more detail how to use Illustrator, refer to *Perspective Warps and Distorts with Adobe Tools, Volume 2*, Chapter 1.

Resources

You can also refer to my books *Graphics and Multimedia for the Web with Adobe Creative Cloud* and *Accurate Layer Selections Using Photoshop's Selection Tools* if you require more detail on those certain tools (`https://link.springer.com/book/10.1007/978-1-4842-3823-3`, `https://link.springer.com/book/10.1007/978-1-4842-7493-4`).

Some other Adobe resources I will mention throughout the book can be found at the Adobe help link: `https://helpx.adobe.com`.

System Requirements

Make sure that when working in Photoshop you have the most up-to-date version of your Creative Cloud desktop and that your system meets the requirements for the latest versions of the applications. I used Photoshop CC 2023 Version 24 on my Windows 10 computer for this book. However, you may be using a newer version of Windows or Mac, so review your system requirements here: `https://helpx.adobe.com/photoshop/system-requirements.html`.

■ **Note** Some features for Windows 11 computers may not be supported at the time of this writing.

With your Creative Cloud desktop subscription active, make sure that you have downloaded Photoshop. From the panel, choose All Apps. To the right of the application name, click Open to launch it. Refer to Figure 1-8.

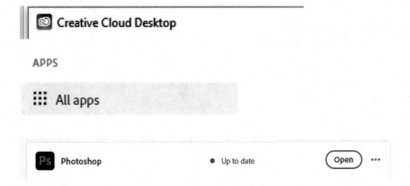

Figure 1-8. *Open Photoshop using your Creative Cloud desktop application*

Setting Up the Workspace and a Review of the Main Panels and Tools

To get started setting up your workspace, from the main menu, Choose File ➤ New. Click the Print tab and use the preset blank document called Letter at 8.5 x 11 inches and 300 ppi. Refer to Figure 1-9.

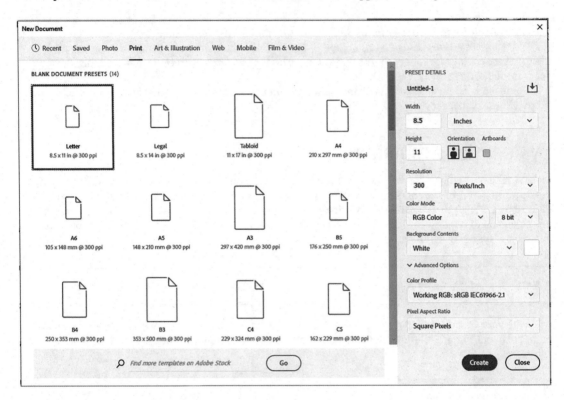

Figure 1-9. *New Document dialog box with a preset of Letter*

Notice in the preset details on the right that the name is currently Untiled -1.

The width is 8.5, the height is 11, and this is in inches, but with the drop-down menu you can choose other measurement settings. Refer to Figure 1-10.

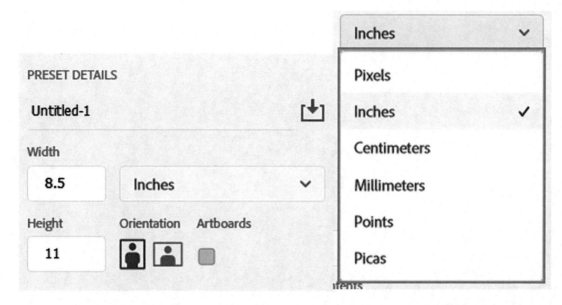

Figure 1-10. *The New Document presets allow you to set other measurement settings besides inches, such as pixels or centimeters*

The orientation is portrait, but it can be switched to landscape by clicking the icon next to it. You can add additional artboards, but let's leave that option unchecked. The resolution is 300 pixels/inches, which is a good resolution for working with photos that will be distorted. With lower resolution images of 72 pixels/inches, certain details might be lost as you later make various adjustments. The color mode is set to RGB (Red, Green, Blue) color, which is the setting to work with for most digital photos. Refer to Figure 1-11.

Figure 1-11. *Set your resolution to 300 pixels/inches and color mode to RGB color*

If you were planning to print, you could set it to CMYK (Cyan, Magenta, Yellow, Black), lab, or even grayscale. However, some of these color modes do not allow access to all of the filters and adjustment layers that we will later be working with, regardless of what warp or distort you choose. Refer to Figures 1-12 and 1-13.

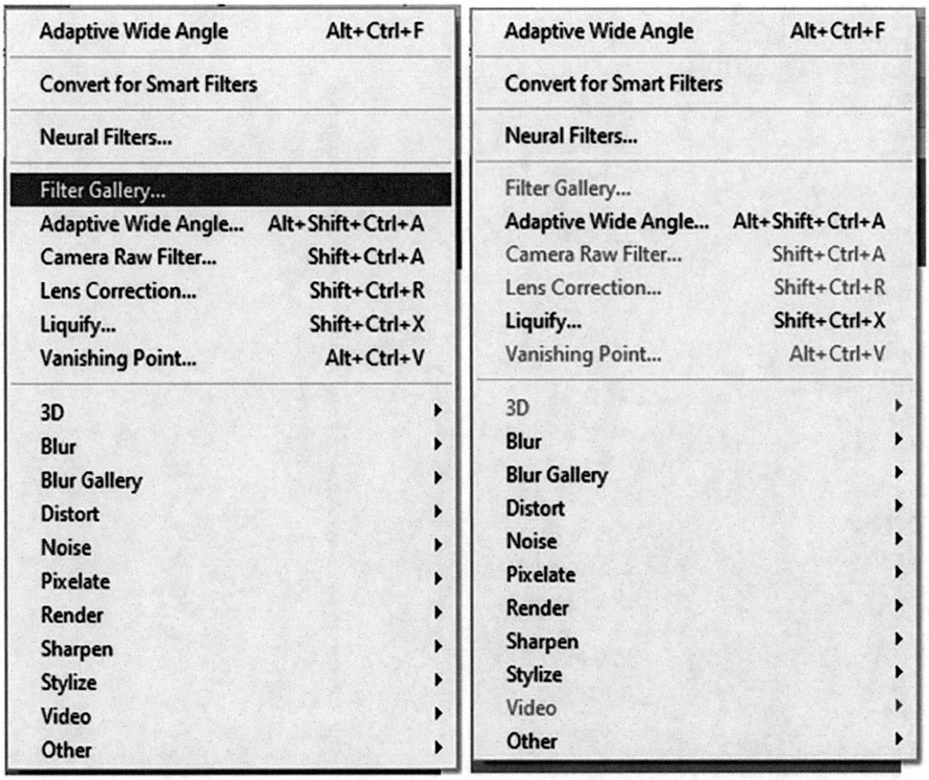

Adaptive Wide Angle Alt+Ctrl+F
Convert for Smart Filters
Neural Filters...
Filter Gallery...
Adaptive Wide Angle... Alt+Shift+Ctrl+A
Camera Raw Filter... Shift+Ctrl+A
Lens Correction... Shift+Ctrl+R
Liquify... Shift+Ctrl+X
Vanishing Point... Alt+Ctrl+V
3D
Blur
Blur Gallery
Distort
Noise
Pixelate
Render
Sharpen
Stylize
Video
Other
Adaptive Wide Angle Alt+Ctrl+F
Convert for Smart Filters
Neural Filters...
Filter Gallery...
Adaptive Wide Angle... Alt+Shift+Ctrl+A
Camera Raw Filter... Shift+Ctrl+A
Lens Correction... Shift+Ctrl+R
Liquify... Shift+Ctrl+X
Vanishing Point... Alt+Ctrl+V
3D
Blur
Blur Gallery
Distort
Noise
Pixelate
Render
Sharpen
Stylize
Video
Other

Figure 1-12. *On the left is the filter selection in RGB color mode. On the right is the filter selection in CMYK color mode*

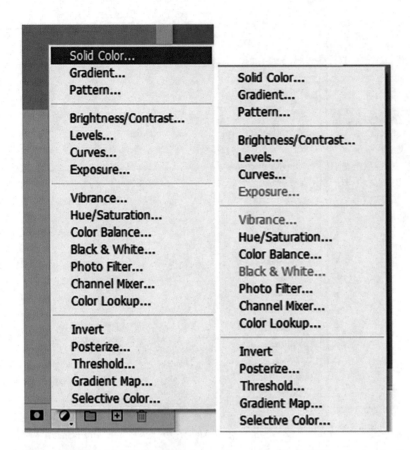

Figure 1-13. *On the left is the adjustment layer selection in RGB color mode. On the right is the adjustment layer selection in CMYK color mode*

I don't always know what direction a project is going to take artistically, so I like to keep all my options open, thus I stay with RGB color mode. I keep the bit setting at 8 bit/channels because higher channels, like 16 or 32 bit, can also affect what filters I can use and can also increase file size. Refer to Figure 1-14.

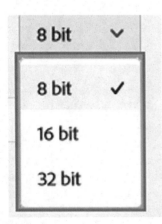

Figure 1-14. *Image bit size options from the drop-down menu*

For information on bit settings, refer to this link: `https://helpx.adobe.com/photoshop/using/bit-depth.html`.

I also leave the Background Contents setting as white. You can change this either via the dropdown menu or the custom color picker on the right. Refer to Figure 1-15.

Figure 1-15. *Background contents and advanced options in the New Document dialog box*

The advanced options set the color profile as Working RGB: sRGB. For your own projects, you may prefer to use a different profile such as Adobe RGB (1998), as this is preferred by some graphic designers for print. Refer to Figure 1-16.

Figure 1-16. *Alternate color profile settings in the New Document dialog box*

Adobe states, "sRGB is recommended when you prepare images for the web, because it defines the color space of the standard monitor used to view images on the web. sRGB is also a good choice when you work with images from consumer-level digital cameras, because most of these cameras use sRGB as their default color space." Adobe also recommends Adobe RGB (1998) for working with documents for conversion between high-end digital cameras and print. However, having said that, a lot of my work has been with my Canon inkjet printers and laser printers, and for this basic type of print work, I have had good success with just the sRGB profile for my portfolio and my clients' work. However, I leave that decision up to you and your print company when it comes to offset print work and the ideal color profile.

For more details on color profile settings, refer to `https://helpx.adobe.com/photoshop/using/color-settings.html`.

Leave the Pixel Aspect Ratio at Square Pixels and then click the Create button. Refer to Figure 1-15.

Photoshop will open a new blank document and the workspace, which we will adjust next. Refer to Figure 1-17.

Figure 1-17. *A new blank document appears in the Photoshop workspace*

You can begin to set up your workspace either using the main menu Window ➤ Workspace or from the Workspace button found on the far right of the Options panel bar. Refer to Figure 1-18.

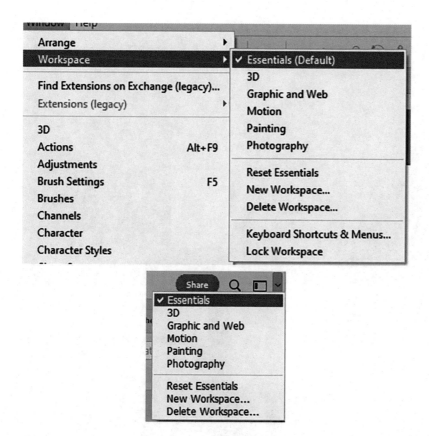

Figure 1-18. *Workspace options in the Window menu and from the right of the Options panel*

For my work, I generally like to choose Essentials (Default) as this gives me all the tools I need in the Tools panel as well as other essential panels. For additional reading, I discuss many of these panels in my book *Accurate Layer Selections using Photoshop's Selection Tools*. Panels can be opened, collapsed, and undocked or docked by dragging them by the tab name to a new location in your Photoshop application. For example, as you work on your project, it may be helpful to separate the Layers panel from the other panels it's grouped with and drag it closer to your canvas. Refer to Figure 1-19.

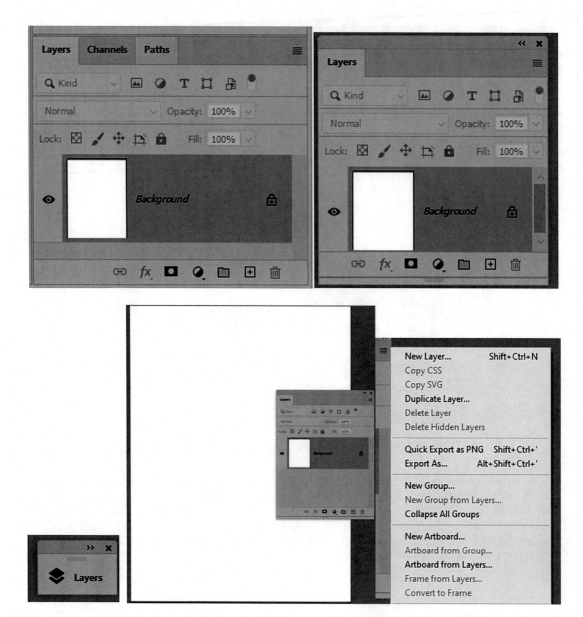

Figure 1-19. *Drag to undock and move your Layers panel or any panel closer to your canvas as you work*

Most panels have their own menu, which provides other options while working with the panel. You can find these panels, as well as additional panels, in the Window dropdown menu.

Tools and Panel Review

This section offers a basic overview of the key panels that are useful from this workspace. In later chapters, some of these tools in panels will be discussed in detail. If your workspaces has become cluttered, you can reset your Essentials workspace by choosing Reset Essentials from the Workspace menu. Refer to Figure 1-18.

Tools

The Tools panel contains all the tools you need to work on your Photoshop projects. There are many. Refer to Figure 1-20.

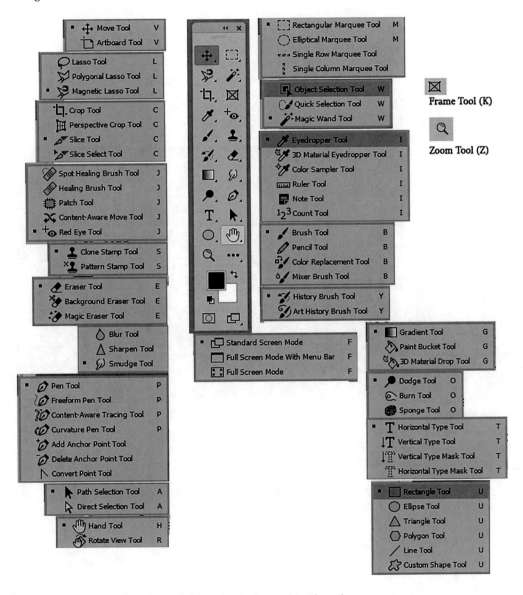

Figure 1-20. Many tools are available in the Tools panel in Photoshop

For the moment, the main tools that you need to know about are the Move tool (V), Zoom tool (Z), and Hand tool (H). Refer to Figure 1-21.

Figure 1-21. *Photoshop's Move tool, Zoom tool, and Hand tool*

We will explore some of the others as they relate to warps and distorts in Chapters 2 through 10.

The Move tool (V) allows you to move objects around on layers with your mouse, and you can drag the contents of a normal layer around. It works with the Layers panel. Try dragging across the locked background layer with the Move tool. An alert message will pop up. In it you can click the Convert to Normal Layer button. This will make it Layer 0 so that you can move it around or off the canvas entirely. It is now a normal or regular layer. Refer to Figure 1-22.

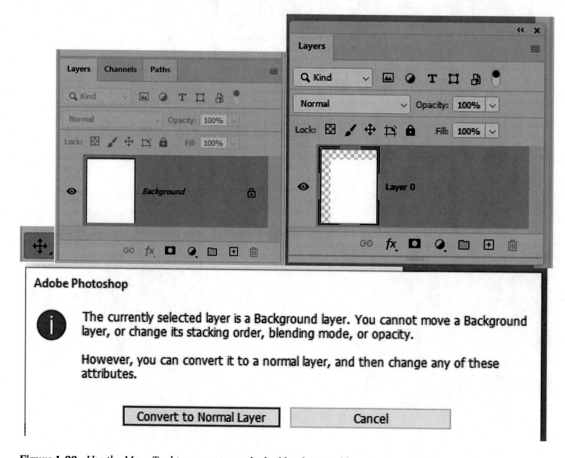

Figure 1-22. *Use the Move Tool to convert your locked background layer to a normal layer*

Alternatively, you can double-click on that background layer first. Then click OK to the name Layer 0 in the New Layer dialog box. Refer to Figure 1-23.

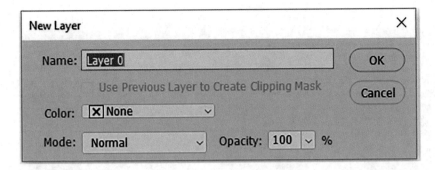

Figure 1-23. *Or double-click on your background layer and use the New Layer dialog box to convert it to Layer 0*

As Layer 0, or any unlocked layer, you can move it around the canvas.

The Zoom tool (Z) allows you to zoom in and out of an image. To zoom in, click once with the tool; to zoom out, hold down the Alt/Option key and click with the tool, or you can use the key commands of Ctrl/CMD and the plus key (+), Ctrl/CMD and the minus key (-), or Ctrl/CMD and 0 to zoom in or out without using the mouse. Once you get to Chapters 4 through 10, knowing how to use these key commands will be extremely helpful because you cannot rely on accessing the tool from the Tools panel when in certain workspaces. Refer to Figure 1-24.

Figure 1-24. *Zoom tool*

Likewise, the Hand tool (H) is great to use when you are zoomed in. Then you can drag and navigate about the canvas without moving or disrupting the layers. If you hold down the spacebar while using the Move tool, you can access this Hand tool. This is a helpful key command to know when you are not able to directly access it from the Tools Panel in certain workspaces, as you will see in Chapters 4 through 10. Refer to Figure 1-25.

Figure 1-25. *Hand tool*

If you find that a tool is missing, it may be hidden under the Edit Toolbar button. Refer to Figures 1-20 and 1-26.

Figure 1-26. *Edit Toolbar button*

To check, click the tool and the Customize Toolbar dialog box will open. Check the right-hand side for your tool. If present, you may need to drag and add it back to the left Toolbar side and then click Done to exit. Refer to Figure 1-27.

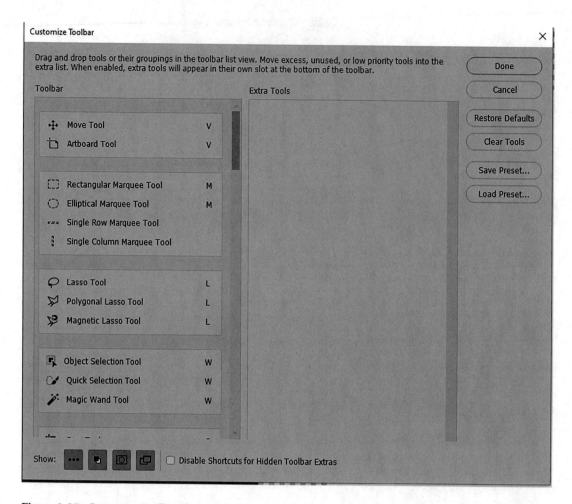

Figure 1-27. *Customize Toolbar dialog box*

However, with the Essentials (default) workspace, all of the tools should be in the Tools panel. Click Cancel to exit the dialog box.

Options

The Options panel works with the Tools panel and the Window ➤ Tools Preset panel when you need to store tool settings or access other tool options, as you can see when you click the Move, Zoom, or Hand tool. Each Options panel-based tool has separate, but sometimes similar, options. Refer to Figure 1-28.

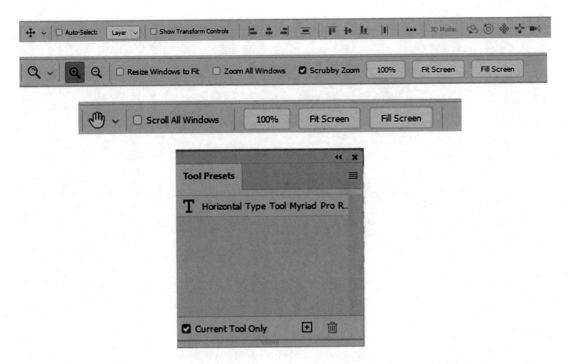

Figure 1-28. *The Options panel changes based on what tools are used. The Tool Presets Panel can store that tool's newly created presets*

History

The History panel records various steps as you perform them on your image. If you make a mistake as you work, you can click back or up a previous step in the History panel to remove that step and try again. You can also use Edit ➤ Undo from the menu, which has the key command of Ctrl/CMD+Z. Knowing this key command will be useful in Chapters 4 through 10 as you may not have access to that sub-change in the History panel while working in various workspaces. Refer to Figure 1-29.

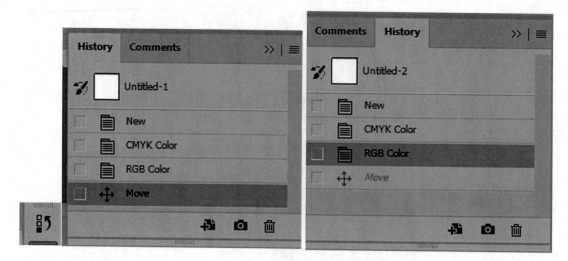

Figure 1-29. *Use the History panel to move back to a previous state in your work*

Comments

Although it appears as one of the Essentials, the Comments panel is not relevant to this book. However, it may be useful if you are working with collaborators on your current project. The comments can be saved as you work in the Creative Cloud for others in your group to view. In this book, you are working alone so you do not need work with this panel in any chapter. Refer to Figure 1-30.

Figure 1-30. *The comments panel is part of the available panels in the Essentials workspace and is used for collaboration with others on the Creative Cloud or send as a link for others to Share for review (Beta) and capture feedback*

Color

The Color panel allows you to click-select colors using its pallet without having to click on the color picker in the Tools panel. The new color is added to the foreground color in the Tools panel. Refer to Figure 1-31.

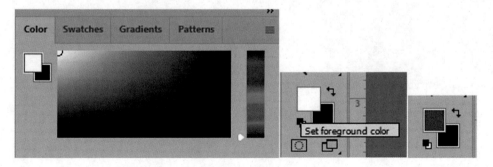

Figure 1-31. *The Color panel can be used to change the current foreground color in the Tools panel*

Note that if you need to reset the Tools panel default to black and white, press the D key. To switch foreground and background colors, press the X key on your keyboard. Refer to Figure 1-32.

Figure 1-32. *Set the current foreground and background colors back to black and white in the Tools panel*

The color panel menu also provides various ways to view the color and alter it. For now, just keep it on the Hue Cube setting. Refer to Figure 1-33.

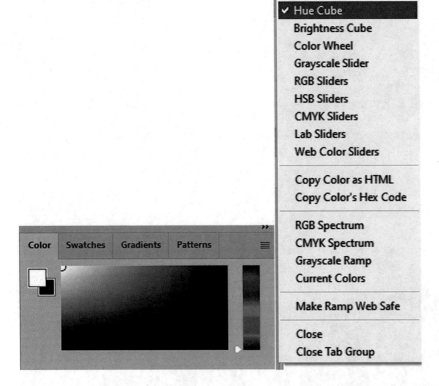

Figure 1-33. *The Color panel menu lets you set the way color is viewed to create a new swatch. Currently, in the menu it is set to Hue Cube*

Swatches

The Swatches panel allows you to store the color swatches in a folder you create after they are acquired from the Tool panel's Color Picker (Foreground or Background Color). You can save or export these folders and later share them with others. They can also be added to the Libraries panel for further collaboration. Swatches can be accessed from the Options panel for the fill or stroke of vector shapes. Refer to Figure 1-34.

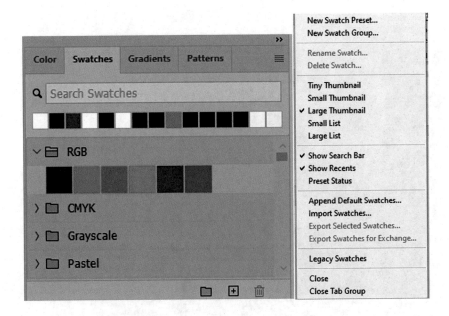

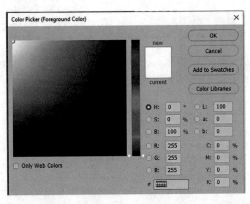

Figure 1-34. *Swatches that are added to the Swatches panel can be created using the Color Picker and then added to folders. These same swatches can be accessed for shapes using the Options panel for fills and strokes*

Gradients

The Gradients panel stores gradients that can be accessed either from the panel or when you use the Gradients tool. You can easily create your own gradients, which can later be applied to a selected area on a layer, a Fill Adjustment layer, or Layer Style. Refer to Figure 1-35.

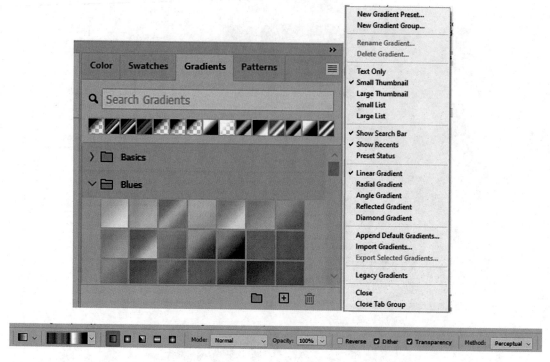

Figure 1-35. *Gradients are stored in the Gradients panel in folders and can be viewed in various ways using the panel's menu and can be accessed using the Gradient Options panel*

Patterns

The Patterns panel stores patterns, which you will discover how to create in Chapter 3. These patterns can later be filled into a selected area on a layer, a Fill Adjustment layer, or even in a Layer Style. You will at that point even see how patterns can be shared. Refer to Figure 1-36.

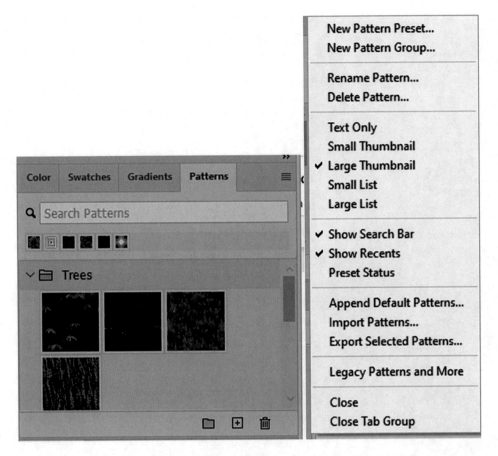

Figure 1-36. *The Patterns panel stores patterns in folder groups and its menu allows you to view, import, or export patterns*

Properties

The Properties panel is in some ways very similar to the Options panel in that it can help you while you are working with a tool as well as with transforming the scale and size of the object on a layer. As you will see in Chapter 4, the Properties panel can also help you with Quick Actions rather than having to remember where in the main menu a command is located. Refer to Figure 1-37.

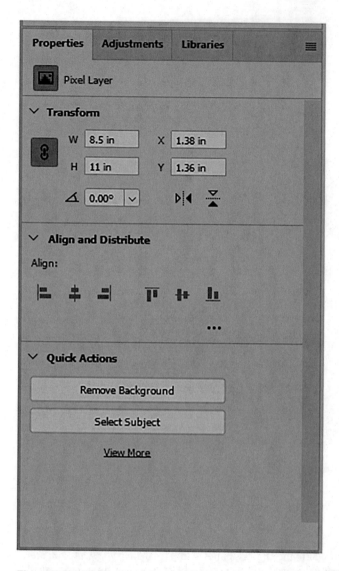

Figure 1-37. *The Properties panel allows you to transform and align layers and work with other Photoshop tools using suggested Quick Actions*

Adjustments

The Adjustments panel provides quick access to many of the adjustment layers found in the Layers panel under the Create New Fill and Adjustment Layer button. Adjustment layers are great for specialized color corrections and hue adjustments, which you can modified using the Brush or Eraser tool on the Layers panel masks (layer and vector). You can also use the Properties panel to move sliders. However, other than if you chose to alter the mask, adjustment layers will not create a distortion to the image itself. Refer to Figures 1-38 and 1-39.

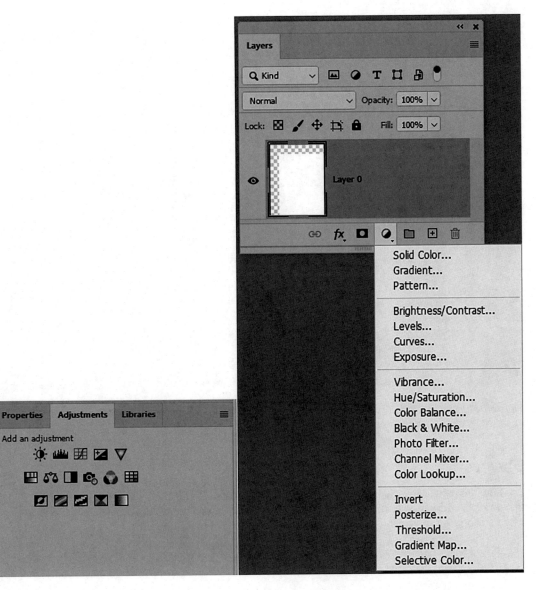

Figure 1-38. *The Adjustments panel allows you to access Adjustment layers as you would from the button in the Layers panel*

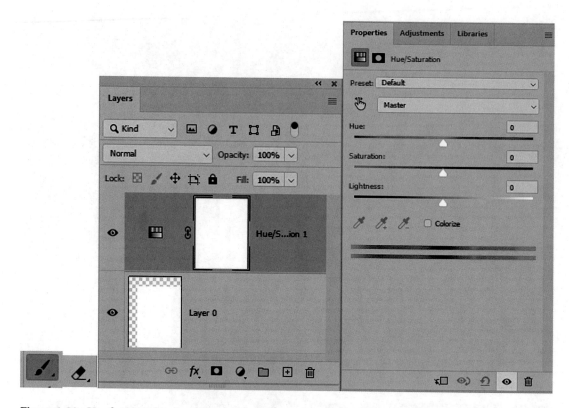

Figure 1-39. *Use the Paint Brush or Eraser tool to paint on an adjustment layer mask or the Properties panel to adjust the slider settings for the adjustment and its mask*

Libraries

The Libraries panel can be used to share your colors, text, patterns, and graphics between Photoshop and Illustrator. In addition, you will see in Chapter 3 that the Photoshop Libraries panel also has a little hidden trick for capturing and creating patterns from your images. Refer to Figure 1-40.

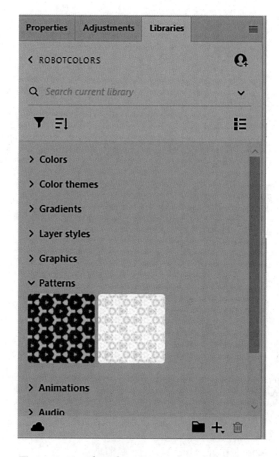

Figure 1-40. *The Libraries panel can be used to store patters and other assets that were created in Photoshop or another Adobe application like Illustrator*

Layers

The Layers panel, along with the Tools and Options panel, is probably the most important panel in Photoshop. The Layers panel stores the background, normal layers, smart objects, text, vector shapes, fills, and adjustment layers along with Layer Styles on separate layers and smart filters. You will see how layers work in the Layers panel in Chapters 2 through 10. There are various options available in its menu for altering specific layers. Refer to Figure 1-41.

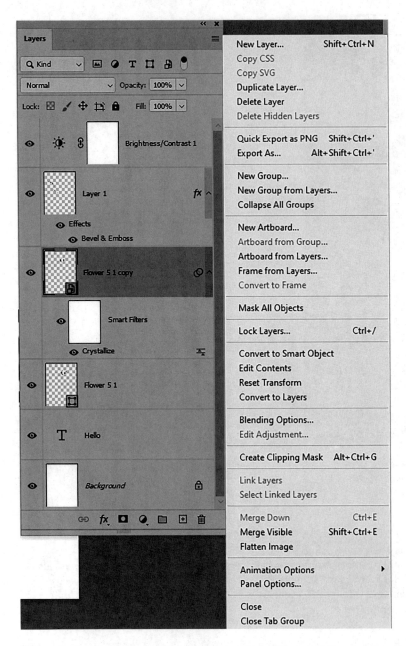

Figure 1-41. *The Layers panel can store a variety of layers and they can be adjusted using its menu. Layers include the (top to bottom) adjustment layer, normal layer with layer style applied, smart object layer with smart filter applied, vector shape layer, text layer, and background layer*

Channels

The Channels panel is a great place to save and store your current selections and later incorporate them into your layer masks. You'll see this briefly in Chapters 7 and 8. For additional reading, I go into greater detail with this in my book *Accurate Layer Selections Using Photoshop's Selection Tools*, although this book is not required to complete the projects within these chapters. Refer to Figure 1-42.

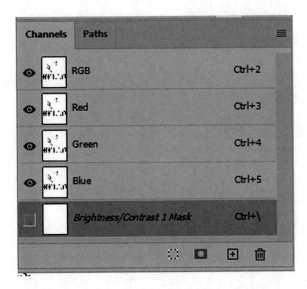

Figure 1-42. *The Channels panel with the active channel hidden*

Paths

The Paths panel is great for working with vector shapes, the Pen tools, and selections. However, it does have a few hidden features that you can use to create patterns, as you will see in Chapter 3, as well as when working with some filters, as you will see in Chapter 8. Path can be stored in the Paths panel for later use. For additional reading, I go into greater detail with this topic in my book *Accurate Layer Selections Using Photoshop's Selection Tools*, although this book is not required to complete the projects within these chapters. Refer to Figure 1-43.

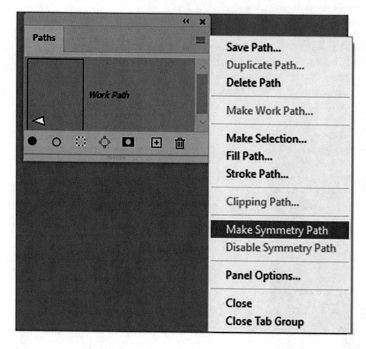

Figure 1-43. *The Paths panel with a newly created work path that is being change to a symmetry path using the panel's menu*

In other chapters, we will look at additional panels such as

- Brushes (refer to Chapter 2)

- Brush Settings (refer to Chapter 2)

- Character (refer to Chapter 5)

- Clone Source (refer to Chapter 2)

- Glyphs (refer to Chapter 5)

- Paragraph (refer to Chapter 5)

- Shapes (refer to Chapter 3)

- Styles (Layer Styles) (refer to Chapter 3 and 5)

- Timeline for Animated GIF (refer to Chapter 8)

If you like, you can open these panels and create your own custom workspace, but for now I recommend keeping them closed. The path is Window ➤ Workspace ➤ New Workspace. Refer to Figure 1-44.

Figure 1-44. *Create a new workspace with the new panels that you frequently use*

In Chapters 6 to 10, we will also be looking at filters and smart filters and how they can apply to warps and distorts in an image.

One other thing you can do while setting up your workspace is to make sure, from the View menu, to choose View ➤ Rulers (Ctrl/CMD+R) in case you need to drag out some guides later when lining up objects on various layers. Go to View ➤ Show ➤ Smart Guides for smarter alignments while moving layers. Refer to Figure 1-45.

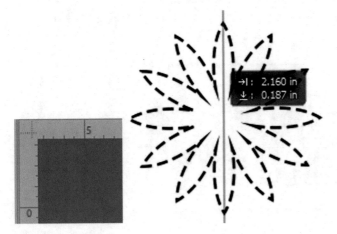

Figure 1-45. *Add rulers to your viewing so that you can add guides or use smart guides for alignment*

After you complete or while working on each project in this book make sure to File ➤ Save (Ctrl/CMD +S), your document as a .psd somewhere on your computer as you are prompted by the dialog boxes until you reach the Save As dialog box . You should do this for all projects in this book. Then you can continue to modify and add more layers to your file at a later date. Click Save and then OK to the Photoshop Format Options dialog box that may appear. Refer to Figure 1-46.

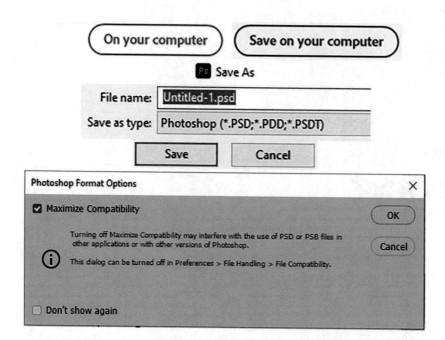

Figure 1-46. *After you save your document for the first time, click OK to the dialog message on maximizing compatibility to complete the saving of the .psd file*

■ **Note** If you are working with one of my project files, after you File ➤ Open (Ctrl/CMD+O), make sure to make an Image ➤ Duplicate so that you can work on a copy without changing the original. In this and all examples in the book, make sure to leave the Duplicate Merged Layers Only checkbox disabled. Click OK and the duplicate is created. Refer to Figure 1-47.

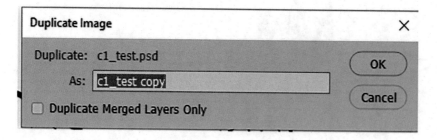

Figure 1-47. *Make an Image ➤ Duplicate of your file when you want to work on a copy without altering the original file*

Summary

This chapter is a starting point for learning about warps and distorts in Photoshop and how to set up your workspace. Now that you know the basics of some of the panels and tools that you will encounter in most chapters, you can begin to work on an actual project. In the next chapter, you will be using various Brush tools, some of which can be used to warp an image.

CHAPTER 2

Basic Warping Tools

Chapter goal: Look at the basic warping tools in the Tools panel in Photoshop.

As you start working on various projects, you may want to touch up various artistic effects in parts of your image. There are a lot of tools for doing so in the Tools panel. But which are the key ones for creating very basic warps and distorts? This chapter looks at this topic and also offers a quick review of tools I discussed in my book *Accurate Layer Selections Using Photoshop's Selection Tools* as they relate to this chapter.

For now, continue to use the file you created in Chapter 1 to first design a custom brush that can be used with other Brush tools.

■ You can find a copy of this file, `brush_test.psd`, as well as other files for this chapter in the Chapter 2 folder.

File ➤ Open this document, and if you want to make a copy, go to Image ➤ Duplicate and press OK in the dialog box. Refer to Figure 2-1.

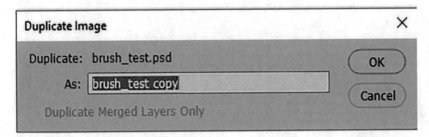

Figure 2-1. Duplicate Image dialog box

Review of Brushes

In my previous book, *Accurate Layer Selections Using Photoshop's Selection Tools*, we looked at several Brush and Eraser tools that could be used to edit an image or clean up broken lines. They included the following:

- Brush tool (B) for creating brush stroke effects
- Pencil tool (B) for creating small, thin pencil lines
- Eraser tool (E) for erasing areas of an image
- Background Eraser tool (E) for erasing background areas of an image
- Magic Eraser Tool (E) for quickly erasing color selections of an image by clicking on an area of color. Refer to Figure 2-2.

J. Harder, *Perspective Warps and Distorts with Adobe Tools: Volume 1*,
https://doi.org/10.1007/978-1-4842-8710-1_2

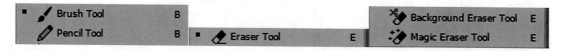

Figure 2-2. *The Tools panel showing the Brush, Pencil, Eraser, Background Eraser, and Magic Eraser tools*

Notice in the Options panel that, except for the Magic Eraser tool, the rest of these tools have access to the Brushes Preset Picker panel. The Magic Eraser tool is not relevant to this book so I will not be discussing it further. We can also eliminate the Background Eraser tool as it does not have access to brush settings panels or additional custom brushes, so we cannot use it to create a custom brush for warp effects. Refer to Figure 2-3.

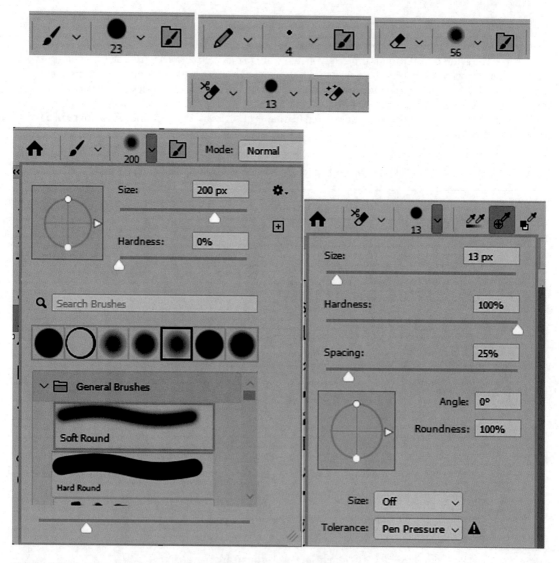

Figure 2-3. *Brush Preset Picker options in the Options panel for Brush, Pencil, Background Eraser, and Magic Eraser tools*

Therefore, the main tool that we will focus on in the following project will be the Brush tool. Afterwards, I will briefly show how the custom brush settings can later be used for the Pencil tool and the Eraser tool. Then we will look at additional tools that can use these brush settings in the panels for basic warping of an image. Refer to Figure 2-4 and Figure 2-5.

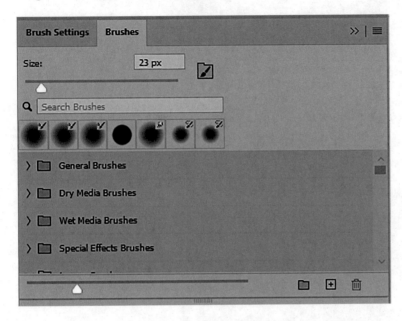

Figure 2-4. *Brushes panel settings with brushes stored in group folders*

Figure 2-5. *Brush Settings Options panel*

It should be noted that the default Brush Presets (see the Brush, Pencil, and Eraser tools options panel dropdown menus) like Soft Round or Hard Round found in the General Brushes folder cannot create artistic warps or distorts without adjusting their brush settings first. Refer to Figure 2-6.

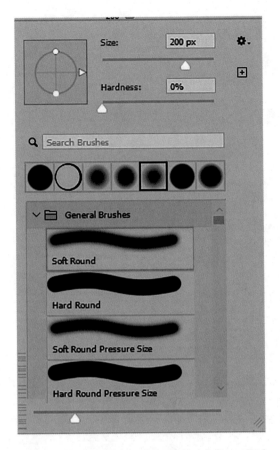

Figure 2-6. *Options panel for the Brush Preset Picker*

At best, the Brush Preset Picker will only adjust for the angle, roundness, size, and hardness to paint or erase the current color on the canvas. Nevertheless, let's look at how to take a default brush setting like Hard Round to create a custom round brush. Later, you'll add a custom shape with the same settings and then move on to other warping tools that could also use those custom brushes, as you will see in this chapter and Chapter 3. Refer to Figure 2-6.

■ **Note**   Under the Brush tool you can find the Color Replacement tool (B) and Mixer Brush tool (B). They are more for replacing a color or painting effects. The Color Replacement tool does not relate to the topic of this book because it does not have access to the Brush Settings panel. However, with the Mixer Brush tool you do have access to the Brush Settings panel. You can use the useful Mixer Brush options to create interesting paint-like smears similar to the Smudge tool, which we will look at later in the chapter. Refer to Figure 2-7.

Figure 2-7. *Options panels for the Color Replacement and Mixer Brush tools. The paint strokes were created with the Mixer Brush tool*

■ For more details on these tools, check out these links:

https://helpx.adobe.com/photoshop/using/replace-colors.html
(See "Use the Color Replacement Tool")

https://helpx.adobe.com/photoshop/using/painting-mixer-brush.html

Creating Custom Brushes and Brush Settings

To begin, let's return to the Brush tool and look at the Options panel. With your duplicate file, brush_test_copy, on your Layers panel, either paint on the background layer to test your brush or click the Create a new layer button in the Layers panel to create a transparent blank layer. Refer to Figure 2-8.

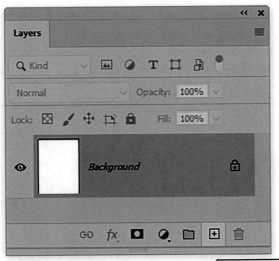

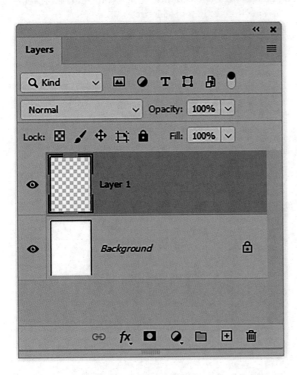

Figure 2-8. *Use the Layers panel to create a new blank layer to paint on*

As I run out of room on the layer, I create another layer to continue painting. This helps me to see the progress of my custom brush creation. I can also turn the layer's visibility off and on to compare past painterly effects. Make sure before you start that your foreground color is set to black in the Tools panel by pressing D on the keyboard. Refer to Figure 2-9.

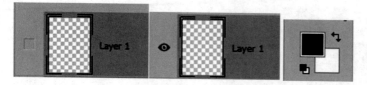

Figure 2-9. *Turn the layer's visibility on and off with the eye icon and set your brush color in the Tools panel to the default of black foreground and white background*

Project: Basic Brush to Custom Brush Settings

Let's take a moment to examine the Brush tool options in the Options panel.

Brush Tool Options

On the left, the Brush tool has a tool preset area where you can save various option settings to reuse on other projects. This is common for all the tools we will be discussing in this chapter. Once you create a preset, you can store it here or click the gear icon for addition preset choices. Refer to Figure 2-10.

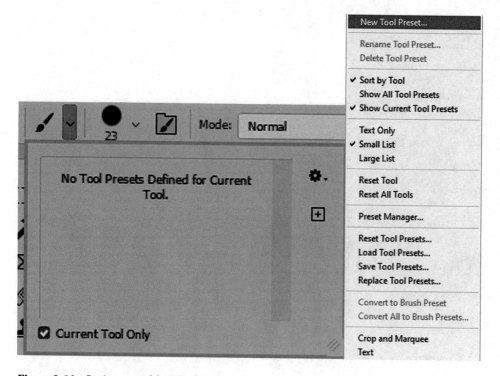

Figure 2-10. *Options panel for Brush tool presets*

We will not be focusing on this area, so let's look at the next section in the Options panel.

Moving right, next to the Presets menu, click the Brush Preset Picker dropdown menu. Refer to Figure 2-11.

Figure 2-11. *The Brush tool's Options panel*

From the Brush Preset Picker dropdown list, choose the General Brushes folder and locate the brush named Hard Round. If you have modified some brushes, you may have added them to this folder as well. You can adjust its current default angle, roundness, size (200 px), and hardness (100%), and this will appear in the text boxes. Use the lower zoom slider if you need to see the brush in more detail. Refer to Figure 2-12.

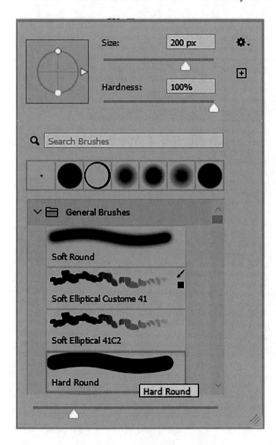

Figure 2-12. *Select a Hard Round brush from the Brush tool's Preset Picker menu*

In this area, you can also search through the most recently used brushes, which are located in the Window ➤ Brushes panel, making it easy to modify your brushes quickly. Open that panel so that you can compare the settings with your Options panel and look at the menu for that panel as well. Refer to Figure 2-13.

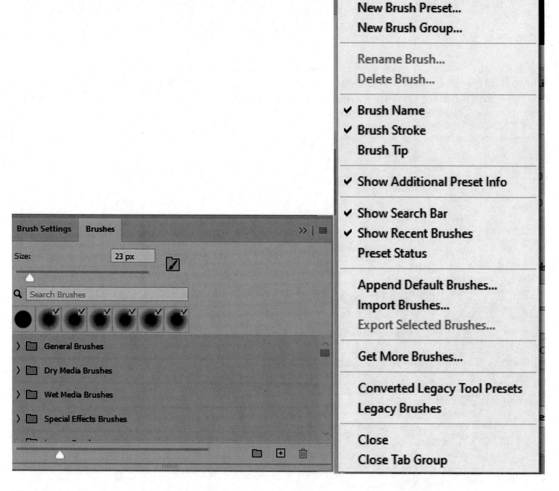

Figure 2-13. *Brushes panel and menu options*

Brushes that were previously created by Photoshop are stored in collapsible group folders. As well, you can create your own and save them in these folders to share with others. Any current brush can be modified and saved as a new brush. This is what you are going to do.

For example, from the General Brushes folder you could select Soft Round for a brush setting of reduced hardness or softer blur around the elliptical boundary. However, let's try something else. While Hard Round is selected, click the tab of the Brush Settings panel or toggle the Brush Settings panel button from the Options panel. This button resembles a folder with a paint brush. Refer to Figure 2-14.

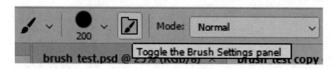

Figure 2-14. *Options panel link to the Brush Settings panel*

Brush Settings Options

The Brushes panel will now flip to the Brush Settings panel. Refer to Figure 2-15.

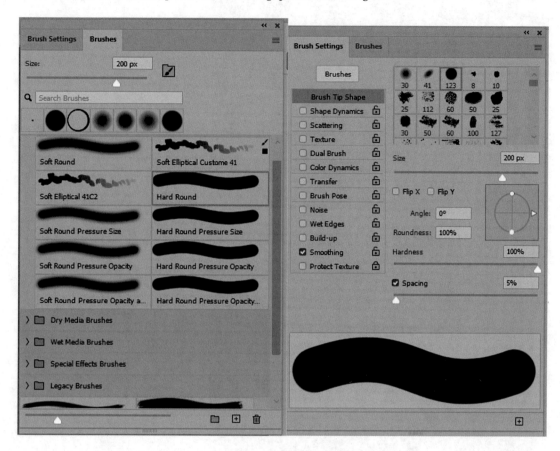

Figure 2-15. *Brushes panel and the link to the Brush Settings panel*

Brush Tip Shape

Under the area below the Brushes button, click the Brush Tip Shape tab. After doing that, you can adjust the following:

- Size of the brush stroke using the slider (1-5000 px)

- Flip on the X or Y axis by enabling one of the check boxes

- Adjust the angle of the brush (-180, 0, 180) degrees

- Roundness of the brush head from 0-100% (use the preview on the right to adjust the angle and roundness)

- Hardness of the brush stroke using the slider (0-100%)

- Spacing of the brush stroke using the slider (0-1000%). The slider is activated when enabled.

Figure 2-16 shows the settings I used to make this a softer brush.

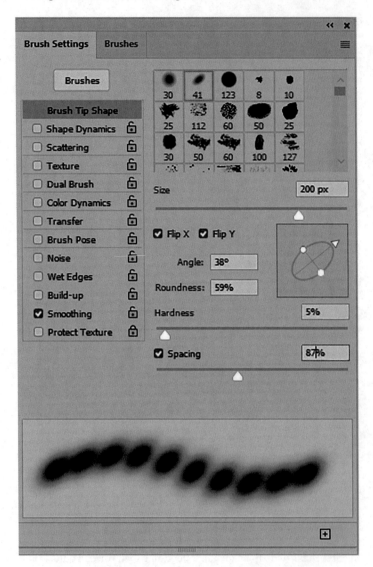

Figure 2-16. *Brush Settings panel showing brush tip shape options*

I set the size to 200 px, enabled flip on X and Y, and set the angle to 38°, the roundness to 59%, the hardness to 5%, and the spacing to 87%. Notice how moving the spacing higher than 25% gives a more dotted appearance because the brush strokes are farther apart.

Make sure, as you build your brushes, to test and move the sliders associated with the next several tabs located on the left. However, for this project, just follow along with me for now as I describe each tab.

Shape Dynamics Tab

Click the Shape Dynamics tab to adjust the shape variation. The check on the tab enables these settings and you can lock the options as well as for the following tabs. Leave them unlocked for now, except for Protect Texture. Refer to Figure 2-17.

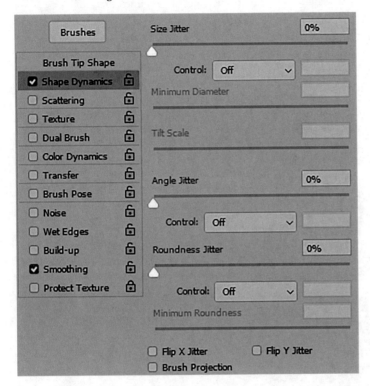

Figure 2-17. *Brush Settings panel showing shape dynamics options*

This area controls the tip shape variation options such as jitter or how each part of the brush stroke will fade, tilt, or spread. Some options will be greyed out or appear as a warning if you do not have a pen or stylus. However, if you do have a stylus, these adjustments can certainly create some interesting angles. Refer to Figure 2-18.

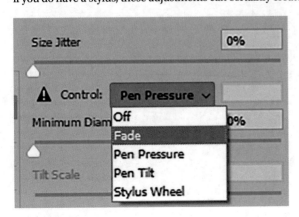

Figure 2-18. *Brush Settings panel in the shape dynamics control options*

51

Things you can control include:

- Size of Jitter randomness: (0-100%) you can keep the dynamic control for size Off or from the dropdown menu choose from the options of Fade, Pen Pressure, Pen Tilt or Stylus Wheel. If you don't have a pen or stylus to work with, Fade is the best option as you will not get a warning message saying you need a tablet that is either an input device with a pressure sensitive tablet, a tilt sensitive tablet or has a tablet with a thumbwheel. Refer to Figure 2-19.

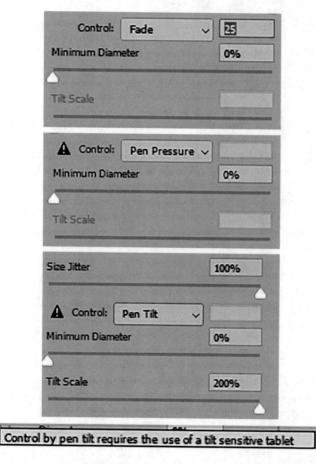

Figure 2-19. *Brush Settings panel showing shape dynamics options and warnings*

With the setting of Fade, you can set the steps of the Fade from 1-9999 and you can alter the minimum diameter from 0-100%. However, only with Pen Tilt can you set the tilt scale from 0-200%.

Let's set the following:

- Size Jitter to 100%

- Contol to Fade: 25

- Minumum Diameter to 0%

Refer to Figure 2-19 and Figure 2-20.

Figure 2-20. *Brush Settings panel with a shape dynamics preview*

- Angle Jitter can be set from 0 to 100%. You have similar dynamic control options for the angle. By default, it is set to Off, but there are options of Rotation, Initial Direction, and Direction. Rotation requires a tablet that supports rotation. Initial direction and Direction give no warning message, but you will not have access to the Fade steps options, which you can set from 1-9999.

Set the Angle Jitter to 32% and the Control to Fade 25. Refer to Figure 2-21.

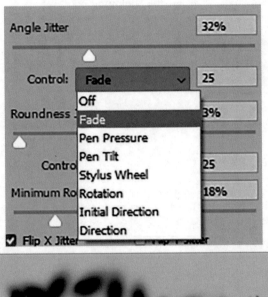

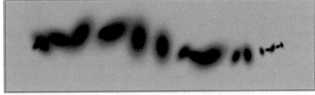

Figure 2-21. *Brush Settings panel showing shape dynamics options and preview*

- The Roundness of Jitter is set from 0-100% and it sets the randomness. You have the same control setting for roundness as the Size Jitter, including rotation. By default, it is set to Off. Fade steps (1-9999) allow you to access the minimum roundness of 1-100%. Refer to Figure 2-22.

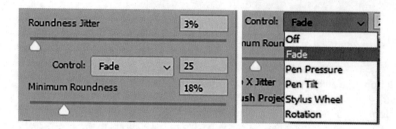

Figure 2-22. *Brush Settings panel showing shape dynamics options*

Set the Roundness Jitter to 3%, the Control to Fade 25, and the Minimum Roundness 18%. Refer to Figure 2-22 and Figure 2-23.

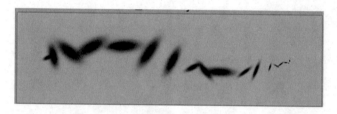

Figure 2-23. *Brush Settings panel showing the shape dynamics preview*

- With the following checkboxes enabled, you can also flip the jitter on the X or Y axis randomly as well as use Brush Projection. Note that Brush Projection disables the Roundness Jitter slider and controls. Refer to Figure 2-24.

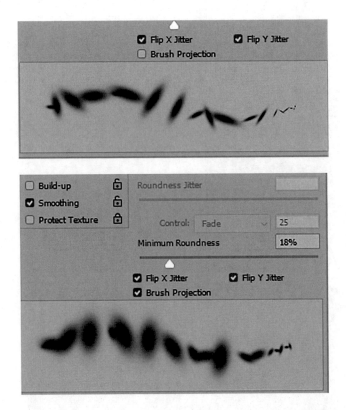

Figure 2-24. *Brush Settings panel showing shape dynamics options and preview*

In this case, just enable the Flip X Jitter option. Refer to Figure 2-25.

Figure 2-25. *Brush Settings panel showing shape dynamics options and preview*

Scattering Tab

Now, in the Brush settings, click the Scattering tab to adjust scattering and count. This tab, when enabled, affects the point at which the brush dots are scattered. Refer to Figure 2-26.

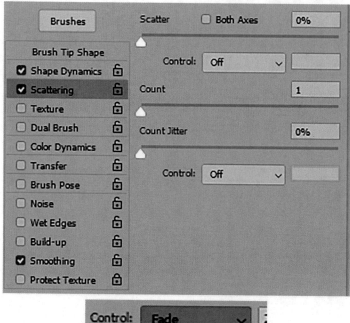

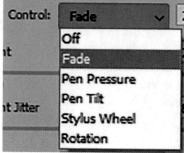

Figure 2-26. *Brush Settings panel in Scattering options*

- The Scatter randomness slider can be set from (0-1000%). The option Both Axes allows for scatter in both directions. It's like Jitter in the Shape Dynamics tab and can be dynamically controled for scatter by choosing a setting from the dropdown menu. The default is Off but you can set to Fade steps (1-9999).

Set Scatter to 123% and Control to Fade 25. Refer to Figure 2-27.

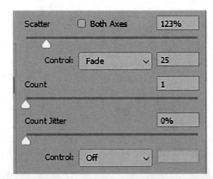

Figure 2-27. *Brush Settings panel in Scatter options and preview*

- Set the Tip Count (1-16) to compress the tips and enlarge the area of scatter as well. Set the Count to 2 as higher settings appear quite congested. Refer to Figure 2-28.

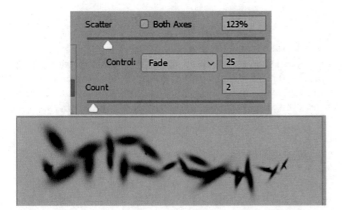

Figure 2-28. *Brush Settings panel in Scatter options and preview*

- Count Jitter sets the randomness of the scatter (0-100%) and also has a dynamic Control for the count dropdown menu with the same settings as Scatter, including Fade steps (1-9999). Set the Count Jitter to 85% and leave the Control set at Off. Refer to Figure 2-29.

Figure 2-29. *Brush Settings panel in Scatter options and preview*

As you drag over the layer on the canvas, the scattering will stop when you reach the end of the scatter.

Texture Tab

Click the Texture tab to adjust texture options. This tab allows you to paint with various rough pattern textures that you create to give the brush a rough edge. These patterns are located in the Patterns panel. We will look at pattern creation in more detail in Chapter 3. In the meantime, select a rough-looking B&W pattern because the rough edges seem to appear more distinctly. Invert, when enabled, allows you to reverse the texture pattern, and the plus icon button allows you to create a new preset from the current pattern. Refer to Figure 2-30.

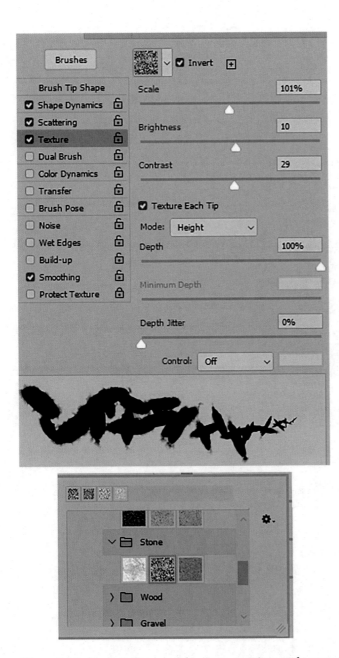

Figure 2-30. Brush Settings panel in Texture options and texture pattern settings

---

■ **Tip** If you cannot locate a rough texture pattern like mine, go to your Patterns panel and, from the menu, make sure to append your Legacy Patterns and more folder. Refer to Figure 2-31.

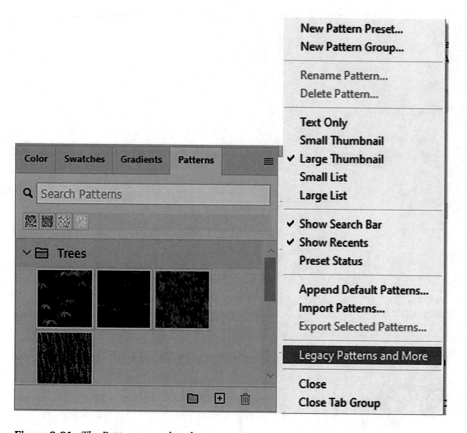

Figure 2-31. *The Patterns panel and menu*

Then return to your Brush Settings panel and, in the Legacy Patterns and More folder, open the 2019 Patterns. Look for the Stone folder and choose Stone_Granite (946 by 946 pixels, Indexed mode). Refer to Figure 2-32.

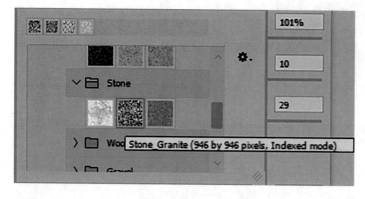

Figure 2-32. *Brush Settings panel in Texture options with the Stone_Granite pattern selected*

In the texture area of the panel, move the sliders or dropdown menus to alter the following settings:

- Scale (1-1000%) alters the size of the texture.

- Brightness (-150, 0, +150) effects the distictness of the texture.

- Contrast (-50, 0, +100) changes the sharpness of the texture.

Set the Scale to 60%, Brightness to -3, and Contrast to 18, making the brush appear like ink bleeds into the canvas. Refer to Figure 2-33.

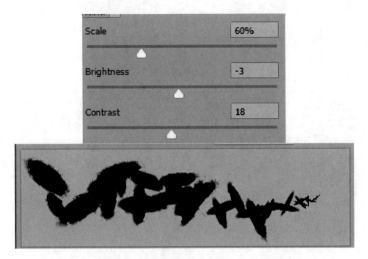

Figure 2-33. *Brush Settings panel in Texture options and preview*

- Texture Each Tip is enabled by default. Set it to blend the texture with each individual tip rather than on the entire stroke. However, when disabled, some settings are not available, such as Depth Jitter. Refer to Figure 2-34.

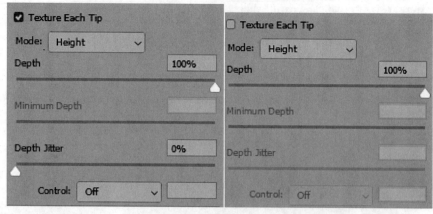

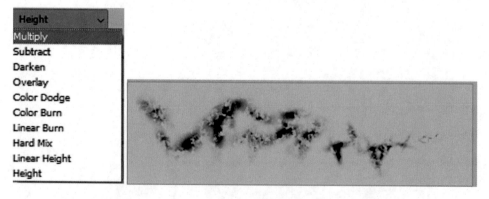

Figure 2-34. *Brush Settings panel in Texture options and previews of the texture of each tip*

Keep this checkbox enabled so the smudge does not smear too much. Refer to Figure 2-34.

- Mode sets a type of texture blending mode or method of interaction between the brush and texture. By default, it is set to Height, but other options include Multiply, Subtract, Darken, Overlay, Color Dodge, Color Burn, Linear Burn, Hard Mix, and Linear Height, each of which gives a slightly different disolved appearance. Note that Height and Linear Height affect texture depth and detail. We will look at some of these other modes in more detail later in the chapter. Refer to the section on brush options and blend modes. Refer to Figure 2-35.

Figure 2-35. *Brush Settings panel in Texture options and preview of mode settings*

Leave it on the Height setting for now. Refer to Figure 2-35 and Figure 2-36.

Figure 2-36. *Brush Settings panel in Texture options and preview of mode height*

- After setting the mode, you can set the Brush Depth (0-100%).

- Mimimum Depth (0-100%) is only available when the Depth Jitter Control area is set to a setting other than the default of Off, such as Fade. Refer to Figure 2-37.

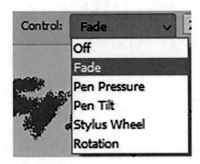

Figure 2-37. *Brush Settings panel in the Texture options Control menu*

- Depth Jitter controls the randomness (0-100%) and has the same control settings for depth as the Shape Dynamics tab including Fade steps (1-9999).

Leave the Depth at 100%, Minimum Depth at 0%, Depth Jitter at 0%, and Control at Fade 25. Refer to Figure 2-38.

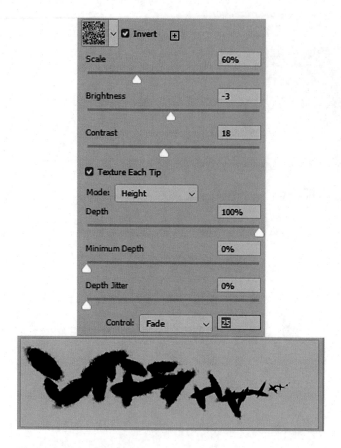

Figure 2-38. *Brush Settings panel in Texture options and preview*

Dual Brush Tab

Select the Dual Brush tab to adjust the dual brush shape. Do you want to use two brushes at the same time? Then this mode is for you. Select another brush from the list to add a more combined and interesting faded effects. I used Soft Round 30 in this figure. Note that with these settings some changes may be more noticeable depending on the chosen brush. Also, higher settings appear to reduce the effectiveness of the dual brush. Refer to Figure 2-39.

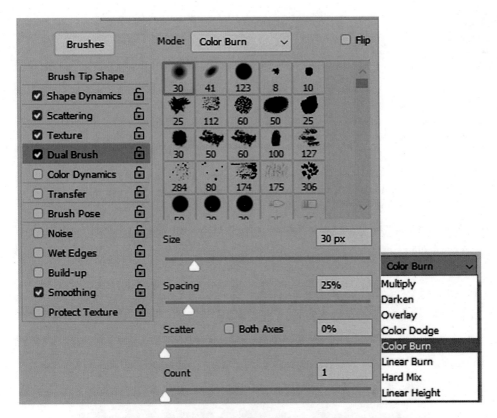

Figure 2-39. *Brush Settings panel in Dual Brush options and preview*

- Blending Mode sets the method of interaction between the primary brush and dual brush. Change to Multiply, Darken, Overlay, Color Dodge, Color Burn, Linear Burn, Hard Mix, or Linear Height. We will review many of these modes later in the chapter. However, in regards to Linear Height, refer to the Note for the Texture tab. By default, the Mode is set to Color Burn. However, a setting of Mutiply can overide the current brush. Refer to Figure 2-40.

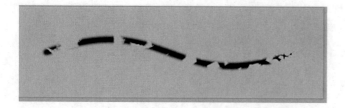

Figure 2-40. *Dual Brush options preview of Mode Multiply*

For now set it back to Color Burn.

- The Flip check box, when enabled, depending on the type of dual brush used, makes the random flip more apparent.

Change other slider settings when a brush is selected, such as

- Size or brush diameter (1-5000 px)

- Spacing (1-1000%)

- Scatter (0-1000%)

- Both axes, to control direction scatter in both directions

- Tip Count (1-16)

Refer to Figure 2-41.

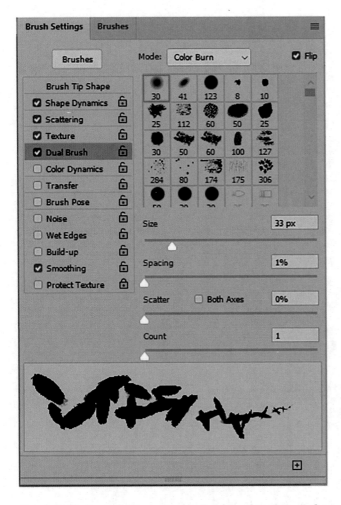

Figure 2-41. Brush Settings panel in Dual Brush options and preview of Color Burn

Change the setting to Size 33 px, Spacing 1%, Scatter 0%, and Count 1. Refer to Figure 2-41.

Color Dynamics Tab

Click the Color Dynamics tab to adjust color variation. These settings will not be apparent until you test the brush on a blank white page, so as you alter the settings in this tab, test often while dragging the brush over the canvas. Refer to Figure 2-42.

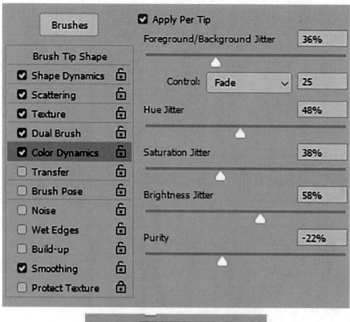

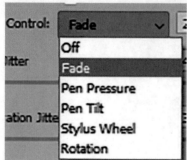

Figure 2-42. *Brush Settings panel in Color Dynamics options*

- Color and fade dynamics can be altered by enabling the checkbox called Apply per Tip. This randomness can also be affected by the current foreground/background jitter or colors in the Tools panel (0-100%). As well, you can use dynamic controls for color from the dropdown menu including Fade steps (1-9999). By default, it is set to Off.

When you paint with a black foreground and a white background, the result is a greyscale pattern. Refer to Figure 2-43.

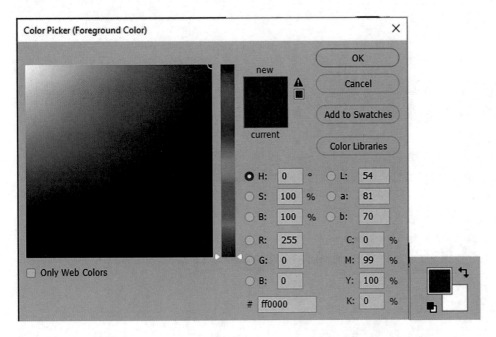

Figure 2-43. *Set your brush to the default black foreground and white background (D) in the Tools panel and paint in grayscale*

At this point, go to the Tools panel and click the foregound color to enter the Color Picker and change it to a red (R: 255 G:0 B:0). Click OK to exit and then paint on the canvas to see the color result. Refer to Figure 2-44.

Figure 2-44. *Set your brush to a red foreground and white background in the Tools panel using the color picker and paint in color*

You get random patterns of color as you paint and this is controled by the following sliders:

- Hue Jitter randomness: (0-100%)

- Saturation Jitter randomness: (0-100%)

- Brightness Jitter randomness: (0-100%)

- Purity: Sets the color shift towards or away from the neutral axis (-100, 0, +100%). A higher number results in brighter colors while lower numbers are more dull and muted.

Set the Foreground/Background Jitter to 36%, Control to Fade 25, Hue Jitter to 48%, Saturation Jitter to 38%, Brightness Jitter to 58%, and Purity to -22%. Refer to Figure 2-42.

Try other slider settings and see how they effect the color as you paint.

Transfer Tab

Click the Transfer tab. This allows you to further adjust the opacity and flow of paint from the brush, as well as the build-up of paint or effect. Refer to Figure 2-45.

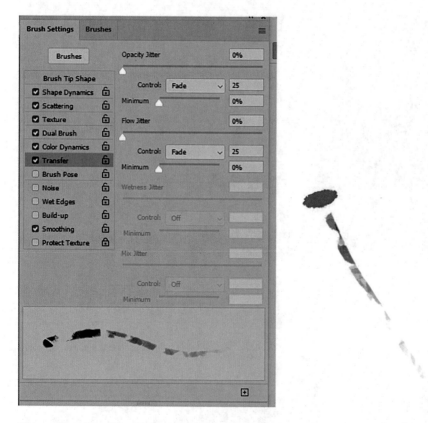

Figure 2-45. *Brush Settings panel in Transfer options and preview with test paint on canvas*

- Opacity Jitter randomness (0-100%) also has dynamic controls for opacity, including Fade steps (1-9999). By defaut, it is Off and Minimum Brush opacity (0-100%). Refer to Figure 2-45 and Figure 2-46.

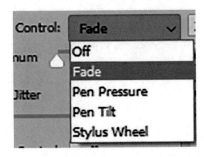

Figure 2-46. *Brush Settings panel in the Transfer options Control dropdown menu*

- Flow Jitter randomess (0-100%) also has dynamic controls for flow, including Fade steps (1-9999). By default, it is set to Off and Minimum Brush flow (0-100%). Refer to Figure 2-45 and Figure 2-46.

- Wetness Jitter randomness is disabled by default and can only be accessed by the Mixer Brush tool, which also has dynamic controls for wetness, including Fade steps (1-9999) and Minimum Brush wetness (0-100%). Refer to Figure 2-47.

- Mix Jitter randomness is disabled by default and can only be accessed if you are using the Mixer Brush tool, which also has dynamic controls for mix including Fade steps (1-9999) and Minimum Brush mix (0-100%) See the earlier Note in the chapter on the Mixer Brush tool. Refer to Figure 2-47.

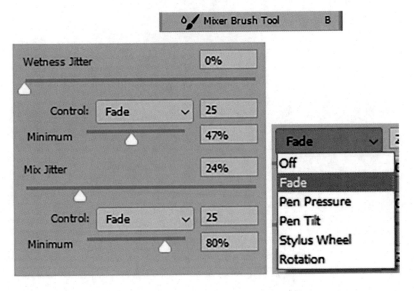

Figure 2-47. *Brush Settings panel in Transfer options that can only be accessed by the Mixer Brush tool*

71

■ **Note**   As you use other tools that use the Brush Settings panel, some options may not be accessible or will be disabled for that tool, as you will see later in the chapter.

I often disable the Tranfer option as I find that it masks some of my smear. This is likey because of my dual brush tab being enabled. But in your case, this might be the exact brush effect you are looking for. Refer to Figure 2-48.

Brush Pose Tab

This Brush Pose tab, while accessable, is more for if you are working with a stylus, one that uses tilt x and y axis, rotation, and pressure. However, if you are just working with a mouse to draw your lines, some of these settings may not be available as you draw. The settings include the following:

- Tilt X (-100,0-100%) sets the default brush stylus X pose.
- Override Tilt X, when enabled, overides stylus tilt X data.
- Tilt Y (-100,0-100%) sets the default brush stylus Y pose.
- Override Tilt Y, when enabled, overides stylus tilt Y date.
- Rotation (0-360°) sets the default brush stylus rotation.
- Override Rotation, when enabled, overrides stylus rotation data.
- Pressure (0-100%) sets the default brush stylus pressure.
- Override Pressure, when enabled, overrides stylus pressure data.

Refer to Figure 2-48.

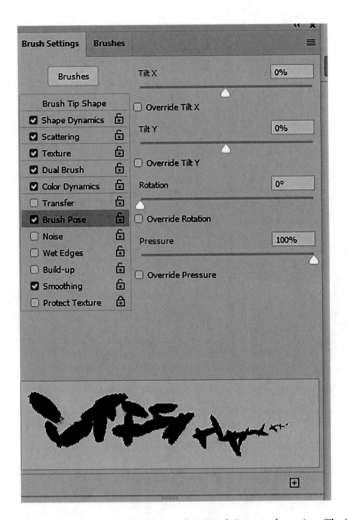

Figure 2-48. *Brush Settings panel in Brush Pose and preview. The Transfer tab disabled*

I leave this tab disabled, but you can adjust the settings if you have a stylus. Refer to Figure 2-53.

Additional Tabs

The last tabs in the Brushes Setting panel do not have additional options. Refer to Figure 2-49.

Figure 2-49. *Brush Settings panel with Noise, Wet Edges, Build-up, Smoothing, and Protect Texture enabled*

They are the following:

- Noise adds noise to the brush tip. Refer to Figure 2-50.

Figure 2-50. *Brush Settings panel in Noise preview with test paint on the canvas*

- Wet Edges emphasizes the edges of the brush stroke, but blends colors as they paint over each other mulitple times. Refer to Figure 2-51.

Figure 2-51. *Brush Settings panel in Wet Edges preview with test paint on the canvas*

- Build-up enables an airbrush-style build-up effect. When you enable this checkbox, look in the Options panel; the Enable airbrush button is also active there. Refer to Figure 2-52.

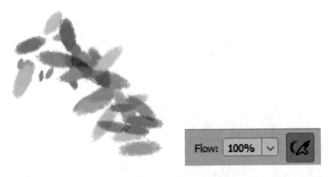

Figure 2-52. *Test of Build-up on the canvas, with the airbrush enabled when this setting is checked in the Brush Setting panel*

- Smoothing is enabled by default and allows for mouse path smoothing.
- Protect Texture preserves the texture pattern while applying brush presets.

Remember, at this point you can turn off or on the check boxes if you need to see how the brush acts with or without certain settings. Figure 2-53 shows the tabs for my brush.

Figure 2-53. *Brush Settings panel with my current options enabled for a custom brush*

Saving the Brush

When you are done adjusting your settings, click the Create new brush button at the bottom of the Brush Settings panel. Refer to Figure 2-54.

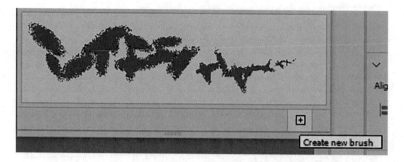

Figure 2-54. *Brush Settings panel preview and the Create new brush button*

The New Brush dialog box will open. Refer to Figure 2-55.

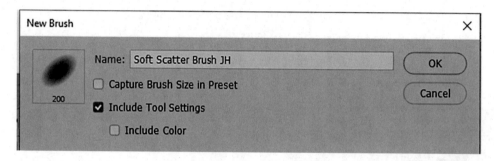

Figure 2-55. *New Brush dialog box with Include Tool Settings enabled*

Change the name of the new brush to a name you will remember. Mine is Soft Scatter Brush JH. I add my intials so I remember that I created the brush.

Then choose whether to capture the brush size in the preset, or to include tool settings to remember the current setting for the brush. Also, enable the Include color check box if you want the current brush color remembered.

In this case, because I want to use the brush with more than one tool, not just the Brush tool, I uncheck the Include Tool Settings option. Then click OK to exit. Refer to Figure 2-56.

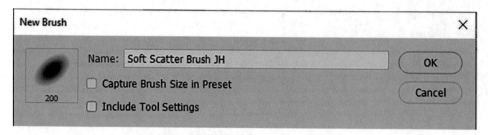

Figure 2-56. *New Brush dialog box with Include Tool Settings disabled*

I add this brush to my General Brushes folder. If you don't like your current brush, you can select it in the Brushes panel and click the trash can icon to delete it. However, in this case, I create a new group brush folder by clicking the New Group Button that looks like a folder. Refer to Figure 2-57.

Figure 2-57. *Brushes Panel's Create New Group, Create New Brush, and Delete Brush buttons*

Name the new group as `Custom Brushes Ch1` and click OK. Then drag the folder to the bottom of your brushes panel if you find that it is inside of the General Brushes panel. Refer to Figure 2-58.

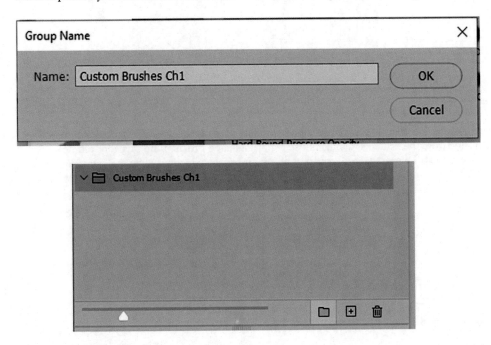

Figure 2-58. *Group Name dialog box for creating a group in the Brushes panel*

Drag your new custom brush, in my case Soft Scatter Brush JH, into the folder to keep it organized. Refer to Figure 2-59.

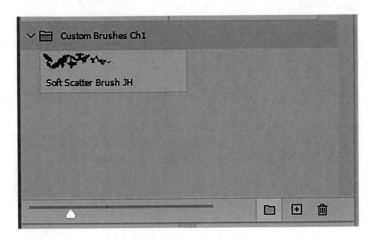

Figure 2-59. *Custom brush dragged into the new group folder in the Brushes panel*

■ **Tip** As you look through the brushes, make sure to use your Brushes menu to add Legacy Brushes for addional options you can modify. Refer to Figure 2-60.

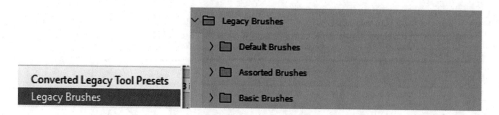

Figure 2-60. *Add Legacy Brushes to your Brushes panel for more options*

Also, as you create new brushes, you can save them outside of Photoshop. Select the folder of brushes you want to save, and from the Brushes menu, choose Export Selected Brushes and save them somewhere on your compter as an (.abr) file so that others can import your brush collection. Refer to Figure 2-61.

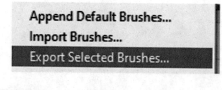

Figure 2-61. *Save and export a brush as a (.abr) file*

Creating a round brush was useful. However, what if you want to create your own custom designed brush that is not round?

Project: Create a Custom Brush

Let's try creating a simple square brush of our own design. Later it can be modified with the Brush Settings panel. In your document, create a new blank layer and turn off all the other layers that you use to paint on the canvas, except for the white background. In my case, the new layer is Layer 3. Refer to Figure 2-62.

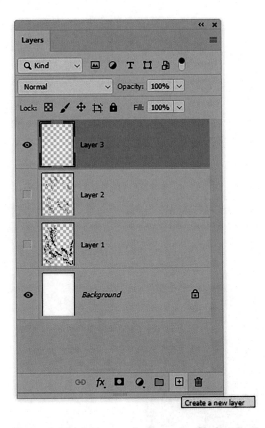

Figure 2-62. *Add a new layer to your file for creating a custom brush*

Using your Tools panel, select the Rectangular Marquee tool (M) in the Options panel and set Style: Fixed Size, Width: 200 px, and Height: 200 px. Make sure the feather is set to 0 px. Refer to Figure 2-63.

Figure 2-63. *Rectangular Marquee tool options panel with Style set to Fixed Size*

Click somewhere on the (Layer 3) white area in the canvas so that you see the marching ants of the selection. Use your Zoom tool if you need to get closer. Refer to Figure 2-64.

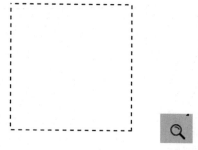

Figure 2-64. *Use the Zoom took to get closer into the selection created*

Now go to Edit ➤ Fill and choose Contents of Black, a Blending of Normal, and an Opacity of 100%. Disable Preserve Transparancy from the dialog box, and click OK. Refer to Figure 2-65.

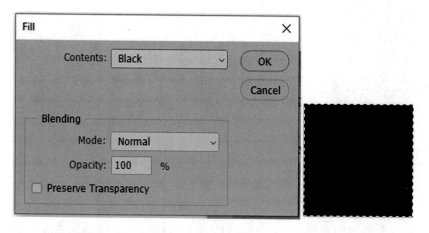

Figure 2-65. *Use the Fill dialog box to fill the selection with black*

You should now have a black square.

Now, with the Elliptical Marquee tool (M) change the fixed size in the Options panel to 175 px and 175 px. Leave Feather at 0 px and click in the center of the black square you already made. Refer to Figure 2-66.

Figure 2-66. *Elliptical Marquee tool options panel with Style set to Fixed Size*

While selected with the Elliptical Marquee tool, you may need to drag the selection around with your mouse to center it more accurately. Refer to Figure 2-67.

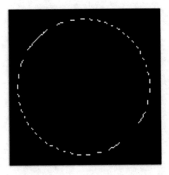

Figure 2-67. *Elliptical selection on top of the square*

Now press the Backspace/Delete key on your keyboard to remove the center. Photoshop generally likes to use black and white shapes for its brushes, but you can use grayscale or transparent areas to enhance faded effects.

Now select the Magic Wand tool (W). Refer to the settings in the Options panel to set Sample Size: Point sample and Tolerance: 32. Enable Anti-alias, enable Contiguous, and optionally you can enable or disable Sample All layers. Refer to Figure 2-68.

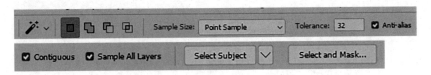

Figure 2-68. *Magic Wand tool*

Click the black area of the square. Refer to Figure 2-69.

Figure 2-69. *Creating a selection of the brush shape*

Go to Edit ➤ Define Brush Preset. Name the brush in the Brush Name panel or use the default name and click OK. A new brush will now be added to your Brushes folder. Refer to Figure 2-70.

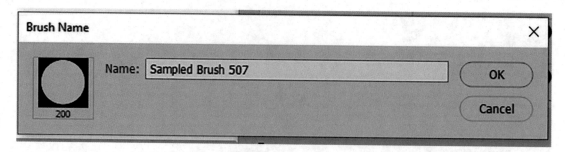

Figure 2-70. *Brush name dialog box for new custom brush with a recorded size of 200 px*

Go to Select ➤ Deselect to exit the selection. Refer to Figure 2-71.

Figure 2-71. *Deselect your custom brush design on the canvas*

Drag the brush into the Custom Brushes Ch 1 folder. Refer to Figure 2-72.

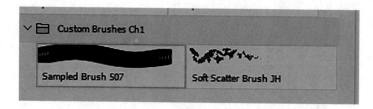

Figure 2-72. *Place the new custom brush in the group folder*

You can now return to the Brushes Settings panel and make some alterations to the brush as you did earlier with the Hard Round brush to create your Soft Scatter brush. In this case, I repeated the same brush settings with this brush. Some of the settings of the Soft Scatter brush may be maintained if it was the last brush you selected before you built this new brush. Note that because this is a custom shape, some settings like Brush Tip Shape Hardness may not be available. Refer to Figure 2-73.

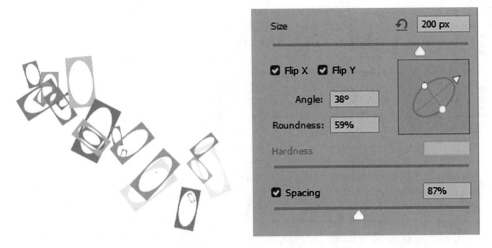

Figure 2-73. *Alter the brush settings for your custom brush, except for Hardness, and paint on the canvas*

Saving Your Custom Brush with New Settings

After you have made your brush setting choices, before you select another brush, make sure to click the New Brush button at the bottom of the Brush Settings panel. Click OK to the message in the New Brush dialog box with both settings disabled. Refer to Figure 2-74.

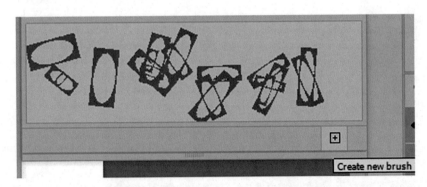

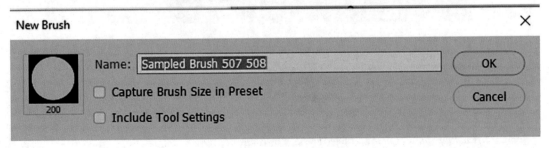

Figure 2-74. *After you have created new settings in the Brush Settings panel, make sure to create a new brush to save those settings*

Then make sure it is in your Custom Brush Ch1 folder or drag it into the folder. Refer to Figure 2-75.

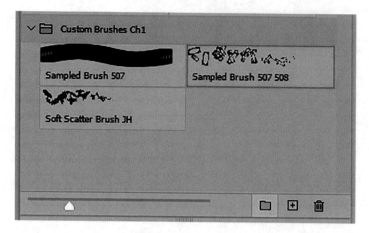

Figure 2-75. *The new brush is added to the group folder in the Brushes panel and is ready to use*

Additional Custom Brush Ideas

For other projects with custom brushes, if you have a black and white image, you can turn that into a brush using the Magic Wand tool to click select black areas of the graphic and choose Edit ➤ Define Brush Preset. Then later Select ➤ Deselect the selection before you begin painting with your new brush. Refer to Figure 2-76.

Figure 2-76. *Create a custom brush from a black and white image*

As you progress though the rest of the book, practice using Shape tools. See Chapter 3 and your Magic Wand tool to make selections for more complex brushes. Refer to Figure 2-77.

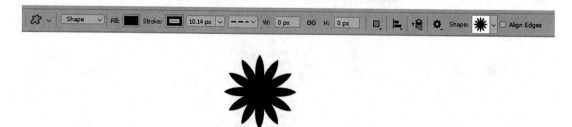

Figure 2-77. *Custom Shape Options panel to create a brush from a custom shape*

Remember, as you build your collection, make sure to save or export. Keep the .abr copies as backup for future projects. In the Chapters folder you will find a copy of the brushes used in this chapter.

Now let's return to the Brushes Options panel.

Brush Options and Blend Modes

In the Options panel, after creating your custom brush, you can paint using various paint blending modes. Some of these blending modes appeared in the various brush settings, as you saw earlier. However, you can add these modes again as you paint. They are simlar to the Layer Blending modes that you can adjust for a specific layer in the Layers panel. Refer to Figure 2-78.

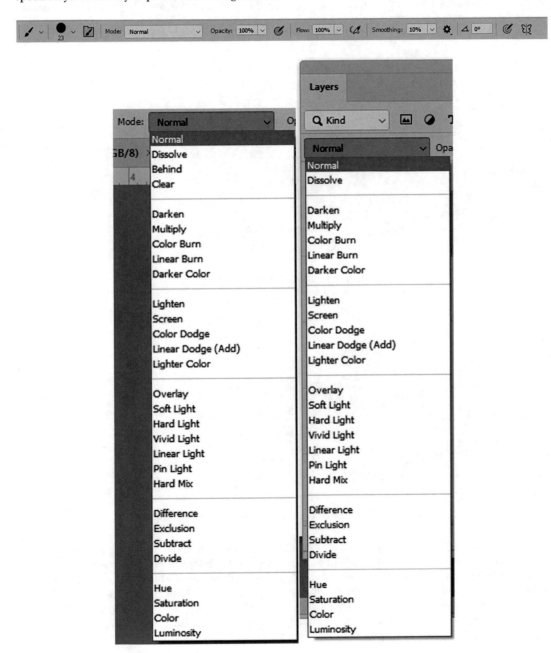

Figure 2-78. *Brush Tool options panel, paint blend modes, and the Layers panel blending modes*

■ **Note** The modes of Height and Linear Height are exclusive to the brush settings of Texture but the brush setting of Dual Brush just uses Linear Height and you can see my earlier reference in the brush settings area.

Blend modes on an image, whether painted or with a layer blend change, work with the base color (original color) plus the blend color (the color being applied with the painting or editing tool) and the result color is the combination of the two. Refer to Figure 2-79.

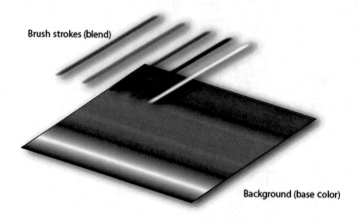

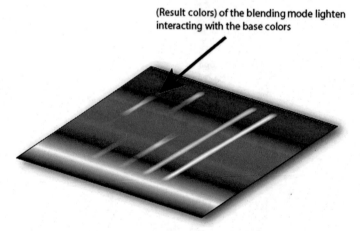

Figure 2-79. *Diagram of how blend and base colors work to create a result color*

Channel: In the following examples, *channel* refers to the RGB or red, green, and blue channels.

The science behind blends and how Adobe determines the blends is quite complicated. For us to see it visually, I experimented and created the following figures so that you can see the difference between painting with the Brush tool, in this case the default general brush of Soft Round, with a specific blending mode in various color hues of red, green, blue, white, and black on the left. I then repeated the steps painting in Normal mode and then appying the Blending mode directly to the layer on the right side. I consider these lines to be the blend color and the gradient background to be the base color. Refer to Figure 2-80.

Brushes with bending mode of Vivid Light applied

Brushes with blending mode of Normal and layer blending mode of Vivid Light applied

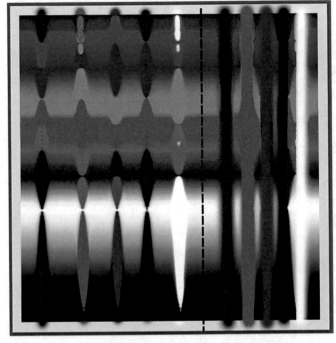

Figure 2-80. *On the left are paint blend modes; on the right are the layer blending modes*

Let's look at these visual examples to get an idea of how blending works.

- **Normal**: Paints the current brush foreground blend color (default). There is no blend because opacity for both is 100%. Refer to Figure 2-81.

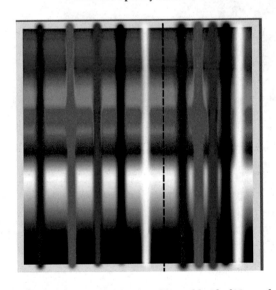

Figure 2-81. *Paint blend and layer blend of Normal*

- **Dissolve**: Paints the current brush foregound blend color, but as a more air brush, random pixilated pattern with some noise distortion arround the soft edges. Refer to Figure 2-82.

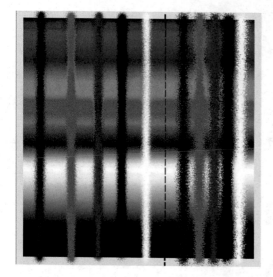

Figure 2-82. *Paint blend and layer blend of Dissolve*

- **Behind**: Edits or paints the current brush foreground blend color only on the transparent areas of the layer. Make sure that Lock transparent pixels for the layer is not enabled when painting in this mode. This blend option is not available for the Layers panel blending modes. It can only be accessed by a Brush, History Brush, Clone Stamp, Pattern Stamp, or Pencil tool. Refer to Figure 2-83.

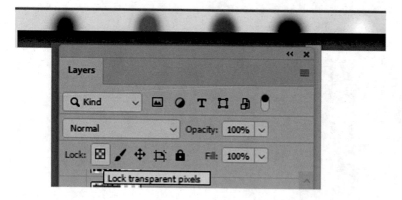

Figure 2-83. *Paint blend of Behind*

- **Clear**: Similar to an Eraser tool, it edits or paints the pixels and makes them transparent. Make sure that Lock transparent pixels for the layer is not enabled when painting in this mode. This option is not available for the Layers panel blending mode, only for the Brush and Pencil tools. Refer to Figure 2-84.

Figure 2-84. *Paint blend of Clear*

- **Darken**: Based on color data from each channel, the base or blend color (whichever is darker) is the result color. Pixels lighter or transparent do not change. White or transparent base areas do not affect the blend color and a white blend has no effect on the base and disappears. Refer to Figure 2-85.

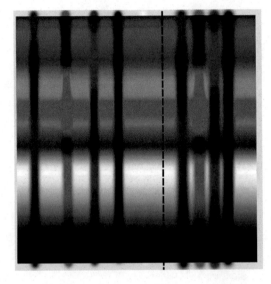

Figure 2-85. *Paint blend and layer blend of Darken*

- **Multiply**: Similar to Darken, based on color data from each channel, the base color is multiplied by the blend color. A darker color results. White or transparent base areas do not affect the blend color and a white blend has no effect on the base and disappears. Refer to Figure 2-86.

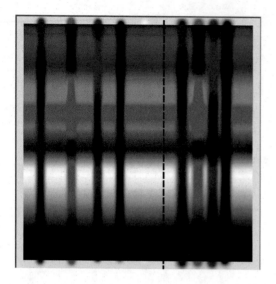

Figure 2-86. *Paint blend and layer blend of Multiply*

- **Color Burn**: Based on color data from each channel, the blend darkens the base color via the blend color by increasing the contrast between them. White or transparent base areas do not affect the blend color and a white blend has no effect on the base and disappears. However, there are slight differences in how the resulant color appears when painting with a brush in this mode or simply changing the above layer's blending mode after painting in Normal mode, as seen on the right of Figure 2-87.

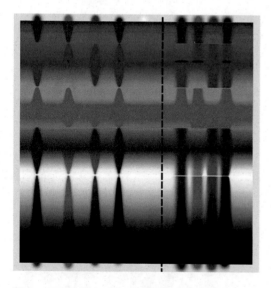

Figure 2-87. *Paint blend and layer blend of Color Burn*

- **Linear Burn**: Based on color data from each channel, the blend darkens the base color and the brightness between the blend and base is decreased. White or transparent blends do not affect the base color and disappear. Refer to Figure 2-88.

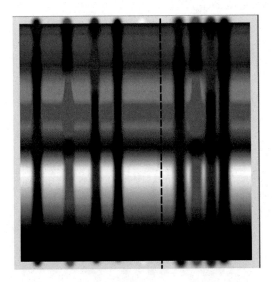

Figure 2-88. *Paint blend and layer blend of Linear Burn*

- **Darker Color**: Compares all the channel values for both the base color and the blend color and displays a lower color value from choosing lower channel values. For example, painting over a black area does not produce a third color and the blend will pass over that area and disappear. Refer to Figure 2-89.

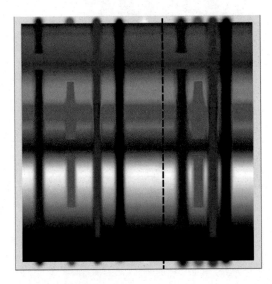

Figure 2-89. *Paint blend and layer blend of Darker Color*

- **Lighten**: Based on the color data from each channel (whichever is lighter, the base or the blend), the result color is created. As the blend is painted over, those base pixels that are darker are replaced by lighter pixels. A white blend is unaffected, and black disappears and does not blend with the base. Refer to Figure 2-90.

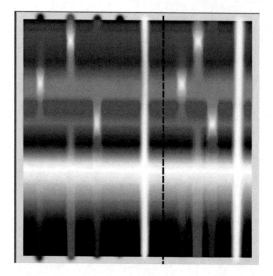

Figure 2-90. *Paint blend and layer blend of Lighten*

- **Screen**: Based on the color data from each channel, the inverse base color is multipled by the inverse of the blend color. A lighter third color results. A white blend is unaffected, and black disappears and does not blend with the base. Refer to Figure 2-91.

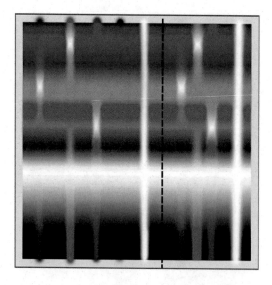

Figure 2-91. *Paint blend and layer blend of Screen*

- **Color Dodge**: Based on the color data from each channel, the base color is brightened to reflect the blend color. The result color is a decreased contrast between the base and blend. Painting with black does not affect the base color and it disappears. Painting on transparent areas does not affect the blend unless you are applying a Layer Blend mode. However, there are slight differences in how the result color appears when painting with a brush in this mode or simply changing above the layer's blending mode after painting in Normal mode. Refer to Figure 2-92.

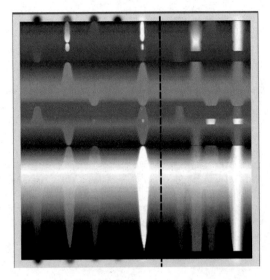

Figure 2-92. *Paint blend and layer blend of Color Dodge*

- **Linear Dodge (Add)**: Based on the color data from each channel, the base color is brightened. The result color is an increased brightness between the base and the blend. Painting with black does not affect the base color and it disappears. Painting on transparent areas does not affect the blend, unless you are applying a Layer Blend mode. There are slight differences in how the result color appears when painting with a brush in this mode or simply changing the above layer's blending mode after painting in Normal mode. Refer to Figure 2-93.

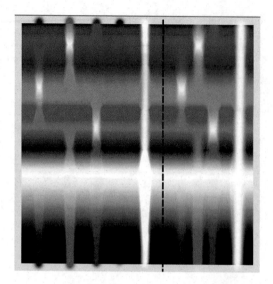

Figure 2-93. *Paint blend and layer blend of Linear Dodge*

- **Lighter Color**: Compares all the channel values for both the base color and the blend and dlsplays a higher color value from choosing highest channel values. A white blend is unaffected, and black disappears and does not blend with the base. Refer to Figure 2-94.

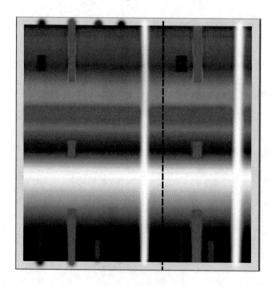

Figure 2-94. *Paint blend and layer blend of Lighter Color*

- **Overlay**: Depending upon the base, the blend color will be multiplied or screened. As the colors overlay the base, the highlights and shadows are preserved, mixing with the blend to preserve the lightness and darkness of the original blend. Refer to Figure 2-95.

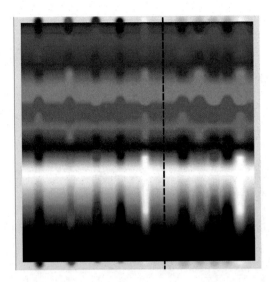

Figure 2-95. *Paint blend and layer blend of Overlay*

- **Soft Light**: Depending on the blend color, the base is lightened or darkened. The color's light is considered diffused or more gentle. If the blend is less than 50% gray, the result is lightened or dodged. If it's more than 50%, the result is like a darker burned area. Painting over colors using black will darken and painting with white will lighten. Refer to Figure 2-96.

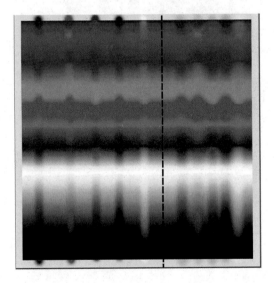

Figure 2-96. *Paint blend and layer blend of Soft Light*

- **Hard Light**: Depending on the blend color, the base is screened or multiplied. The color's light is considered harsh or more intense. If the blend is less than 50% gray, the result is lightened or screened. If it's more than 50%, the result is like multiply. Blend colors of black and white over a black or dark base will cover and no blend will result. This blend is more apparent when woking with more dull or muted hues that have a mixture of RGB not 100% pure. Refer to Figure 2-97.

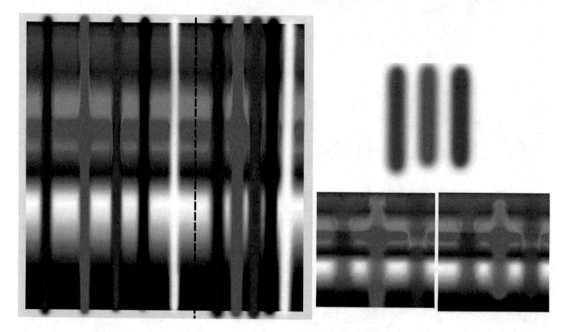

Figure 2-97. *Paint blend and layer blend of Hard Light is more apparent with muted colors*

- **Vivid Light**: Depending on the blend color, a burn or dodge occurs when the contrast is increased or decreased. If the blend is less than 50% gray, the result is lightened or there is a decrease in contrast. If it's more than 50%, the result is darkened or there is an increase in contrast. Vivid light can give a more blurred or smeared appearance when painted with a blend over the base. However, the result using a brush verses later appying the blending mode to the layer after painting in Normal mode can be dramatically different. Refer to Figure 2-98.

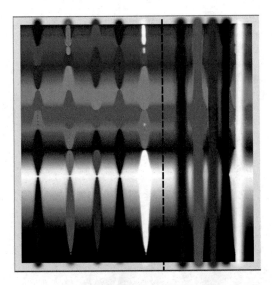

Figure 2-98. *Paint blend and layer blend of Vivid Light*

- **Linear Light**: Depending on the blend color, a burn or dodge occurs when the brightness is increased or decreased. If the blend is less than 50% gray, the result is lightened or increased brightness. If it's more than 50%, the result is darkened or decreased brightness. Linear light can give a more blurred or smeared appearance when painted with a blend over the base. However, the results vary when using a brush versus later applying the blending mode to the Layer after painting in Normal mode. Refer to Figure 2-99.

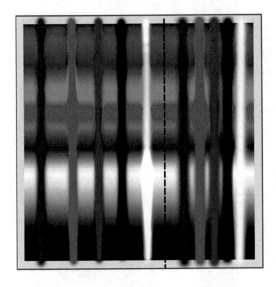

Figure 2-99. *Paint blend and layer blend of Linear Light*

- **Pin Light**: Depending on the blend color, colors are replaced. If the blend is less than 50% gray, the result is that the darker base colors are replaced and the lighter the blend color is unchanged. If it's more than 50% gray, the result is that lighter base colors are replaced and the darker the blend color is left unchanged. This is more apparent in the green and red channels and the brush strokes appear slightly pinched. This blend is more apparent when woking with more dull or muted hues that have a mixture of RGB that is not 100% pure. Refer to Figure 2-100.

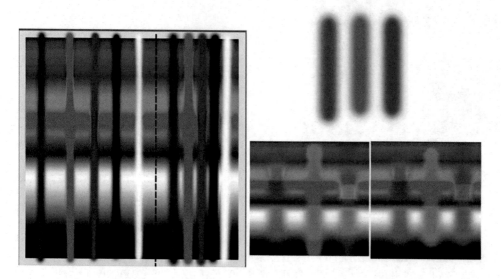

Figure 2-100. *Paint blend and layer blend of Pin Light, which is more apparent with muted colors*

- **Hard Mix**: Add the RGB channel values of the blend color to the same channels of the base color. Each channel has a value of 0-255, and when combinined, the channel will either be 0 or 255, resuting in a harsh contrast of one range or the other. However, the results vary when using a brush versus later applying the blending mode to the layer after painting with the Brush in Normal mode. Refer to Figure 2-101.

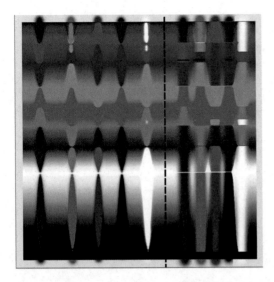

Figure 2-101. *Paint blend and layer blend of Hard Mix*

- **Difference**: Based on the color data from each channel, either the base or the blend is subtracted from the other and can produce a black or darker result over similar colors. This choice is dependant upon which has the greatest brightness value. White causes an inverse result while a black blend produces no change to the base and disappears. Refer to Figure 2-102.

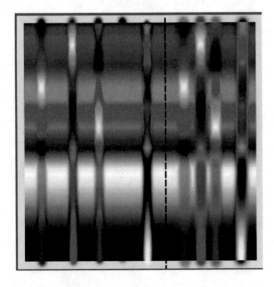

Figure 2-102. *Paint blend and layer blend of Difference*

- **Exclusion**: Creates a blend similiar to Difference, but with a lower contrast. Like Difference, white can cause an inverse result, while a black blend produces no change to the base and disappears. Refer to Figure 2-103.

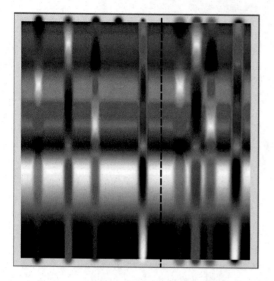

Figure 2-103. *Paint blend and layer blend of Exclusion*

- **Subtract**: Based on the color data from each channel, the result is that the blend is subtracted from the base. White painted over a color turns black while a black blend produces no change to the base and disappears. Refer to Figure 2-104.

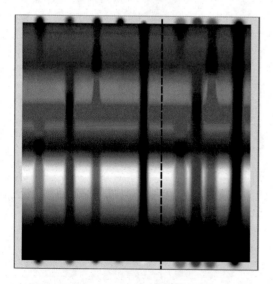

Figure 2-104. *Paint blend and layer blend of Subtract*

- **Divide**: Based on the color data from each channel, the blend is divided from the base color. Black painted over certain colors turns white and a white blend does not effect the base color and disappears. Refer to Figure 2-105.

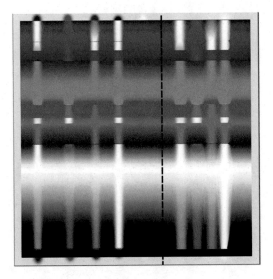

Figure 2-105. *Paint blend and layer blend of Divide*

- **Hue**: The base color's luminance and saturation plus the blend color's hue equals the result color, often in shades of gray. Note that areas of grey are unaffected by the blend color and it disappears. Refer to Figure 2-106.

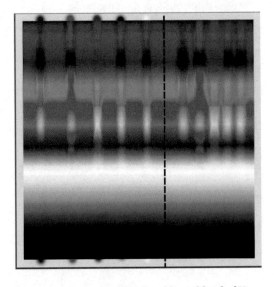

Figure 2-106. *Paint blend and layer blend of Hue*

- **Saturation**: The base color's luminance and hue plus the blend color's saturation equals the result color. Areas of no satauration and just gray are unaffected by the blend. Red, green, and blue blends produce little or no result, while black and white do produce a grey result in colorful areas. Refer to Figure 2-107.

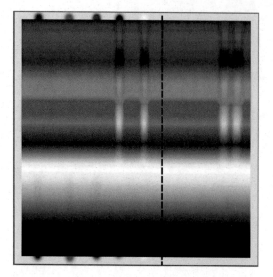

Figure 2-107. *Paint blend and layer blend of Saturation*

- **Color**: The base color's luminance plus the blend color's hue and saturation equals the result color. Gray levels in the dark and light range are preserved and are ideal for tinting black and white images. Note that some RGB color will appear in the mid-tone grayscale range. Refer to Figure 2-108.

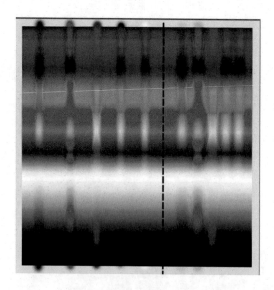

Figure 2-108. *Paint blend and layer blend of Color*

- **Luminosity**: The base color's hue and saturation plus the blend color's luminance equals the result color. It is an inverse of the Color mode and produces a result in various grayscale shades. White and black do not blend into the base. Refer to Figure 2-109.

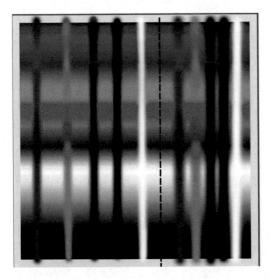

Figure 2-109. *Paint blend and layer blend of Luminosity*

As you can see, each blend color, depending on how it passes over a base color, produces a different result. If you use a custom brush rather than a soft brush, this can enhance the look further as you paint over your artwork or a photo. Here is an an example using my soft scatter brush that I created earlier over a gradient backgound. See file Ch2_gradient.psd and make an image duplicate for practice. Refer to Figure 2-110.

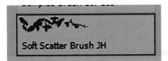

Figure 2-110. *A custom brush in the Brushes panel selected*

Make sure to set a color using your Color Picker and Tools panel for a foreground like red to see more blends. Then paint on the background layer, trying each brush option and blending in Painting mode, one at a time. Refer to Figure 2-111.

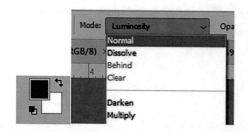

Figure 2-111. *Painting with a custom brush with red in various panting blend modes directly over the gradient*

Depending on where you paint, the colorful brush changes.

Remember to use your History panel and go back a step as required. Refer to Figure 2-112.

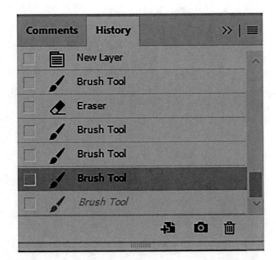

Figure 2-112. *History panel for undoing steps with the Brush tool*

Then paint on a blank layer and adjust the blending mode of the layer and see what difference it makes to the custom brush strokes. Refer to Figure 2-113.

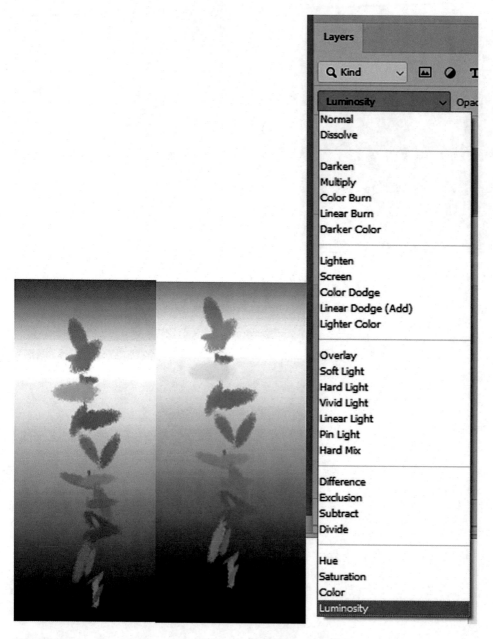

Figure 2-113. *Paint with the brush in normal paint blending mode and then change the blending mode of the layer itself to another mode like Luminosity*

For more details on blending modes, refer to this link and see the modes on other images: `https://helpx.adobe.com/photoshop/using/blending-modes.html`.

Brush Options Continued

In the next section of the Options panel you can set the brush's opacity (1-100%). Opacity can interact with the blending mode as well.

Always use presure for opacity when enabled. When off, the Bush Preset controls presure. Set the Flow rate (1-100%) for the stroke to enable airbrush-style build-up effects

Smoothing (1-100%): Set the smoothing for the stroke. Use higher values to reduce the shakiness of brush strokes.

Under the gear, enable smoothing options for the brush while painting, which include Pull String Mode, Stroke Catch-up, Catch-up on Stoke End, and Adjust for Zoom. Refer to Figure 2-114.

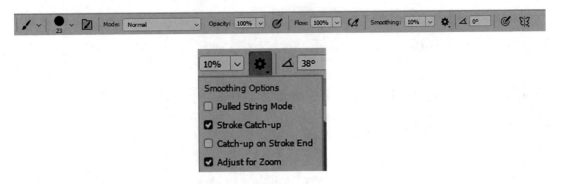

Figure 2-114. Brush tool Options panel and Smoothing options

Then set the brush angle, which is the same as if you set the angle in the Brush Preset Picker and spun the brush preview in a 360-degree spin. It sets the equvalant number between -180, 0, and 180. Refer to Figure 2-115.

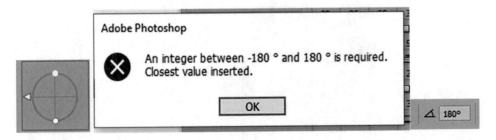

Figure 2-115. The Brush Preset Picker angle preview and angle in the Options panel are the same setting and must be set to a value between -180 ° and 180 °

The second to last button is "Always use Pressure for Size. When off Brush Preset controls pressure." Note the last button, Symmetry Paint; we will look at it in Chapter 3. Refer to Figure 2-116.

Figure 2-116. Pressure button icon in the Options panel next to the Brush Symmetry Paint menu

If you want to create a straight line from one point to the next, remember to click and then hold down the Shift key as you drag. Or click and then Shift+Click to the next location to get the brush to spread from one point to the next. Refer to Figure 2-117.

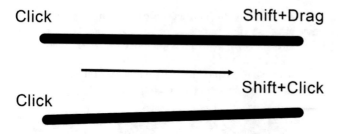

Figure 2-117. *Create straight lines using your Brush tool*

Using Your Custom Brushes with Other Tools to Warp Your Artwork Further

After you have created a warped brush tip, you do not have to limit yourself to using just the Brush tool. You can test it with the Pencil or Eraser tool as well.

If you use the current brushes settings that you set for your brush, you will not have access to all of the brush settings for that brush. This includes the following:

Pencil: Wet Edges, Build-up, and some sliders in Shape Dynamics, Texture, and Transfer are disabled. Refer to Figure 2-118.

Figure 2-118. *Available brush setting options for the Pencil tool*

Eraser Tool: Wet Edges, Color Dynamics, and some sliders in Shape Dynamics, Texture, and Transfer are disabled. Refer to Figure 2-119.

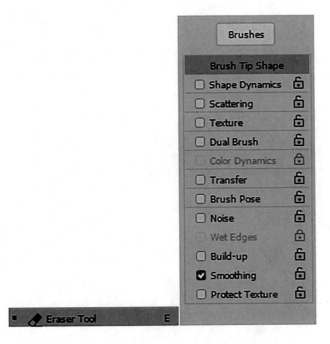

Figure 2-119. *Available brush setting options for the Eraser tool*

Test your custom brush with these tools.

Pencil Tool Options (Review)

In the Options panels are the following settings that are like your Brush tool, from left to right: Tool Preset, Brush Preset Picker, Brush Settings Panel, Blending Paint Mode, Opacity, Opacity Pressure, Smoothing, Smoothing Options, Angle, Always use Pressure for Size, and Symmetry Paint (See Chapter 3). Note that Auto Erase, when enabled, draws the background color over the previously painted foreground color. Refer to Figure 2-120.

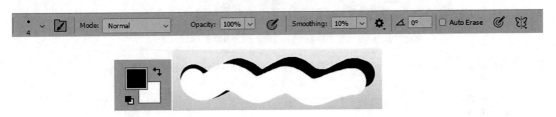

Figure 2-120. *The Pencil tool's Options panel. You can paint over a foreground with a background color when Auto Erase is enabled*

Eraser Tool Options (Review)

In the Options panel, moving from left to right, after the Tool Preset, Brush Preset Picker, and Brush Setting Panel, you can set the Eraser tool mode. For the Eraser tool to use your brushes settings, you can only erase in either Brush or Pencil mode. Block mode only creates a square eraser, which is not useful for this topic. Brush mode is best to use, and like the Brush tool, you have access to the same brush settings mentioned earlier in the chapter. Next are Opacity, Opacity Pressure, Flow Rate, Enable Airbrush Style Build-Up Effects when enabled button, Smoothing, Smoothing Options, Angle, Erase to History, and Always use Pressure for Size button. The last button is Symmetry Paint, which we will look at in Chapter 3. Refer to Figure 2-121.

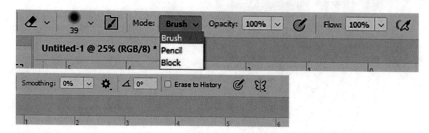

Figure 2-121. *The Eraser tool's Options panel. Set the mode to either Brush or Pencil to work with a custom brush*

However, when enabled, Erase to History allow you to erase areas from a designated history state in the History panel, such as to when the document was first opened. We will look at history brushes later in the chapter. Refer to Figure 2-122.

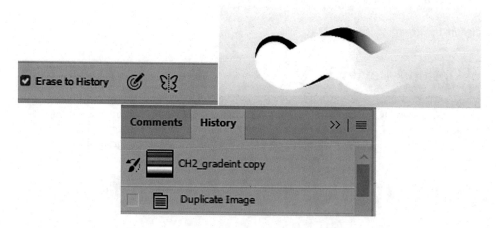

Figure 2-122. *Erase to History, when enabled in the Options panel, works with the History panel*

Let's now move on to the other tools you can test using your new brush tip to create some actual painterly distorts.

Garden Project

File ➤ Open CH2_IMG_3348.psd and use this image to practice the next set of tools. Make an Image➤ Duplicate of the image for practice. Click OK to the message. Refer to Figure 2-123.

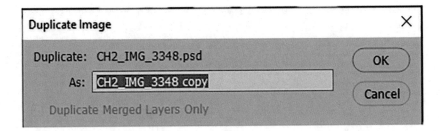

Figure 2-123. *Duplicate Image dialog box*

This is a picture of a flower I took as a macro shot (or close up) in a local garden. Nature is full of potential images to which you can add painterly effects. Refer to Figure 2-124.

Figure 2-124. *A picture of a Venidium "Zulu Prince" flower in a garden*

Remember to use your Zoom tool to get closer to an area and your Hand tool (spacebar) to move around the image when working with other tools. Refer to Figure 2-125.

Figure 2-125. *Zoom tool and Hand tool in the Tools panel*

First, we will explore three tools that are grouped together, as well as their options in the Options panel. Refer to Figure 2-126. They are the following:

- Blur tool

- Sharpen tool

- Smudge tool

Figure 2-126. *Blur, Sharpen, and Smudge tools in the Tools panel*

■ **Note** Before we use a custom brush, first we will test on the image with one of the Brush Preset Picker general brushes to see the difference in effects. I'll first use a Soft Round. Refer to Figure 2-127.

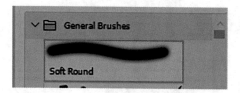

Figure 2-127. *General Brushes folder with Soft Round in the Brush Preset Picker*

In the Layers panel, create a new blank layer so that you will not alter the background while painting. Refer to Figure 2-128.

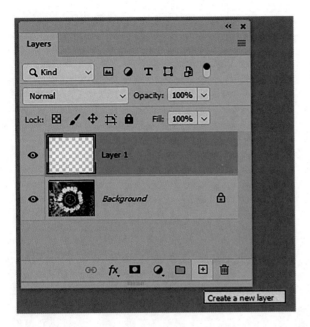

Figure 2-128. *Layers panel and the Create a new layer button*

Rename the layer as Blur by double-clicking the name and typing Blur and then clicking on the thumbnail on the layer to commit. Refer to Figure 2-129.

Figure 2-129. *Renaming a layer*

Blur Tool

The Blur tool allows you to blur or make fuzzy areas in an image, so that those areas appear out of focus. I like the way the camera created the background blur, but maybe I want to blur some other areas as well.

Blur Options

Look at the Options panel from left to right. Refer to Figure 2-130.

Figure 2-130. *The Blur tool's Options panel*

As with the Brush tool, the first section is used to store the tool presets, if there are any. If you have made certain changes to your Options panel, you can save and store them here to use on other projects. Currently this area contains no tool presets. Refer to Figure 2-131.

113

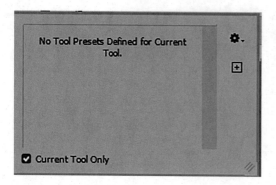

Figure 2-131. *Blur tool preset are empty*

Next, as you saw with the Brush tool, is the Brush Preset Picker. It allows you to change the size, hardness, angle, and roundness of the brush head. You can search for brushes, as well as create a new brush from your settings or a brush group just as you would from the Brushes panel. Often a bigger brush will result in a more visible blur. Refer to Figure 2-132.

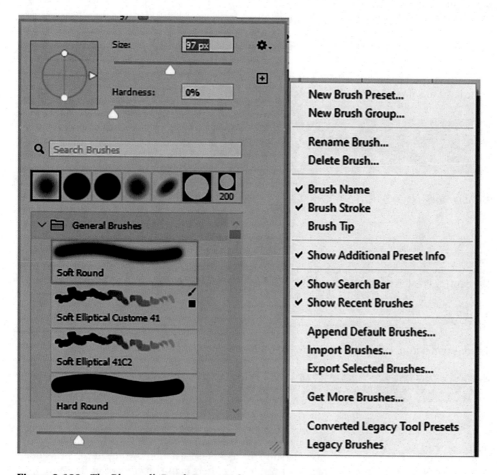

Figure 2-132. *The Blur tool's Brush Preset Picker options panel*

Select Soft Round with a Size of 97 pixels and Hardness of 0%.

The next button allows you to adjust the Brush settings in that panel. Refer to Figure 2-133.

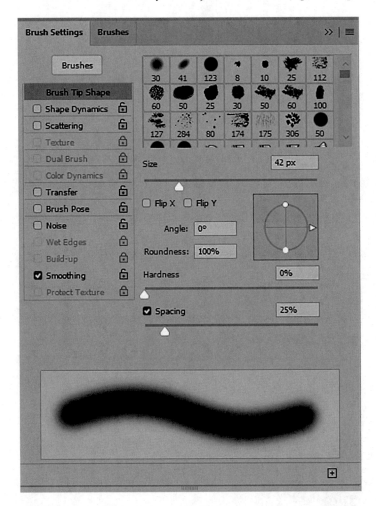

Figure 2-133. *Brush settings panel for the Blur tool*

Notice that some areas are greyed out and are not accessible, as they were with the Brush tool. You do, however, have access to the settings of Brush Tip Shape, Shape Dynamics, Scattering, Transfer, Brush Pose, Noise, and Smoothing. For details on those tabs, refer to earlier in the chapter about creating custom brush settings. Likewise, the accessible settings that you created earlier with your custom brush should be retained as you paint with the Blur tool.

The next section is for the mode or painting mode. This is similar to a brush and layers blending mode, but in this case for painting a blur. Refer to Figure 2-134.

Figure 2-134. *Blur tool options for painting blend mode*

You can review the previous brush blending modes earlier in the chapter, but here is an overview of the settings as they apply to the Blur tool:

- **Normal**: How the tool normally blurs

- **Darken**: Blurs and darkens the colors

- **Lighten**: Blurs and lightens the colors

- **Hue**: Blurs and alters the hue of the colors

- **Saturation**: Blurs and greys the colors

- **Color**: Blurs and alters the color to blend

- **Luminosity**: Blurs and alters the brightness of the colors

Let's paint in Normal mode for now.

Next, you can set the Strength for the blur stroke. By default, it is 50% but it can be reduced to 1% or increased to 100%. This will allow the blurring to appear slower or faster, increasing or reducing the amount of time you click and drag over an area holding down the mouse key. Refer to Figure 2-15.

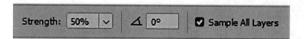

Figure 2-135. *Blur tool options for Strength, Angle, and Sample All Layers*

The angle is the same as what is set in the Brush Preset Picker dropdown menu (-180, 0, 180) when you alter the angle of the brush.

Sample All Layers is a very useful option in that you can work on a blank layer and paint your blur, without damaging the pixels on the background layer. This why the blank layer was created. Enable the checkbox and paint on the Blur layer with the Blur tool around the edge of the flower's petals, and you can then turn on and off the visibility of that layer to review the before and after. Refer to Figure 2-135 and Figure 2-136.

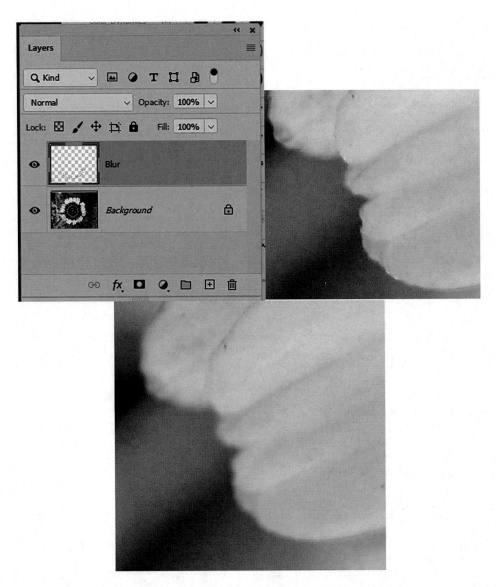

Figure 2-136. *Painting on the Blur layer when Sample All Layers is enabled so I don't alter the background layer. Without Blur and with Blur on the image*

■ **Note** Use your Zoom tool if you need to get closer to the flower. If you find that you are not noticing enough of a blur, then move the strength up to 80%. You may need to paint by dragging over an area a few times. Refer to Figure 2-137.

Figure 2-137. *Get closer to the image with the Zoom tool and increase the strength of the blur if it is not fast enough*

The last button in the Options panel is The Always use Pressure for Size button. This can be used to adjust the pressure of the blur and when off, the original brush preset will control the pressure instead. Click this button as well and continue to paint over the edge of the white petals. Refer to Figure 2-138.

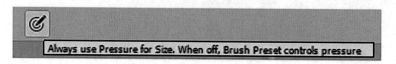

Figure 2-138. *Blur tool options for Pressure for Size*

■ **Tip** As with the Brush tool, you can click and then Shift+Click in a new location if you want a blur in a straight, direct line from point to point. Or you can hold down the Shift key and drag. Refer to Figure 2-139.

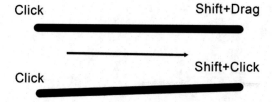

Figure 2-139. *Paint a straight line with the Blur tool*

Continue to paint around the edge of the flower to achieve the subtle blur you want. Then try some of the Blend modes to see if they improve the blur. They will be quite subtle compared to the Brush tool. Then set the Blend mode back to Normal. Refer to Figure 2-134.

Now try one of your custom brushes and see how it affects the blurring. I tried my Soft Scatter Brush, and it created a scattering of random blur areas on the blur layer. Refer to Figure 2-140.

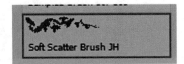

Soft Scatter Brush JH

Figure 2-140. *Painting a custom blur with the custom brush*

■ **Tip** Blurring can be localized if you use selection tools such as the Magic Wand tool when Sample All Layers is enabled in the Options panel and then click and Shift+Click on the image to create the selection and then add a layer mask. The layer mask can then be edited further with the Brush or Eraser tools, which I discuss regarding masks in more detail in my Photoshop Selections book. Refer to Figure 2-141.

Figure 2-141. *Use a selection to restrict or a layer mask to hide part of the blur*

■ **Note** If you set your Eraser tool to erase from history, then you can add to the blur in areas from a previous state. See Eraser tool options for more details. Refer to Figure 2-142.

Figure 2-142. *Remove part of the blur with your Eraser tool set to Erase to History*

You will see more intense blur-related filters in Chapter 8.

For now, turn off the visibility of the Blur layer and create a new layer and rename it Sharpen. Refer to Figure 2-143.

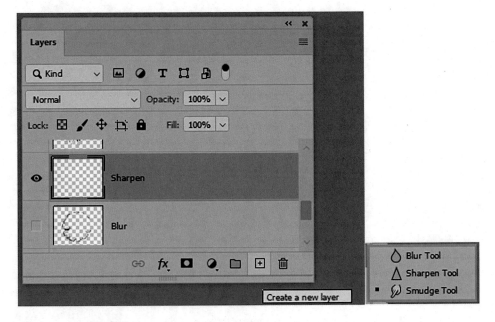

Figure 2-143. *Adding a new layer to test the Sharpen tool*

Select the Sharpen tool. Refer to Figure 2-143.

Sharpen Tool

The Sharpen tool, while not really used to create a warp or distort, can be used to adjust or correct blurs and make pixels appear slightly clearer. However, sometimes sharpening too much can make the image appear grainy and pixelated.

Sharpen Tool Options

Much of what you saw in the Blur tool's Options panel is the same for the Sharpen tool. I will just point out the key differences, and you can refer to the Blur tool for more details. Look at the Options panel from left to right. Refer to Figure 2-144.

Figure 2-144. *Options panel for the Sharpen tool*

The first section allows you to save and store presets for your tool.

After the Sharpen tool presets is the Brush Preset Picker, which has the same settings as the Brushes panel. Often a bigger brush will result in a more visible sharpen. Set the Size to 97 px and Hardness to 0% so that the sharpening is gradual and not too distinct along the edges and use a General Brushes brush of Soft Round. Refer to Figure 2-145.

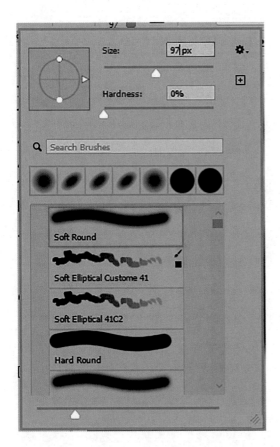

Figure 2-145. *Brush Preset Picker setting for the Sharpen tool*

Brush settings are the same as for the Blur tool. Likewise, the accessible setting that you created earlier with your custom brush should be retained as you paint with the Sharpen tool. Refer to Figure 2-146.

Figure 2-146. *Brush settings available for the Sharpen tool*

The next section is for the mode or painting mode. You can review the following brush blending modes earlier in the chapter, but here is an overview of the settings as they apply to the Sharpen tool. Refer to Figure 2-144

- **Normal**: How the tool normally sharpens
- **Darken**: Sharpens and darkens the colors
- **Lighten**: Sharpens and lightens the colors
- **Hue**: Sharpens and alters the hue of the colors
- **Saturation**: sharpens and greys the colors
- **Color**: Sharpens and alters the color to blend
- **Luminosity**: Sharpens and alters the brightness of the colors

Let's paint in Normal mode for now.

Next, you can set the strength for the sharpen. By default, it is 50% but it can be reduced to 1% or increased to 100%. This will allow the sharpen to appear slower or faster, increasing or reducing the amount of time you click and drag over an area. Let's leave it at 50% so you can see the sharpen happen gradually as you hold down the mouse and drag around the center of the flower image or other areas you want to sharpen. Refer to Figure 2-147.

Figure 2-147. *Sharpen options for Strength, Angle, Sample All Layer, and Protect Detail*

The angle is the same as what is set in the Brush Preset Picker dropdown when you alter the angle of the brush.

Sample All Layers is a very useful option in that you can work on a blank layer and with paint without damaging the pixels on the background layer. Now paint on the Sharpen layer in the center of the flower with the Sharpen tool and then turn on and off the visibility of that layer to review the before and after. Refer to Figure 2-148.

Figure 2-148. *The Sharpen tool before and after use on the center of flower*

You will notice that the image now appears clearer and sharper in the center and even brighter than before.

Make sure to keep Protect detail enabled so that you minimize pixelation while protecting details. Refer to Figure 2-147.

The last button in the options panel is Always use Pressure for Size. This button can be used to adjust the pressure of the sharpen. When off, the original brush preset will control the pressure instead. Refer to Figure 2-149.

Figure 2-149. *Sharpen tool option called Always use Pressure for Size*

Click this button to compare how it effects the sharpening. The change may be subtle, depending on what brush is used.

■ **Tip** As with the Brush tool, you can click and then Shift+Click in another location if you want a blur in a straight, direct line from point to point. Refer to Figure 2-139.

As with the Blur tool, sharpening can be localized, if you use selections such as the Elliptical Marquee tool and add a Layer Mask, which I discuss in more detail in my Photoshop Selections book. Refer to Figure 2-150.

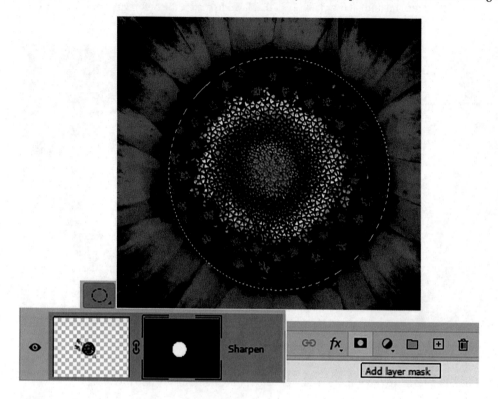

Figure 2-150. *Use a selection to restrict or a layer mask to hide part of the sharpened area*

Now, as you did with the Blur tool, try one of your custom brushes with different painting blending modes to see how they affect the sharpening. I tried my Soft Scatter Brush and it created a scattering of random areas of sharpening on the sharpen layer. I found some blending modes to be more subtle in sharpening, so I will return back to the Normal blend mode. Refer to Figure 2-151.

Figure 2-151. *Painting a custom sharpen with the custom brush*

You will see other sharpening-related filters briefly in Chapter 8.

For now, hide the visibility of the Sharpen layer and create a new Layer in the Layers panel and name it Smudge. Then select the Smudge tool. Refer to Figure 2-152.

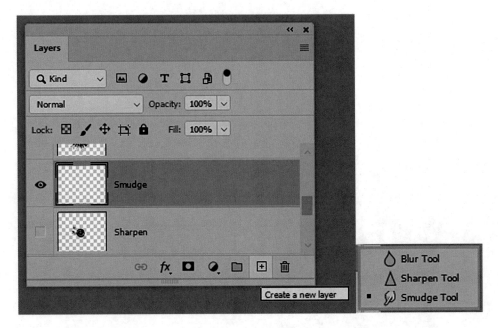

Figure 2-152. *Adding a new layer to test the Smudge tool*

Smudge Tool

The Smudge tool is definitely a tool for warping and distorting parts of an image. It is in some ways like the Mixer Brush tool I mentioned briefly earlier in the chapter. Refer to Figure 2-152 and Figure 2-153.

Figure 2-153. *The Mixer Brush tool shares some similarities to the Smudge tool but smears color, not pixels*

The difference is that it alters pixels, rather than foreground colors from the Tools panel or color picker. You will drag the mouse up and down on the petals to smudge.

Much of what you saw in the Blur tool options panel is the same for the Smudge tool. I will just point out the key differences, and you can refer to the Blur tool for more details.

Smudge Tool Options

Moving from left to right, the first section allows you to save and store presets for your tool. Refer to Figure 2-154.

Figure 2-154. *Options panel for the Smudge tool*

Next is the Brush Preset Picker, which has the same settings as the Brush Tool options panel. Often a bigger brush will result in a more visible smudge. Set up the General Brushes Brush as Soft Round and a Size of 97 px and a Hardness of 0% for a nice smooth smudge. Refer to Figure 2-155.

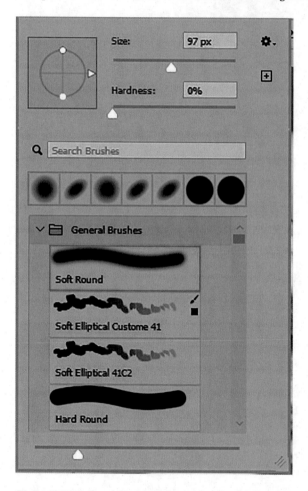

Figure 2-155. *Brush Preset Picker setting for the Smudge tool*

Brush settings are the same as for the Blur tool. Likewise, the accessible setting that you created earlier with your custom brush should be retained as you paint with the Smudge tool. Refer to Figure 2-156.

Figure 2-156. *Brush settings available for the Smudge tool*

The next section is for the mode or painting mode. You can review the following brush blending modes from earlier in the chapter, but here is an overview of the settings as they apply to the Smudge tool. Refer to Figure 2-154.

- **Normal**: How the tool normally smudges

- **Darken**: Smudges and darkens the colors

- **Lighten**: Smudges and lightens the colors

- **Hue**: Smudges and alters the hue of the colors

- **Saturation**: Smudges and greys the colors

- **Color**: Smudges and alters the color to blend

- **Luminosity**: Smudges and alters the brightness of the colors

Keep the mode on the setting of Normal for now.

Next, you can set the strength for the smudge stroke. By default, it is 50% but it can be reduced to 1% or increased to 100%. This will allow the smudge to appear slower or faster, increasing or reducing the amount of time you click and drag over an area. Keep it at the default of 50%. Refer to Figure 2-154.

Sample All Layers is a very useful option in that you can work on a blank layer and paint your smudge without damaging the pixels on the background layer. On your Smudge layer, use the Smudge tool on the petals and try smearing them outward gradually one at a time. Then you can then turn on and off the visibility of that layer to review the before and after. Refer to Figure 2-154 and Figure 2-157.

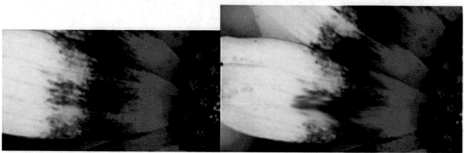

Figure 2-157. *Drag outward with your smudge brush to create a smudge of color*

Enabling the Finger Painting checkbox creates a darker yet more fluid smear. By default, it is disabled so you can uncheck it afterwards to return to normal smearing. Refer to Figure 2-158.

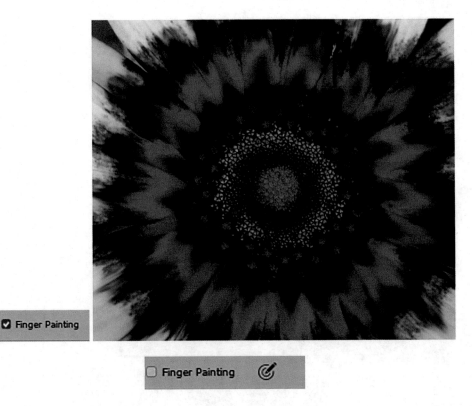

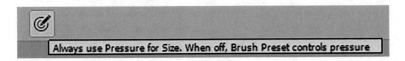

Figure 2-158. *Enable Finger Painting mode in the Options panel for a more dramatic smudge*

The Always use Pressure for Size button can be used to adjust the pressure of the smudge; when off, the original brush preset will control the pressure instead. Refer to Figure 2-159.

Figure 2-159. *Smudge Tool option of Always use Pressure for Size*

Click this button to compare how it affects the smudging. The change may be subtle depending on what brush is used.

■ **Tip** As with the Brush tool, you can click and then Shift+Click in a new location if you want a smudge in a straight, direct line from point to point. Refer to Figure 2-139.

Like the Blur tool, smudges can be localized if you use selections like the Elliptical Marquee tool and add a Layer Mask, which I discuss in more detail in my Photoshop Selections book. The selected layer mask can also be inverted. (Ctrl/CMD+I). Refer to Figure 2-160.

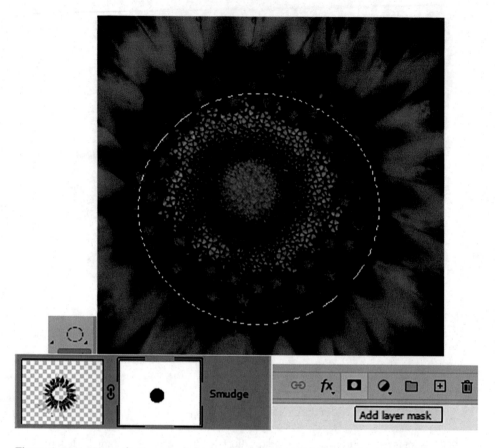

Figure 2-160. *Use a selection to restrict or a layer mask to hide part of the smudged area*

Now try one of your custom brushes and some different blending modes to see if it improves the smudge. I used the Soft Scatter Brush I created earlier in the chapter. This created some subtle, pointy smears. I found some blending modes to be very subtle so I will go back to the Normal blend mode. Refer to Figure 2-161.

Figure 2-161. *Painting a custom smudge with the custom brush*

You can at this point File ➤ Save Ctrl/CMD+S your document as a .psd file so that you can review the changes you made on each layer. You can refer to `CH2_IMG_3348_final.psd` to see my progression. Refer to Figure 2-162.

Figure 2-162. *Flower with Blur, Sharpen, and Smudge painting on separate layers*

You will see other smudge-related filters in Chapters 8 and 9.

Other Tools to Enhance or Correct Distorts

While working with the Brush, Eraser, Blur, and Smudge tools you can use other tools that help you adjust your colors after creating these distorts. They include the Dodge (O), Burn (O), and Sponge (O) tools. Refer to Figure 2-163.

Figure 2-163. *Tools panel showing the Dodge, Burn, and Sponge tools*

They too can use some of the brush settings we created earlier. But keep in mind that they cannot work on blank separate layers, only on the current layer that contains pixels. So, if you are not sure how the results will look on your image, I recommend painting with them on a duplicate layer by dragging the layer over the Create a new layer icon or by creating a copy of your file. Refer to Figure 2-164.

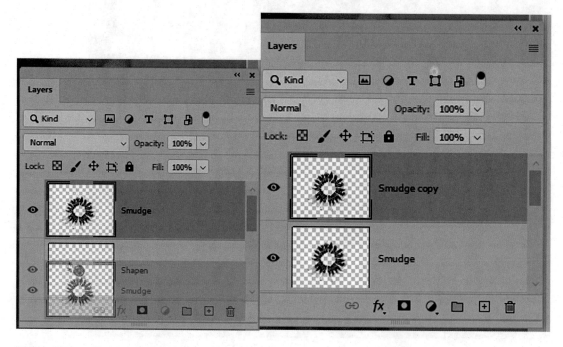

Figure 2-164. *Create a duplicate of the layer in the Layers panel to test tools*

And use the History panel if you need to revert a step while practicing with these tools. Refer to Figure 2-165.

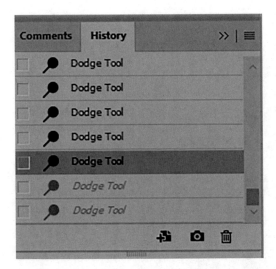

Figure 2-165. *Use your History panel to go back a step or two while practicing with a tool*

I will just talk briefly about these three tools and uses. You can view their settings in the Options panel when you select each tool.

■ **Note** If you want to test these next tools, just make copies of your smudge layer and test the tools one at a time. Make sure to rename each layer to remind yourself what current tool is you are using.

Dodge Tool

The Dodge tool is used to lighten the areas of an image without affecting the hue or saturation. You can see the options in the Options panel from left to right.

Dodge Tool Options

After the Tool presets and brush preset picker is the Brush Settings panel area, and it has many of the options of the Brush tool except for working with color dynamics, which is not accessible. Refer to Figure 2-166.

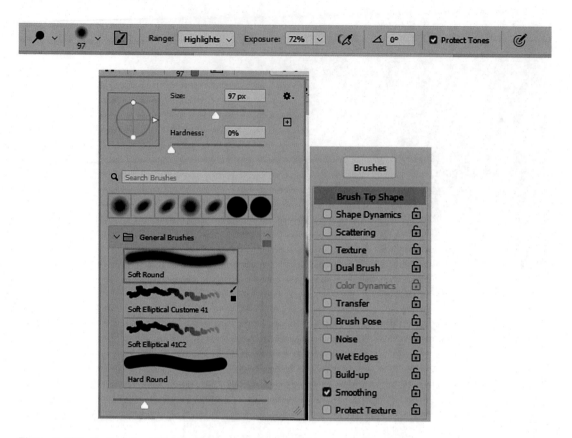

Figure 2-166. *Options panel for the Dodge tool and its brush presets and available settings*

For range or painting mode, you set what you want to target the highlights, midtones, or shadows and then you click and drag over the image. The exposure of the stroke can be set from 1-100%; by default, it is set to 72%. In this example, I used the mode setting of Highlights to brighten up the yellow I recently smudged. Refer to Figure 2-166 and Figure 2-167.

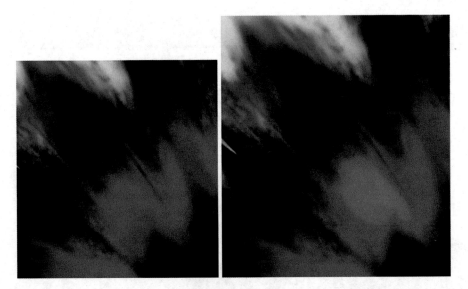

Figure 2-167. *Before and after using the Dodge tool to brighten the yellow area of the flower*

Then enable the airbrush style to build up effects as you would with the Brush tool.

The angle is the same as what you set in the Brush Preset Picker. Refer to Figure 2-166.

The Protect Tones option, when enabled, minimizes clipping in shadows and highlights, and keeps the color from shifting hue. Refer to Figure 2-168.

Figure 2-168. *Smudge tool options for Protect Tones and Always use Pressure for Size*

The Always use Pressure for Size button can be used to adjust the pressure of the dodge; when off, the original brush presets control the pressure instead.

For more details on using this tool, refer to this link: `https://helpx.adobe.com/photoshop/using/tool-techniques/dodge-tool.html`.

Now try your custom brush or just use a General Brushes: Soft Round Brush to create the dodge.

Burn Tool

The Burn tool does the opposite of the Dodge tool and is used to darken the areas of an image without affecting the hue or saturation. You can see the options in the Options panel.

Burn Tool Options

After the tool presets is the Brush Preset Picker. The Brush Settings panel area has many of the same options as the Brush tool except for working with color dynamics, which is not accessible. Refer to Figure 2-169.

Figure 2-169. *Options panel for the Burn tool*

For range or painting mode, you can set what you want to target the highlights, midtones, or shadows when you click and drag over the image. The exposure of the stroke can be set from 1-100%. The default is 50%. I dragged the Burn tool around the purple-red areas to darken this area slightly in the midtones. Refer to Figure 2-170.

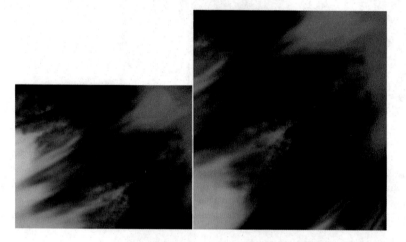

Figure 2-170. *Before and after using the Burn tool to darken the purple-red area of the flower*

Then enable the airbrush style to build up effects as you would with the Brush tool.

The angle is the same as what you set in the Brush Preset Picker. Refer to Figure 2-169.

Protect Tones, when enabled, minimizes clipping in the shadows and highlights, and keeps the color from shifting hue. Refer to Figure 2-171.

Figure 2-171. *Burn tool options for Protect Tones and Always use Pressure for Size*

The Always use Pressure for Size button can be used to adjust the pressure of the burn; when off, the original brush presets control the pressure instead. Refer to Figure 2-171.

For more details on the using this tool, refer to this link:

https://helpx.adobe.com/photoshop/using/tool-techniques/burn-tool.html.

Now try your custom brush or just use a General Brushes: Soft Round Brush to create the burn.

Sponge Tool

The Sponge tool is used to saturate or desaturate color in an image. You can see the options in the Options panel.

Sponge Tool Options

After the tool presets is the Brush Preset Picker. Next is the Brush Settings panel area, which has many of the same options as the Brush tool except for working with color dynamics, which is not accessible. Refer to Figure 2-172.

Figure 2-172. *Options panel for the Sponge tool*

For range or painting mode, you can set whether you want to saturate or desaturate from the list. Saturate brightens and desaturate dulls.

The flow rate of the stroke saturation change can be set from 1-100%. It is at the default of 50%.

Then enable the airbrush style to build up effects as you would with the Brush tool.

The angle is the same as what you set in the Brush Preset Picker. Refer to Figure 2-172.

Vibrance, when enabled, minimizes clipping for fully saturated or desaturated colors. Refer to Figure 2-173.

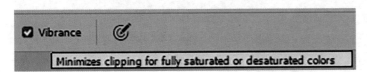

Figure 2-173. *Sponge tool options for Vibrance and Always use Pressure for Size*

The Always use Pressure for Size button can be used to adjust the pressure of the sponge; when off, the original brush presets control the pressure instead. Refer to Figure 2-173.

For more details on using this tool, refer to this link:

https://helpx.adobe.com/photoshop/using/change-color-saturation-sponge-tool.html.

Now try your custom brush or just use a General Brushes: Soft Round Brush to create the sponge effect.

Make sure to File ➤ Save your files at this point. You can refer to my file CH2_IMG_3348_final.psd and the Layer Smudge DBS to compare to the original smudge layer. Refer to Figure 2-174.

Figure 2-174. *Before and after using the Dodge, Burn, and Sponge tools on various areas of a copy of the Smudge layer*

History Brushes

Whether touching up or adding a distort, there are two other brush-related tools that are very useful. However, as a beginner, you may not be familiar with these tools or may have rarely used them. These tools work best on the background layer or the layer you are currently painting on with pixels. Refer to Figure 2-175. They are the following:

- History Brush (Y)
- Art History Brush (Y)

Figure 2-175. *Tools panel History and Art History Brush tools*

Let's look at what makes them different than the Brush tool.

History Brush

The History Brush tool can be used after you have already painted with other tools, to paint back or erase certain effects. Like the History Eraser setting, it restores the image back to an earlier state. Refer to Figure 2-176.

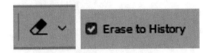

Figure 2-176. *Eraser tool options panel with Erase to History enabled*

History Brush Options

Many of the same options that are found in the Brush tool are found in the History Brush panel. I will just mention a few key differences. Look at the Options panel from left to right. Refer to Figure 2-177.

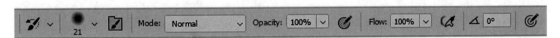

Figure 2-177. *Options panel for the History Brush*

First is the tool presets. Next is the Brush Preset Picker where you can set the brush size, hardness, angle, and roundness. Set a Size of 72 px and Hardness of 0% with a Soft Round Brush. Refer to Figure 2-178.

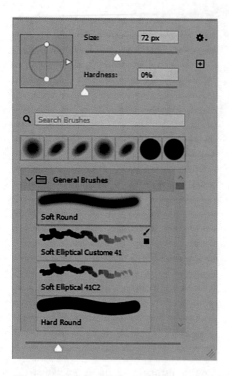

Figure 2-178. *Brush Preset Picker for Brush History panel*

Next is the link to the Brushes Settings panel. In this panel, you can use all of the settings of your custom brush except for color dynamics. Refer to Figure 2-179.

Figure 2-179. *Available brush settings for the History Brush*

As with the Brush tool, you can use the modes to try various blending painting modes; the default is Normal. Refer to the brush options and blend modes section of this chapter if you need to review the blending modes. Refer to Figure 2-180.

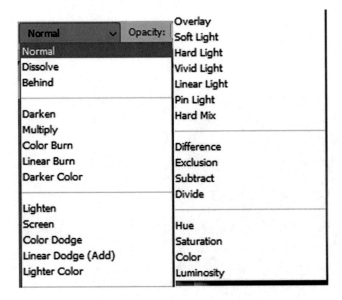

Figure 2-180. *History Brush paint blend mode options*

You can set the Opacity (1-100%), Always use Presure for Opacity when enabled, Flow rate for stroke (1-100%), Enable airbrush style build-up effects when enabled, and Brush Angle (-180, 0, +180°), which is the same as in the Brush Preset Picker.

The last option is Always use Pressure for Size; when off, the brush preset controls pressure. Refer to Figure 2-177.

■ **Tip** For a straight line, click and then Shift+Click in the next location. Refer to Figure 2-139.

To test, create a copy of your Smudge layer (drag over the Create new layer icon) and paint with a custom brush like the Soft Scatter one you created earlier with a size of 127 px. In areas where there are pixels, it will try to paint back to the orginal of the last history state found in the History panel. Refer to Figure 2-181.

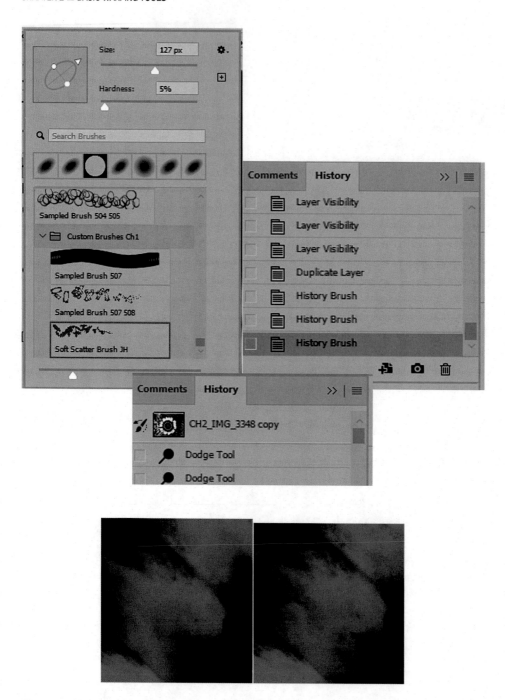

Figure 2-181. *Paint back parts of an image using your custom brush and the History panel's last state*

Make sure to File ➤ Save your files at this point.

And you can refer to my file CH2_IMG_3348_final.psd and the Smudge History layer to compare to the original Smudge layer normally and Smudge History 2 layer where I repeated the steps with different brush blending modes, some of which have more noticeable blends than others. Refer to Figure 2-182.

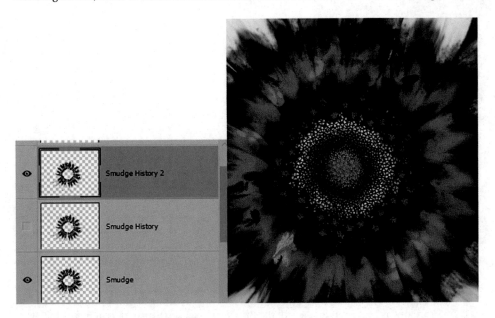

Figure 2-182. *Added brush effects using the History Brush tool and a custom brush on a copy of the Smudge layer*

Art History Brush Tool

The Art History Brush tool has many similarities to the Brush tool and the History Brush tool. Like the History Brush tool, it can restore a pixelated area to a previous state after using other brush tools first, but in a more spreading, artistic way. After you have created a custom brush, there are a few surprising effects the longer you hold down the brush with your mouse key.

Look at the Options panel from left to right. Refer to Figure 2-183.

Figure 2-183. *Options panel for the Art History Brush tool*

Art History Tool Options

First is the tool preset. The next is the Brush Preset Picker where you can set the brush size's hardness, angle, and roundness. Refer to Figure 2-183.

Then you see the link to the Brushes Settings panel. In this panel you can uses many of the settings except for Scattering, Dual brush, and Build-up. However, you can use Color Dynamics, which is not available to some previously mentioned Brush tools. Refer to Figure 2-184.

Figure 2-184. *Available options in the Brushes Settings panel for the Art History Brush*

As with the Brush tool, you can use the painting mode to try various painting blending modes. The default is Normal. There are not as many modes as with the Brush and History Brush tools. It has a similar amount to the Blur, Sharpen, and Smudge tools. You have access to Darken, Lighten, Hue, Saturation, Color, and Luminosity. Refer to the brush options and blend modes section of this chapter if you need to review the blending modes. Refer to Figure 2-185.

Figure 2-185. *Options for paint blending modes of the Art History Brush tool*

You can set the Opacity for the stroke (1-100%), and the Always use Presure for Opacity option. Refer to Figure 2-183.

The next section allows you to paint with a style to control the paint stroke's shape. There are various options of Tight, Loose, Medium, Long, Dab, and Curl strokes which, depending on the brush used, create different results. Refer to Figure 2-186.

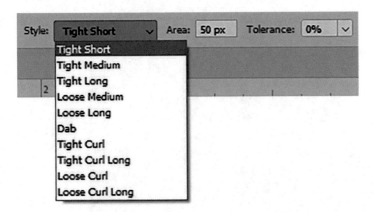

Figure 2-186. *Style, Area, and Tolerance options for the Art History Brush*

The Area is the painting area diameter of 0-500 px, and the Tolerance can be set from 0-100% to limit where the paint strokes will be applied.

Brush angle (-180, 0, +180°) is the same as in the Brush Preset Picker. Refer to Figure 2-183.

The last button is the Always use Pressure for Size button. When off, the brush preset controls the pressure. Refer to Figure 2-187.

Figure 2-187. *Art History Brush option named Always use Pressure for Size*

■ **Tip**   According to Adobe, the best way to work with the tool is to use the History panel and click the left column of the state or snapshot to use as the source for the History Brush and Art History Brush tool. A brush icon appears next to the source history state. Refer to Figure 2-188.

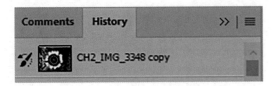

Figure 2-188. *History panel last state for the Art History Brush tool*

Working from a history state or snapshot then allows you to use your Eraser tool to erase from history.

For more details, go to https://helpx.adobe.com/photoshop/using/painting-stylized-strokes-art-history.html.

To test the Art History Brush, make a copy again of the Smudge Layer (drag the layer over the Create new layer icon) and use the custom Soft Scatter Brush at a size of 127 px and Hardness of 5%. Refer to Figure 2-189.

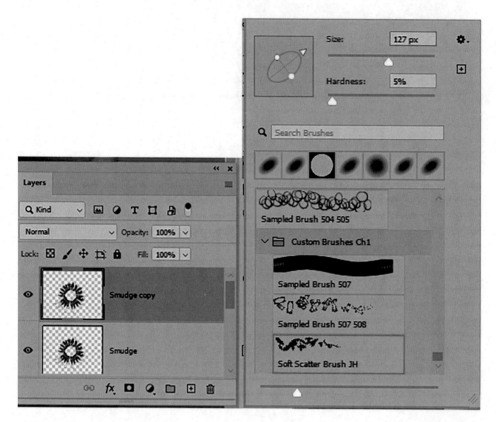

Figure 2-189. *Paint on a copy of the Smudge layer with your custom brush to test the Art History Brush tool*

Click once here and there over areas with the brush to create a scattering of color in Normal mode first, and then try other blend modes and styles, creating a colorful center like confetti. Refer to Figure 2-190.

Figure 2-190. *Before and after painting with the Art History Brush tool using various styles*

Make sure to File ➤ Save your document at this point.

You can refer to my file CH2_IMG_3348_final.psd and the Smudge Art History layer to compare to the original smudge layer.

Stamp and Healing Brush-Related Tools

The last set of tools that you can use with custom brushes are the Stamp tools. Refer to Figure 2-191. They include the following:

- Clone Stamp tool (S)

- Pattern Stamp tool (S)

Figure 2-191. *Clone and Pattern Stamp tools*

Clone Stamp Tool

The Clone Stamp tool is very similar to a brush. However, it is used to paint large or small areas of pixels from a cloned source. To select a source, you hold down the Alt/Option key and click the image on either the current layer or with a setting of Sample: current layers and below to gather the sample to paint the cloned pixels on the currently selected layer. Click elsewhere to cover the area you want with the source. I go into more detail in my book *Accurate Layer Selections Using Photoshop's Selection Tools* on its settings in the Options panel but the information you need to know now is in this chapter. Refer to Figure 2-192.

Figure 2-192. *Clone Stamp tool cloning a source location and then clicking in a new location to add the clone source pixels*

Clone Stamp Tool Options (Review)

From left to right, like the Brush tool after the tool presets, you can use many of the same options in the Brush Preset Picker and Brush Settings panel except for the Color Dynamics and Smoothing options. Refer to Figure 2-193.

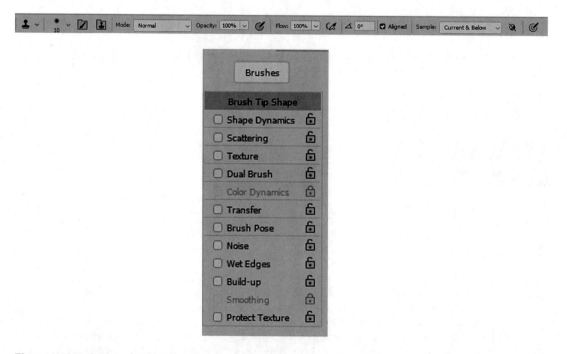

Figure 2-193. *Options for the Clone Stamp tool and available brush settings*

In addition, you can also use the Clone Source panel and have up to five cloning locations in other open documents, and you can set the rotation of the clone for a more realistic blend. Refer to Figure 2-194.

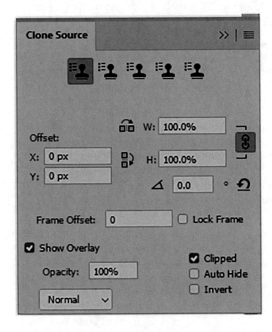

Figure 2-194. *Clone Source panel*

Like other brush tools, there is also a blending effect mode that can affect how the clone appears when stamped. Refer to the brush options and blend modes section of this chapter if you need to review the blending modes. Refer to Figure 2-195.

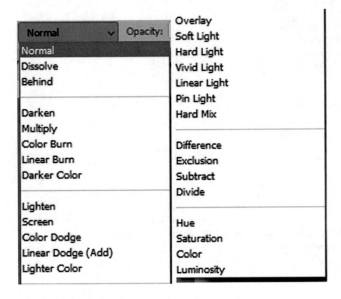

Figure 2-195. *Effect Blending Mode options for the Clone Stamp tool*

Next you can set the Opacity for Stroke (1-100%) and then Always use pressure for Opacity when enabled, Flow rate for stroke (1-100%), Enable airbrush style build-up effects when enabled, and Brush angle (-180, 0, +180), which is the same as the Brush Preset Picker. Aligned, when enabled, allows for same offset for each stroke when painting with the clone source. Refer to Figure 2-196.

Figure 2-196. *Clone Stamp options*

The last section list menu is Sample from either: Current layer, Current and Below, or All Layers. Beside this list is the currently disabled icon "Turn on to ignore adjustment Layers when Cloning." The last button is Always use Pressure for Size. When off, the brush preset controls pressure. Refer to Figure 2-196.

Here you can see how stamping with a custom brush on a blank new layer using the sample area of Current & Below and then Alt/Option clicking on a location with the custom Soft Scatter Brush created earlier, and then clicking in a new location, can cause a scattering of color and image depending on what effect blending mode is used. Refer to Figure 2-197.

Figure 2-197. *Testing the Clone Stamp tool with a custom brush and effect blending modes*

Make sure to File ➤ Save your document at this point.
You can refer to my file CH2_IMG_3348_final.psd and the Clone Stamp layer.

Pattern Stamp Tool

The Pattern Stamp Tool allows you to stamp a pattern with your custom brush, and we will look at this tool in Chapter 3. However, it has many of the same options as the Brush tool including tool presets, Brush Preset Picker, Brush Settings link, Effect blending modes (see the brush options and blend modes section), Opacity for stroke (1-100%) and its pressure icon, flow rate (1-100%), Airbrush icon, Brush Angle (-180, 0, +180), and Control Pressure for Size on the far right. Refer to Figure 2-198.

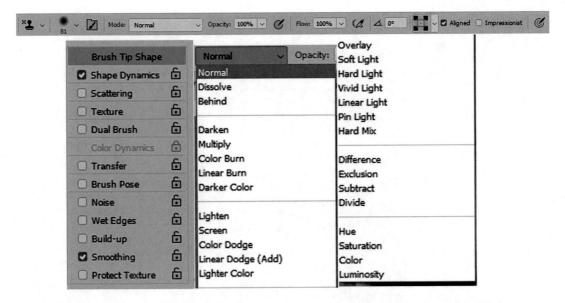

Figure 2-198. *Options panel for the Pattern Stamp tool, available brush settings, and effect blend modes*

In Chapter 3, we will look at pattern, alignment, and the impressionist settings.

Notes on Healing Tools

Then there is another set known as the Healing tools, but not every tool uses brushes. Refer to Figure 2-199.

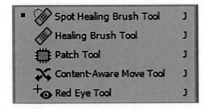

Figure 2-199. *Tools panel showing the Spot Healing Brush, Healing Brush, Patch, Content-Aware Move, and Red Eye Tools*

The Spot Healing Brush Tool (J), while it might appear to be part of the stamp collection, cannot use any of the Brushes settings, only the Size, Hardness, Spacing, Angle Adjustment, and Roundness of the Brush. Refer to Figure 2-200.

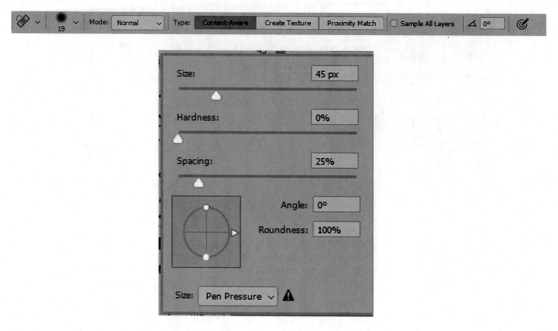

Figure 2-200. *Options panel for the Spot Healing tool and Brush options*

The Healing Brush tool (J), while it might appear to be part of Stamp collection, cannot use any of the Brush settings only the Size, Hardness, Spacing, Angle Adjustment, and Roundness of the brush. However, you can use the Clone Source panel with this tool. We will revisit this tool in more detail in Chapter 3 as it relates to patterns. Refer to Figure 2-201.

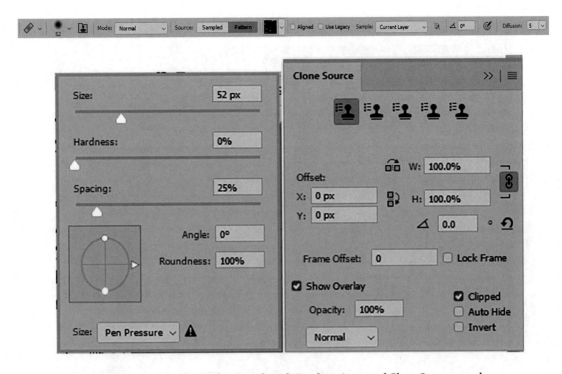

Figure 2-201. *Options panel for the Healing Brush tool, Brush options, and Clone Source panel*

Finally, it should be mentioned that while the Patch Tool, Content-Aware Move Tool, and Red Eye Tool are a part of the healing tool collection for cosmetic touch-ups, they do not use any brush tool settings and are not relevant to this chapter. However, the Patch tool will be briefly mentioned in Chapter 3 as it relates to patterns. You'll explore the Content-Aware tool in Chapter 7 and the Red Eye tool in Chapter 9.

For reference on healing tools, refer to `https://helpx.adobe.com/photoshop/using/retouching-repairing-images.html`.

Project: A Review of the Perspective Crop Tool

In my book *Accurate Layer Sections using Photoshop's Selection Tools*, I talk about selection tools as well as how to use the Crop tool to reduce the size of the page. I also demonstrate the Perspective Crop tool, which you can review in detail in Chapter 4 of that book. It is very useful for when you want to correct a distort rather than create one, as I will demonstrate here.

File ➤ Open the file `CH2_IMG_2577_Chicken_painting.psd` and Image ➤ Duplicate for practice. Click OK to the dialog box message. Refer to Figure 2-202.

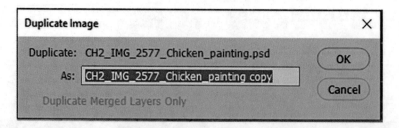

Figure 2-202. *Duplicate Image dialog box and a painting of chickens with a slight keystone distortion*

Select the Perspective Crop Tool (C) from the Tools panel. Refer to Figure 2-203.

Figure 2-203. *Tools panel showing the Crop tool and Perspective Crop tool*

Perspective Crop Tool Options

Refer here to the Options panel and look from left to right. In this area, you can adjust the preset, width, height, swap the width and height measurements, and change the resolution to pixels/inches or pixels/cm from the dropdown menu.

The Front Image button uses values from the front image. The Clear button allows you to reset the width, height, and resolution values and you have the option of showing or hiding the grid with the checkbox. Refer to Figure 2-204.

Figure 2-204. *Options panel for the Perspective Crop tool*

In this example, besides cropping, we can see a slight keystone distortion and a slight angle tilt because I was not able to photograph the image straight on without my shadow getting in the way. I did, however, make sure to take a picture of this artwork on a grid so that it would help me to line up the sides better. I also used the grid lines in my camera so that it was not too misaligned. Nevertheless, the keystone effect makes the picture appear trapezoid rather than rectangular, so we need to correct this.

To do so, do not enter any settings in the Options panel. Instead, on the canvas, just click the four points as shown in the diagram and then adjust each bounding box point to match mine in the picture by dragging each corner individually. Refer to Figure 2-205.

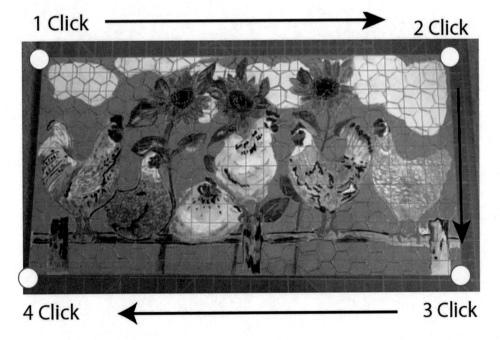

Figure 2-205. *Click out the grid with the Perspective Crop tool*

■ **Note** If you need to zoom in to adjust the bounding box handles, do not use the Zoom tool or you may get a warning message. Click Cancel to remain with the Perspective Crop tool if you do this by accident. Refer to Figure 2-206.

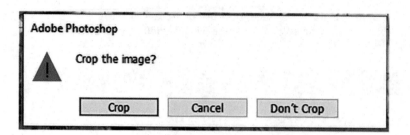

Figure 2-206. *Warning message if you select another tool while using the Perspective Crop tool*

■ Instead, use the key commands of Ctrl/CMD+ + and then hold down the spacebar to access the Hand tool and move around without disturbing the grid. Use Ctrl/CMD + – or Ctrl/CMD +0 to zoom out again. Refer to Figure 2-207.

Figure 2-207. *Use a key command instead if you need to access the Hand tool rather than selecting it from the Tools panel*

In the Options panel, two new button icons will appear on the right; the circle with the slash through it will cancel the crop. Click the check to commit the crop. Refer to Figure 2-208.

Figure 2-208. *Click the check in the Options panel to commit the perspective crop*

You can now see how this stretched the images in some areas, and corrected the keystone distort and angle while cropping the image at the same time. Refer to Figure 2-209.

Figure 2-209. *The keystone effect is removed from the chicken painting and the image is cropped*

File ➤ Save your document as a .psd file with your initials and click Save to commit. Refer to Figure 2-210.

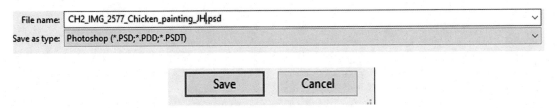

Figure 2-210. *Make sure to save your work as you complete each project with the Save As dialog box*

You can see my final file, CH2_IMG_2577_Chicken_painting_final.psd.

Later, you will look at more complex distorts in Chapters 4 through 8. In Chapter 9, you will look at advanced lens correcting filters for distortion.

___

■ **Note**   I saved a copy of the brushes used in this chapter as an .abr file that you can find in this chapter's folder.

___

Summary

In this chapter, you looked at several brush settings and how they relate to custom brush creation. After creating custom brushes, you also looked at many of the brush tools that can utilize these brush setting presets, such as Blur, Sharpen, Smudge, History Brushes, and Clone Stamps. They allow you to continue to warp and distort in different artistic ways based on choices made in the tool's Options panel. You saw how to use many of these brushes in a non-destructive way by painting on a blank or copy layer so that the original was not destroyed. Finally, you looked at the Perspective Crop tool as another basic warping tool that you can use to correct basic keystone and angle distorts at the same time. In the next chapter, you will look at some more tools and hidden features for pattern creation.

CHAPTER 3

■ ■ ■

Warping with Patterns

Chapter goal: Look at different ways that repeating patterns can be created and then warped.

Pattern creation is probably one of the more interesting and novel things you can do with a program like Photoshop. Patterning can be used for a variety of projects, including but not limited to

- Backgrounds for websites and printed materials

- Surfaces of parts of a selection of a design

- Styles that can be applied to text or lettering

So, what are some tools that can be used to create patterns?

In this chapter, you'll look at the Options panel for some tools that you should now be familiar with from the previous chapter (the Brush, Pencil, and Eraser tools) and you'll look at how they can be used with the symmetry paint option and the Paths panel. Then you'll do a brief review of the Pen tools, Path Selection tools, and Shape tools, and see how vector shapes can be made into a pattern. Next, you'll take a scanned pattern and use the Offset filter and Clone Stamp tool to adjust the pattern. Then you'll look at how the Libraries panel can be used for pattern generation. After creating the patterns, you'll then look at how to reuse stored patterns, either for patterned backgrounds or textures in adjustment fill layers or layer styles. Lastly, you will look at how patterns can be used with some tools and then look at how to create a custom texture for the Filter Gallery, which you'll explore in Chapter 8.

■ **Note**   You can find the projects for this chapter in the Chapter 3 folder.

File ➤ Open the blank file CH3_SymmetryPaint.psd and make an Image ➤ Duplicate as you did in Chapter 2 to practice. Refer to Figure 3-1.

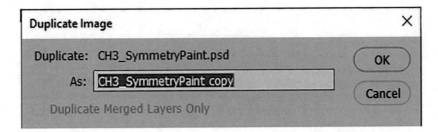

Figure 3-1. *Duplicate Image dialog box*

This file has a blank layer for you to paint on, but you can create more if you need to while painting and testing patterns. Refer to Figure 3-2.

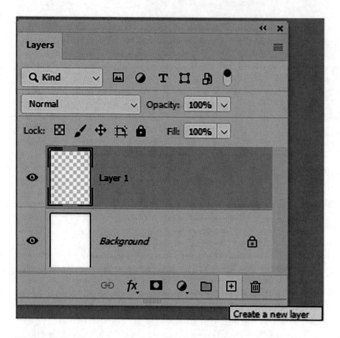

Figure 3-2. *Create a new layer in the Layers panel to paint on*

Basic Pattern Creation

The first tool we are going to use for pattern creation may not be very obvious at first. In the Tools panel for the Brush tool (B), Pencil tool (B), and Eraser tool (E), look for the symmetry paint icon (the butterfly) that is found in Options panel in the far right. Refer to Figure 3-3.

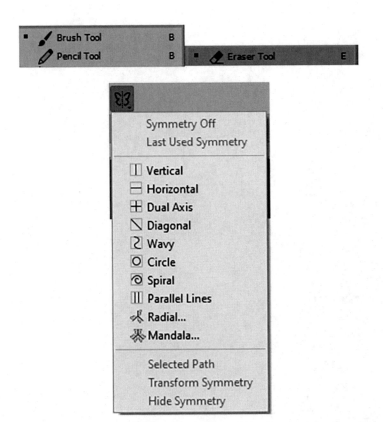

Figure 3-3. *Symmetry paint options for the Brush, Pencil, and Eraser tools*

As you know, the Brush and Pencil tools are for drawing and the Eraser tool is for removing parts of the painting. However, when a choice of symmetry paint is made from the dropdown menu, you can begin to create a pattern. To start, select your Brush tool from the Tools panel and first use a Brush Picker Preset of General Brushes Hard Round. Refer to Figure 3-4.

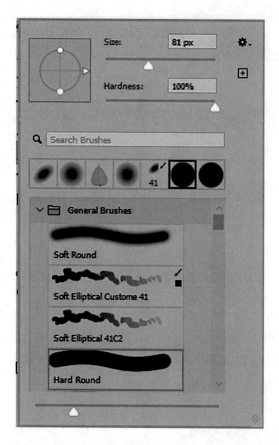

Figure 3-4. *Brush Preset Picker and Hard Round Brush selected*

As you progress with symmetry paint, you can alter the size, hardness, roundness, angle, or switch to a custom brush that you created in Chapter 2. Everyone's pattern will be different.

To start using symmetry paint, just choose settings from your Brush Options panel as you did in Chapter 2. Then change your foreground color in the Tools panel using the Color Picker. When you click on the color in the Tools panel, choose a color and click OK to exit. Refer to Figure 3-5.

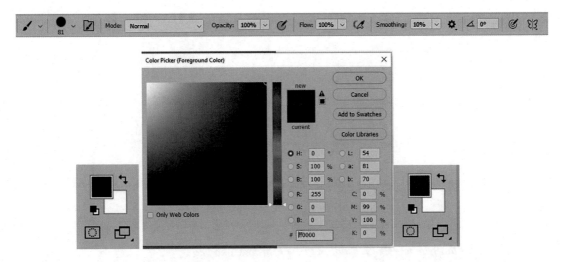

Figure 3-5. *Options panel for Brush and changing the foreground color in the Tools panel with the Color Picker*

I will keep the Painting mode on Normal and Opacity at 100%, Flow at 100%, and Smoothing at 10% with the other icon buttons for pressure disabled and for the moment paint with a black foreground (Press D), but later I'll use my Color Picker to switch to other colors. Refer to Figure 3-5.

Then choose one of the symmetry paths. The default options are

- Vertical

- Horizonal

- Dual Axis

- Diagonal

- Wavy

- Circle

- Spiral

- Parallel Lines

- Radial

- Mandala

For example, if you choose the first option of Vertical, temporarily the Transform options of the Path will open. We will be looking at the Transform Options panel more in Chapter 4. I will just give a quick overview here. Refer to Figure 3-6.

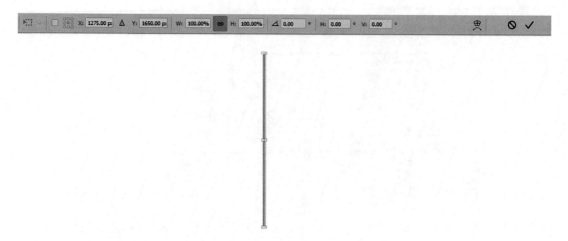

Figure 3-6. *Setting the Symmetry Paint Guide in the Transform Option panel*

This area allows you to move, scale, and rotate the path, and you can use your mouse and bounding box handles to do that as well. You can even warp the path by switching from the warp transform options, which will be looked at more in Chapter 4, and continue to move the bounding box handles to add a curve. Refer to Figure 3-7.

Figure 3-7. *Options panel in Warp settings to warp the path*

In this case, just click the check to commit the default transform settings in the Options panel for now. Refer to Figure 3-8.

Figure 3-8. *Click the check in the Options panel to commit the settings for the path*

Then, with the vertical path, begin to paint your symmetry path on your blank Layer 1. I made a crisscross pattern that resembles a shoelace. Refer to Figure 3-9.

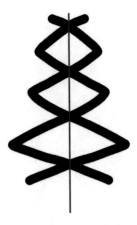

Figure 3-9. *Brush painting vertical symmetry path*

If at any point you need to alter the path from the menu, choose Transform Symmetry to enter the transform dialog options again. Refer to Figure 3-10.

Figure 3-10. *Transform Symmetry path option selected*

Now take a moment on the new layer to try painting some of the other symmetry paths. Just select another from the list and click the check in the Transform options to commit. Remember to show or hide the visibility of your layer to compare your results and you can rename them (double-click the name and type) to keep track of your progress. Refer to Figure 3-11.

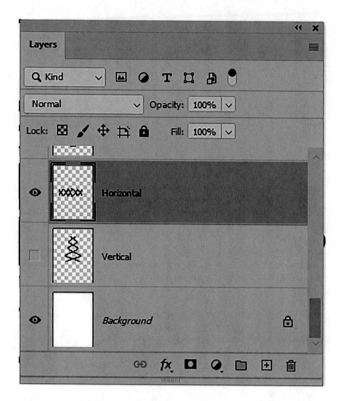

Figure 3-11. *Painting a different symmetry path on a new layer to test it*

Below are my results using Horizontal, Dual Axis, Diagonal, Wavy, Circle, and Spiral. Refer to Figure 3-12.

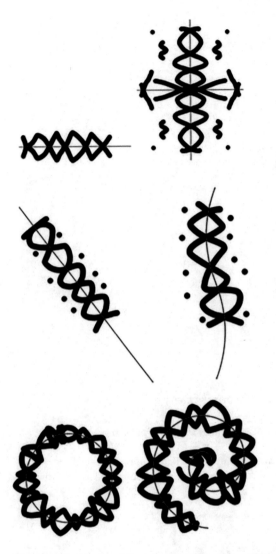

Figure 3-12. *Testing different symmetry paths with the Brush tool*

You may notice at this point that while straight or wavy lines are more predictable, a closed path can be unpredictable and if you try creating a straight line (Click and then Shift+Click in a new location) you can sometimes end up with unpredictable results. You may need to practice a few times to master a closed path like a circle. I find it is just better to drag slowly along the path in single strokes. And use your History panel to go back a step if you make a mistake. Refer to Figure 3-13.

Figure 3-13. *Use the History panel to undo steps as you paint with a symmetry path*

Create two more blank layers, one for Radial and the other for Mandala, and paint one at a time on those layers as you select either option.

Each of these layers will ask you what segment count you want to use. Radial allows 2-12, Mandala 3-10. Choose a number and click OK and then click the check in the Options panel to commit. Refer to Figure 3-14.

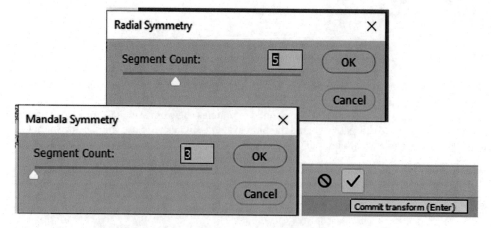

Figure 3-14. *Radial and Mandala Symmetry dialog boxes. Click in the Options panel to commit the transformation of the path*

Radial brushes will repeat a single brush stroke around the center point or radial axis. Refer to Figure 3-15.

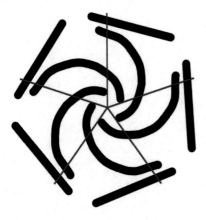

Figure 3-15. *Radial symmetry paint with Brush tool*

The mandala, while like the radial, first mirrors and then repeats a single brush stroke around the center point or radial axis. Refer to Figure 3-16.

Figure 3-16. *Mandala symmetry paint with Brush tool*

■ **Note** If you are working with the paths and need to hide them temporarily, choose Hide Symmetry from the list and Show Symmetry to make visible. Refer to Figure 3-17.

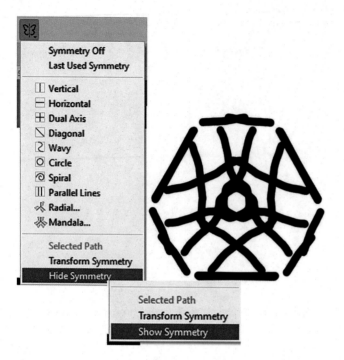

Figure 3-17. *Hide and show options for the symmetry paint path*

The Last Used Symmetry option will return to the previous used symmetry path (in this case, radial) if you want to switch symmetry paths. I tried it with a new brush color on a duplicate layer of my Mandala pattern. Refer to Figure 3-17 and Figure 3-18.

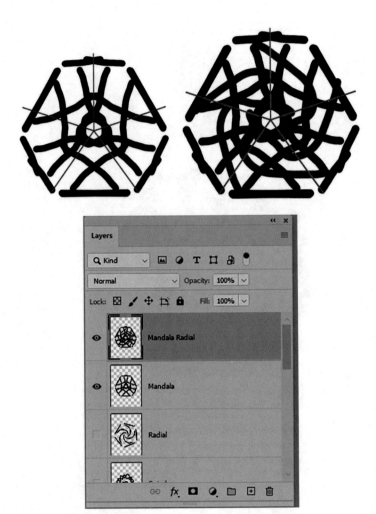

Figure 3-18. *Continue to paint on a layer with the last used symmetry path*

If you need to erase part of your path in a symmetry mode, switch to your Eraser tool or Pencil tool to draw some thinner lines. I also changed to a 10-segment count rather than the default 5. Refer to Figure 3-19.

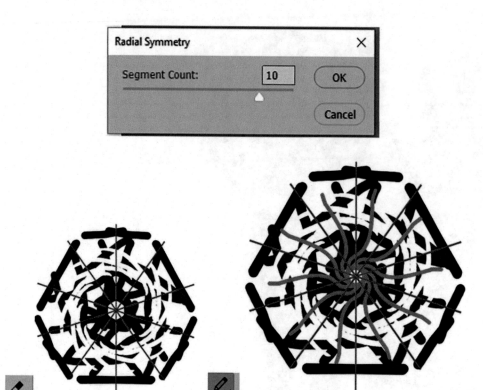

Figure 3-19. *Paint with a new radial symmetry path with your Eraser or Pencil tool*

You can even paint with the custom brushes you created in Chapter 2. Refer to Figure 3-20.

Figure 3-20. *Paint a new symmetry path with your custom brush*

When you are done using the symmetry paths, choose Symmetry Off to return to normal brush, pencil, or eraser modes. Refer to Figure 3-21.

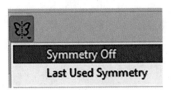

Figure 3-21. *Select the Symmetry Off option in the Options panel to return to normal paint mode*

However, we will just keep it on symmetry paint for the moment as we work on the next part of the project.

Project: Create a Custom Symmetry Paint Path

After experimenting with default symmetry paint paths, you may want to create a custom path. Another way this can be done is by using the Paths panel.

Use your Brush tool again with a General Brushes of Hard Round. Refer to Figure 3-22.

Figure 3-22. *Options panel for the Brush tool*

To create a path, you need to make sure that you have the Paths panel visible and the Pen tool selected. Refer to Figure 3-23.

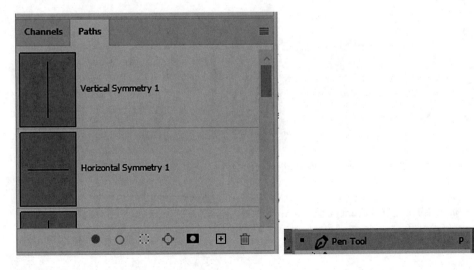

Figure 3-23. *Use the Paths panel and the Pen tool to create a custom path*

I talk about path creation in detail in my book *Accurate Layer Selections Using Photoshop's Selection Tools.*

To create a simple open or closed path, make sure that the mode of the Pen tool is set to Path in the Options panel. Refer to Figure 3-24.

Figure 3-24. *Options panel for the Pen tool set to Path mode*

Then refer to the Paths panel. In your case, you may have several paths already in the Paths panel if you were experimenting with symmetry paint. Refer to Figure 3-25.

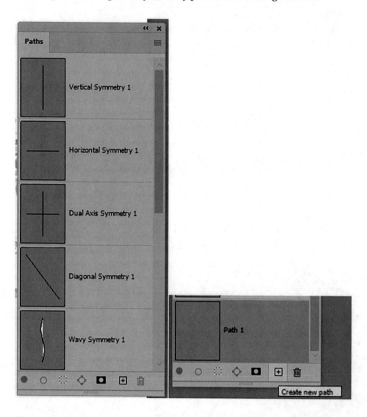

Figure 3-25. *Create a new path and select it in the Paths panel*

Click the Create new path button and select the Path 1 path only. Refer to Figure 3-25.

Create a new blank layer in the Layers panel and turn off the visibility of your other test layers, other than the background layer. Refer to Figure 3-26.

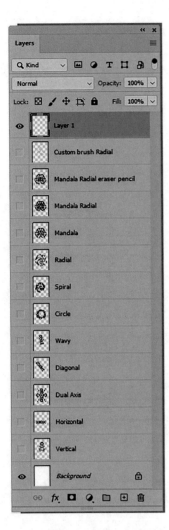

Figure 3-26. *Create a new blank layer before you create your custom path*

With the Pen tool, click out a similar closed path like I have made here, like a triangle. Then, from the Paths panel menu, choose Make Symmetry Path. Refer to Figure 3-27.

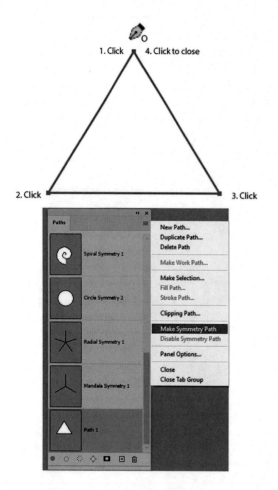

Figure 3-27. *Once the path is created with the Pen tool, from the Path menu choose Make Symmetry Path*

You may get a warning message saying that the symmetry path is not supported by the Pen tool or other unsupported tools and may be hidden. Click OK. Refer to Figure 3-28.

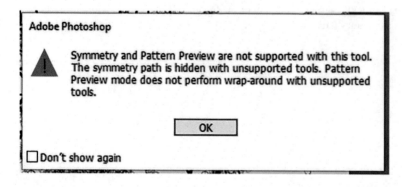

Figure 3-28. *Alert message about using a symmetry path while using the Pen tool*

This makes the Path 1 into a custom symmetry path. You can see that by the small butterfly symbol in the thumbnail in the lower right. Refer to Figure 3-29.

Figure 3-29. *Symmetry path icon in the Paths panel*

Now return to the Brush tool with symmetry paint on and try painting out the path on a new layer in a color of your choice. Refer to Figure 3-30.

Figure 3-30. *Use the Brush tool to paint with the new closed symmetry path*

Each path has its unique characteristics when working with symmetry paint. So, with closed paths you may need to experiment several times on a new layer or use your History panel or Edit ➤ Undo or Ctrl/CMD+Z until you feel comfortable using this new path.

■ **Note** If you notice that more than one path is selected while you are working and that your custom path has been deselected, first click on the path you want to use. Refer to Figure 3-31.

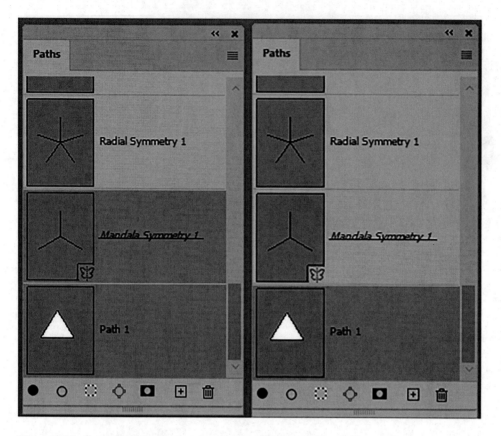

Figure 3-31. *Reselecting the custom symmetry path in the Paths panel*

■ Then, choose Selected Path from the Options panel Symmetry menu so that only the currently selected Path 1 is selected. This option will also turn any selected path into a symmetry path. Refer to Figure 3-32.

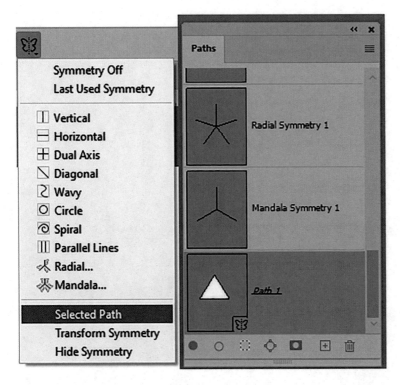

Figure 3-32. *Reselecting the custom symmetry path in the Paths panel and choosing the Selected Path option*

■ Now click the Commit Transform check in the Options panel and then continue painting with it on a new layer. Refer to Figure 3-33.

Figure 3-33. *Click the check in the Options panel to commit the transformed symmetry path*

If you no longer want it to be a symmetry path, you can choose Disable Symmetry Path from the Paths menu. Refer to Figure 3-34.

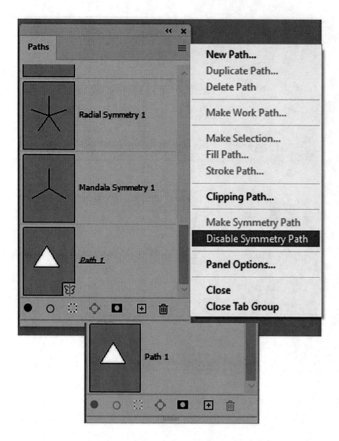

Figure 3-34. *Disable the custom symmetry path in the Paths panel to return it to a normal path*

You can see how this is the beginning of a custom pattern layer in Photoshop.

After you are finished painting with the Brush, Pencil, or Eraser tool, select Symmetry Off from the Options menu. This returns the tools to normal mode and the paths are now disabled in the Paths panel. Refer to Figure 3-35.

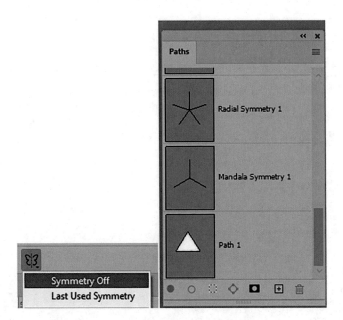

Figure 3-35. *Turn the symmetry mode off in the Options panel to disable all symmetry paths in the Paths panel*

We will continue to look at paths later in the chapter as well as in Chapters 5 and 8.

Make sure at this point to File ➤ Save your document. You can refer to file CH3_SymmetryPaint_final.psd if you need to review the layers so far.

Defining the Custom Pattern

Make an Image ➤ Duplicate of your file so far. Make visible a layer or layers of your choice. I am using the Mandala Radial eraser pencil Layer I created. Make sure that it and the background are also visible but turn off the visibility on other pattern layers that you do not want to use as part of the pattern. Then, from the menu, choose Flatten Image. Click OK to the warning message. Refer to Figure 3-36.

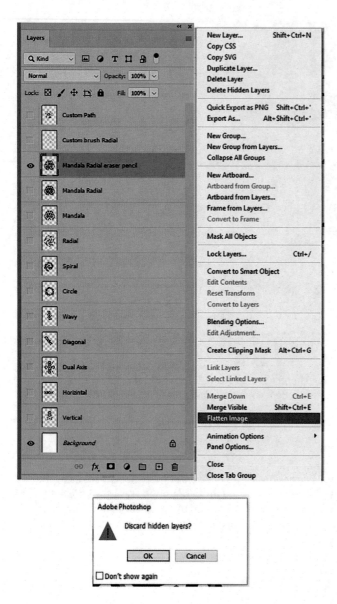

Figure 3-36. *Flatten the layers in a copy of your file before you define a pattern and discard hidden layers*

Now use your Rectangular Marquee tool with a Style of Normal and drag a new selection around the area you want as part of the pattern. Refer to Figure 3-37.

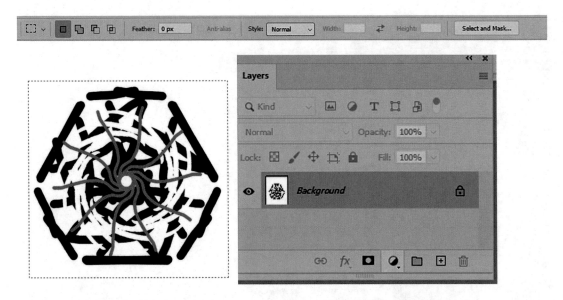

Figure 3-37. *Use the Rectangular Marquee tool to select your pattern from the background*

From the main menu choose Edit ➤ Define pattern. In the Pattern Name dialog box, give the pattern a name and then click OK. I called mine Colorful Symmetry Paint. Refer to Figure 3-38.

Figure 3-38. *Pattern Name dialog box*

Now the pattern is stored in the Patterns panel. There are other default patterns stored in there as well as patterns created from earlier projects. Refer to Figure 3-39.

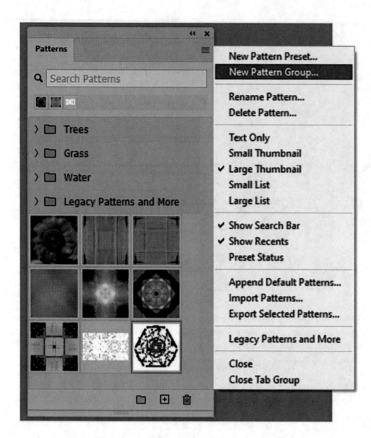

Figure 3-39. *Patterns panel with menu*

We will use the Edit ➤ Define Pattern command a few more times again later in the chapter and then look at how they can be used with various tools.

Choose Select ➤ Deselect to deselect the pattern.

To keep the patterns organized, you can create new group folder or new pattern group. Name the folder as Ch3 Patterns. Click OK and then click and then drag the patterns into that folder so they are part of the collection. Refer to Figure 3-40.

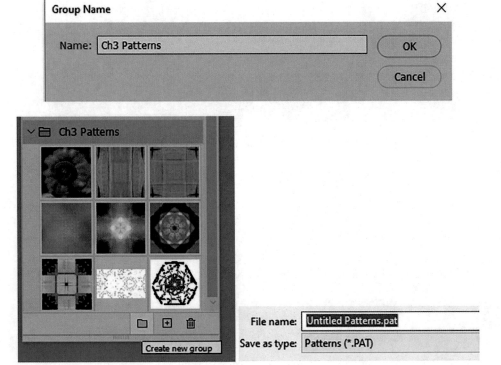

Figure 3-40. *Group Folder dialog box created for the Patterns panel and file format to save your patterns for use by others*

■ **Note** Patterns can be saved or exported by selecting the folder, and from the menu choosing Export Selected Patterns. They are saved as a .pat file and then can be imported by choosing from the menu Import Patterns. In this chapter's project folder, I have saved the current patterns we are using if you want to use them as well. Refer to Figure 3-40.

Later, we will apply the patterns to various backgrounds.

You can close the copy of your flattened file without saving changes but save your layered .psd files for future reference.

Vector Shape Patterns

When you want to create geometric patterns with vector shapes, it should be noted that the Pen tool and Selection tools along with the paths panel can be used for a few other unusual warps and distorts for selections and masks, which I discuss in more detail in my Photoshop Selections book mentioned earlier in the chapter. For more details and resources, see Chapter 10 of that book for work in the Path mode. The Paths panel will be used again later in the chapter and then in Chapter 8 when working with certain filters to create distorted trees and flames. However, regarding to the Pen, Selection, and Shape tools, they can also be used to create vector shapes that can be part of a pattern. So, let's take a quick review of these tools. Refer to Figure 3-41.

Figure 3-41. *Tools panel collections of Pen tools, Path Selection tools, and Shape tools*

While working in this section, if you need to practice, File ➤ Open CH3_SymmetryPaint.psd as it is just a blank file for you to create layers on and make an Image ➤ Duplicate of the file for practice.

Pen and Shape Tools Review

The Pen tool, besides creating paths, also can be used to create shapes and vector shape layers. After the tool presets, if your Pen tool is set on Path mode, change it now to Shape mode. Refer to Figure 3-42.

Figure 3-42. *Options panel for the Pen tool set from Path mode to Shape mode*

Pen Tools

There are seven related pen tools in this collection. I will briefly discuss each one with a few tips regarding shapes. Refer to Figure 3-43.

Figure 3-43. *The Pen tool collection*

Pen Tool (P)

This tool can create paths that are open and closed as well as custom shapes. Tip: If you need to draw a straight line, Click and then Shift+Click in a new location. Refer to Figure 3-44.

1. Click   **2. Shift + Click**

Figure 3-44. *Use the Pen tool to draw a straight line*

Click and Click+Drag when you want to create a curve or curves in a certain direction. Refer to Figure 3-45.

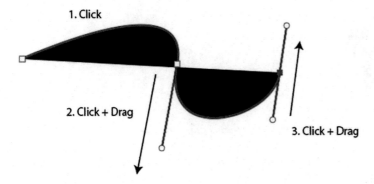

Figure 3-45. *Use the Pen tool to draw curves*

Click again on the same point, holding down the Alt/Option+ Click point, when you want to change from a curved to a straight path and click in a new location. Or after you Alt/Option+Click, you can drag out the handle as well and change direction and then click the next point. Refer to Figure 3-46.

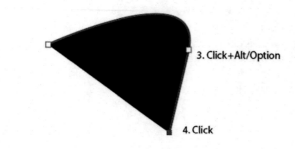

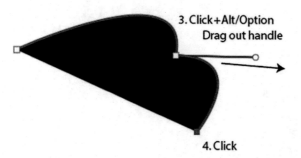

Figure 3-46. *Use the Pen tool to draw a straight or a curved line that changes direction*

To close the path, make sure the pen has a zero icon beside it when you return to the original point and then Click or Click+Drag for a curve. Refer to Figure 3-47.

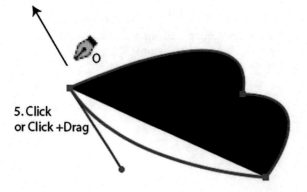

Figure 3-47. *Use the Pen tool to close the open path for your shape*

Once the path is closed, a vector shape layer is created. You can then use the Pen tool Options panel to modify the selected shape layer. Refer to Figure 3-48.

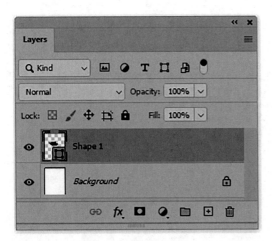

Figure 3-48. *Vector shape layer in the Layers panel*

Pen Tool Options

Look at the Options panel from left to right. After the tool presets is the Mode menu. With the pen in Shape mode, as you create the shape, you can set a fill color or stroke color from colors from the Swatches panel. Refer to Figure 3-49.

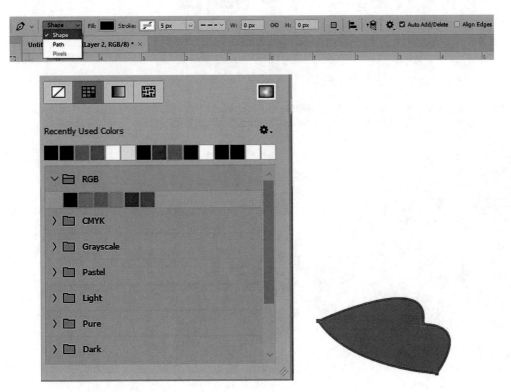

Figure 3-49. *Options panel for the Pen tool. Use the dropdown menu to change the swatches color for a fill or stroke of the shape*

When using the Set shape fill or stroke type, besides the solid swatches found in the group folders, you can either set the stroke or fill to

- No Color (square with red slash)

- A gradient from the list and alter the gradient's slider order (color and opacity stops, opacity midpoint), opacity (0-100%), style (Linear, Radial, Angle, Reflected, Diamond), angle (-180, 0, 180), reverse gradient colors, scale (1-1000%), Align with Layer, and Method (Perceptual, Linear, Classic). These gradients can be found in the Gradients panel. Refer to Figure 3-50.

Figure 3-50. *Options panel for the Pen tool. Use the dropdown menu to change the gradient color for the fill or stroke of the shape*

- Or a pattern and alter the scale (1-1000%) and angle (-180, 0, 180). These patterns can be found in the Patterns panel. Refer to Figure 3-51.

Figure 3-51. *Options panel for the Pen tool. Use the dropdown menu to change the pattern for the fill or stroke of the shape*

Alternatively, you can choose a color from the Color Picker on the far right of the menu. The gear menu on the right will change options according to the type of fill or stroke chosen. Recently used items are displayed in a row depending on whether swatch, color, gradient, or pattern. Refer to Figure 3-51.

For now, set the fill and stroke back to a solid color. Refer to Figure 3-42.

Next, you can set these stroke options:

- **Size**: 0 px - 1200 px

- **Shape stroke type**: This menu includes various stroke options. They allow you to align the stroke and add caps and corners to the stoke. The gear menu allows you to save custom strokes. Click the More Options button and the dashed line check box if you want to create a dashed and gapped preset line. Otherwise, by default, the line will be solid. Refer to Figure 3-52 and Figure 2-53.

Figure 3-52. *Stroke color, width, and style in the Options panel*

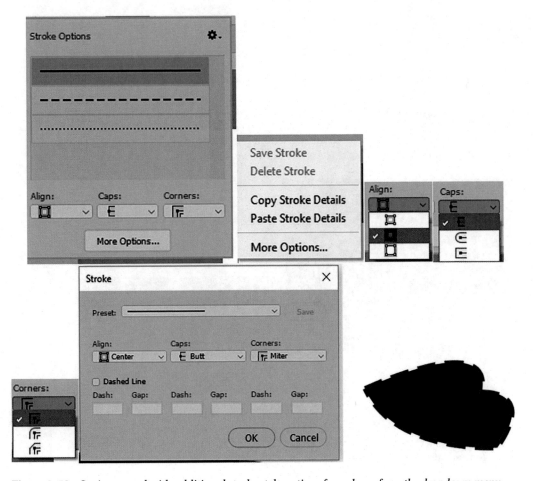

Figure 3-53. *Options panel with additional stroke style options for a shape from the dropdown menu*

The next section allows you to alter the width and height of the shape on the layer. It can be linked to keep the scaling proportionate. Right-click a text box if you want the scaling to be in increments other than pixels. Refer to Figure 3-54.

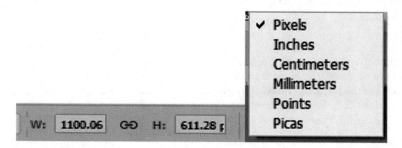

Figure 3-54. *Set the unit of increments for the shape's width and height and link to scale proportionality*

The next sections allow you work with two or more shapes that are present on the same layer. Refer to Figure 3-55.

Figure 3-55. *Options panel menus for path operations, alignment, and arrangement*

Otherwise, if only one, then the options are grayed. To see how this works, create a duplicate layer of the current shape (drag over the Create a new layer icon). Use the Move tool to move the shape on the layer over. Then Shift+Click and select both layers and then from the Layers menu choose Merge Shapes or Ctrl/CMD+E. You should now have two shapes on one layer. Refer to Figure 3-56.

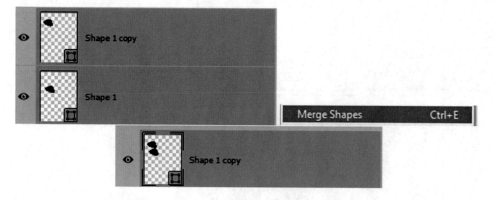

Figure 3-56. *Merge two or more shapes layers onto one layer so they share the same attributes*

- The path operations are New Layer, Combine Shapes, Subtract Front Shape, Intersect Shape Areas, Exclude Overlapping Shapes, and Merge Shape Components. This works similarly to the Properties Pathfinders area to create live shapes, which we'll look at later. Refer to Figure 3-57.

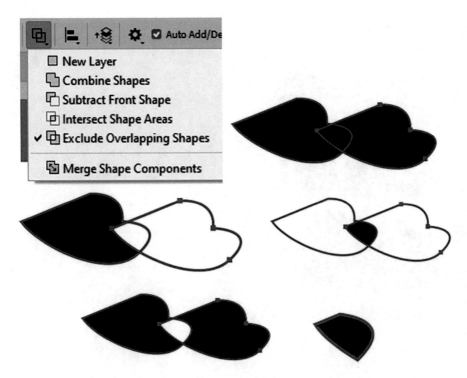

Figure 3-57. *Options panel for path operations: Combine, Subtract, Intersect, Exclude, and Merge Shape Components from Intersect Shape areas*

- **Path Alignment**: When two or more shapes are selected, you can align the shapes (left edges, horizontal centers, right edges, top edges, vertical centers, bottom edges) or distribute the spacing vertically or horizontally by clicking one of the options in the menu. To create and select more duplicate paths on one layer, you need to use the Path Selection tool, which we will review in the next section of this chapter. Refer to Figure 3-58.

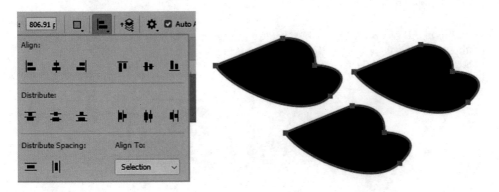

Figure 3-58. *Use path alignment on two or more selected shapes*

- **Path arrangement**: When paths overlap on a shape layer, you can change the order, bring a shape to front, forward, or send a shape backward or to the back of the stack. Refer to Figure 3-59.

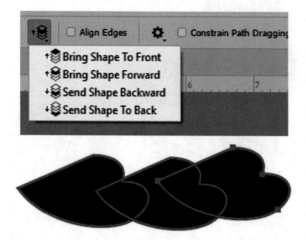

Figure 3-59. *Bring and send shapes when one shape is selected*

Next, the gear path options allow you to adjust the guides for viewing the guide path of the shape (Thickness, Color, Rubber Band). Refer to Figure 3-60.

Figure 3-60. *Path Options for the Pen tool*

The next checkbox in this section, when enabled while creating the path, allows you to add or delete anchor points without selecting those tools in the menu. Just hover over an active point to delete it or over a path to add a point. See "Add Anchor, Delete Anchor, and Convert Point Tools" later in this section. Refer to Figure 3-60 and Figure 3-61.

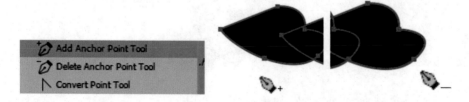

Figure 3-61. *Auto add or auto delete points rather than using those tools in the Tools panel*

196

The last checkbox allows you to align vector shape edges to the pixel grid when drawing. To show/hide the grid, go to View ➤ Show ➤ Grid. Refer to Figure 3-62.

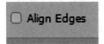

Figure 3-62. *Align Edges check box option*

Freeform Pen Tool (P)

The Freeform Pen tool is like the Pen tool. It binds to edges of selection if the magnetic option is chosen; otherwise, you can drag in a circular motion to create a path.

Freeform Pen Tool Options

The Freeform Pen basically has all of the options of the Pen tool, except for when you draw freehand or drag a path, you can choose either to move and draw as you would, like a using a Brush or Lasso tool, or enable the magnetic options to allow the points to attach and stick to edges of shapes as you draw. To close a path, make sure that you double-click when you reach the final point of the shape you are drawing. Refer to Figure 3-63.

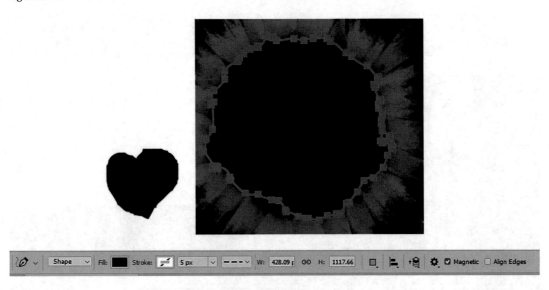

Figure 3-63. *Options panel for the Freeform Pen tool and drawing with the tool on an image with normal or magnetic settings*

This tool is not relevant to the topic of this book, and I prefer to use it in Path mode so that I can see the image below for a more accurate trace, before turning it into a shape. But if you would like more details on how to use it for paths, you can refer to my Photoshop Selections book mentioned earlier the chapter. This book shows how a path can be turned into a new shape layer while in Path mode.

Content-Aware Tracing Tool (P)

Like the Pen tool, you can attempt to draw a path around a distinct shape and image with the Content-Aware Tracing tool, and while you draw, it creates a preview selection of the path before you click the next location.

Content-Aware Tracing Tool Options

In Shape mode, this tool contains many of the path panel settings already mentioned for the Pen tool. Refer to the Pen tool for more details. Refer to Figure 3-64.

Figure 3-64. *Options panel for the Content-Aware Tracing tool*

However, in the next section, there are additional tracing options that include creating paths from detected edges, extending currently selected paths with detected edges, and trimming traced paths.

You can then set the tracing mode for the types of edges to detect (Detailed, Normal, Simplified), the detail settings (1-100%) for edge detection, and Auto Trim, which will automatically trim selected paths and detect edges to minimize gaps with extending traced paths. It works best with shapes with distinct edges to guide you as you create the shape and preview selection. Refer to Figure 3-65.

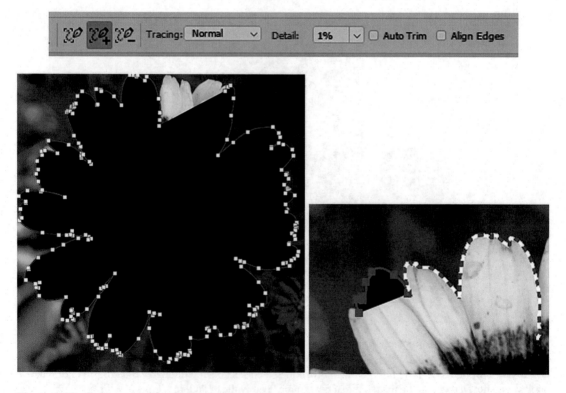

Figure 3-65. *Options panel for the Content-Aware Tracing tool's additional options and preview of trace as you draw the shape*

See the Pen tool for details on the Align Edges check box.

This tool is not relevant to the topic of this book, and I prefer to use it in Path mode so that I can see the image below for a more accurate trace, before turning it into a shape. If you would like more details on how to use it for paths, you can refer to my Photoshop Selections book mentioned earlier the chapter. This book shows how a path can be turned into a new shape layer while in Path mode.

Curvature Pen Tool (P)

Like the Pen tool, the Curvature Pen tool allows you to create curved paths around a drawing to create a closed path.

Curvature Pen Tool Options

The Curvature Pen tool has basically the same options as the Pen tool for shape creation. So refer to the Pen tool for more details. Refer to Figure 3-66.

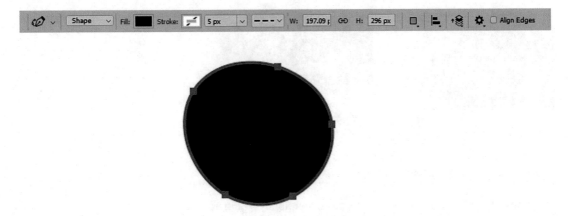

Figure 3-66. *Options panel for the Curvature Pen tool and a shape drawn with the tool*

This tool is not relevant to the topic of this book, and I prefer to use it in Path mode so that I can see the image below for a more accurate trace, before turning it into a shape. If you would like more details on how to use it for paths, you can refer to my Photoshop Selections book mentioned earlier the chapter. This book shows how a path can be turned into a new shape layer while in Path mode.

Add Anchor, Delete Anchor, and Convert Point Tools

The last three tools in this Pen collection can be used at any time with the Pen tool as well as the other three previously mentioned pen tools. Refer to Figure 3-67.

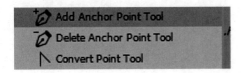

Figure 3-67. *Add Anchor, Delete Anchor, and Convert Point Tools*

Add Anchor Point tool: Adds an anchor point to a path. Refer to Figure 3-68.

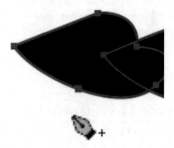

Figure 3-68. *Add an anchor point to a path*

Delete Anchor Point tool: Deletes an anchor point from a path. Refer to Figure 3-69.

Figure 3-69. *Delete an anchor point from a path*

Convert Anchor Point tool: Converts an anchor point on path from curved to straight by clicking on the point, or from straight to curved if you drag on the point to bring out two handles. Then you can create a curved-to-straight transition by dragging on a single handle. Refer to Figure 3-70.

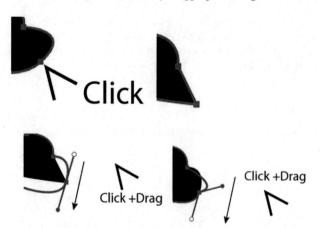

Figure 3-70. *Convert an anchor point to either straight or curved*

If you find one of your anchor points is twisted while drawing, the Convert to Anchor Point tool is the best option to use to untangle it. Just click and drag in the opposite direction.

■ **Note** The Add Anchor Point, Delete Anchor Point, and Convert Anchor Point tools do not have additional options in the Options panel. Refer to Figure 3-71.

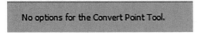

Figure 3-71. *The Options panel has no additional options for the Add Anchor, Delete Anchor, and Convert Point tools*

Path Selection Tools

Once points are created for vector shapes on the layers, they can be selected and modified with the following tools:

- **Path Selection tool (A)**: Move or transform the entire path or shape
- **Direct Selection tool (A)**: Move a point or handles to distort or adjust the path. Refer to Figure 3-72.

Figure 3-72. *Tools panel with Path Selection and Direct Selection tools*

Path Selection Tool Options

Many of the tool options that were available with the Pen tool are available with the Path Selection tool, so you can refer to the Pen Tool for more details. I will just point out a few key differences. When you select a shape, you can choose to select All layers or All Active Layers. Then, as with the Pen tool, you can at this point modify your selected shape's fill, stroke, stroke width, stroke type, and adjust the scale of the width and height or link to constrain proportions. Refer to Figure 3-73.

Figure 3-73. *Options panel for the Path Selection tool*

The next section allows you to set Path Operations, Path Alignment, and Path Arrangement, and this I find is easier to do with the Path Selection tool rather than then Pen tool. However, refer to that section for more details. Refer to Figure 3-73.

■ **Tip**   To duplicate a shape on the same layer for use with various path operations, while the path is selected, hold down the Alt/Option key and drag out a new shape. Refer to Figure 3-74.

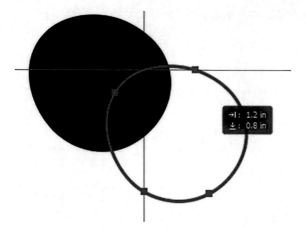

Figure 3-74. *Creating a duplicate shape with the Path Selection tool*

When you want to select more than one shape, drag and draw a rectangular marquee around the items you want to select or Shift+Click on each one at a time. Then you can use the various path operations and alignment options mentioned earlier. Refer to Figure 3-75.

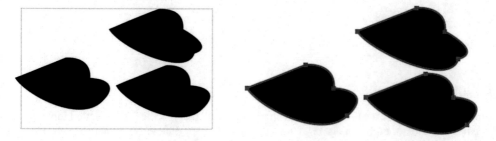

Figure 3-75. *Selecting multiple shapes with the Path selection tool by dragging a marquee around them*

The next section allows you to align vector shape edges to the pixel grid. The gear icon contains the path guide options for thickness and color. The Constrain Path Dragging, if enabled, is a legacy option for path dragging. You can keep this option unchecked. Click elsewhere on the canvas to deselect all the shapes. Refer to Figure 3-76.

Figure 3-76. *Path options for the Path Selection tool*

Direct Selection Tools Options

The same options as the Path Selection tool are available here when working with selected paths, except you use this tool to select individual points rather than the whole shape. Refer to Figure 3-77.

Figure 3-77. *Options panel for Direct Selection tool*

When you want to select more than one point, drag to draw a rectangular marquee around the items you want to select or Shift+Click on each point one at a time. Refer to Figure 3-78.

Click elsewhere on the canvas to deselect the shapes.

Figure 3-78. *Selecting multiple points with the Direct Selection tool by dragging a marquee around them*

Shape Tools

Shape tools allow you to create basic default or custom shapes by dragging them out on the artboard while that tool is in Shape tool mode. Refer to Figure 3-79.

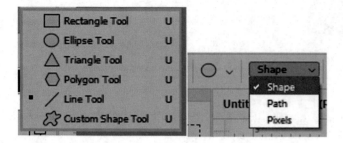

Figure 3-79. Shape tools in the Tools panel and the Options panel set to Shape mode

---

■ **Note** In this chapter, we will not be using Pixels mode because I consider these shapes to be difficult to scale and manipulate later. However, in this mode, shapes act like brushes and you can use blending modes. See "Brush Options and Blend Modes" in Chapter 2 for reference. Refer to Figure 3-80.

Figure 3-80. Options panel for a shape either set to Pixels or Shape mode

---

Coming back to Shape mode, let's review the next six tools.

Rectangle tool: It creates rectangles or squares as you drag out a shape on the canvas. To create a square, hold down the Shift key as you draw, or click on the canvas to enter the Create Rectangle options dialog box for more width, height, and radii options for rounded rectangles or squares. With the link disabled, you can set a separate radii for each side. From Center, when enabled, creates the rectangle from a center point of where you clicked in the canvas. Click OK and once the rectangle is created and selected with your Path Selection tool, use the bounding box handles for further moving, scaling, and rotation. Use the live corners widgets to round the rectangle. Refer to Figure 3-81.

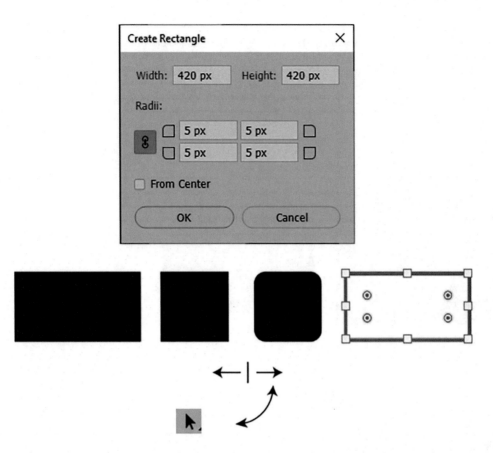

Figure 3-81. *Create Rectangle dialog box and various created rectangles and squares that can be further transformed with the Path Selection tool when the cursor changes shape*

Ellipse tool: It creates ellipse ovals or circles as you drag out a shape on the canvas. To create a circle, hold down the Shift key as you drag. Or click on the canvas to enter the Create Ellipse options dialog box for more options for width and height. From Center, when enabled, creates the ellipse from a center point of where you clicked in the canvas. Click OK and once the ellipse is created and selected with your Path Selection Tool, use the bounding box handles for further moving, scaling, and rotation. Refer to Figure 3-82.

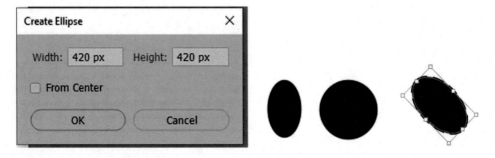

Figure 3-82. *Create an Ellipse dialog box and various created ellipses and circles that can be further transformed with the Path Selection tool*

Triangle tool: It creates triangles as you drag out a shape on the canvas. Or hold down the Shift key to create an equilateral triangle. Click the canvas to enter the Create Triangle options dialog box for more options for width and height, to make the triangle equilateral, or to adjust the corner radius for a rounded triangle. From Center, when enabled, creates the triangle from a center point of where you clicked in the canvas. Click OK, and once the triangle is created and selected with your Path Selection tool, use the circle (live corners widget) to adjust the radius and the bounding box handles for further moving, scaling, and rotation. Refer to Figure 3-83.

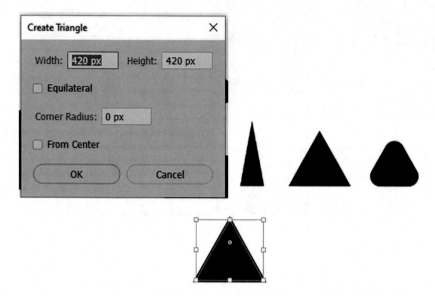

Figure 3-83. *Create a Triangle dialog box and various created triangles that can be further transformed with the Path Selection tool*

Polygon tool: It create polygons with multiple sides and stars as you drag out a shape on the canvas. Hold down the Shift key for more symmetric shapes. Click the canvas to enter the Create Polygon options dialog box for more options to set width and height, make the polygon symmetrical, change number of sides (3-100), adjust the corner radius for a more rounded shape, and use the star ratio to make a star. Smooth Star Indents is only available when the star ratio is set to 99% or less. Refer to Figure 3-84.

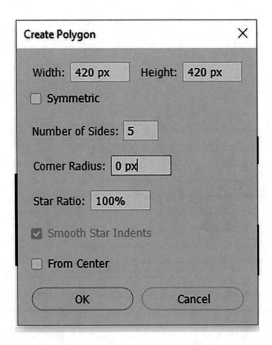

Figure 3-84. Create a Polygon dialog box and various created polygons and stars that can be further transformed with the Path Selection tool

From Center, when enabled, creates the polygon from a center point of where you clicked in the canvas. Click OK and once the Polygon is created and selected with your Path Selection tool, use the circle (live corners widget) to adjust the radius and the bounding box handles for further moving, scaling, and rotation. Refer to Figure 3-84.

Line tool: It creates basic lines and arrowheads. Click at point 1 and then hold down the Shift key while dragging to create a straight line. There is no additional dialog box when you click on the canvas, and you must make adjustments using the Options panel, as you will see shortly. Use the Path Selection tool or Direct Selection tool to adjust the path. Refer to Figure 3-85.

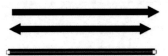

Figure 3-85. Lines creates with the Line tool. Some have arrow heads

Custom Shape tool: It's a collection of custom shapes that are stored in the Window ➤ Shapes panel. Hold down the Shift key as you drag if you want a proportionate shape. For additional shapes, make sure to add your Legacy Shapes and More folder from the Shapes menu. Refer to Figure 3-86.

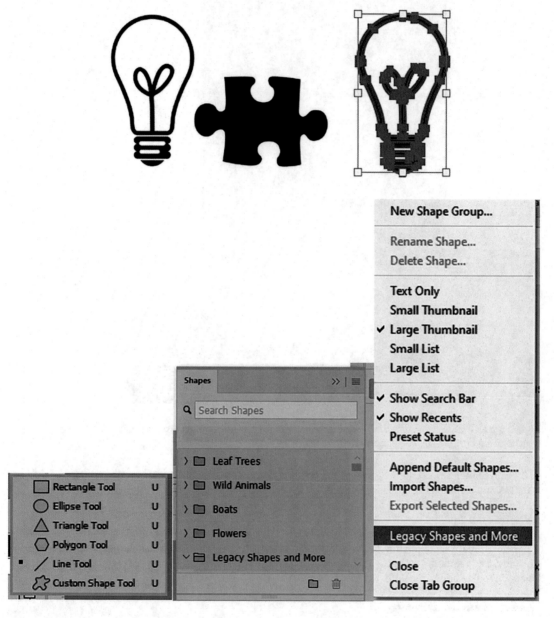

Figure 3-86. *Custom shapes created with the Custom Shape tool and custom shapes stored in the Shapes panel and additional options in its menu*

Once the custom shape is created and selected with your Path Selection tool, use the bounding box handles for further moving, scaling, and rotation. Refer to Figure 3-86 and Figure 3-87.

Figure 3-87. *Path Selection and Direct Selection tools*

To select individual points, use your Direct Selection tool. Refer to Figure 3-87.

Shape Tool Properties

Since many of the Shape tool properties are similar for most tools when in Shape mode, as with the Pen tool, I will just look over the main key differences for each tool. Otherwise, refer to the Pen tool for more details.

Rectangle Tool Options and Properties

Look at the Options panel from left to right. Many of the same settings are found with the Pen tool. You can set a fill or stroke to a fill of No color, Solid, Gradient, or Pattern. Refer to Figure 3-88.

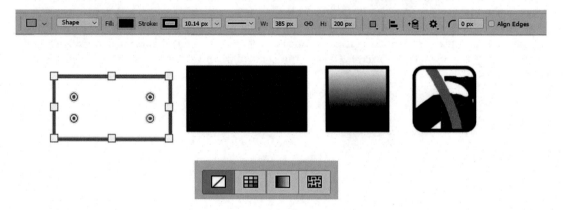

Figure 3-88. *Options panel for the Rectangle tool and various rectangles and squares with various fill and stroke settings*

Next, adjust the stroke width and style type options as well as the shape's width and height and link proportionately. Refer to Figure 3-89.

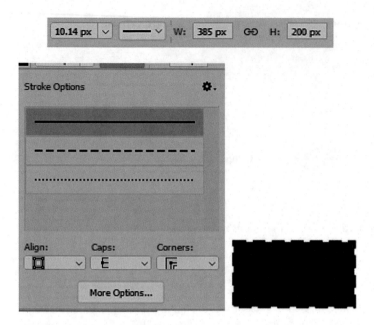

Figure 3-89. *Options panel for Rectangle tool stroke width, styles, width, and height with a link to constrain proportions and a custom rectangle with fill and stroke*

Like the Pen and Selection tools, you can use the Path Operations and Path Alignment options if there are two or more shapes on the same layer. Or Path Arrangement when a single shape is selected on the layer. Refer to Figure 3-90.

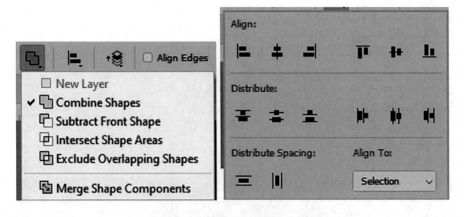

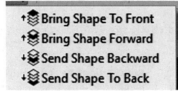

Figure 3-90. Options panel for Rectangle tool path operations, alignment, and arrangement for various rectangles and squares with similar fill and stroke settings on a single layer

---

■ **Tip** To put similar shapes on one layer, use your Path Selection tool to Alt/Option+Drag duplicate shapes. To combine different shapes that are on separate layers, Shift+Click each the layer in the Layers panel and choose Merge Shapes from the Layers panel menu or Ctrl/CMD+E. Refer to Figure 3-91.

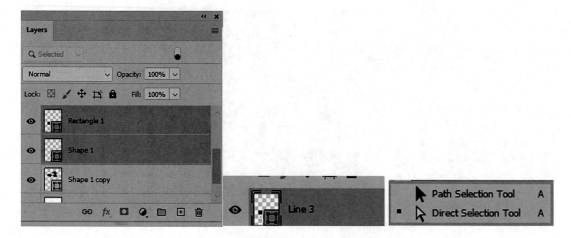

Figure 3-91. *Layers panel with two shape layers merged or use Path Selection tool to duplicate shapes*

However, this will cause the shapes to take on the same options and attributes. If you want to use basic path alignment options without combining layers, after you have Shift+Clicked each separate layer, select your Move tool and use the layer alignment options instead. Refer to Figure 3-92.

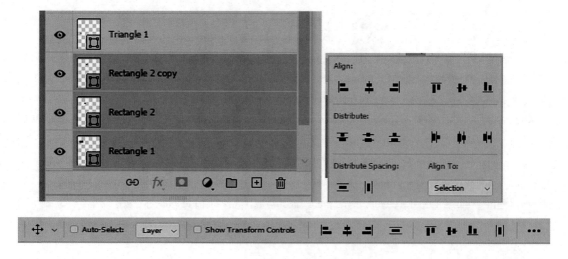

Figure 3-92. *Use the Move tool Options panel to move shapes on separate layers when selected*

However, from the Rectangle tool Options panel, additional path options, constrains, and From Center options can be found under the gear icon for adjusting the shape of the rectangle as you draw a new shape. On the far right you can round the radius of each side of the rectangle as well prior to dragging out the shape. Refer to Figure 3-93.

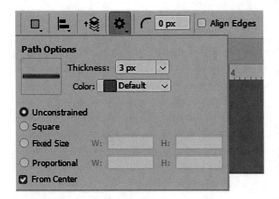

Figure 3-93. *Rectangle tool Path Options menu*

The last checkbox, when enabled, allows you to align edges to the pixel grid. See View ➤ Show ➤ Grid.

Additional Properties Panel Options

Once you have dragged out and drawn the shape, you can go to your Properties panel and do additional things to the shape, such as transform the shape further in scale or position, alter the angle, or flip the shape vertically or horizontally. Then, as in the Options panel, you can alter the appearance of the fill, stroke, stroke width, stroke type, stroke align type, stroke cap height, and stroke join type. Then you can set each individual side of the rectangle's radius or keep all the sides the same with the link. All corner radius values are displayed. Refer to Figure 3-94.

213

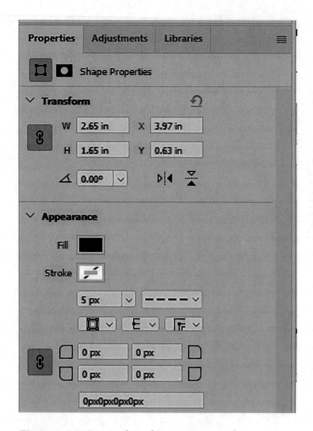

Figure 3-94. *Rectangle tool Properties panel*

Lastly, you can use the Pathfinder options to alter how the shapes combine. Similar settings are also located in the options panel above as Path Operations.

As you drag a new shape, most of them can also be used with key commands to combine another shape to the currently selected shape and the cursor changes:

- Combine shapes (Shift)
- Subtract front shape (Alt/Option)
- Intersect shape areas (Shift +Alt/Option)
- Exclude overlapping shapes (does not appear to have a key command, so just use the button in the properties or Path Operations dropdown in the Options panel)

Refer to Figure 3-95.

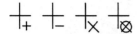

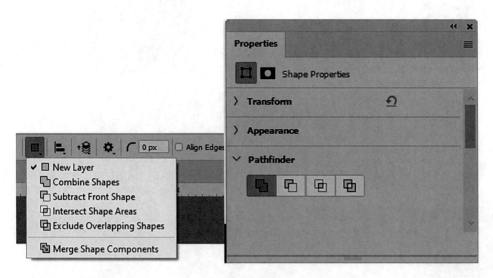

Figure 3-95. *Options panel and Pathfinder options for live shapes in the Properties panel. Cursor icons change when you combine, subtract, intersect, or exclude overlapping shapes*

Alternatively, you can use the Live Pathfinder Properties icons on selected shapes on the same layer or on separate layers. However, they must overlap to see the effect, and layer order is important. Refer to Figure 3-96.

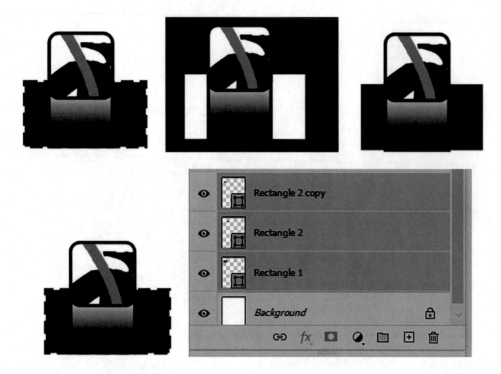

Figure 3-96. *Selected layers when Pathfinder settings of combine, subtract, intersect, or exclude are enabled*

■ **Note** Live Pathfinder options are not available for shapes created with the Pen tool.

Ellipse Tool Options and Properties

The Ellipse Tools options and properties are like the Rectangle tools and Pen tools, so refer to those earlier notes as you look from left to right in the Options panel. However, different additional path options can be found under the gear icon for path options, constrains, and From Center options to alter the ellipse as you draw a new shape. Refer to Figure 3-97.

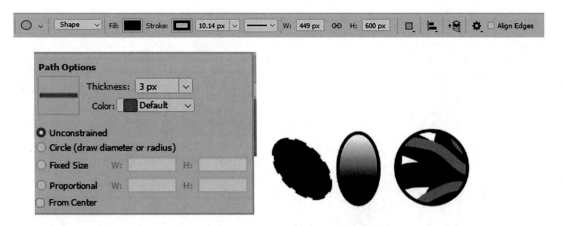

Figure 3-97. *Options panel for the Ellipse tool, path options and various ellipses and circles with various fill and stroke settings*

The last checkbox, when enabled, allows you to align edges to the pixel grid. See View ➤ Show ➤ Grid. Like the Rectangle tool, similar options are available in the Properties panel. Refer to Figure 3-98.

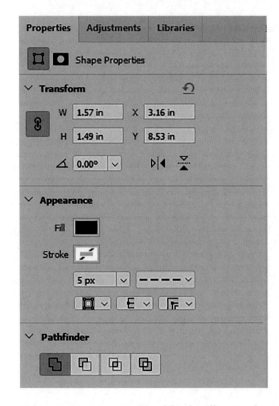

Figure 3-98. *Properties panel for the Ellipse tool*

Triangle Tools Options and Properties

The Triangle tools options and properties are like the Pen and Rectangle tools. As you look from left to right in the Options panel, refer to those earlier notes. Additional path options, constrains, and From Center options can be found under the gear icon for path options to alter the triangle as you draw a new shape. You can also set the round radius from the Options area prior to dragging out the new shape. Refer to Figure 3-99.

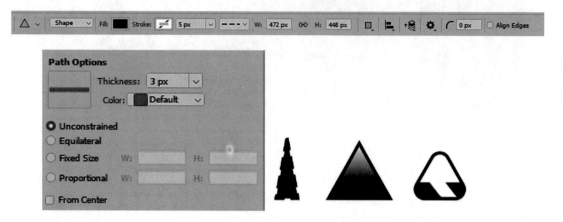

Figure 3-99. *Options panel for the Triangle tool, path options, and various triangles with various fill and stroke settings*

The last checkbox, when enabled, allows you to align edges to the pixel grid. See View ➤ Show ➤ Grid. Like the Rectangle tool, similar options are available in the Properties panel. Refer to Figure 3-100.

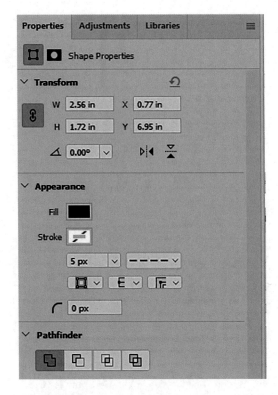

Figure 3-100. *Properties panel for the Triangle tool*

Polygon Tools Options and Properties

The options and properties for the Polygon tools are similar to the Pen and Rectangle tools. As you look from left to right in the Options panel, refer to those earlier notes. Additional path options can be found under the gear path options icon as well as constrain options and From Center, including for star ratio and smooth star indents. The setting you make here will affect how the shapes appear as you draw them. In the Options panel, you can set the number of sides and the radius for round corners prior to dragging out the polygon. Refer to Figure 3-101.

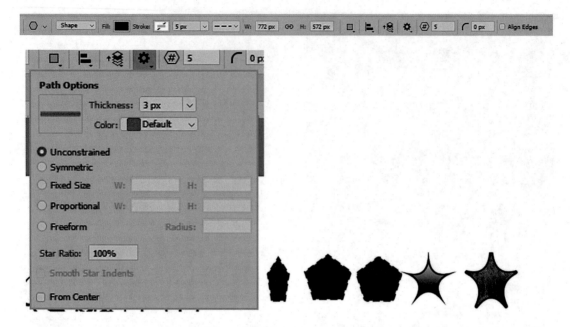

Figure 3-101. *Options panel for the Polygon tool, path options, and various polygons and stars with various fill and stroke settings*

The last checkbox, when enabled, allows you to align edges to the pixel grid. See View ➤ Show ➤ Grid.

Like the Rectangle tool, similar options are available in the Properties panel. You can adjust the shape's number of side as well as set star settings, and more options can be found under the dotted ellipse for smooth star indents, if enabled, but the star ratio must be less than 99%. Refer to Figure 3-102.

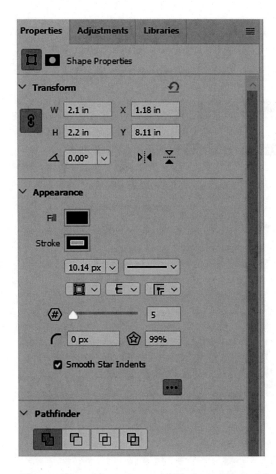

Figure 3-102. *Properties panel for the Polygon tool*

Line Tool Options and Properties

The options and properties for Line tools are like the Pen and Rectangle tools. As you look from left to right in the Options panel, refer to those earlier notes. However, to work with arrows, you need to adjust the line width. Additional path options can be found under the gear icon; they include live shape controls and arrowheads settings for start and end, width, length, and concavity. In the Options panel, the line weight allows for rectangular shapes with arrowheads and a visible fill. The weight by default is set to 0 px. Refer to Figure 3-103.

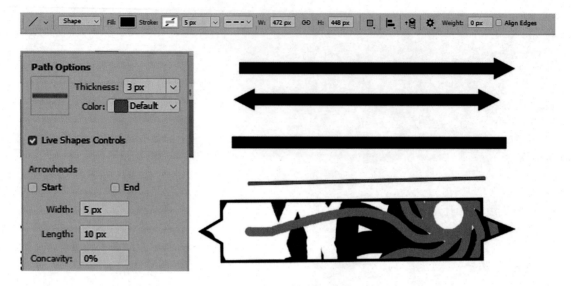

Figure 3-103. *Options panel for the Line tool, path options, and various lines with various fill and stroke settings*

The last checkbox, when enabled, allows you to align edges to the pixel grid. See View ➤ Show ➤ Grid.

Like the Rectangle tool, similar options are available in the Properties panel. However, arrowhead options are only found in the Options panel gear icon menu. Refer to Figure 3-103 and Figure 3-104.

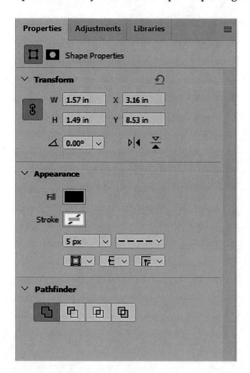

Figure 3-104. *Properties panel for the Line tool*

Custom Shape Tool Options and Properties

The options and properties for custom tools are like the Pen and Rectangle tools. As you look from left to right in the options panel, refer to those earlier notes. Additional path options, constrains, and From Center options can be found under the gear icon. Refer to Figure 3-105.

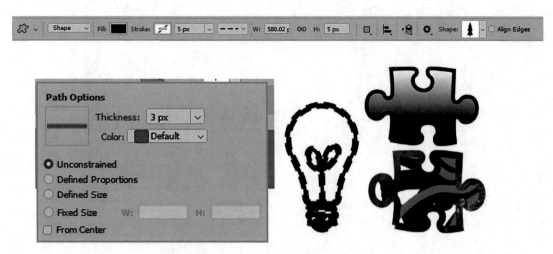

Figure 3-105. *Options panel for the custom shape tool, path options, and various shapes with various fill and stroke settings*

You can select your custom shapes from the Options panel, which are linked to the Window ➤ Shapes panel. Refer to Figure 3-106.

Figure 3-106. *The custom Shapes dropdown menu is the same as the Shapes panel*

The last checkbox, when enabled, allows you to align edges to the pixel grid. See View ➤ Show ➤ Grid. Refer to Figure 3-106.

Like the Rectangle tool, similar options are available in the Properties panel. Refer to Figure 3-107.

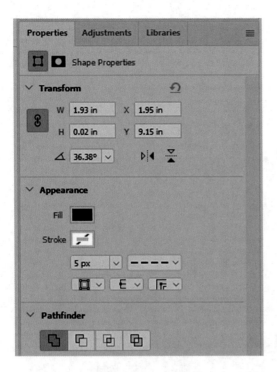

Figure 3-107. *Properties panel for the custom shape tool*

■ **Tip** If you have shapes on one layer that have attributes that you want to add to another shape on a different layer, you can use the Layers panel to right click on a layer. From the pop-up menu, choose Copy Shape Attributes and then select another layer and then right-click and paste the shape attributes. Refer to Figure 3-108.

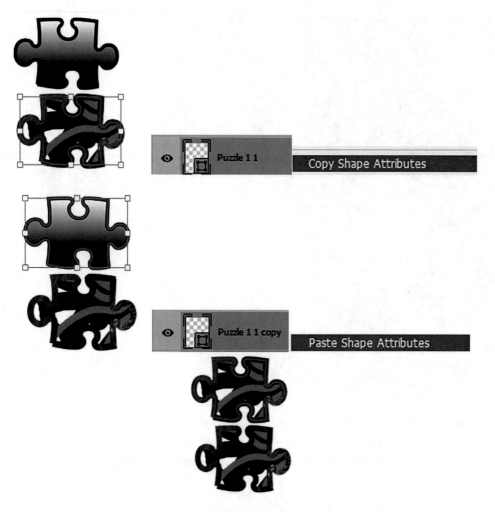

Figure 3-108. *Use the Layers panel to copy and paste attributes from one selected shape to another*

Use your History Panel or Edit ➤ Undo or Ctrl/CMD+Z if you need to undo this step. Refer to Figure 3-109.

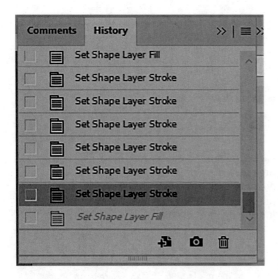

Figure 3-109. *Use the History Panel to undo steps*

After practicing creating shapes with your Pen tools, Selection tools, and Shapes tool, make sure to File ➤ Save your document as a .psd file. You can refer to file shapes.psd to see my progress.

Project: Create a Custom Shape and Then Turn It into a Pattern or Brush

Once you have created some shapes with your shape tools, you can then create a custom shape. Let's try that now.

File ➤ Open the file Ch3_CustomShape.psd. This file is square 500 px by 500 px because a square area is best to create my eventual pattern. Make an Image ➤ Duplicate of the file for practice.

This file contains one small ellipse that is a vector shape layer. Refer to Figure 3-110.

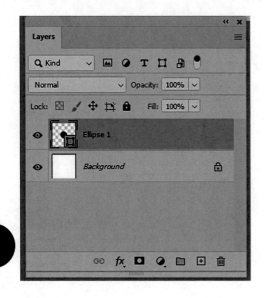

Figure 3-110. *Shape layer in the Layers panel*

Use the Ellipse tool and make sure in the Ellipse tool options to keep the fill and stroke at black as shapes are stored as black and white images, which you can color later on. And keep the stroke solid. Refer to Figure 3-111.

Figure 3-111. *Ellipse tool options*

Hold down the Shift key and drag out to draw and add several more circles in varying sizes and then use the Move tool or Alt/Option+Drag with your Path Selection tool to move and duplicate them and add them around the first ellipse to arrange them into a pattern. It does not have to be the same as mine.

To scale a shape with the Path Selection tool, select the shape and then hold down the Shift key to constrain proportions with the bounding box handles. Alt/Option+Shift will allow you to scale from the current center point.

■ **Note**   When a shape is selected with the Path Selection tool, you can also use the arrow keys on your keyboard to nudge it into place.

As you build the shape, make sure that you do not get too close to the edge as you do not want the shape to break off when it becomes a pattern. Here is my pattern so far. You can see how some shapes are together on one layer or on separate layers. You may have a different number of layers. Refer to Figure 3-112.

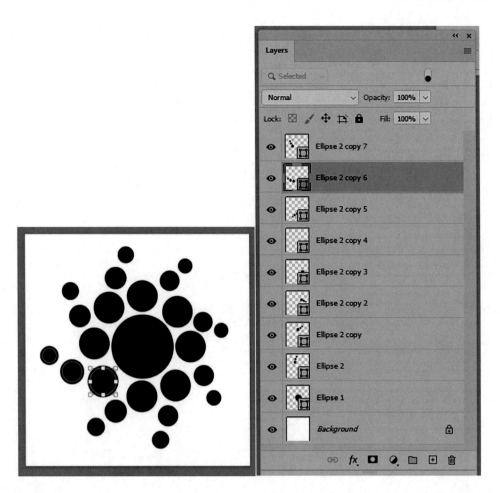

Figure 3-112. *Multiple ellipses on various layers in the Layers panel and moved with the Path Selection tool*

Add a few more shapes like a rectangle or triangle around the design in a stroke and fill of black. Just make sure it does not go to the edge of the canvas. With your Path Selection tool, select the shapes and use the bounding box handle corners to rotate and scale. Refer to Figure 3-113.

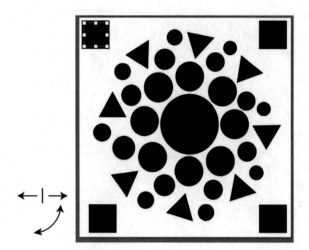

Figure 3-113. *Use the Path Selection tool when a shape is selected to scale or rotate further*

Now, to make sure that all the shapes will be part of the custom shape, in the Layers panel you must select all the layers that you want to have as part of the shape. With the Path Selection Tool selected, Shift+Click all your shape layers in the Layers panel. Refer to Figure 3-114.

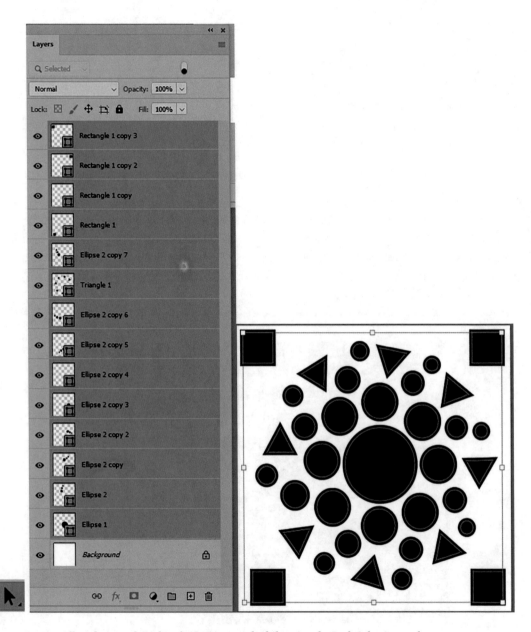

Figure 3-114. *All paths are selected in the Layers panel while using the Path Selection tool*

Now with the Shape Layers selected, choose Edit ➤ Define Custom Shape. Name the shape or keep the default name and Click OK. Refer to Figure 3-115.

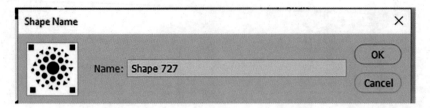

Figure 3-115. *Shape Name dialog box*

The shape is now added to the Shapes panel with any other shapes that were created by yourself or others.

■ **Note** Once a shape has been created, you can return to the Layers panel and continue to create more shapes. As you create your custom shapes, create a group folder and, as you did with the brushes (Chapter 2) and patterns earlier (I called mine Ch3 Custom Shapes), click OK and drag the shapes into the folder to store them. Refer to Figure 3-116.

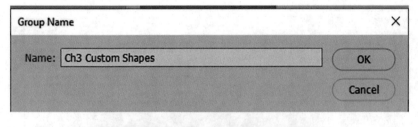

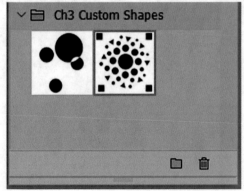

Figure 3-116. *Create a group folder to store custom shapes*

■ Like brushes and patterns, shapes can be stored as .CSH files and saved for other projects when you select the folder and from the Shapes panel menu, choose Export Selected Shapes. You can then share and load shapes created by others when you choose Import Shapes from the menu. You can find my custom shapes file in the chapter's project folder. Refer to Figure 3-117.

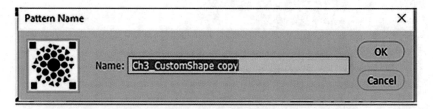

Append Default Shapes...
Import Shapes...
Export Selected Shapes...

Figure 3-117. *Export or import custom shapes from the Shapes panel menu*

Now, while the shape is still selected, try Edit ➤ Define Pattern to create a new pattern and store it in the Pattern panel with your earlier patterns. Click OK. Refer to Figure 3-118.

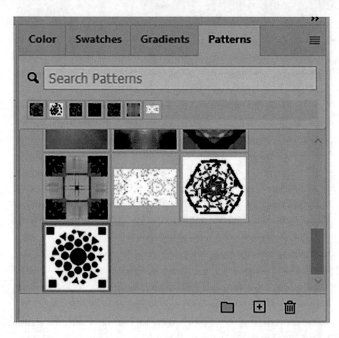

Figure 3-118. *Add a custom pattern to the group folder in the Patterns panel*

You can even do one more thing, as in Chapter 2, but this time choose Edit Define ➤ Brush Preset to make this same pattern into a custom brush and click OK and store it in your folder of custom brushes. Refer to Figure 3-119.

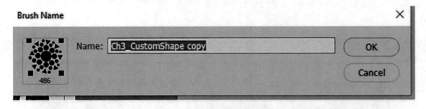

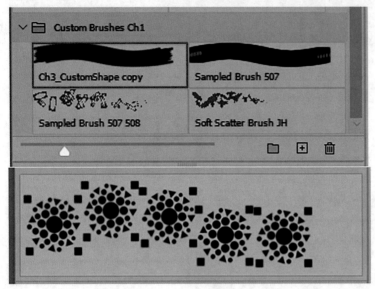

Figure 3-119. *Add a custom brush to a group folder in the Brushes panel and preview with the Brush Settings panel*

Wow! One pattern can be used in three different tools! That's good value.

File ➤ Save your custom shape file at this point. You can refer to my file, Ch3_CustomShape_final.psd. And you will find the files for the custom shapes, patterns, and brushes in the chapter's project folder.

Project: Patterns with the Offset Filter

Once you have created various designs with your brushes and shapes, you can see how they can be defined as patterns. However, maybe you have a photo of a textile or a pattern that you created and then made a photo or scan. How can you create a seamless pattern from an image? To create seamless patterns that flow correctly, you need to find a way to check how the pattern appears at the edges so that one side flows into the other. You can do that in two ways. The first is to use the Offset filter.

File ➤ Open file Pattern6.psd in the Chapter 3 Cloth_Patterns folder and make an Image ➤ Duplicate of the file as you did in Chapter 2 and click OK.

In this case, I'm using a pattern I created from thread and then scanned and straighten using the Perspective Crop tool. See Chapter 2 if you need to review. Refer to Figure 3-120.

Figure 3-120. *A custom cross-stitch pattern with texture*

Currently this pattern is 827 pixels wide by 745 pixels high. For this project, I need a square pattern so using Image ➤ Image Size, I am going to distort the pattern slightly to force it to be square. Refer to Figure 3-121.

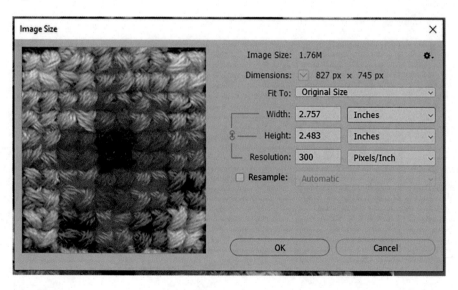

Figure 3-121. *Image Size dialog box settings*

In the Image size dialog box, disable the link between the width, height, and resolution by enabling the Resample button. Refer to Figure 3-122.

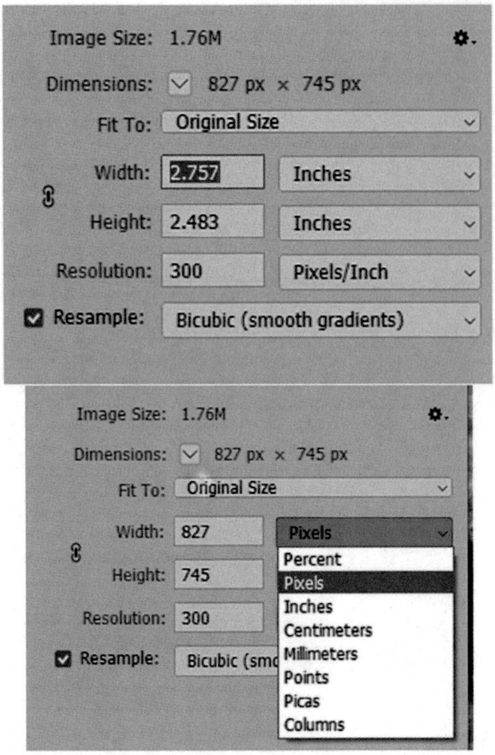

Figure 3-122. *Changing the Image Size dialog box settings from inches to pixels*

Change the units of measurement from inches to pixels. For the moment, relink the width and height and type in an even number for the width of 828 pixels. Refer to Figure 3-123.

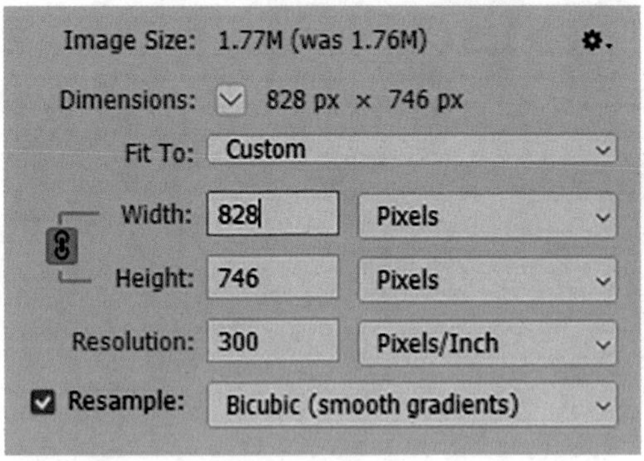

Figure 3-123. *Increasing the image size's width and height proportionately*

Disable the link again and make the height 828 pixels as well. There will be a slight height distortion but this is what this book is all about. Bicubic (smooth gradients) is OK. You will see an example of resampling in Chapter 4 where I explain this in more detail for the perspective and interpolation. Click OK to exit the dialog box. Refer to Figure 3-124.

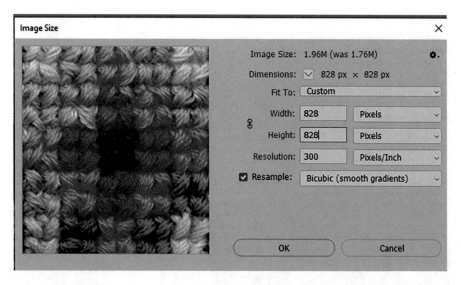

Figure 3-124. Making the pattern square by stretching and increasing the height slightly

This pattern is now 828 px wide and 828 px high. The resolution is 300ppi for print. Remember that if you are planning to use your pattern for a website, then after you create the background, set the resolution to 72ppi. While not relevant to the topic of this book, you can see example files of that resolution in my book *Graphics and Multimedia for the Web with Adobe Creative Cloud*. However, I think it is best to create the initial pattern at 300ppi because, depending on your project requirements, later you can use the background for a variety of print or web projects and are not restricted to one media.

Also, always keep a backup of your original pattern in an undistorted state. This is why we are working on a copy: in case we want to use this pattern for a different project.

Now I want to create a repeating pattern with seamless edges. I prefer working with a square canvas that has an even number of pixels. It makes the math in the next step easy to figure out. However, depending on the complexity of your pattern, you can make your file dimensions larger or smaller than mine or use a rectangular pattern instead. Just make sure each side has an even number of pixels.

Offset Filter

In the menu, go to Filter ➤ Other ➤ Offset. In the Filter Offset dialog box, set Horizontal: +414 pixels right and Vertical: +414 pixels down. This is because the design is 828 px by 828 px, so you want to break it in half to correct the edge. Then for the Undefined Areas, select Wrap Around. If set to Transparent or Repeat Edge Pixels, this will not give the result you want and only place the pattern in the corner of the canvas. Make sure that Preview is checked so you can see what is happening to your pattern on the canvas. Refer to Figure 3-125.

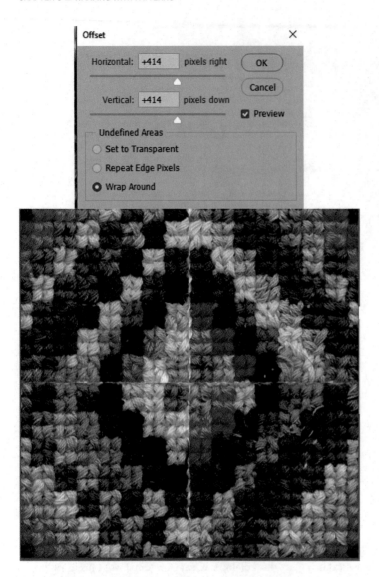

Figure 3-125. *Offset filter and preview of current pattern*

You willl notice that there are a few lines where the edges are not meeing correctly. This is due to some of the canvas that borders where I stitched and it cannot be helped with handmade items. In the Offset dialog box, click OK.

Touching Up the Pattern

In the Layers panel, create a new layer called Layer 2. Refer to Figure 3-126.

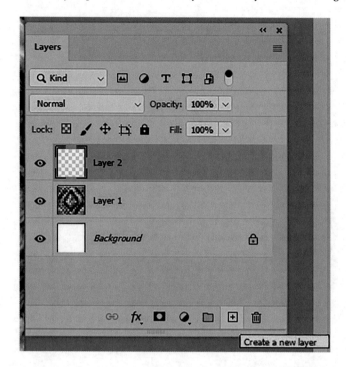

Figure 3-126. *Create a new layer to work with the Clone Stamp tool*

Then select your Clone Stamp tool (S). We talked about this tool in Chapter 2. Refer to the Options panel to adjust your settings. Use a brush preset of Soft Round Brush with a small Size like 36px and Hardness 0%. The brush should be soft so that you can blend in the threads in a natural way. Leave the Effect Mode at normal and Opacity 100% and Flow at 100%. Make sure Aligned is enabled and Sample is Current & Below. Refer to Figure 3-127.

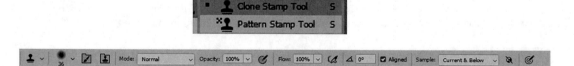

Figure 3-127. *Clone Stamp tool and its Options panel*

Alt/Option+Click to select an area to clone and then click on a location to cover that area along the seam to make sure that the pattern has a smooth transition. From the Brushes Preset Picker you can vary your bush size to smaller sizes from 36 px down to 15 px as required and Alt/Opiton+Click if you need to select a new sample area again. Also remember to use your Zoom tool and Hand tool (spacebar) if you need to move arround and get closer to the image. Refer to Figure 3-128.

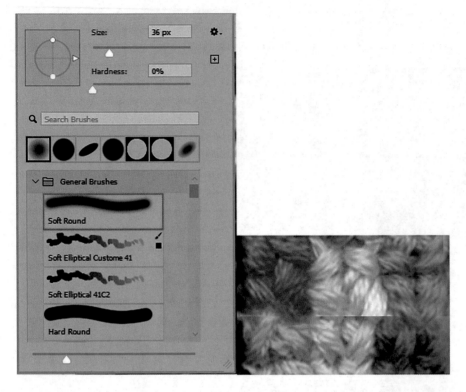

Figure 3-128. *Options panel for Brush Picker Presets for clone stamp and cloning covering parts of the seam on the new layer*

Also make sure to use your Eraser tool (E) with a Soft Round Brush so that you can clean up any mistakes or added seams and vary the size of the soft brush as well. Refer to Figure 3-129.

Figure 3-129. *Options panel for Eraser tool*

Be careful when you get near the edges with your Clone Stamp tool. Don't clone too closely to the side as that will reflect as a defect later on when the pattern is repeated at that seam. Refer to Figure 3-130.

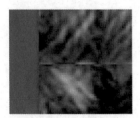

Figure 3-130. *Close-up of edge of pattern that is being cloned with the clone stamp*

Turn on and off the Layer 2 visbity eye as you work so that you can see if you have blended in the seam accurately with your Clone Stamp and Eraser tools. Refer to Figure 3-131.

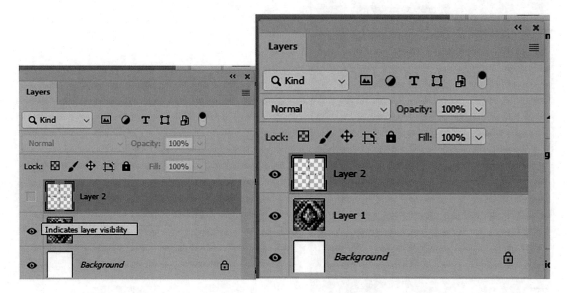

Figure 3-131. *Turning off and on the visibility of the area being cloned on the new layer*

When you are happy with the results, then from the Layers menu, rather than choose Flatten Image, try the key command of Shift+Ctrl/CMD+Alt/Option+E. This merges all visible layers but creates a copy of them on a new layer (in this case, Layer 3). Your background pattern square should be complete. Refer to Figure 3-132.

241

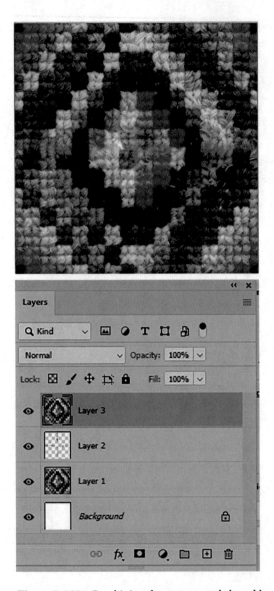

Figure 3-132. *Combining the pattern and cloned layers as a new merged and complete layer*

At this point File ➤ Save your document as a .psd file. You can refer to my file so far, Pattern6_final.psd.

Pattern Preview

If you don't want to view your pattern again in the Offset filter, another way to check it is to use View ➤ Pattern Preview. You may get a warning message that you need to use a smart object, but in this case clicking OK will allow you to see a display of the pattern as it would appear if were tiled. Refer to Figure 3-133.

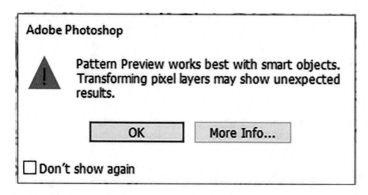

Figure 3-133. *Pattern preview info warning*

Use the Zoom tool or Ctrl/CMD+- to zoom out to see more of the pattern tiled at once. Refer to Figure 3-134.

Figure 3-134. *Pattern in Pattern Preview with thin blue guide indicating center*

The thin blue line is where your original canvas area is. Looks good to me.

For more details on how to use Pattern Preview, refer to this link: https://helpx.adobe.com/photoshop/using/pattern-preview.html.

To get out of this view, choose View ➤ Pattern Preview again.

■ **Note**   I'll start talking more about smart objects and their uses in Chapter 4 and other filters in Chapters 8 to 10.

Defining a Pattern

To complete your pattern creation, from the menu choose Select ➤ All (Ctrl/CMD+A) and then Edit ➤ Define Pattern. Give it a name like Pattern 6 and click OK to add it to the Patterns panel. Refer to Figure 3-135.

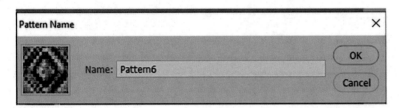

Figure 3-135. *Pattern Name dialog box*

Then drag the pattern into your group folder. Refer to Figure 3-136. File ➤ Save and close your file.

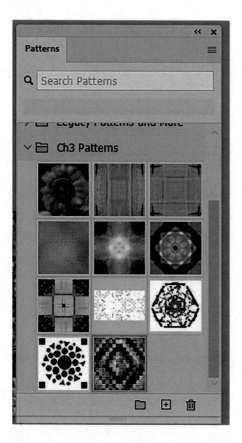

Figure 3-136. *Pattern added to the group folder in the Patterns panel*

■ **Note** If you enjoyed this pattern creation process, I have five other patterns in the `Cloth_Patterns` folder you can practice with and repeat these steps.

Earlier in the chapter you saw how to add patterns to vector shapes. Later in this chapter we will start using our patterns in backgrounds to fill areas. However, before we do that, I will show you a second way to create a unique repeating pattern from any image.

Libraries Panel: Adobe Sensei Capture Extract from an Image to a Pattern

The Libraries Panel is used by Creative Cloud to transfer different assets from Photoshop to Illustrator and other Adobe apps without having to File ➤ Open each item. Once you have added items to your panel, just drag and drop on the canvas and they can be linked to the cloud folder or embedded in the new file. The types of assets that Photoshop can create or accept are

- Colors and color themes

- Gradients

- Character styles

- Layer styles

- Brushes

- Graphics

- Patterns

Refer to Figure 3-137.

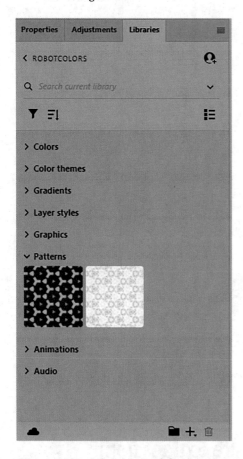

Figure 3-137. *Libraries panel that stores various assets including patterns*

You can learn more about the Libraries panel as Adobe updates it frequently. Refer to these related links to explore how additional assets can be used in libraries with other Adobe apps: https://helpx.adobe.com/photoshop/using/cc-libraries-in-photoshop.html and https://helpx.adobe.com/illustrator/using/creative-cloud-libraries-sync-share-assets.html.

Most libraries in other Adobe apps have similar importing and exporting features. However, Photoshop appears to be the only one so far that has an Adobe Sensei Capture Extract from Image to create patterns from any image. Let's see how that works.

Project: Patterns from Cloth Pattern Part 2

To start, make sure that you have your Photoshop Libraries panel visible. If you don't have a library, create one first or use one of the current libraries you have open for this project.

To create a library, click the Create new library icon or choose this option from the menu. Refer to Figure 3-138.

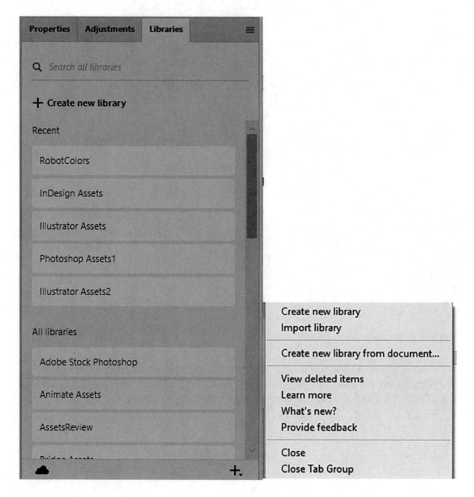

Figure 3-138. *Creating a new library to add patterns to*

Give your library a name like Photoshop Patterns and click to create. Refer to Figure 3-139.

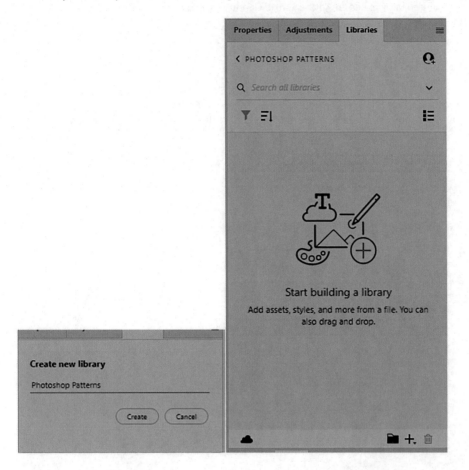

Figure 3-139. *Creating a new library in the Libraries panel*

You can now start building and adding assets in your library by dragging layers into the library or, when a layer is selected from the plus menu, choosing Extract from Image. Let's try that with an Image ➤ Duplicate copy of the file Pattern2.psd found in the Cloth_Patterns folder. Refer to Figure 3-140.

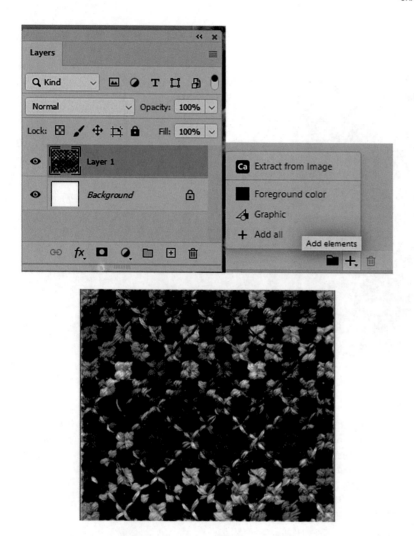

Figure 3-140. *Selecting a layer and choosing to extract from images in the Libraries panel*

To create a pattern, make sure your current background layer is visible and Layer 1 is selected. Then, from the Libraries panel, click the plus icon (add elements). Rather than choosing the graphic or the current foreground color, choose the option Extract from Image.

This brings up the Extract from Image dialog box for Adobe Capture. Refer to Figure 3-141.

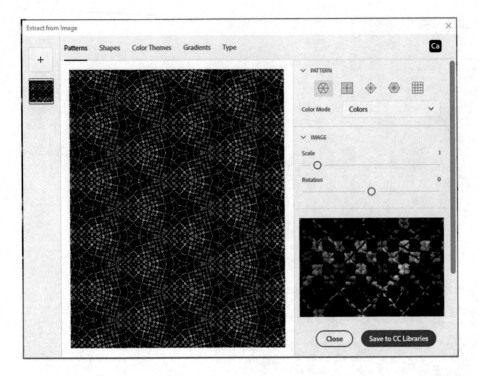

Figure 3-141. *Extract from Image dialog box*

The first tab which we will be looking at is the Patterns Tab. However, if you want to create and clean up a graphic shape, add swatches for custom Color Themes or Gradients, or find similar Type fonts make sure to check out those options on your own afterwards as it is not part of the topic of this book.
https://helpx.adobe.com/photoshop/using/capture-extension-in-libraries-panel.html
https://www.adobe.com/products/capture.html

Returning to the Patterns tab, on the left side the current pattern is stored you. When you click the plus icon, you can open and select other file formats to add to the list:

- PNG (.png)
- JPEG (.jpg and .jpeg)
- SVG (.svg)
- Bitmap (.bmp)
- ICO (.ico)
- Webp (.webp)

Refer to Figure 3-142.

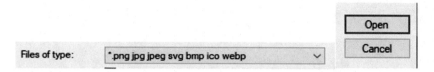

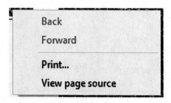

Figure 3-142. *File formats that can be opened in the Extract from Image dialog box*

Click Cancel to this dialog box if you do not want to do this or click Open to add the file to the list. You cannot remove this file from the list until you click the Close button in the dialog box, but you can right-click the thumbnail to print the current graphic pattern for reference. Refer to Figure 3-143.

Figure 3-143. *You can print a preview of your current pattern in the Extract from Image dialog box*

In the middle of the Patterns tab is the pattern live preview. Refer to Figure 3-141 You can make modifications on the right of this area under the Patterns tab. Refer to Figure 3-144.

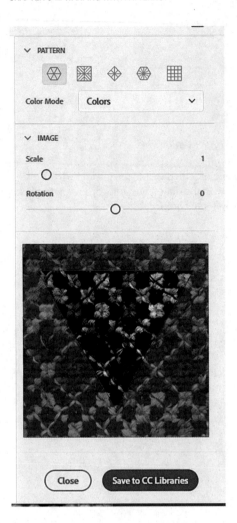

Figure 3-144. *Pattern and image options*

There are five options for tile patterns: traditional triangular, square, diamond, and hexagonal grids that create a kaleidoscope effect, like what you saw when working with symmetry paint. Refer to Figure 3-144 and Figure 3-145.

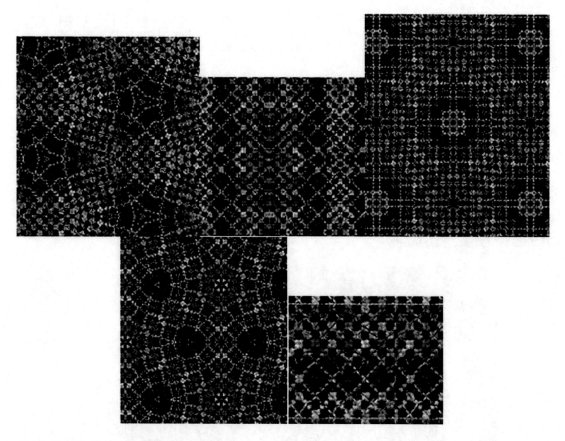

Figure 3-145. *Five different pattern variations*

You can then set the color mode for your pattern either to appear in colors or grayscale from the dropdown menu. Refer to Figure 3-144 and Figure 3-146.

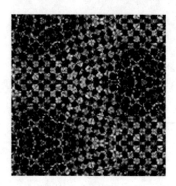

Figure 3-146. *Change the color mode from color to grayscale*

The image can then be scaled (0.1 - 10) or rotated (-180, 0, +180°) using the sliders and you can preview this in the image on the left as well as the Pattern Tile Preview area lower down. Here you can drag your image in the Pattern Preview to regenerate the pattern and see a different view or image slices. Refer to Figure 3-147.

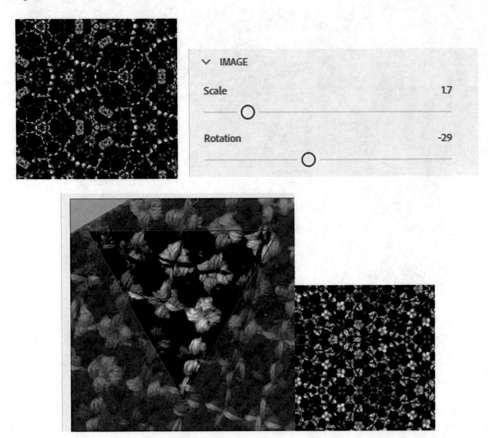

Figure 3-147. *Change the image scale, rotation, or Pattern Preview area*

Take some time to move the patterns around and move the sliders.

Once you are happy with the pattern you have created, click on the Save to CC Libraries button and the pattern will be added to your current open library as a pattern asset. Refer to Figure 3-148.

Figure 3-148. *Save your pattern to the selected CC library in the Libraries panel*

To generate more patterns from your currently selected image, drag the pattern around or adjust the sliders. For each new pattern, click the Save to CC Libraries button and then click the Close button to exit the Extract from Image dialog box.

OK, you now have a pattern or maybe several patterns. However, they may not be showing up in the Patterns panel for you to use in your current project.

Adding a Library Pattern to the Patterns Panel

While a pattern is selected in the Libraries panel, double-click it to add it to the Layers panel as an adjustment layer called Pattern Fill. Refer to Figure 3-149.

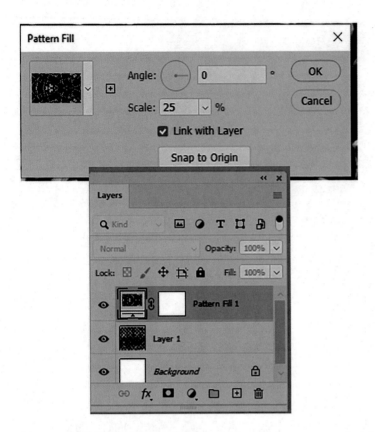

Figure 3-149. *Use the Pattern Fill dialog box to move your new pattern to your Layers panel from the Libraries panel*

A preview of the pattern appears in the dialog box while selected in the dropdown list. Click the plus icon next to the preview to create a new preset from this pattern. This will now add it to the Patterns panel. Refer to Figure 3-150.

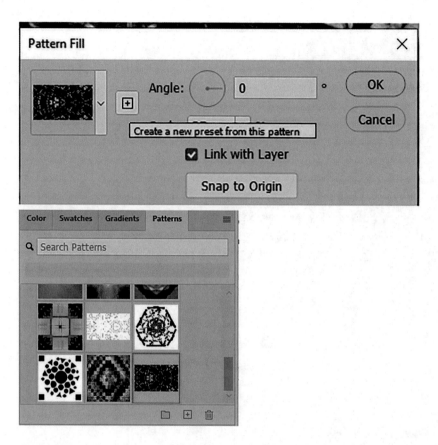

Figure 3-150. *Use the Pattern Fill dialog box to move your new pattern to your Patterns panel*

Click OK to the default message in the dialog box. We will look at this dialog box in more detail shortly. At this point, you can close the copy of the Pattern2.psd file without saving changes.

With a few extra steps, Creative Cloud library pattern assets can also later be used in Adobe Illustrator, and you can see that in Volume 2, should you want to extend the use of your patterns in only the Illustrator application.

■ **Note** If you want to save a copy of your library to share with others, in the menu, choose Export "Library Name" and it will be saved as a .cclibs file that you can save in a selected desktop folder and then later others can use when they import the library. Refer to Figure 3-151.

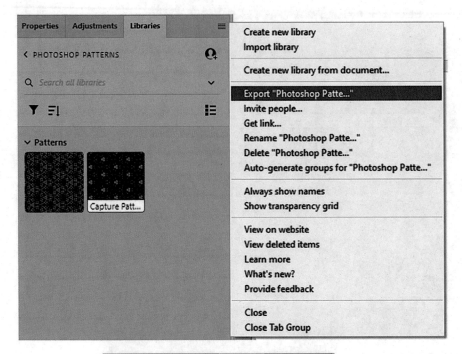

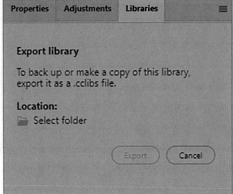

Figure 3-151. *Export patterns from the Libraries panel to share with others*

You can find a copy of this current library in this chapter's project folder, which you can from the menu load when you choose Import Library and locate the file in your folder. See the file `Photoshop Patterns.cclibs`. Refer to Figure 3-151.

Reusing Patterns or Textures

Once you have created your patterns using the various methods described earlier, there are several dialog boxes and tools that you can use them in, so let's explore them next.

For practice, you can use the blank file that you opened earlier, CH3_SymmetryPaint.psd, and make an Image ➤ Duplicate. And then, in the Layers panel, create a new layer before the next dialog box. Refer to Figure 3-152.

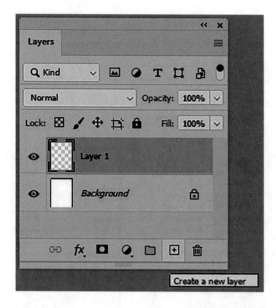

Figure 3-152. *Create a new layer in the Layers panel for practice*

Fill Dialog Box

When you want to fill a background or selection area on a layer quickly with a solid color swatch, you can use the Fill dialog box. However, did you know that you can also use it to fill an area with a custom pattern?

On a blank new layer, go to Edit ➤ Fill and from the contents list, this time choose Pattern. Refer to Figure 3-153.

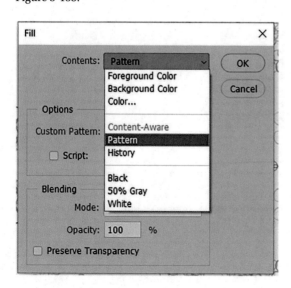

Figure 3-153. *Fill dialog box with the Pattern option*

From the Options presets Custom Pattern List, choose a pattern from the dropdown menu, which is the same as the Patterns panel, and click OK. This will make the pattern appear at its current scale across the entire layer. Refer to Figure 3-154.

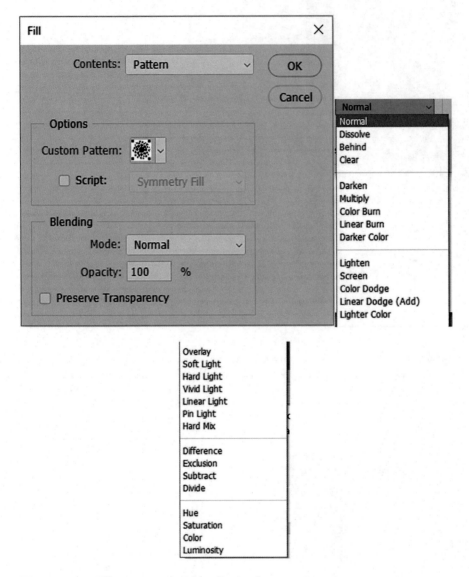

Figure 3-154. *Fill patterns can use blending modes*

Alternatively, for altered colors you can also set the blending mode (refer to Chapter 2). Here I tried a mode of Multiply. It will affect how the pattern applies itself over areas already painted on that layer. Refer to Figure 3-155.

Figure 3-155. *Fill patterns can use blending modes to affect how they fill on the canvas over previously painted areas on the same layer. These are Normal and Multiply examples*

For blending, you can also set Opacity (1-100%). Preserve Transparency can be enabled if present in the patterns.

However, the drawback of creating a background this way is that you can't scale the pattern if you find that the pattern is too large or small without destructively altering the resolution or now creating an area of missing pattern on one or more sides of the canvas. You can see how this looks when I use the Move tool and enable the Show Transform controls for scaling the pattern on the layer using the bounding box handles. Refer to Figure 3-156.

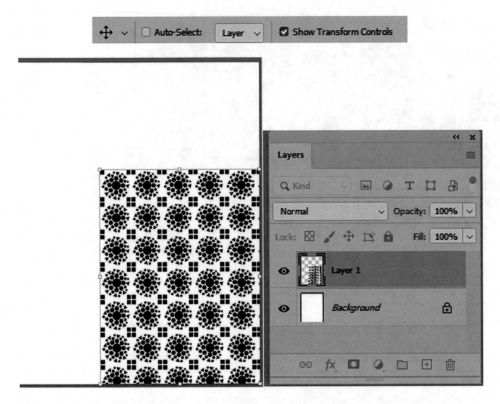

Figure 3-156. *Scaling a pattern on a normal layer with the Move Tool results in blank areas*

Later, we will scale the pattern using an adjustment fill layer instead.

Click the Cancel icon in the Options panel to undo this step for now. We'll explore this type of transformation in more detail in Chapter 4 and then disable the Show Transform Controls checkbox in the Options panel. Refer to Figure 3-157.

Figure 3-157. *In the Options panel, cancel the transform in the Move tool's Options panel and deselect Show Transform Controls*

Fill Pattern Scripts

In the Layers panel, turn off the visibility of fill Layer 1 and create a new layer. Refer to Figure 3-158.

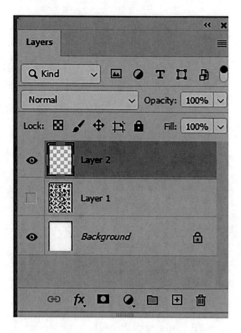

Figure 3-158. *Create a new layer in the Layers panel for practice*

Return to Edit ➤ Fill for the moment and set the blending mode back to Normal Opacity: 100% and uncheck Preserve Transparency.

Try a different pattern with more colors.

Another hidden feature in the Fill options panel is Script. Enable this checkbox if you want to experiment with this feature. Refer to Figure 3-159.

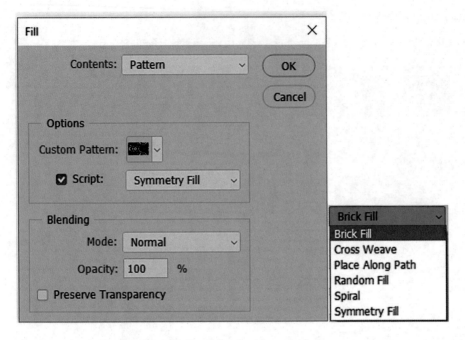

Figure 3-159. *Fill dialog box with the Script checkbox enabled*

There are six custom scripts with their own settings and previews. To enter each dialog box, select one from the list and click OK to enter the next dialog box. However, you can only apply these options one at a time, so as you test them, create a new layer and name them for each one so that you can see the difference and then return to Edit ➤ Fill and test the next one.

Your design may be different than mine depending on what pattern you choose.

Here are the details on the six custom scripts.

Brick Fill: It allows you to create a further brick-like design. Every other row is shifted by half a tile. Refer to Figure 3-160.

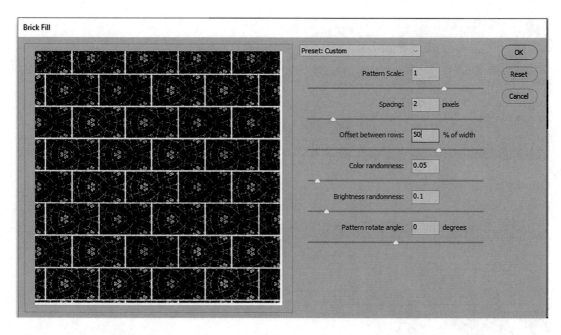

Figure 3-160. *Brick Fill dialog box*

Adjust your pattern with various sliders that affect

- **Pattern Scale (0.1 - 1.25)**: Makes the pattern larger or smaller.

- **Spacing in pixels (-1292, 0, 7980)**: Often a small spacing is best, as too high a number makes the space too great, and too low a negative number can make the pattern difficult to see. The range of spacing can vary depending on the pattern used.

- **Offset between rows percentage of width (-100, 0, 100%)**: The default is 50% and gives the best brick spacing.

- **Color randomness (0-1)**: Alters the color of the bricks with higher settings. Refer to Figure 3-161.

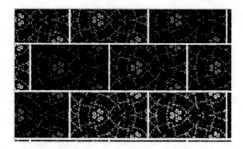

Figure 3-161. *Color randomness preview*

- **Brightness randomness (0-1)**: Alters the brightness of some of the bricks. A setting of 1 makes some bricks black. Refer to Figure 3-162.

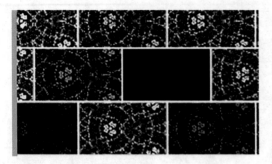

Figure 3-162. *Brightness randomness preview*

- **Pattern rotate angle in degrees (-180, 0, 180°)**: changes the angle of the bricks, creating a zig-zag like pattern. For example, with 113° degrees, refer to Figure 3-163.

Figure 3-163. *Pattern rotate preview*

I tried a Pattern scale: 0.34, Spacing of 10 pixels and Offset between rows 50% of width, Color randomness of 0.05, Brightness randomness of 0.1, and Pattern rotate angle of 0 degrees.

When done, you can click OK or you can reset the pattern by clicking the Reset button if you do not like the new settings. Refer to Figure 3-164.

Figure 3-164. *Click OK to commit the pattern settings or Reset to set back to the default*

■ **Note** Additional presets can be loaded as an .xml file and saved from this menu when altered. The current preset is Custom. Or you can reset by choosing Default from the list. Refer to Figure 3-165.

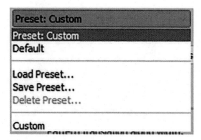

Figure 3-165. *Set the preset from custom to default or load, save, or delete a preset*

If you find that the pattern does not have the adequate spacing you are looking for, go back a step in your History panel to remove the fill and then return to the Edit ➤ Fill dialog box to adjust. Refer to Figure 3-166.

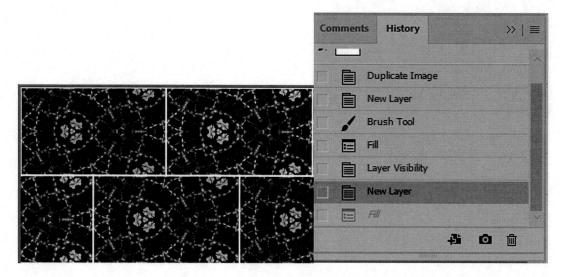

Figure 3-166. *Use your History panel if the pattern fill is not to your liking and enter the Fill dialog box again*

On a new layer, you can try the next fill script setting. Go to Edit ➤ Fill. Refer to Figure 3-167.

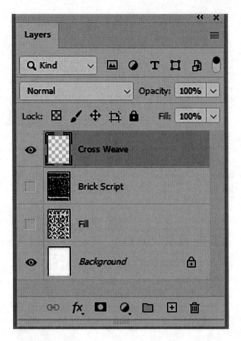

Figure 3-167. *Create a new layer in the Layers panel for practice and name the layers to keep track of your progress. Turn off the visibility of some layers to see that blank layer clearly*

Cross Weave: Allows you to create a more woven or block-like pattern with more gaps. The tiles are rotated at right angles. In this case, the tiles should be square or gaps may emerge. However, for your design, maybe rectangular is what you want. Also, tiles with a grain in one direction will have a more apparent design change rather than uniform tiles. Similar setting to a brick fill can be found, so refer to that script for more details.

- Pattern Scale

- Spacing in Pixels

- Color randomness

- Brightness randomness

Refer to Figure 3-168.

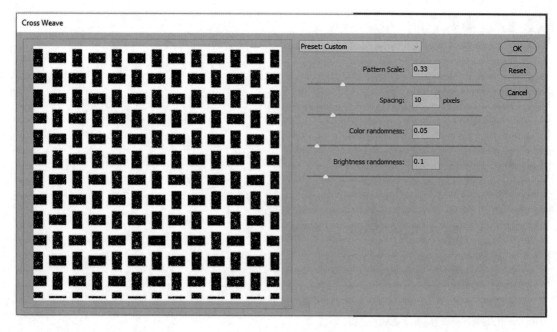

Figure 3-168. *Cross Weave dialog box*

I set my setting to Pattern Scale: 0.33, Spacing: 10 pixels, Color randomness: 0.05, and Brightness randomness: 0.1. Spacing often varies slightly from what is seen in the preview so you may need to use your History panel and enter the Fill dialog box a few times before you get the exact cross weave pattern you want. Refer to Figure 3-169.

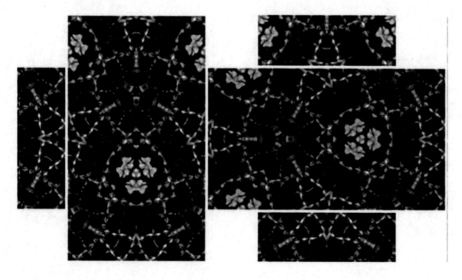

Figure 3-169. *Cross Weave pattern generated*

On a new layer, you can try the next fill script setting. Go to Edit ➤ Fill. Refer to Figure 3-170.

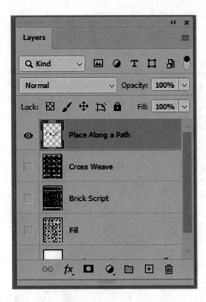

Figure 3-170. *Create a new layer in the Layers panel for practice and name the layers to keep track of your progress and keep only the new layer visible*

Place Along Path: This type of fill can only be used if you have already created a path with the Paths panel. Otherwise, you will get a warning alert. Refer to Figure 3-171.

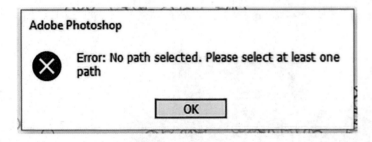

Figure 3-171. *Warning message reminds you to create a path first before using the script*

Use your Pen tool in Path mode to create a simple path. In this case, an open path is fine. Refer to Figure 3-172 and Figure 3-173.

Figure 3-172. *Pen tool options in Path mode*

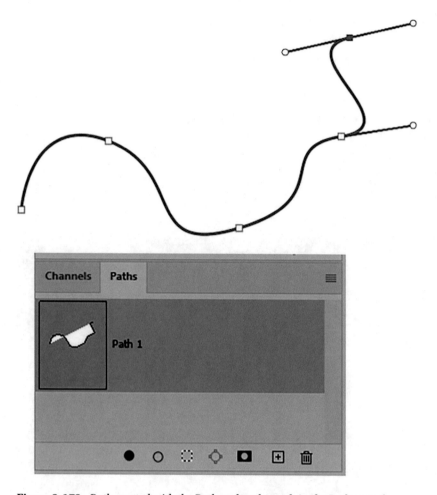

Figure 3-173. *Path created with the Path tool and a path in the Paths panel*

To review that, refer to "Project: Create a Custom Symmetry Paint Path" and the Pen tool sections of this chapter.

Once a path is created and selected in the Paths panel, then choose Edit ➤ Fill again and then the pattern and a script of Place along Path and click OK. This script fill allows you to set the following options:

- **Pattern Scale (0.1-1.25)**: Makes the pattern larger or smaller. Often smaller, less detailed patterns are best for this dialog box to render, or you may get a warning message.

- **Spacing in pixels (-2660, 0, 7980)**: Often a small spacing is best, as too high a number makes the space too great and too low a negative number can make the pattern difficult to see. This setting range may vary depending on what pattern was chosen.

- **Adjust spacing to fit**: Click the checkbox to enable

- Angle from path in degrees (-90,0,90)

- **Distance from path in pixels (0-2000)**: This setting range may vary depending on what pattern was chosen.

- **Alternate patterns**: On the path, click the checkbox to enable. It is enabled by default.

- Scale progression percentage (90-110%)

- **Skip symbol rotation**: When this checkbox is enabled, it disables the spacing and angle from the path options parts of the pattern and they will not be rotated.

- **Color randomness (0-1)**: Alters the color of the tiles with higher settings.

- **Brightness randomness (0-1)**: Alters the brightness of some of the tiles; a setting of 1 makes some tiles black. Refer to Figure 3-174.

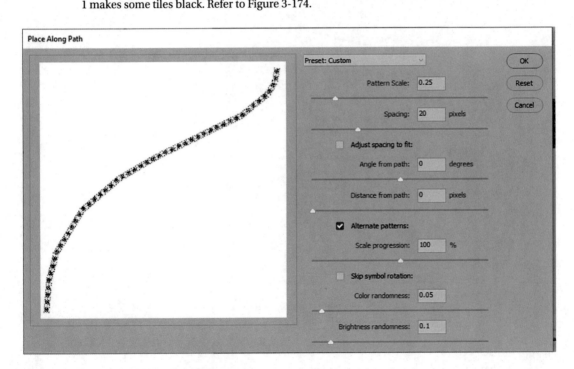

Figure 3-174. Place Along Path dialog box

■ **Note**   What you see in the preview may be slightly different than what appears on your custom path and may require you to use your History panel a few times to get the tiles on the path to your liking.

In my example, I kept the default settings and only adjusted the pattern scale to 0.25 and spacing to 20 pixels; however, depending on the pattern you created and path you made, it may look very different. Refer to Figure 3-175.

Figure 3-175. *Pattern on Path*

Make sure to deselect your path in the Paths panel by deselecting it in the Paths panel it so that you can see the path clearly. Refer to Figure 3-176.

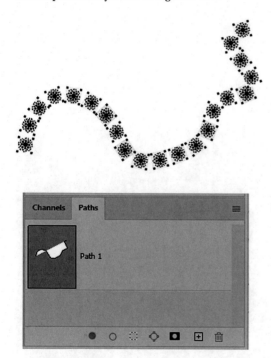

Figure 3-176. *Pattern on Path, path deselected in the Paths panel*

On a new layer you can try the next fill script setting. Go to Edit ➤ Fill. Refer to Figure 3-177.

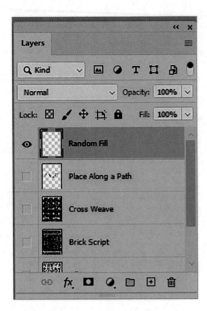

Figure 3-177. *Create a new layer in the Layers panel for practice and name the layers to keep track of your progress and make only that layer visible*

Random Fill: Creates an almost jumbled appearance of tiles of varying sizes. Refer to Figure 3-178.

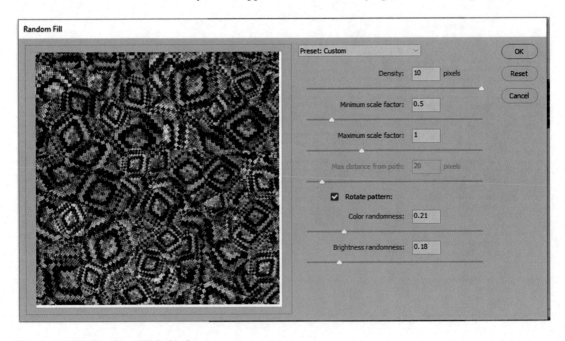

Figure 3-178. *Random Fill dialog box*

This fill allows you to set the following options:

- **Density pixels (0.1-10):** How many tiles fill the area without leaving gaps

- **Minimum scale factor (0.1-3):** Works with the minimum scale factor to alter the size of the tiles

- **Maximum scale factor (0.1-3):** Works with the minimum scale factor to alter the size of the tiles

- **Max distance from paths in pixels (0-250):** This setting is only available if a path is enabled. See "Place Along a Path Script" earlier for more details on how to create a path. Refer to Figure 3-179.

Figure 3-179. *Pattern on a Path when a path is selected prior to entering the dialog box*

- **Rotate Pattern:** When this checkbox is enabled, it causes the pattern to rotate. When disabled, the pattern can be at random sizes but are now square. Refer to Figure 3-180.

Figure 3-180. *Rotate Pattern disabled for random fill*

275

- **Color randomness (0-1)**: Alters the color of the tiles with higher settings.

- **Brightness randomness (0-1)**: Alters the brightness of some of the tiles; a setting of 1 makes some tiles black.

In this example, I set the following: Density of 10px, Minimum scale factor of 0.5, Maximum scale factor of 1, enabled Rotate Pattern, color randomness of 0.21, and brightness randomness of 0.18. Refer to Figure 3-181.

Figure 3-181. *Random fill pattern generated*

On a new layer, you can try the next fill script setting. Go to Edit ➤ Fill. Refer to Figure 3-182.

Figure 3-182. *Create a new layer in the Layers panel for practice and name the layers to keep track of your progress and make only that layer visible*

Spiral: Creates a pattern that spirals outward from the middle. Refer to Figure 3-183.

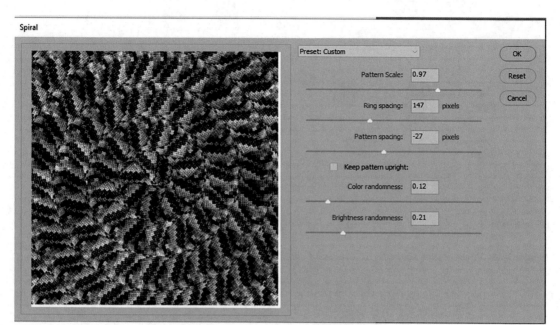

Figure 3-183. *Spiral script dialog box*

This fill allows you to set the following options:

- **Pattern Scale (0.1-1.25)**: Alters the size the pattern tiles collectively.

- **Ring spacing in pixels (-708, 0, 1656)**: Depending on the pattern, this setting may make little difference to the spacing of the spiral. Spacing range may vary due to what image is chosen.

- **Pattern spacing in pixels (-708, 0, 828)**: Bring the spacing either closer together or farther apart. Spacing range may vary due to what image is chosen.

Figure 3-184. *Keep Pattern Upright disabled and enabled*

- **Keep Pattern Upright**: When this checkbox is enabled, the pattern does not rotate with the spiral. Refer to Figure 3-184.

- **Color randomness (0-1)**: Alters the color of the tiles with higher settings.

- **Brightness randomness (0-1)**: Alters the brightness of some of the tiles; a setting of 1 makes some tiles black.

In this example, I used a Pattern scale of 55px, Ring spacing of 0 pixels, Pattern spacing of -27 pixels, disabled Keep Pattern Upright and used a color randomness of 0.12 and a brightness randomness of 0.21. Refer to Figure 3-185.

Figure 3-185. *Spiral fill pattern generated*

On a new layer, you can try the last fill script setting. Go to Edit ➤ Fill. Refer to Figure 3-186.

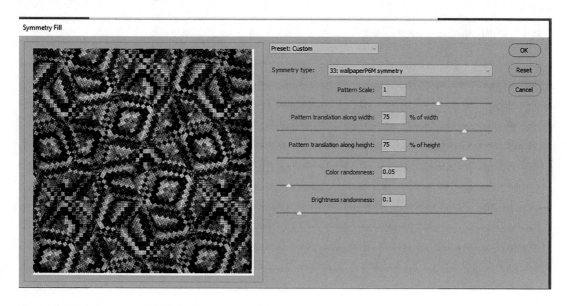

Figure 3-186. *Create a new layer in the Layers panel for practice and name the layers to keep track of your progress and make only that layer visible*

Symmetry Fill: The most complex of the six scripts, it has 33 different symmetry types to chose from. Refer to Figure 3-187 and Figure 3-188.

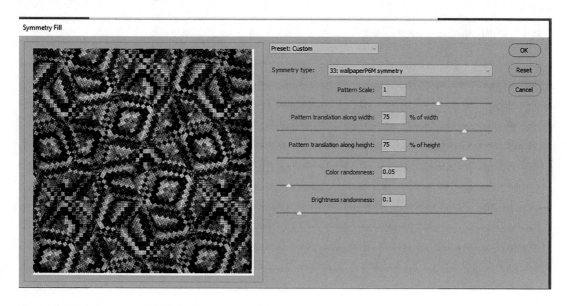

Figure 3-187. *Symmetry Fill dialog box*

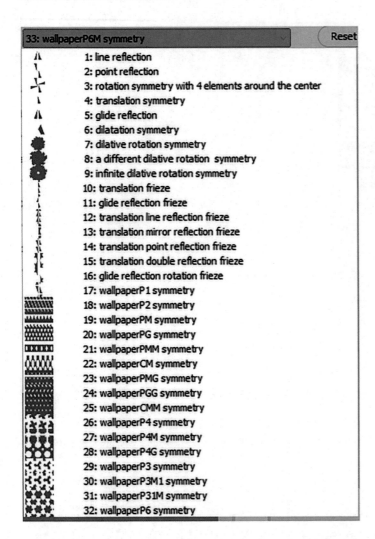

Figure 3-188. *Symmetry type options*

Take some time to preview each of the symmetry fills on your own and see which ones look best for your pattern. Every one is very different.

The one that I like the best is 7: dilative rotation symmetry. It can give some unusual effects similar to a Droste-like pattern appearing within a pattern and spiralling inwards like the center of a flower. Refer to Figure 3-189.

Figure 3-189. *Symmetry fill pattern number 7 generated*

Then for whichever symmetry type you choose, you can set the options:

- **Pattern Scale (0.25-1.25)**: Alters the size the pattern tiles collectively

- **Pattern translation along the width percentage of width (-100, 0, 100%)**: Alters the complexity of the pattern along the width

- **Pattern translation along the height percentage of height (-100, 0, 100%)**: Alters the complexity of the pattern along the height

- **Color randomness (0-1)**: Alters the color of the tiles with higher settings.

- **Brightness randomness (0-1)**: Alters the brightness of some of the tiles a setting of 1 makes some tiles black.

In this example, I used a Pattern scale of 0.9, set the Width translation to 75%, Height translation to 75%, Color randomness of 0.05, and Brightness randomness of 0.1. Refer to Figure 3-187.

Click OK to commit to exit the dialog box. And make sure to File ➤ Save your document. You can review mine in CH3_PatternFill_Finals.psd. Refer to Figure 3-190.

Figure 3-190. *Various Fill script layers in the Layers panel*

■ **Note** There are limits to how much you can scale these fills. Something you can do to avoid having areas chopped off at the edge is to make your canvas size a bit larger before you fill with a script. Another way that I have found around the resolution issue is to make sure that the file that I am creating the random or symmetry fill in is set to 600ppi. Then, if I must copy the background into a file at 300ppi, I find I can get a larger, better quality graphic if scaling is required.

Adjustment Pattern Fill Layers

Earlier, while working with the Libraries panel, you saw that you could easily create an adjustment layer pattern fill. Now we will look at that dialog box a bit further. From the Layers panel, choose Pattern from the Create New Fill and Adjustment Layers list. Refer to Figure 3-191.

Figure 3-191. *Create an adjustment layer pattern fill*

This creates a pattern fill and will hold the current pattern selected from the Patterns panel. Refer to Figure 3-192.

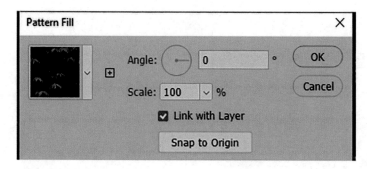

Figure 3-192. *Pattern Fill dialog box*

You can change the pattern here from the drop-down preview list if you want a different pattern. Refer to Figure 3-193.

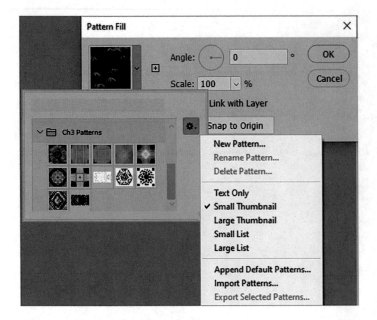

Figure 3-193. *Pattern dropdown menu and options*

Set an angle for the pattern (-180, 0, 180) and scale the pattern (1-1000%) if you find it is too large or small, which is something you could not do with Edit ➤ Fill after the pattern filled the layer. Refer to Figure 3-194.

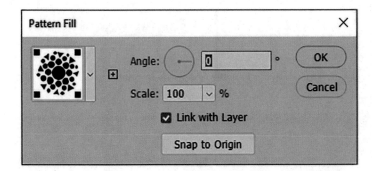

Figure 3-194. *Pattern Fill dialog box options for scale and rotation*

You can also enable the option Link with Layer as this will force the pattern to move with the layer if you use the Move tool outside of the dialog box. Use Snap to Origin to reset the pattern position if you have, while in the dialog box, adjusted the position of the pattern. If you look at your Options panel area, there is a Move tool hint to remind you that you can move and drag the pattern. Refer to Figure 3-195.

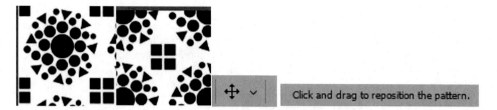

Figure 3-195. *Use the Move tool to move your pattern*

And after adjusting the settings, click OK to exit. Refer to Figure 3-194 and Figure 3-196.

Figure 3-196. *Enter the Pattern Fill adjustment layer anytime from the Layers panel*

These features are non-destructive to the pattern fill, and you can double-click the pattern fill layers thumbnail at any time to enter it and make adjustments.

As with any layer in the Layers panel, when selected you can alter the blending mode and opacity. This especially useful if you plan to have a text layer over a pattern. Lowering the opacity of a busy background layer makes the text easier to read. Refer to Figure 3-197.

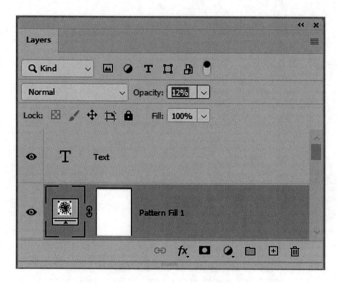

Figure 3-197. *For readability, lower the opacity of your Pattern Fill layer if text is to be over it*

We'll look at text in more detail in Chapter 5.

Also, you can paint on and edit the layer mask if you want remove part of the pattern with your brush or a selection on the layer mask thumbnail. And you can make further edits by feathering the selection in the Properties panel. Also, for more resources and details on masks, you can refer to my Photoshop Selection book that I mentioned earlier in the chapter. Refer to Figure 3-198.

Figure 3-198. *Use the Pattern Fill layer mask to hide part of the pattern*

■ **Note**   To see the options of a selected fill or adjustment layer, you need to click on the mask and refer to the Properties panel. Refer to Figure 3-199.

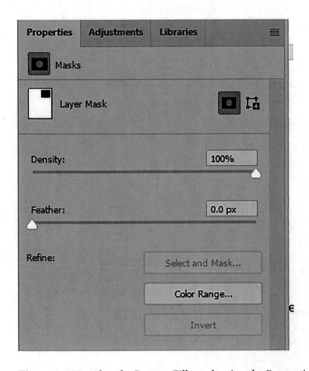

Figure 3-199. *Alter the Pattern Fill mask using the Properties panel to set Density and Feather*

Later you can apply additional adjustment layers on top of your current pattern fill for additional color enhancement.

Layer Styles with Patterns and Textures

Layer styles are great to add as embellishments to shapes as well as text. In this example, use one of the shape tools that you used earlier in the chapter and drag out a shape. I am going to Shift+Drag out a circle with the Ellipse tool. It will have a fill of white and a stroke of black in the Options panel. Refer to Figure 3-200.

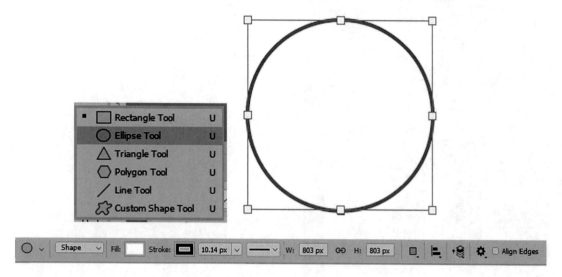

Figure 3-200. *Use a Shape tool to create a shape and the Options panel to edit before you add layer styles with patterns and textures*

While your vector shape layer is selected from the Layers panel, choose the Add a Layer Styles dropdown menu. Refer to Figure 3-201.

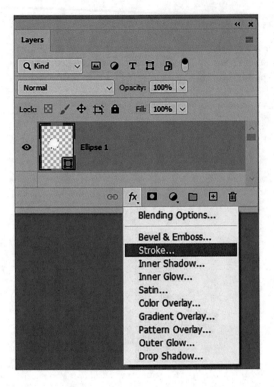

Figure 3-201. *From the Layers panel, add a layer style to your vector shape layer*

Layer styles include

- Blending Options

- Bevel & Emboss

- Stroke

- Inner Shadow

- Inner Glow

- Satin

- Color Overlay

- Gradient Overlay

- Pattern Overlay

- Outer Glow

- Drop Shadow

Most layer styles rely on a combination of opacities, blending modes, colors, and gradients to get the effect you are looking for. However, there are a few layer styles like Bevel & Emboss, Texture, Stroke, and Pattern Overlay that allow you to reuse your patterns in unique ways.

While you should experiment with all layer styles, let's focus on where to add the pattern or texture to the three I just mentioned.

To start from the list, choose Bevel & Emboss to enter the Layer Style dialog box. Refer to Figure 3-202.

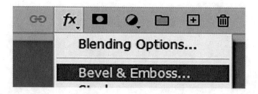

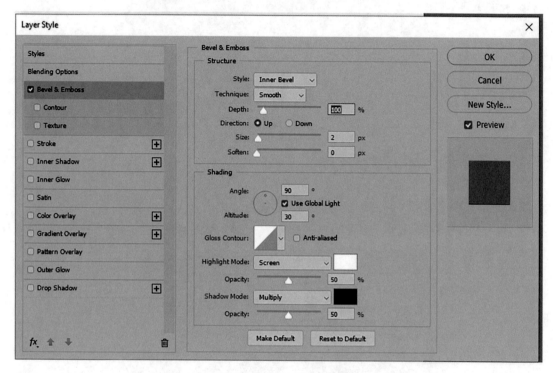

Figure 3-202. *From the Layers panel, enter the Layer Style dialog box*

■ **Note**   While in this area, you can use your Hand tool and Zoom tool key commands of Ctrl/CMD++ or Ctrl/CMD+– if you need to zoom in and out of an area.

Bevel and Emboss – Texture

In the Layer Styles dialog box, below Bevel & Emboss are two submenus of Contour and Texture. Enable the check of Texture and select it. Refer to Figure 3-203.

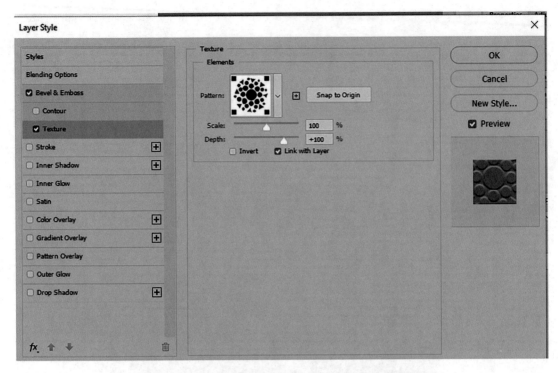

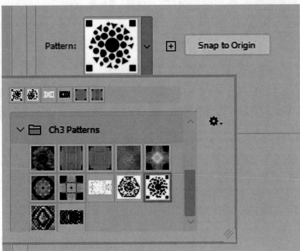

Figure 3-203. *Layer Style options for Bevel & Emboss - Texture*

From here, in the elements, you can choose a pattern that becomes an embossed texture. As with other patterns, you can add a new preset pattern to the Patterns panel using the plus icon.

With your Move tool, you can drag on the pattern on the canvas and then reset it with the Snap to Origin button. Refer to Figure 3-203 and Figure 3-204.

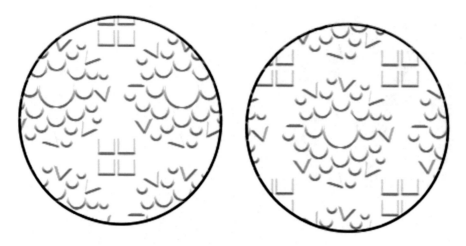

Figure 3-204. *Texture applied to shape*

Then, with the sliders, adjust the scale size (1-1000%) of the texture or texture depth (-1000, 0, +1000%). Refer to Figure 3-205 and Figure 3-206.

Figure 3-205. *Texture scale and depth adjustments*

With the checkboxes enabled, you can invert the texture pattern and link the texture with the current layer, so that it moves along with the shape once you exit from the dialog box. Refer to Figure 3-206.

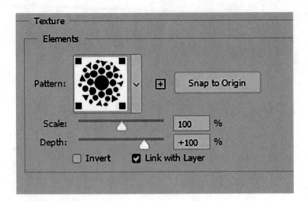

Figure 3-206. *Texture settings*

■ **Note** If you do not see the same texture setting, return to the Bevel & Emboss tab make sure that the Structure Style tab is set to Inner bevel, as Outer Bevel affects the stroke area and may cause the texture bevel to disappear inside the shape but appear on the stroke instead. Other style settings like Emboss and Pillow Emboss make the texture appear on the fill and stroke. Refer to Figure 3-207.

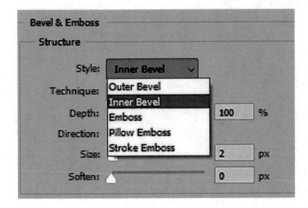

Figure 3-207. *Bevel & Emboss settings adjusted for Style*

Stroke

Click the Stroke tab in the Layer Style dialog box. At first, it might be hard to find where you can add pattern to a stroke but look in the fill type menu and change it from Color or Gradient to Pattern. Refer to Figure 3-208.

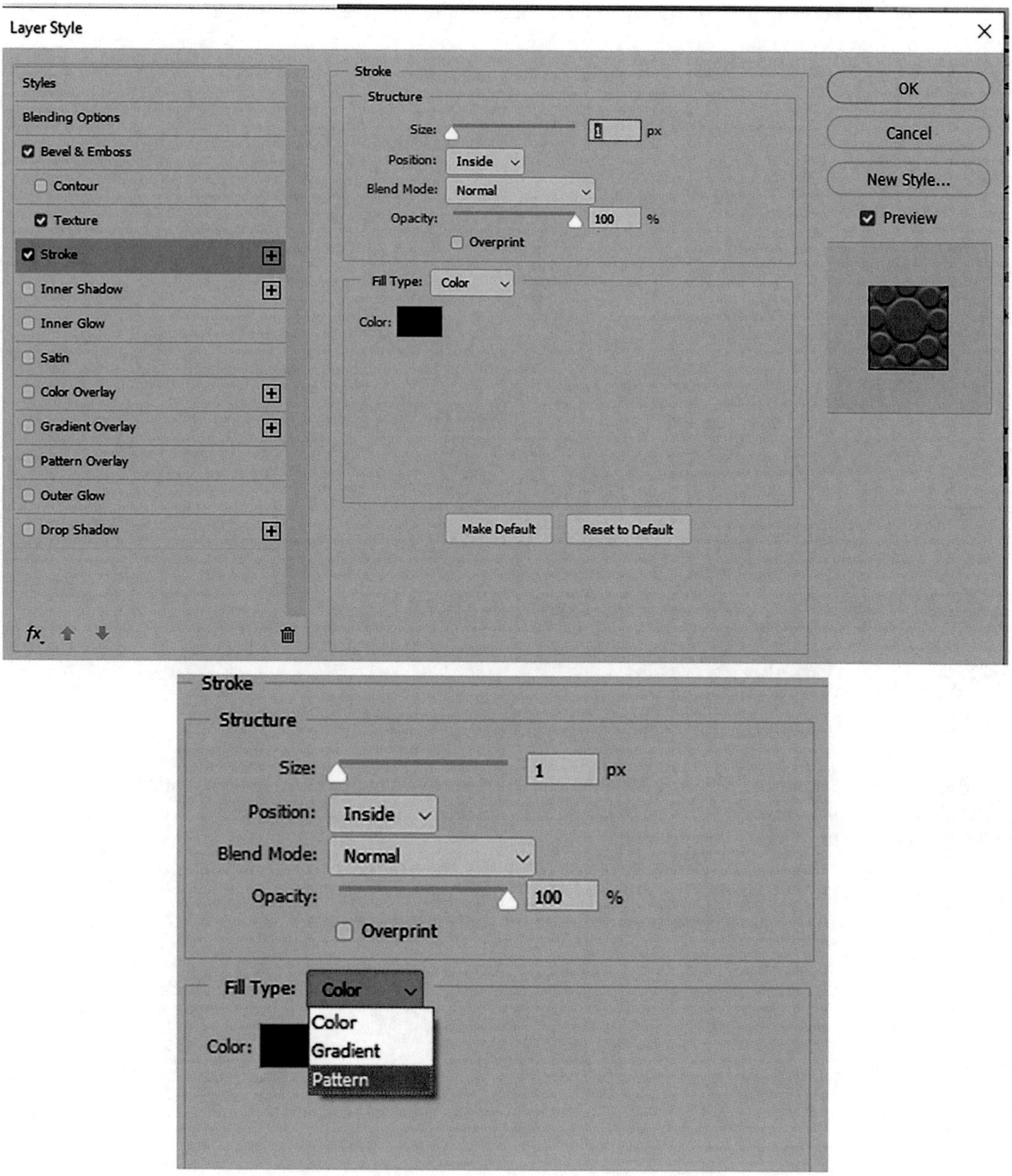

Figure 3-208. *Layer Style options for Stroke*

This will load a default pattern and the related fill type options. Refer to Figure 3-209.

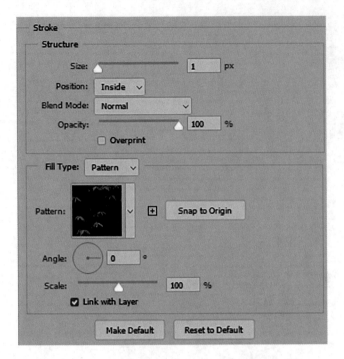

Figure 3-209. *Layer Style options for Stroke with Pattern*

As with Bevel & Emboss - Texture, you have the same options to change the pattern. Create a new pattern preset. Snap to origin if the pattern is moved, alter the angle, change the scale size, and link with layer so that the pattern moves together with the shape.

If you can't see the pattern, adjust the Stroke Structure areas of Size (1-250) px, Position to Outside, Inside, or Center, Blend Mode (see note on Blend Mode in Chapter 2), and set the Opacity (0-100%) and Overprint (blend stroke against current layer contents). Refer to Figure 3-210.

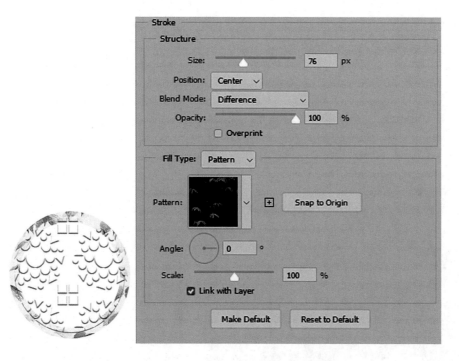

Figure 3-210. *Preview and Layer Style options for Stroke with Pattern*

In my test, I set the Stroke structure to Size: 76 px and Position to Center so that only part of the earlier texture appeared on the stroke. I set the Blend Mode to Difference, Opacity to 100%, and Overprint disabled. The pattern I used was Tree Tile 4 from the default Pattern Trees folder. I kept the angle at 0° and Scale: 100% and Link with Layer. Refer to Figure 3-210 and Figure 3-211.

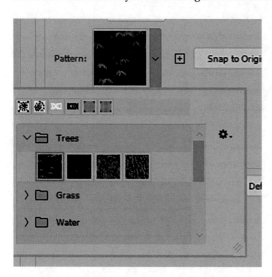

Figure 3-211. *Layer Style options for Stroke with Pattern, changing the pattern to a new pattern*

One additional feature with strokes is that you can add more than one in the Layer Styles dialog box. By clicking the plus symbol, you can add more than one stroke with a pattern over each other. Just vary the structure size, position, blend mode, and opacity, and then the pattern. Refer to Figure 3-212.

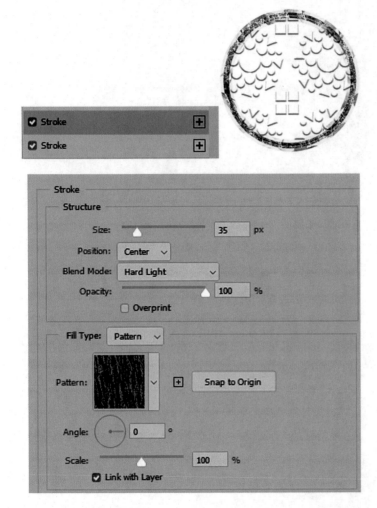

Figure 3-212. *Preview and Layer Style options for Stroke with Pattern, adding another stroke called Tree Tile 4*

■ **Note** Not all layer effects can be used multiple times; only those with a plus symbol. You can select and click the trash can icon if you need to remove a style from the list. Refer to Figure 3-213.

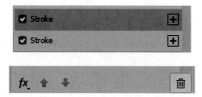

Figure 3-213. *With two stokes, use the Trash can icon to select one and remove it if required*

Pattern Overlay

Click the Pattern Overlay tab in the Layer Styles dialog box. Refer to Figure 3-214.

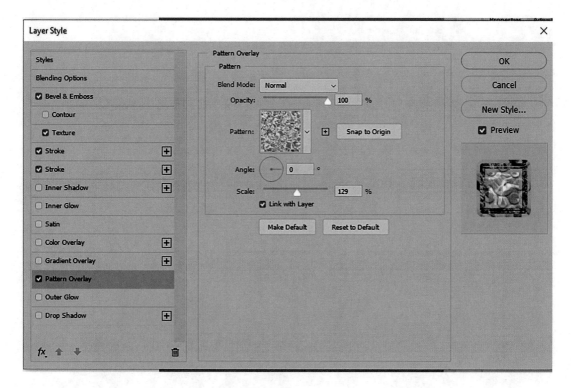

Figure 3-214. *Layer Style options for Pattern Overlay*

Pattern overlay allows you to add a pattern overtop of the shapes or text. It will cover the currently applied fill pattern, gradient, or solid color with the custom pattern you choose from the list. As with Bevel & Emboss - Texture and Stroke, you can set a Blend Mode, Opacity, Pattern, New Pattern preset, Snap to Origin if you have moved the pattern with your Move tool, Angle (-180, 0, 180), Scale (1-1000%) and Link with Layer to allow the pattern to move with the shape. Refer to Figure 3-215.

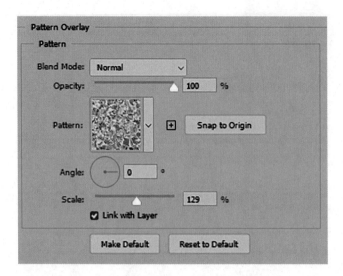

Figure 3-215. *Layer Style options for Pattern Overlay*

I'll change the pattern to one of my custom patterns. I'll leave the Blend Mode at Normal, Opacity 50%, Angle 0°, and scale at 129%. Refer to Figure 3-216.

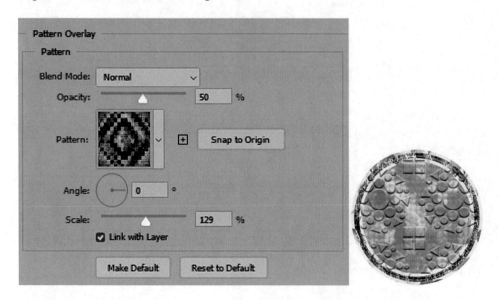

Figure 3-216. *Layer Style options for Pattern Overlay, new Pattern and Preview*

After adjusting your styles, add some layer styles such as Drop Shadow or Outer Glow to complete your style effect. Refer to Figure 3-217.

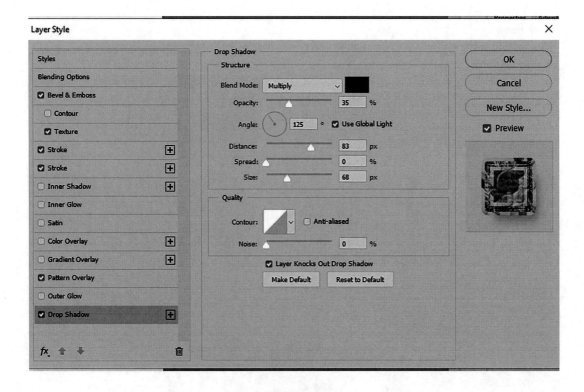

Figure 3-217. *Layer Style options for Drop Shadow and Preview*

You can then click the New Style button, name the style, and just enable the Include Layer Effects. Keep the checkboxes Include Layer Blend Options and Add to my Current Library unchecked. Click OK. Click OK to exit the Layer Styles dialog box. This will store your texture pattern and styles as a new layer style in the Window ➤ Styles panel. Refer to Figure 3-217 and Figure 3-218.

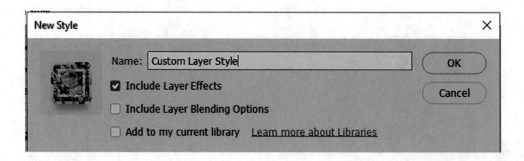

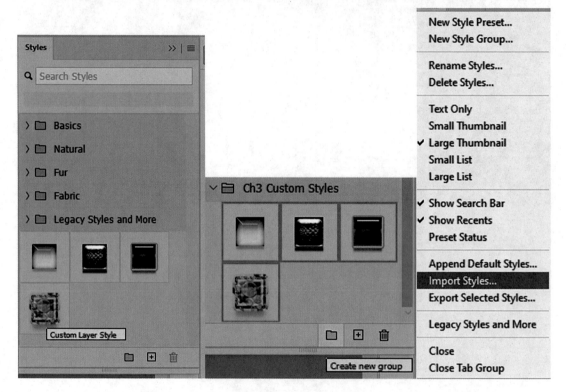

Figure 3-218. *Save your new style and store it in the Styles panel in a group folder and then you can export the style later for others to use*

Other layers styles with additional patterns can be found here as well, which you can modify for your project. We'll talk more about layer styles again in Chapter 5. However, as with the Patterns panel, you can create a group folder to store your styles in and later Save (Export Selected Styles) as an .ASL file that others can Load (Import Styles) and reuse.

You can take a look at this shape with the styles applied in my file CH3_PatternFill_Finals.psd as layer Ellipse 1. Refer to Figure 3-219.

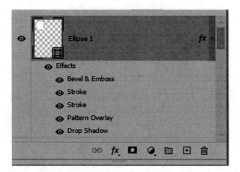

Figure 3-219. *Layer styles applied to the vector shape layer in the Layers panel*

Tools That Use Patterns

In Chapter 2, I mention that there are a few tools in the Tools panel that also use patterns, Let's look at them here. Create a new layer in your file to test. Refer to Figure 3-220.

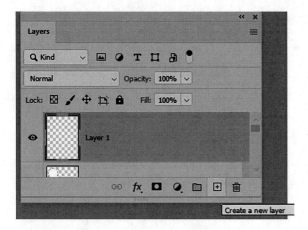

Figure 3-220. *Create a new layer in the Layers panel for practice and name the layers to keep track of your progress*

Pattern Stamp Tool (S)

Under the Clone Stamp tool in the Tools bar is a lesser-known tool called the Pattern Stamp tool (S). It's main purpose, rather than to heal or clone an area, is to act as a paint brush to stamp a pattern on a layer. Refer to Figure 3-221.

Figure 3-221. *Pattern Stamp tool*

Pattern Stamp Tool Options

Look from left to right in the Options panel. After setting your tool presets, you can set your Brush Preset Picker options and Brush Settings as mentioned in Chapter 2 in the Stamp and Healing Brushes related tools area. Refer to Figure 3-222.

Figure 3-222. *Options panel for Pattern Stamp tool*

However, after setting your blending mode (refer to Chapter 2), opacity, pressure, flow, enabling airbrush, and brush angle, then you can choose a pattern. Refer to Figure 3-223.

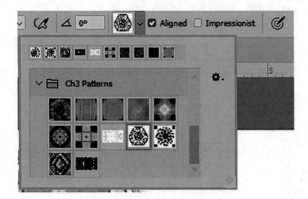

Figure 3-223. *Patterns options for Pattern Stamp tool*

On a new layer, paint a pattern. Try varying your brush from a default General Brushes of Soft Round to one of your custom brushes you created in Chapter 2. Refer to Figure 3-224.

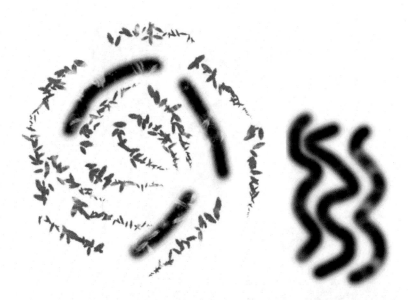

Figure 3-224. *Paint with the Pattern Stamp tool with your custom brushes or the Impressionist option*

Aligned, when enabled, uses the same offset for each stroke as you lift your brush; that same pattern still remains, and a new pattern does not start. Impressionist, when enabled, has a soft blurry effect and works best with brushes with a lower hardness. The last button icon in the Options panel, Always use Pressure for Size, is affected by the current brush settings. When off, it is controlled by the brush preset. Refer to Figure 3-223 and Figure 3-224.

■ **Tip** You can also use a Pattern Stamp tool to paint on a layer mask. This can add a mottled appearance, revealing hidden features from the image behind. This works well on a solid color fill adjustment layer. Refer to Figure 3-225.

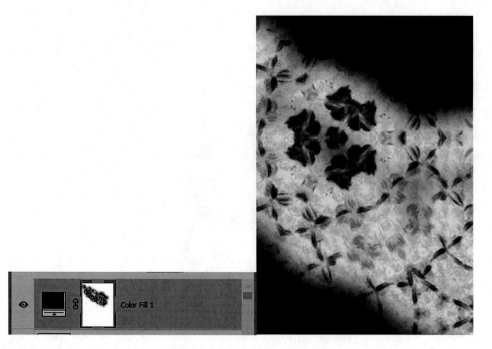

Figure 3-225. *Paint on a Color Fill mask with the Pattern Stamp tool*

You can alter the color fill at any time with the mask pattern applied.

Paint Bucket Tool (G)

The Paint Bucket tool found under the Gradient Tool is not just for filling the current foreground color into a selection but also for filling with patterns. To use with a pattern, switch the Source for Fill area to Pattern. Refer to Figure 3-226.

Figure 3-226. *Paint Bucket tool and options in the Options panel currently set to Foreground but choosing the Pattern option*

Paint Bucket Tool Options

Look from left to right in the Options panel. After the preset Tools area, you can set the source from Foreground to Pattern. Refer to Figures 3-226 and 3-227.

Figure 3-227. *Options panel for Paint Bucket tool now set to the Pattern option*

Choose a pattern from the Pattern Picker List. This time I'll just use one of the default patterns from the Water folder like Water-Pool. Refer to Figure 3-228.

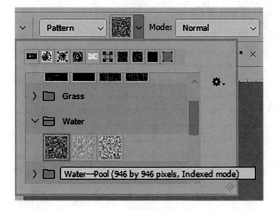

Figure 3-228. *Pattern options for Paint Bucket tool*

You can set the fill blending mode. Refer to the custom brush section in Chapter 2 if you need to review the blending modes. Refer to Figure 3-229.

Figure 3-229. *Fill Blend Mode options for Paint Bucket tool*

Set your Opacity (1-100%), Tolerance or Range of colors to fill (0-255), enable Anti-alias for a smoother blend and Contiguous for filling touching pixels. All Layers, when enabled, will affect how the paint bucket fills on the current layer; leave this setting unchecked. Refer to Figure 3-229.

Now use your Rectangular Marquee tool or any selection tool (which you can learn more details about in my Photoshop Selection book) and drag out the selection on a new layer. Refer to Figure 3-230.

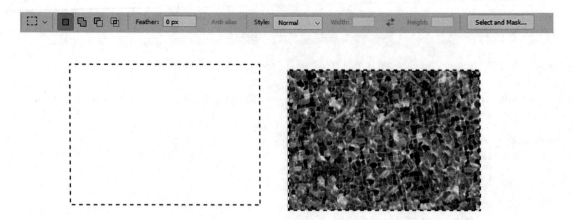

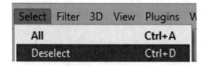

Figure 3-230. *Rectangular Marquee options and selection filled with a pattern from the Paint Bucket tool*

Select the Paint Bucket tool and click inside the selection to fill with your chosen pattern. Otherwise, it will fill the whole layer.

Then, from the menu, Select ➤ Deselect to remove the selection. Refer to Figure 3-231.

Figure 3-231. *Deselect the selection after you fill it with pattern*

■ **Tip** You can also use a paint bucket pattern to paint on a layer mask as well, which can add a mottled appearance, revealing hidden features from the image behind. Refer to Figure 3-232.

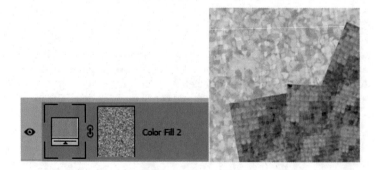

Figure 3-232. *Use the Paint Bucket tool on a mask on a Color Fill layer*

Healing Brush Tool (J)

The Healing Brush tool, which was briefly mentioned in Chapter 2, is more for cosmetic touch-ups on images and models and is often used with the other brushes and tools in the collection, such as the Spot Healing Brush and Patch tool. Its main purpose is to blend the texture, lighting, transparency, and shading of the sampled pixels to the current pixels that you are trying to "heal." Refer to Figure 3-233.

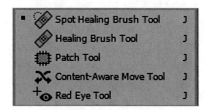

Figure 3-233. Healing Brush tool

However, once the Healing Brush tool is selected, you will discover that it also has a pattern option hidden in the source area of the Options panel. Refer to Figure 3-234.

Figure 3-234. Options panel for Healing Brush tool set to Sampled and Pattern

Healing Brush Tool Options

Look at the Options panel from left to right. Like the Brush tool, after the tool preset area, you can set your Brush Preset Picker options of size, hardness, spacing, angle, and roundness. Refer to Figure 3-234.

However, unlike the brush, which contains brush settings, the next icon allows you to access the Clone Source panel when in Sampled mode. See the Clone Stamp tool for more details. Refer to Figure 3-235.

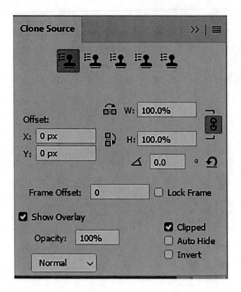

Figure 3-235. *Clone Source panel*

You can set a painting blending mode (Normal is the default, Multiply, Screen, Darken, Lighten, Color, and Luminosity). Refer to the "Brush Options and Blending Modes" section of Chapter 2 if you need to review the blending modes. Refer to Figure 3-236.

Figure 3-236. *Options panel for Healing Brush tool's Painting Blending modes*

■ **Note**   Unlike the other blending modes, Replace is used to preserve noise, film grain, and texture at the edges of the brush stroke when using a soft-edge brush and you will not have access to the Options panel's diffusion settings. Refer to Figure 3-236 and Figure 3-237.

Next, switch from the source of Sampled to Pattern and choose a pattern from the pop-up Patterns panel menu. I used one from the Trees folder, Tree Tile 4. Refer to Figure 3-237.

Figure 3-237. *Options panel for Healing Brush tool switched from Sampled to Pattern*

Aligned, when enabled, allows you to align the same offset for each stroke.

The Use Legacy setting is from an older Photoshop version (CC2014). This option will also disable the Diffusion option.

You can sample image data from the current layer, current and below, or all layers including adjustment layers. Click this button next to this menu to exclude adjustment layers while healing. Refer to Figure 3-238.

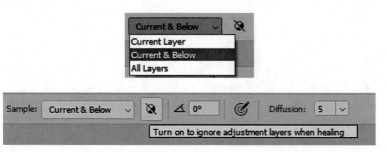

Figure 3-238. *Options panel for Healing Brush tool Sample options*

The next section allows you to set the brush angle, which is the same as what is set in the Brush Preset Picker. The next button is Always use Pressure for Size or let the brush preset control the pressure. And a Diffusion (1-7) slider. This slider and number controls how quickly the pasted region adapts to the surrounding image. Adobe recommends you select a lower value for images with grain or fine details and a higher value for smooth images.

Depending on the choice of brush, blending mode, or pattern, this can create some unusual blur and pattern effects.

I made a copy of my Symmetry Fill layer (drag over the Create new layer icon in the Layers panel) and then tested the tool on it with a pattern.

While in Pattern source, you do not need to Alt/Option+Click to retrieve a sample for the heal; simply paint with your brush and create a pattern covering.

I recommend working on a new layer when using this tool, so that you can later fade the layer's opacity or alter its blending mode as required.

Everyone's design will turn out differently. You can review my example in CH3_PatternFill_Finals. psd. I kept the following layers visible to create this effect. Refer to Figure 3-239.

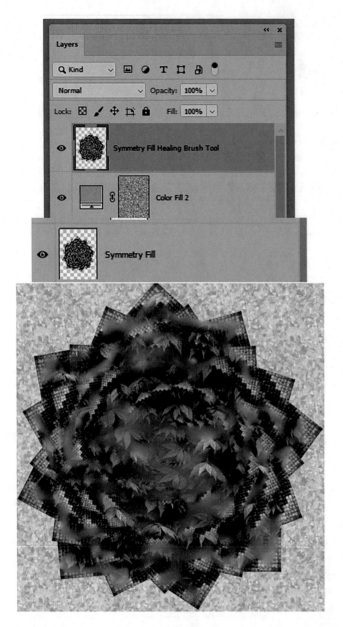

Figure 3-239. *Painting with the healing brush on a copy of the symmetry fill layer and a patterned color fill mask behind*

For more detail on healing brush topics, you can refer to these links: https://helpx.adobe.com/photoshop/using/retouching-repairing-images.html and https://helpx.adobe.com/photoshop/using/healing-examples.html.

Patch Tool (J)

The other healing tool I will mention is the Patch tool. If you do not use this tool, often you may be unaware that it can use patterns as well for basic cosmetic touch ups and artistic effects. To locate this setting in the Options panel, switch the Patch dropdown menu from Content-Aware to Normal. I created a copy of the layer Symmetry Fill again to work with this tool. Refer to Figure 3-240.

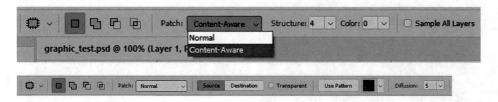

Figure 3-240. *Options panel for the Patch tool set from Content-Aware to Normal Patch mode*

Patch Tool Options

After the tool presets area, use this tool now to make a new selection with the tool, dragging in a loop shape with the new selection option. Refer to Figure 3-241.

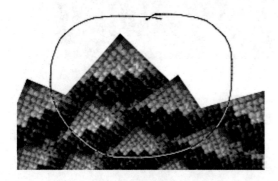

Figure 3-241. *Create a selection*

Additional selection options after you have made a new selection are

- Add to selection (Shift+Drag)

- Subtract from selection (Alt/Option+Drag)

- Intersect with selection selections (Alt/Option +Shift+Drag)

I talk about selections in detail in my previously mentioned book. Patch is set to Normal in the drop-down menu. When the Source tab is on, drag the selection to get the selected clone area from the new sample source. This will add or blur that new information into the selection. Refer to Figure 3-240 and Figure 3-242.

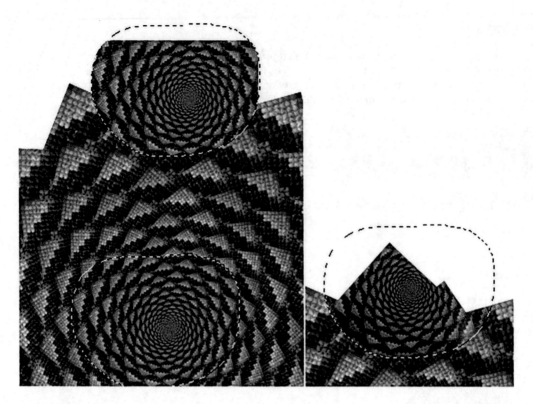

Figure 3-242. *Move the selection as a source*

Or choose the Destination tab and drag to move the selection sample to that area you want to cover. Refer to Figure 3-243.

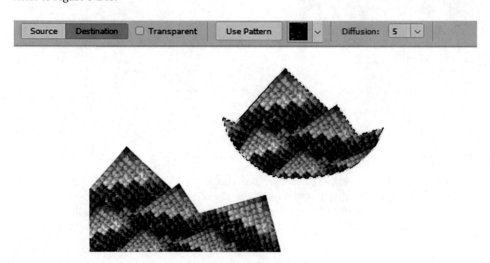

Figure 3-243. *Move the selection as a destination*

Enable the Transparency checkbox to use transparency when blending. This is good for extracting texture with a transparent background from sampled areas. Disable it if you want to fully replace the target with sampled image. Refer to Figure 3-244.

***Figure 3-244.** Transparent option enabled and disabled*

In the next section, select a pattern from the Pattern dropdown menu and click the Use Pattern button. This will affect the blur of the blend based on the pattern chosen from the Patterns panel menu. Refer to Figure 3-245.

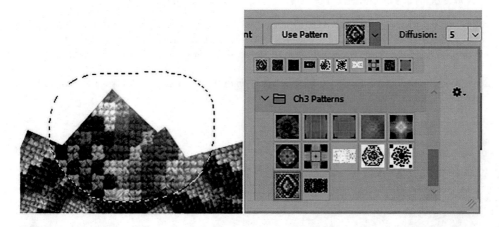

***Figure 3-245.** Options panel for the Patch tool. Click the Use Pattern button to add the pattern to the patch*

In the last section, as with the Healing Brush tool, you can also set the degree of diffusion from 1-7. See the Healing Brush tool for more details on this option. Refer to Figure 3-245.

Click elsewhere on the canvas to remove the selection, or Select ➤ Deselect, or Ctrl/CMD+D.

Everyone's design will turn out differently. You can review my example in CH3_PatternFill_Finals.psd. Refer to Figure 3-246.

***Figure 3-246.** Edited layer using the Patch tool*

■ **Note** In Normal mode, I had to work directly on the layer to sample and use the pattern. I could not use the Sample All Layers option that would have been available had the Patch mode been set to Content-Aware. Refer to Figure 3-247.

Figure 3-247. *Options panel for the Patch tool in Content-Aware mode*

For details on content-aware features, you can check out in this link (it also applies to the spot healing brush and content-aware move tools): `https://helpx.adobe.com/photoshop/using/content-aware-patch-move.html`.

Make sure to File ➤ Save your document at this point.

Project: Create a Texture for the Filter Gallery

While custom patterns and textures seem interchangeable when it comes to layer styles and some healing tools, this is not the case when it comes to filters, as you will see in Chapter 8 when you work in the filter gallery. In this gallery, you will not have access to the Patterns panel and must instead create a file to load a texture.

We can create that quickly here. File ➤ Open `Pattern4.psd` found in the `Cloth_Patterns` folder. Make an Image ➤ Duplicate. Refer to Figure 3-248.

Figure 3-248. *Cross-stitch pattern to be used for texture*

This file is currently in RGB mode. Convert it to Image ➤ Mode ➤ Grayscale and from the warning message choose Flatten. In the next message, choose Discard. Refer to Figure 3-249.

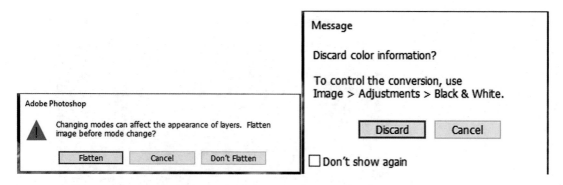

Figure 3-249. *Warning message when changing a file from RGB color mode to grayscale*

The reason I made the pattern in grayscale is that I really do not care about the color, only the texture of the threads, so a grayscale image is just what I need. This is best when you want to do certain types of embossing with textures because you need the shadows and highlights. Refer to Figure 3-250.

Figure 3-250. *Grayscale pattern*

At this point, to make the pattern seamless, you could use the Offset filter. We will do that in Chapter 8. But instead, I will just use my Crop tool to move the bounding box handles inward and take a bit off the sides and then click the Commit check to commit the crop. Refer to Figure 3-251.

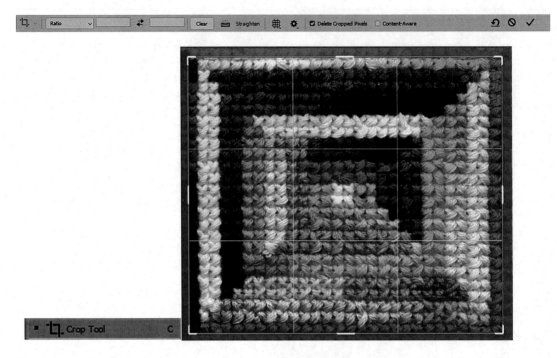

Figure 3-251. *Grayscale pattern cropped using the Crop tool and its Options panel*

Then with my View ➤ Pattern preview, I'll check to see how it looks. Click OK to any warning message. Refer to Figure 3-252.

Figure 3-252. *Testing the texture pattern in Pattern Preview*

316

The texture now looks good. Click View ➤ Pattern Preview again and click the Move tool to exit the Crop tool.

Make sure to File ➤ Save this as a .psd file such as Pattern4_Texture.psd. You can find my example in the folder Cloth_Patterns. Keep it aside in your project folder for now. In Chapter 8, we'll look at this custom texture again and how to load it and test whether it is seamless.

■ **Tip** You can also use Patterns found in the Patterns panel and in the Layers, panel rasterize the Pattern Fill adjustment layer when you right-click on it and from the pop-up men choose Rasterize Layer and then repeat this project to re-use those patterns as a texture.

In this current version of Photoshop, you can also create additional patterns using the new Window ➤ Materials panel for Substance Materials which you can learn more about here:

https://helpx.adobe.com/photoshop/using/substance-3d-materials-for-photoshop.html

Folders containing Brushes (.abr), Library files (.cclibs), Patterns (.pat), Shapes (.csh) and Layer Styles (.asl) used in this Chapter can be found in the Chapter's folder and you can import them using that panels menu.

Summary

In this chapter, you looked at the many ways to create patterns and use them with other tools such as the Pen and Shape tools and then dialog boxes, the Offset filter, and the Layers panel. While working with patterns can involve many tools, in the next chapter you will look at a collection of editing tools that affect the transformation of an object on a layer, either in a destructive or non-destructive way, depending on the type of layer that is used.

CHAPTER 4

■ ■ ■

Transform Your Layers in a Non-Destructive Way with Smart Objects

Chapter goal: Using the Edit ➤ Transform menu, you will first work with a layer that is not a smart object and then see how it is better to work with smart object layers so that the edits stay non-destructive until you are ready to flatten a copy of the image.

Photoshop's Edit menu, besides allowing you to Edit ➤ Undo (Ctrl/CMD+Z), Redo (Shift+Ctrl/CMD+Z), Copy (Ctrl/CMD+C), and Paste (Ctrl/CMD+V), has additional tools that are not found in the Tools panel. They include various transformations or commands for the Free Transform and Transform, which in the submenu includes

- Scale

- Rotate

- Skew

- Distort

- Perspective

- Warp

In this chapter, we will focus on these Transform commands and later explore other Edit menu commands in Chapters 5, 6, and 7.

Refer to Figure 4-1.

© Jennifer Harder 2023
J. Harder, *Perspective Warps and Distorts with Adobe Tools: Volume 1*,
https://doi.org/10.1007/978-1-4842-8710-1_4

Undo Brush Tool	Ctrl+Z
Redo	Shift+Ctrl+Z
Toggle Last State	Alt+Ctrl+Z
Fade Brush Tool...	Shift+Ctrl+F
Cut	Ctrl+X
Copy	Ctrl+C
Copy Merged	Shift+Ctrl+C
Paste	Ctrl+V
Paste Special	▶
Clear	
Search	Ctrl+F
Check Spelling...	
Find and Replace Text...	
Fill...	Shift+F5
Stroke...	
Content-Aware Fill...	
Content-Aware Scale	Alt+Shift+Ctrl+C
Puppet Warp	
Perspective Warp	
Free Transform	Ctrl+T
Transform	▶
Auto-Align Layers...	
Auto-Blend Layers...	
Sky Replacement...	
Define Brush Preset...	
Define Pattern...	
Define Custom Shape...	
Purge	▶
Adobe PDF Presets...	
Presets	▶
Remote Connections...	
Color Settings...	Shift+Ctrl+K
Assign Profile...	
Convert to Profile...	
Keyboard Shortcuts...	Alt+Shift+Ctrl+K
Menus...	Alt+Shift+Ctrl+M
Toolbar...	
Preferences	▶

Again	Shift+Ctrl+T
Scale	
Rotate	
Skew	
Distort	
✔ Perspective	
Warp	
Split Warp Horizontally	
Split Warp Vertically	
Split Warp Crosswise	
Remove Warp Split	
Convert warp anchor point	
Toggle Guides	
Rotate 180°	
Rotate 90° Clockwise	
Rotate 90° Counter Clockwise	
Flip Horizontal	
Flip Vertical	

Figure 4-1. *The Photoshop Edit menu contains the Free Transform tool and its submenu*

■ **Note** You can find the projects for this chapter in the Chapter 4 folder.

Project: The Warped Vase

File ➤ Open the file vase_1.psd. Make an Image ➤ Duplicate of the file as you did in previous projects to practice on.

This project contains two layers, one that contains an illustrated vase object that was marquee selected in Adobe Illustrator with its Selection tool (V) and then Edit ➤ Copy (Ctrl/CMD+C) from Illustrator into Photoshop via Edit ➤ Paste (Ctrl/CMD+V). Then I chose the option of Paste As Pixel for a normal rasterized Layer 1 and then repeated the steps for the other layer that was pasted as a vector smart object layer. Then I clicked OK. Refer to Figure 4-2 and Figure 4-3.

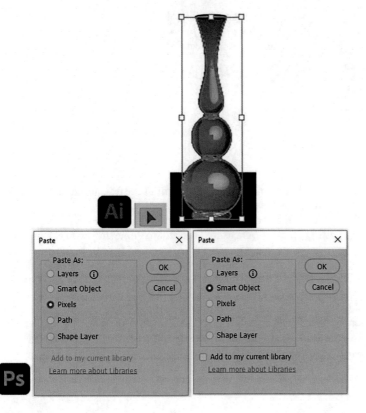

Figure 4-2. *Images that are pasted from Illustrator into Photoshop have several different paste options in the dialog box*

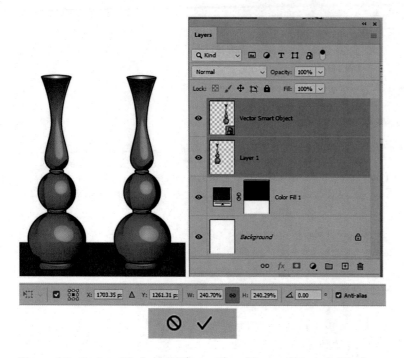

Figure 4-3. *Paste as Pixels on left (Layer 1) and Smart Object on right (vector smart object) in the Layers panel*

To complete the paste in each case, I then had to move, scale, and commit the transformation using the Options panel and you can see the results in the Layers panel. Refer to Figure 4-3.

For a more detailed review of Illustrator itself, you can check out Volume 2 of this book. However, I will just mention that if you need to copy a path, shape, or layers from Illustrator to Photoshop, you can use those Paste as options. Refer to Figure 4-2. Note that some layers may become rasterized (pixels) in the process, so that is why I prefer to paste as a smart object. Also, if you want your items to be added to the Creative Cloud Libraries panel, enable the option called Add to my current Library. For this project, I left that checkbox disabled.

Come back to the copy of the file vase_1.psd. For the first part of the project, I will demonstrate what happens when we use a normal layer (consider pixel or rasterized) before we use the smart object layer. Then we will continue the project with the smart vector object only. As you'll see, a smart object layer is considered non-destructive, and I will explain my reasons for doing so throughout the chapter.

Remember, as you work with each Move or Transform command, refer to Options panel to adjust the settings.

Move Tool Review

When working with layers and doing transformations to an object on a layer, generally the first tool that you work with is in your tools panel is the Move Tool, which we looked at briefly in Chapter 1 and again when we needed to transform a fill pattern that was scaled in Chapter 3. Once you have moved an object into place, you may then want to transform it in some way such as scaling or rotating. To do that, you could, from the Options panel, choose to enable the Show Transform Controls check box. Refer to Figure 4-4.

Figure 4-4. *Options panel for the Move tool*

Let's try that now. Select the Move tool and Layer 1 in the Layers panel and from the Options panel, enable the Show Transform Controls option. Refer to Figure 4-5.

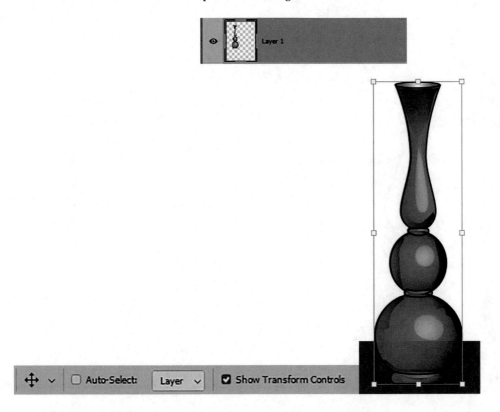

Figure 4-5. *Use the Move tool Options panel to scale your vase on Layer 1*

Now use your Move tool to drag and move the vase around on the canvas. Then use the bounding box handles to scale or rotate the vase. Your mouse cursor will change to different shapes indicating what task you can perform, as you saw when you worked with shapes in Chapter 3. Refer to Figure 4-6.

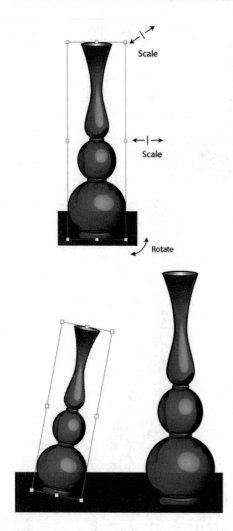

Figure 4-6. *Scaling and rotating an item on a layer with the Move tool*

Free Transform with Rasterized Layers

Hold down your mouse key and drag to move the bounding box handles on the Layer 1 object and the Free transform options panel opens. Refer to Figure 4-7.

Figure 4-7. *Options panel for Free Transform*

We will explore this options panel in a moment. However, once you have completed your transformation, click the check icon on the far right to commit the transformation and return to the Move tool. Uncheck the Show Transform Controls box if you no longer want to see the bounding box. Refer to Figure 4-8.

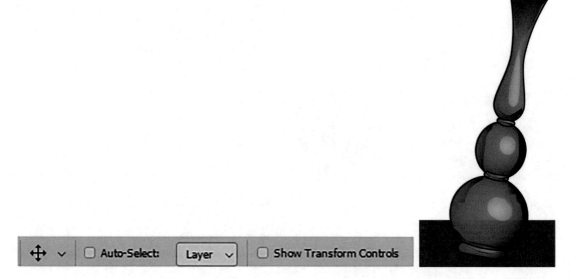

Figure 4-8. *Options panel Move tool with check box Show Transform Controls disabled and bounding box around vase hidden*

Another way to get to this menu without enabling this checkbox is to select the Layer 1 layer, which is rasterized in the Layers panel, and choose Edit ➤ Free Transform.

■ **Note** Background layers first must be double-clicked on to convert them to normal layers. Click OK in the New Layer dialog box and they become Layer 0. Refer to Figure 4-3 and Figure 4-9.

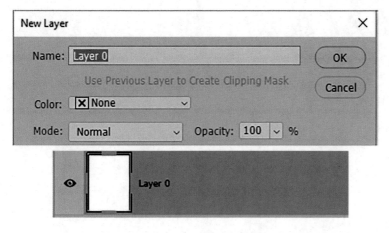

Figure 4-9. *New Layer dialog box after double-clicking on a background layer*

However, if you keep entering the Free Transform Command options and scaling your layer repeatedly, this causes your pixels and detail on your layer over time to become more and more blurry. This is true when you decide to scale a very small image suddenly larger after you have saved the file. With rasterized layers, each time you save, close the file, and then open it again to scale in the Free Transform panel and click the check to commit, the quality of the graphic degrades, and information is lost. Refer to Figure 4-7 and Figure 4-10.

Figure 4-10. *After scaling the vase multiple times, Layer 1 pixels start to become fuzzy and less crisp*

So, scaling normal pixelated layers is not a good option when you're undecided as to what your exact size of the object on your layer should be.

To return Layer 1 back to its previous state, use your History panel. Refer to Figure 4-11.

Figure 4-11. *Use the History panel to undo multiple steps*

Let's see from now on how working with a vector smart object layer is a better solution and non-destructive when working with Free Transform commands and related options.

Tip: In your own projects, if you want to select more than one layer for transformation. Either Ctrl/CMD click on non-sequential layers or Shift+Click to select the contiguous layers. Refer to Figure 4-12.

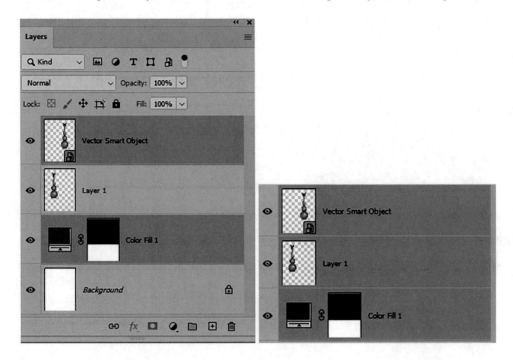

Figure 4-12. *Select multiple layers in the Layers panel*

Likewise, you can also transform layers in a group folder or linked layers at the same time. If only part of a normal layer, then on the selected layer, drag a rectangular marquee with the Rectangular Marquee tool around the area you want to select and then choose Edit ➤ Free Transform. This last selection option will not work with smart object layers. Refer to Figure 4-13.

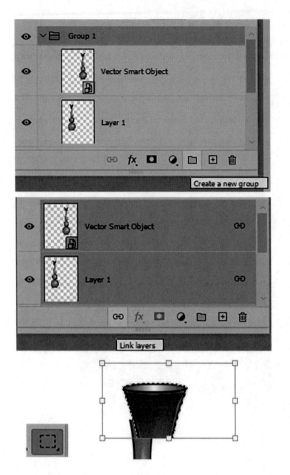

Figure 4-13. *Group and linked layers can be scaled in unison, but only a normal layer can allow you to scale part of a selection*

Free Transform with a Smart Object Layer

Now we will focus on using the Vector Smart Object layer to make changes and alterations to the vase. Select the layer and choose Edit ➤ Free Transform. Refer to Figure 4-14.

Figure 4-14. *Select the Vector Smart Object layer in the Layers panel*

Free Transform (Ctrl/CMD+T) allows you to move, scale, rotate, skew, and warp your shape very easily.

■ **Note** While you are in the transformation, you will not be able to undo or go back a step with your History panel, so make sure to use Edit ➤ Undo (Ctrl/CMD+Z) from the menu if you make any mistakes. While working, if you need to zoom in and out, use key commandsCtrl/CMD + +, Ctrl/CMD + −, and Ctrl/CMD + 0. Use the spacebar to access the Hand tool. If you try clicking on any of these tools in the Tools panel, it will cause you to exit the transform area while working. While we work with this Free Transform command and its related tools, there are other useful key combinations you will discover.

Free Transform Options

Let's look at the Options panel. Refer to Figure 4-15.

Figure 4-15. *Options panel for Free Transform*

The tool's presets area is greyed out as each transformation is unique, and because it is not a tool found in the Tools panel, you cannot add additional tool presets here. The first section allows you add a toggle reference point. Click the check if you want to enable this option. Most times, by default, you want to scale or rotate from the center, but in other cases you may want to pivot from a left, right, top, or bottom edge or corner, as you will try later in a project in this chapter. Refer to Figure 4-16.

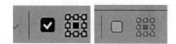

Figure 4-16. *Options panel for Free Transform to enable and disable reference points*

For now, I will leave the center reference point option disabled or enabled at center point.

The next section allows you to find where on your canvas you use your x and y coordinates from your reference point. Refer to Figure 4-17.

Figure 4-17. *Options panel for Free Transform to set your X and Y coordinates*

You can then click and drag in the center of the object on your layer and move, as you would with the Move tool, the object around on the canvas. The change will be reflected in those text boxes. Refer to Figure 4-18.

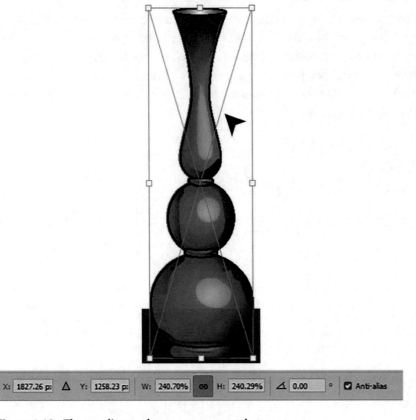

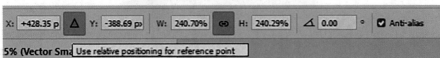

Figure 4-18. *The coordinates change as you move the vase*

The triangle shape between the x and y coordinates, when clicked, allows you to set the relative positioning for the reference point based on the object's position. Also, when you right-click on an x or y coordinate text area, you can select a change in units of measurement, for example from pixels to inches or another unit you prefer to work with. Refer to Figure 4-19.

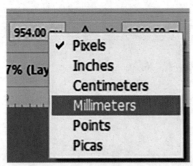

Figure 4-19. *Change the units of measurement and use relative positioning for the reference point*

Scale

The next section involves width and height scaling to make the object on the layer larger or smaller, and using the bounding box handles to scale from the top, left, right, or bottom.

■ **Note**   In newer versions of Photoshop, you do not have to hold down the Shift key to scale proportionally while the Maintain Aspect Ratio link is enabled. In this case, holding down the Shift key will scale disproportionally. Refer to Figure 4-20.

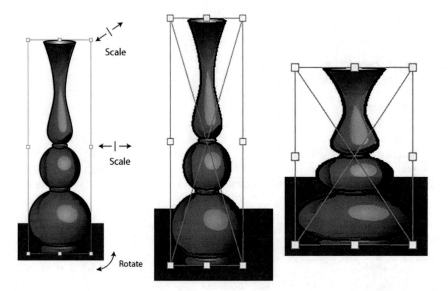

Figure 4-20. *Scale the vase proportionately or disproportionately using the bounding box handles*

Hold down the Alt/Option key when you want to scale from the center of the object rather than from the opposite anchor point. Use Alt/Option+Shift when you want to scale disproportionally from the center of the object on the layer. Refer to Figure 4-21.

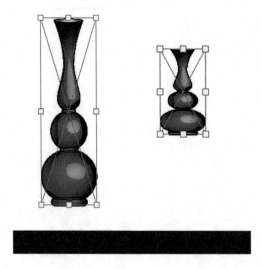

Figure 4-21. *Scale the vase using various key commands*

Likewise, you can type in the percentage of scale directly into the text box for the width and height in percentage or a different unit of measurement when you right-click first on the dialog box. Clicking the link in the center allows you to maintain the aspect ratio while scaling or, when not highlighted disproportionally, scale the width and height separately. In this case, I prefer to keep the aspect ratio linked. Refer to Figure 4-22.

Figure 4-22. *Scale using the Options panel's width and height text boxes*

If your only focus is to scale the object on the layer, then use Edit ➤ Transform ➤ Scale. Now you can only scale as you drag the shape; however, the Options panel will remain the same. Two other scale options you can use from the Edit ➤ Transform menu are to flip your object horizontally or vertically. This may show negative scaling numbers.

■ **Note**   If you want to switch to the legacy transformation option of using the Shift key to scale proportionately, go to Edit ➤ Preferences ➤ General, and enable Use Legacy Free Transform under Options and Click OK to commit or Cancel to continue with the current new settings used in this book. Refer to Figure 4-23.

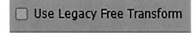

Figure 4-23. *The Legacy Free Transform option is disabled by default in the Preferences dialog box*

In my case, I left it disabled and clicked Cancel to exit the Preferences dialog box.

Rotate

The next section in the Free Transform options panel allows you to rotate or spin the object from the reference point. In this case, it is the center. Refer to Figure 4-24.

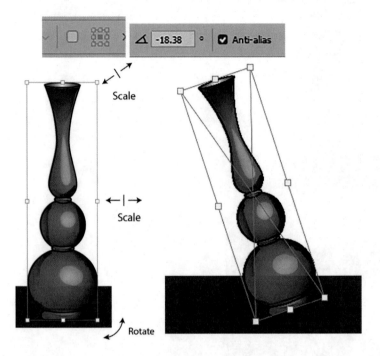

Figure 4-24. *Rotate the vase using either the Free Transform Options in the Options panel or your bounding box handles*

You can rotate by moving near a bounding box handle and waiting until the icon changes to a curved two-sided arrow and then mouse drag from 0° to -180 or 180 degrees. Another way is to type the number directly into the text area.

If you want to ensure that rotation is the only transformation that is occurring, choose Edit ➤ Transform ➤ Rotate. However, the Options panel will remain the same. Hold down the Shift key if you want to constrain the rotation by 15 degree increments.

You can also, from this area of the Edit ➤ Transform submenu, choose three other preset rotate options: Rotate 180°, Rotate 90° Clockwise, or Rotate 90° Counter Clockwise. Refer to Figure 4-25.

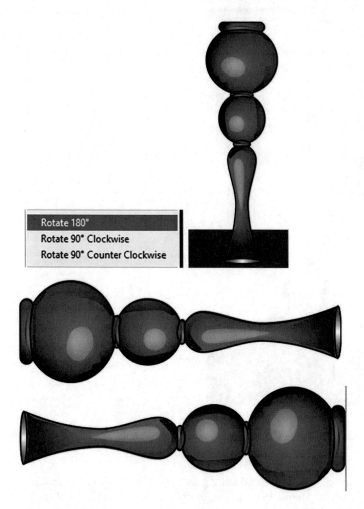

Figure 4-25. *Rotate the vase using default options in the Edit ➤ Transform submenu*

In this example, the last check box in the Options panel is Anti-alias. This helps smooth the edges as you scale.

I scaled my vase to 150% for width and height and left the rotation at 0 degrees. Refer to Figure 4-26.

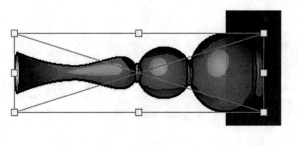

Figure 4-26. *Settings in the Options panel for the Free Transform update if the smart object on the layer has been moved scaled or rotated*

At this point, you can either cancel the transformations, or in this case, click the check to commit. Refer to Figure 4-27.

Figure 4-27. *Cancel or commit your Free Transform using the icons in the Options panel*

The last settings that you use will be maintained even after you save the file, and you can enter Edit ➤ Free Transform anytime and continue to scale or rotate your Illustrator vector smart object without loss of quality.

■ **Tip** If you need to reset your transformation while working outside of the Free Transform workspace back to 100%, right-click on the layer and from the Layers panel menu and choose Reset Transform. Refer to Figure 4-28.

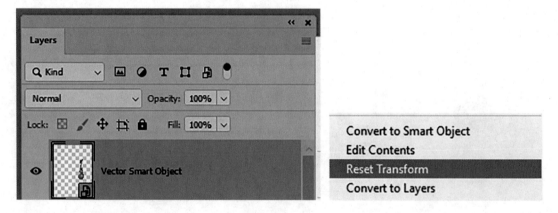

Figure 4-28. *Use the Layers panel menu when you need to reset a transform back to default*

Before we continue with the next transformation, here is a fun idea you can try with just Free Transform Scale and Rotate.

Project Idea: Reference Point

File ➤ Open vase_2.psd and make an Image ➤ Duplicate for practice. In this example, there are eight vases on separate layers. I created an image duplicate by dragging it over the Create a new layer button. Select the layer Vector Smart Object Copy. Some of the above layers' visibility will be turned off for now. Go to Edit ➤ Free Transform. Refer to Figure 4-29.

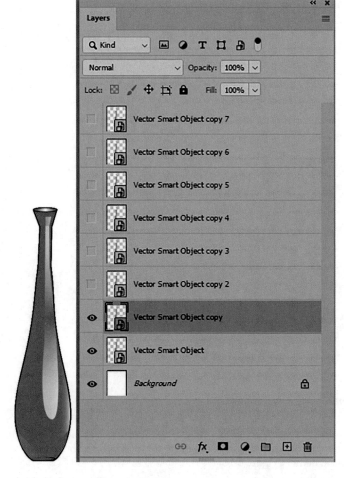

Figure 4-29. *Vector Smart Object copy layer selected in the Layers panel*

In the Options panel, go to your Reference point location, and rather than center, choose center bottom. Refer to Figure 4-30.

Figure 4-30. *Changing the reference point location in the Free Transform options panel*

Scale width and height to 175% and rotate 45 degrees. Refer to Figure 4-31.

Figure 4-31. *Type in new scale and rotation settings in the Free Transform options panel and enable the anti-alias setting*

Click the check to commit. Refer to Figure 4-32.

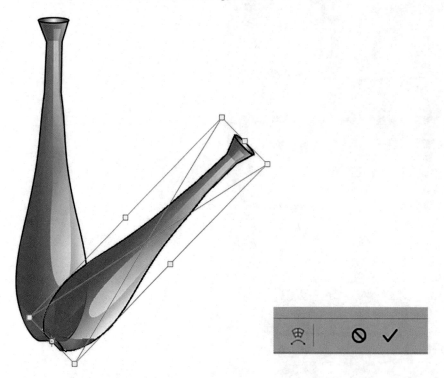

Figure 4-32. *Click the check icon in the Options panel to commit the new scale and rotation*

Now select and turn on the visibility for the Vector Smart Object copy 2 layer and choose Edit ➤ Free Transform. Again, set the same reference point location, this time scaling to 150% for width and height and an angle of 90°, and click the check to commit. Refer to Figure 4-33.

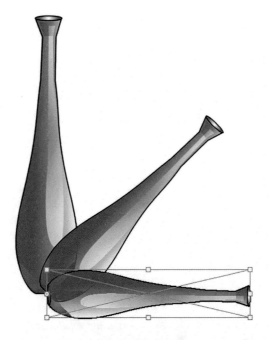

Figure 4-33. Repeat the rotation for the next vase and click the check to commit

Now repeat these steps for the next five layers. Here is the breakdown:

- Layer Vector Smart Object copy 3: Width and Height 125%, degrees 135

- Layer Vector Smart Object copy 4: Width and Height 100%, degrees 180

- Layer Vector Smart Object copy 5: Width and Height 75%, degrees -135

- Layer Vector Smart Object copy 6: Width and Height 50%, degrees -90

- Layer Vector Smart Object copy 7: Width and Height 25%, degrees -45

Refer to Figure 4-34.

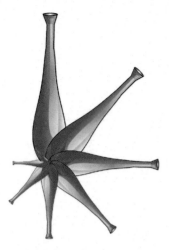

Figure 4-34. *Several vase layers have been rotated to create a spiral design*

This creates a spiral-like Droste effect with the vases getting smaller and smaller almost to nothing. However, now let's fill in the gaps.

At this point, Shift+Click to select all the layers except the background and click the Create a New Group folder button to group them together. Refer to Figure 4-35.

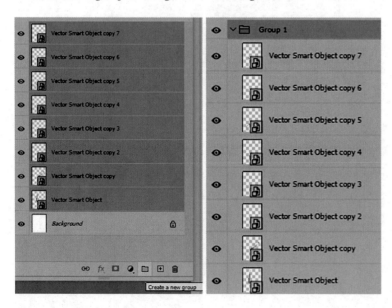

Figure 4-35. *Shift+Select all your vase Vector Smart Object layers and create a group folder to store them in*

Now drag the group folder over the Create a new layer button to create a duplicate group folder. Refer to Figure 4-36.

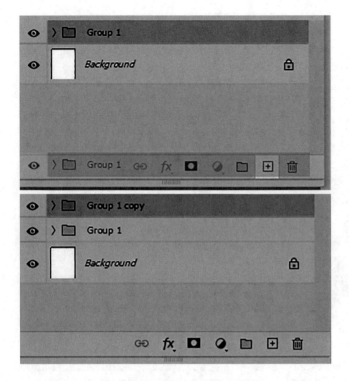

Figure 4-36. *Create a duplicate of the Group 1 folder in the Layers panel*

Select the Group 1 copy layer and Choose Edit ➤ Free Transform. Drag and move your reference point to a custom location near where the bottom of all the vases touch. Refer to Figure 4-37.

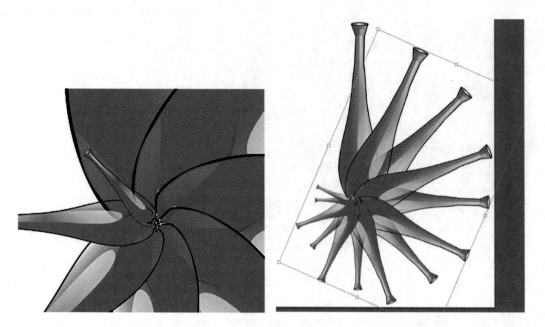

Figure 4-37. *Select the duplicate group folder and set a custom reference point for scale and rotation*

Then rotate all the bottles about 22.5 degrees and scale about 88% for width and height. Because we are dealing with a collective group, the scaling is different, and you may notice some additional options in the Options panel; we'll talk about those shortly. Refer to Figure 4-38.

Figure 4-38. *Rotate your selected group layers and then scale the width and height using the Free Transform options*

You may have to drag and move your vases so that they sit in the center. To check, you can change your Group folder's opacity in the Layers panel and use your keyboard arrow keys to nudge into place. Refer to Figure 4-39.

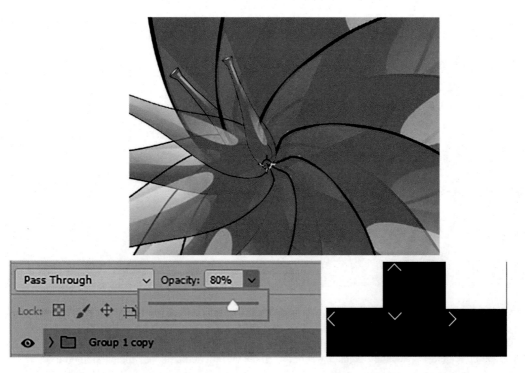

Figure 4-39. *Alter the Group 1 copy folder's opacity to see your transformation and use the arrow keys on your keyboard to nudge your group into place*

Then click the check to commit the transformation and return your group folder's opacity to 100% if you have not already done so. Refer to Figure 4-40.

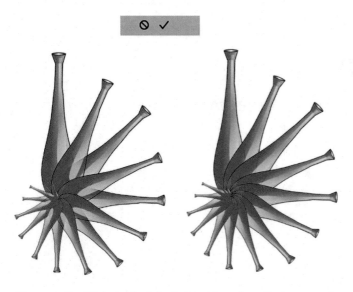

Figure 4-40. *Click the check in the Free Transform Options panel to commit scale and rotation, and then move your layers from one group folder to the other to rearrange the order of the vases*

Then you can spend time reordering your layers by moving them into other group folders and renaming them. You can see my final example in vase_2_final.psd. Refer to Figure 4-40 and Figure 4-41.

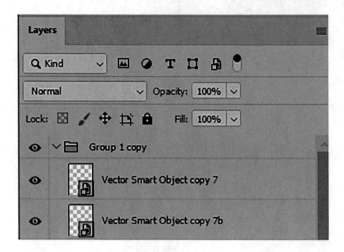

Figure 4-41. *Reorder and rename your Vector Smart Object Layers in the Layers panel*

■ **Note** Group folders, unlike smart objects, will not keep the current numbers that you created on the transform, only the smart objects themselves.

Then on an Image ➤ Duplicate copy of the file from the Layers menu, you could choose to flatten the image and choose Edit ➤ Define Pattern for future use, as you saw in Chapter 3. Refer to Figure 4-42.

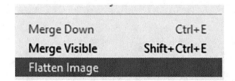

Figure 4-42. *From the Layers panel, choose Flatten Image to flatten layers you want to turn into a pattern*

Continue with Free Transform

As mentioned, while working in the Transform panel with the group folder, you may have noticed a few options that weren't there before. Let's return to the vase_1.psd copy that we are currently working on.

Make a duplicate of your Vector Smart Object layer by dragging it over the Create a new layer button and choose Edit ➤ Transform ➤ Flip Vertical to create a mirror reflection of the vase. Refer to Figure 4-43.

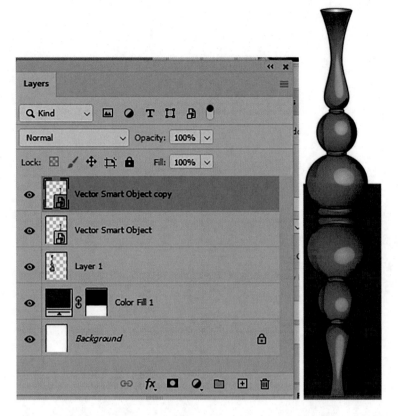

Figure 4-43. Create a reflection of the vase by creating a copy of the Vector Smart Object layer and rotating it

---

■ **Tip**　Choose Edit ➤ Transform ➤ Flip Horizontal when you want a side-by-side mirror.

It's OK if some of the vase goes off the canvas. Set the layer's opacity to about 34%. Refer to Figure 4-44.

Figure 4-44. *Change the layer's opacity in the Layers panel so that appear to reflect into the shiny surface*

Usually, at a certain point the reflection kind of dissolves so in this case add a layer mask. Refer to Figure 4-45.

Figure 4-45. *Add a layer mask to the Vector Smart Object copy layer in the Layers panel*

Press D and then X if you need to reset your foreground and background colors in the Tools panel to a white foreground and black background. Now with your Gradient tool (G), set to the Gradient basics of Foreground to Background and the settings in the Options panel. The panel from left to right contains the tool presets, the Gradient Preset from the Gradients panel, five gradient options (Linear, Radial, Angle, Reflected, and Diamond), Blending Mode (see Chapter 2), Opacity, Reverse Gradient Colors, Dither to reverse banding, Transparency, and Method for displaying gradients on the canvas (Perceptual, Linear, or Classic). Refer to Figure 4-46.

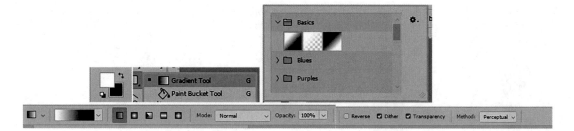

Figure 4-46. *Tools panel, Gradient panel, and Gradient Options Panel for the Gradient tool and setting the default colors in the Tools panel D and X to swap*

Drag downward on the layer mask while holding the Shift key. Start at the base of the vase and drag to the edge of the canvas to make part of the vase invisible. Refer to Figure 4-47.

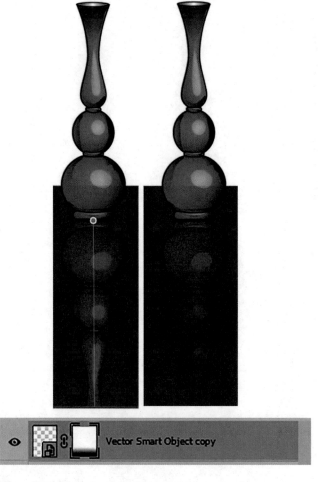

Figure 4-47. *Creating a gradient on the layer mask*

Now return to Edit ➤ Free Transform to give the vase a slightly distorted reflection. I Shift+Dragged it upwards so that it touched the edge of the canvas. The width is 100% but height is about 85.76%. Refer to Figure 4-48.

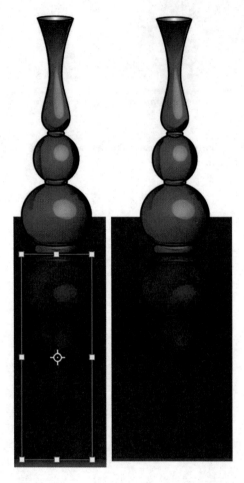

Figure 4-48. *Use Free Transform to scale the layer and the layer mask together*

Now you will see that by adding the layer mask we have a new section for Skew, Interpolation, and Warp. We'll look at those in the next sections. Refer to Figure 4-49.

Figure 4-49. *Adding a layer mask adds options to the Free Transform in the Options panel*

These options are available because the layer mask must transform as well. For now, click the check to commit your settings. Refer to Figure 4-49.

File ➤ Save your document at this point. You will notice that the mask has altered slightly as well to compensate for the scale. You can look at my Vase_1_final.psd file for reference. Refer to Figure 4-50.

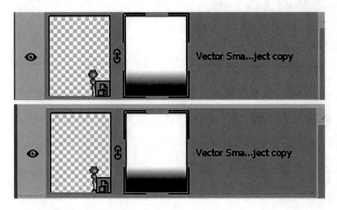

Figure 4-50. *The mask alters after it has been scaled along with the vector mask smart object with Free Transform*

■ **Tip**   Keep both your smart object and layer, as linked while scaling, so that they both commit to the transformations.

Skew

Let's try a skew in a new file. File ➤ Open vase_3.psd. Refer to Figure 4-51.

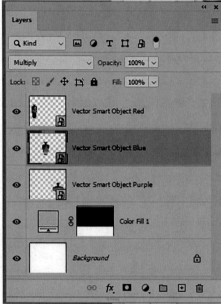

Figure 4-51. *Three vases that are smart object layers in the Layers panel with different blending modes to improve transparency*

In this example, I set the red and blue vase vector smart object layers from Illustrator to a blending mode of Multiply because I found that it improved the transparent effect. However, the purple vase was fine with the transparency intact.

I rotated a copy of each vase and added a shadow/reflection layer by creating a duplicate layer (by dragging over the Create a new layer icon). Then I chose Edit ➤ Transform ➤ Flip Vertical to mirror the layer and lowered the opacity to about 43%. I then added a layer mask and used the Gradient tool to create a slight graduation to give a reflection. You can review those earlier steps if you want to try this for your own project. I renamed some of the layers for clarification. Refer to Figure 4-52.

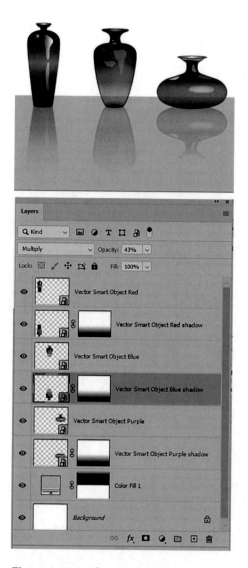

Figure 4-52. *In the Layers panel, layers were duplicated and rotated, and a layer mask with a gradation was applied to create a reflection that will become a colorful shadow*

So that looks OK for a shiny surface, but with a transparent vase maybe I want it not to be a reflection but rather a shadow, as shadows with transparent items often involved some color. To create that, I am first going to try a skew.

Make an Image ➤ Duplicate of the file to practice on, as you did in previous chapters.

Shift+Click select layers Vector Smart Object Red and Vector Smart Object Red Shadow. With the Move tool, move the shadow and the vase down to the middle of the image. Refer to Figure 4-53.

Figure 4-53. *Move two layers in unison when you Shift+Click and use the Move tool*

It's OK if some of the shadow of the vase is hidden and the layer mask is altered.

Now just select the layer Vector Smart Object Red Shadow. Make sure to select the layer's thumbnail image and not the mask, and keep the layer and layer mask linked. Refer to Figure 4-54.

Figure 4-54. *Select the layer Vector Smart Object Red shadow in the Layers panel*

Go back now to Edit ➤ Free Transform. We will look at the next section of the Options panel. Refer to Figure 4-55.

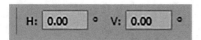

Figure 4-55. *Free Transform for Skew Horizontal and Vertical*

The next section in the Free Transform lets you skew or slant in degrees along the horizontal and vertical. You can create this skew in several ways:

- Type the numbers into the text box area for Horizonal (H) and Vertical (V) in degrees from (-180, 0, +180)

- Hover over the H or V next to the text boxes in the Options panel and drag with the mouse left or right to see the skew change in small amounts of a tenth of a degree.

- Ctrl/CMD+Shift while dragging from the middle left or middle right, or top center and bottom center bounding box handles. Adding the Shift key will turn off the Constrain proportions link to maintain the aspect ratio in the Options panel. Refer to Figure 4-56.

Figure 4-56. *Link icon (maintain aspect ratio) in the Free Transform options panel enabled and disabled*

- To ensure that only the skew option is active while using the bounding box handles, choose Edit ➤ Transform ➤ Skew. This will allow you to easily drag and skew individual corners, but still set other areas of the Free Transform Options panel at the same time. The Options panel will remain the same as Free Transform.

So, let's try that now. Go to Edit ➤ Transform ➤ Skew and move your handles in the lower area horizontal to the left to skew and then move the shadow back to the right with the upper handles. Or use your arrow keys on your keyboard to nudge the whole transformation into place, so that it remains under the vase. This creates a rather long shadow that kind of disappears off the page. Refer to Figure 4-57.

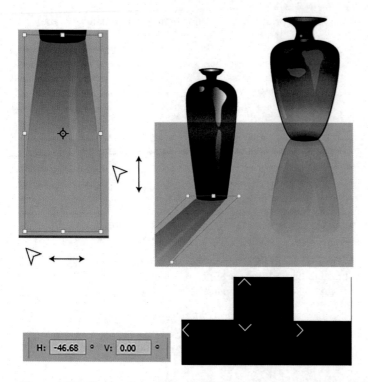

Figure 4-57. *Skew settings update in the Free Transform Options panel as the bounding box handles are moved. You can use the arrow keys on your keyboard to move your item in small increments*

Interpolation

The next area in the Options panel is for interpolation, or how the pixels on a normal pixel layer (or in this case, how the Layer mask) will adjust during the transformation process.

For a normal rasterized pixelated layer, if I am altering it, this is destructive once I click the commit check in the Options panel. It cannot be undone unless I choose Edit ➤ Undo right away. But as we have seen with smart objects, we can continue to edit and enter the transformation any time. Refer to Figure 4-58.

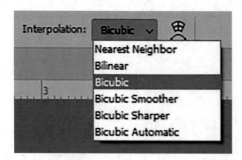

Figure 4-58. *Interpolation options in the Free Transform Options panel*

The options of Interpolation (or pixel replication) when scaling include

- **Nearest Neighbor**: Used for illustrations and line drawing to preserve hard edges

- **Bilinear**: Looks at the pixels surrounding the area and adds pixels by averaging the color value

- **Bicubic**: More precise than Bilinear and Nearest Neighbor and relies on a more detailed evaluation of the surrounding pixels

- **Bicubic Smoother**: Used for enlarging images and produces smoother results

- **Bicubic Sharper**: Used for reducing the size of the image to keep the image detailed and sharp (alternatively you can use Bicubic if the image appears over-sharpened)

- **Bicubic Automatic**: Chooses how the resampling will occur based on if the object is scaled up or down

---

■ **Note**   You can find these same interpolation settings in the Image ➤ Image Size dialog box when you are scaling an entire image and not just a layer.

For more details on Interpolation, check out `https://helpx.adobe.com/photoshop/using/resizing-image.html`
and my book *Graphics and Multimedia for the Web with Adobe Creative Cloud*.
In this example, I will leave it on the default Bicubic setting.
For now, Click the check in the Options panel to commit the transformation. Refer to Figure 4-59.

Figure 4-59. *Click the commit icon in the Free Transform Options panel*

As you can see, the mask is also altered. Refer to Figure 4-60.

Figure 4-60. *The skew is updated and the mask is updated as well after exiting the Free Transform options*

■ **Note**   To work with Skew, you do not need to have a layer mask. However, adding the mask to an Illustrator smart object does allow you to interact with the Skew options in the Options panel.

Just keep in mind that if you need to reset the Skew for your Illustrator vector smart object, when you enter the Free Transform area the skew degree numbers may be set back to 0. Refer to Figure 4-61.

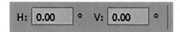

Figure 4-61. *After exiting and entering again, Free Transform options for Skew may be reset to 0*

Remember to reset your smart object entirely from the Layers menu by choosing Reset Transform. Or in this case use your History panel to undo the current Skew and try again if you made a mistake. Refer to Figure 4-62.

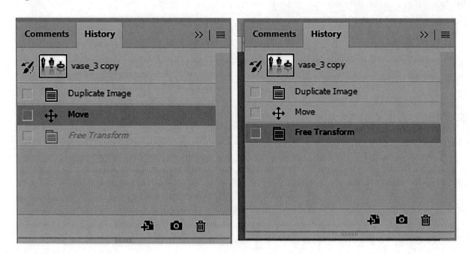

Figure 4-62. *Use your History panel when you need to undo a step and enter Free Transform again*

Now, with your Gradient tool, you can return to your layer mask and remove some of your gradient so that it does not fall off the page. Press the D key to reset your gradient to a white foreground and black background and drag from the base of the vase outward to the edge of the canvas. Refer to Figure 4-63.

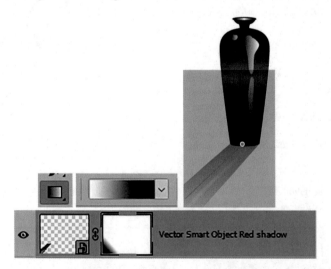

Figure 4-63. *Use your Gradient tool and its options to update the layer mask*

Distort

Now that you have progressed through most of the Free Transform options in the Options panel, another similar transformation to a skew that you may want to apply is a distort, which will stretch the shape on the layer in more than one direction.

Select the layer Vector Smart Object Blue shadow. Refer to Figure 4-64.

Figure 4-64. *Select the layer Vector Smart Object Blue Shadow in the Layers panel*

However, when you go to Edit ➤ Free Transform it may not be clear where the Distort option is located as Scale, Rotate, and Skew seem to be the only options available.

When I go to Edit ➤ Transform ➤Distort, this option, as well as the Perspective and Warp options, appear to be grayed out and unavailable. Refer to Figure 4-65.

Transform ▶	Again	Shift+Ctrl+T
Auto-Align Layers...	Scale	
Auto-Blend Layers...	Rotate	
Sky Replacement...	Skew	
Define Brush Preset...	Distort	
Define Pattern...	Perspective	
Define Custom Shape...		
	Warp	

Figure 4-65. *In the Transform submenu, Distort, Perspective, and Warp are unavailable*

On a normal pixelated layer, these options would be available, but again, as you edit a rasterized layer in Free Transform, this would be destructive.

Strangely, not all smart objects are created equal as well. In this case, we are working with an Illustrator smart object layer so Distort, Perspective, and Warp are greyed out.

However, to activate them, here is a trick you can try.

From the Layers menu, choose Convert to Smart Object. Refer to Figure 4-66.

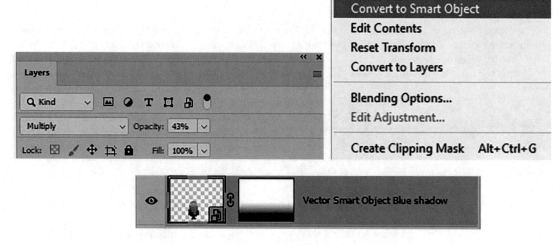

Figure 4-66. *Convert your Illustrator smart object layer to a Photoshop smart object layer using the Layers menu*

This wraps the vector Illustrator smart object and its layer mask within a Photoshop smart object. See my notes at the end of the chapter explaining this. Refer to Figure 4-67.

Figure 4-67. *The layer as a Photoshop smart pbject*

You will see that Edit ➤ Transform ➤ Distort and the other transforms are now available. Refer to Figure 4-68.

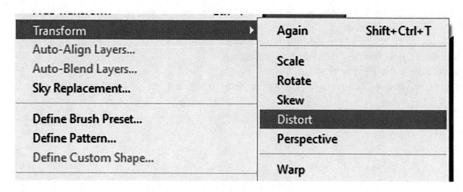

Figure 4-68. *After the smart object conversion, Distort, Perspective, and Warp are now available in the Transform submenu*

Photoshop smart objects, although they appear identical to Illustrator smart objects in a Layers panel, are different on the inside and have access to more options.

Now choose Edit ➤ Free Transform. There are no additional options added to the Options panel. Refer to Figure 4-69.

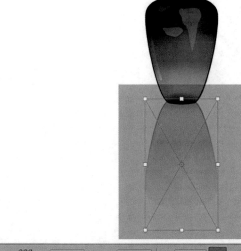

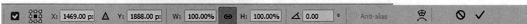

Figure 4-69. *Options panel for Free Transform Distort with a bounding box around the shape on the layer*

■ **Note**   You may not see the Skew options if no layer mask is applied to the Photoshop smart object.

To alter the distort on one of the bounding box corner handles,

- Hold down Ctrl/CMD and drag on the bounding box corner handles

- Ctrl/CMD+Shift, which will turn off the constrain proportions link in the options panel. However, it will allow you to move the handle in a straight line. Refer to Figure 4-70.

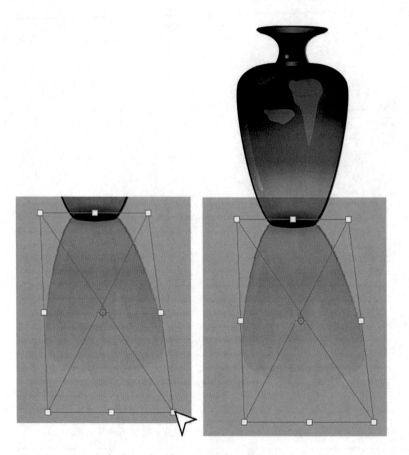

Figure 4-70. *Use the bounding box corner handles to create a distort*

- Or choose Edit ➤ Transform ➤ Distort. You can move the corner points rather than the center handles. The Options panel will remain the same as Free Transform.

In the Transform Distort option, click and drag on the lower left and right handles one at a time and expand the shape. Then, on the upper right and left handles, move them inward if you need to move the bottom of the shadow closer to the reflection. Then click the check in the Options panel to commit. Refer to Figure 4-71.

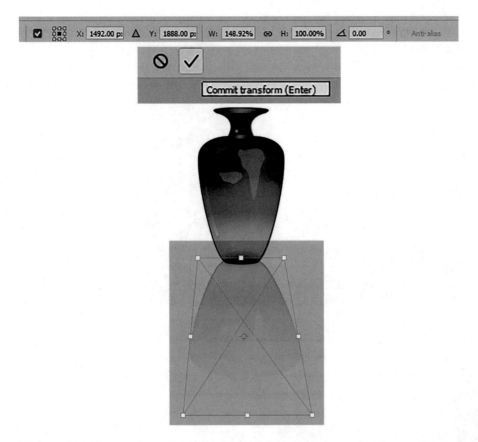

Figure 4-71. *After creating a distort, the Free transform Options panel updates and you can click the check to commit the transform*

If you do not want as much of the layer to be visible again, you could add another layer mask. Use the gradient tool and its panel, as you saw earlier with the vase_1.psd project. Drag downward holding the Shift key with the gradient tool on the layer mask, in this case, from the base of the vase to the edge of the canvas. Refer to Figure 4-72.

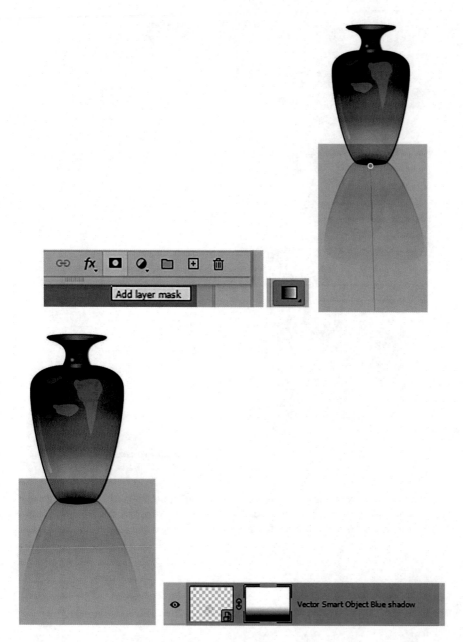

Figure 4-72. *Create a new layer mask for your vector smart object layer and edit it using the Gradient tool*

Then, if you need to update the distort some more, select the layer's thumbnail again and go to Edit
➤ Transform ➤ Distort and make further adjustments if required. I moved my lower right and left handles
outwards a bit more. This time you can see the Skew settings because of the added layer mask. I then clicked
the check to commit. Refer to Figure 4-73.

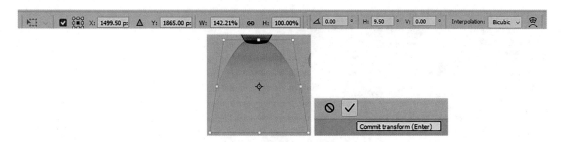

Figure 4-73. Enter Free Transform again with the layer mask. The skew options are now available. Commit any transformations

And the mask updated as well. Refer to Figure 4-74.

Figure 4-74. If adjustments are made, the layer mask will update as well upon exit of Free Transform

At this point, with your Move tool selected, use your Arrow keys on your keyboard if you need to nudge the shadow under the vase slightly. Refer to Figure 4-75.

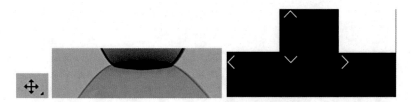

Figure 4-75. Use your arrow keys with the Move tool if you if you need to nudge a shape on a layer

Perspective

Now that you know a bit more about smart objects, this time select your layer Vector Smart Object Purple shadow and drag the layer mask to the trash can icon, as you can recreate it later. Refer to Figure 4-76.

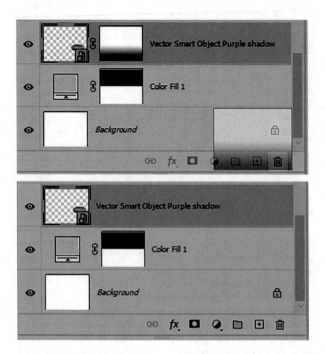

Figure 4-76. *Drag the layer mask to the trash icon for layer Vector Smart Object Purple shadow*

Now with that layer selected From the Layers menu, choose Convert to Smart Object. Refer to Figure 4-77.

Figure 4-77. *Convert layer Vector Smart Object Purple shadow to a Photoshop smart object*

As mentioned with the transformation of Distort, we need to do this step to convert the Illustrator smart object layer into a Photoshop smart object layer so that now we have access to the Perspective options. I will add a blank layer mask back to the layer and edit it later. Refer to Figure 4-78.

Figure 4-78. *Add a new layer mask to the Photoshop smart object layer*

Now with the layer's thumbnail selected, go to Edit ➤ Free Transform. Refer to Figure 4-79.

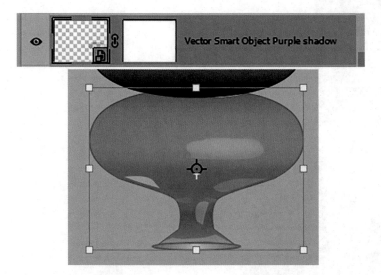

Figure 4-79. *Enter Edit free transform so that you can use the bounding boxes*

You will find that the Transform options in the Options panel have not changed. Refer to Figure 4-80.

Figure 4-80. *Options panel for Free Transform Perspective*

Perspective will allow you to apply a one-point perspective to the object on your layer. Here are some ways to use it:

- While in Free Transform, hold down the Ctrl/CMD+Alt/Option+Shift keys and drag on the center and corner bounding box handles. The center handle acts like a skew while the corner handles act like a distort, but on both sides at the same time.

- Or instead, choose Edit ➤ Transform ➤ Perspective. which I find easier to use rather than holding down multiple keys while dragging on handles. Refer to Figure 4-81.

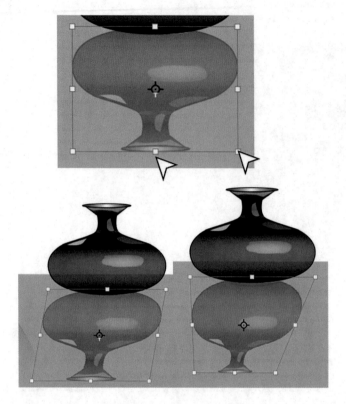

Figure 4-81. *Drag on the bounding box handles to alter the perspective of the shadow*

Perspective can also be useful when lining up shapes against a background or floor and part of image is moving into the distance or toward you. In these situations, you can move the bounding box handles to points on the wall so that they match up and appear like the object was painted onto the surface.

We will look at some more complex ways to apply perspective in Photoshop in Chapters 7, 9, and 10.

However, in this case, using Edit ➤ Transform ➤ Perspective, I moved my shadow over and to the right using my lower center handle and then dragged on my lower left or right handle to expand the shadow slightly to make it appear like it was resting on the table. Refer to Figure 4-82.

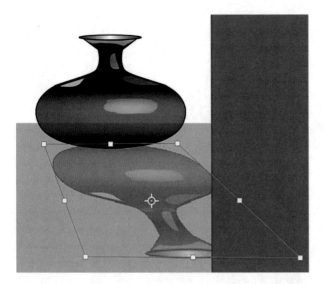

Figure 4-82. *Drag on the bounding box handles to alter the perspective of the shadow to the right*

The width and height scaling as well as the angle are altered in the Options panel along with the skew when a layer mask is preset. Refer to Figure 4-83.

Figure 4-83. *Options panel for Free Transform Perspective updates with changes*

When done, click the check in the Options panel to commit. Refer to Figure 4-84.

Figure 4-84. *Click the check to commit the changes in the Free Transform Options panel*

Now, on my layer mask, I will add with my gradient tool a new gradient to hide part of the vase and make it fade out. Remember to press D and X on your keyboard if you need to reset your gradient colors to white foreground and black background and from the Options menu, chose Basics: Foreground to Background. Refer to Figure 4-85.

Figure 4-85. *Adjust the setting for the Gradient tool in the Options panel and Tools panel*

This time with the Gradient tool I only dragged a bit downward holding down the Shift key, and this gave me only a slight shadow of color under the vase. Refer to Figure 4-86.

Figure 4-86. *Use the Gradient tool to change the gradient shadow in the Layers panel layer mask*

Now, if you want return to your red vase back up to be level with the other vases, with the Move tool make sure to Shift+Click on both the Vector Smart Object Red and shadow layers and move them into place. Refer to Figure 4-87.

■ **Note**   If you are having difficulty doing this from the rulers, drag down a guide using your Move tool. Guides can now be custom colored as well. Go to https://helpx.adobe.com/photoshop/using/grid-guides.html.

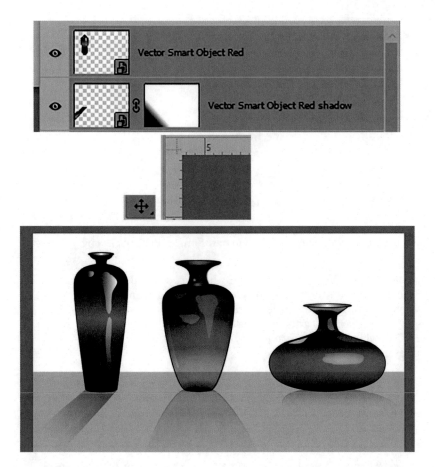

Figure 4-87. *Use the Move tool and your rulers to create guides when you need to line up two selected layers with the other vases in the image*

Later you can remove the guide by choosing View ➤ Clear Guides.

File ➤ Save your work at this point. You can see my example in vase_3_final.psd.

Before we look at the Warp transformation area, I will just give a few additional transformation tips:

- If you do not want to use your settings, in the Free Transform options panel, you can click the cancel (Esc) or if you do commit click the check to commit your transformation (Enter/Return).

- If you want to repeat a similar transformation, you can then Use Edit ➤ Transform ➤ again (Shift+Ctrl/CMD+T) to repeat the transformation. Refer to Figure 4-88.

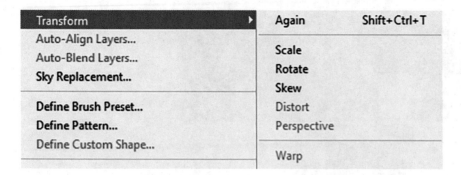

Figure 4-88. *Use Edit ➤ Transform ➤ Again when you need to repeat a transformation*

- Use Ctrl/CMD+Alt/Option+Shift+T when you want to transform again but on a copy or duplicate layer.

- Another hidden trick is to try Ctrl/CMD+Alt/Option+T when on a selected rasterized layer. Then, while in the transformation area, Alt/Option drag inside the bounding box handles and this will create a duplicate layer copy for you to do your transformations on without having to exit Free Transform. However, dragging again with the Alt/Option key will not create a second copy. This does not appear to work with smart object layers.

Warp

When you want to manipulate and distort your smart object layer further, use the Warp command. You will find it at the end of the Free Transform options panel. This toggle button makes it easy to switch to the Warp options.

Click the toggle button to switch between Free Transform and Warp or Choose Edit ➤ Transform ➤ Warp. Refer to Figure 4-89.

Figure 4-89. *Use the Options panel Free Transform toggle button to switch to the Warp options*

When working with Warp, as with Distort and Perspective, if you find this area grayed out in the menu, it is likely that you are working with an Illustrator smart object. You need to convert it to a Photoshop smart object using your Layers panel.

File ➤ Open the file furniture_warp.psd. Make an Image ➤ Duplicate of the file for practice. Refer to Figure 4-90.

Figure 4-90. *An illustration of a custom cabinet that I want to warp*

Then select the layer in the Layers panel and choose Convert to Smart Object from the menu to Convert from an Illustrator to Photoshop smart object. Refer to Figure 4-91.

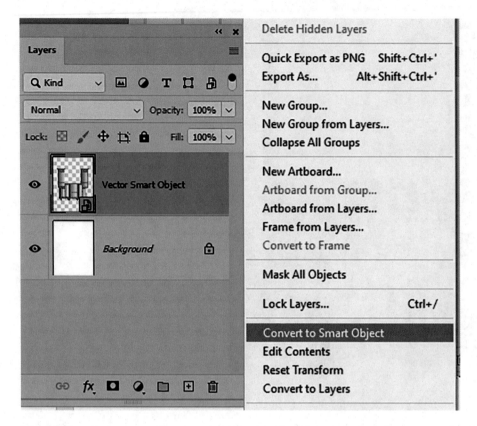

Figure 4-91. *Convert your Illustrator Vector Smart Object layer to a Photoshop Smart Object layer using the Layers menu*

Now from the menu, choose Edit ➤ Free Transform and then click on the switch between Free Transform and Warp modes. Refer to Figure 4-92.

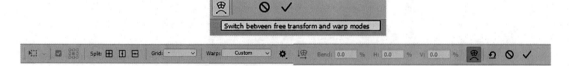

Figure 4-92. *Switch to the Options panel settings for Warp*

You will then see your cabinet surrounded by a different set of handles. Warp works by dragging on one of the eight handles or controls point handles to bend and stretch around and mold the object on the layer. Likewise, you can manipulate and move one of four default corner points on the outside or move the grids within the mesh. Refer to Figure 4-93.

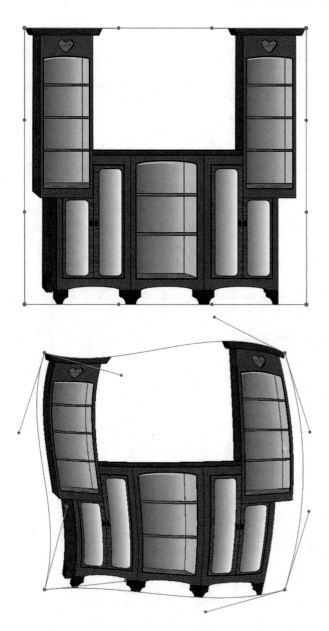

Figure 4-93. *Warping with the point handles*

When you use the Options panel, you can add additional anchor points to cause further stretches in the grid.

Warp Transformation Options

Look at the Warp Options panel from left to right. Refer to Figure 4-94.

Figure 4-94. *Options panel for Warp*

In the Warp transform area you can now choose from several different options. Note that your tool presets are grayed out and your toggle reference point is locked; it can only be accessed if you return to the Free Transform Options panel. Currently, it is at center point, which is what you want. Refer to Figure 4-95.

Figure 4-95. *Options panel for Warp. The reference point is locked*

The next section allows you to split the warp. This area can also be accessed from the Edit ➤ Transform menu or by right-clicking for options on the new warp. Refer to Figure 4-96.

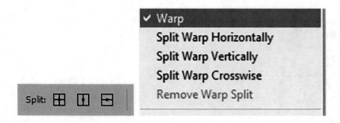

Figure 4-96. *Warp Transform split options*

Here is what each item does:

- **Split the warp crosswise**: Select and click a point in the bounding box where you want to place a vertical and horizontal grid line warp. Or Ctrl/CMD+Click without selecting from the option options menu. Refer to Figure 4-97.

Figure 4-97. *Cursor for split warp crosswise*

- **Split the warp vertically**: Select and click a point in the bounding box where you want to place a vertical grid line warp. Refer to Figure 4-98.

Figure 4-98. *Cursor for split warp vertically*

- **Split the warp horizontally**: Select and click a point in the bounding box where you want to place a horizontal grid line warp. Refer to Figure 4-99.

Figure 4-99. *Cursor for split warp horizontally*

- From the menu or right-click on the Warp again and choose Remove Warp Split to delete it from the mesh. Refer to Figure 4-100.

Figure 4-100. *Menu options for splitting a warp with Remove Warp Split selected*

As you see the grid while warping, you can from the Options menu choose various grid size options. They are Default, 1x1, 3x3, 4x4, and 5x5. Or you can choose a custom size of columns and rows from the dialog box and click OK to commit. Note, if you cannot see you guides, refer to the guide option (gear) section in this chapter. Refer to Figure 4-101.

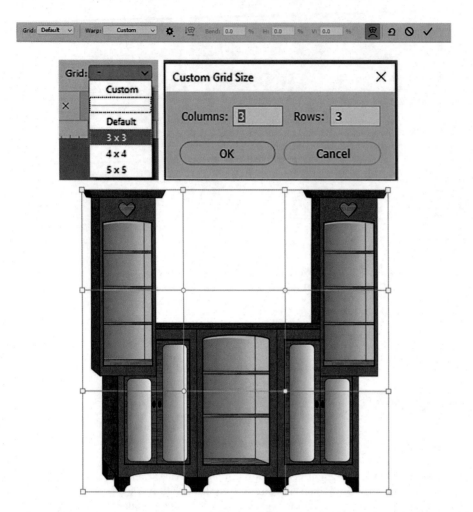

Figure 4-101. *Options panel custom grid size options and dialog box with grid visible on cabinet*

I will leave the grid at the default setting as it will become custom later as I add rows and columns to the grid.

Drag on a grid line to activate the control point and alter the warp or, on the anchor point, move and drag it around to manipulate further. I started by warping to a general shape. Refer to Figure 4-102.

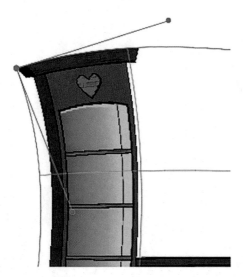

Figure 4-102. *Drag on the handles to twist and warp the cabinet*

To keep it level, I dragged in my guides on the left and right. Refer to Figure 4-103.

Figure 4-103. *Move the right and left handles in to create a warp*

Click inside to add some additional vertical and horizontal guide gridlines here and there to create a similar look to mine. Refer to Figure 4-104.

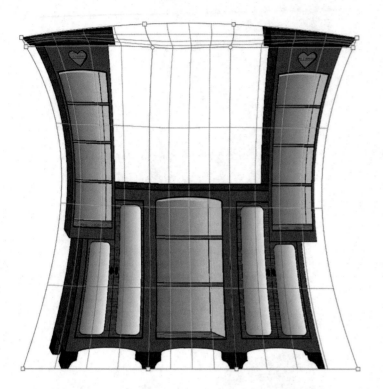

Figure 4-104. *Add some more gridlines and points to warp the grid further*

Shift+Click if you need to select multiple points, and when the points are selected, you can move them in unison now as you drag them about. Refer to Figure 4-105.

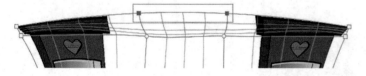

Figure 4-105. *Shift+Click select multiple points to move them in unison*

A rectangle bound appears around the area while dragging. You can continue to Shift+Click to add more points and drag the selected area around in unison. Refer to Figure 4-106.

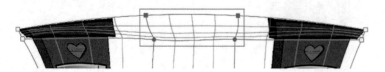

Figure 4-106. *Shift+Click on more points to add them to the grid*

To deselect point, Shift+Click on an already selected point. Refer to Figure 4-107.

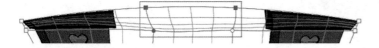

Figure 4-107. *Shift+Click on a point in a selection to deselect it*

Or click outside of the grid to deselect all points.

Remember, you can choose Edit ➤ Transform ➤ Remove Warp Split if you need to remove part of the warp. Refer to Figure 4-108.

Figure 4-108. *A vertical blue gridline on the right was removed, which slightly altered the warp*

Choose Edit ➤ Undo or Ctrl/CMD+Z to undo that last step if it was not your intent.

When a point in the mesh is selected, choose Edit ➤ Transform ➤ Convert Warp anchor point. Refer to Figure 4-109.

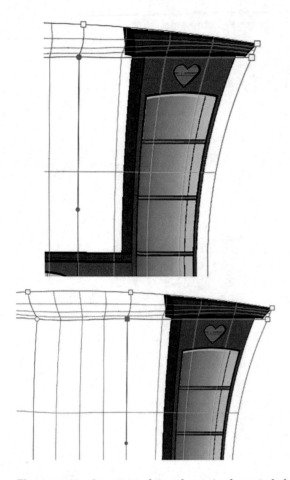

Figure 4-109. *Converting the anchor point from circle (unison) to square (independent)*

There are two kinds of anchor points:

- Unison points have all handles moving together and the points appear as circles.

- Independent points have each handle move without affecting the other handles and these points appears as squares. Refer to Figure 4-110.

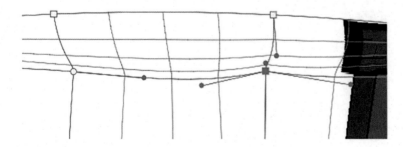

Figure 4-110. *Unison and independent anchor points*

Alt/Option+Click on a point to toggle it between unison and independent. Refer to Figure 4-110 and Figure 4-111.

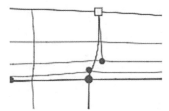

Figure 4-111. *Toggle between unison and independent anchor points*

By default, your corner and side point are set as independent, while the interior anchor points are set to unison.

Keep on adding points and grid lines to straighten or curve areas of your grid. Also, drag out guidelines from your ruler if you are trying to line up and straighten various lines in your custom warp. Refer to Figure 4-112.

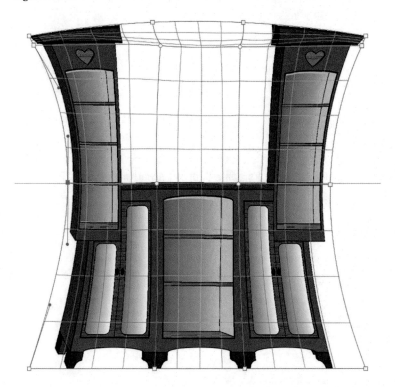

Figure 4-112. *Drag down guides when you need to line up areas of the warp grid*

So far you have created a custom warp, but from the options menu you can choose preset warps. The options are Arc, Arc Lower, Arc Upper, Arch, Bulge, Shell Lower, Shell Upper, Flag, Wave, Fish, Rise, Fisheye, Inflate, Squeeze, Twist, and Cylinder. Refer to Figure 4-113.

Figure 4-113. *Options panel for Warp preset options*

■ **Note** If you choose these while working on a custom warp, you will receive a warning message. Refer to Figure 4-114.

Figure 4-114. *Alert message when you change from a custom warp to a preset option*

Click Cancel for now and proceed with your custom warp.

Guide Options

Use Edit ➤ Transform ➤ Toggle guides when you need to see the guides in more detail or hide the detail. Refer to Figure 4-115.

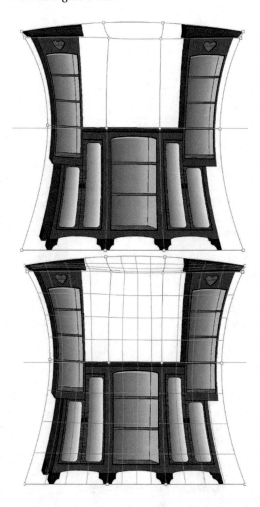

Figure 4-115. *Viewing the cabinet warp without and with the guides*

Various guide options are found under the gear. They allow you to set the color of the guide, guide opacity, and density of guidelines and when to show the guides (Auto, Always, or Never). Refer to Figure 4-116.

Figure 4-116. *Options panel for Guide Options*

By default, the setting is on Auto, but when working on more complicated shapes, I prefer the Always Show Guides setting.

If you had chosen a preset warp from the earlier list, then you could use the next set of options. Refer to Figure 4-117.

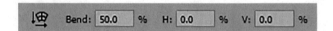

Figure 4-117. *Options panel for Warp preset options for Orientation, Bend, and Horizontal and Vertical distortion*

Change the warp preset orientation for preset warps to

- Bend: (-100, 0, 100%)

- X or horizontal distortion (H): (-100, 0, 100%). Type in number or drag over the H left and right to lower or raise the settings

- Y or vertical distortion (V): (-100, 0, 100%). Type in number or drag over the V left and right to lower or raise the settings.

- Click again on the Warp preset orientation button if you want to change the warp orientation from vertical to horizontal. Refer to Figure 4-117.

- Drag on the square handle on the warp grid to adjust the warp further, which will update the calculations of the bend in the text boxes. This option is not available when the horizonal and vertical distortion is set above 0%. Refer to Figure 4-118.

***Figure 4-118.** Adjust the preset warp on your image with the square handle*

- Fisheye, Inflate, Twist, and Cylinder will not allow you to adjust the warp orientation. Additionally, the new Cylinder option will not allow you to type in a bend or set a horizontal or vertical distortion. You must make these adjustments manually on the object itself using the five additional handles to control corners and curvature. Refer to Figure 4-119.

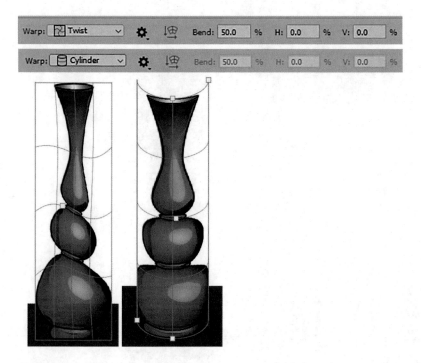

***Figure 4-119.** The warp preset orientation is unavailable for some preset warp options*

You can find some examples of a vase that I experiment on in the file `vase_4.psd`. Refer to Figure 4-120.

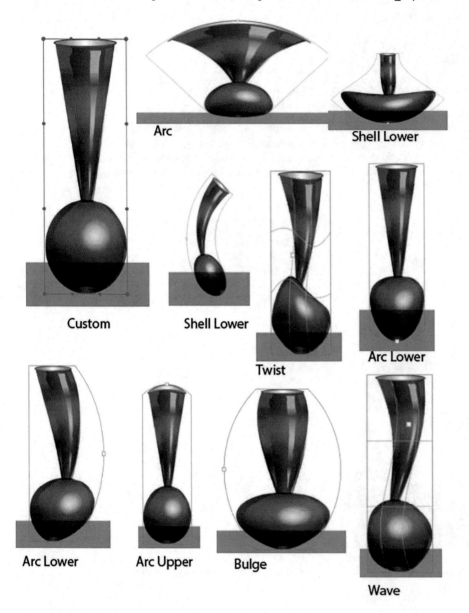

Figure 4-120. *Various examples of preset warps on a smart object vase*

I turned the image into a Photoshop smart object first and then tested different preset warps from the list in the Options panel.

■ **Note** For additional options on how to use the New Transform Warp Cylinder Option, you can visit the following link: `https://helpx.adobe.com/photoshop/using/warp-images-shapes-paths.html` (see Transform Warp: Cylinder).

However, we will be talking about this option again in Chapter 5 and how it relates to warp text and creating warped labels on bottles compared to a custom warp preset.

A custom preset, like the one you are creating, will not let you enter these numeric values, and this area will be grayed out. Refer to Figure 4-121.

Figure 4-121. Warp presets are collectively unavailable when creating a custom preset

If at some point you need to return to your previous transformations, use the toggle button to go back to Free Transform mode. Refer to Figure 4-122.

Figure 4-122. Toggle back to Free Transform in the Options panel to scale, skew, or rotate if required

While in that mode, your warp guides and points will become hidden. But you will see the general shape of your warp while you scale, rotate, skew, distort, or adjust perspective. In this case, we will remain in the warp transformations area. Refer to Figure 4-123.

Figure 4-123. *Switch mode, reset, or cancel the warp or click the check in the Options panel to commit to the warp for the cabinet*

The last section allows you to reset the entire warp, cancel the warp, or commit the warp to exit the transform area. Refer to Figure 4-123.

When you are happy with the warp you created, click the check to commit the warp.

If at any point you need to adjust your warp again, go to Edit ➤ Transform ➤ Warp and Photoshop remembers your warp from the last edit.

One final note about warps that I want to mention is if your smart object layer contains a layer mask. Refer to Figure 4-124.

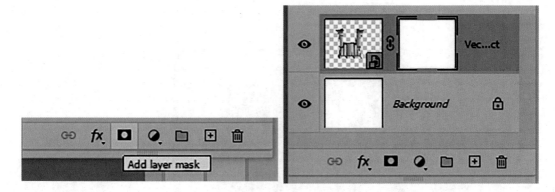

Figure 4-124. *Add a layer mask if you need to hide areas of your warp*

Even if you have not edited the mask, you will get a warning when you try to enter the Warp transformation. Refer to Figure 4-125.

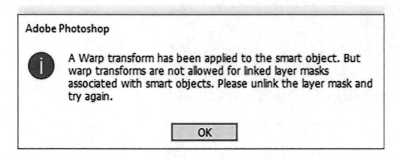

Figure 4-125. *Layer masks cannot be linked while creating a Warp on a smart object*

In a situation like this, unlink the layer mask, select the layer's thumbnail image, and you will be able to enter the Warp transformation area. Refer to Figure 4-126.

Figure 4-126. *Unlink your layer mask to enter the transform for Warp*

After your transformation, you must update your layer mask by hand with your Brush or Eraser tool. In my case, I will not add a layer mask to my warped image and will remove it using the History panel. Make sure to File ➤ Save your document at this point.

Alternatively, for your own projects, after you complete your file, you could make an Image ➤ Duplicate and then choose from the Layers menu ➤ Flatten Image so that you can save it either as a .jpg image for the web or print it for your portfolio. Just make sure if you plan to print to set your Image ➤ Mode to CMYK color, although your home inkjet printer may be fine with the file in RGB color mode.

My final file is furniture_warp_final.psd and I added a few vases for decoration to some of the shelves. Refer to Figure 4-127.

Figure 4-127. *I added the warped cabinet to a room after I completed the warp*

You can see how, with a few selections, patterns, shapes, and layer styles like Bevel & Emboss or Drop Shadow, you can begin to create a room for your furniture piece.

We will look at warping text in Chapter 5 and the Puppet Warp in Chapter 6.

Should You Create Free Transforms and Warps with Normal or Smart Object Layers?

To review, working with normal layers can be OK for some projects, if you know exactly how much you want to transform the layer and it will not be repeated multiple times. However, this is destructive when working with multiple transformations that you want to return to or edit. So, as you saw in this chapter, it is a better idea is to use smart object layers instead. Smart object layers can protect the layer graphic from degrading when being scaled up and down in size and are ideal when working with layer masks as well. Refer to Figure 4-128.

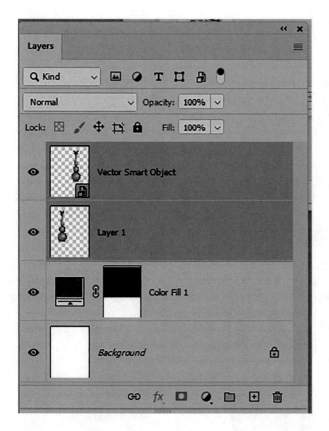

Figure 4-128. *Normal pixel Layer 1 and Vector Smart Object layer in the Layers panel*

Here are a few tips to review for working with smart objects:

Before you start working on a normal layer, you will need to convert your layer to a smart object layer. Select the layer that you want to scale or transform in some way and choose Convert to Smart Object from the Layers menu. Refer to Figure 4-129.

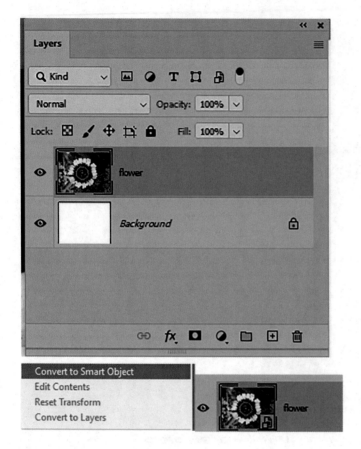

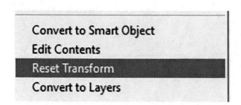

Figure 4-129. *Converting an image to a smart object in the Layers panel using the menu is a good idea before scaling*

Now you do not have to worry that if you make a transformation to that layer, you are degrading it. You can return any time to the transformation of your choice and adjust it. Or, from the Layers menu, choose Reset Transform to reset the smart object at any time back to its original state without using the History panel. Refer to Figure 4-130.

Figure 4-130. *Use your Layers panel menu to reset your transform to default if required*

Now I will explain in more detail that there are two kinds of smart objects discussed in this book: those that are created in Photoshop and those that are generated when you paste from Illustrator. Refer to Figure 4-131.

Figure 4-131. *Possible application sources for a smart object layer*

Two Kinds of Smart Objects

A Photoshop smart object can easily be created from a photographed image or scanned drawing that was created in Photoshop by using the Layers panel. Refer to my file CH4_IMG_3348_smartObject.psd.

If you double-click the thumbnail of the layer after you created it, it will open as a .psb file (or Photoshop big or Large Document Format). It will take on the name of whatever the layer was called before it became a smart object. Refer to Figure 4-132.

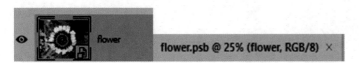

Figure 4-132. *A Photoshop embedded smart object is a .psb file inside*

You can then edit this original file in a destructive way, such as painting with a brush or a scale transformation, or a non-destructive way such as adding a layer mask. Refer to Figure 4-133.

Figure 4-133. *You can edit the .psb by adding a layer mask or other layers*

Once you have finished your edits, File ➤ Save the .psb file, close the file, and then the smart object layer is updated in the .psd file. Refer to Figure 4-134.

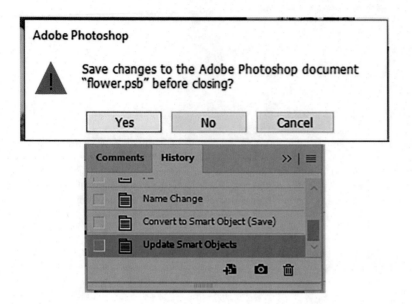

Figure 4-134. Save your changes by clicking Yes after you alter your .psb file and return to the .psd file, as seen in the History panel

You should then save your .psd file just to commit the change. Refer to Figure 4-135.

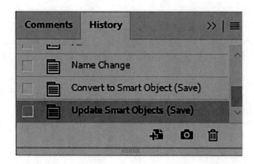

Figure 4-135. Save your .psd file to commit the changes to the smart object layer, as seen in the History panel

And any transformations that were applied to the smart object are maintained. This smart object is embedded in the file, as you can see in the Properties panel. Refer to Figure 4-136.

Figure 4-136. *Properties panel when the Photoshop smart object layer is selected*

■ **Note**   With photos in smart objects, if they are a low resolution like 72ppi, if you scale, let's say, over 200%, they may be slightly blurry at that size, but this is not a degrade from multiple scale, only an initial and unfortunate resolution choice. The image will not degrade further if you scale back up or down again. That is why it is best to start with high res or large images because you have more options as to how large you can scale your image.

The second kind of smart object is the Illustrator smart object. This is when, in Illustrator, you use the Selection tool and drag a rectangular marquee around some shapes or a logo to select it. Then you choose Edit ➤ Copy (Ctrl/CMD+C). Refer to Figure 4-137.

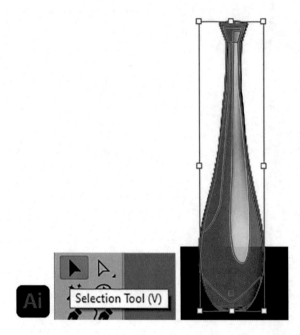

Figure 4-137. Copying a selection of a vase from Adobe Illustrator with its Selection tool

Then return to Photoshop and choose Edit ➤ Paste (Ctrl/CMD+V), as you saw in the beginning of this chapter. You will be presented with several paste options from the dialog box in this chapter; choose the Smart Object option and click OK. The shape is placed on the page, and you have the opportunity to scale it using the bounding box handles and the Options panel and then click the check to commit. Refer to Figure 4-138.

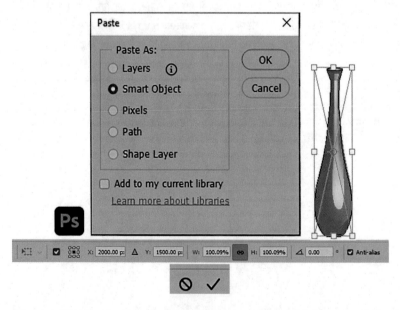

Figure 4-138. Pasting the selected vase as a smart object and then committing the transformation as a smart object by clicking on the check in the Free Transform Options panel

This just became an Illustrator embedded smart object as seen in the Properties panel. Refer to Figure 4-139.

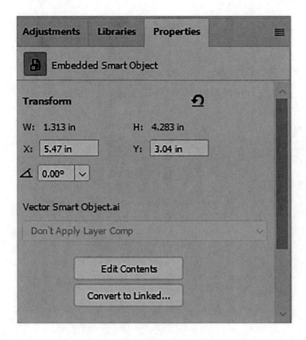

Figure 4-139. *The Properties panel when the Illustrator smart object is selected*

Unlike the Photoshop smart object, it is not resolution-dependent and can be scaled to large sizes without concern of the pixels per inch.

When you double-click this layer's thumbnail, you will be taken directly to Illustrator where you can edit the current embedded file (.ai). Refer to Figure 4-140.

Figure 4-140. *Entering the Illustrator smart object to edit the .ai file*

When you have completed the changes, choose File ➤ Save and then close the file. The smart object is updated in the Photoshop (.psd) file. Refer to Figure 4-141.

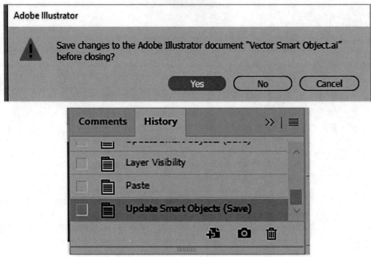

Figure 4-141. *Save your .ai file before returning to your .psd file and then save the .psd file as seen in the History panel*

Make sure to File ➤ Save your .psd file at this point to commit the changes.

As you saw in this chapter, there are two kinds of smart object layers that don't operate in the same way.

A Photoshop smart object can instantly use all the Free Transforms we talked about: Scale, Rotate, Skew, Distort, Perspective, and Warp. However, when you select to transform an Illustrator smart object, the Distort, Perspective, and Warp choices are grayed out and you cannot use them. Refer to Figure 4-142.

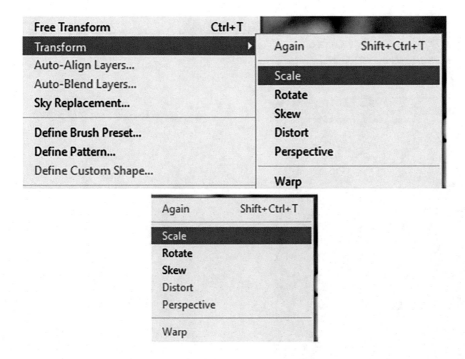

Figure 4-142. *Illustrator smart objects have less Transform options than Photoshop smart objects*

In this chapter, you used the work-around. It is to select your Illustrator smart object layer and this time, choose Convert to Smart Object from the menu. This makes it an official Photoshop smart object (.psb) file. Now all the transformation options in this chapter will be available to you. Refer to Figure 4-143.

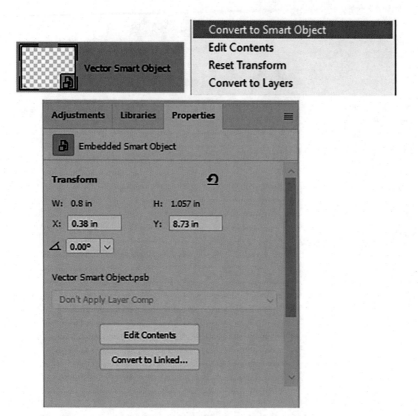

Figure 4-143. *Once the Illustrator smart object is converted to a Photoshop smart object, you can see how it appears in the Properties panel*

■ **Note** You can still edit your vector smart object in Illustrator but now you will have to double-click once to enter the .psb file and then once inside, double click again to enter the .ai file. Save and close each time as you progress back to your original .psd file. Refer to Figure 4-144.

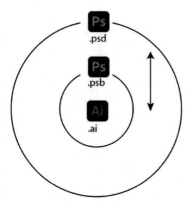

Figure 4-144. *The progression of the Illustrator smart object as it is turned into a Photoshop smart object*

Also keep in mind that when an .ai file is inside a .psb smart object, it does become resolution-dependent when scaled inside the .psd file. So, to ensure that the resolution is clearer at larger sizes, enter the .psb to scale the Illustrator smart object first to a larger size to avoid blurriness. Refer to Figure 4-145.

Figure 4-145. *When an Illustrator smart object is inside a Photoshop smart object, you may have to enter the .psd file and scale your Illustrator vector smart object to improve the quality of the image*

Embedded or Linked Smart Objects

Besides being embedded, a smart object (Photoshop or Illustrator) can be linked. This link could be to a file somewhere on your computer or to the Creative Cloud Libraries panel. Once a smart object layer is created, you can choose Convert to Linked from the Properties panel and locate your file. Refer to Figure 4-146.

Figure 4-146. *Use the Properties panel to convert an embedded smart object to a linked smart object*

Or you can link to a graphic asset file somewhere in one of your libraries in the Creative Cloud Libraries panel. Refer to Figure 4-147.

Figure 4-147. *Use the Creative Cloud Libraries panel to link to a smart object*

You can learn more about cloud linkage for Adobe's CC Libraries with Photoshop at the following link: https://helpx.adobe.com/photoshop/using/cc-libraries-in-photoshop.html.

Either way, the image in the layer can later be embedded using the Properties panel. Refer to Figure 4-148.

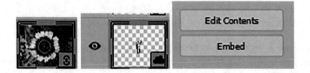

Figure 4-148. *Whether a smart object is linked to a document or your computer or the Libraries panel, once you click Embed in the Properties panel, the link to the external file is broken*

Linked or embedded layers each have their own benefits. A linked layer can lower the .psd file size. Also, if you update the file in one location, all other files are updated. The one drawback is that if you lose the file or delete it from the CC library, the link is broken, and file layer may be difficult to restore. When you embed the image in the .psd, the file size becomes larger, and you can be sure the link will not be broken. However, you must manually update each instance of that graphic in all other files if you make a major change. So, depending on the project, you need to consider your options of whether to link or embed and choose a method for your workflow.

■ **Note** All layer duplicates that you create of a smart object within your .psd file that are embedded are linked together. When you enter and make a change to one, you affect the other. Refer to Figure 4-149.

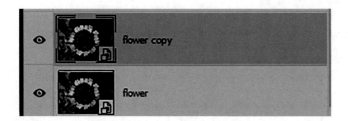

Figure 4-149. *This smart object layer was entered and an adjustment layer was added and the .psb file saved. Notice that it affected both layers, as one was duplicated from the other*

A way around this is rather than drag the smart object layer over the Create a new layer button in the Layers panel, right-click on the smart object layer and choose New Smart Object via Copy from the pop-up menu. Refer to Figure 4-150.

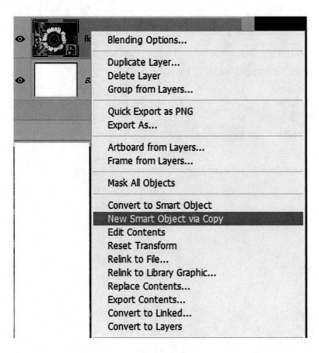

Figure 4-150. *To create a separate smart object, right-click select and choose New Smart Object via Copy from the pop-up menu in the Layers panel*

A new layer is now created with a separate embedded smart object that you can enter and edit without affecting the other. Refer to Figure 4-151.

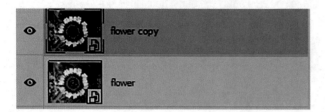

Figure 4-151. *An adjustment layer was added to the .psb file of the layer called flower copy and saved upon exit, but that did not alter the flower smart object layer*

Smart Objects from CMYK to RGB

When you copy/paste an Illustrator graphic that is in CMYK color mode graphic to an RGB .psd as a smart object file, keep in mind that there might be a slight color shift, so it is always best to start with the file in RGB mode first before your copy the graphic into Photoshop.

■ **Note** If you notice that your Illustrator file was in CMYK, you can create a copy of that file and choose Document Color Mode ➤ RGB Color from the Illustrator File menu. Refer to Figure 4-152.

Figure 4-152. *To avoid color shifts, make sure that the .ai file you are copying from is in RGB document color mode*

After you have read this book, I suggest exploring Adobe Illustrator in more detail in Volume 2.

Using Layer and Vector Masks with Smart Object Layers and Free Transforms

Also, whether you are using a normal pixel layer or a smart object layer, remember that you can use layer masks and vector masks in combination with selections to block out or cover areas of your image you want to hide. I talk about these two kinds of masks in detail in my Photoshop Selections book. However, in this example, I am using a layer mask that I created using the Elliptical Marquee tool and dragged out a selection and added as a layer mask using the Add layer mask button in the Layers panel. Refer to Figure 4-153.

Figure 4-153. *Add a layer mask to your smart object layer*

However, as you saw in this chapter, one major benefit with working with smart objects is that the layer mask can be altered along with the layer as you make various transformations. This is true for scaling, rotation, skew, distortion, and perspective. You can continue to paint on your layer mask and, as long as it is linked, it will scale with the smart object and either the mask or thumbnail can be selected as you work. Refer to Figure 4-154.

Figure 4-154. *Free Transform scale the layer and layer mask when linked*

If you only want to transform the layer mask, you can unlink it, select only the mask, and choose Edit ➤ Free Transform. This is the same for the smart object layer if you want to scale it separately from the layer mask and then unlink it. Refer to Figure 4-155.

Figure 4-155. *Free Transform scale the layer and layer mask separately when unlinked*

This is what you must also do if you want to use the Warp transformation.

Smart Object Layers and Warp

With smart object layers, whether or not you have already painted on the layer mask, and you Choose Edit ➤ Transform ➤ Warp, you may receive this warning. Refer to Figure 4-156.

Figure 4-156. *Warning alert that appears when you try to warp a smart object with a linked layer mask*

Click OK and unlink the layer mask before you attempt the warp, either on the object or the mask itself.

Alternatively, keep the mask linked and place the smart object inside another smart object and then perform the warp, this time with the mask contained. Refer to Figure 4-157.

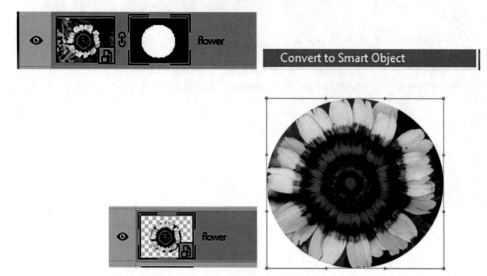

Figure 4-157. *If you want to keep the masked linked, convert that Photoshop smart object layer into a Photoshop smart object layer again from the Layers panel so that the mask is within the new smart object layer*

We'll look at layer masks again in Chapters 6 and 7 and how to apply them when working with these smart filter commands.

Vector Masks and Transformation

As mentioned, vector mask can also be added to a layer and transformed. They can be added from the Paths panel after you have created a path with the Pen tool. When selected, and then in the Layers panel on the selected layer, click the Mask icon again if a layer mask is already preset or Ctrl/CMD+Click the icon to add without adding a layer mask first. Refer to Figure 4-158.

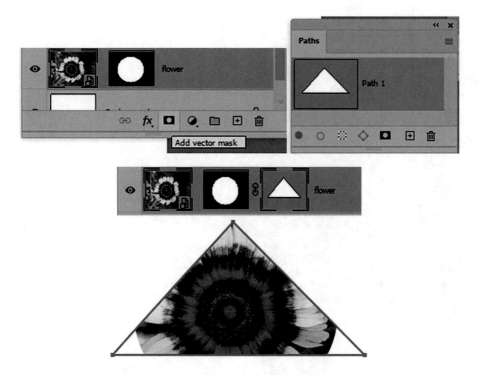

Figure 4-158. *Adding a vector mask to the smart object layer using the Paths panel*

However, when vector masks are selected, whether linked or not, from the menu you will now have the option to Edit ➤ Free Transform path as well as the option to warp the path. Refer to Figure 4-159.

Free Transform Path	Ctrl+T		
Transform Path	▶	Again	Shift+Ctrl+T
Auto-Align Layers...			
Auto-Blend Layers...		Scale	
Sky Replacement...		Rotate	
		Skew	
Define Brush Preset...		Distort	
Define Pattern...		Perspective	
Define Custom Shape...			
		Warp	

Figure 4-159. *Vector masks have all of the Transform options to edit the path*

To Free Transform them together (smart object, layer mask and the vector mask path), make sure that the path is deselected in the Paths panel by clicking below the path. Refer to Figure 4-160.

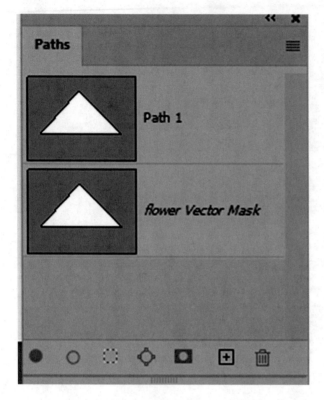

Figure 4-160. *Deselect the paths in the Paths panel when you want to Free Transform the smart object and the layer and vector masks*

In the Layers panel, select either the layer mask or smart object thumbnail and make sure they are linked and then choose Edit ➤ Free Transform or one of the mentioned transformations, except for Warp. Refer to Figure 4-161.

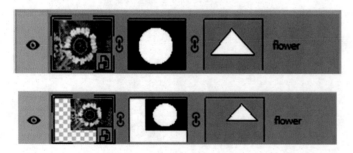

Figure 4-161. *The smart object thumbnail on the layer is scaled and so is the layer mask and vector mask*

Keep in mind these steps learned in this chapter as you return to the previous chapters to transform and warp, if you have ideas for

- Brush creation (Chapter 2)
- Patterns (Chapter 3)

- Vector shapes (Chapter 3)

- Layer styles when applied to shapes (Chapter 3)

For example, use these steps in regard to layer styles, when you draw a shape such as a rectangle and then apply a layer style layer like Drop Shadow. Refer to Figure 4-162.

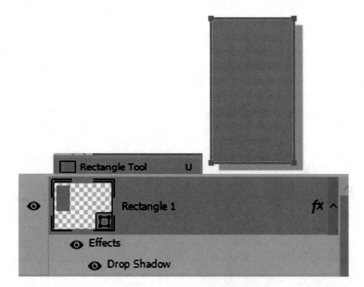

Figure 4-162. *Apply a layer style to a shape*

Now you can use the Path Selection tool and the Direct Selection tool, as in Chapter 3, or, as in this chapter, one of the Edit ➤ Free Transform Path commands or Transform Path ➤ Warp to scale your vector shape and the layer style will scale along with it. Refer to Figure 4-163.

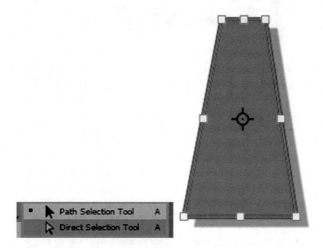

Figure 4-163. *Use the Path Selection tool, Direct Selection tool, or Free Transform to edit the shape*

When you click the check in your Options panel, you will get this message. Refer to Figure 4-164.

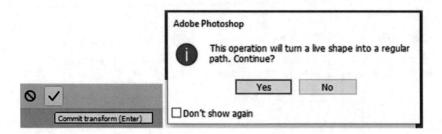

Figure 4-164. *Click the check in the Options panel to commit the shape transformation and Yes to the alert message and change from a live shape to a regular path*

You can click Yes and continue to edit the shape and notice how the layer style updates to match the new path.

■ **Note** For shapes or a path when a single point on a path is selected with the Direct Selection tool, the menu changes to Edit ➤ Free Transform points and only for Transform Points are the Scale, Rotate, and Skew options are available. Refer to Figure 4-165.

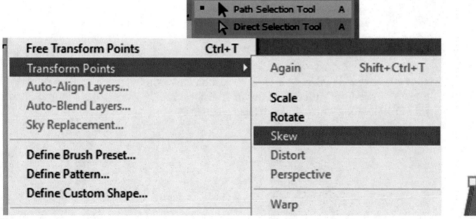

Figure 4-165. *You can also Free Transform selected points on a shape*

You will learn more about smart objects in Chapters 5 through 10.

Summary

In this chapter, you looked at the various Free Transform options that you can use to scale, rotate, skew, distort, and alter perspective. Then you looked at how to warp your layers. You also looked at some of the benefits of using smart objects as well as how to alter layer masks, vector masks, and shape layers with layer styles. In the next chapter, you will look at how this can be applied to warping text.

Warping Text

Chapter goal: Learn different ways you can alter your text with various warps.

While it's fun to transform layers, whether the layers are smart objects, a normal layer, or vector shapes, you can use what you learned in Chapter 4 about transformation on type layers as well.

In this chapter, we will be exploring how to use the Horizontal and Vertical Type tools along with their related panels for additional options to warp text and then look at how to create a path for text to flow on.

■ **Note** You can find the projects for this chapter in the Chapter 5 folder.

Working with Type Tools to Create a Text Warp

Photoshop has text tools in the Tools bar panel for working with type: the Horizontal Type tool and the Vertical Type tool. However, if you want to create selections of type for a mask, you can also use the Vertical and Horizontal Mask Type tools, which I discuss in detail in my book *Accurate Layer Selections Using Photoshop's Selection Tools*. In this book, our focus is on the first two tools for text warping. Although they will not be mentioned further in this book, you can also use the Type Mask tools for your projects, as much of what you will learn here can be applied to those tools. Refer to Figure 5-1.

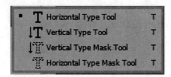

Figure 5-1. *Horizontal and Vertical Type tools in the Tools panel*

Project: The Circus Tent Poster

To warp text, you first need to create a type layer. File ➤ Open the file Circus_Poster_start.psd. Make an Image ➤ Duplicate of the file for practice. Refer to Figure 5-2.

© Jennifer Harder 2023

J. Harder, *Perspective Warps and Distorts with Adobe Tools: Volume 1*,
https://doi.org/10.1007/978-1-4842-8710-1_5

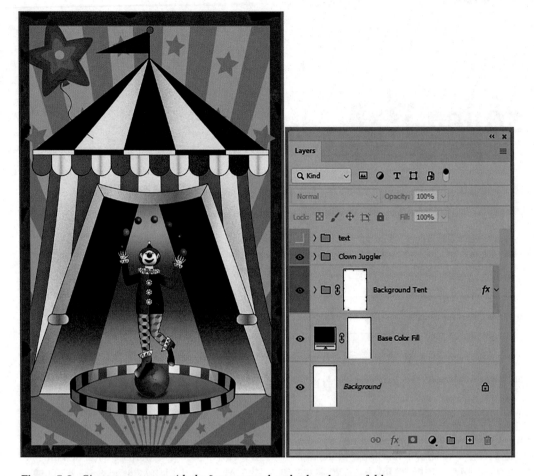

Figure 5-2. *Circus tent poster with the Layers panel and colored group folders*

In this example, I colored some of my group folders so to organize some of my smart objects and layers. Right-clicking a group folder's visibility eye will allow you to change the color of the folder. Refer to Figure 5-3

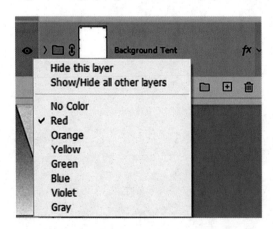

Figure 5-3. *How to color a group folder*

The Background Tent red group folder has some layer styles globally applied to it as well as a layer mask that is used to affect those layers collectively with a blending mode of Pass Through. This is like working with a clipping mask, which I talk about in more detail in my previously mentioned book regarding how to affect other layers with a mask. We will not be focusing on clipping masks in this book but you can explore that topic on your own. The Clown Juggler group folder in green contains the clown and the balls he juggles while he balances on the Earth ball in the ring with the spotlight shining down on him. Take some time to explore these folders on your own as you explored many of these layer types in the last four chapters. The only one we have not talked about is the Smart Filter, which we will look at in the coming chapters. Refer to Figure 5-4.

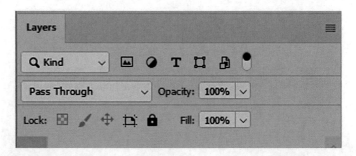

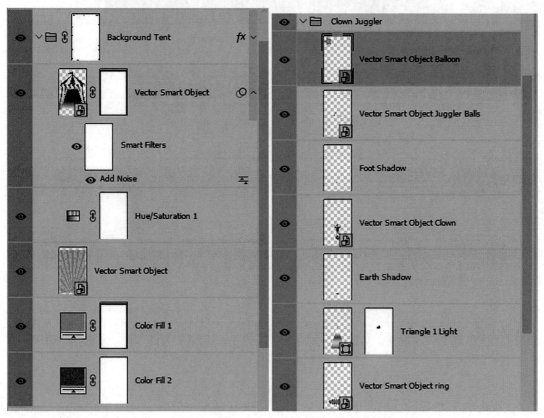

Figure 5-4. *The Background Text folder has a layer style and mask set to a blending mode of Pass Through. The green folder contains the clown and other layers*

However, other than an Edit ➤ Free Transform of Scale, no other distortion has been applied to these smart objects, so you can keep these folders collapsed for now.

The other folder called text, which is blue, contains most of the text that will be warped in this poster. For now, the visibility has been turned off. We will look at that text later and warp it. So, keep the visibility of this group folder off for now and collapse it. Refer to Figure 5-5.

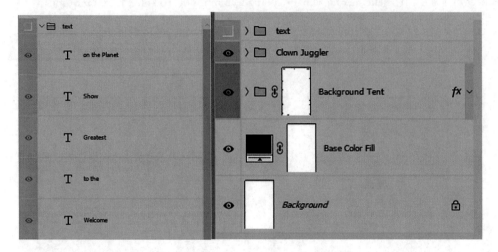

Figure 5-5. *Layers in the Text folder are currently hidden*

Make sure at this point none of your layers are selected.

From the Tools panel, select the Horizontal Type tool. It changes the Options panel. Refer to Figure 5-6.

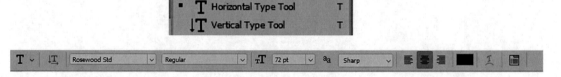

Figure 5-6. *Horizontal Type tool and the Options panel*

Then click on the canvas. If you just want a straight line of text, at whatever point you clicked some default text will appear at that location in the current font that you have chosen. In this case, I was working with Rosewood Std, so that appears on the screen. Refer to Figure 5-7.

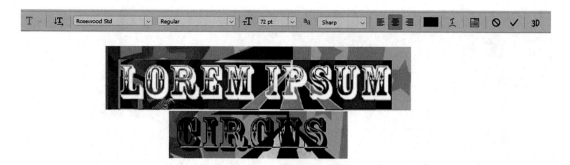

Figure 5-7. Horizontal Type tool Options panel. The text point highlighted, and a new word is typed in

I could start typing my text on the line. However, in this case, I want a text block. Click the cancel symbol icon in the Options panel to unto this last step; the temporary layer is removed. Refer to Figure 5-8.

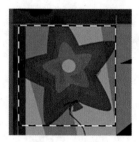

Figure 5-8. Click the Cancel icon in the Options panel

When you want to create a text box with the same tool, drag out a rectangular marquee. This will create an area for the text to fill rather than be on one single path. In this case, I dragged out a square text box around the star balloon. Refer to Figure 5-9.

Figure 5-9. Dragging with the Horizontal Type tool to create a type block

This created a type Layer 1 at the top of the Layers panel. The type bounding box surrounds the text. Refer to Figure 5-10.

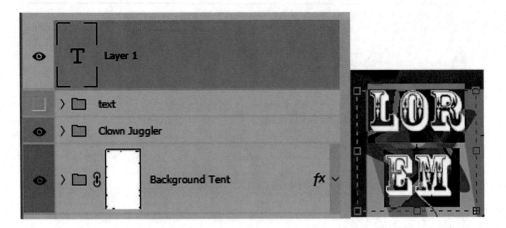

Figure 5-10. *The type layer is created in the Layers panel and the default text is highlighted on the canvas*

While the default text is selected and highlighted, let's use the Options panel to alter it.

Horizontal Type and Vertical Type Tool Options

Now look at the Horizontal Type tool Options panel. The first section is the tool preset where you can store options for this tool. Before you clicked on the canvas with the tool, you would have had access to this area and would have been able to save a preset based on the settings chosen in the Options panel. Now, however, while the text is selected, it is grayed out. Refer to Figure 5-11.

Figure 5-11. *Options panels for the Horizontal and Vertical Type tools, which can be toggled between*

The next section is the toggle text orientation. Clicking this button allows you to change the text from the Horizontal to the Vertical Type tool. There are really no differences between these two tools other than how the text flows or aligns. Left, Center, Right changes to Top, Center, Bottom. Refer to Figure 5-11 and Figure 5-12.

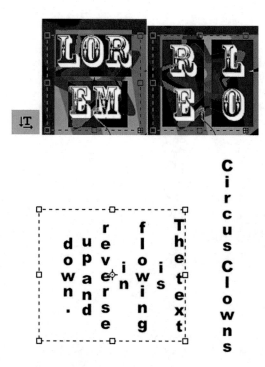

Figure 5-12. *Use the toggle to switch between horizontal and vertical text orientations*

Vertical type is often more common with Asian characters and writing where the text must flow up and down and right to left. Nevertheless, if you need text to flow downward on a vertical path, it can be a useful tool.

■ **Note**   While the Vertical Type tool is selected, refer to the Properties panel for East Asian Features and Middle Eastern Features options if you need to make additional text adjustments. Refer to Figure 5-16.

Return to the horizonal type orientation if you clicked on this toggle.

The next section allows you to search and select fonts from the dropdown menu. When you drag highlight the text, you can then choose a new font from the menu. It may be from the current fonts on your computer or one you acquired from Adobe Fonts via the Creative Cloud. Refer to Figure 5-13.

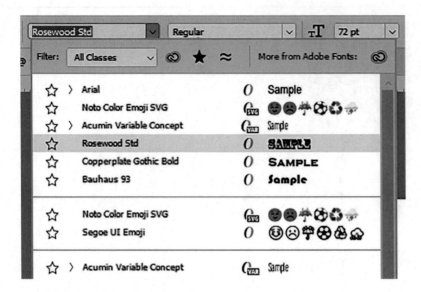

Figure 5-13. *Choose a font from the dropdown list*

By default, the fonts are filtered by all classes and the most recently used are at the top. However, you can filter them further by choosing an option from the filter list. To the right of the menu are other filter options such as Show Adobe Fonts (which is currently active), Favorite fonts, and Similar fonts, if present. You can also browse Adobe Fonts online. Refer to Figure 5-14.

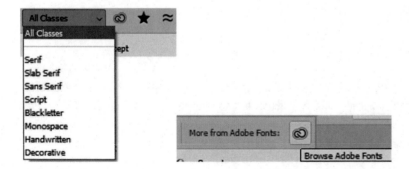

Figure 5-14. *Sort the kinds of fonts you want to see*

The next section allows you to set the font style for that font while the text is highlighted. They can also be viewed in the search area if you open the triangle by the font. Most fonts either have one style or the four main styles such as regular, italic, bold, and bold italic. But other fonts, like Acumin Variable Concept, can have a much larger family of options including condensed, light, and black. Refer to Figure 5-13 and Figure 5-15.

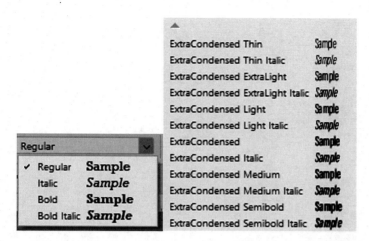

Figure 5-15. *Choose a font style for that font from the Options menu*

■ **Note** To work with Variable Concept fonts further, you can use your Properties panel to adjust the weight, width, and slant. Many of these same features are also found in your Window ➤ Character Panel. Refer to Figure 5-16.

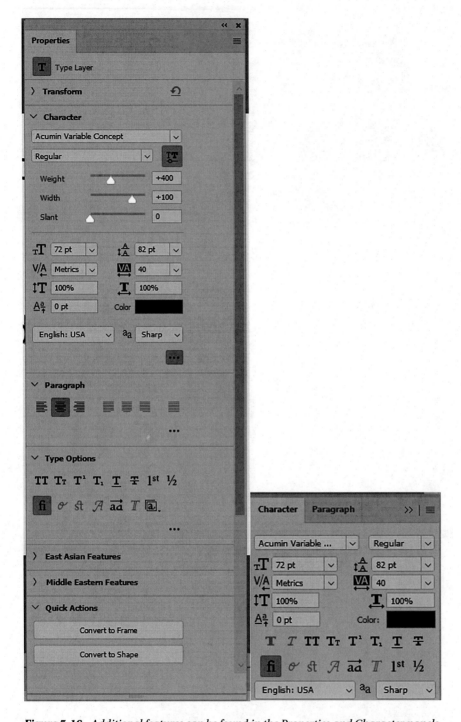

Figure 5-16. *Additional features can be found in the Properties and Character panels*

At this point, change your font to whatever it is currently set to, a font like Arial and a style of black. If you don't have this font, use a similar sans serif font like Helvetica Bold. Refer to Figure 5-17.

Figure 5-17. *Change to the font Arial Black*

The next section in the Options panel allows you to control the font size. While the text is highlighted, you can either type in a point size or choose one from the dropdown list. Sizes larger than 72 pt must be typed in. However, if the size is highlighted in this text box, you can use the up and down arrow keys on your keyboard to raise or lower the size. Refer to Figure 5-18.

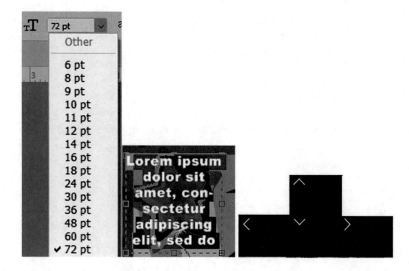

Figure 5-18. *Change the font size in the Options panel*

Select a point size by typing in 21.62; this fills the area with text. Now type the words Buy Tickets Now! and press the Enter/Return key to make a hard return as you type each word so each word is on its own line. Refer to Figure 5-19.

Figure 5-19. *Type in a new font size and then unhighlight the text to view it*

You can at this point scale the text box as well as rotate it. If you make it too small, some words will disappear and a plus symbol will appear in the lower corner bounding text box handle, so you will need to increase the size of the box to accommodate this text. Refer to Figure 5-20.

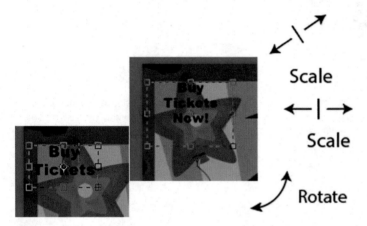

Figure 5-20. *Scale your text box so that you can see all of the text*

I scaled my text box and will move and rotate it later on. Highlight the text again by dragging your cursor over it. Refer to Figure 5-21.

Figure 5-21. *Highlight text when you want to make changes*

When the text is highlighted, the Properties and Characters panel, after you set a size, allow for many other sizing options including scaling vertically and horizontally, as well as various spacings between the letters like leading, kerning, tracking, and baseline shift. We will explore some of these options later when we work with text on a path. Refer to Figure 5-22.

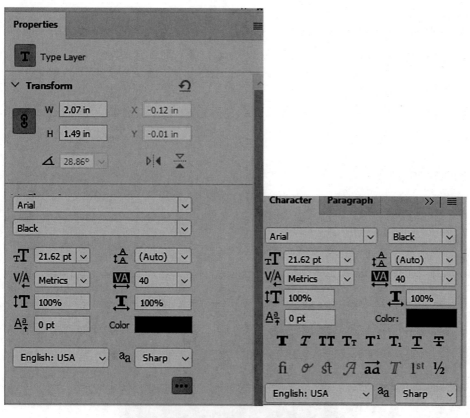

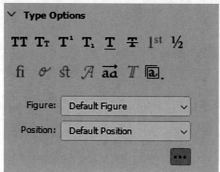

Figure 5-22. *Use the Properties or Character panels to make additional changes to your highlighted text*

Returning to the Options panel, the next section allows you to set the anti-aliasing method. This affects how the edges of the text appear. It can be set to None, Sharp (default), Crisp, Strong, Smooth, or for Windows or MAC computers, for the screen. This same setting is also found in the Properties (click the ellipse button) and Character panels. Refer to Figure 5-23.

Figure 5-23. *Anti-aliasing dropdown menu*

I left the setting at the default of Sharp, but you may prefer another setting if you need your text to blend into the background more smoothly.

The next section in the Options panel is for Text alignment. If horizontal, it can be left align text, center text, or right align text, and if switched to the Vertical Type tool, top align text, center text, or bottom align text. Further paragraph alignment options, as well as indents, spacing, and hyphenation can either be found in the Properties panel or in the Paragraph panel. Refer to Figure 5-24.

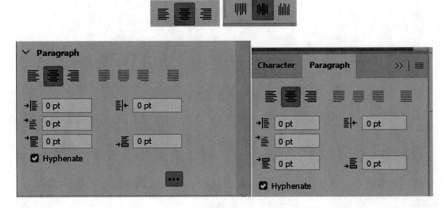

Figure 5-24. *Options panel for text orientation for a text block for the Horizontal and Vertical Type tools settings found in the Properties and Paragraph panels*

In my case, because I am using the Horizontal Type tool, I have in the Options panel set the text to Center. Do that now if your text is currently not on that setting so that it looks the same as mine. Refer to Figure 5-25.

Figure 5-25. *Center align the text using your Properties panel*

424

The next section in the Options panel allows you to alter or set the base text color using the Color Picker and the option of the Eye Dropper tool to select a color from your image and click OK. Click the color icon to enter the Color Picker for the text color. This color icon can also be found in the Properties or Character panel. Refer to Figure 5-26.

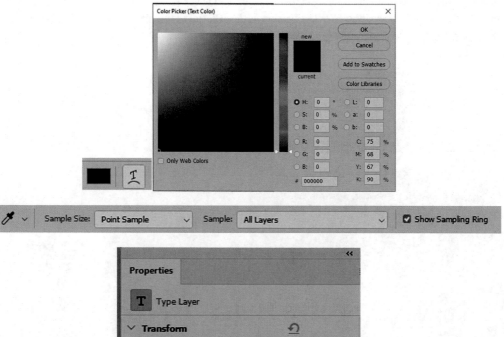

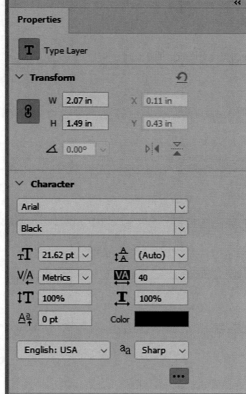

Figure 5-26. *Options panel for current text color, Color Picker dialog box, and Properties panel settings for the Character color*

In this case, let's leave the text at the default black color.

■ **Note** If you're working on text portions of highlighted text that have two colors, a (?) question mark symbol will appear in the swatch location. You either need to highlight that single line of text or highlight all the lines and click the Color Picker to select one color like black and click OK to exit the dialog box. Then the text will have the same consistent color. Refer to Figure 5-27.

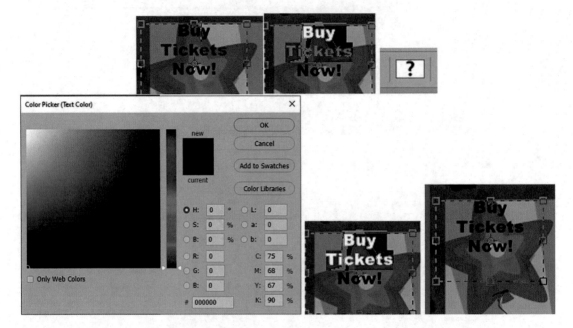

Figure 5-27. *When highlighted text has more than one color in a text box, a (?) appears in the Options panel. Select it and use the Color Picker to make the text one color*

■ **Note** To create graduated multicolored or patterned text, you can add a layer style, such as Gradient Overlay or Pattern Overlay, after you have committed your setting or converted the text to a smart object layer before applying the layer styles. We'll look at this later in the chapter.

In the Options panel, the next section allows you create the text warp. Likewise, you can also choose from the menu Type ➤ Warp Text to bring up the same dialog box. Refer to Figure 5-28.

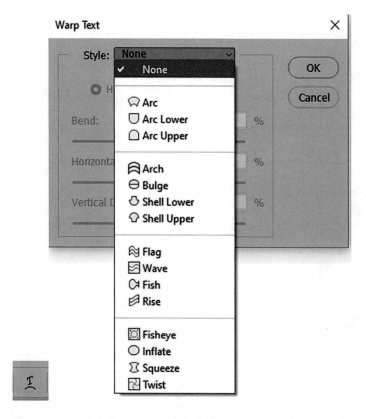

Figure 5-28. *Click the text warp icon in the Options panel to enter the dialog box and set a style option other than None*

Warps can be used with the Horizontal and Vertical Type tools.

The Warp Text dialog box has many of the same settings as Edit ➤ Transform ➤ Warp, which you saw in Chapter 4, and I will comment on this later in the chapter. It can warp a line or an entire block of text, as we are currently doing. However, when you want to warp text in the dialog box, you must change the style from the default setting of None to Arc, Arc Lower, Arc Upper, Arch, Bulge, Shell Lower, Shell Upper, Flag, Wave, Fish, Rise, Fisheye, Inflate, Squeeze, and Twist. Depending upon your style selection, you can preview and then adjust the horizontal, vertical, bend percent, and horizontal or vertical distortion. Refer to Figure 5-29.

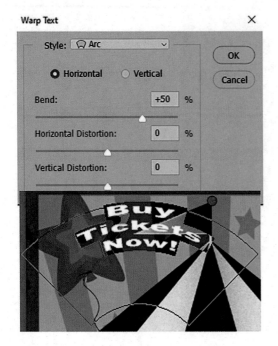

Figure 5-29. *A style of Arc is applied to the text box and text with the dialog box and previewed*

■ **Note** Fisheye, Inflate, and Twist have the horizontal and vertical warp orientation radio buttons disabled and you can only set Bend and Horizontal and Vertical Distortion. Also, currently in the Warp Text dialog box you will not find the new Cylinder style mentioned in Chapter 4. To access and use this feature for type, you must use Edit ➤ Transform ➤ Warp and select the Cylinder option from the Options menu. Refer to Figure 5-28 and Figure 5-30.

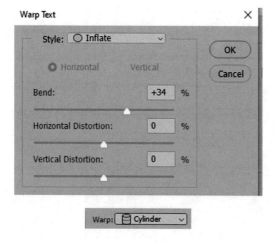

Figure 5-30. *The Warp text style is set to Inflate. Only in the Transform Warp Options panel can you find the Cylinder option for type—not in the dialog box*

After experimenting with the various warps for text, in the Warp Text dialog box, choose Inflate and set the bend to 34%, leaving the Horizontal and Vertical Distortion sliders at 0%. Drag and move the inflated text over the star and click OK to close the dialog box. Refer to Figure 5-30 and Figure 5-31.

Figure 5-31. *Current inflated text*

The last section of the Options panel, when clicked, allows you access to the Character and Paragraph panels if you need to make further settings to the fonts, and as mentioned, you can find these settings in the Properties panel, including Type Options, East Asian Features, and Middle Eastern Features. Refer to Figure 5-32 and Figure 5-33.

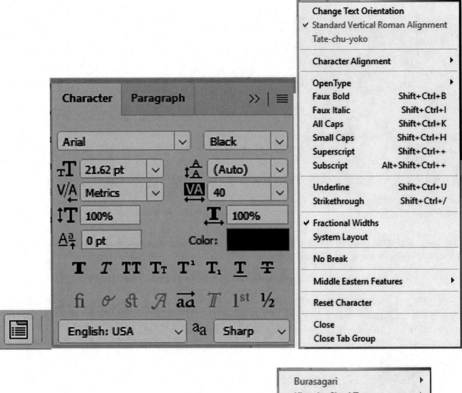

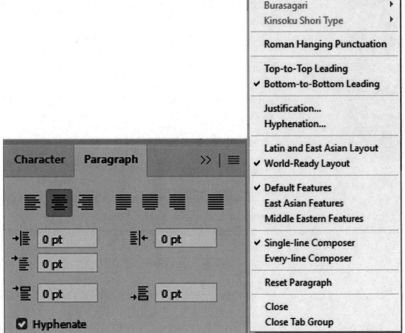

Figure 5-32. *Accessing the Character and Paragraph panels through the Options panel and viewing their menus for additional options*

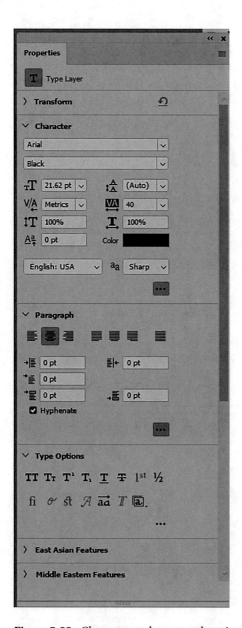

Figure 5-33. *Character and paragraph options in the Properties panel*

For more details on working with Character and Paragraph panels as well as type styles, go to https://helpx.adobe.com/photoshop/using/formatting-characters.html and
https://helpx.adobe.com/photoshop/using/formatting-paragraphs.html.

■ **Note**   In this chapter, when you adjust these panels, the settings are stored until the next time you type. So, make sure to, from both Panel menus, choose both Reset Character and Reset Paragraph to reset your tracking back to 0 or scaling to 100% before you type your next layer, or you may get some unusual results the next time you type a line of text. Refer to Figure 5-32 and Figure 5-34.

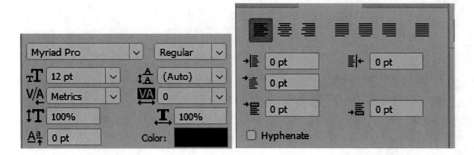

Figure 5-34. *Character and Paragraph options reset in their panels after a project*

However, for now in the Options and Properties panels keep the following settings: Arial, Black, 21.62 pt, Anti-aliasing, Sharp, and Text Aligned Center. For the highlighted text, set the Leading: (Auto), Kerning: Metrics, and Tracking to 40. The Vertical and Horizontal Scale are both at 100% and the Baseline Shift at 0 pt. Vertical and horizontal scale are useful if you need to make your highlighted type taller or wider. Refer to Figure 5-35.

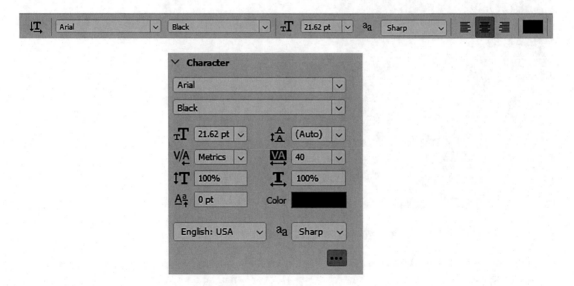

Figure 5-35. *Current Character and Paragraph settings in the Options panel and additional settings in the Properties panel's Character tab*

Once you have made your text adjustment, you can either cancel or commit them. To commit, click the check to commit your settings. Now you will see that the Layers panel has updated the layer name with the new text and has a text warp symbol applied to it. Refer to Figure 5-36.

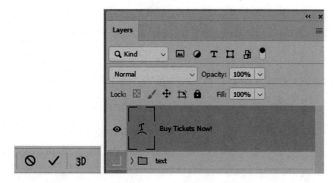

Figure 5-36. *Click the check to commit your type settings*

■ **Note** In past versions of Photoshop, another popular way to warp text was to use the Create from 3D Text button option. However, this and other 3D features are gradually being moved to the Substance Collection, so I will not discuss that feature in this chapter. Refer to Figure 5-36 and Figure 5-37.

Figure 5-37. *Adobe apps to use for 3D design*

However, you can still create 3D warped text and shapes in Illustrator, as you will see in Volume 2, should you want to explore that topic further. These creations can then be copied as a smart object layer into Photoshop. For example, the ball that the clown is standing on with the Earth map art applied is a 3D effect from Illustrator. Refer to Figure 5-38.

Figure 5-38. *3D ball created in Adobe Illustrator*

However, in book you will not be creating any 3D objects.

You can then use your Move tool to move the text area into place if you find it is partially off the canvas. Refer to Figure 5-39.

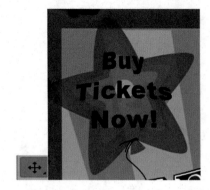

Figure 5-39. *Use the Move tool to shift your text on your Type layer*

■ **Tip** Besides the main text characters that you use in most fonts, make sure to search for more unusual characters that you can locate using your Window ➤ Glyphs panel. These include Color fonts like EmojiOne or the more recently added Noto Color Emoji SVG. You can Highlight text and then in your Options panel to apply this font and then using the Glyphs panel while the default text is highlighted, double-click on a symbol to add it to your path or text box. And these can be warped as well. Refer to Figure 5-40.

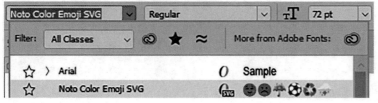

Figure 5-40. *Color fonts from the Glyphs panel turn to one color when text warp is used*

■ However, they will only take on the current base color and not full color when a warp is applied. We'll look at a work-around for this in a moment. So, for now, if you want to use the color font, keep the warp at None.

Deselect your type layer called Buy Tickets Now! for the moment and select and turn on the visibility of the blue group folder, text. Open the folder to view all the layers. Refer to Figure 5-41.

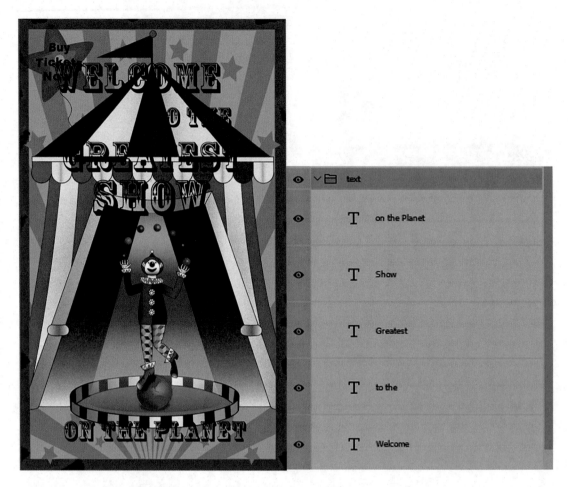

Figure 5-41. *Turn on the visibility for the text group folder in the Layers panel and preview the work*

This text has already been created and I have set the font, style, and size as Adobe Font Rosewood Std Regular. Refer to Figure 5-42.

Figure 5-42. *Current font, style, and font size for one of the selected layers*

Check your computer to see if you have this font. If you don't, you may get a warning message that you do not have this font in your computer and a request to replace with a different font. Or a warning icon may appear on your font layer. I have included a copy of this font in the Fonts folder or, if you do not have permission to use this font, use a similar font found on your computer. You can also activate this font from your Creative Cloud subscription when you choose More from Adobe Fonts and then locate that font when you search. In some cases, if the font is available through Adobe Creative Cloud, it will automatically be activated when the file opens. Refer to Figure 5-42 and Figure 5-43.

Rosewood Std Regular </>

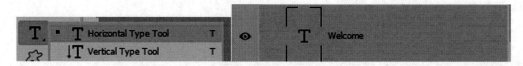 Activate font

Figure 5-43. *Warning icon you might see if font is missing. You can use Creative Cloud Adobe Fonts to activate it*

Rosewood Std, I find, gives a carnival circus-like feel to the poster.

Now, with the Horizontal Type tool in the Layers panel, select the type layer named Welcome. Refer to Figure 5-44.

T.	▪	T	Horizontal Type Tool	T
		↓T	Vertical Type Tool	T

◉   T   Welcome

Figure 5-44. *Just select the type layer if you want to warp the text*

From the Options panel, choose the text warp button. Choose the Style of Rise, Horizontal, Bend of +50% with the Horizontal and Vertical Distortion at 0% and click OK. Refer to Figure 5-45.

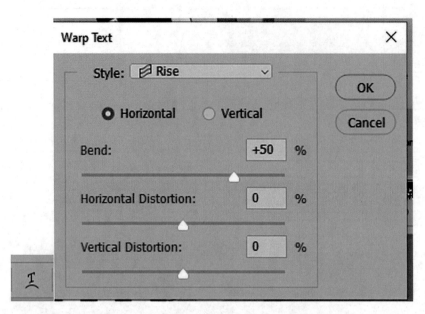

Figure 5-45. *The word Welcome rises upwards when the style of Rise is chosen in the Warp Text dialog box*

The text is a bit hard to read at this moment, but we will fix that later. For now, you can see the text has more movement, almost like a flag waving in the wind.

Skip over the type layer called to the, as not every layer in a poster must have a warp. Sometimes less is more, and I want the text to stay nudged under the word Welcome. Refer to Figure 5-46.

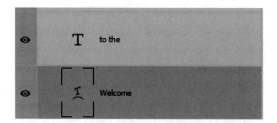

Figure 5-46. *The Welcome type layer thumbnail shows that the text is warped but the layer above it is not*

Now select the type layer named Greatest. Choose a Style of Arc, Horizontal, and Bend of +16% with the Horizontal and Vertical Distortion at 0% and click OK. Refer to Figure 5-47.

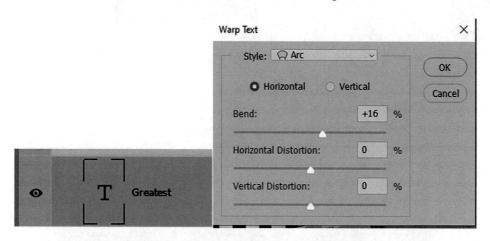

Figure 5-47. *Use the Warp Text dialog box to warp the next layer of type with an arc*

Now select the type layer named Show and choose a Style of Arc, Horizontal, and Bend of +24% with the Horizontal and Vertical Distortion at 0% and click OK. Refer to Figure 5-48.

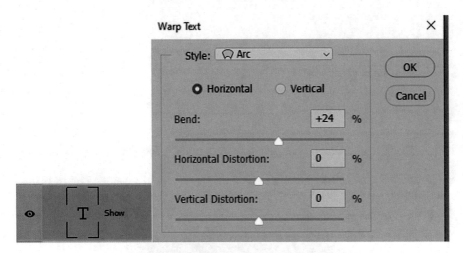

Figure 5-48. *Use the Warp Text dialog box to warp the next layer of type with an arc but a different setting*

Lastly, select the type layer called on the Planet and choose a style of Arch, Horizontal, and Bend of -16% with the Horizontal and Vertical Distortion at 0% and click OK. Refer to Figure 5-49.

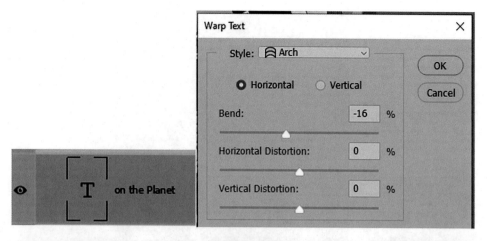

Figure 5-49. *Use the Warp Text dialog box to warp the next layer of type with an arch*

This will cause the text to appear as though it is slightly bending around the ring.

On your own, you can try other warp combinations. However, in this lesson, let's make the text appear a bit clearer on the image. This text has a lot of transparent areas that need to be filled. Turn off the visibility of the Clown Juggler folder, Background Tent folder, and the fill layer named Base Color Fill so that you can make a selection. Refer to Figure 5-50.

Figure 5-50. *How the text currently appears with the background folders and layers visibility turned off*

With your Magic Wand tool, click and hold down the Shift key to select multiple selections of the white areas including the diamond shapes inside of the lettering and the ring in the R and P, but not the hole in the center of the letters; it may take you a few minutes to do so. Currently in the Tools panel the foreground is set to black and the background to white. Refer to Figure 5-51.

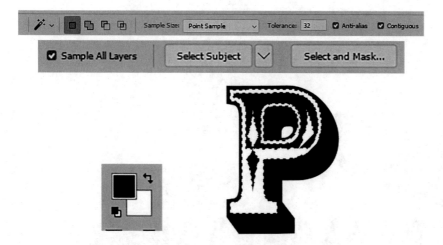

Figure 5-51. *The tools panel with default settings and the magic wand tool and one of the letter's white areas selected*

Make sure in the Options panel that Sample All Layers is enabled as you make this selection of all the letters on other layers. Use your Zoom tool and Hand tool (spacebar) if you need to zoom in and move around to make a more accurate selection. Refer to Figure 5-52.

Figure 5-52. *Zoom in and move about with the Hand tool while using the Magic Wand to select the white areas of the text*

Now select the type layer named Welcome while the section is still active and the from the Layer panels choose a Fill Adjustment layer of Solid color and choose white (R:255, G:255, B:255) from the Color Picker dialog box and click OK. Refer to Figure 5-53.

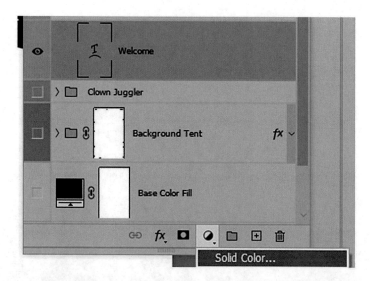

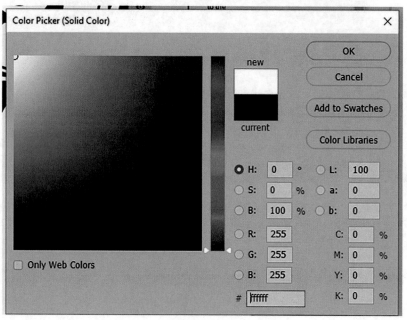

Figure 5-53. *Choosing a solid fill color of white from the layers panel to create a white selection from the font*

This adds a white fill mask (color fill) to fill in the gaps between the letters. Then drag this fill layer below the Welcome Type layer so it is below all the type and turn on the visibility for the Clown Juggler folder, Background Tent folder, and color Base Color Fill layer. Zoom out if you need to view your work as a whole. Refer to Figure 5-54.

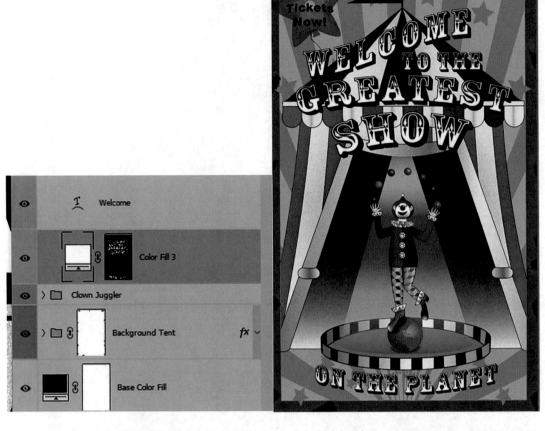

Figure 5-54. *Drag the white fill area below the lettering so that it makes the text less transparent*

Now you can collapse the Text Group folder and then apply a layer style of Satin to all the text in that folder. Refer to Figure 5-55.

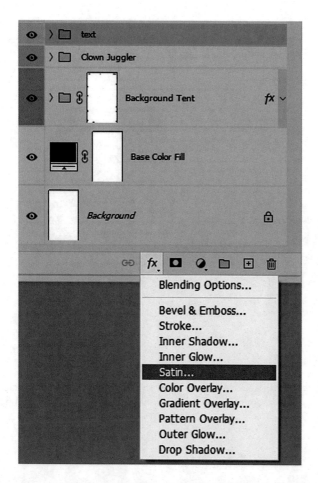

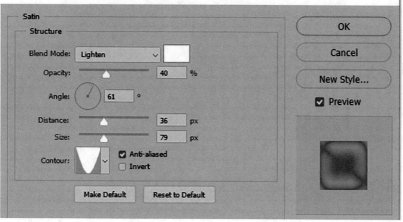

Figure 5-55. *Adding a layer style of Satin to the Text folder*

A layer style of Satin with a Structure: Blending Mode Lighten, White (R:255 G:255 B:255), Opacity of 40% angle of 60 degrees, Distance of 36 px, and Size of 79 px with a Contour of Cone-Inverted and Anti-alias enabled and Invert disabled can give the black area of the letters almost a softer air brush effect. I think it makes the letters appear more 3-D like collectively. Click OK to commit your settings and exit the dialog box. Refer to Figure 5-56.

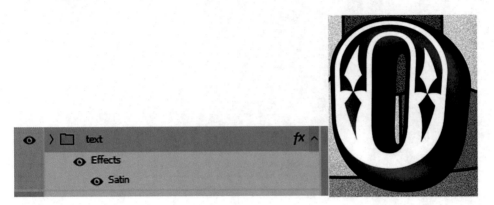

Figure 5-56. *Satin layer style applied to the letter O and all other type in the group folder*

Another Way to Warp Text

Let's return back to the type layer called Buy Tickets Now. I like the warp, but the letters are not exactly on the star balloon as I would like them to be. Use your Zoom and Hand tools if you need to look at the layer close up. Refer to Figure 5-57.

Figure 5-57. *Select your layer to continue to Free Transform it*

So far, you have seen how to warp text using the Text panel. However, as mentioned, you can still use your Edit ➤ Free Transform options of Scale, Rotate, Skew, and Warp. Refer to Figure 5-58.

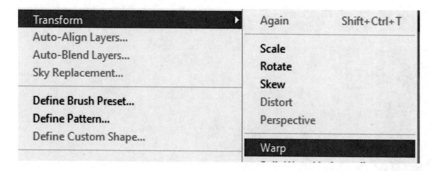

Figure 5-58. *Free Transform options in the Edit menu*

■ **Note**   Because it is not a smart object layer, the Distort and Perspective Transforms are grayed for type layers.

First, choose Edit ➤ Transform ➤ Rotate and rotate about -16.44 degrees. Remember to use the arrow keys on your keyboard as you did in Chapter 4 to nudge your text into place. Then click the check in the Transform panel to commit. Refer to Figure 5-59.

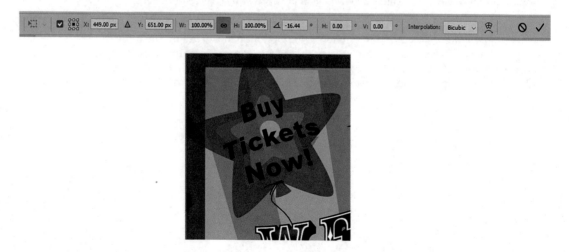

Figure 5-59. *Text is rotated using the Free Transform options*

Now go to Edit Transform ➤ Warp. This options panel allows you to use the same warp settings you saw in Chapter 4. And you do not need to use the dialog box. However, you will not have access to the split options to create a custom warp, but you can toggle back to your other Transform settings to scale, rotate, and skew. Refer to Figure 5-60.

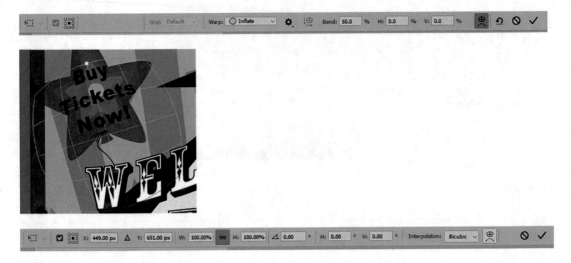

Figure 5-60. *After rotation, the text is warped or scaled if required by toggling between the two options panels of Free Transform and Warp*

■ **Note** As well with text, you can hold down the Shift key to scale disproportionately.

To cancel the warp, click the Cancel button in the Options panel to exit the dialog box for now.

To the Buy Tickets Now layer I added a layer style of Stroke with Structure: Size of 6px, Position Outside, Blend Mode Normal, Opacity 100%, Overprint disabled, and a Fill Type of Color: White (R:255 G:255 B:255), which you can enter into the Color Picker when you click the swatch. Refer to Figure 5-61.

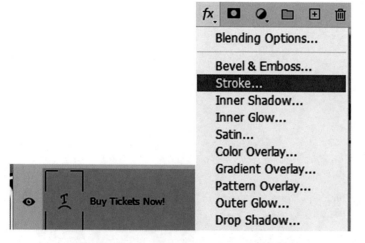

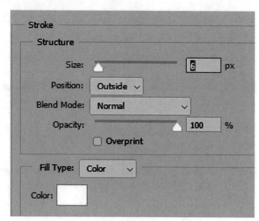

Figure 5-61. *Applying a layer style of Stroke to the text*

Click OK to exit the Layer Styles dialog box and you can see how the stroke bends around the warped text.

Refer to Chapter 3 if you want to know how to apply a patterned stroke. Refer to Figure 5-62.

Figure 5-62. *The completed warped text on the balloon*

File ➤ Save your work at this point.

Warping Text Continued

So, what do you need to do create a custom warp for text or have access to all the transformation settings, including distort and perspective?

There are several ways to can do this, which I will discuss next. They are not part of this circus poster project.

Converting Text to a Path or Shape Layer

Text can be converted to a path by choosing the type layer and then, from the menu Text ➤ Create Work Path, the text will remain in the Layers panel and a path is created and stored in the Paths panel. Refer to Figure 5-63.

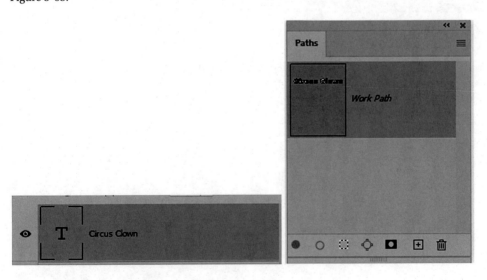

Figure 5-63. *Text converted to a path is found in the Paths panel*

These kinds of paths can prove useful later when you want to use render filters, as you will see in Chapter 8. Paths, as noted in Chapter 4, can use the Free Transform Path options, including Distort and Perspective.

However, a better option to create a visual effect is to choose, either from the menu Type ➤ Convert to Shape or from the button from the Properties panel Quick Actions menu while the layer is selected with the Horizontal or Vertical Type tool. Refer to Figure 5-64.

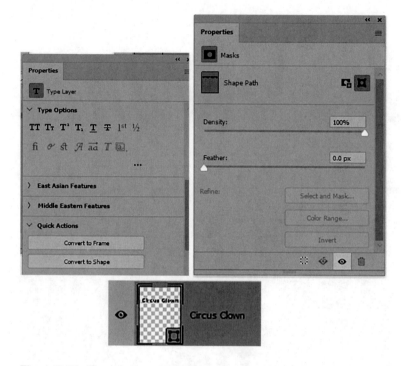

Figure 5-64. *Use your Properties panel when you want to convert text to a shape*

Once the type is a shape layer, you will then have access to all of the transform features, including the ability to Edit ➤ Transform Path ➤ Warp to custom warp the shape. Refer to Figure 5-65.

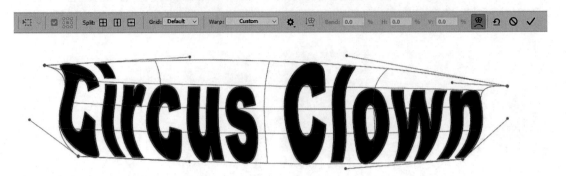

Figure 5-65. *You can easily custom warp text when it becomes a shape*

However, because it is no longer a type layer, the text is no longer editable and could be an issue if the client wants to change the lettering later.

In this case, before I custom wrap any text shape, I create a copy of the Type layer (drag over the Create new layer icon) so that I still have access to the original text. Then, on the copy, I choose Convert to Shape from the Properties panel and then Free Transform the shape path on that layer. Refer to Figure 5-66.

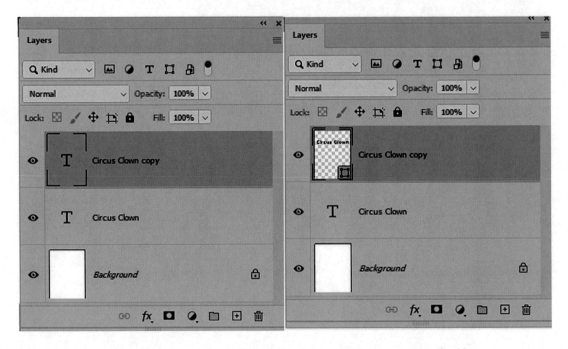

Figure 5-66. *Convert a type layer to a smart object layer when you want it to remain editable*

Project: Bottle Label Warp

While the shape layer option was helpful for some type projects, there are situations where being able to warp the actual type is a much better solution. In that case, turning your text into a smart object layer and being able to edit it is a better option.

File ➤ Open the file named AppleCider_Label_pattern.psd and make an Image ➤ Duplicate to use for practice.

The font used here was Algerian Regular, which I have included in the project folder. If you get an error message, you can use a similar font if you need to replace it as this is not an Adobe font. Refer to Figure 5-67.

Figure 5-67. *Label for a bottle that contains text*

This file contains layers and a group folder with various layer styles and advanced blending modes applied to give the appearance that the lettering and the logo are part of the wood, as seen in an example in Chapter 1. Refer to Figure 5-68.

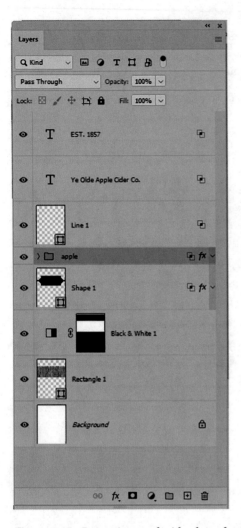

Figure 5-68. *Properties panel with a layer for the label*

For this example, if you double-click the advanced blending layer option icon for the type layer Ye Olde Apple Cider Co., you will see that in the Layer Styles dialog box, under blending options, I have split and moved part of the black slider for Underlying Layer. I slid it up to the 40 mark. Refer to Figure 5-69.

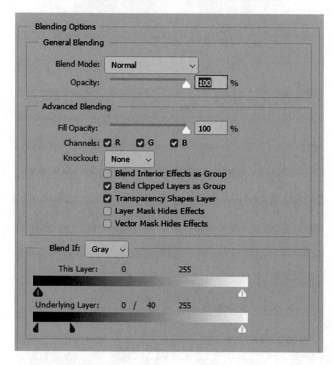

Figure 5-69. *Blending options applied to text*

■ **Note** To split a slider, hold down the Alt/Option key and click right in the center of the slider to split it. Then the left and right can move freely, and when they touch, they can join back together. In this case, the split slider on the underlying layer allows some of the underlying wood grain to show through the layer in the dark area, giving a worn appearance, like the paint is peeling or cracking due to age. A layer mask in this case is not necessary to achieve this effect. Refer to Figure 5-69 and Figure 5-70.

Figure 5-70. *The text appears worn when layer style blending modes are applied*

Because I have already adjusted the setting for the layer style for both the layers and the group folder, just click Cancel to exit the Layer Styles dialog box, but for your own projects you would click OK. Refer to Figure 5-71.

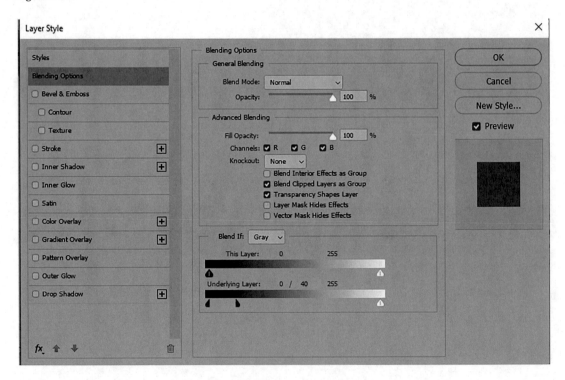

Figure 5-71. *Layer Style Blending Options applied to text*

Take a moment to review the file and study the layers and their blending modes.

Then Shift+Select the layers in the Layers panel, except for the background layer, as this layer is not part of the label. Refer to Figure 5-72.

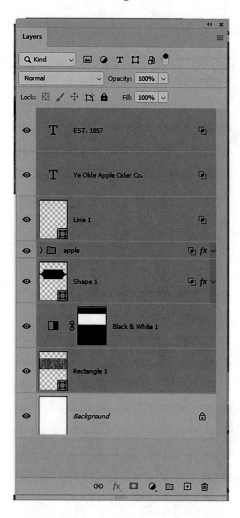

Figure 5-72. *Shift+Select more than one layer when you want them to be a part of the smart object*

Convert Text to Smart Object

Now, from the Layers panel menu, choose Convert to Smart Object. This packs all the layers into one smart object, in this case, named by the top type layer EST. 1857. Refer to Figure 5-73.

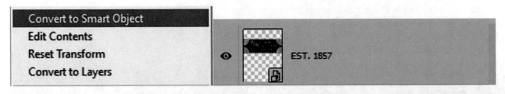

Figure 5-73. *Sometimes layer styles alter when they are confined to a new smart object space*

During this process you may notice a slight color shift that happened with the layer style for the group folder apple. This can sometime happen to layer styles when they are packaged into a smart object; a gradient can shift or reset. This is a good reason to work on a copy of your original image while making adjustments. To correct this, double-click the smart object thumbnail to enter it and access the .psb file.

Locate the apple group folder and double click on the layer style (fx) icon. Refer to Figure 5-74.

Figure 5-74. *The apple group folder is where you will have to correct the layer style*

Once in the Layer Style dialog box, select the Gradient Overlay Tab. Refer to Figure 5-75.

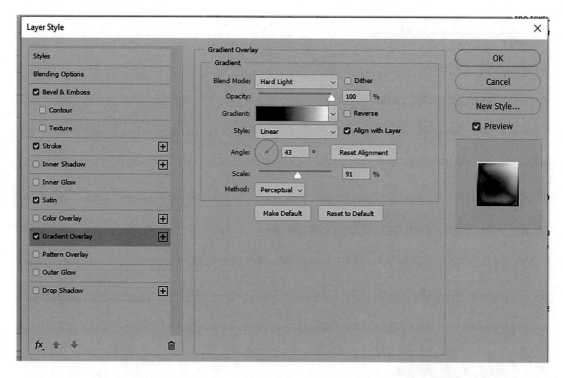

Figure 5-75. *Layer Style dialog box for the apple group folder and Gradient Overlay settings*

Nothing has changed here, but what you need to do, while in the dialog box, is in your image, drag the apple gradient down and to the left to reset the starting position of the gradient. This lightens it but the settings in this area do not change. Refer to Figure 5-76.

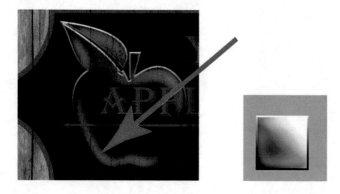

Figure 5-76. *Correct your gradient overlay by moving it while that tab in the dialog box is active*

When done, click OK in the dialog box to commit the changes. Now File ➤ Save your .psb file, File ➤ Close the file, and then return to the .psd file and it should be updated.

At this point, you can save the .psd file so that you can continue to the next part of the project. I added my initials to the file name and clicked the Save button to commit. Refer to Figure 5-77.

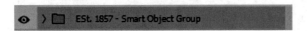

Figure 5-77. *Save your files after you make your changes to the duplicate file*

■ **Tip** If you ever need to unwrap a smart object layer, you can right-click on the layer, and from the pop-up menu, choose Convert to Layers. This unpacks the smart object inside the .psd file as a group folder. But keep in mind, as you saw earlier, this may reset some of your layer styles so you may need to reset them after unpacking. Refer to Figure 5-78.

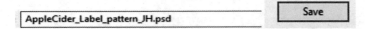

Figure 5-78. *Unpacking a smart object makes it appear inside a group folder in the .psd file*

Now that the layer is a smart object, File ➤ Open the document `AppleCider_Bottle_start.psd` and make an Image ➤ Duplicate of the file for practice. Refer to Figure 5-79.

Figure 5-79. *The apple cider bottle sitting on a table*

Return to your edited version of the `AppleCider_Label_pattern.psd` file, and with the smart object layer selected, choose Edit ➤ Copy. Refer to Figure 5-80.

Figure 5-80. *The apple cider label smart object*

Then return to the file `AppleCider_Bottle_start.psd`. and choose Edit ➤ Paste. This adds the smart object layer to this file. Refer to Figure 5-81.

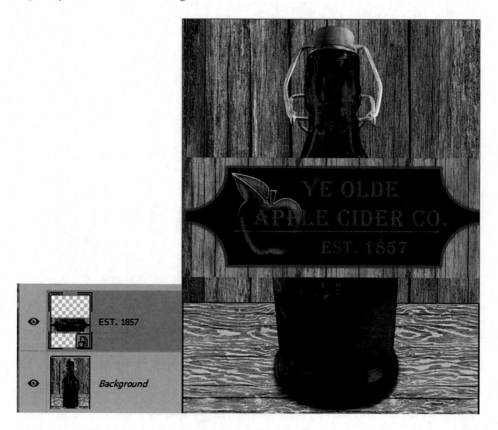

Figure 5-81. *The label is added to the file containing the bottle*

Use your Move tool if you need to move the label down a bit to the area where you roughly want the label to sit. Now it's time to Free Transform and Warp.

Now that the type is part of a smart object, you can use all of the Free Transformation features as seen in Chapter 4.

Edit ➤ Transform ➤ Scale to place the label where you would like it to appear on the bottle. Then toggle to the warp area of the Options panel. You must create a custom warp as the bottle is not perfectly cylindrical. To curve the label around the bottle, making it appear like it is wrapped but not with too much distortion, you may need to toggle back and forth several times and drag guides down from your ruler to get the label to look balanced and lined up. Lower the opacity of your layer so that you can see the background layer more clearly while you scale and warp. Refer to Figure 5-82.

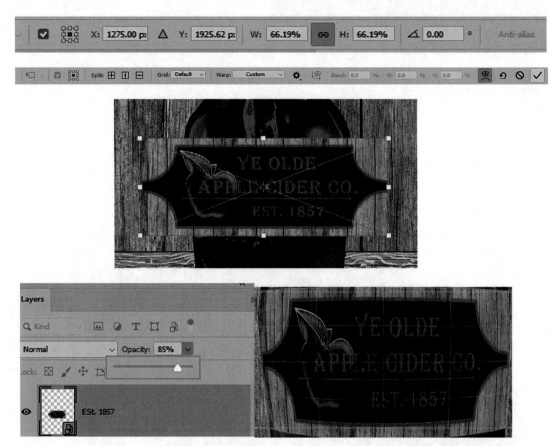

Figure 5-82. *Free Transform Scale, lower the layer's opacity, and then toggle in the Option panel to warp the label*

Remember, because this is a smart object layer, Scale settings and Warp settings are saved so that you can edit and correct as required.

Remember to hold down the Shift key while scaling. In this case, it will correct letters that now appear stretched and disproportionate vertically.

How you wrap the label will be based on the angle and perspective for your own project. So, try to get it as close as possible to mine. Refer to Figure 5-83.

Figure 5-83. *Close-up of the warped label with Free Transform Scale and custom warp settings in the Options panel*

Then click the check in the Warp options panel to commit the change. Raise the Opacity of the layer to 100%, if you have not already done so and File ➤ Save your document. Refer to Figure 5-84.

Figure 5-84. *Final custom warped label on the bottle and how the same label could be used on a more perfectly cylindrical bottle*

■ **Note**   Because this bottle was not perfectly cylindrical, we could not use the new preset warp of Cylinder, so we had to create a custom warp instead. Keep this in mind when you need to apply labels or type to different botte shapes. (See file `AppleCider_Bottle_Cylinder.psd`). Refer to Figure 5-84 and the following link for more details on how to use this new warp and its controls: `https://helpx.adobe.com/photoshop/using/warp-images-shapes-paths.html` (see Transform Warp: Cylinder).

At this point, if you need to change text or alter something on your label, you can double-click the smart object thumbnail to enter the .psb to find the type layer such as EST. 1857. Refer to Figure 5-85.

Figure 5-85. *Enter the smart object .psb file to alter a layer*

With the Horizontal Type tool, highlight part of the date and change it to 1858 or some other date of your choice and commit the change in the Options panel. Refer to Figure 5-86.

Figure 5-86. *Use the Horizontal Type tool to change a date in the text*

■ **Note**   Another change I made in the file was to select my adjustment layer called Black & White 1. I noticed that during the transition, the mask did not expand enough and some of the brown wood was showing on the left and right side when the wood should appear gray. Refer to Figure 5-87.

Figure 5-87. *Correct color issues on your adjustment layer mask*

Do not worry about the transparent pixels on the edge of the image as this will not be noticeable in the warp.

With the mask selected, go to Edit ➤ Fill and choose a fill of white. Click OK and this should correct the gap. Refer to Figure 5-88.

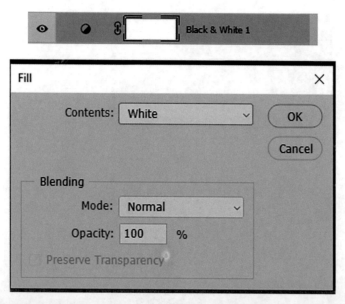

Figure 5-88. *Fill in missing areas on the black and white adjustment layer mask with the Fill dialog box*

Once you have completed your adjustment, File ➤ Save your .psb file and File ➤ Close and the text will be updated in the smart object, along with the warp. File ➤ Save the .psd file. Refer to Figure 5-89.

Figure 5-89. *Final warped label on a bottle with date and color changes*

If required, you can then further edit the warp using my Edit ➤ Free Transform Tools and commands.

At this point, to make the label appear more realistic, you can add some layer style effects such as Gradient Overlay and Drop Shadow. You can review my settings in the file `AppleCider_Bottle_final.psd`. Refer to Figure 5-90.

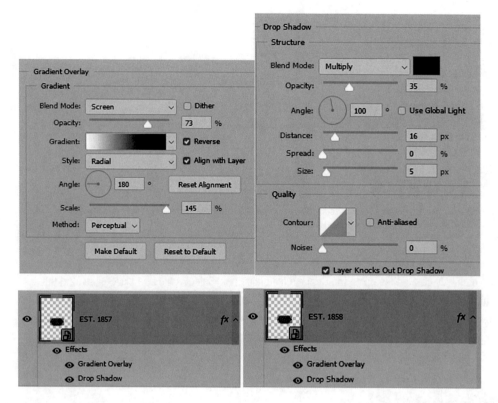

Figure 5-90. *Additional layer style settings for the label. Rename the label in the Layers panel to reflect the changes to the date*

You can then rename the layer, if required, but this will not affect the file name of the .psb file within the smart object.

■ **Tip** If you ever need to replace the label entirely, just make sure that you build the label to the exact same size as the original smart object. Select the smart object layer, right-click, and choose Replace Contents. Refer to Figure 5-91.

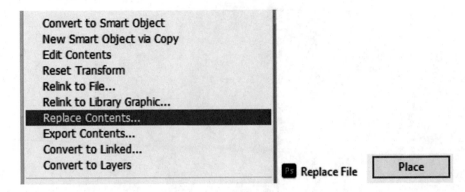

Figure 5-91. *Use your pop-up menu to replace the contents of a smart object when required. The files do not have to be a .psb file; you can select other formats*

■ Then locate the newly created file using the Replace file dialog box. Select a file and click Place, and the contents will update but the warp will be maintained. Refer to Figure 5-91. If you want to have both labels in the file for the client to compare, select the smart object layer first, then right-click and from the menu choose New Smart Object via Copy, as seen in Chapter 4, and then replace the contents of the copied layer. Refer to Figure 5-92.

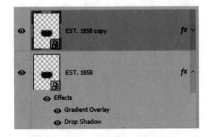

Figure 5-92. *Create alternate labels for the client to view*

File ➤ Save your document at this point and you can close the apple cider project files.

Adding Additional Layer Styles and Color to Warped Text

As you have seen, layer styles can be applied to text whether you have added a text warp to them or not. This can improve the design, such as adding a drop shadow or even a gradient or texture pattern within the lettering. For example, Pattern Overlay blends can be set to Blend Mode of Normal.

However, keep in mind that if you apply a layer style to text or a shape, this does not guarantee that when you apply a pattern overlay that the pattern is going to warp as well. Refer to Figure 5-93.

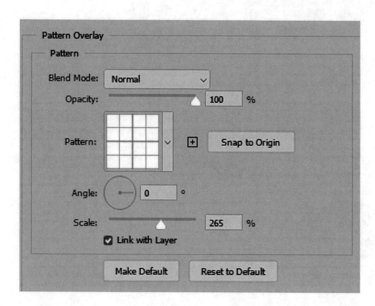

Figure 5-93. *Type can have layer styles of a pattern overlay applied but the pattern may not warp*

So how can you ensure that the pattern overlay or any layer style will appear warped? The answer is to convert the text layer to a smart object before warping by using the Layers panel menu. Refer to Figure 5-94.

473

Figure 5-94. *Turn your type into a smart object layer when you want it to warp*

Use Edit Transform ➤ Warp and you will see that you can easily warp the text and texture or patterns at the same time. And you can enter the smart object layer any time, as you saw in the earlier example, and make edits. Then you save the .psb, close it, and the edits will update in the .psd file.

Keep this idea in mind if you need to work with glyphs and color fonts, as you saw earlier in this chapter, as now the color will be preserved during the warp. Refer to Figure 5-95.

Figure 5-95. *Warp colored fonts when you turn them into smart object layers*

Making text into a smart object is also useful when you want to apply certain smart filters, as you will see in Chapters 6, 7, and 8.

■ **Note** With smart objects you can alter text or shapes in Illustrator smart objects as well. For information on working with text in Illustrator, refer to Volume 2. However, you can follow the steps mentioned in this chapter and Chapter 4 if you need to edit your Illustrator smart object text.

Converting Text to Frames

Another feature that you may have noticed in the Properties panel under Quick Actions is that you can convert text to a frame. Refer to Figure 5-96.

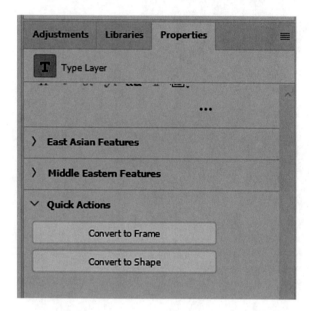

Figure 5-96. *Use your Properties panel to Convert type layers into frames quickly*

To get more detail about how to work with frames, you can check out the following link: https://helpx.adobe.com/photoshop/using/place-image-frame-tool.html.

However, I will just point out that you can make your text into frames that are like a clipping mask when you want a picture to show through, in this case after you have warped your text using the Horizontal Type tool Options panel. Refer to Figure 5-97.

Circus Clown

Figure 5-97. *Warped type created using the Horizontal Type tool options*

From the Properties panel or from the Layers menu, choose Convert to Frame. Name the frame and leave the width and height at the default and click OK. Refer to Figure 5-98.

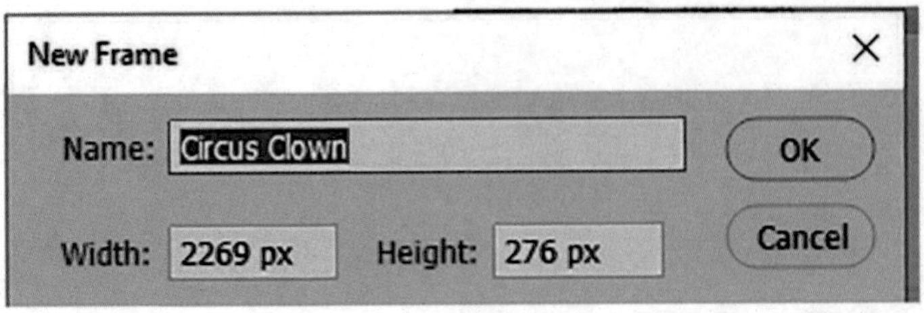

New Frame ✕

Name: Circus Clown   OK

Width: 2269 px   Height: 276 px   Cancel

Figure 5-98. *New Frame dialog box*

At this point, the frame is created in the Layers panel. Refer to Figure 5-99.

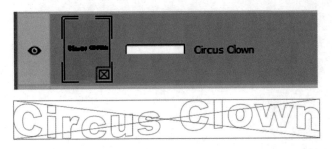

Figure 5-99. *New frame layer created*

Like a path, it does not have an image linked into it, so it is blank inside and has a white fill. From the Properties Panel menu Inset image, select either Place from Local Disk Embedded or Linked. I chose to embed. Refer to Figure 5-100.

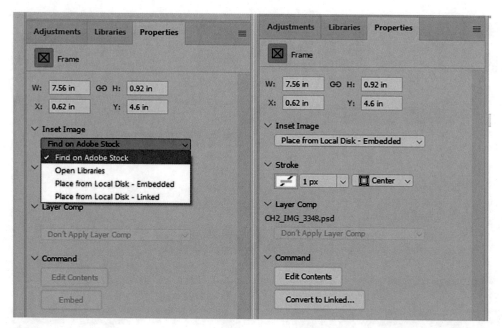

Figure 5-100. *Adding an image to a frame layer*

Locate an image using the dialog box and click Place. Refer to Figure 5-101.

Figure 5-101. *Once you locate the file, click the Place button in the dialog box*

This places the image inside the new frame. However, keep in mind that once again the frame may be warped but not the image within. To ensure the image bends with the warp, as with previous example, start with the text layer with no warp applied and then create the frame. While other Free Transform options could be applied to the frame, the option to Warp is unavailable, so the smart object transformation is necessary before a warp can be applied. Refer to Figure 5-102 and Figure 5-103.

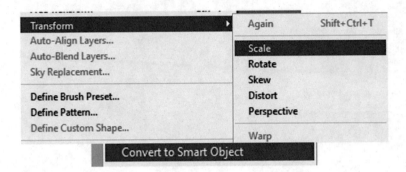

Figure 5-102. *Convert the frame layer to a smart object when you want to warp the text and image*

Figure 5-103. *Transform the warp text and smart object layer*

You can see that a certain order in steps must be followed to achieve the look you want.

■ **Tip**　In addition, for your smart object layer you could further use your Properties panel to fade, add layer masks, or even use your Layers panel blending modes to improve the look of the text on the layer.

Project: The Circus Clown

Let's return back to the copy you have been working on of the Circus_Poster_start.psd file. I saved my file with my initials earlier so that I could come back and complete the file. Refer to Figure 5-104.

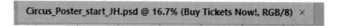

Figure 5-104. *Open your circus poster file to complete it*

Type on a Curved Path

Make sure to select your Buy Tickets Now! layer. Create a blank layer above it and select it. Then select your Pen tool. Refer to Figure 5-105.

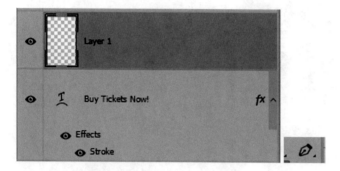

Figure 5-105. *Use the Pen tool on a new layer to create a text path*

In the Options panel, make sure that the pen is in the Path mode so that you do not create a shape by mistake, and make sure that your Paths panel is also visible. Currently, there should be nothing in the Paths panel. Refer to Figure 5-106.

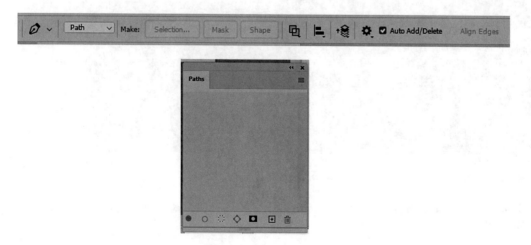

Figure 5-106. *Pen tool options and Paths panel*

One further feature you can try is getting your type to go on curved path. Use Ctrl/CMD++ to zoom in closer to the clown's head and the round balls he is juggling. Refer to Figure 5-107.

Figure 5-107. *Look at the juggler to begin creating your new type path*

Create a work path with your Pen tool. Click point 1 on the left. Click+Drag Point 2 in the center and then click point 3 on the right to create a curved open path. It will appear in the Paths panel. Refer to Figure 5-108.

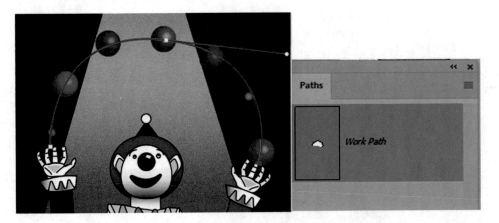

Figure 5-108. *Create a work path that appears in the Paths panel*

While the path is selected, with the Horizontal Type tool options, set to Arial Black 18pt, Sharp, Center Text Align, and White text. Refer to Figure 5-109.

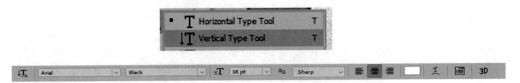

Figure 5-109. *Use the Horizontal Type tool to begin creating your path*

Click somewhere on the path, in this case the center. The Blank Layer 1 will now become a text layer. When your baseline indicator appears, you can begin to type. This creates a type path in the Paths panel. Refer to Figure 5-110 and Figure 5-111.

Figure 5-110. *Click on the path in the center to begin typing the text*

In all capitals, type the word JUGGLER. Refer to Figure 5-111.

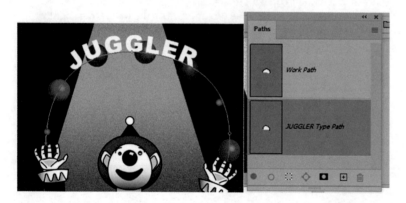

Figure 5-111. *Type the text and a new path in the Paths panel appears*

With the text highlighted, use the Properties Character panel and set the Tracking to 1140. Refer to Figure 5-112.

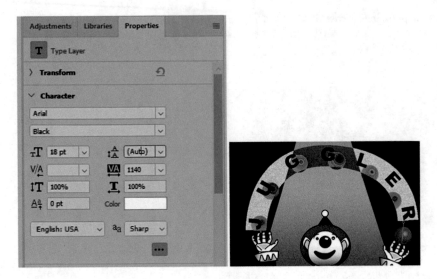

Figure 5-112. *Use the Properties panel Character tab to make further adjustments to the highlighted text*

This spreads the text farther apart so that it match up with the balls.

You can use your Path Selection tool to make sure that all the text appears on the path. Drag slightly above your path on the text. This adjusts the I-beam with an arrow to move the position left or right or have the text appear up or down. Dragging along the path will move the text as well, backwards or forwards. Refer to Figure 5-113.

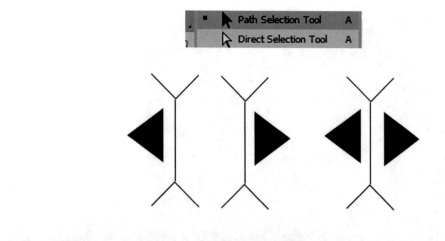

Figure 5-113. *Use your Path Selection tool to move the text around on the path sot that it is distributed correctly as the cursor changes*

You can then use your Direct Selection tool to select and adjust individual points on the path. Refer to Figure 5-114.

Figure 5-114. *Use the Direct Selection tool to adjust individual points on the path*

I used my Pen tool afterwards to add two more points to the path so that the letters would sit on the balls and continued to use my Direct Selection tool until the text was over the balls. I then clicked the check in the Type Options panel to commit the transform. Refer to Figure 5-115.

Figure 5-115. *The competed path with a few additional points. In the Options panel, click the check to commit the transform*

Afterwards, I added some layer styles to my type layer such as Inner Shadow and an Advanced Blending mode, so it appears like the letters are on the balls. Refer to Figure 5-116.

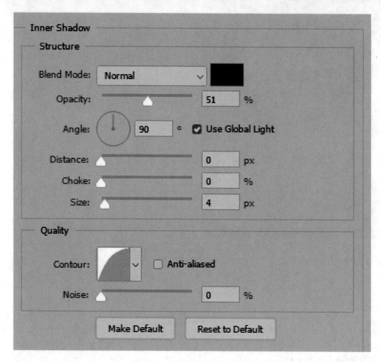

Figure 5-116. *Juggler type layer with Blending Options and Inner Shadow layer style added*

Set the Dark Blending Options Underling Layer slider to 104, Inner Shadow Structure Blend Mode to Normal, Black, Opacity 51%, Angle 90, Use Global Light enabled, Distance: 0 px, Choke: 0%, Size of 4 px, Quality: Half round contour, Anti-alias disabled, and leave Noise at 0%. Click OK to exit the Layer Style dialog box.

File ➤ Save this document and File ➤ Close any of the projects you have open at this point as the projects are complete. You can refer to my file `Circus_Poster_final.psd` if you need to see a copy of the work done here. Refer to Figure 5-117.

Figure 5-117. *Final circus tent poster*

Type on a Closed Path

Type on a path can also be created with shape paths that are closed, such as circles or polygons. Again, make sure to click on the path with the type tools baseline indicator; if you click inside the path, it becomes a text box area, which can be useful for other projects. Use your History panel if you did this by accident. Refer to Figure 5-118.

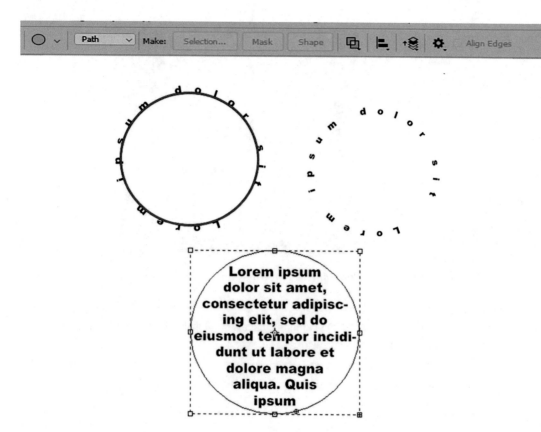

Figure 5-118. *Type on a path or in a custom text box shape with default text*

The type on a path can also be adjusted further with the Horizontal or Vertical Type tools or using the property of character baseline shift. With baseline shift, use positive numbers to raise the text and negative numbers to lower the text on the path. As mentioned, you can also use vertical or horizontal scaling to apply an additional stretching to the text. Refer to Figure 5-119.

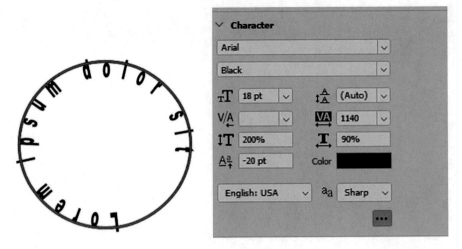

Figure 5-119. *Type on a path altered further with the Properties panel Character tab*

■ **Note**   Remember to reset your Character and Paragraph panels using their menus for your next project before you start, or you might include a previous warp setting.

To transform the Text path for the text to reflow on, use Edit ➤ Free Transform Path or Edit ➤ Transform Path ➤ Warp.

While not required for this book, if you would like to know how to use text paths in Illustrator, refer to Volume 2.

Summary

In this chapter, you looked at how to lay out some text and then warp it. You can also see that text by itself has some limitations, but you can add layer styles or convert it to smart objects or frames. Text within a smart object layer can use all the Free Transform commands, and specifically the custom warp command, when you want the patterns or images within the text to appear more realistic. In the next chapter, you will explore another tool in the Edit menu that is also a smart filter. It is known as Puppet Warp.

For recent updates on the change of EmojiOne to Noto Color Emoji SVG font refer to this link:
`https://helpx.adobe.com/photoshop/using/fonts.html#support-emoji-glyphs`

CHAPTER 6

■ ■ ■

Working with Puppet Warp

Chapter goal: Focus on the Puppet Warp and how it can be used to alter photos, shapes, gradients, types, and smart objects.

In the previous two chapters, you use the various Free Transforms and Warps on normal layers, vector shape layers, smart object layers, and type layers. However, the Edit menu has a few more warping tools and commands that you can use to improve your images and text. Refer to Figure 6-1.

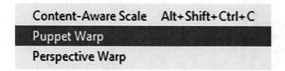

Figure 6-1. *The Edit menu contains the Puppet Warp*

In this chapter, we are going to look at Puppet Warp and its Options panel. Puppet Warp is more advanced than the Transform ➤ Warp, and with its meshes and pins you can use it to stretch and further mold your shapes in a variety of ways. In many ways the mesh is like puppet strings or a spider's web. After you have applied other Free Transforms like scale, the Puppet Warp tool can be used to apply further warps. Refer to Figure 6-2.

© Jennifer Harder 2023

J. Harder, *Perspective Warps and Distorts with Adobe Tools: Volume 1*,
https://doi.org/10.1007/978-1-4842-8710-1_6

Figure 6-2. The Puppet Warp alters the shape of a photograph

■ **Note**   You can find the projects for this chapter in the Chapter 6 folder.

Project Puppet Warp: Cover a Bowl with a Pattern

To see how Puppet Warp works, File ➤ Open the document bowl_puppetwarp_start.psd. Make an Image ➤
Duplicate to practice with. Refer to Figure 6-3.

Figure 6-3. *A bowl on a wooden table with a very warped shape*

Here you can see a bowl that is on a wooden table, and you are looking down into its center. The bowl has many twists and curves. The original bowl was colorful but because we are going to cover the bowl with a new, colored pattern, I made the bowl into a grayscale image so that later we could add some blending modes to different layers, in order for some of the bowl's original reflections and shadows to show through.

The original file I created had a layer mask applied to the bowl, so that the photo background could be hidden, and I added a layer-style drop shadow so that it appeared liked it was resting on the table. Then, from the Layers menu, I choose to Merge Visible so that the bowl and table are one image.

In this case, to make the project less cluttered I saved the selection in the Channels panel (Select ➤ Save Selection) as Bowl Selection, which we will access later to add a layer style to select layers as we build the Puppet Warp. Refer to Figure 6-4.

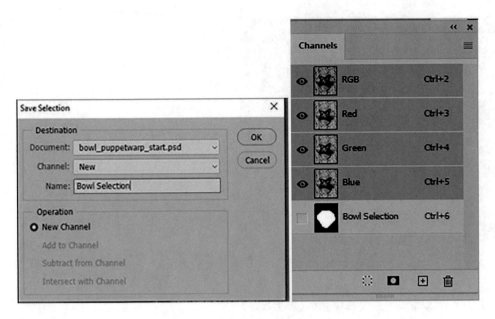

Figure 6-4. *A selection of the bowl was saved in the Channels panel for future use*

■ **Note** Selections can be made in a variety of ways including using the Magic Wand tool.

Currently, the visibility for the Illustrator Vector Smart Object layer is hidden. Click the layer visibility eye to show the visibility. This is a sunflower pattern that I created in Illustrator using various geometric shapes and patterns. For your own project, you could use a photograph and then convert it to a smart object layer so that whether your image starts out as a photo or as an illustration from Adobe Illustrator it does not really matter. Just make sure to convert to a smart object layer first. You can review those steps in Chapter 4. We will use this layer to cover the bowl. Refer to Figure 6-5.

Figure 6-5. *In the Layers panel, show the visibility for the Vector Smart Object layer*

Scale the Pattern

First, we need to scale the pattern so that it roughly fits to the bowl's borders. As you did in Chapter 4, select the Move tool and then Edit ➤ Transform ➤ Scale. Now scale the image using the Options panel down to about 37.9% or 38% for both the width and height. Refer to Figure 6-6.

Figure 6-6. *Select the Move tool and then Edit* ➤ *Transform Scale to use the Options panel to scale the pattern*

Hold down the Alt/Option key while you scale and drag the bounding box handles if necessary to keep the image centered. Move into place, and as you cannot see your transformation clearly over the bowl, lower the layer's opacity to about 35% while you work. Refer to Figure 6-7.

Figure 6-7. *Lower the opacity of the layer using the Layers panel to help you scale your pattern on the bowl*

After the scale and movement is complete, return the opacity of the layer back to 100% and click the check in the Free Transform Options panel to commit the scale. Refer to Figure 6-8.

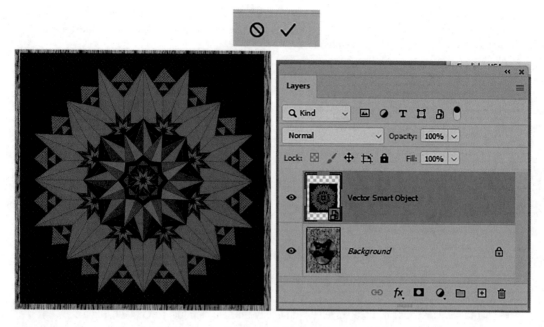

Figure 6-8. Commit the scale using the Options panel check and return the layer opacity to 100%

Using the Puppet Warp Smart Filter

Now, while the Vector Smart Object layer is selected, choose Edit ➤ Puppet Warp. Refer to Figure 6-9.

Figure 6-9. The pattern with the Puppet Warp mesh covering it

One of the reasons I prefer to use the Puppet Warp on smart object layers is because the pins and mesh order of the warp are then remembered by Photoshop. I can close and open my file again the next day and continue to edit my warp if I need to make changes.

■ **Tip** When you only want to warp part of the image or objects found on a background layer, here is what you should do: double-click the layer to convert it to Layer 0 using that dialog box and click OK. Refer to Figure 6-10.

Figure 6-10. *Change the background layer into a normal Layer 0 to begin a Puppet Warp*

It's always best to have that specific area selected with one of the selection tools and made into a copy on a separate layer using Ctrl/CMD+J (Layer via Copy) rather than trying to warp each item on one layer. Each new layer should then be turned into a smart object before using the Puppet Warp. Refer to Figure 6-11 and Figure 6-12.

Figure 6-11. *Attempting to Puppet Warp too many images on a single layer cause all images to be affected, so it is better to copy images onto their own layers*

Figure 6-12. *Convert each image layer into a smart object layer when you want to warp it separately from the other images*

Remember, when in Puppet Warp mode, to use your key commands of Ctrl/CMD++ or Ctrl/CMD+- or your Hand tool (spacebar) as you move around the canvas to edit the warp. Use Edit ➤ Undo or Ctrl/CMD+Z to undo steps if you make a mistake. Do not click on other tools in the Tools panel because you will get a warning. Click Cancel and continue to use the key commands. Refer to Figure 6-13.

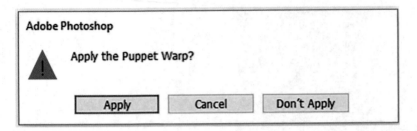

Figure 6-13. Warning message you may encounter if you try to use tools in the Tools panel while in the Puppet Warp workspace

Puppet Warp Options

Before we edit the mesh, let's look at the Puppet Warp options. As with the Free Transform, you will notice that the Pin tool presets are greyed out as every transform is different. Refer to Figure 6-14.

Figure 6-14. Options panel for Puppet Warp

Mode: Controls elasticity of the mesh distortion from the dropdown menu and has three settings.

- **Normal**: Default rigidity two-dimensional warp across a large area

- **Rigid**: More rigid for warping in two dimensions

- **Distort**: Best for correcting distortion in three dimensions, controlling the distortion and scaling. Distort, once pins are added, can depend on the shape of the warp and can increase or decrease the size of the smart object.

Refer to Figure 6-15.

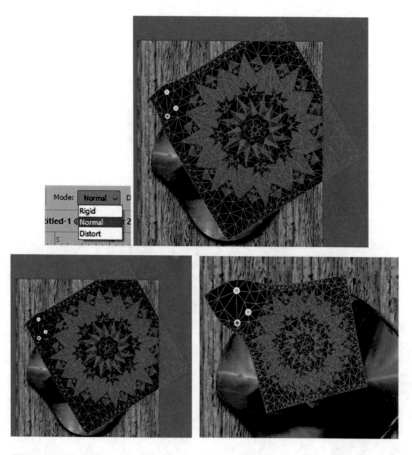

Figure 6-15. *Options panel for Puppet Warp and mode options of Rigid, Normal, and Distort when pins are present*

I generally leave my setting on the default of normal.

Density: Sets the space of the points of the mesh to control the quality of the transformation. From the dropdown menu you can set it to Fewer Points for a faster warp that is not as precise, Normal for an average warp, or More Points for a slower but more detailed warp. Refer to Figure 6-16.

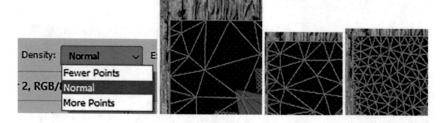

Figure 6-16. *Options panel for Puppet Warp showing Density options of Fewer Points, Normal, and More Points*

When working, I find that leaving it on Normal Density is best for the number of pins I use. However, you may be doing more detailed work, so More Points may be a better setting for you. Leave it on the Normal setting for now.

Expansion: Allows you to expand or contract the area of the mesh transformation. By default, it is set to 2 px, but it can be set from -20 px to 100 px. Leave it at the 2 px settings. Refer to Figure 6-17.

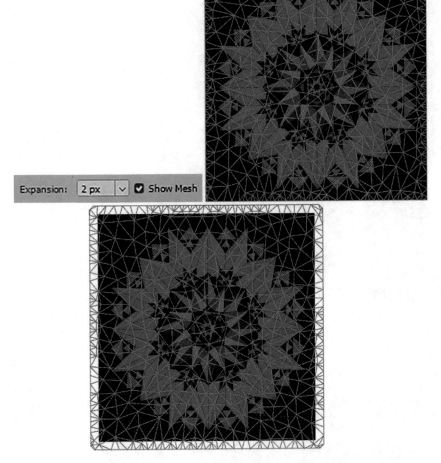

Figure 6-17. *Options panel for Puppet Warp showing Expansion and Show mesh options. Expansion preview at 2 px and 79 px*

■ **Tip**   Always plan your Density and Expansion settings right away because if you decide to alter them while setting down pins, some of the pins may get dropped during the alteration of the mesh. Refer to Figure 6-18.

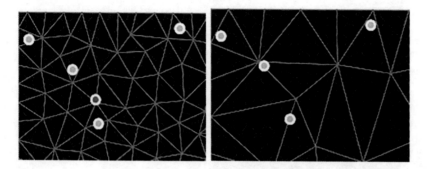

Figure 6-18. *A Density of More Points. Setting the Density down to Normal drops pins*

Enable the Show mesh checkbox when you want to see a preview of the mesh. This is the same as Ctrl/ CMD+H to hide the mesh while you continue to place pins. Press and hold down the H key if you want to temporarily hide placed pins. We will look at how to place pins in a moment. Refer to Figure 6-17 and Figure 6-19.

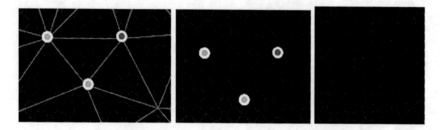

Figure 6-19. *Pins with mesh, mesh hidden, pins and mesh hidden*

Pin Depth: Pins can be moved up or down to set the pin depth and these buttons can be clicked multiple times to resolve any overlap. The first button in this section is to set a pin forward, and if you don't want to click multiple times in the options panel to resolve the overlap, press the right bracket on your keyboard (]) instead. The other button is to set a pin backward, and you can press the left bracket on your keyboard ([). Often, on simple Puppet Warps, I find the pins are far enough apart, so this option is not often required when working with smart objects. Refer to Figure 6-20.

Figure 6-20. *When no pins are present, the options are grayed out*

Currently there are no pins and so this area will be grayed out until you add one to your mesh.

What Are Pins?

Pins resemble push pins that you would use on a bulletin board. They are basically used to act as anchor points that, when selected and dragged, allow you to move parts of your shape or warp. If you don't add an adequate number of pins, then parts of your image may rotate or move where you do not want them to. Refer to Figure 6-21.

Figure 6-21. *Two pins have been added to the Puppet Warp. One is selected and the other is not*

A blue pin with a white outline is selected and a gray pin with a white outline is deselected.

Placing Pins

Click the tip of the yellow flower petal to add a blue pin on the mesh.

One pin will not create much of a change, even though you can drag the object around by clicking the pin and dragging it. Ctrl/CMD+Z if you moved the shape. Refer to Figure 6-22.

Figure 6-22. *Click to place a pin on the tip of the petal*

Pins, as mentioned, can act as anchors to hold part of the shape in place but they can also assist in stretching and warping the shape.

On the mesh, place another pin. The pin cursor will have a pin shape and a plus symbol next to it. Refer to Figure 6-23.

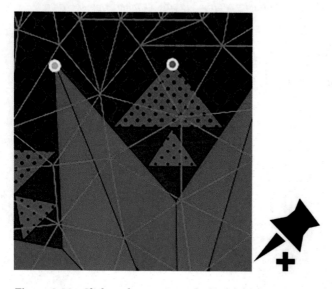

Figure 6-23. *Click to place a pin on the leaf shape tip*

In my case, I started by placing multiple pins along the points of my flower petals; these are the areas I want to stretch around the bounds of my bowl. Then I lowered the layer's opacity to about 35% so that I could see better where I need to move and stretch the pins. Refer to Figure 6-24.

Figure 6-24. *Once you place some pins, lower the layer's opacity so that you can see where they should be dragged to meet the edges of the plate*

Drag the pins one at time, moving them to the edge of bowl. Remember to zoom in (Ctrl/CMD++) and use your Hand tool (spacebar) to move around. Notice, when you drag one pin, how it interacts with the other pin, causing an area of the shape to warp and stretch. Refer to Figure 6-25.

Figure 6-25. *Dragging and moving one pin can affect other parts of the pattern connected to the pins in the vicinity*

Once you have dragged and stretched the points of the petals and leaves, either inward or outward to meet the edge of the bowl, zoom out (Ctrl/CMD+0) to see your work so far. Note that you may have to look around your shape a few times, as when you stretch one pin, sometimes another moves. Refer to Figure 6-26.

Figure 6-26. *The pins have been dragged and moved to the edge of the bowl*

Now continue to add another circle of pins near the joins of the petals to cause further warping and stretching in select areas. This will create a more accurate molding of areas of the object. Refer to Figure 6-27.

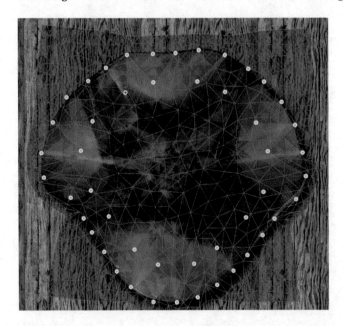

Figure 6-27. *More pins have been added to the Puppet Warp to further manipulate the pattern*

Drag those pins slightly outward to create the roundness of the edge. Refer to Figure 6-28.

Figure 6-28. *These pins have been dragged closer to the other pins to add pattern on the bowl's rim*

Then add some more pins to the inner petals and drag them a bit more inward, creating the feeling of contour to the inner part of the bowl. Refer to Figure 6-29.

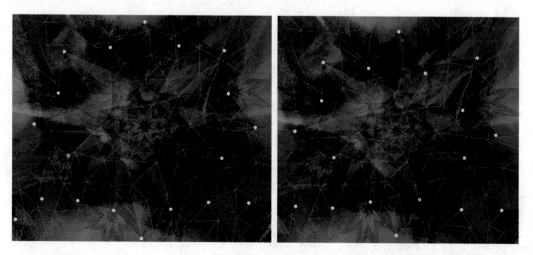

Figure 6-29. *More pins have been added to drag the pattern inward and downward into the bowl*

I added a collection of 12 points to the center and pulled them slightly inward to give the bowl more depth. Refer to Figure 6-30.

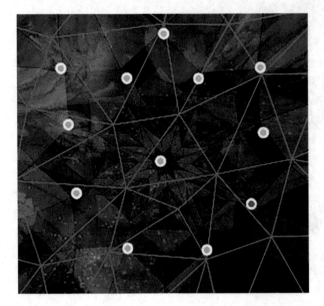

Figure 6-30. *More pins have been added to the center or lowest part of the bowl*

Tips About Pins

Pins can be added on intersections or paths of the mesh. Shift+Click on multiple pins so that you can move them as a unit. To select all pins, right-click on a pin and choose Select All Pins from the pop-up menu. Shift+Click on a selected pin in a group to deselect it. Refer to Figure 6-31.

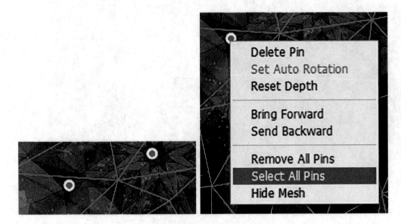

Figure 6-31. *You can select more than one pin using key commands or the right-click pop-up menu*

Depending on the density of the mesh, when you try to add another pin too close to one, you may get a warning message. Click OK and try adding a pin farther away from the other pin, or next time you make a Puppet Warp, try setting the density to More Points before you start to work on the warp. Refer to Figure 6-32.

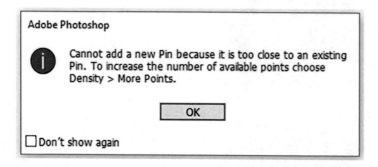

Figure 6-32. Warning message you may encounter if you add a pin too close to an existing pin. On some density settings, this will not work and the pin will not be added

To remove a pin, hold down the Alt/Option key as you hover over the pin. The cursor changes into a scissor pointer; click and the pin is removed from the mesh. Or, if you have selected one pin or Shift-Clicked on several pins to select them, you can press the Delete/Backspace key on your keyboard. Refer to Figure 6-33.

Figure 6-33. The cursor changes to this shape when you want to delete a pin while holding down the Alt/Option key

Complete the Placing of the Pins

At this point, just add the number of pins shown in Figure 6-34 and drag to stretch the warp to match mine. It does not have to be perfect. Sometimes turning off the mesh makes it easier to visualize the positioning. You can also refer to my completed file, which I will mention at the end of the chapter, if you need to compare or modify your Puppet Warp. Refer to Figure 6-34.

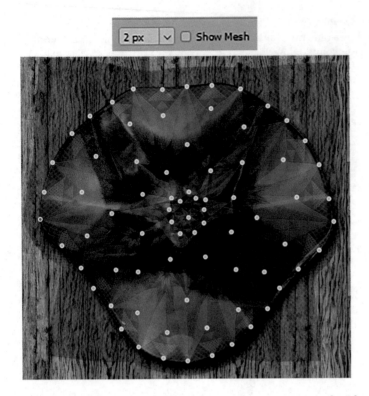

Figure 6-34. *Hiding the mesh sometimes makes it easier to work with a Puppet Warp*

Return to the Puppet Warp Options

Look back at the Options panel again.

Rotate: Selected pins can be rotated. They are either set to fixed or auto degrees between -179, 0, and 180. Refer to Figure 6-35.

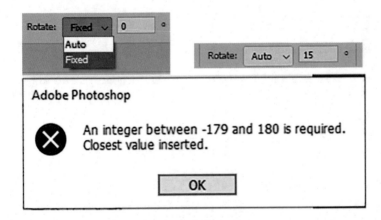

Figure 6-35. *Options panel for Puppet Warp, Rotate options, and a warning message if you try to enter an incorrect rotation of degrees*

Auto will cause the area where the pin is to scrunch or twist slightly as you drag because the application assumes the pin rotation should occur.

Another way to rotate the pin is to hold down the Alt/Option key, but do not click on the actual pin because doing so will delete it. Instead, slightly move away from it. This will make a rotation preview appear around the pin and then you can drag and rotate the pin clockwise or counter-clockwise manually by the handles to create the twist or straighten in the shape. Refer to Figure 6-36.

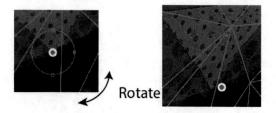

Figure 6-36. *Rotate the pin when you hold down the Alt/Option key and move the mouse a bit away from the pin*

This sets the rotation to Fixed so the angle of rotation does not change while dragging on that pin or another. Refer to Figure 6-37.

Figure 6-37. *Options panel for Rotate set to Fixed*

To set a pin back to Auto, click to select the pin and return to the Options menu and change the setting to Auto in the Rotate dropdown menu. Refer to Figure 6-38.

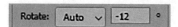

Figure 6-38. *Rotate option reset to Auto*

In the Options panel, you have the option to reset the entire Puppet Warp by clicking the Remove All Pins button (alternatively, you can right-click on the mesh or a pin for this option). Refer to Figure 6-39.

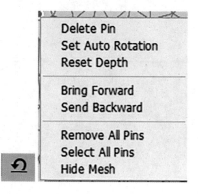

Figure 6-39. *Option to remove all pins or use the right-click pop-up menu for the same options*

If you have tried this, use Edit ➤ Undo or Ctrl/CMD+Z to undo that last step. The other options allow you to cancel and exit without saving changes to the Puppet Warp and the check allows you to commit your Puppet Warp settings. Refer to Figure 6-40.

Figure 6-40. *Options panel to cancel or commit the Puppet Warp*

After you have completed adding your pins and dragging them into the correct locations, click the check to commit the Puppet Warp and a new Puppet Warp option will be added to the layer, which is a Puppet Warp smart filter and mask. Refer to Figure 6-41.

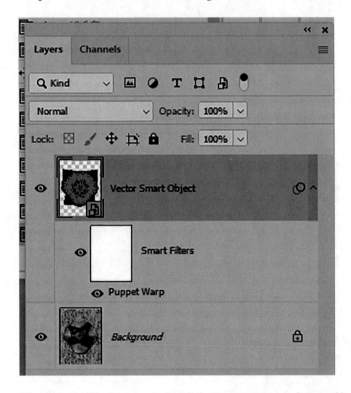

Figure 6-41. *The Layers panel with the Puppet Warp and smart filter added*

■ **Note**   If you apply a Puppet Warp to a normal layer rather than a smart object layer, this smart filter won't be added, and the warp will be permanent unless you Edit ➤ Undo right away.

Make sure to change your Vector Smart Object layer's opacity back to 100%. Refer to Figure 6-42.

Figure 6-42. *The completed warp of the pattern hiding the bowl*

Smart Objects Smart Filter and Filter Effects Mask

Since this layer is an Illustrator smart object layer, the Puppet Warp is applied as a smart filter with a mask. You can see this if you click the filter icon arrow on the right of the layer to see the details. Refer to Figure 6-43.

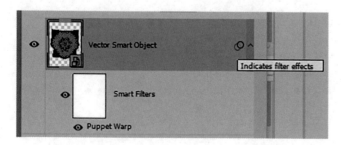

Figure 6-43. *The Vector Smart Object layer now has a smart filter and the Puppet Warp applied*

You can enter the smart filter any time by double-clicking the name "Puppet Warp" and editing the Puppet Warp using the pins and the Options panel. It is always editable even if you close the file.

In the Layers panel, you can turn the visibility of the Puppet Warp on and off to see the before and after. Refer to Figure 6-44.

Figure 6-44. *The layer's visibility eye will allow you to hide (disable) or show (enabled) the Puppet Warp*

The smart filter mask is not the same as a layer or vector mask, which can be applied to the smart object separately, and we will do so in a moment. Refer to Figure 6-45.

Figure 6-45. *The smart filters mask is separate from a layer mask and a vector mask*

It only applies to all smart filters on that layer, and in this case, the current Puppet Warp filter that you applied. However, like a layer mask, you can paint on it with your Brush or Eraser tool with your paint set to the default base colors (D) in the Tools panel to reveal or hide part of the Puppet Warp. You can also turn the mask's visibility on or off with the eye icon to compare the before and after. Refer to Figure 6-46.

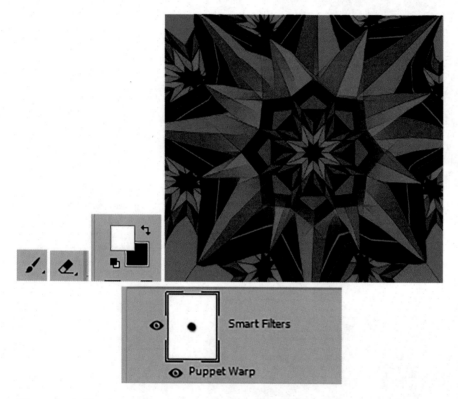

Figure 6-46. *You can paint on a smart filter mask to reveal the original pattern behind the warp*

Edit ➤ Undo that last step if you painted on the mask by mistake or use your History panel to go back a few steps. Refer to Figure 6-47.

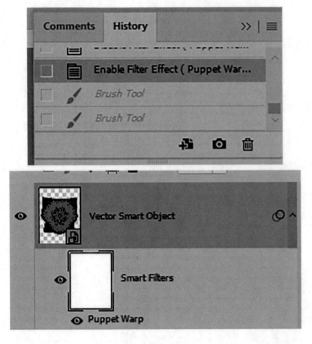

Figure 6-47. *Use the History panel if you painted on the smart filter mask by mistake to return it back to its original state*

■ **Note** The smart filter mask is disabled when entering the Puppet Warp transformation area. Refer to Figure 6-48.

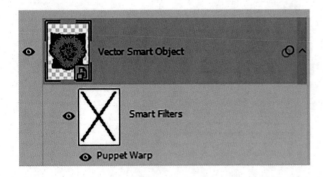

Figure 6-48. *Smart filter masks are disabled when working in the Puppet Warp workspaces*

You can also use the Properties panel to further edit your smart filter mask, including Density and Feather sliders, Refine the selection using color range or invert the selection. Refer to Figure 6-49.

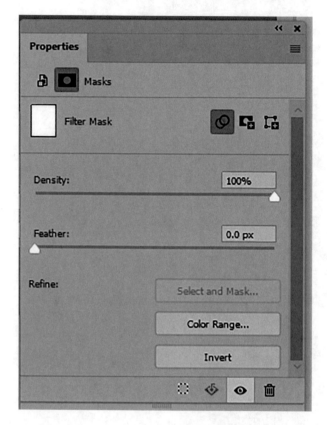

Figure 6-49. *Smart filter masks can be edited further using the Properties panel*

We will look at smart filters again later in Chapters 7 to 10. Some can be used to enhance Puppet Warps as well.

Adding a Layer Mask

To cover areas of the pattern that we don't want to go over the bowl, let's apply a layer mask. As mentioned, prior or creating a layer mask, selections can be saved in the Channels panel while they are active, and you can choose Select ➤ Save Selection and fill in the information in the dialog box and click OK. In this case, I have already done that. Ctrl/CMD+Click the thumbnail of the Bowl Selection in the Channels panel I created earlier. A selection will be generated. Refer to Figure 6-50.

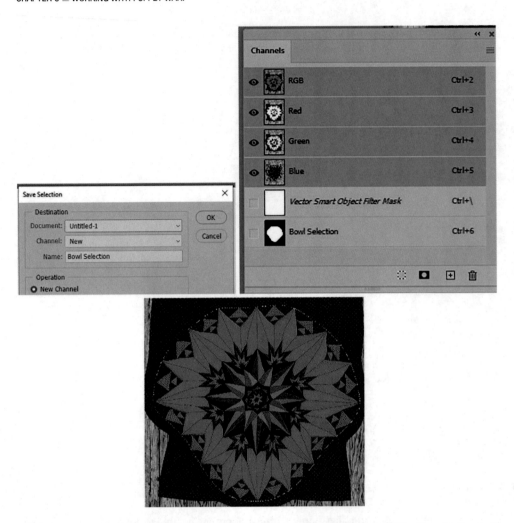

Figure 6-50. *A selection was saved earlier with the Save Selection dialog box. Use the selection in the Channels panel to add a selection over the pattern for a layer mask*

Then return to the Layers panel and select the Vector Smart Object layer and click the Add Layer mask icon. This covers the excess areas of the Puppet Warp we do not want to see. Refer to Figure 6-51.

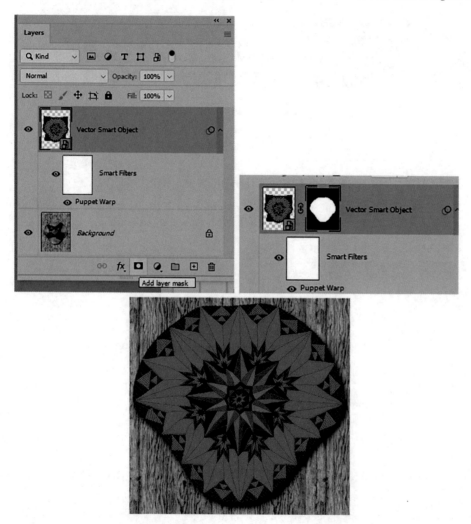

Figure 6-51. *Use the Layers panel to add a layer mask from the selection that now covers part of the pattern and conforms the pattern to the shape of the bowl*

When you apply a layer mask to a smart object layer, you will notice that the Edit ➤ Puppet Warp option is greyed out in the menu. Refer to Figure 6-52.

Content-Aware Scale	Alt+Shift+Ctrl+C
Puppet Warp	
Perspective Warp	

Figure 6-52. *When a layer mask is selected, Puppet Warp is not available*

In this case, make sure that the image thumbnail is selected and not the layer mask. Then you will have access to the Puppet Warp again. Refer to Figure 6-53.

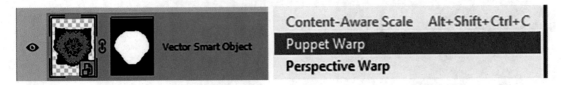

Figure 6-53. *Select the smart object layers thumbnail and Puppet Warp is available again*

The layer mask will unlink itself when entering the Puppet Warp.

Using Free Transform Options After a Puppet Warp Has Been Applied

Also, notice you will not be able to access some Free Transform options such as Distort, Perspective, and Warp once the Puppet Warp smart filter has been applied. It does not matter if the smart object comes from Illustrator or Photoshop. Refer to Figure 6-54.

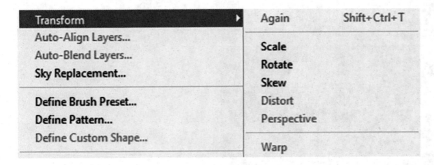

Figure 6-54. *After using Puppet Warp, some Free Transform options are disabled*

Situation 1: When a Transform ➤ Warp Has Previously Been Applied

Trying to access the Warp through Free Transform for Scale, Rotate, and Skew will just lead to other alert messages if a warp has already been applied. Click OK. Refer to Figure 6-55.

Figure 6-55. *If a Transform Warp was applied before creating a Puppet Warp, you may get a message that you need to unlink the layer mask*

In this case, you need to temporarily unlink your layer mask to continue with the Free Transform warps, which will produce the next warning message found in Situation 2. Refer to Figure 6-56.

Figure 6-56. *Unlink the layer mask because a Transform Warp was earlier applied*

Situation 2: When a Free Transform of Scale, Rotate, or Skew Has Already Been Applied, but not Warp

However, as in this project, no additional Transform Warp has been applied, so keep the layers linked and then choose Edit ➤ Free Transform. You will be reminded that the Puppet Warp smart filter will be turned off while working in Free Transform. Click OK and then you can enter the Free Transform options for scale, rotate, and skew. Refer to Figure 6-57.

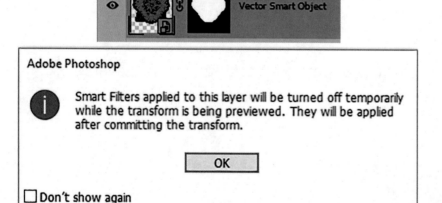

Figure 6-57. *You can keep layers linked to apply a free transform to both the layer and then the mask, but the smart filters will be turn off temporarily while the transform is being previewed but reapplied after you commit the transformation*

This will allow you to scale the shape and layer mask, if it is linked, using the Options panel or the bounding box handles around the object. Refer to Figure 6-58.

Figure 6-58. *Free Transform Options panel with Warp disabled*

Then commit your transformations in the Options panel. Refer to Figure 6-59.

Figure 6-59. *Click to cancel or commit your transformation in the Options panel*

In your own project, if the layer was unlinked (see Situation 1), you relink the layer mask so that it will move with the layer thumbnail.

■ **Note** If you need to use the Free Transform options of Perspective, Warp, and Distort, you need to select the Puppet Warp to delete it by dragging it to the trash can icon in the Layers panel or select the Smart Object layer and from the Layers menu and choose the Convert to Smart Object option, keeping the Puppet Warp contained within the smart object. Refer to Figure 6-60.

Figure 6-60. *You will have to wrap your smart object with the Puppet Warp in another smart object if you want to add additional Free Transform options*

Returning to the Current Project and Working with the Layer Mask

In this current project, just click the Cancel icon in the Free Transform panel because no further scaling is required.

For now, let's just focus on the vector smart object and its layer mask. Refer to Figure 6-61.

Figure 6-61. *Smart object layer linked with a layer mask*

With a layer mask on the current layer, there may be a point at which you need to edit the image underneath but not the mask. In this case, unlink the mask. Refer to Figure 6-62.

Figure 6-62. *Smart object layer with a layer mask unlinked*

Right-click the mask itself and choose Disable Layer Mask; this turns off the layer mask's visibility. Refer to Figure 6-63.

Figure 6-63. *Right-click the mask to disable the layer mask*

While the layer mask will unlink itself when entering the Puppet Warp, do this step anyway just to make sure nothing on the mask shifts.

Now you can double-click the Puppet Warp name in the Layers panel to enter the workspace and adjust without the layer mask blocking your view. Refer to Figure 6-64.

Figure 6-64. *Enter the Puppet Warp. The layer mask is enabled on the right and disabled on the left*

Commit any further changes you make by clicking the check in the Options panel, and then right-click and select Enable Layer mask and relink it. Refer to Figure 6-65.

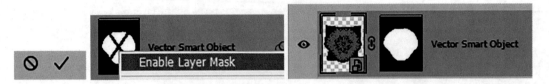

Figure 6-65. *After you click the check in the Options panel to commit the Puppet Warp, right-click the layer mask to enable it and relink it to the smart object*

■ **Note** Puppet Warps also allow you to have vector masks present, but make sure that you select the layer thumbnail first to enter the Puppet Warp. Refer to Figure 6-66.

Figure 6-66. *Vector masks can also be added to smart object layers that have a Puppet Warp, but the layer thumbnail needs to be selected before entering the Puppet Warp*

Blending Modes and Layer Styles

To complete the project and make it look more realistic, here are a few things you can do.

To make some of the color from the bowl underneath show through the pattern, select your Vector Smart Object layer, and from the Layers panel, click the Add Layer Style of Blending Options. Refer to Figure 6-67.

Figure 6-67. *Choosing Layer Style Blending Options*

Blending Options

In the Layer Styles dialog box, change the General Blending to Hard Light. Keep the Opacity at 100%, Fill Opacity at 100%, and leave all the Channels (RGB) check boxes enabled. Knockout is set to None in the dropdown menu. Refer to Figure 6-68.

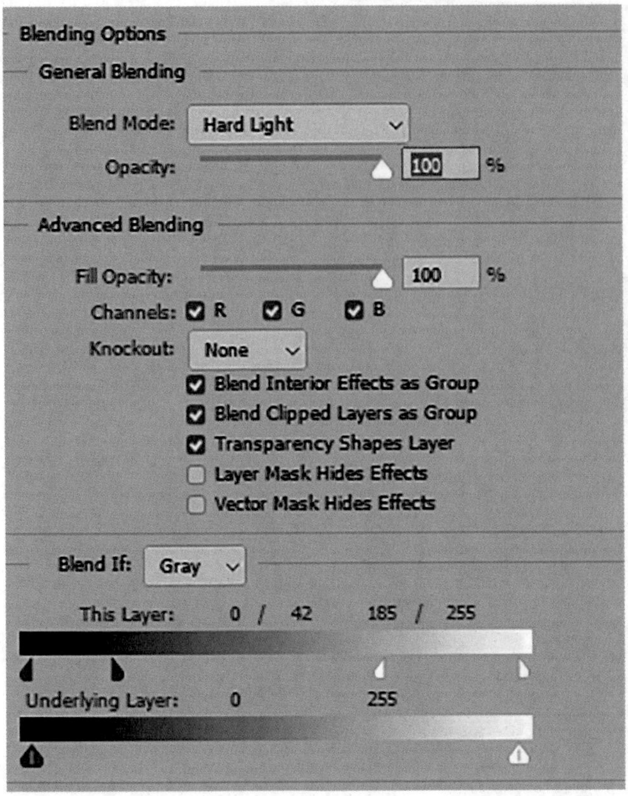

Figure 6-68. *Blending Options dialog box*

Enable the check boxes of Blend Interior Effects as Group, Blend Clipped Layers as a Group, and Transparency Shapes Layers. Leave the other check boxes for Layer Mask and Vector Mask Hides Effects disabled.

Set Blend If: Gray. For This Layer, Alt/Option+Click the black slider and move the inner part it to the 42 mark and then Alt/Option+Click the white slider and move the inner part to 185. Do not alter the Underlying Layer slider.

Bevel and Emboss

Now select and add a Bevel & Emboss.

Structure: Style: Inner Bevel, Technique: Chisel Soft, Depth: 386%, Direction: Up, Size: 3 px, Soften: 0 px

Shading: Angle: 90°, enable the Use Global Light check box, Altitude: 30°, Gloss contour linear

Highlight Mode: Screen, white (R:255, G:255, B:255), Opacity: 50%

Shadow Mode: Multiply, black (R:0, G:0, B:0), Opacity: 50%

Refer to Figure 6-69.

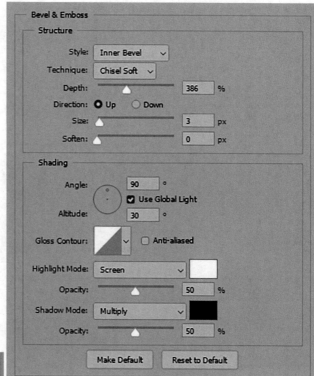

Figure 6-69. *Bevel and Emboss options*

Inner Glow

Then select and add an Inner Glow.

Structure: Blend Mode: Screen, Opacity: 35%, Noise: 0%, Color: White
Elements: Technique: Softer, Source: Edge, Choke: 20%, Size: 125 px
Quality: Contour: Linear, disable the Anti-aliased option, Range: 34%, Jitter: 19%
Refer to Figure 6-70.

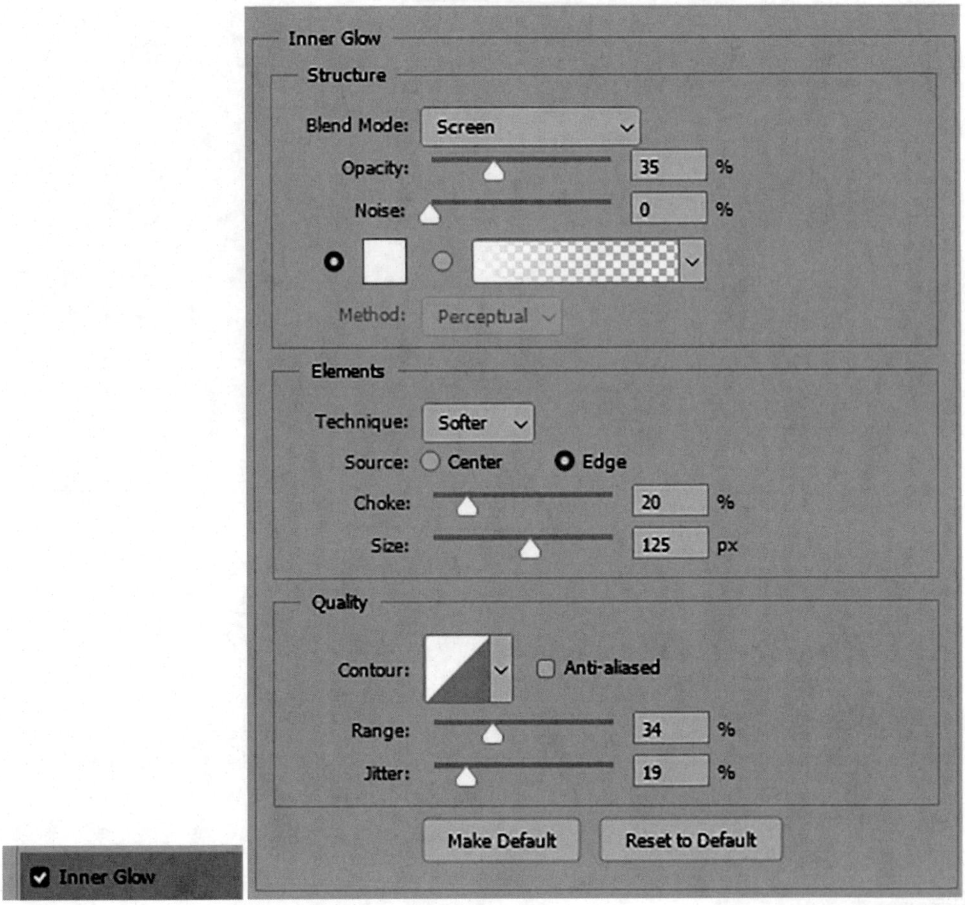

Figure 6-70. *Inner Glow options*

To commit your settings, click OK to exit the dialog box. And you can see, I added some shine to the bowl and made some of the pattern from the original bowl show through. Refer to Figure 6-71.

Figure 6-71. Click OK to exit the New Layer Style that has been applied to the bowl

Creating and Puppet Warping a Gradient Fill

Now Ctrl/CMD+Click on the Vector Smart Object layer mask to create another selection around the bowl. Refer to Figure 6-72.

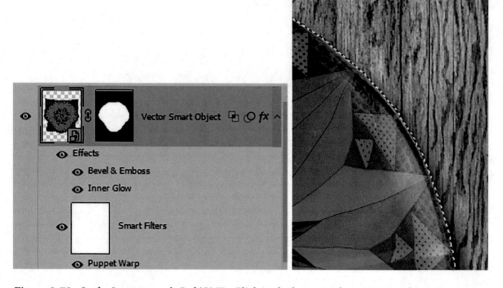

Figure 6-72. In the Layers panel, Ctrl/CMD+Click in the layer mask to create a selection

Next, add a New Adjustment Gradient Fill layer. This added the mask right away. Refer to Figure 6-73.

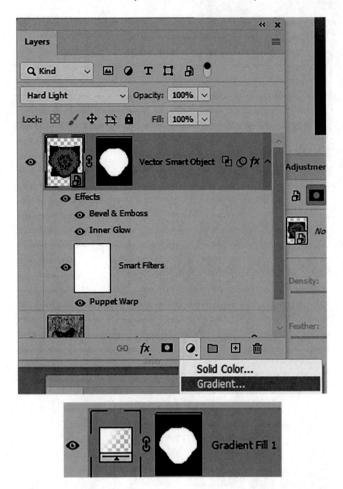

Figure 6-73. *While the selection is active, use the Layers panel to choose a Gradient Fill adjustment layer with a layer mask*

Here are the settings for the custom gradient. We will edit the gradient in a moment.

Style: Radial, Angle 90°, Scale 133%, Reverse and Dither check boxes are disabled, enable Align with Layer and Method is Perceptual check boxes.

Refer to Figure 6-74.

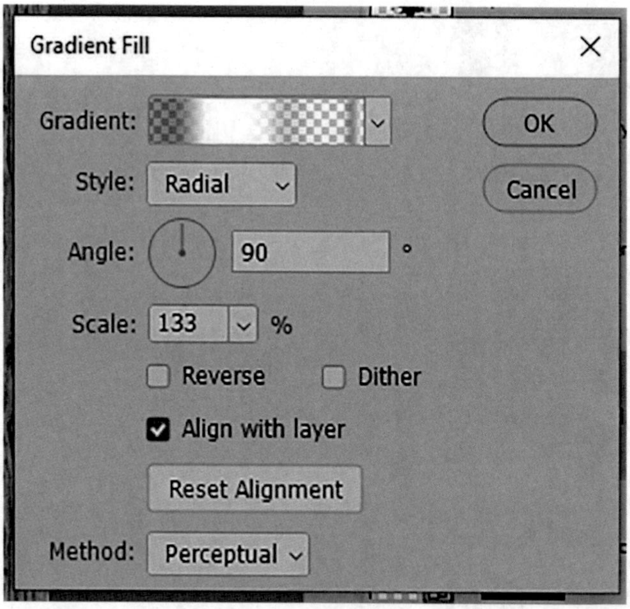

Figure 6-74. *Gradient Fill dialog box*

Click in the gradient to enter the Gradient editor. In the dialog box, create a custom gradient. You can start with a preset of one of the basic gradients and then click and add additional stops to the bar. Refer to Figure 6-75.

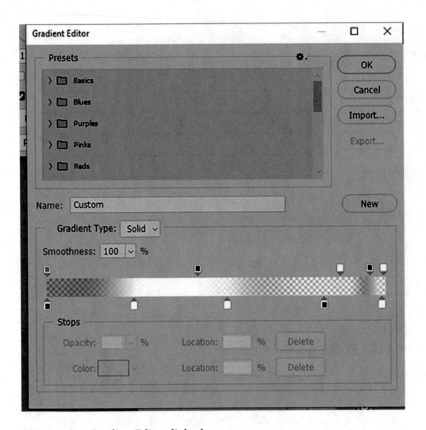

Figure 6-75. *Gradient Editor dialog box*

Gradient Type: Solid
Smoothness: 100%
In the upper area are five Opacity stops. Their details can be entered in the Stops area. Refer to Figure 6-76.

Figure 6-76. *Add opacity stops to the gradient bar and enter their details in the text boxes*

- Opacity stop: 57% Opacity, Location: 0%

- Opacity stop: 100% Opacity, Location: 45%

- Opacity stop: 0% Opacity, Location: 87%

- Opacity stop: 100% Opacity, Location: 96%

- Opacity stop: 0% Opacity, Location: 100%

In the lower part of the slider are five color stops. Their details can be entered in the Stops area. Refer to Figure 6-77.

Figure 6-77. *Add color stops to the gradient bar and enter their details in the text boxes*

- Color stop: Black location: 0%

- Color stop: White location: 26%

- Color stop: White location: 54%

- Color stop: Black location: 82%

- Color stop: White location: 99%

■ **Tip**   To remove a stop, drag it off the gradient preview. To edit a stop, select it first. Also, all mid-point siders were left at the location of 50% between the stops.

Once complete, click OK to exit the Gradient Editor dialog box and OK to exit the Gradient Fill dialog box. Refer to Figure 6-75 and Figure 7-74.

The gradient highlight was a bit too bright for me but I will fix that. Refer to Figure 6-78.

Figure 6-78. *The completed gradient on the bowl*

And now set the Blending mode of the layer Gradient Fill to Multiply. Refer to Figure 6-79.

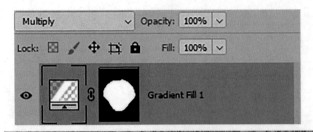

Figure 6-79. Applying a blending mode of Multiply to the gradient on the bowl

This adds a bit more shine to the bowl to show how it bends over the tri-corner edges.

Now it would be very nice to warp this gradient layer so that it's less radial and conform to the bowl. The problem is this a Fill Adjustment layer and gradients only appear to have five "flavors," so what to do? Refer to Figure 6-74 and Figure 6-80.

Figure 6-80. Gradients only come in five options: Linear, Radial, Angle, Reflected, and Diamond

Adding a gradient overlay layer style to the layer mask just didn't look right to me. The solution is to convert the Gradient Fill adjustment layer to a smart object. Make a duplicate copy of this adjustment layer (drag it over the New Layer icon) and turn off the visibility for the original. Then select the copy, and from the Layers menu, choose Convert to Smart Object. Refer to Figure 6-81.

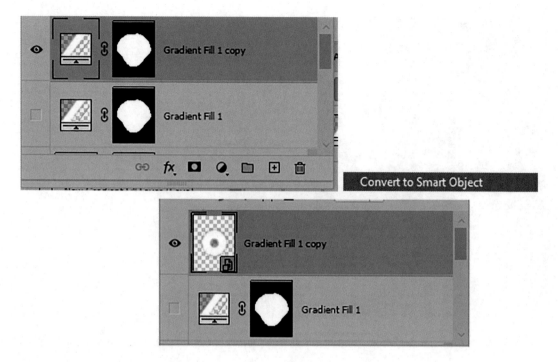

Figure 6-81. *Convert your copy of the Gradient Fill adjustment layer to a smart object layer using the Layer's menu and hide the visibility of the original Gradient Fill layer*

Set the smart object layer Gradient Fill 1 copy to a blending mode of Multiply, if it has not already been set. Refer to Figure 6-82.

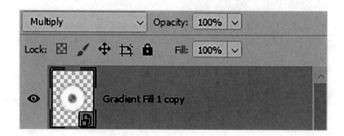

Figure 6-82. *Make sure the smart object layer is set to a blending mode of Multiply*

Now we can edit the Puppet Warp so that it better conforms to the shape of the bowl.

Go to Edit ➤ Puppet Warp and drag your pins like mine, stretching the gradient to mold to the shape. Refer to Figure 6-83.

Figure 6-83. *Use Puppet Warp to mold the gradient around the bowl so that is it is no longer radial in shape*

Click the Commit check in the Options panel and look at the Layers panel. Refer to Figure 6-84.

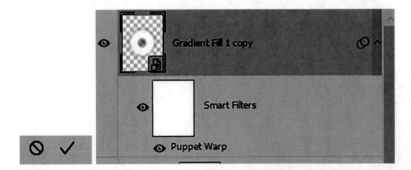

Figure 6-84. *Click the check to commit your Puppet Warp in the Options panel and view the smart object in the Layers panel*

Adding Paint Layers

Now, in the Layers panel, create a new layer (Layer 1).

To finish on the new blank Layer 1, set with a blending mode of Multiply and an Opacity of 21%. Use the Brush tool and paint with a Soft Brush (Size: 155 px and Hardness 0%) of black and switch to white to add soft shadows and highlights to the bowl. Paint around the mid area of the bowl, as seen in the figure. Remember to press the D key for the default colors and then the X key to switch from foreground to background colors as you paint. Refer to Figure 6-85.

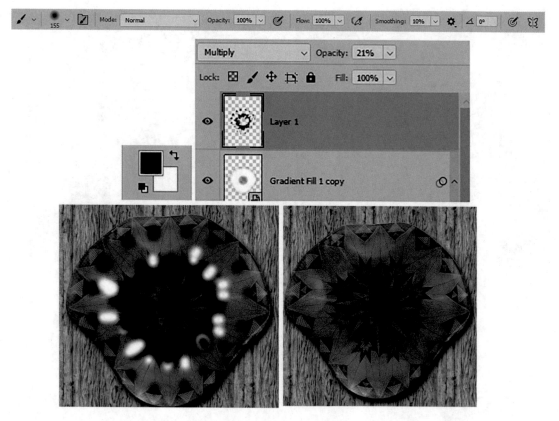

Figure 6-85. *Brush tool Options panel and colors set in the Tools panel. Paint on the new layer and then adjust the layer's blending mode and opacity*

Use the Eraser tool with similar Soft Brush settings if you need to erase areas of paint. Refer to Figure 6-86.

Figure 6-86. *Eraser tool Options panel*

Then create another new layer (Layer 2) and paint with the Brush tool using the Soft Brush but this time paint a white ring roughly where the red petals spread outward to add a more highlighted curve. For Layer 2, set the blending mode to Overlay with an Opacity of 45%. Refer to Figure 6-87.

Figure 6-87. *Paint on another layer and set the blending mode and opacity*

File ➤ Save your document. You can refer to my example bowl_puppetwarp_final.psd or the file bowl_puppetwarp_final_RGB.psd if you need to compare brush strokes and colors. If you need to review bushes, refer to Chapter 2.

Puppet Warp for Type and Shape Layers

Type layers can have a Puppet Warp applied to them. But first you will get a warning. Refer to Figure 6-88.

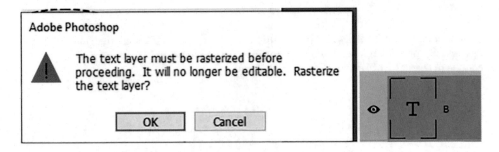

Figure 6-88. *If you plan to Puppet warp a type layer, you may receive the following message asking you if you want to rasterize the type/text layer first*

Rasterizing a type layer is destructive, and the text will be un-editable so click Cancel and instead convert your type layer into a smart object first. You can see here how I took a single letter and made it appear like it was stretched over a ball. The letter is not a complex shape so this time I only used four pins, one at each corner, the mode of Distort, and a Density of fewer points. Refer to Figure 6-89.

Figure 6-89. Turn the type layer into a smart object layer first before you commit the Puppet Warp

Likewise, shape layers can have a Puppet Warp applied to them if they are converted into a smart object layer and you can apply similar mode settings. Refer to Figure 6-90.

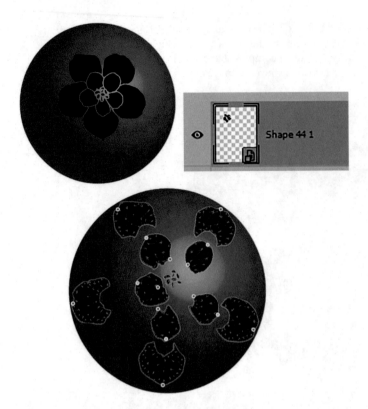

Figure 6-90. *Shape layers can be made into smart object layers as well, and if they have transparent areas, you can Puppet Warp segments separately*

■ **Note**   If the custom shape is in separate pieces on a transparent background, you can use a Puppet Warp to move and break apart the shape and apply separate warps to individual parts. You can see this in my file puppet_warp_TextShape.psd. This is also true for a full word of type; each letter will be separate in the Puppet Warp. Refer to Figure 6-91.

Figure 6-91. *Turn the type layer into a smart object layer, and if there are transparent areas between each letter, you can Puppet Warp letters separately*

For additional resources on how to use the Puppet Warp tool in Illustrator, you can check out Volume 2. In that book I compare the Illustrator Puppet Warp to what we just looked at in Photoshop. However, you do not need to use that tool in Illustrator in the previously mention examples.

Summary

In this chapter, you looked at the several ways to use the Puppet Warp smart filter to warp a vector pattern, a gradient, type, and a shape. Puppet Warps are extremely useful in situations where you need to adjust areas of a logo or image to move or blend on a curved shape. However, sometimes you need to add more detail and then you need to rely on layer mask selection, blending modes, opacity, layer styles, and the Brush tool. In the next chapter, you will look at another smart filter warp for perspective and then you'll use content-aware to scale and discover how to replace the sky in an image.

CHAPTER 7

■ ■ ■

Perspective Warp and Content-Aware Scale

Chapter goal: Learn how to correctly use the features of the Perspective Warp, Content-Aware Scale, and Sky Replacement

So far, as you've seen, Photoshop's Edit menu is full of transformation tools and commands that are not in the tools panel itself. In this chapter, we will look at three more, Perspective Warp, Content-Aware Scale, and Sky Replacement. We will also look briefly at a few other related content-aware tools. Refer to Figure 7-1.

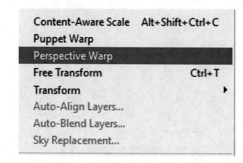

Figure 7-1. *Edit menu options with Perspective Warp selected*

■ **Note** You can find the projects for this chapter in the Chapter 7 folder.

Perspective Warp

Perspective Warp is more advanced than Transform ➤ Perspective, which was talked about in Chapter 4. With that Free Transform command, you could only do one point perspective. However, with Perspective Warp you can now create and edit multiple perspectives. This is also useful when there is a distortion on an item in an image or you want to correct the perspective of a structure in the image. Shortly, we will use Edit ➤ Perspective Warp and look at the Options panel. Refer to Figure 7-2.

Figure 7-2. *Perspective Warp can be used in a variety of ways*

■ **Note** If this tool does not function correctly, make sure that under Edit ➤ Preferences ➤ Performance ➤ Use Graphics Processor is enabled and that you have adequate video RAM, at least 512 MB. Adjust your advanced settings, if required, and click OK. In my case, I have plenty of RAM, so I clicked Cancel to exit the dialog box. Refer to Figure 7-3.

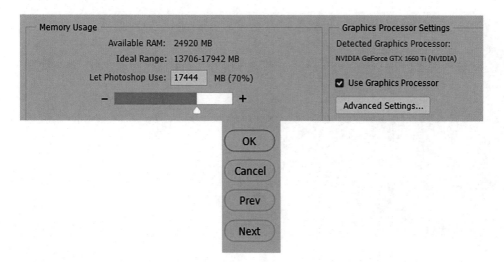

Figure 7-3. *Preferences dialog box. Check memory usage if Perspective Warp is not functioning correctly*

Project: Cherry Blossom Box

File ➤ Open Box_with_images_start.psd. Make an Image ➤ Duplicate to practice with. This is a box that we are going to apply two images to, one to each side of the box. Rather than use Edit ➤ Transform ➤ Perspective, we are going to use Perspective Warp twice, once for each side. Refer to Figure 7-4.

Figure 7-4. *The box image we are going to cover with cherry blossom images found in the Layers panel*

I copied some images of cherry blossoms to this file by first selecting the whole image in my original photo via Select ➤ All. Then I used Edit ➤ Copy and Edit ➤ Paste in the new document in layers over top of the box. I converted each of these layers into smart object layers and then I used Edit ➤ Transform ➤ Scale. For this project, refer to the layers **2589 1 point** and **2593 1 point**, which have been scaled to 64% in width and height. Refer to Figure 7-4 and Figure 7-5.

Figure 7-5. *Options panel for Free Transform Scale*

In this first example, we will first focus on one point perspective in which we will perspective warp the two sides separately; this is ideal when you are working with boxes that you want to cover with multiple pictures such as a photo cube. In this example, the box is our photo cube.

Make visible in the Layers panel the smart object layer **2589 1 point**. We will use this image to cover the right side. As mentioned, it has already been scaled so that it will fit on the box. Refer to Chapter 4 if you need to review how to do that. Refer to Figure 7-6 and Figure 7-7.

Figure 7-6. *Image scaled while in Free Transform*

In this chapter, as in Chapter 6, we are again working with a smart object layer. This is because with a normal layer we do not have access to the smart object smart filter features and the Perspective Warp would be permanent and destructive and you would not be able to edit it later on. Refer to Figure 7-7.

Figure 7-7. *One of the cherry blossom layers is made visible in the Layers panel*

Now with the layer selected, go to Edit ➤ Perspective Warp.
Refer to the Options panel.

Perspective Warp Options

In the Perspective Warp Options panel, the preset area is grayed out as each warp is different. By default, you are on the Layout tab for laying out quad shapes. Refer to Figure 7-8.

Figure 7-8. *Options panel for Perspective Warp*

Step 1: Click and drag points to define planes. In this case, we are just going to work with one plane at a time. Later in the chapter, I will show you how to snap two or more planes together to define corners or to correct the distortion of the warp slightly.

Click once on the artboard so that you can start with one grid. In this example, I clicked on the upper left-hand corner. It is very similar to working with the Perspective Crop tools as you did in Chapter 2. Refer to Figure 7-9.

Figure 7-9. *Adding a plane over the cherry blossom image in the upper left*

Then drag and move the four corners of the grid, as the pointer changes to a pin, and set them, in this case, to the edges the image, which you will later align to the sides of the box. Refer to Figure 7-10.

Figure 7-10. *Moving the four pins in Layout mode*

You can drag on the outer point edges of the grid path to scale or drag in the center to move the whole grid to a new location.

Remember to zoom in (Ctrl/CMD++) so that you can see the points more clearly in order to move them closer to edge of the image and use your Hand tool (spacebar) if you need to move around without shifting the Perspective Warp. Refer to Figure 7-11.

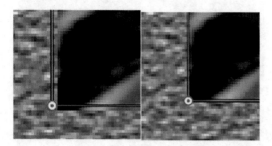

Figure 7-11. *Zooming in closer lets you accurately move the pins over the image*

When done creating the plane and checking that your four perspective points are aligned at the corners of the image, you can zoom out (Ctrl/CMD+- or Ctrl/CMD+0) and in the Options panel switch to the Warp tab for adjusting pins and warping the image. Refer to Figure 7-12.

Figure 7-12. *Once the pins are in place, use the Options panel to switch to Warp mode*

You will then be presented with Step 2. It may take a moment to load.

Step 2: Move the warp pins to manipulate the perspective. In this case, we are only working with one quad plane. Refer to Figure 7-13.

Figure 7-13. *Message that appears when you switch to Warp mode*

To do this accurately, lower the opacity of the layer to about 33%. Refer to Figure 7-14.

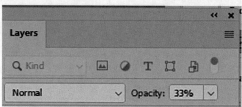

Figure 7-14. *Lowering the opacity of the cherry blossom layer helps you see the box below so that you can place the pins accurately*

On this image, move the black pins one at a time over the image to match the edges of the box as closely as possible. It's OK if there is some overlap on the rim of the box because we will correct that with a layer mask later. Refer to Figure 7-15.

Figure 7-15. *Move in closer so that you can place the pins in the correct location*

■ **Note** For your project, you can switch back to the Layout button anytime while warping if you discovered you did not line up the pins correctly while working and correct them. Refer to Figure 7-16.

Figure 7-16. Switch to Layout mode if you need to correct the pin placement

For now, remain in Warp mode. Refer to Figure 7-17.

Figure 7-17. Use Warp mode to complete your project

As you move each pin, the object on the layer moves with it and you can start to conform to the shape of a box. If you don't want to use a custom build, there are three settings available to the right of the warp button:

- Automatically straighten near vertical lines. Refer to Figure 7-18.

Figure 7-18. Preview of automatically straighten near vertical lines option

- Automatically Level near horizontal lines. Refer to Figure 7-19.

Figure 7-19. *Preview of automatically straighten near horizontal lines option*

- Auto warp to horizontal and vertical. Refer to Figure 7-20.

Figure 7-20. *Preview of auto warp to horizontal and vertical option*

These settings can be clicked multiple times in the Options panel while working to continue to correct the straightening. You can undo steps with Edit ➤ Undo (Ctrl/CMD+Z) or to reset all steps; click the Remove Warp button and drag out the layout again. Refer to Figure 7-21.

Figure 7-21. *Reset and remove the warp*

In this case, let's create the custom warp. Refer to Figure 7-22.

Figure 7-22. *Completed custom warp*

Once you have completed the single plane, you can then either click the Cancel icon to cancel the warp without applying the change, or in this case, what you want to do is click the check to commit the Perspective Warp. Refer to Figure 7-23.

Then raise the layer's opacity back to 100%.

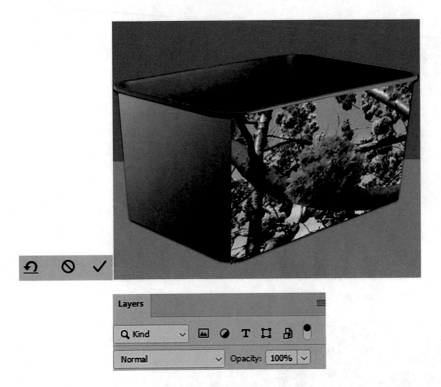

Figure 7-23. *Commit the warp and then rase the layer's opacity*

Smart Objects Smart Filter and Filter Effects Mask

The Perspective Warp and smart filter are now applied to the layer. Refer to Chapter 6 for notes on what the smart filter can do in more detail. You can enter the Perspective Warp any time by double-clicking on the name "Perspective Warp." You can enter the workspace and edit both the layout and the warp. During that time, before you commit your changes, the smart filter mask will be disabled. Refer to Figure 7-24.

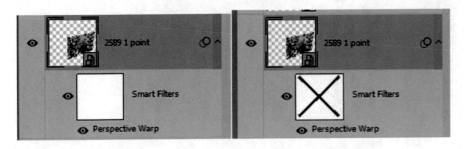

Figure 7-24. *Enter the Perspective Warp. The smart filters are disabled*

Now repeat the same Perspective Warp steps with the left side using layer **2593 1 point**. Turn on that layer's visibility. Refer to Figure 7-25.

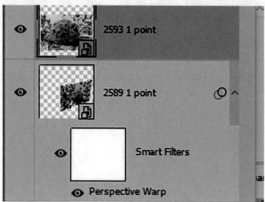

Figure 7-25. *Second image of cherry blossoms to warp on the left side of box*

Remember, Edit ➤ Perspective Warp. In Layout mode, click and drag out the grid points over the image. Refer to Figure 7-26.

Figure 7-26. *Use your options panel and pins to create a layout grid over the image*

Switch to Warp mode. Lower the opacity of the layer to about 33% and then drag your four warp pins into place on the left side of the box. Then click the check to commit and raise the layer opacity to 100%. Refer to Figure 7-27.

Figure 7-27. *Once the Perspective Warp is complete and committed with the check button, raise the opacity of the layer to review the completed result*

Adding a Layer Mask Using the Channels Panel

You will notice that there are some ragged edges that are covering part of the box lid or even sticking out on the sides. Refer to Figure 7-28.

Figure 7-28. *Some of the image is covering the rim of the lid and the corners of the box*

When I created the box for this project, I made sure to save some of the selections that I needed in my Channels panel. Refer to Figure 7-29.

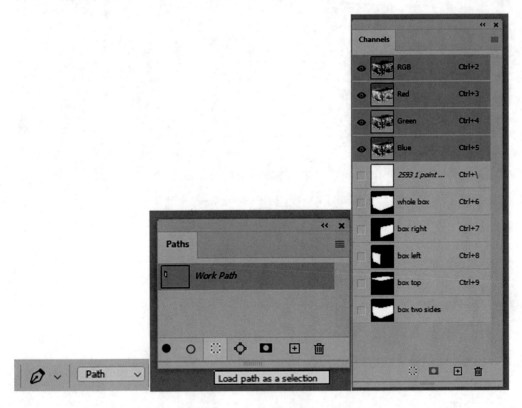

Figure 7-29. *The Channels panel is storing multiple saved selections that were previously paths created with the Pen tool*

I discussed how to save selections in Chapter 6 briefly and in much more detail in my book *Accurate Layer Selections Using Photoshop's Selection Tools*. These selections were created using the Pen tool in Path mode, as seen in the Paths panel, and then loaded as a selection before being saved in the Channels panel, but there are many ways to create a selection. In this case, that part of the work is done for you.

For this project, use the selections I created. In the Layers panel, select the layer **2589 1 point.** Refer to Figure 7-30.

Figure 7-30. *Select the layer to which you want to add a layer mask*

In the Channels panel, Ctrl/CMD+Click on the selection thumbnail **box right** to load the selection, and then from the Layers panel, click the Add layer mask button. Refer to Figure 7-29 and Figure 7-31.

Figure 7-31. *Load a selection and add the layer mask to the image*

This adds the mask. Now the sides are rounded, and the image is no longer overlapping the rim. Refer to Figure 7-32.

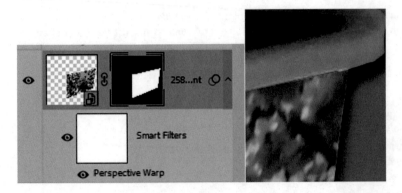

Figure 7-32. *The layer mask covers the area of the image that you do not want over the rim*

Repeat these steps with the image on the right side. Select **Layer 2593 1 point**, but this time Ctrl/CMD+Click the selection from the Channels panel of **box left** to load it. Refer to Figure 7-29 and Figure 7-33.

Figure 7-33. *Load a selection for the second selected image*

Use your Layers panel to add the layer mask. Refer to Figure 7-34.

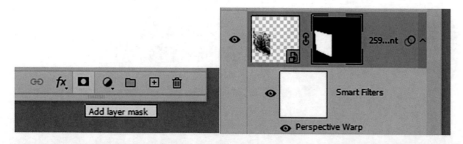

Figure 7-34. *Add the layer mask using the selection for the section image on the left*

■ **Note** When the layer's thumbnail image is selected, upon entering the Perspective Warp the layer mask will temporarily unlink so that the warp is not affected. Refer to Figure 7-35.

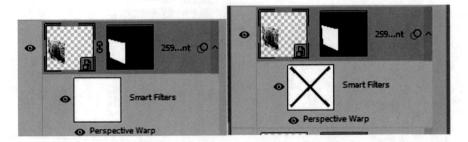

Figure 7-35. *Entering the Perspective Warp will disable the smart filter and unlink the layer mask*

However, as mentioned in Chapter 6, you can, prior to entering the Perspective Warp, unlink and disable the layer mask (right-click the mask) in your project if you find it is hiding certain areas while working. Refer to Figure 7-36.

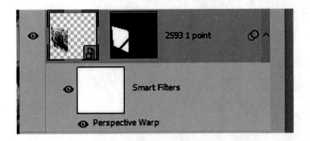

Figure 7-36. *Disabling and unlinking the layer mask is useful before you adjust the Perspective Warp*

Then just remember, after you have completed your Perspective Warp, to enable the layer mask again (right-click the mask) and relink it again. Refer to Figure 7-37.

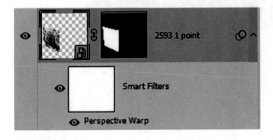

Figure 7-37. *Enable and relink the layer mask upon exiting Perspective Warp*

Adding a Layer Style to Create Some Shadows

Select layer **2593 1 point** again, and from the Layers panel this time apply a layer style of Gradient Overlay. Refer to Figure 7-38.

Figure 7-38. *Choosing a layer style of Gradient Overlay from the Layer menu*

Here are the settings I used in the Layer Styles dialog box.

Gradient Blend Mode: Hard Light, Dither disabled, Opacity: 17%. The gradient was Basics Foreground to Background. Other settings are Reverse disabled, Style: Linear, Align with Layer enabled, Angle: 43°, Scale: 91%, and Method: Perceptual. Refer to Figure 7-39.

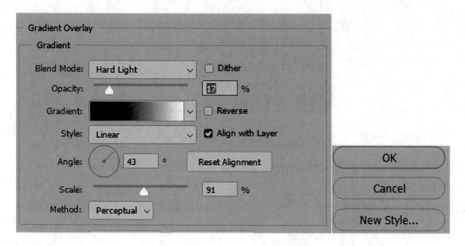

Figure 7-39. *Gradient Overlay options. Click OK to commit*

Click OK to exit the dialog box, then right-click the Layer Style dialog Layer Style effect and choose Copy Layer Style. Refer to Figure 7-40.

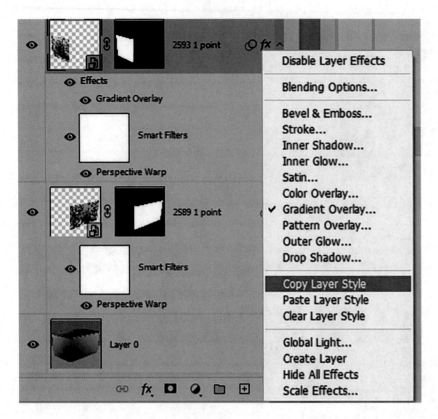

Figure 7-40. *Copy a layer styles from one layer*

Select layer **2589 1 point** and right-click and choose Paste Layer Style. Refer to Figure 7-41.

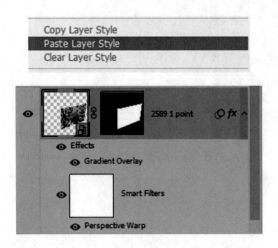

Figure 7-41. *Paste a copy of the layer style setting onto another layer*

You can see that this layout looks alright for two images. Refer to Figure 7-42.

Figure 7-42. *The perspectives for two images are completed on the cherry blossom box*

We'll add some more shadows to the box later. However, in other situations, you may want to have the images warp around.

File ➤ Save your project at this point as a .psd file, as in previous projects. You can add you initials to the file name. Now let's try another way of making a warp in the second part of this project.

Project: Cherry Blossom Box Part 2

Continue with the copy you made of the file Box_with_images_start.psd. This time, select and make visible the layer **2593 2 point wrap**. Hide the visibility for the layers **2593 1 point** and **2589 1 point** since you do not need these layers for this part of the project. Refer to Figure 7-43.

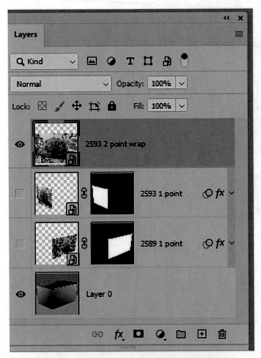

Figure 7-43. *Use one image from the Layers panel to wrap an image around the box while the other blossom images are hidden*

In this situation, you want one image to wrap around the box. This is ideal for this box because it has rounded corners. This smart object layer has already had a Transform ➤ Scale of 66.62% for width and height. Refer to Figure 7-44.

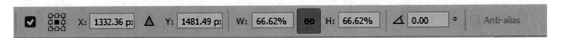

Figure 7-44. *Options panel for Free Transform Scale*

Go to Edit ➤ Perspective Warp. Lower the layer's opacity to about 33%. Refer to Figure 7-45.

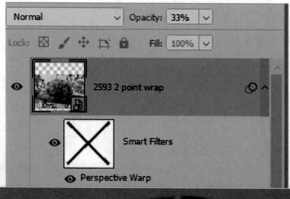

Figure 7-45. *Layers panel with layer's opacity lowered*

In Layout mode, as you did earlier, click out one perspective plane and move the points into place. In this case, I am creating my left side first and will match it up with the box's corner edge where the two planes meet. Refer to Figure 7-46.

Figure 7-46. *Adding a layout grid while in Perspective Warp*

Remain in Layout mode. Now click elsewhere on the canvas outside the current grid to create a second grid to warp another portion of the art. When working with two grids, this is known as creating quad shapes or quadrants. You may see this instructional message appear as you begin to work on the second quad shape. Refer to Figure 7-47.

Figure 7-47. Adding another quad-shaped grid plane

After you create the second quad shape for the right side, you can then drag the second quadrant grid so that it touches the first grid on its left and becomes blue and attached after you drag the second point so that both sides join together on release of the mouse key. This is good as you are going around a second side of the box. Refer to Figure 7-48.

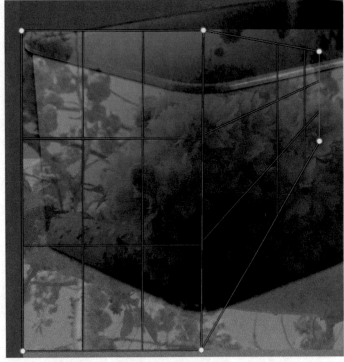

Figure 7-48. *Connecting the two quad shapes*

Now drag the other two pins to the right on the right of the image's edge. Refer to Figure 7-49.

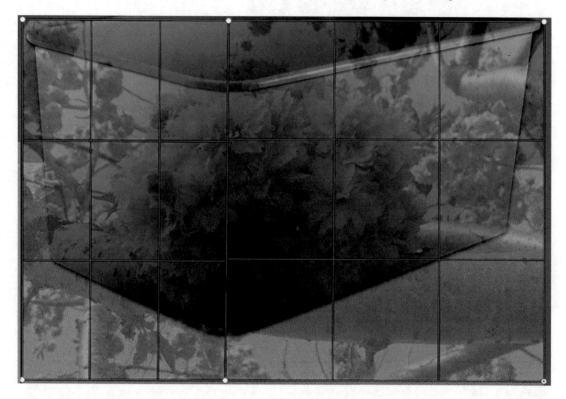

Figure 7-49. *Moving the points of the second quad shape to the other side of the image*

■ **Tip**　You can hold down the Shift key to lengthen or shorten one of the two connecting quad grid planes or one of the planes sides in unison horizontally or vertically in a straight line. If you do not hold down the Shift key, the grid will bend at the join, which in this case is not what you want. Refer to Figure 7-50.

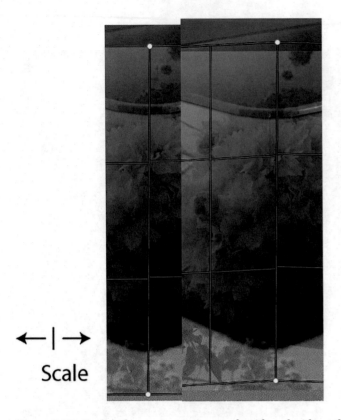

Figure 7-50. Scaling the two connecting quads with and without the Shift key while dragging

---

■ **Note**   For your own projects, you can keep adding more grids and join all or some of them and then, when you are ready to start warping, click the Warp button and you will see the next step 2.

In this case, for now we will work with just two, but later I will show why adding a third quad shape might improve the distort.

Now click the Warp Button in the Options panel. Refer to Figure 7-51.

Figure 7-51. Switch to Warp mode to complete the warp

Step 2, as you saw earlier in the chapter, is to move the warp pins to manipulate the perspective. Make sure to touch the sides of the box. Reduce the layer opacity to 33%. This should assist you if you are having difficulty lining up the sides of the box. Refer to Figure 7-52.

Figure 7-52. *Viewing the warp pins that will be moved to complete the warp*

Remember to Ctrl/CMD++ when you need to zoom in to get a closer view of your pins. Refer to Figure 7-53.

Figure 7-53. *Moving the six warp pins into place*

Remember, you can use the three options previously mentioned in the Options panel for straightening warp lines if you do not want a custom warp. Refer to Figure 7-54.

Figure 7-54. *The straightening warp line options in the Options panel*

However, there are other key commands you can try as well.
For example,

- Hold down the Shift key and click on a connection side of the grid. It will turn yellow, and that side will be straightened, linked, and anchoring both planes. They and the two pins can now be moved together. You can Shift+Click multiple sides. Refer to Figure 7-55.

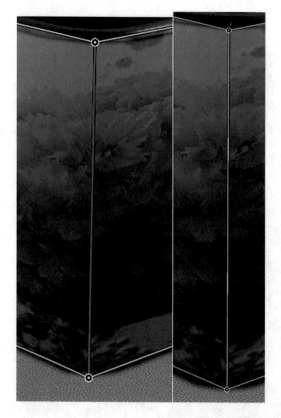

Figure 7-55. *Linking (yellow) and unlinking (gray) anchoring planes*

- Shift+Click again to deselect it from the group, so it is no longer yellow. And you can move the two plane pins separately while still joined. Refer to Figure 7-55.

Other key combinations that you can use to adjust the perspective include the following:

- Use your arrow keys on your keyboard to nudge a selected quad pin. Refer to Figure 7-56.

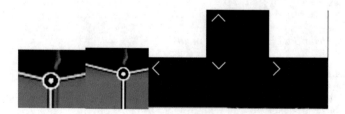

Figure 7-56. *Nudging pins using the keyboard arrow keys*

- In Warp mode, you can press H to hide the grid temporarily and H again to reveal it. Refer to Figure 7-57.

Figure 7-57. *Hiding the grid lines so that you can see the image below*

- Press L to switch to Layout mode and W to switch to Warp mode. Refer to Figure 7-58.

Figure 7-58. *Key commands can be used to switch from Layout to Warp mode*

- Pressing the Enter/Return key while in Layout mode will also move you to Warp mode but pressing this key again will commit the warp.

In this case, once you have completed your warp, click the check in the Options panel to commit the warp. Refer to Figure 7-59.

Figure 7-59. *Click the check to commit the warp*

580

And then raise the layer's opacity back to 100%. Refer to Figure 7-60.

Figure 7-60. *The completed warp with its opacity raised to 100%*

Can You Detach or Delete One Quad Shape Plane?

Currently, in this version of Photoshop, it does not appear in Layout mode that you can tear off or drag a quad off to detach or if you want to delete it. So, if you attached or created an extra quad grid by mistake, make sure to Edit ➤ Undo right away. Or while in Layout mode, to remove all grid layouts at once, click the Remove all quads button and recreate them again before returning to the Warp button tab. Refer to Figure 7-61.

Figure 7-61. *The Options panel will only let you delete all the quad shape planes but not separate ones or detach them*

Improving the Perspective Warp

Upon inspecting the warp after committing, you may feel that part of the warp along the long right side of the box is a bit too stretched. You can minimize that by adding one more quad shape plane. This is like when working with a Free Transform Warp where sometimes you need to adjust the grid.

In this case, create a duplicate layer. Drag layer **2593 2 point wrap** over the Create a new layer button to create a copy. Refer to Figure 7-62.

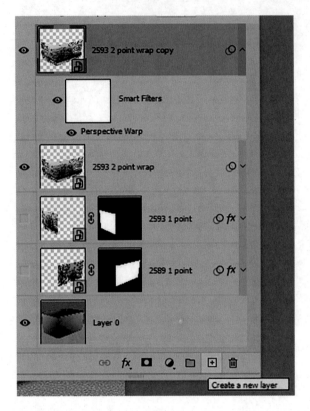

Figure 7-62. *Create a duplicate layer using the Create a new layer button when you want to create a second version of a Perspective Warp*

You did this so that you can see the difference in distortion when a new quad plane shape is added. Turn off the visibility of the original, then select the copy and lower the layer opacity down to 33% and double-click on the Perspective Warp name to enter/edit the warp. Refer to Figure 7-63.

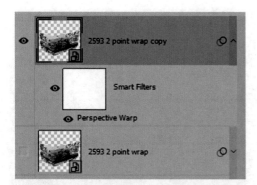

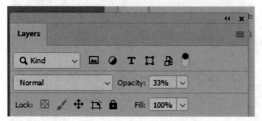

Figure 7-63. *Turn off the visibility of the original layer and lower the opacity of the copy*

Switch to the Layout tab button, hold down the Shift key, and move/scale the right side of second quad plane to the left over to about the middle of the right side of the box. Refer to Figure 7-64.

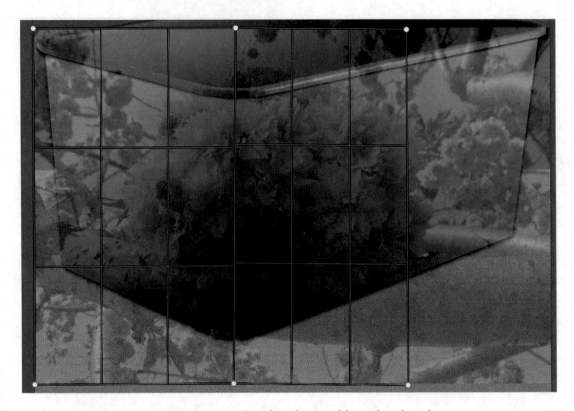

Figure 7-64. *In Perspective Warp Layout mode, reduce the size of the grid on the right*

Then click to add another quad plane to the right and drag to connect it, as seen in Figure 7-65. This divides the area into thirds over the image. Remember, you can hold down your Shift key and drag between two planes if you need to move them over in a straight horizontal direction. Refer to Figure 7-65.

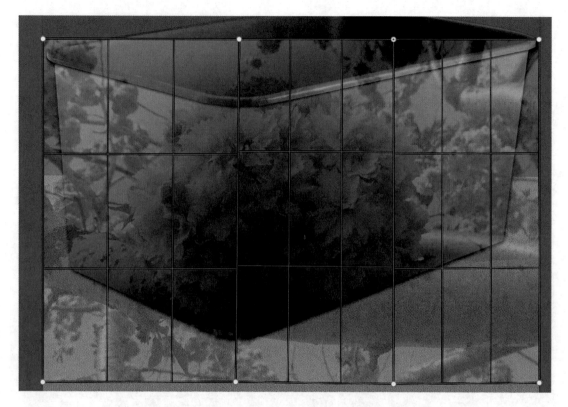

Figure 7-65. Add another quad plane shape to the right and move the pins to complete the grid over the image

Then switch to Warp mode and readjust the warp over the box. Refer to Figure 7-66.

Figure 7-66. *Switch to Warp mode and move the pins into place along the shape of the box*

Hold down the Shift key if required while moving pins or dividers between the quad shapes. Then click the check in the Options panel to commit the Perspective Warp. Raise the layer's opacity back to 100%. Refer to Figure 7-67.

Figure 7-67. *Raise the layer's opacity to view the new Perspective Warp*

If you turn on and off the visibility of the original and copy layers, you can see how creating another quad shape improved the distortion and there is less of a pull on the right as it goes around the curve. Refer to Figure 7-68.

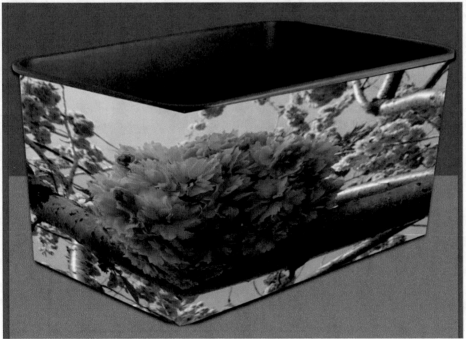

Figure 7-68. *Turn on and off the layer's visibility in the Layers panel to compare the original (top image) and copy (bottom image). Notice that the warp on the right side is now not as intense*

As you did in the earlier part of the project, you can then add a layer mask. Select the layer **2593 2 point wrap copy** and then, using the Channels panel, Ctrl/CMD+Click on the channel selection **box two sides** to load the selection. Refer to Figure 7-69.

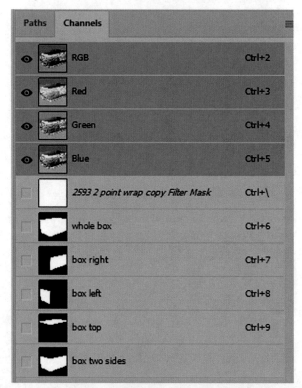

Figure 7-69. *Load a selection from the Channels panel for the copy layer*

589

Then, in the Layers panel, click Add layer mask. Refer to Figure 7-70 and Figure 7-73.

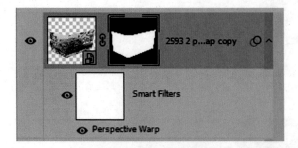

Figure 7-70. *Add a layer mask to the copy layer to cover parts of the image that are over the rim and the base of the box*

Adding Layer Styles

Then, using the Layers panel, add some layer styles. Click the fx icon to add the styles of Inner Shadow and Gradient Overlay to the layer **2593 2 point wrap copy**. Refer to Figure 7-71.

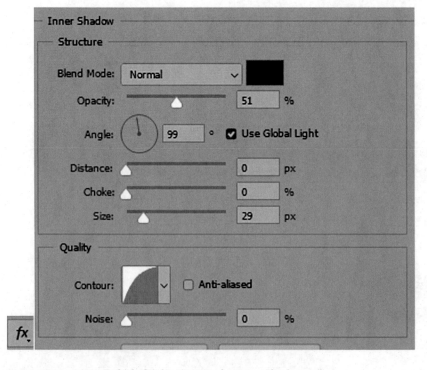

Figure 7-71. *Layer Style dialog box options for Inner Shadow Tab*

Inner Shadow: Structure: Blend Mode Normal Black, Opacity: 51% Angle: 99°, Use Global Light enabled, Distance: 0 px, Choke: 0%, Size: 29 px, Quality: Contour: Half round, Anti-aliased disabled, Noise: 0%. Refer to Figure 7-71.

Gradient Overlay: Gradient: Blend Mode: Multiply, Dither disabled, Opacity: 13%. Gradient was Basics Foreground to Background. Reverse disabled, Style: Radial, Align with Layer enabled, Angle: 43°, Scale 127%, and Method: Perceptual. Refer to Figure 7-72.

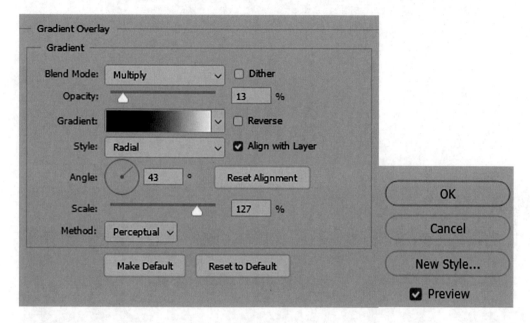

Figure 7-72. *Layer Style dialog box options for Gradient Overlay Tab, click OK to exit*

Click OK to commit and exit the dialog box. This added a bit more shadow to the edges and under the lid of the box. Refer to Figure 7-73.

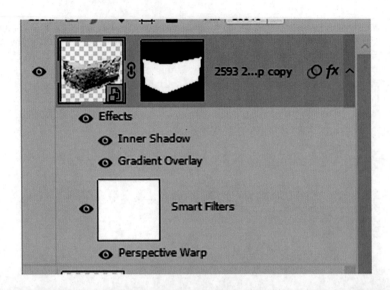

Figure 7-73. *The completed box with a layer mask and layer style (fx) applied*

Then I created two new layers above **2593 2 point wrap copy**. Refer to Figure 7-74.

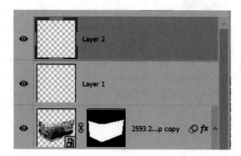

Figure 7-74. *Two more layers above the other layers*

On Layer 1, I used my Brush tool and with a large soft brush about size 86 px and hardness 0%, I painted a straight black line (Shift+Click and Drag) to make an edge for the box. To create a shadow, I also used my Eraser tool with a size of 66 px and hardness of 100% to erase some of the detail on the left and then lowered the layer's opacity to about 25%. Refer to Figure 7-75 and Figure 7-76.

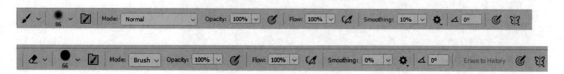

Figure 7-75. *Options panels for Brush and Eraser tools*

Figure 7-76. Layer 1 with brush paint and then opacity lowered to 25%

Lastly, on Layer 2, while selected, I then CTRL/CMD+Clicked on the selection in the Channels panel of **box left** to load the selection. Refer to Figure 7-77.

Figure 7-77. Layer 2 and loading a selection from the Channels panel

Then to Edit ➤ Fill, I chose a Contents of Black and clicked OK. Refer to Figure 7-78.

Figure 7-78. *Use the Fill dialog box to fill the selection with Black*

I lowered the opacity of Layer 2 to 15% and used Select ➤ Deselect (Ctrl/CMD+D) to remove the selection. Refer to Figure 7-79.

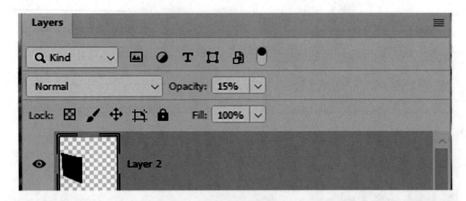

Figure 7-79. *Lower the opacity of Layer 2 and view the completed box*

File ➤ Save your document at this point. You can view file Box_with_images_final.psd as a reference.

■ **Note** These last two added layers can improve the shadow of the first part of the project as well, and you could add them both to a group folder and apply a layer style of Inner Shadow to them as a group, as you saw in Chapter 5 with group folders. See file Box_with_images_final.psd and refer to Figure 7-80.

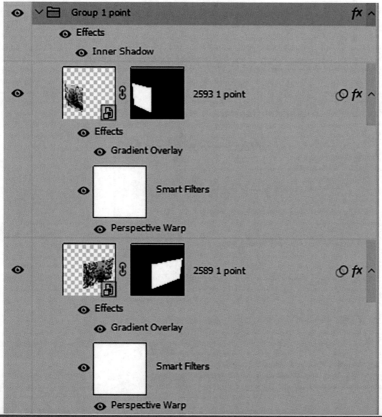

Figure 7-80. *Same box from first project with layers in a group folder and an inner shadow added*

Using the Free Transform, Warp, or Puppet Warp Option After Applying Perspective Warp

On a Photoshop smart object, whether or not it has a layer mask applied after a Perspective Warp, you still have access to the Free Transform and Warp menu options that we looked at in Chapter 4. Remember that an Illustrator smart object has less options (only Scale, Rotate, Skew) but still can use the Perspective Warp. However, as with the Puppet Warp, when you choose one of them, you will get an info message that the smart filter will be temporarily turned off during the transform. Refer to Figure 7-81.

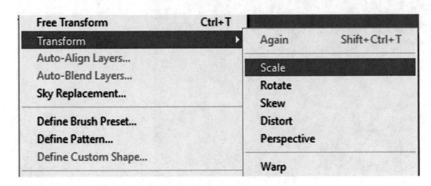

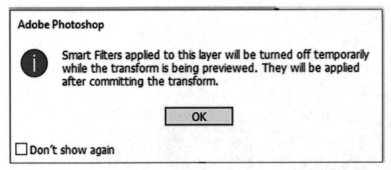

Figure 7-81. *Free Transform options and info message that appears when you try to edit them after Perspective warp has been applied*

Click OK and then continue to use your Free transform tools. Once done, click the check to commit in the Free Transform Options panel. The smart filter for Perspective Warp will be restored and updated with the current changes that affect the Perspective Warp. Refer to Figure 7-82.

Figure 7-82. *Click the check in the Free Transform Options panel to commit the transformation*

If you want to remove the Perspective Warp and smart filter, drag the name to the trash can icon in the Layers panel. Refer to Figure 7-83.

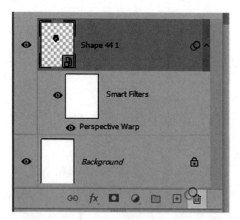

***Figure 7-83.** To remove the Perspective Warp, drag it over the trash can icon*

■ **Note**   As with Puppet Warp, the Perspective Warp can only be applied to the smart object and not to a layer mask or vector mask. If a mask is selected, the Perspective Warp option will be greyed out, so click the layer's image thumbnail to access those options from the menu again. Refer to Figure 7-84.

***Figure 7-84.** Layer masks will not be transformed with Perspective Warp*

Also, if trying to apply either an Edit ➤ Transform ➤ Warp to the mask of the layer or the smart object, as with the Puppet Warp, make sure to unlink the mask from the layer before you start the Transform ➤ Warp. The Perspective Warp will be temporarily turned off until the settings are committed. Refer to Figure 7-85.

***Figure 7-85.** Unlink the mask if you need to transform warp after a Perspective Warp has been applied*

Perspective Warp for Type and Shape Layers

As with the Puppet Warp, you can alter type layers with the Perspective Warp. However, to keep them in a non-destructive state, make sure to convert the type layer to a smart object first using the Layers panel menu. Refer to Figure 7-86.

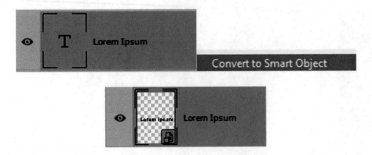

Figure 7-86. *To keep type layers editable, they need to be converted to a smart object first before you can use Perspective Warp*

In the case of a type layer, if you do not convert it to a smart object first, you will get a warning message asking if you want to rasterize the type. Click Cancel and then convert to a smart object. Refer to Figure 7-87.

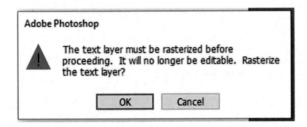

Figure 7-87. *Warning message if you try to perspective warp a type layer*

Shape layers must be converted to a smart object layer first before you have access to the Perspective Warp options.

In Chapter 10, we'll be looking at another type of Perspective filter known as Vanishing Point and see how there are similarities and differences between these two filters when we create a more complex perspective.

For more details on Perspective Warp, you can view this link: `https://helpx.adobe.com/photoshop/using/perspective-warp.html`.

Project: Touch Up Your Images After Using the Perspective Warp with the Content-Aware Move Tool

Earlier, you saw that sometimes a flat photo may need more than one quad shape plane to warp correctly around another object on a different layer. However, there are situations where may be working on just a flat photo on a single layer where two planes are moved within the image. But doing so can result in a type of warp around the areas similar to what you saw with the Puppet Warp. Refer to Figure 7-88.

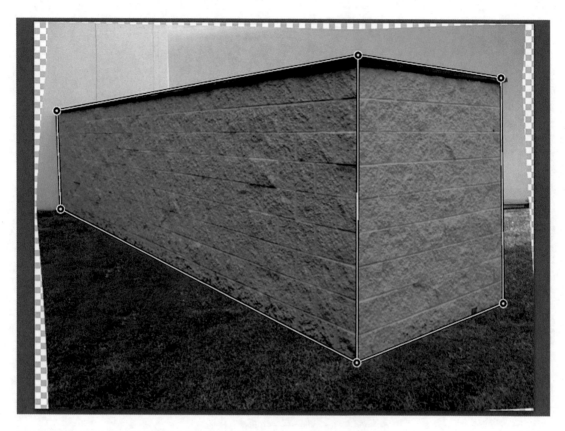

Figure 7-88. *Warping a wall to make it straight and correct lens distortion*

File ➤ Open the wall_start.psd file and make an Image ➤ Duplicate if you want to practice. Refer to Figure 7-89.

Figure 7-89. *Smart object wall with some lens distortion*

In this example, we are looking at a slightly distorted wall; this can happen sometimes due to the type of lens that was used to take the photo, as well as the distance and angle at which you stood.

We will look at advanced filters for lens correction in Chapter 9.

However, using Perspective Warp we can now fix the warp and use guides to help us straighten the wall and adjust the thickness of the wall.

Make sure that View ➤ Rulers is on, as mentioned in Chapter 1, and then on the smart object layer, go to Edit ➤ Perspective Warp. This time, in Options panel for Layout mode, create two quad planes than match the sides of the wall. Refer to Figure 7-90.

Figure 7-90. *Wall with new quad grid applied in Layout mode*

Now go to Warp mode and drag out some guides at least three from your Rulers on the document so that you can straighten the wall. Refer to Figure 7-91.

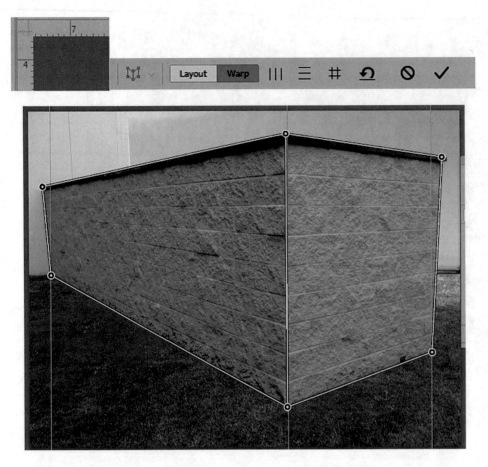

Figure 7-91. *Use your rulers and guides to assist you while in Warp mode*

Move the pins to straighten the walls. You may need to zoom in (Ctrl/CMD++) and use the Hand tool (spacebar) to move about as you straighten the lines. Refer to Figure 7-92.

Figure 7-92. *Line up the pins in the guide while in Warp mode*

For some added interest, you could also narrow the wall. Try that now. First drag another guide about to the 8.5-inch mark on the image, and then move the pins on your plane again and place them on the new guide narrowing the right face of the wall. Refer to Figure 7-93.

Figure 7-93. *Add another guide and move the pins over to change the warp of the wall*

Then click the check in the Options panel to commit. Refer to Figure 7-94.

Figure 7-94. *Click the check to commit the warp of the wall*

After you edit with Perspective Warp, you can see that there are some gaps on the edge of the image due to how the image was restretched, similar to when dealing with Puppet Warp. Refer to Figure 7-95.

Figure 7-95. *The wall with distortion corrected has some gaps on all sides*

■ **Tip** Use Ctrl/CMD+H to hide your guides for the moment if you do not want to see them while working. Ctrl/CMD+H again when you want to reveal them.

Let's look at four options for correcting the gaps.

Option 1: Use the Original Photo

To fill in the gaps on your own project, you could use your original photo and use the pixels from the base or background layer below the smart object layer. However, that may not be ideal in all situations. It may leave strange gaps on the edge and the sky may not match. Refer to Figure 7-96.

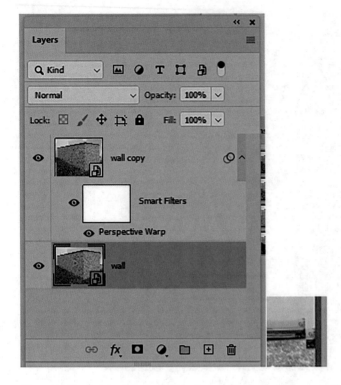

Figure 7-96. *Layers panel with two layers. The lower un-warped layer does not fill in the missing areas very well*

Option 2: Content-Aware Fill Workspace

You can use tools found in the Edit ➤ Content-Aware Fill workspace, which I talk about in my Photoshop Selections Book in Chapter 7. In this example, use the Magic Wand tool and Shift+Click on the gap areas, making selections of all the gaps. For the magic wand, make sure the Sample All Layers checkbox is enabled in the Options panel. Then create a blank layer above. You can try that as an option on this project by entering the Content-Aware Fill workspace previewing the change. I used a sampling area option of Rectangular and left the other settings of Show sampling area and Fill settings at the defaults. Output the settings for your fixes to a new layer or the current layer and click OK. Refer to Figure 7-97.

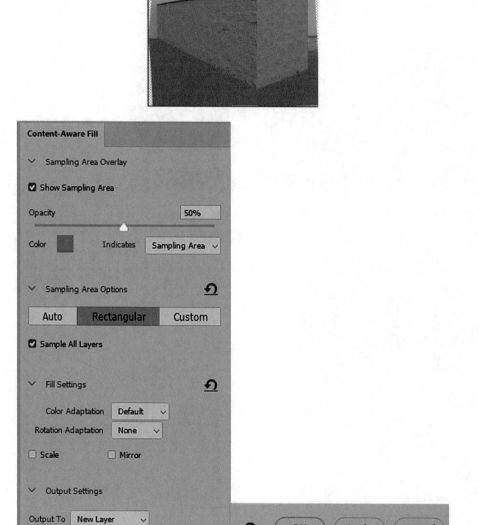

Figure 7-97. *Use the Magic Wand tool to add selections and then enter the Content-Aware Fill workspace to fill in the gaps while previewing the sampling area in green*

This option is fairly accurate, but still requires a bit of correcting with the Clone Stamp tool afterwards to cover minor gaps and you can do that on your new layer. Just make sure that the sampling option of Current & Below is set. Refer to Figure 7-98.

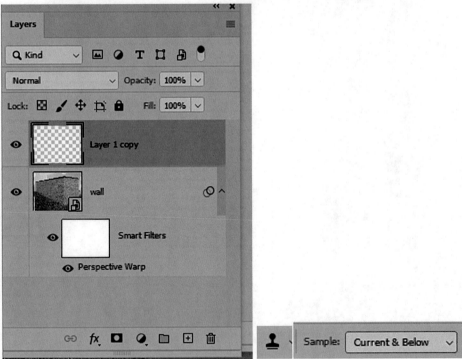

Figure 7-98. *New layer with missing gaps added that were content-aware-generated. Edit the layer further with the Clone Stamp tool*

Option 3: Content-Aware Fill Dialog Box

You can also use this method after you have Shift+Clicked in the gap areas with your Magic Wand tool to create a selection. Then try Edit ➤ Fill (Shift+F5) and from the Contents menu choose Content-Aware. Refer to Figure 7-99.

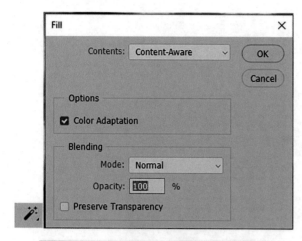

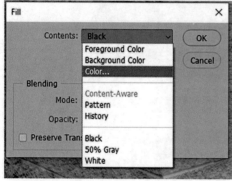

Figure 7-99. *Use the Magic Wand tool to create selections and the Fill dialog box to add content to fill in the gaps with Content-aware but only on normal layers*

However, this option will only work on a normal layer, or you could first rasterize a copy of the smart object layer, using the Layers panel menu for this option to work correctly. This will not work with a smart object layer where maybe you need to maintain the warp. Refer to Figure 7-100.

Figure 7-100. *Content from the Fill dialog box can only be added to a normal Layer*

The quality in this case is similar to Option 2 Content-Aware Fill Workspace and fills in the gaps, but there are no adjustment options and the fills are combined into one layer rather than separate layers.

Option 4: Content-Aware Move Tool (J)

When you need to make minor edits, there is a fourth option. It is the Content-Aware Move tool found in the Tools panel, which I will briefly demo here. Refer to Figure 7-101.

Figure 7-101. *Content-Aware Move tool*

Create a new layer for the copy of the `wall_start` file and then use the Rectangular Marquee tool to create an area that you want to clone. Refer to Figure 7-102.

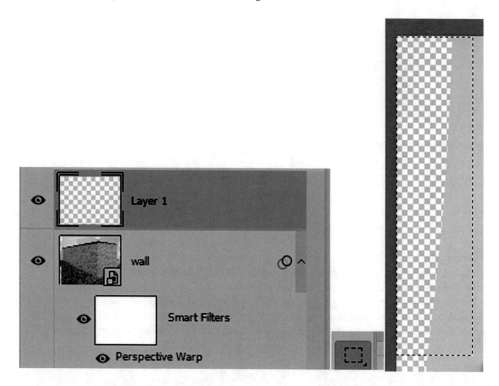

Figure 7-102. *New layer created and using the Rectangular Marquee tool to make a selection*

Then, still with your Rectangular Marque tool active, drag at the edge of the selection and move it over into the area that contains content. Refer to Figure 7-103.

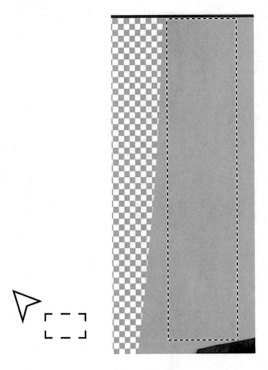

Figure 7-103. *Move the selection over the content you want to clone*

Choose the Content-Aware Tool. Let's look at the Options panel first, viewing from left to right. Refer to Figure 7-101.

Content-Aware Move Tool Options

After the tool presets area are options for selections to Create a new selection, Add to selection (Shift), Subtract from selection (Alt/Option), or Intersect with selection (Alt/Option +Shift). However, because we have created the selection already using the Rectangular Marquee tool, we can ignore this area. I find that often the selection created with this tool does not always accurately cover the area I want to clone but creating a selection ahead of time with my Rectangular Marquee selection tool is much easier. However, if you were to use this tool to create a selection, you would need to drag and draw a selection manually, which in this case would not create the exact selection I just made. Refer to Figure 7-104.

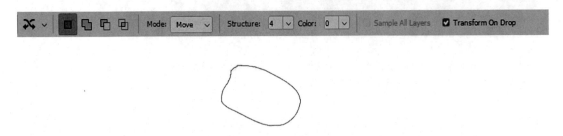

Figure 7-104. *Content-Aware Move tool Options panel and a selection you can make with that tool*

614

Change the Remix mode from Move to Extend and make sure that Sample all Layers is enabled.

Move will move the selection from one place to another, but in this case, we want to scale and expand the selection as we move. Refer to Figure 7-105.

Figure 7-105. *Change the mode from Move to Extend*

Then Click+Drag, holding onto your selection, moving it over to the area you want to scale; get the edges into the areas to fill the gaps. If the selection becomes deselected and disappears, you will have to redraw you selection again with the Rectangular Marquee tool. Refer to Figure 7-106.

Figure 7-106. *The Content-Aware Move tool allows you to clone, move, and extend the selection*

Once in place, click the check in the Options panel to commit the selection. And return to the other options in the Content-Aware Move tool. Refer to Figure 7-107.

Figure 7-107. *Click the check in the Options panel to commit the selection and reuse the selection in another location*

In the Options panel, keep the structure at a setting of 4. It can be between 1-7. This controls how strictly the source structure is preserved. The higher the number, the more strongly the selection patch conforms to the current image patterns. Color is at 0 but you can set it up to 10. Higher numbers may improve the color blend and adjust how much of the source color can be modified. Refer to Figure 7-108.

Figure 7-108. *Content-Aware Move tools Options panel*

When working on a new layer above a smart object, make sure you enable Sample All Layers to enable a remix of all layers during the cloning. Enable Transform on Drop to allow rotation and scaling (expansion and contraction) of the selection, should that be required. Refer to Figure 7-108.

Continue to work on Layer 1, switching between the Rectangular Marquee Tool creating rectangular selections and then using those selections with your Content-Aware Move tool. With that tool, after moving, drag on the selection area to resize the bounding box handles to scale and expand and then drag to fill in the gaps. Refer to Figure 7-109.

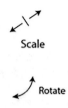

Figure 7-109. *With Extend mode, current selections can be scaled and rotated as they are moved into place*

When complete, click the check in the Options panel to commit. Select ➤ Deselect your last section.

Try any one of these options mentioned and see what works best for your project as there is never any one way of doing things for all projects.

In my project, afterwards I used the Clone Stamp tool and Eraser tool to touch up or blend in areas, so the grass did not appear to be copied. Refer to Figure 7-110 and Figure 7-111.

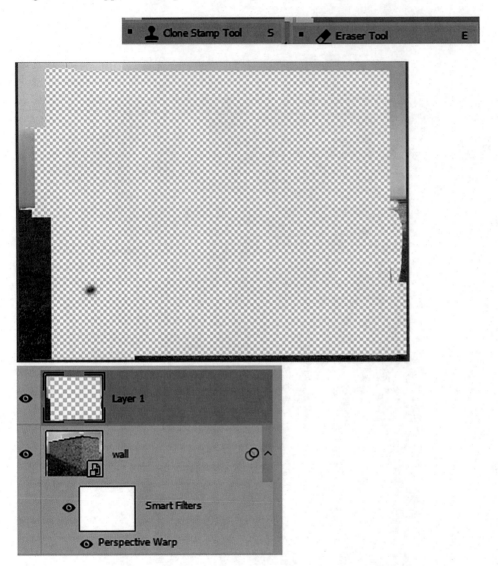

Figure 7-110. *Use the Clone Stamp or Eraser tool on Layer 1 to clean up any areas that you did not like that the Content-Aware Move tool selection created*

Figure 7-111. *The completed wall*

File ➤ Save your document at this point. You can compare your project to my file, `wall_final.psd`.

■ **Tip** For alternative options for working with filling gap areas using Content-Aware and the Object Selection Tool refer to the link:

`https://helpx.adobe.com/photoshop/using/making-quick-selections.html#one-click-delete-fill`

Afterwards, on your own, you may want to use plants or shrubs that you have from other projects and dress up the wall. You could copy and paste part of another photo and scale and rotate or even use the Clone Stamp tool and the Clone Source panel mention in Chapter 1 to assist when you Alt/Option+Click areas out of another image. Just be aware of the angle and perspective of the wall so that the flow is correct and then later paint in shadows with your Brush tool or use Layer styles and layer blending modes where required, varying the layer opacity. You can see an example of this in `wall_start_grasses_copy.psd`. Refer to Figure 7-112.

Figure 7-112. *Adding flowers and shrubbery around the wall*

Content-Aware Scale

In the previous section, you saw a few tools that rely on content-aware functionality to fill in gaps and even scale at the same time. However, there is one more content-aware command in the Edit menu, Content-Aware Scale.

Some images can become disproportionate if not scaled correctly and then they're not visually pleasing. Using content-aware scale can help us correct this in some situations, such as when a smaller item in an image needs to be enlarged. However, it can also be used to create some very uniquely distorted images when we reduce the scale. Refer to Figure 7-113.

Figure 7-113. *Strange warps can be created when you scale with the Content-Aware Scale command*

As well, in some cases, there are areas in the image that you may want to protect from scaling smaller using a previously create selection that was saved and placed in the Channels panel. Refer to Figure 7-114.

Figure 7-114. *You can use a selection in the Channels panel to protect areas from unusual scaling*

File ➤ Open mask_start.psd and make an Image ➤ Duplicate to practice with.

In the Layers Panel, double-click the background layer and click OK to the message in the New Layer dialog box to leave it at Name: Layer 0. Refer to Figure 7-115.

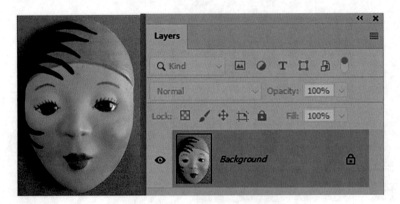

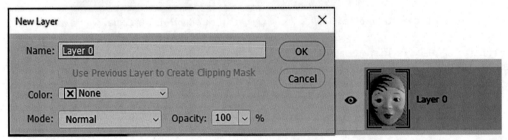

Figure 7-115. *Scale the doll face, but first you need to change it from a background layer to a normal layer*

■ **Note** This Scale tool is not available for smart object layers, masks, type, or vector shape layers. So work on a duplicate copy of the file or layer if you want to refer to the original image afterwards.

Choose Edit ➤ Content Aware Scale (Alt/Option+Shift+Ctrl/CMD+C). This is very similar to the Free Transform Tools for scale that we used in Chapter 4. Refer to the Options panel.

Content-Aware Scale Options

Here you can adjust relative position from the center reference point, as well as set a horizontal (X) and vertical (Y) position for reference point scale. The Trangle, as with Free Transform options, allows you to use the relative positioning for the reference point, based on current image positoning. Refer to Figure 7-116.

Figure 7-116. *Content-Aware Scale Options panel*

You can also scale by percentage for width and height and maintain the aspect ratio link. Hold down the Shift key if you want to scale disproportionately and unlink the aspect ratio. You cannot rotate using these options as it is for scaling only. However, you can change the scale increments if you right-click the text box. Refer to Figure 7-117.

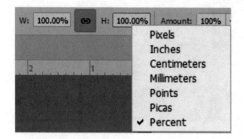

Figure 7-117. *Change the units of measurement in the Options panel*

Amount (0-100%): Lets you set the threshold for content-aware scaling to minimise distortion. Type a number in the text box or move the slider. A higher number causes the distortion to happen fairly quickly while lower numbers slow down the distorion as the image is smaller or larger. Refer to Figure 7-118.

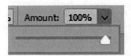

Figure 7-118. *Change the amount of distortion in the Options panel. The settings for this image were scale width and height 72.25% at an amount of 100% and same width and height scale with an amount of 16%*

Protect: None or choose a channel to specify which areas to protect. This relies on the Channels panel having a selection present (in this case, Alpha 1). Refer to Figure 7-119.

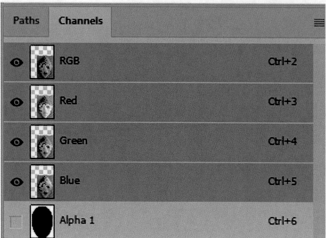

Figure 7-119. *When a selection from the Channels panel is enabled, it can protect areas of the distortion and make it more symmetrical*

Protect skin tones: The icon looks like a liitle person. Use this to keep skintone colors accurate. This can depending on the picture, create other distortions if the amount silder is not adjusted as well. Refer to Figure 7-119 and Figure 7-120.

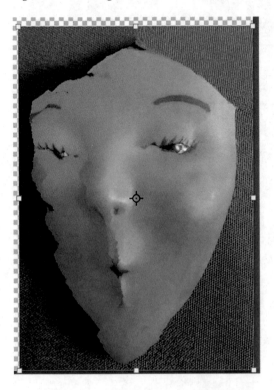

Figure 7-120. *Enabling the Protect skin tones option can also alter the content when you scale*

The last buttons allow you to cancel the transform or commit the transform. If you commit the transform, note that because you are working with a Normal layer, the results are permanent, so always work on a copy. In my case, I clicked cancel and closed the file. Refer to Figure 7-121.

Figure 7-121. *Click the check in the Options panel to commit*

Some other funny faces that you can try with this Content-Aware Scale are your pets. Their reactions to their daily interaction can be enhanced. Refer to Figure 7-122.

***Figure 7-122.** Now the cat can really show how she feels inside*

We'll look at another way to distort images using the Liquify filter in Chapter 9.

Project: Sky Replacement

While not exactly a warping tool, after you have scaled and transformed your image correctly, you may want to replace the sky in an image. And rather than creating your own a separate images or masks and selections, this unique content-aware tool can help you do that quickly. You can use a normal or smart object layer for this project as your background.

File ➤ Open Sky_replacement_start.psd. Make an Image ➤ Duplicate for practice. It's a rather overcast day at the wildlife sanctuary, yet there are some hikers walking the trails in the distance over the river. I would like the sky to be a bit more dynamic as I think that would enhance the scene. Refer to Figure 7-123.

Figure 7-123. *Walking the trails on an overcast day with a boring sky*

To begin, you can make a selection of the sky using the Magic Wand or another selection tool, or you can let the Sky Replacement tool detect the sky for you.

From the Edit menu, choose Sky Replacement. This opens the dialog box. It may take a few moments for the sky to be detected. Let's take a moment to explore the tools in the dialog box. Make sure that Preview checkbox is enabled. Refer to Figure 7-124.

Figure 7-124. Sky Replacement dialog box

Tools: There are four tools. Refer to the Option panel area at the same time for more options as you look at the dialog box.

- **Sky Move tool(V):** Moves the sky around on the canvas to the area you want it to start and stop. Refer to Figure 7-125.

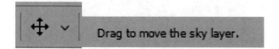

Figure 7-125. Sky Replacement dialog box and Sky Move tool and Options panel

- **Sky Brush tool (B):** Extends or reduces the sky. To reduce, you can also hold down the Alt/Option key and paint, as you saw earlier with the Brush tool in various blending modes. See Chapter 2 for more details on blending modes. You can set the Opacity (1-100%) for the blend. This is another location where you could use your pattern brush. From the menu, you can set the angle, size, and hardness as well. In this case, I use a Soft Round Brush, the Mode is set to Overlay and Opacity to 50%. If you do paint, the change may not be overly noticeable with certain blend modes and opacities. Refer to Figure 7-126.

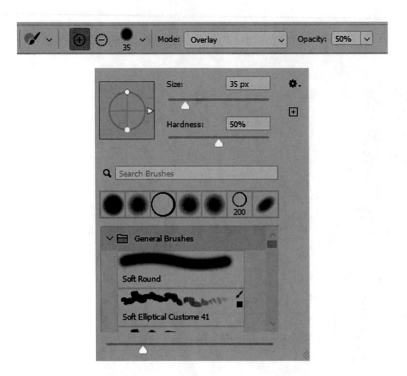

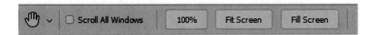

Figure 7-126. Sky Replacement dialog box, Sky Brush tool, and Options panel

- **Hand tool (H)**: Use to move around the image without moving the sky by accident. It has three zooming presets. Refer to Figure 7-127.

Figure 7-127. Sky Replacement dialog box for Hand tool and Options panel

- **Zoom tool (Z)**: Zoom in or Alt/Option Zoom to Zoom out. You can also use similar zoom presets as found in the Tools panel Zoom options. Refer to Figure 7-128.

Figure 7-128. Sky Replacement dialog box for Zoom tool and Options panel

Now move to the right of the panel:

- Sky Presets: From the dropdown menu you can find and select a preset sky from the folder. Many are available. They include Blue Skies, Spectacular, and Sunsets. The most recently used skies are seen above the folders for easy access. Refer to Figure 7-129.

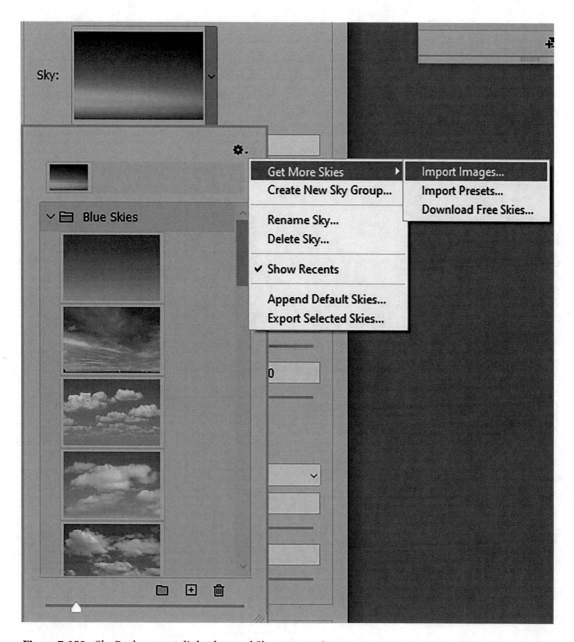

Figure 7-129. *Sky Replacement dialog box and Sky menu options*

In this case, I will select Blue Sky0006 by Photoshop the Blue Skies folder. It has a bit of a stormy atmosphere, but it makes the scenery appear brighter. Refer to Figure 7-129.

■ **Note** From the gear menu, you can manage your presets further, such as get more free skies from Adobe Creative Cloud or import images from your desktop. They can be saved in a new sky group and exported for others to share. Further down on the drop-down menu, you can zoom in on the skies to see them in more detail using the slider and use the buttons to create a new sky group folder, import sky images, or delete selected skies. Refer to Figure 7-129 and Figure 7-130.

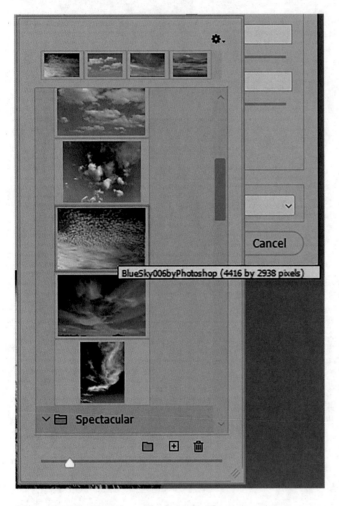

Figure 7-130. Choosing a sky from the Sky menu options

Using the Sky Move tool, you can move it down a bit in the scene. We do not need to use the Sky Brush as it appears that the sky area has been detected correctly. Refer to Figure 7-131.

Figure 7-131. *Move the sky so that you can see the clouds you want*

Just don't move the sky to the left or right as you may get a strange broken off gap in the clouds. The sliders and text boxes below let you edit the following:

- **Shift Edge**: Expand or contract the sky and foreground boundary (-100, 0, +100) where the sky and original images begin. Set to 5.

- **Fade Edge**: Soften sky and foreground boundary (0-100) edges between the sky and the original image. Set to 48. Refer to Figure 7-132.

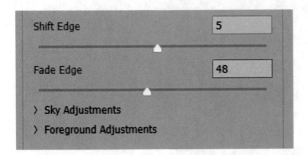

Figure 7-132. Sky Replacement dialog box for Shift and Fade Edge sliders

- **Sky Adjustments**: Open the tab to see the options and control these settings:

  Brightness (-100, 0, +100): Controls the brightness of the replacement sky. Set to 26.

  Temperature (-100, 0, +100): Controls how warm or cool the colors appear in the replacement sky. Set to 34.

  Scale: Adjust the size of replacement sky (50-400). Set to 107.

  Flip sky horizontally to reverse when enabled. Keep unchecked. Refer to Figure 7-133.

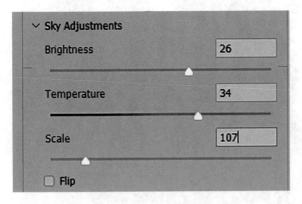

Figure 7-133. Sky Replacement dialog box, Sky Adjustment sliders, and Flip check box

- Foreground Adjustments:

  Lighting Mode: Sets the blending mode of Lighting mode to Multiply or Screen. I set it to Multiply.
  Foreground Lighting: Controls the opacity values of the lighting adjustment applied to the foreground (0-100%), set to 62.
  Edge Lighting: Where the sky blends with the original image (0-100%) to preserve lighting along the edges and reduce halos by controlling opacity values, set to 64.
  Color adjustment: Controls the opacity values of color harmonizing applied to the foreground (0-100%), set to 50. Refer to Figure 7-134.

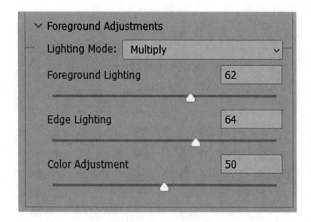

Figure 7-134. *Sky Replacement dialog box, Foreground Adjustmentss, menu, and sliders*

- **Output**: This replacement sky can be output to new layers or a duplicate layer. New Layers creates a group folder that contains the sky layer with a mask, a gradient foreground light with a mask, and a curves adjustment layer for foreground with a mask. Duplicate Layer automatically applies all the settings to a duplicate copy layer of the smart object as a normal layer that essentially has been merged and flattened. Refer to Figure 7-135.

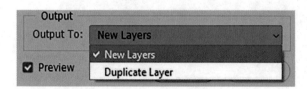

Figure 7-135. *Sky Replacement dialog box Output options*

Click OK to commit or Cancel to exit. Refer to Figure 7-136.

Figure 7-136. *Click OK to commit the changes for the new sky and exit the dialog box*

In this case, I chose New Layers and clicked OK.

When you choose the Output New Layers option, a Sky replacement group folder is created. You can edit the masks and adjustment layers further with your Brush or Eraser tools to improve the replaced sky if required. Also, within the group folder, new Edge Lighting Group is added as well.

Adjustment layers, when selected, can also be altered in the Properties panel. Refer to Figure 7-137.

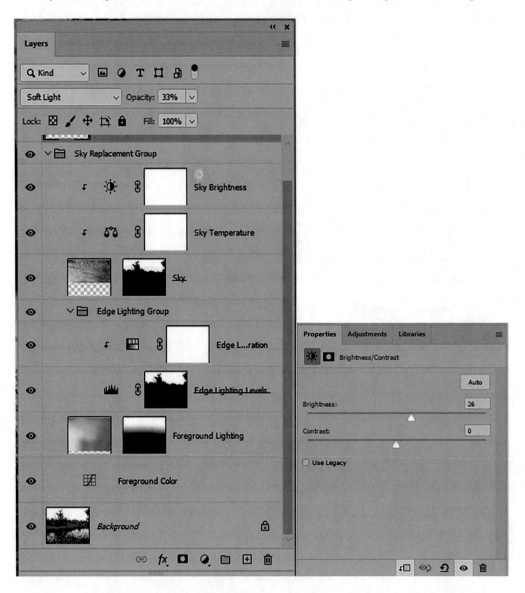

Figure 7-137. *A group folder and layers that are generated in the Layers panel. Adjustment layers can be altered afterwards using the Properties panel*

To discover how you can get more skies, visit this link:

`https://helpx.adobe.com/photoshop/using/replace-sky.html.`

File ➤ Save your document at this point. You can look at my file, Sky_replacement_final.psd. I added a blank layer where I painted, with the Brush tool, some blue foreground color (R: 77, G: 130, B:155) on areas of the water and used a layer blending mode of Soft Light and an Opacity of 33%. Refer to Figure 7-138.

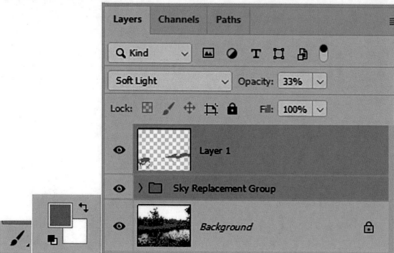

Figure 7-138. *The completed sky with a new layer added above with some blue added to the water with a color similar to the sky*

This made it appear like some of the blue sky was reflecting onto the water as well, now that the sky has been altered.

Summary

In this chapter, you explored more tools and commands in the Edit panel and how they can be used to warp perspective and scale an image. You also looked at some of the content-aware features as well as the Content-Aware Move tool that can be used to fill in missing gaps after warping. Lastly, you toured the Sky Replacement dialog box and saw how you can use it to improve the look of your image. In the next chapter, you will look at a few basic filters that can also be smart filters that you can use to further warp and distort an image.

CHAPTER 8

■ ■ ■

Basic Filters and Smart Filters

Chapter goal: While there are many filters in Photoshop, not all can be considered true warps and distorts. Some are more alterations of color. This chapter will focus on select filters that either distort or correct distortion in an image. The focus here is on basic filters that can be used to create unusual, distorted backgrounds for your projects. Refer to Figure 8-1.

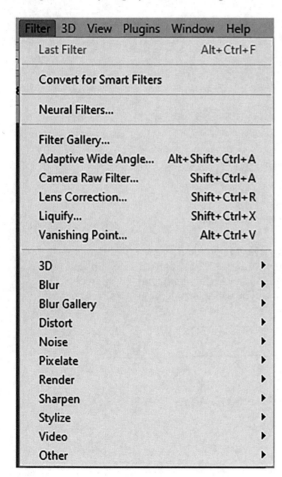

Figure 8-1. *Photoshop Filter menu*

© Jennifer Harder 2023
J. Harder, *Perspective Warps and Distorts with Adobe Tools: Volume 1*,
https://doi.org/10.1007/978-1-4842-8710-1_8

■ **Note** You can find the projects for this chapter in the Chapter 8 folder.

Long-term Photoshop users know that this application has many filters that have been added to the program over the years. Some have remained a constant of Photoshop. However, others have been removed. And then there are some that have been improved upon over time, such as Oil Paint, which we'll look at in this chapter, and the Liquify filter, which we will look at as an advanced filter in Chapter 9. More recently, Adobe has added new filters called Neural Filters, some of which are experimental or in beta format, as well as the options of third-party plugins from other companies. We'll look at them in Chapter 10.

In this chapter, I want to look at some of my favorite basic filters that I think are great to use for warps and distorts. In the past, I used them on normal layers, which could be considered destructive. When I did that, I made a duplicate of the layer and then, after I used the filter on the layer, I added a layer mask and then erased or hid the area on the layer mask that I did not want to have filtered. Refer to Figure 8-2.

Figure 8-2. *Layers panel with a duplicate layer with a layer mask added*

You can still do that now with your own projects. However, the problem for me with this approach was then I could not go back and tweak my settings for the filter after it was applied to the duplicate layer. Happily, with smart object layers this is not a problem. As you saw in Chapters 6 and 7, a smart object layer can have a smart filter and a filter mask applied to it. And, as you will see, multiple smart filters can be combined. Refer to Figure 8-3.

Figure 8-3. *Smart object layer with a various smart filters applied and a filter mask*

We'll try that first with the Filter Gallery and then look at some basic filters outside the Filter Gallery. So, let's take a look at some of my basic filter favorites.

As mentioned in Chapter 1, make sure that you are working in an RGB Color mode so that you have access to all the filters I am discussing. If you try to convert your color mode to CMYK, when some smart filters are applied, you may get a warning message and some filters may no longer be accessible. So always do your final color conversion to CMYK on an Image ➤ Duplicate after you have flattened the copy of the image, and keep the original as a backup. Refer to Figure 8-4.

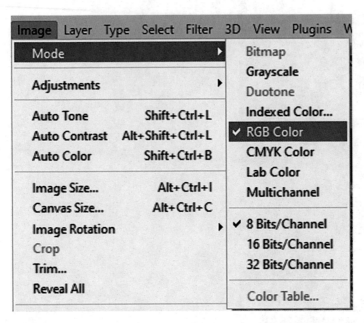

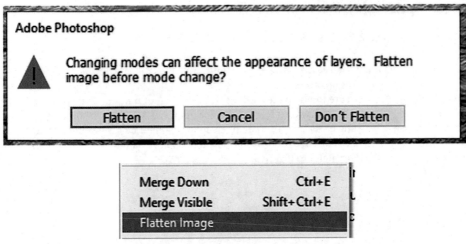

Figure 8-4. *When you want to use all the filters, you should be in Image ➤ Mode> RGB Color. If you choose CMYK, you have to decide whether to flatten the layers in the image*

Also, to practice with your own files in this chapter, convert the normal layer to a smart object layer. Choose Filter ➤ Convert for Smart Filters and click OK to the message. Or just use your Layers menu as you did in the past and Choose Convert to Smart Object. In this chapter, you can use Illustrator or Photoshop smart object layers. Refer to Figure 8-5.

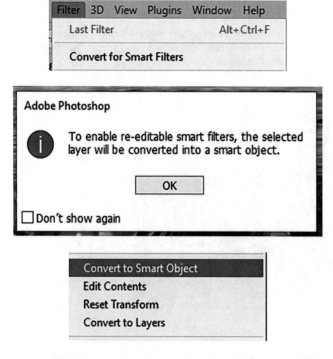

Figure 8-5. *Convert a layer to a smart object using either the filter menu with the information message or use the Layers panel menu*

Lastly, in this chapter you'll take what you have learned about filters and discover how this can be applied to a GIF animation.

Basic Filters

A basic filter, in my opinion, is meant to have very few settings that you must alter to achieve an effect.

A collection of these filter can be found in the Filter Gallery workspace. While I am not going to explore in detail every single filter in this area, let's look at the ones I feel are best used for warping and distorting, and then look at how one filter can be combined with another to create a blend. Go to Filter ➤ Filter Gallery. Refer to Figure 8-6.

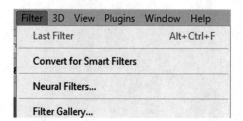

Figure 8-6. *Use the Filter menu to access the Filter Gallery*

Project: Working with Various Backgrounds and Filters

In this part of the gallery and when using other filters outside the gallery, I am going to demo images that I have in the Chapter 8 folder. I will reference them and before entering the filter, you can File ➤ Open then and Make an Image ➤ Duplicate so that if you like an effect, you can save copies of the file for a potential background pattern for a personal project. Or you can use your own image. In this first example, open file water_feature_start.psd. Refer to Figure 8-7.

***Figure 8-7.** Work on a smart object layer when using the Filter Gallery*

Select the smart object layer Background Copy and go to Filter ➤ Filter Gallery. Refer to Figure 8-7 and Figure 8-8.

***Figure 8-8.** Filter Gallery dialog box workspace*

Working in the Filter Gallery

The Filter Gallery is divided into six folders or categories: Artistic, Brush Strokes, Distort, Sketch, Stylize, and Texture. You can look at each of the filters in these areas by opening the folder and clicking one of the filters to see how it previews on the image left of the workspace. In Figure 8-8, I am looking at the Artistic folder and I've selected Pallet Knife, which I'll discuss in a moment.

To navigate the Preview area, use the plus, minus, or navigational dropdown menu to zoom in or out (Ctrl/CMD++ or Ctrl/CMD+-) or just hold down the Ctrl/CMD key to click and zoom in. Then drag over the area (the Hand tool appears on preview) to move to the location to preview how it appears with the filter. Holding down the Alt/Option key will also bring up the Zoom tool to zoom out quickly. Refer to Figure 8-9.

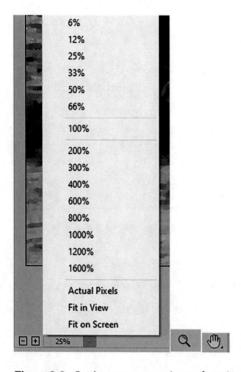

Figure 8-9. *Setting your zoom size and navigating in the Filter Gallery*

■ **Note** If you cannot see the filter thumbnails, make sure to click the double arrow button near the OK Button to hide and show filters in your workspace. This is useful when you need more room for your preview. Make sure, for now, that the filters are visible. Refer to Figure 8-10.

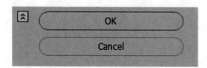

Figure 8-10. *Show and hide your Filter Gallery options*

You can spend time on your own testing the filters, but I will talk about each briefly here. The two folders that I will be focusing on are Distort and Texture. Any one of the other filters from the Gallery can be added to enhance the distort, as you will try in a moment. Refer to Figure 8-11.

Figure 8-11. *Filters are stored in the six folders in the Filter Gallery*

■ **Note**   Some filters may take longer to render than others, so keep an eye on the progress bar near the lower navigation area and wait a few moments as the filter adjusts. Refer to Figure 8-12.

Figure 8-12. *Check the progress of the chosen filter in the gallery as it renders in the preview*

Artistic Folder

For now, open the Artistic Folder triangle. There are 15 filters. Select Plastic Wrap. Refer to Figure 8-13.

Figure 8-13. *Apply a Plastic Wrap filter from the Artistic folder in the Filter Gallery and preview the result*

By adjusting the sliders for Highlight Strength (0-20), Detail (1-15), and Smoothness (1-15), this can give the impression of a distorted contour and a type of bevel and embossing that you would see on the edges to make the object appear more three-dimensional as if wrapped in shiny clear plastic. Refer to Figure 8-13.

Other filters in this folder, like Colored Pencil, Cutout, and Neon Glow limit the colors or posterize the image. Refer to Figure 8-14.

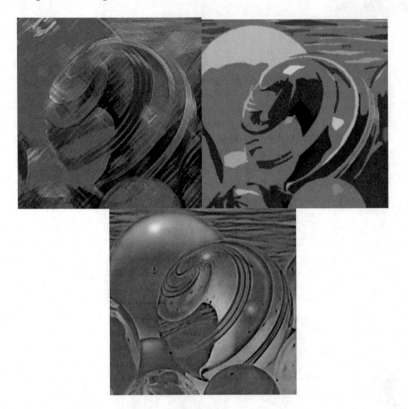

Figure 8-14. *Examples of Artistic filters: Colored Pencil, Cutout, and Neon Glow*

Some give more painterly and blurry effects and soften features, such as Dry Brush, Paint Daubs, Palette Knife and Smudge Stick. Refer to Figure 8-15.

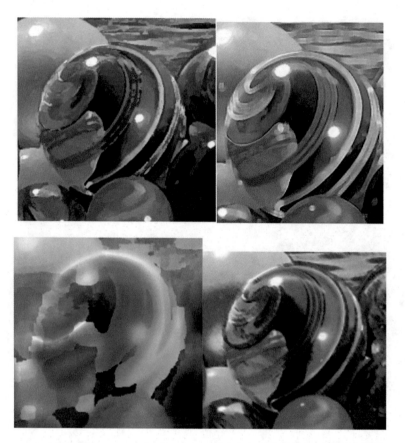

Figure 8-15. *Examples of Artistic filters: Dry Brush, Paint Daubs, Palette Knife, and Smudge Stick*

Fresco, Poster Edges, and Watercolor, while not distorts, can sharpen or darken and make an image stand out. Refer to Figure 8-16.

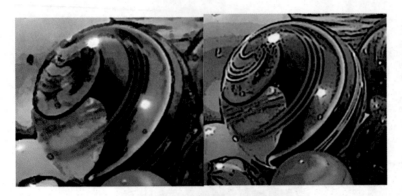

Figure 8-16. *Examples of Artistic filters: Fresco, Poster Edges, and Watercolor*

Film Grain, Rough Pastels, Sponge and Under Painting can overlay a more textured effect. Refer to Figure 8-17.

Figure 8-17. *Examples of Artistic filters: Film Grain, Rough Pastels, Sponge, and Under Painting*

■ **Note**   Neon Glow and Colored Pencil will be different colors, depending on what the foreground or background colors are in the Tools panel as you enter the Filter Gallery. So, use your Color Picker dialog box first when you click on the swatch, to set the colors before you enter the Filter Gallery. Otherwise, make sure to reset the colors by pressing D and then X to toggle between a black background and white foreground. In my case, before I entered the Filter Gallery, I had my foreground set to white and my background to black, but if it had been reversed or another color, I would have gotten different results. Refer to Figure 8-18.

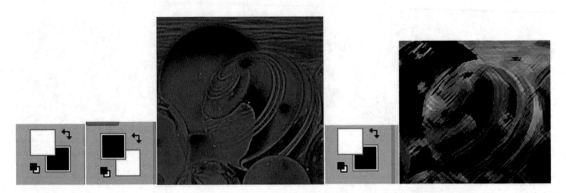

Figure 8-18. *Set your foreground and background colors in the Tools panel to affect how certain filters interact*

Take a moment to explore each filter and adjust sliders, checkboxes, and drop-down menus. Neon Glow is the only option that lets you access the Color Picker for the glow color.

Brush Strokes Folder

Let's look at the next folder in the Gallery. There are eight filters. Refer to Figure 8-19.

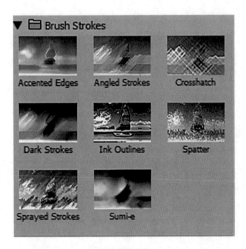

Figure 8-19. *Brush Strokes filters*

In the Brush Strokes folder, Angled Strokes, Crosshatch, Spatter, and Sprayed Strokes can give unusual blurs and jaggedness. Refer to Figure 8-20.

Figure 8-20. *Examples of Brush Stroke filters: Angled Strokes, Crosshatch, Spatter, and Sprayed Strokes*

Accented Edges and Ink Outlines can define corners and edges very distinctly. Refer to Figure 8-21.

Figure 8-21. *Examples of Brush Stroke filters: Accented Edges and Ink Outlines*

Dark Strokes and Sumi-e can blur and darken an image. Refer to Figure 8-22.

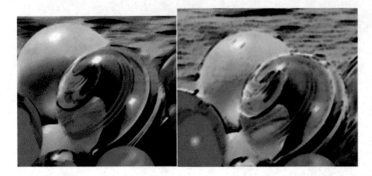

Figure 8-22. *Examples of Brush Stroke filters: Dark Strokes and Sumi-e*

Take a moment to explore each filter and make adjustments to sliders and drop-down menus.

Distort Folder

The Distort folder has three filters: Diffuse Glow, Glass, and Ocean Ripple. Refer to Figure 8-23.

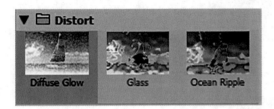

Figure 8-23. *Distort filters*

Diffuse Glow can be used to blur or make an image grainy by setting the level of Graininess from 0-10. Refer to Figure 8-24.

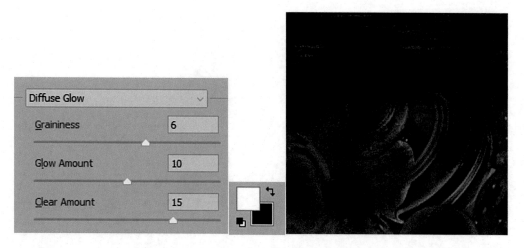

Figure 8-24. *Diffuse Glow options are also affected by current background color in Tools panel*

The Glow Amount (0-20) sets how much white or black is added to the image and this is based on what you set as the current background color earlier in your Tools panel. Clear amount (0-20) will also set the amount of whiteness. Refer to Figure 8-25.

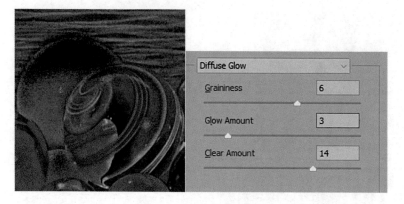

Figure 8-25. *Diffuse Glow options altered to make it appear less black*

If you have the wrong background or foreground color applied to the filter in a smart object, you cannot correct it inside the Filter gallery. Exit the Filter Gallery by clicking the Cancel button and then change the background or foreground color using the Color Picker. Press X to swap. Refer to Figure 8-26.

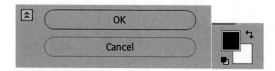

Figure 8-26. *Click Cancel to exit without committing changes and make the background in the Tools panel white by pressing X*

Then, to reapply, you need to go back into the Filter ➤ Filter Gallery, and then the new background color will appear for Diffuse Glow. Click OK to commit. Refer to Figure 8-27.

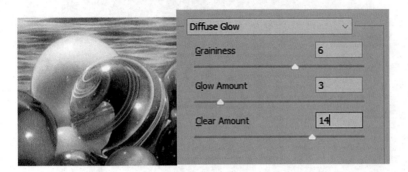

Figure 8-27. *Diffuse Glow options also affected by current background color in Tools panel upon entering the Gallery again*

However, if you already applied the filter earlier in the Layers panel, then select the older, lower Diffuse Glow (Filter Gallery) smart filter and drag it to the trash icon, so only the new smart filter is applied.

Double-clicking the older smart filter will not alter the background or foreground color, only retain what you originally used the first time you entered the filter. Refer to Figure 8-28.

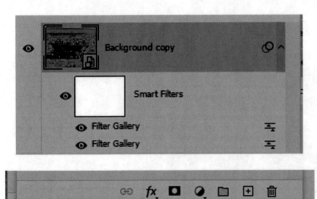
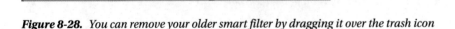

Figure 8-28. *You can remove your older smart filter by dragging it over the trash icon*

Glass is in some ways like the brush stroke of Spatter, but with more rounded contours to resemble older glass with its mottled appearance. Refer to Figure 8-29.

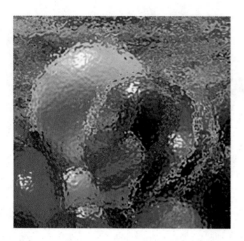

Figure 8-29. *Glass option set as Frosted Glass*

You can set the sliders for Distortion (0-20). The higher the distortion, the less visible the image is. For Smoothness (1-15), the higher the smoothness, the less textured it is. Refer to Figure 8-30.

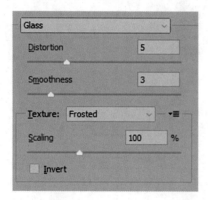

Figure 8-30. *Glass options set to a texture of frosted glass*

For the actual Texture setting, you can use the preset textures of Blocks, Canvas, Frosted, and Tiny Lens. In Figure 8-29, you are looking at Frosted. Each texture creates a unique distortion. Refer to Figure 8-29 and Figure 8-31.

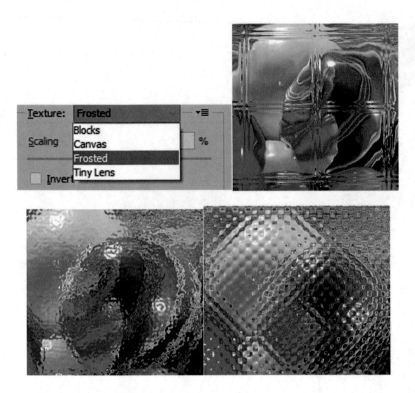

Figure 8-31. *Textures for Blocks, Canvas, and Tiny Lens*

Beside these texture options is a small menu called Load Texture. Here you can add your own custom create textures like the grayscale one we created as a .psd at the end of Chapter 3. Refer to Figure 8-32.

Figure 8-32. *Option to load a custom texture*

You will look at that texture setting and how to test and use it successfully a bit later in the chapter in this Filter Gallery section in the Texture folder Texturizer. However, note that earlier filters you may have previewed on your own in the Artistic folder such as Rough Pastels and Under Painting also allow you to add a texture of your own, which is a great way to customize your filter. Refer to Figure 8-33.

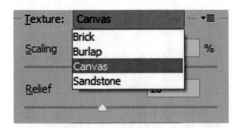

Figure 8-33. *Other filters in the Filter Gallery allow you to use defaults or add custom textures*

Next, you can set the Glass Filer Scaling (50-200%) and invert the glass reflections when the checkbox is enabled. This affects the pattern. Refer to Figure 8-34.

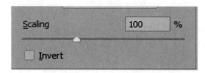

Figure 8-34. *Options to Scale and Invert*

Ocean Ripple is very similar to Glass and the brush stroke named Filter Spatter. However, it gives more of a water effect, and it lets you set the Ripple Size (1-15) and Ripple Magnitude (0-20). Refer to Figure 8-35.

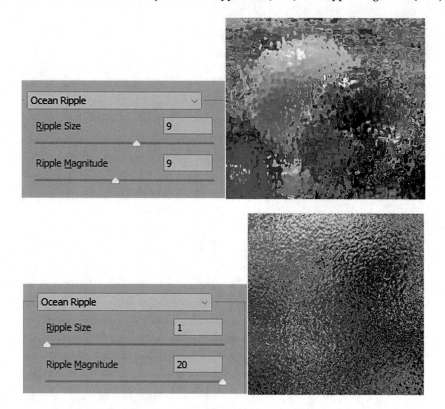

Figure 8-35. *Ocean Ripple options and examples*

Other filters outside of the Filter Gallery, which you'll see later, can achieve similar effects including Wave and Crystalize.

Sketch Folder

This folder is more for creating black and white sketch images. There are 14 filters. Currently, I am using a black foreground and white background color while in the Gallery. Refer to Figure 8-36.

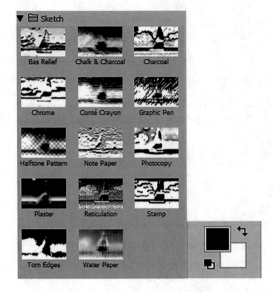

Figure 8-36. *Filter Gallery Sketch filters. Most are affected by the current foreground and background colors in the Tools panel*

Bas Relief, Photocopy, and Plaster create more of an embossed effect. Refer to Figure 8-37.

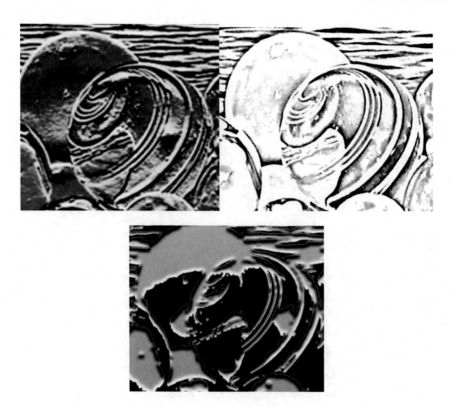

Figure 8-37. *Examples of Sketch filters: Bas Relief, Photocopy, and Plaster*

Chalk and Charcoal, or just Charcoal, offer more of a smeared or hand-drawn texture. Refer to Figure 8-38.

Figure 8-38. *Examples of Sketch filters: Chalk and Charcoal and Charcoal*

Other filters that create a textured effect included Graphic Pen, Halftone Pattern (dot, line, and circle), Note Paper, and Reticulation. Refer to Figure 8-39.

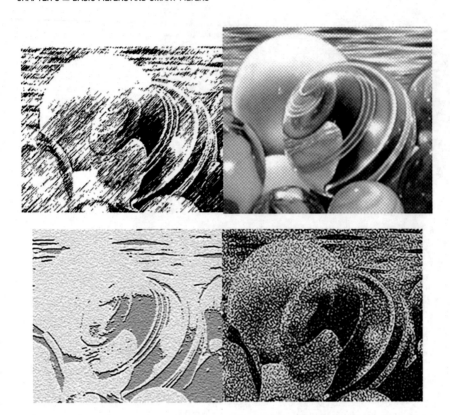

Figure 8-39. *Examples of Sketch filters: Graphic Pen, Halftone Pattern, Note Paper, and Reticulation*

Conté Crayon also allows you to alter or add custom textures, which you will see as we will look at further in the Filter Gallery's Texture folder. Refer to Figure 8-40.

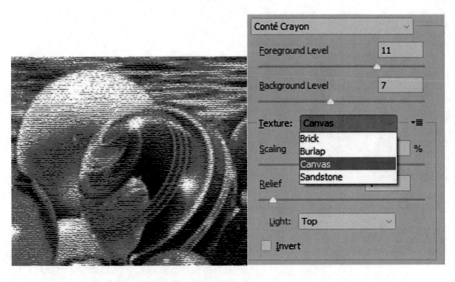

Figure 8-40. *Examples of Sketch filters: Conté Crayon and filter settings*

Chrome, like Plastic Wrap in the Artistic folder, gives a shinier appearance and is great for creating twisted metal effects. You adjust the Detail (0-10) and Smoothness Sliders (0-10). Altering the settings can make the chrome appear more liquid. Refer to Figure 8-41.

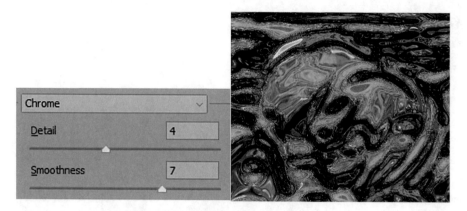

Figure 8-41. *Examples of Sketch filters: Chrome with filter settings*

Stamp and Torn Edges create images that are either black or white with no grayscale blend. Refer to Figure 8-42.

Figure 8-42. *Examples of Sketch filters: Stamp and Torn Edges*

Water Paper is the only color filter in this folder and is good for creating a fibrous blurred watercolor effect. Refer to Figure 8-43.

Figure 8-43. *Example of Sketch filters: Water Paper*

■ **Note** Except for Chrome and Water Paper, all the other filters in this folder, based on what your current foreground and background colors are in your Tools panel, affect the colors as you use the filter. The foreground appears to control the shadows or darker areas of the current Stamp image and the background controls the highlights and brighter colors. Refer tov Figure 8-44.

Figure 8-44. *The foreground and background colors currently in the Tools panel effect the Stamp filter*

See notes on Artistic folder and Diffuse Glow in the Distort folder and how background and foreground colors affect them.

Stylize Folder

Only one filter exists in this area, Glowing Edges. With the sliders, you can set the Edge Width (1-14), Edge Brightness (0-20), and Smoothness (1-15). Refer to Figure 8-45.

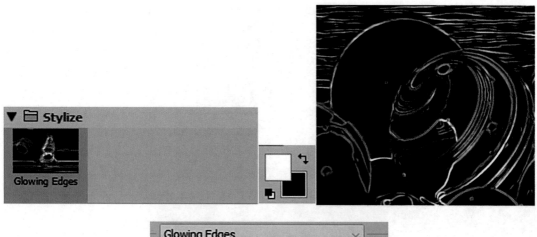

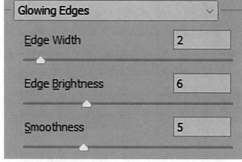

Figure 8-45. *Example of Stylize filter: Glowing Edges and its settings, and the current foreground and background colors in the Tools panel*

Texture Folder

The last folder is the Texture folder. It contains six filters: Craquelure, Grain, Mosaic Tiles, Patchwork (tiles), Stained Glass and Texturizer. Refer to Figure 8-46 and Figure 8-47.

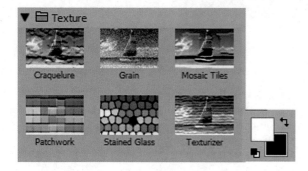

Figure 8-46. *Texture filters. Some are affected by the current foreground and background colors in the Tools panel*

Figure 8-47. *Examples of Texture filters: Craquelure, Grain, Mosaic Tiles, Patchwork, Stained Glass, and Texturizer*

Stained glass, though it does not have any extra options for texture, is interesting as it does let you create an almost organic cell-like structure. Use the sliders to adjust Cell Size (2-50) and Border Thickness (1-20). The border color is the current foreground color in the Tools panel. Light Intensity (0-10) is radial from the center of the image. See the note earlier for Diffuse Glow to know how to change your background or foreground color for a smart filter. Refer to Figure 8-47 and Figure 8-48.

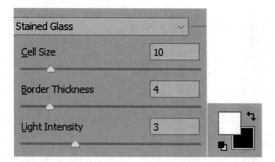

Figure 8-48. *Stained Glass options are affected by the current foreground color*

Adjusting Textures

With most of these filters you are limited by the menu as to what texture you can use to create depth. However, Texturizer, besides allowing you to use its default textures (Brick, Burlap, Canvas and Sandstone), does allow you to use your own custom texture. Refer to Figure 8-49.

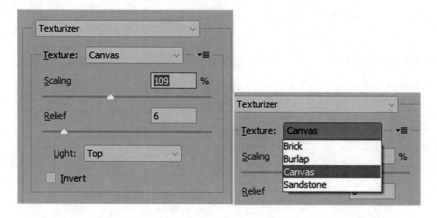

Figure 8-49. *Texturizer allows you to alter its settings and set a default texture*

To review the process of how a grayscale custom texture could be created, see the section in Chapter 3 and then follow the next steps to review how it can be created. In this case, we will use a copy of that texture, found in the Chapter 8 folder. See file Pattern4_Texture.psd. Next, we will load the texture and see if what we created then is working correctly in the Filter Gallery. Refer to Figure 8-50.

Figure 8-50. *We can use a grayscale texture that was created in Chapter 3*

Project: Loading a Custom Texture to Create Another Distortion

After reviewing Chapter 3, make sure that you have located the grayscale texture you created, and from the drop-down menu, choose Load texture from the Texturizer menu. Refer to Figure 8-51.

Figure 8-51. *Load a custom texture for the Texturizer filter*

In the Load Texture dialog box locate the pattern I am using, the one in the Chapter 8 project folder called Pattern4_Texture.psd. Refer to Figure 8-52.

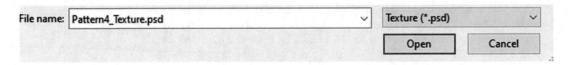

Figure 8-52. *Locate the texture .psd file and then click open in the dialog box and apply it*

Select the file and click Open. This overlays that repeating pattern.

Take a moment to scale the pattern (50-200%) and adjust the relief (0-50). I set the Scaling to 55% and the Relief to 31. Refer to Figure 8-53.

Set the Light to Top. There are several options to choose from to set your lighting angle, either to the bottom, left, right, top, or somewhere in between.

Enabled the Invert check box. This affects whether the texture is embossed or debossed. Refer to Figure 8-53.

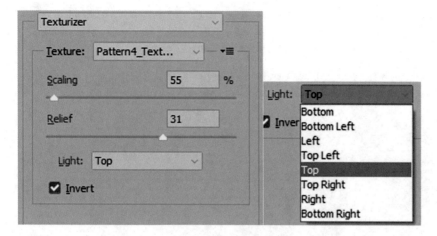

Figure 8-53. *Texturizer options and Light settings*

This creates a stitched quilt effect that covers the image.Refer to Figure 8-54.

Figure 8-54. *An extra line is appearing in the texture that should not be there*

However, if you zoom in close, you may notice an issue that does not seem to go away no matter what settings you use.

Correcting Textures

A slight issue with this custom pattern texture is that there is a thin black or white pixilated line appearing horizontally where each part of the pattern tiles or joins. But it does not appear vertically unless you change the lighting direction. When we created it in Chapter 3, it appeared OK, and if used as a pattern fill for an adjustment layer, you would not notice any dark border seam issue or, at the very least, it would appear that each square is touching the other, creating a block pattern. Refer to Figure 8-55.

Figure 8-55. *The texture file looks OK as a .psd, but not when it's a texture in the Filter Gallery*

However, in the Filter Gallery, Photoshop adds a pixelated edge to one side, creating an annoying thin horizontal grid even though there are no black pixels along the edge of the original pattern. To correct this issue, exit the Filter Gallery without making changes. Click Cancel to exit the Filter Gallery. Refer to Figure 8-56.

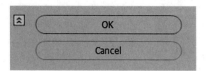

Figure 8-56. *Click Cancel to exit the Filter Gallery to correct the texture file*

Now File ➤ Open your texture currently in your Chapter 8 project folder, Pattern4_Texture.psd. Make an Image ➤ Duplicate. As in Chapter 3 with your colorful pattern, to ensure that your pattern is seamless, go to Filter ➤ Other ➤ Offset and set the Horizontal to +418 pixels right, Vertical +359 pixels down, and Undefined Areas to Wrap Around. And click OK. Refer to Figure 8-57.

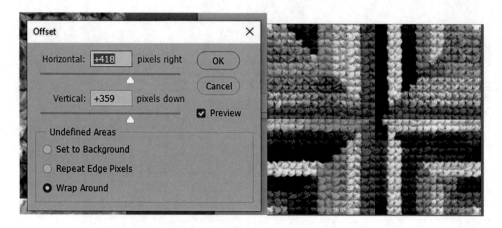

Figure 8-57. *Use the Offset filter on a copy of the texture to correct the seam*

Create a new blank layer for working on. Refer to Figure 8-58.

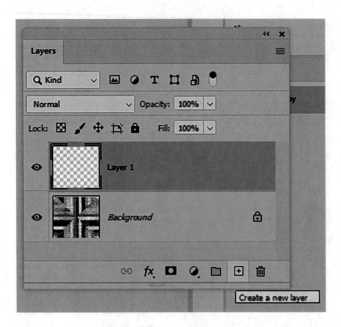

Figure 8-58. *In the Layers panel, create a new layer*

Then use your Clone Stamp tool, as you did in Chapter 3, and Alt/Option+Click a clone location and then, on the new layer, click and cover the seam so that the threads blend in; it does not have to be perfect as it will be in black and white. I used a 39px soft brush (Hardness 0%). Sample Options are set to Current & Below. Refer to Figure 8-59.

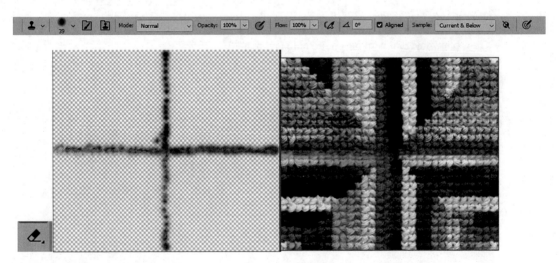

Figure 8-59. *Use your Clone Stamp and Eraser tools on a new layer to cover the seam*

You can use your Eraser tool with a soft brush if you need to clean up any fibers.

Then, when you're done using the Layers panel menu, flatten the image so that it is a single background layer again. Refer to Figure 8-60.

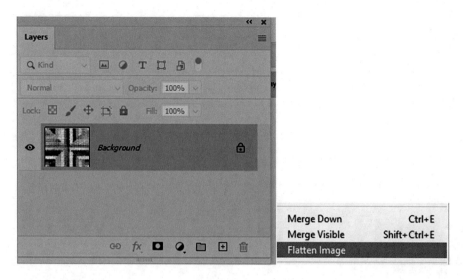

Figure 8-60. Once complete, use your Layers panel menu to flatten the image again

File ➤ Save this copy file as a .psd file. I saved mine as Pattern4_Texture_r2.psd so that I could compare. Close the file.

Return to your copy of your file water_feature_start copy. Make sure you are still on the smart object layer.

Go to the Filter Gallery again and return to the Texturizer filter. This time, load the new texture you created. The strange horizontal black line should be gone, and the overall pattern should be seamless. Refer to Figure 8-61.

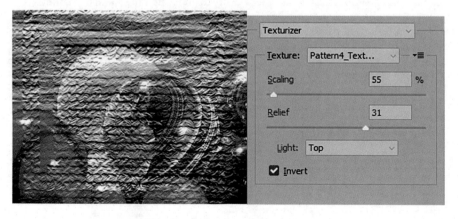

Figure 8-61. Apply the new texture to the Texturizer filter

■ **Note** This may not be an issue for all texture patterns that you build. However, this is why you must test your custom textures in the Filter Gallery after creating them and zoom in close to preview any issues if they arise. In this case, the Offset filter and Clone Stamp were the best way to correct the issue on a copy of the original file.

■ **Tip** Try this same texture on the Glass, Rough Pastels, Underpainting, or Conté Crayon filters.

You can see how a custom texture adds interest to a background.

More information about filters in the smart gallery can be found here: `https://helpx.adobe.com/photoshop/using/filter-basics.html` and `https://helpx.adobe.com/photoshop/using/filter-effects-reference.html`.

Combining Gallery Filters

After setting your options with the sliders for your filter and before clicking OK, you can choose to add another filter. Refer to Figure 8-62.

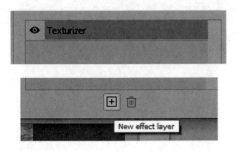

Figure 8-62. *Currently only one filter is applied in the Filter Gallery, but you can add more with the New effect layer button*

Click the New layer effect button (plus icon) in the Filter Gallery to duplicate a filter, and then from either the folders or the dropdown menu, choose another filter such as Brush Strokes ➤ Crosshatch and see how this enhances the effect. Refer to Figure 8-63.

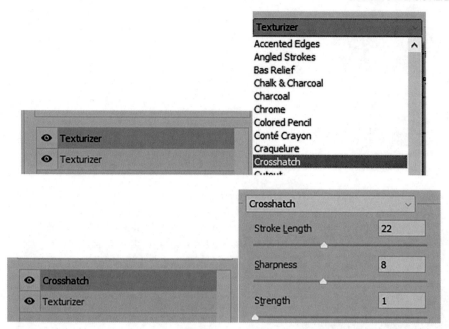

Figure 8-63. *Once a filter is duplicated, you can then select another filter to change it and then alter its options*

Any combination of filters can be changed to another once it is selected in the list. But not all work well together. Refer to Figure 8-64.

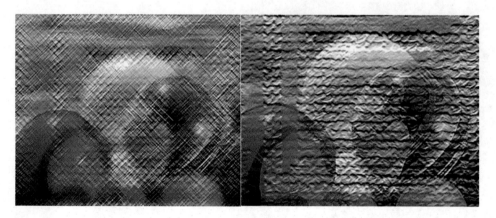

Figure 8-64. *Applying more than one filter can affect how the preview image appears*

You can drag one filter above or below another and see if it improves the effect. And turn on or off the visibility eyes. Refer to Figure 8-65.

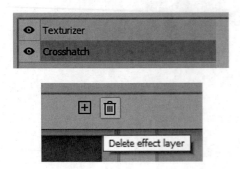

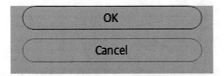

Figure 8-65. *You can change the filter order or delete a filter effect layer*

If you don't like a filter effect, you can select it and use the trash can icon to delete a filter or effect layer.

Once you have made your choices, click OK to exit the Filter Gallery. The filter is added as a smart filter to the smart object in the Layers panel. Refer to Figure 8-66.

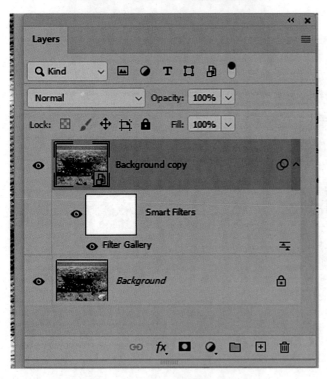

Figure 8-66. *Click OK and your smart filter is added to the layer*

As you did in Chapters 6 and 7, you can double-click the Filter name to enter the Filter Gallery to alter your settings or to reset and create a new Filter Gallery. Choose Filter ➤ Filter Gallery, as mentioned earlier, when you need to correct your background and foreground colors. See Diffused Glow.

Adjusting Filter Masks

The smart filter mask is for all smart filters regardless of if they are inside or outside the Filter Gallery, and you can turn off the visibility eye for both the mask or filter to compare the before and after. Refer to Figure 8-67.

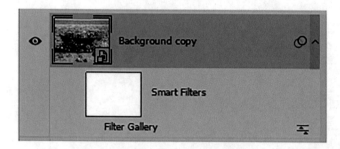

Figure 8-67. *Turn off the visibility for both the filter and the filter mask when you don't want to see them*

Click the smart filter mask and now look at the Properties panel Masks tab icon. If you have worked with layers and masks in the past, you will know that this is where you can add an additional vector mask after your layer mask has been added to your normal or smart object layer. As mentioned in Chapter 6, as with the layer mask and vector mask, you can make adjustments to the filter mask after painting on the filter mask using the sliders for Density (0-100%) and Feather (0-1000 pixels). You can use two of the Refine Selection Options: Color Range for a more accurate selection based on color and invert to reverse the selection. However, Select and Mask are grayed out and can only be used for layer masks. Refer to Figure 8-68.

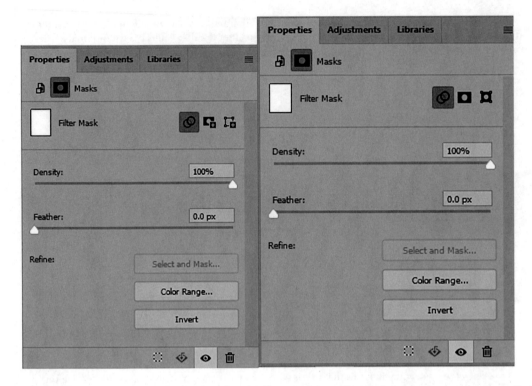

Figure 8-68. *Use the Properties panel to alter the filter mask as well as the layer and vector masks applied to a layer*

Isolating a Selection on a Smart Filter Mask

To keep your smart filter isolated to a select location before you apply the filter, you can drag out a selection with a selection tool such as the Rectangular Marquee tool or load a selection from your Channels panel (Ctrl/CMD+Click the Channel thumbnail). The smart object layer is selected first before entering the Filter Gallery and this will add that mask to the filter mask when you click OK. Refer to Figure 8-69.

Figure 8-69. *You can create an isolated area or selection on your smart filter that hides part of the filter*

Then, if the selection is the reverse of what you expect, select the smart filter mask and use the key combination Ctrl/CMD+I to invert the mask or press the Invert button in the Properties panel. Refer to Figure 8-70.

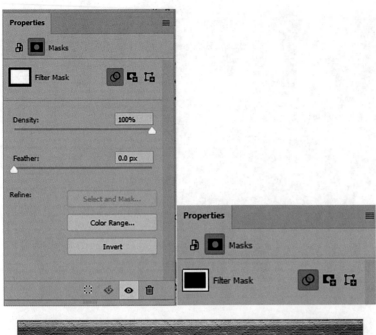

Figure 8-70. *Use your Properties panel to invert part of the mask*

Like a layer mask, a filter mask allows you to use the selection tools that I talk about in my other book, *Accurate Layer Selections Using Photoshop's Selection Tools*. From the menu, you can set the filter mask's color and opacity masking options. This color mask is visible when the visibility eye in the Channels panel is turned on. Refer to Figure 8-71 and Figure 8-72.

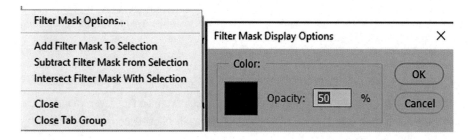

Figure 8-71. *Your Properties panel menu has additional filter mask options when that mask is selected*

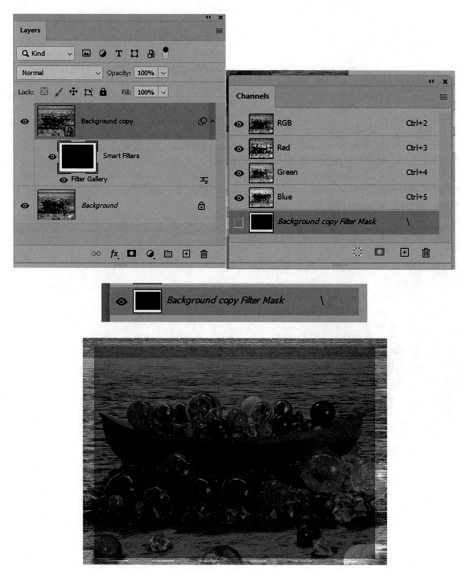

Figure 8-72. *The mask, when selected, appears in the Channels panel and can be used to create a selection or view in mask mode*

Here you can see I earlier used the Rectangular Marquee tool on my smart filter mask and made a selection. That same selection appears in the Channels panel. Turn off the visibility eye of that channel if you do not what to see the red mask. Refer to Figure 8-72.

■ **Note**   A smart filter mask only covers over parts of the filter on a smart object layer and does not target one specific area of the image. If you want to apply a filter to a targeted selection area on the layer, you need to work on a normal layer rather than a smart object layer, although doing so, as mentioned, permanently effects the layer, so work on a layer copy if you need to keep the original.

Smart Filter Blending Modes

One other feature of smart filters is that they can have a separate blending mode applied and this can be altered when you click the filter-blending mode options icon and then when you double-click it to enter the dialog box. This dialog box is for the Filter Gallery. You can set a Blend mode and Opacity (0-100%) options. They are separate from the layer bending mode. In this case, I changed my blend mode from Normal to Difference. See Chapter 2 for more details on Blending Modes. You can also go to this link: https://helpx.adobe.com/photoshop/using/blending-modes.html.

Alter the options and then click OK to commit. Refer to Figure 8-73 and Figure 8-74.

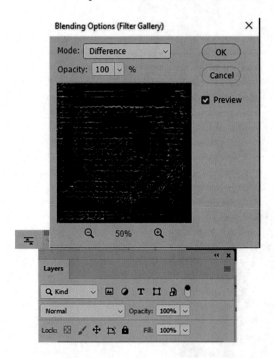

Figure 8-73. *Most filters can have their own separate blending modes and opacity options*

Figure 8-74. *An altered blending mode of a filter could be used as a type of a border on an image*

■ **Note** If you are using a normal layer, alternatively exiting the gallery, you could use Edit ➤ Fade but this is destructive, while the blending options for smart object layers can be entered and adjusted anytime. Refer to Figure 8-75.

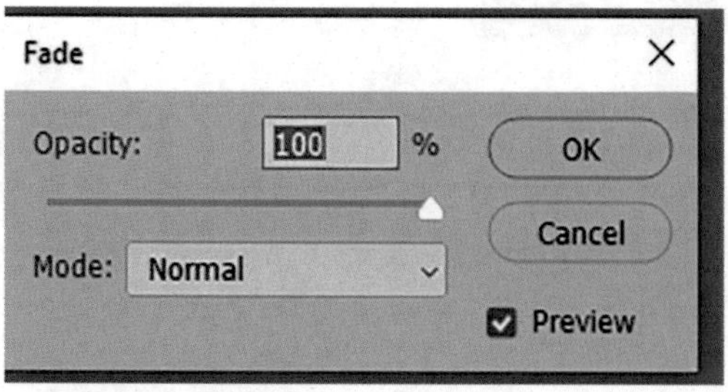

Figure 8-75. *When working on normal layers, you can use the Edit ➤ Fade option to effect a blending mode after applying a filter*

683

■ **Tip** In some situations, rather than piling all your filters from the gallery into one Filter Gallery set, you may want to create a Filter Gallery separately for each filter and see if this produces different results as well as separate blending modes. Refer to Figure 8-76.

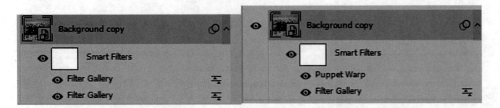

Figure 8-76. *You can apply some filters more than once, and some filters will not have the blending mode option*

It should be noted that not all filters outside of the Filter Gallery have additional blending modes (see Puppet Warp, Perspective Warp, or Blur Gallery). When used in combination and upon entering another filter, you may see this warning message. They may be disabled temporarily while you adjust the blend mode or another filter. Refer to Figure 8-77.

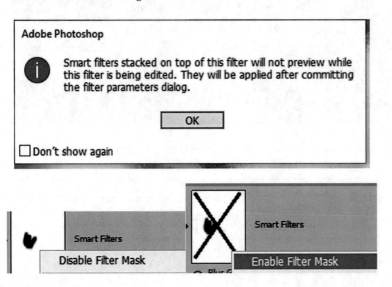

Figure 8-77. *Some filters will be disabled when entering another smart filter, and you can disable and enable the smart filter mask*

You can also temporarily disable a filter mask by right-clicking it. Right-click it again to enable it. Refer to Figure 8-77.

■ **Note**   If you drag your filter mask to the Layers panel trash icon by mistake, you can either go a step back in your History panel to return to the original mask or right-click the smart filter and choose Add Filter Mask and this will add a new filter mask. Refer to Figure 8-78.

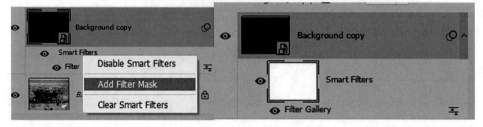

Figure 8-78. *If a smart filter mask is deleted, you can restore it using your History panel or the Layers panel pop-up menu*

File ➤ Save your .psd document at this point. We will use other images for demonstrations of the filter mask. See my water_feature_final.psd file

Basic Filters Continued

Now we will look at filters that are not part of the Filter Gallery but still can be added as smart filters for smart object layers.

We will not be looking at 3D filters as they are not the topic of this book. For working with the filters Adaptive Wide Angle, Camera Raw Filter, Lens Correction, Liquify, see Chapter 9. For working with Vanishing Point and Neural Filters, see Chapter 10. Refer to Figure 8-79.

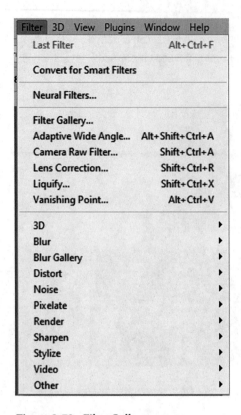

Figure 8-79. *Filter Gallery menu*

Blur (Radial Blur and Shape Blur)

Like the Blur tool in Chapter 2, most blurring is done for cosmetic reason to hide an area of a picture or make it appear hazy. The Blur submenu has several ways to blur an image:

- **Average (no dialog box)**: Finds the average color

- **Blur (no dialog box)**: Removes noise where major color transition occurs

- **Blur More (no dialog box)**: Like blur, but 3-4 times stronger

- **Box Blur**: Creates a box-like blur based on colors of neighboring pixels radius (1-2000), based on an adjustable amount

- **Gaussian Blur**: An overall blur and smoothing of the image based on an adjustable amount of radius (0.1-1000 px)

- **Lens Blur**: Cannot work with smart objects and is a workspace to create more complex blurs using a depth map (none, transparency, layer mask, channel) to create a narrow-field depth. Additional options of Iris, Specular Highlights, Noise, and Distribution are used enhance the blur. For settings to work with smart object layers with a similar blur, refer to the Filter ➤ Blur Gallery. See the "Blur Gallery Workspace" section of this chapter for more details.

- **Motion Blur**: Used to create an angled blur in motion, based on an adjustable amount of distance (1-2000 px) and angle (-180, 0, 180)

- **Radial Blur**: The blur radiates out from the center, based on a set method. See the "Radial Blur" section of this chapter for more details.

- **Shape Blur**: Custom shapes create blur, based on an adjustable amount of radius. See the "Shape Blur" section of this chapter for more details.

- **Smart Blur**: Dialog allows for more options to blur so that the blur is more accurate, based on an adjustable amount of radius (0.1-100), threshold (0.1-100), quality (low, medium, high), and mode options (Normal, Edge Only, Overlay Edge).

- **Surface Blur**: Assists in blurring the surface of areas of the image, but attempts to preserve edges, based on an adjustable amount of radius in pixels (1-100) and threshold levels (2-255)

However, other than blurring an image, most are not very useful when warping and distorting. Only two in this section stand out for that purpose: Radial Blur and Shape Blur. Refer to Figure 8-80.

Figure 8-80. *Blur filters*

Radial Blur

This filter does not come with a preview, but if you are working with a smart object layer, you can enter the smart filters as many times as you need to get it to the settings you need.

Set the Amount (1-100) and observe how the blur center preview changes. Higher numbers create a greater blur.

Set the blur method using the radio buttons to either spin to blur along the concentric lines or zoom (like motion blur out from the center).

Then adjust the amount and then set the Quality to Draft, Good, or Best for a smoother blur. Draft will add a bit of noise or graininess to the blur. Best may take longer to render so I left it on the default setting of Good, which looks the same as best. The point of blur origin can be move by dragging around the blur center pattern.

Hold down the Alt/Option key when you want to reset the current options and the blur center and click OK to exit the dialog box. You can use this reset option for other filters as well. Refer to Figure 8-81.

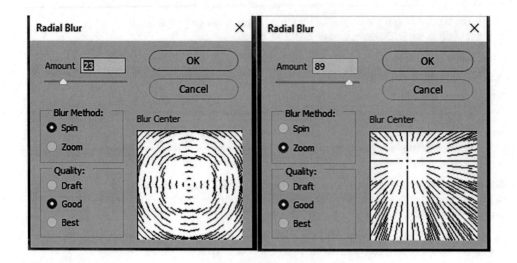

Figure 8-81. *Radial Blur options*

In this example, I experimented with a copy of the file star_plate_start.psd and tried various blurs on the smart object layer, changing the point of origin. Refer to Figure 8-82 and Figure 8-83.

Figure 8-82. *Effects of the Radial Blur on a plate of paper stars*

Figure 8-83. *Quality settings of the Radial Blur of Draft, Good, and Best*

■ **Tip**   If you have entered (double-click) and exited the smart filter several times and made adjustments, you can also use your History Panel to go back several smart filter steps if you want to reset to an original state. This is true for other smart object filters as well. Refer to Figure 8-84.

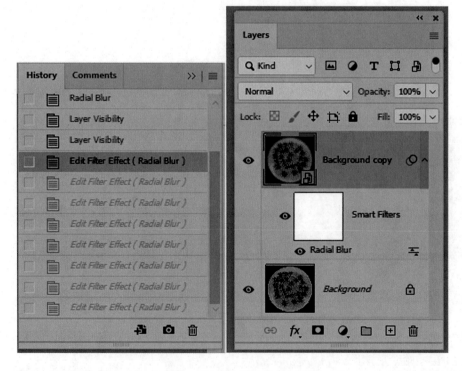

Figure 8-84. *Reset your Radial Blur using the History panel if you have entered the dialog box several times*

Shape Blur

Shape Blur is a newer blur that you may not have tried before. It creates a blur based on shapes called kernels, found in the Shapes panel. See Chapter 3. Shapes can be selected from the folders or imported using the gear dropdown menu.

Not all shapes work well for Shape Blur. The simpler and more basic the shape, the better the blur. With others you may see no difference between a complex shape and a regular blur, depending on the radius settings chosen 5-1000px.

For example, a blur with the legacy default shapes of diagonal lines, grid lines, or circles and a blur radius of 300-500 pixels will make the blur more distinct while other blurs will show no distinct visible result other than a blur.

Make sure that the Preview check box is enabled while working and the click OK to commit changes and exit the dialog box. Refer to Figure 8-85.

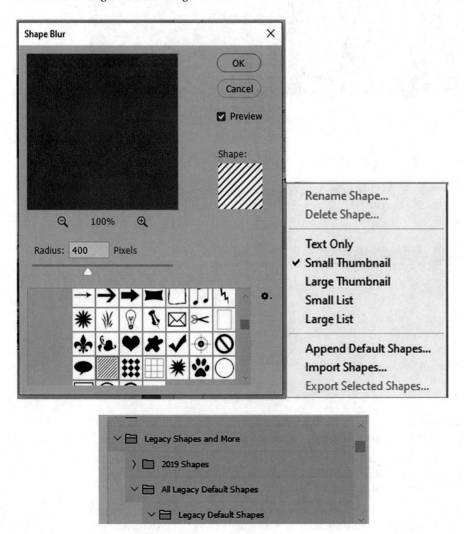

Figure 8-85. *Shape Blur dialog box and its settings and shapes from the Shapes panel*

691

Again, I used a copy of star_plate_start.psd and tried various shapes at a radius of about 400 pixels. Refer to Figure 8-86.

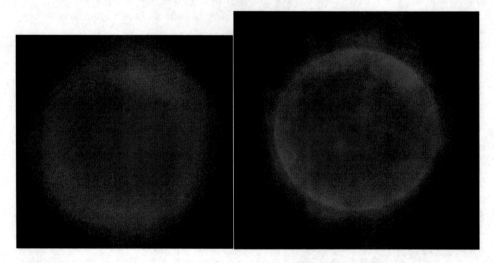

***Figure 8-86.** Examples of the plate of stars affected by blurs of diagonal lines and circles*

Blur Gallery Workspace (Spin Blur, Path Blur)

As mentioned, the Blur Gallery can be used on smart objects and has more features than the Lens Blur, which only works with normal layers. I will use a copy of star_plate_start.psd and select the smart object layer. Refer to Figure 8-87.

***Figure 8-87.** Blur Gallery filters in the submenu*

Five different blurs can be found in the Blur Gallery workspace:

- **Field Blur**: Blurs out the whole image from the center field. This can be set multiple times in different locations. The blur range is 0-500 px.

- **Iris Blur**: Keeps the elliptical inner center field clear, but everything else around is blurred. This sets a shallow depth field and can be set multiple times in different locations. The blur range is 0-500 px.

- **Tilt-Shift**: A straight plain or angled area remains clear but then blurs outward. It is like a tilt-shift lens and is used in the simulation of miniature items. It can be set multiple times in different locations. The blur range is 0-500 px, distortion is (-100, 0, 100%) and you can enable or disable symmetric distortion for both directions of the blur.

- **Path Blur**: Like Motion Blur, this directs the angle of the blur along a path. See the section on Path Blur for more details.

- **Spin Blur**: Like radial blur, but more accurate and you can preview while you work. See the section on Spin Blur for more details.

All five blurs are found together in the Blur Gallery workspace, and you can use them together on a single image. In this case, we will use Spin Blur and later look at Path Blur.

As the workspace opens, you will notice that it has an Options panel along the top and a Blur Tools panel on the right and additional panels for Effects, Motion Effects, and Noise. Refer to Figure 8-88.

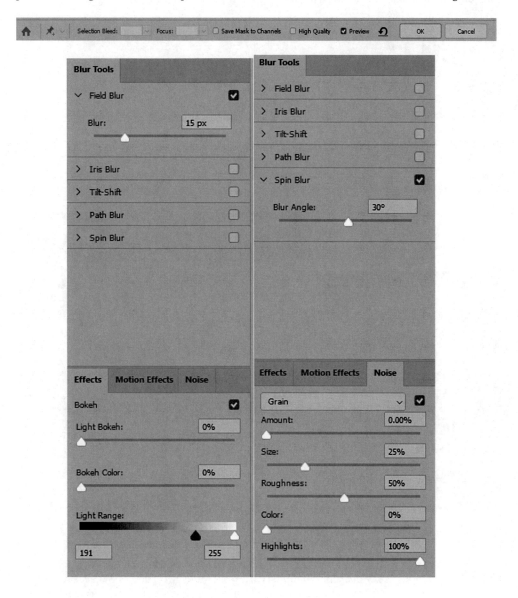

Figure 8-88. *Options panel and other panels found in the Blur Gallery*

First, to create any blur, make sure to enable the check box in the Blur Tool panel that you want to work with. Then you need to set a pin somewhere on the preview and adjust the setting for that blur. By default, one pin will be set for you. Uncheck any blur types you don't want to use or hide. In this case, let's check the Spin Blur first. Refer to Figure 8-88.

Spin Blur

Spin Blur is much more accurate than Radial Blur in that you can set a very specific area that you want to spin and set the Blur Angle of 0-360°. Refer to Figure 8-89.

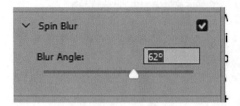

Figure 8-89. *Spin Blur options*

Or use the blur ring controls surrounding the pin on the preview and drag to increase the tightness of the spin. Refer to Figure 8-90.

Figure 8-90. *A spin blur is applied to the center of the star plate and the blur ring altered*

You can also scale the spin with the square handle. And rotate the spin on the circle handles and make it more angled and flatten by adjusting the ellipse boundary. The four inner larger circles will also allow you to scale the blur. The angle ring in the center rotation point will also allow you to adjust the blur angle as you drag on it. Refer to Figure 8-91.

Figure 8-91. *Modifying the blur ring*

Additionally, you can pin other areas to spin by clicking in other locations. Refer to Figure 8-92.

Figure 8-92. *Adding more spin blurs to the image when the cursor changes to a pin with a plus symbol*

Select a spin by clicking in the center of the spin and dragging to move it. To remove a spin while selected, press the Backspace/Delete key. To duplicate a spin, Alt/Option +Ctrl/CMD+Drag to create a copy. Refer to Figure 8-93.

Figure 8-93. *Use the blur ring to alter the spin or drag it off center*

Alt/Option+Drag will move a rotation point off center. Refer to Figure 8-93. Hold down the H key to hide the controls and pins.

■ **Tip**   Use Ctrl/CMD+Z to undo steps, and as with other workspaces, you can use your key combinations of Ctrl/CMD+-, Ctrl/CMD++, and the Hand tool (spacebar) to get closer, farther away, and control navigation in the preview.

As mentioned, when you want to hide the blurs, use the checkbox to turn the blur on or off as you preview it in the workspace. Refer to Figure 8-94.

Figure 8-94. *Spin Blur enabled and Spin Blur disabled*

There are several panels that are available as well.

Effects Panel

The Effects panel that appears is not available to Spin or Path Blur. It is only enabled for the blurs of Field, Iris, and Tilt-Shift. It is for working with Light Bokeh: (0-100%), Bokeh Color:(0-100%), and Light Range:(0-255) settings when those blurs are enabled with the checkbox. Refer to Figure 8-95.

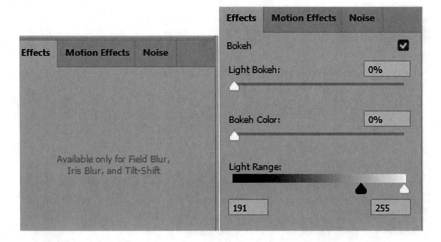

Figure 8-95. *The Spin Blur Effects panel is disabled here but is available for other filters using Bokeh*

When rendering out-of-focus points of light using Bokeh options, you must consider what is pleasing or displeasing to the eye. Some tips about Bokeh can be found here: www.adobe.com/creativecloud/ photography/discover/bokeh-effect.html.

Noise Panel

The Noise panel lets you, from the Dropdown menu, restore the noise/grain type of the blur for Spin Gaussian, Uniform, or Grain. You can disable this setting with the check box.

With the sliders, you can set the following options:

Amount: Of noise added to blurred areas (0-100%) to match the noise in non-blurred areas

Size: Of noise grain (0-100%)

Roughness: Or coarseness of noise grain texture (0-100%). Less than 50% the grain is more uniform and more than 50% the grain is less even.

Color: Variation added to the blurred area (0-100%) controls how the noise is colored. 0% is considered the least amount of color.

Highlights: Noise applied to the image highlights or reduced from highlights and shadow areas (0-100%). Refer to Figure 8-96.

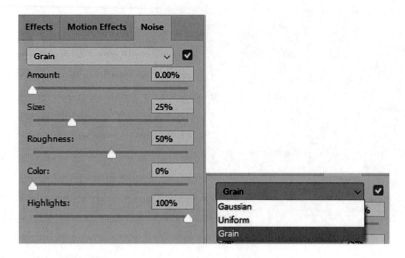

Figure 8-96. *Spin Blur Noise panel and it options*

Motion Effects Panel

The Motion effects panel allows you to set various slider options. Refer to Figure 8-97.

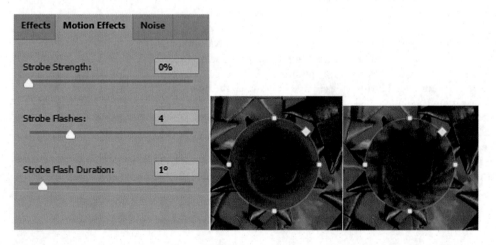

Figure 8-97. *The Blur Motion Effects Panel and its options can affect the blur based on slider settings*

Strobe Strength (0-100%): Controls the ratio of ambient light to strobe (flash) light, so 0% means no strobe and 100% means full strobe.

Strobe Flashes (1-100): Controls the number of strobe flash instances and alters the blur slightly.

Strobe Flash Duration (0-20 degrees): Adjusts the finite duration of each strobe flash for Spin Blur. The value is represented in amount of angle on the circumference of the blur circle.

For the moment, I will turn off and disabled the spin blur and then enabled the Path Blur. Refer to Figure 8-98.

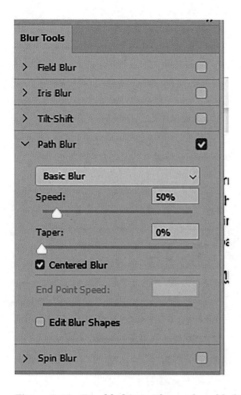

Figure 8-98. *Disabled Spin Blur and enabled Path Blur*

Path Blur

For Path Blur, the settings can be a Basic Blur, Rear Sync Flash blur, or custom on a created custom path or paths. Refer to Figure 8-99.

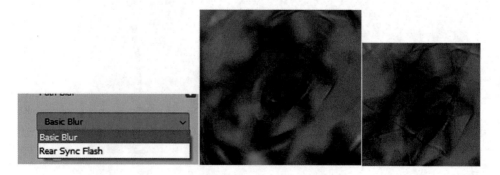

Figure 8-99. *Path Blur settings of Basic Blur and Rear Sync Flash*

Click the preview and then click and drag to create a path curve and double-click to exit the created path. You will find this very similar to working with the Pen tool, as in Chapter 3. Refer to Figure 8-100.

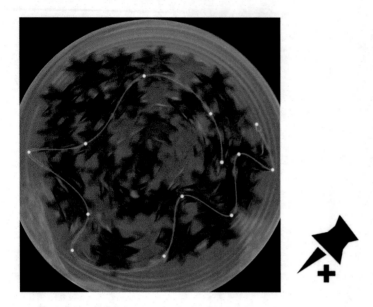

Figure 8-100. *Click with the pin cursor to add and then edit paths*

Notice how the blur warp now follows a path.

You can then set additional settings such as the speed to control the blur amount for all paths from 0-500%. Refer to Figure 8-101.

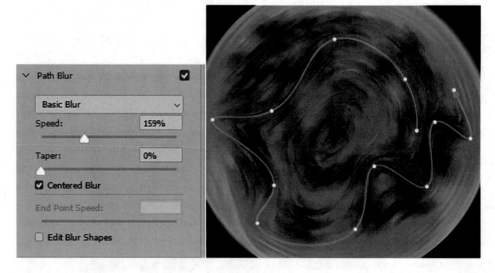

Figure 8-101. *The Path Blur setting can alter the preview of the blur*

Taper: Adjust the fading edges of the blur (0-100%). Refer to Figure 8-102.

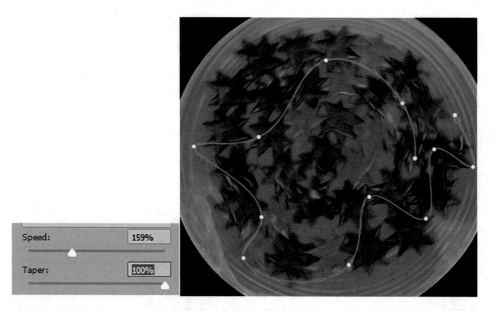

Figure 8-102. *Path Blur setting adjusted for Speed and Taper*

Centered Blur: When enabled, it samples from both sides of pixel; when disabled, it's from one side of pixel. Refer to Figure 8-103.

End point speed: Controls the blur amount for a selected end point and the ability to edit the blur shape at its end point when the Edit Blur Shapes check box is enabled. Range is 0-2000 px. Refer to Figure 8-103.

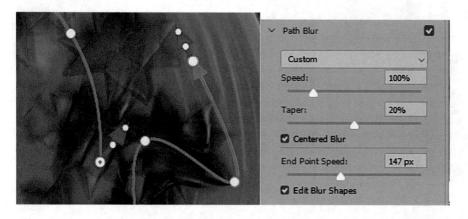

Figure 8-103. *Red arrowheads for Blur shape editing, based on the setting for the Path Blur*

Edit Blur Shapes: Shows and controls the editable blur shape at each end point. This must be enabled for End Point Speed to be adjusted. Refer to Figure 8-103.

Here are some additional tips for working in the Blur Gallery:

- Drag part of a path and end point, the blue or red arrow, if you want to lengthen part of the blur path. Alt/Option+Click on a point to change it from curved to corner point and back. Refer to Figure 8-104.

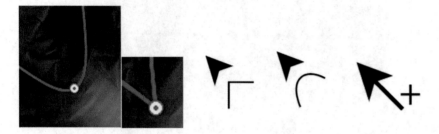

Figure 8-104. *Alter the points on the path from square to curved or add points*

- Click the path to add more points when the arrow adds a plus symbol. Refer to Figure 8-104.

- To remove a single selected point on a path or the whole path, select and press the Backspace/Delete key.

- Shift+Click and Drag on the red blur arrows to blur the shape and path together. Refer to Figure 8-105.

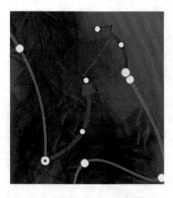

Figure 8-105. *Alter the red blur arrow by dragging on it*

- Ctrl/CMD+Clicking on a point will set the end point speed of the blur back to 0%. Ctrl/CMD+Click again to return it back to your settings. Refer to Figure 8-106.

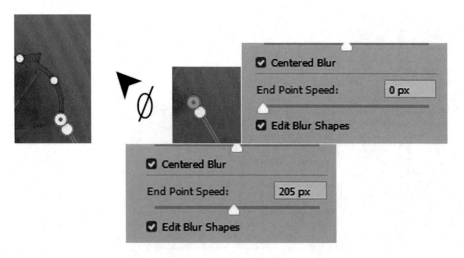

Figure 8-106. *Alter the end point speed of each side of the blur*

- Ctrl/CMD+Drag to move the blur path. To duplicate, use Ctrl/CMD+Alt/
  Option+Drag.

■ **Note**   All Noise Panel effects for Spin Blur are available for Path Blur. However, in the Motion Effects panel, all effects are available except Strobe Flash Duration. The Effects panel is not available. You can review those option details in the previous Spin Blur section. Refer to Figure 8-107.

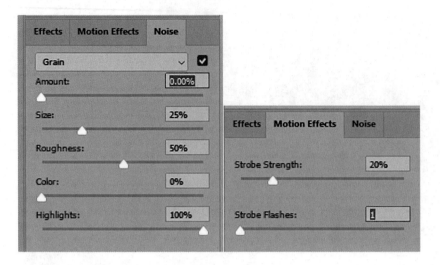

Figure 8-107. *Noise Panel setting for Path Blur*

For more details on other blur gallery settings for the other blurs (Field, Iris, and Tilt-Shift), refer to Figure 8-108 and visit `https://helpx.adobe.com/photoshop/using/blur-gallery.html`.

Figure 8-108. *You can enable or disabled other blurs as you work in the Blur Gallery*

Spin and Path Blur Options

In the Options panel for the Spin and Path Blurs, l do not have access to text boxes, Selection Bleed (the amount of blur that filters into selected regions), or Focus (1-100%) (the amount of blur in a protected region of a pin) when I am working on smart object layers for Iris and Tilt-Shift to affect focus; these are also for normal layers. Refer to Figure 8-109.

Figure 8-109. *Blur Gallery Options panel*

With the few other options available, you can save a copy of the blur mask to your channels panel. Hold down the M key to preview the mask while the blurs are active. Refer to Figure 8-110.

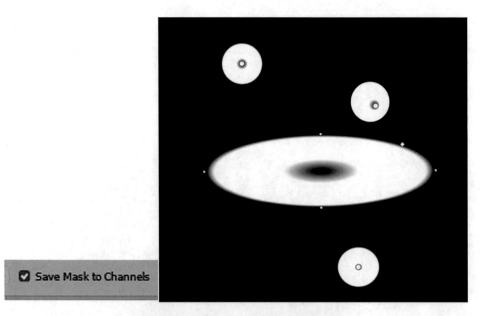

Figure 8-110. *Enable the option to save your Blur Gallery mask to the Channels panel*

This channel can later be turned into a layer mask that you can use to enhance the area of your image, using adjustment layers. I will uncheck the box for now as I don't need the selection.

Next, you can enable high quality for more accurate Bokeh, but this may affect performance. I left it unchecked as it is not relevant to these blurs. Make sure that Preview is enabled while you edit your blurs. Refer to Figure 8-111.

Figure 8-111. *The Blur Gallery Options panel lets you adjust quality, preview, and reset pins. Click OK or Cancel to exit the gallery*

The next button, resembling a counterclockwise arrow, is the Remove all pins button. It allows you to reset the blurs back to 0. Click OK to commit the blur or blurs or Cancel to exit.

When done make, sure both the path and Spin Blur are enabled. Click OK to exit and view the Layers panel and the final blurs of Spin and Path. Refer to Figure 8-112.

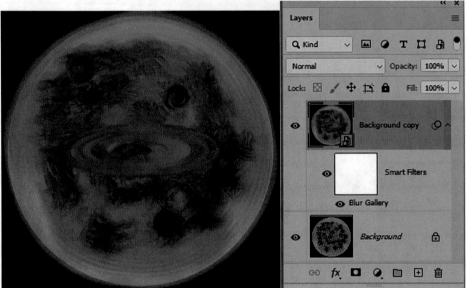

Figure 8-112. *Make sure your Path and Spin Blur are enabled if you want to see both as you exit the Blur Gallery*

■ **Tip** Just as you would with other smart filters (example: see Filter Gallery) or normal layers, you can load a selection prior to entering the Filter Gallery to restrain where the blur will be applied. This restriction will appear on the smart filter mask, showing only a portion of the blur. Refer to Figure 8-113.

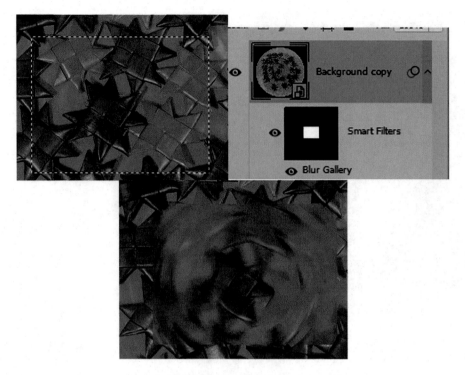

Figure 8-113. *Areas of the Blur Gallery are covered by the smart filter mask*

Distort Filters

Not to be confused with the Distort folder in the Filter Gallery, this area contains nine separate filters that you can use on your smart object layers.

Use an Image ➤ Duplicate of the file Glass_Start.psd and select the smart object layer to practice on. Refer to Figure 8-114.

Figure 8-114. *Use your smart object layer of broken glass to try different distorts*

Go to Filter ➤ Distort and choose either Displace, Pinch, Polar Coordinates, Ripple, Shear, Spherize, Twirl, Wave, or ZigZag. I will discuss each in more detail next. Refer to Figure 8-115.

Figure 8-115. *Distort filters*

■ **Note**   If you choose one after another on the same smart object layer, they will be added collectively.

Displace

Displace is used to move part of an image around to another location based on the horizontal or vertical scale. You can set the displacement map to Stretch to fit or Tile, then Undefined Areas, which can then be either Wrap Around or Repeat Edge Pixels. In this case, you need to have a displacement map created first for this to work. Click OK and then select a .psd file by navigating to it in the dialog box and click Open. See my project in Chapter 3 on how to create a texture for the Filter Gallery. You can use a similar grayscale image to create a displacement map. In this case, you do not need to use the Offset filter to correct the texture as you did in the Filter Gallery. Locate the file displace_map.psd and you can use it here for practice. Click Open and the filter is applied. Refer to Figure 8-116 and Figure 8-117.

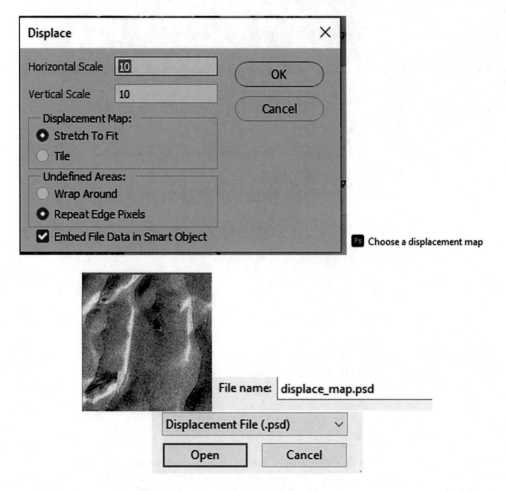

Figure 8-116. *Displace Dialog box and example of a grayscale displacement map and how to load the map*

709

Figure 8-117. *Before the displacement map and after adding the displacement map to the smart object layer example*

■ **Note**   For the smart object, the file data is embedded. Refer to Figure 8-116.

Pinch

The Pinch filter only has one slider to set the amount from -100 to 100% to either bring the pinch outward or inward from the center. In some ways, it is very similar to the Spherize filter, which we will look at in a moment. As you drag the slider, you can use the two previews to see how the pinch will look, and you can zoom in or out using the zoom navigation area or drag the image around to see how it previews before you click OK. This filter is not available for images larger than 11500 px by 11500 px. Refer to Figure 8-118.

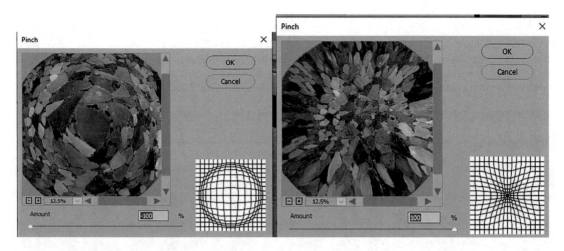

Figure 8-118. *Pinch filter dialog box options with a preview of a Pinch*

Polar Coordinates

Polar coordinates can either rotate or stretch an image out of proportion. There are only two options: rectangular to polar or polar to rectangular. You can use the zoom area to increase or decrease the level of zoom and drag around the preview screen to see the before and after. Choose an option and then click OK to commit. Refer to Figure 8-119.

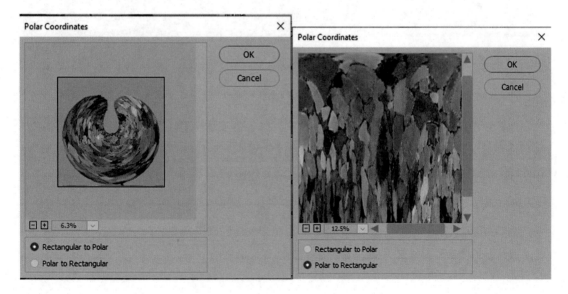

Figure 8-119. *Polar Coordinates filter dialog box options with a preview*

Ripple

In the Filter Gallery, you can find a similar ripple called Ocean Ripple. For greater control, refer to the Wave filter. This Ripple dialog box allows you to set the Amount: -999, 0, 999% and a Size of Small, Medium, or Large. You can use the zoom area to increase or decrease the level of zoom and drag move around the preview screen to see the before and after. Then click OK. Refer to Figure 8-120.

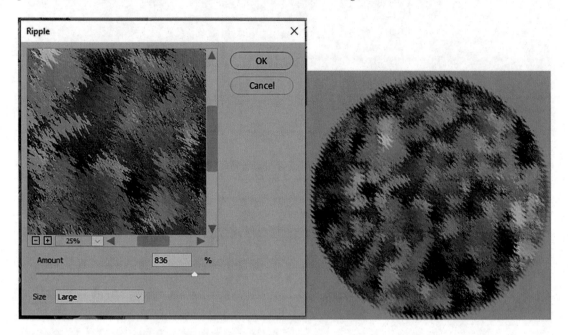

Figure 8-120. *Ripple filter dialog box options with a preview*

Shear

The Shear filter has some similarities to Transform ➤ Warp (Chapter 4) and Puppet Warp (Chapter 6) and lets you set an angled curve on a layer. You can set the undefined areas to either wrap around or repeat edge pixels. You can add more points to the shear and drag them to bend or drag off the grid to delete. The shear end points cannot be pulled upwards or downwards to join. Then click OK to exit. Refer to Figure 8-121.

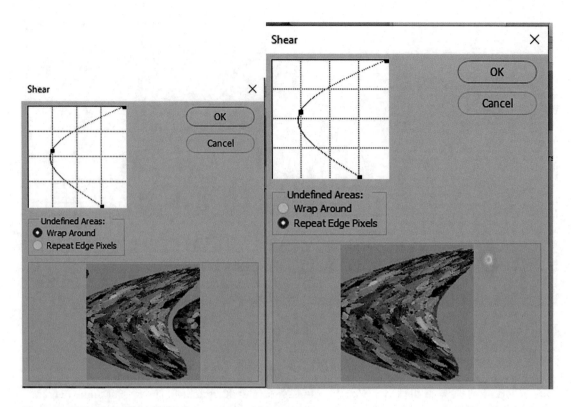

Figure 8-121. *Shear filter dialog box options with a preview*

Spherize

As mentioned, Spherize is like the Pinch filter where you can move the center inwards or outwards by dragging on the slider or typing in a percentage amount of -100, 0 ,100%. However, you can also set the Mode to Normal for the sphere shape or Horizontal Only or Vertical Only for a more rectangular stretch. You can use the zoom area to increase or decrease the level of zoom and drag to move around the preview screen to see a before and after. Then click OK. This filter is not available for images larger than 11500 px by 11500 px. Refer to Figure 8-122.

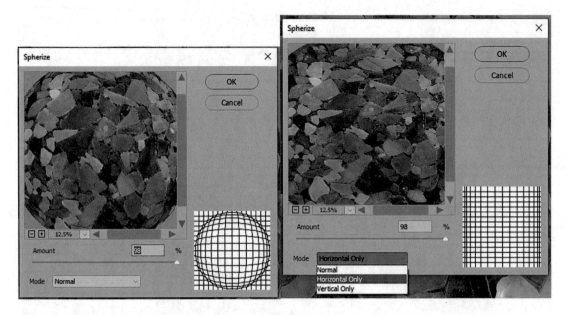

Figure 8-122. *Spherize filter dialog box options with Preview*

Twirl

The Twirl filter is in some way similar to the Spin Blurs and lets you spin the image without blurring, either counterclockwise (-999°) or clockwise (999°) by setting the angle with the slider. The twist becomes tighter in the center. You can use the zoom area to increase or decrease the level of zoom and drag move around the preview screen to see the before and after. Then click OK. This filter is not available for images larger than 11500 px by 11500 px. Refer to Figure 8-123.

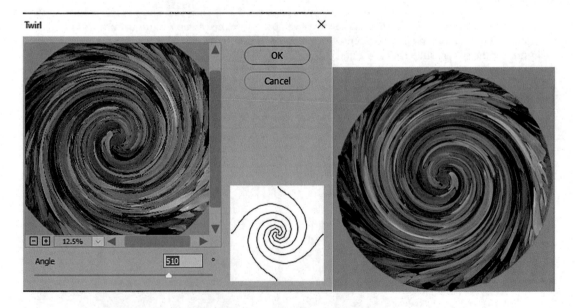

Figure 8-123. *Twirl filter dialog box options with a preview of clockwise and counterclockwise*

Wave

The Wave is the most complex of all the Distort filters and I find the most interesting. It's kind of like a visual sound wave. Refer to Figure 8-124.

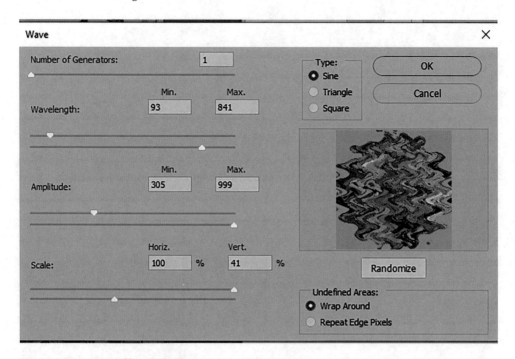

Figure 8-124. *Wave filter dialog box options with a preview*

Wave has three types: Sine, Triangle, and Square. Refer to Figure 8-124 and Figure 8-125. Once you choose a type, you can then set with the slider the following:

- **Number of Generators**: (1-999)

- **Wavelength**: Min (1-998) and Max (2-999)

- **Amplitude**: Min (1-998) and Max (2-999)

- **Scale**: Horizontal (1-100%) and Vertical (1-100%)

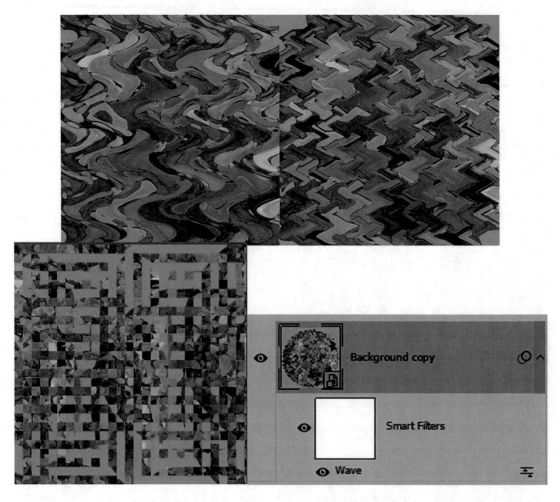

Figure 8-125. *Wave types of Sine, Triangle, and Square and a filter applied to the smart object layer*

You can then click the Randomize button as many times as you want to see the pattern change. There are many possibilities. Refer to Figure 8-124.

Then you can set the Undefined Areas to either Warp Around or Repeat Edge Pixels.

Then click OK to commit the changes.

ZigZag

The last filter in this area is ZigZag. It lets you set the Amount (-100, 0,100), Ridges (0-20) and Style: Around Center, Out from Center, and Pond Ripples. It has some similarities to the filters Spherize, Pinch, and Twirl. You can use the zoom area to increase or decrease the level of zoom and drag move around the preview screen to see the before and after. Then click OK to commit the changes. This filter is not available for images larger than 8000 px by 8000 px. Refer to Figure 8-126.

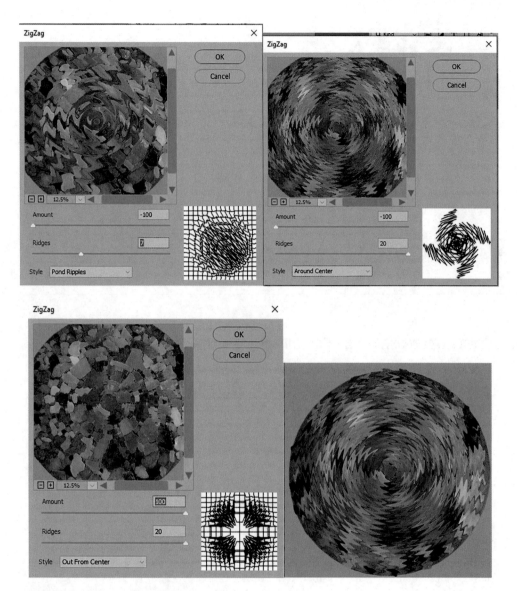

Figure 8-126. *ZigZag filter dialog box options with a preview*

Noise Filters

While useful for adding or removing noise from an image, the noise filters are not relevant to this chapter topic and are more for image touch up and do not create warps and distorts. They include Add Noise, Despeckle, Dust & Scratches, Median, and Reduce Noise. Some can blur, like Median, or even sharpen the image, like Reduce Noise. Except for Despeckle, all of these filters have dialog boxes that allow you to preview and adjust settings. Refer to Figure 8-127.

Figure 8-127. *Noise filters and an example of Add Noise*

■ **Note**   The Add Noise Filter was used in Chapter 5 for the clown poster and gave the cloth on the tent a textured effect.

Pixelate (Crystalize, Mosaic, and Pointillize)

Under Filter ➤ Pixelate are seven filters for color adjustment and distortion:

- **Color Halftone**: Creates a halftone dot effect with a Max radius (4-127 px), similar to a printed image with four channels screen angles for (CMYK) from an offset press. The dots are larger, more exaggerated, and create a screened effect or each print plate. This is sometimes used to simulate the feel of an image in a comic book. This filter has no preview so it's best to work with a smart object layer to make adjustments.

- **Crystalize**: Creates a blurry patterned effect, with detail based on cell size. See the Crystalize section of this chapter for more details.

- **Facet (no dialog box)**: Turns the pixels into a mottled effect as seen in some paintings, but in high-resolution images the filter is not that noticeable.

- **Fragment (no dialog box)**: Creates a more broken, blurry effect, like a mosaic, but in high-resolution images the filter is not that noticeable.

- **Mezzotint**: Turns the image into a random pattern of black, white, and highly saturated dots, lines, or strokes depending on the type chosen in the dialog box.

- **Mosaic**: Creates blur of square blocks. the detail is based on cell size. See the Mosaic section of this chapter for more details.

- **Pointilllize**: Randomly places dots. The detail is based on cell size. See the Pontilllize section of this chapter for more details. Refer to Figure 8-128.

Figure 8-128. *Pixelate filters*

Here are details on a few that I like to use for my distortions.

Crystalize

This filter is like some of the brush strokes in the Filter Gallery as well as Texture Stained Glass. You can adjust the cell size from 3-300. You can use the zoom area to increase or decrease the level of zoom and drag move around the preview screen so you can see a before and after. Then click OK to commit the settings and exit the dialog box. Refer to Figure 8-129.

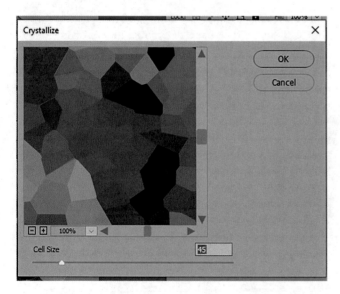

Figure 8-129. *Crystalize dialog box options and preview*

Mosaic

Like Patchwork in the Filter Gallery, you can set the cell size from 2-200 squares, and it is another way to blur images. You can use the zoom area to increase or decrease the level of zoom and drag move around the preview screen to see a before and after. Make sure Preview is checked if you want to see the preview on the canvas. Then click OK to commit the settings and exit the dialog box. Refer to Figure 8-130.

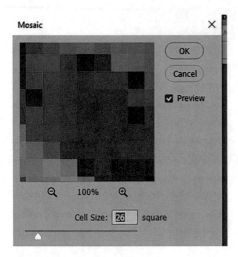

Figure 8-130. *Mosaic dialog box options and preview*

Pointillize

Similar to the Stained Glass filter in the Filter Galley and Crystalize, the shapes with the Pointillize filter are rounded and without a border. But the background color in the Tools panel determines the canvas color between dots. See the Filter Gallery on that topic. The cell size can be set from 3-300 and creates a random dot pattern and blurs the image. Refer to Figure 8-131.

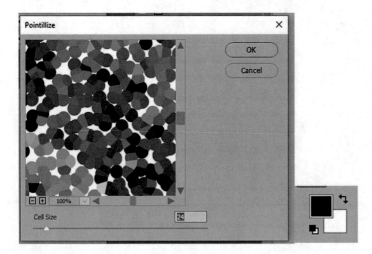

Figure 8-131. *Pointillize dialog box options and preview. The color is affected by the background color in the Tools panel*

Render Filters

Under Render filters this area is divided into two sections. I will point out how the first three filters in section one (Flame, Picture Frame, and Tree) can be used to create distorts and give a few tips on how to use them. However, these filters can only be used on a normal or background layer and not a smart object layer. Refer to Figure 8-132.

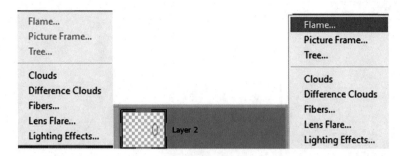

Figure 8-132. *Render filters cannot be used on smart object layers, only normal layers*

Flame

The Flame filter is very useful for creating fire-like effects for rockets and various burning effects where you want a lot of fire.

However, I also mentioned in this chapter you can warp a flame around a path or text turned into a path. Let's look at how this is done. To work with this filter, first some sort of path must be created using the Paths panel. Photoshop will warn you about this if you try to enter the filter. You can review how to create a Path with your Pen or Shape Tools in Chapter 3. Refer to Figure 8-133.

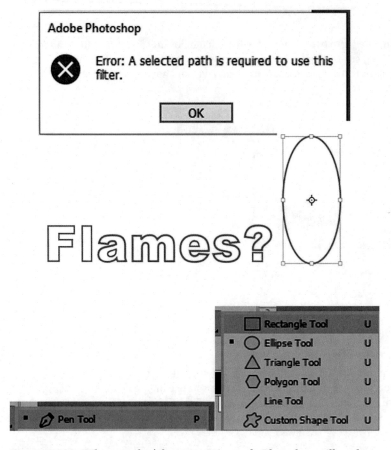

Figure 8-133. *When you don't have an active path, Photoshop will not let you use the Flame Filter, so you must create one with your Pen or Shape tools*

Project: Ring of Fire for Clown to Jump Through

File ➤ Open the circus image of flame_jump_start.psd. This file has many other layers stored in a group folder and one of the clowns in the circus is performing a dangerous stunt. First, without the flames, but he's got to take a leap of faith at some point. Make an Image ➤ Duplicate of the file for practice. Refer to Figure 8-134.

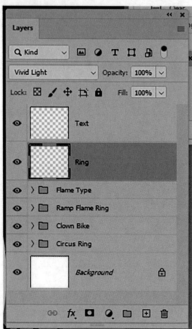

Figure 8-134. *An image of a clown jumping through a ring and the blank ring layer selected in the Layers panel*

Select the blank normal layer named Ring to start.

Earlier, using my Ellipse tool set to Path Mode, I dragged out an ellipse to match the shape of the ring the clown jumps through. This created a work path in my Paths panel, which I double-clicked and renamed Ring in the Save Path dialog box and clicked OK. Refer to Figure 8-135.

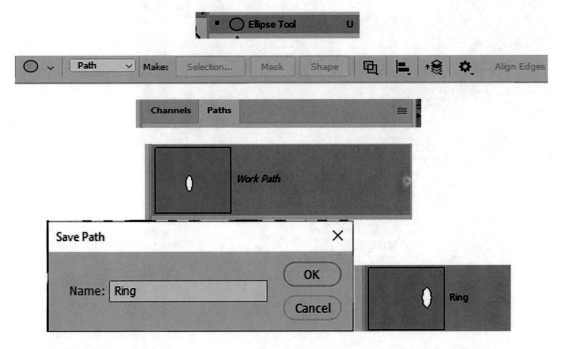

Figure 8-135. *Use the Ellipse tool in Path mode in the Options panel to create a work path in the Paths panel and then save the path with a new name*

I then used my Path Selection tool and then moved and scaled it into place using the bounding box handles. Refer to Figure 8-136.

Figure 8-136. *Use the Path Selection tool to move or scale the path if required*

In this project, just refer to the Paths panel now and select the Ring path. Refer to Figure 8-137.

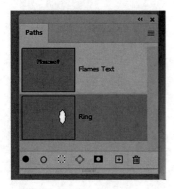

Figure 8-137. *The Ring Path is selected in the Paths panel*

While the path is selected, make sure you are still on the Ring layer in your Layers panel. Now go to Filter ➤ Render ➤ Flame.

I'll just give a quick tour and instruction as well. Refer to Figure 8-138.

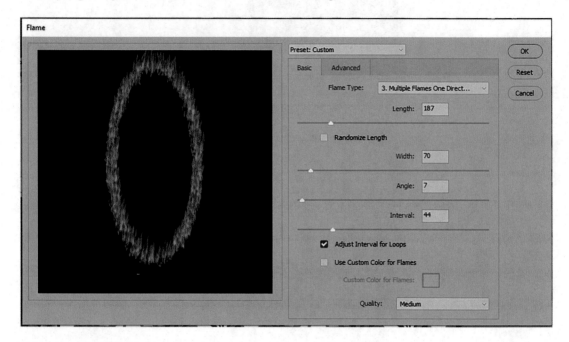

Figure 8-138. *Flame dialog box*

Under the Basic tab are six flame type options you can choose from. Some types will have more options and other options will be grayed out depending on the choice. In this case, I am using number 3: Multiple Flames One Direction but take a moment to review each one as they may give you ideas for your own projects. Refer to Figure 8-139.

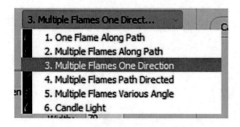

Figure 8-139. *Flame Type options*

The other basic tab options include the following (refer to Figure 8-141):

- Flame Length (20-1000). I set mine to 187.

- Randomize Length, when enabled makes the flame appear more random on the path. I disabled this setting.

- Width (5-1000). I set it to 70.

- Angle (0-360). I set it to 7 to make it appear the flame was blowing a bit.

- Interval (10-200) controls spacing of flame. I want the flames fairly close, so I set it to 44.

- Adjust interval for loops, when enabled, controls how the flame sits on the ring. I enabled the checkbox.

- Use Custom Colors for Flames. In this case I went with the default flame color and kept this option disabled. But maybe you want blue or red flames. In that case, you would enable the check box and then click Use Custom Color for Flames from the computer system's Color Picker. Click OK to commit the new color. Refer to Figure 8-140 and Figure 8-141.

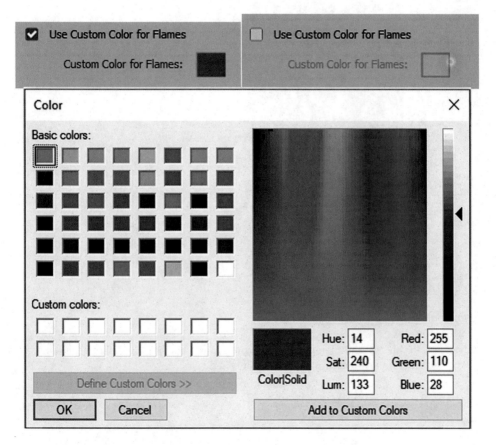

Figure 8-140. *Choose a new color flame using you computer's Color Picker*

For now, I'll click Cancel and just keep the orange flame (R: 255 G:110 B:28) and disable the option.

- Flame Quality: Draft (Fast), Low, Medium (Default), High (Slow), Fine (Very Slow). The higher the quality, the longer it takes to render. So just leave at the default of Medium. Refer to Figure 8-141.

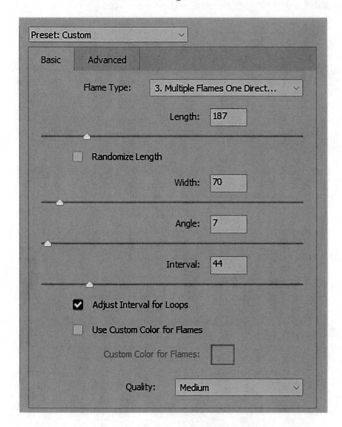

Figure 8-141. *Flame dialog box Basic tab settings*

Under the Advanced tab you can control more options of the flame by moving the sliders or entering numbers in the text boxes and dropdown menus. Refer to Figure 8-142.

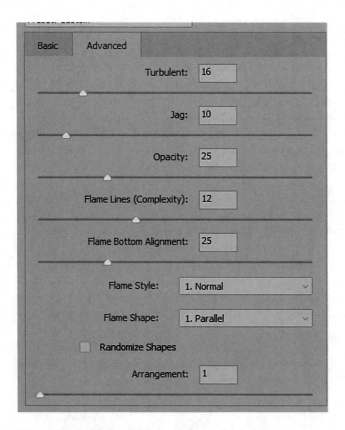

Figure 8-142. *Flame dialog box Advanced tab settings*

They include the following:

- Turbulent (0-100) controls turbulence. I left it at 16 so I could still see the flame shape.

- Jag (0-100) movement and jaggedness of flame edges. I left it at 10 to maintain the flame shape.

- Opacity (0-100) for overall opacity and brightness of flame. I set it to 25 so that you could see through the flame in some areas.

- Flame Lines Complexity (2-30) for details for flame. I set it to 12.

- Flame Bottom Alignment (0-100) for how the flame aligns to the bottom of a path or spreads out. I set it to 25 so that it gives the flame some movement on the ring.

- Flame Style (Normal, Violent, Flat). Flat is blurrier in appearance, so I kept it at the default of Normal. Refer to Figure 8-143.

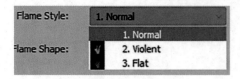

Figure 8-143. *Flame dialog flame style options*

- Flame Shape: Parallel, To the center, Spread, Oval, and Pointing. It gives the flame different widths and sizes. I left at the default of Parallel. Refer to Figure 8-144.

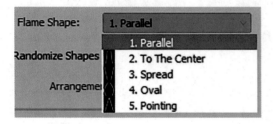

Figure 8-144. *Flame dialog flame shape options*

- Randomize shapes when the checkbox is enabled makes the flames more random. I left it unchecked for this example. Refer to Figure 8-142.

- Arrangement (1-100): Changes the arrangement of the flame. I left it at a setting of 1. Refer to Figure 8-142.

As you make alterations, the preset of the flame becomes custom. You have the options of loading or saving these presets for other users as an .xml file. Refer to Figure 8-145.

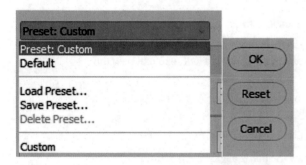

Figure 8-145. *A preset can be reset (default), loaded, saved, deleted, and made into a custom option*

■ **Note**   If you need to reset your flames while working, you can press Reset or choose the Default option to return back to Photoshop's original Flame settings. Refer to Figure 8-145.

Once you have built the flame you want, you can click OK or Cancel without saving change. Upon clicking OK the flame is rendered on a layer (in this case, Ring). Now, in the Paths panel, deselect your path by clicking in the blank area of the Paths panel so that you can see the flame more clearly. Refer to Figure 8-146.

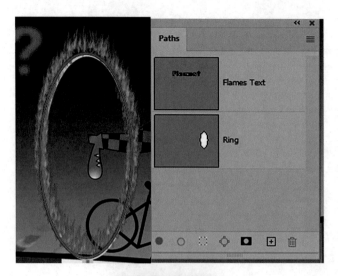

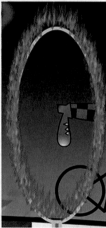

Figure 8-146. *You can deselect your path by clicking in the black area in the Paths panel below the paths*

It's always best to render your flame on a normal blank layer as you can then use your Move tool to move them around into place. Then set the layer blending mode to Vivid Light for an even hotter flame. Refer to Figure 8-147.

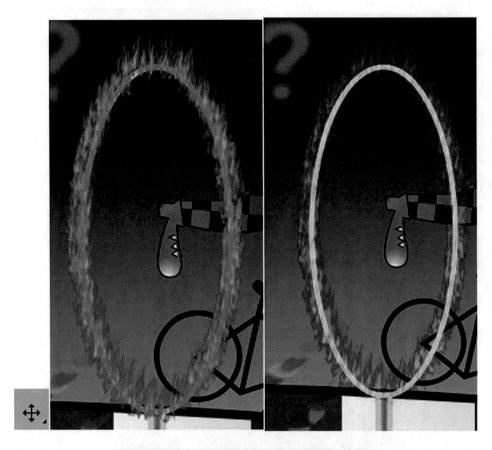

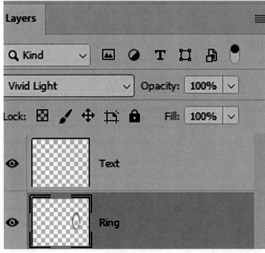

Figure 8-147. *Use the Move tool if you need to move the path over the flame and alter its layer blending mode*

Likewise, you can use your Path Selection tool to move the path and then render in the same or different location. Or use your Direct Selection tool to alter the path to create a new shape for the flames when you apply the filter again on another blank layer. Refer to Figure 8-148.

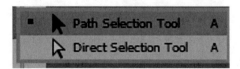

Figure 8-148. *Use your Path Selection or Direct Selection tools when you need to move or alter a path*

■ **Tip** For your own projects, remember a path can be a closed shape created with a shape tool or open, and you can use your Pen tool in Path mode to do that. Refer to Figure 8-149.

Figure 8-149. *Use the Pen tool when you want to create custom paths*

Just make sure to create a new work path while no other paths are selected and then repeat the earlier steps you used with the closed path on a new blank Layer. Refer to Figure 8-150.

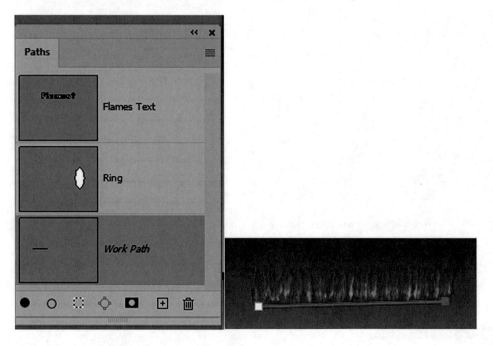

Figure 8-150. *Paths can be close like an ellipse or open like a line*

Flame Type

However, an even better example of this is to use type and multiple paths. Try this now with the word "Flames." A bold type Like Arial Black or Arial Bold is best. Refer to Figure 8-151.

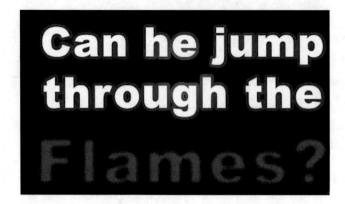

Figure 8-151. *You can apply a flame to text paths*

To turn text into type, I earlier selected my type layer "Flames?" found in the Group folder Flame Type. Refer to Figure 8-152.

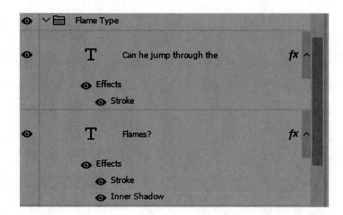

Figure 8-152. *Select the text that you want to turn into a path*

Then, from the menu, I chose Type ➤ Create Work Path or right-clicked the type layer and chose this option from the menu. Refer to Figure 8-153.

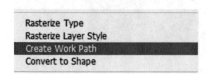

Figure 8-153. *Select Create Work Path from the menu options*

A path for the type appears in the Paths panel. I double-clicked the name and renamed it in the Save Path dialog box to Flames Text so that the path was saved and clicked OK. Refer to Figure 8-154.

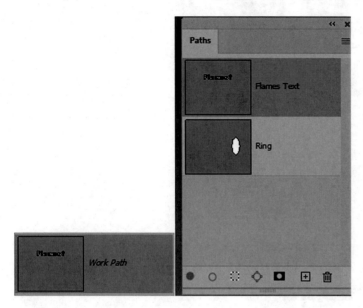

Figure 8-154. *There is now a work path created in the Paths panel that you can rename and save*

In this example, just select the Flames text path and in the Layers panel select the blank text layer so that you do not get the following warning when you select the Flame filter. You do not want the type layer to be selected because it is not a normal layer. Click OK and select the text layer. Refer to Figure 8-155.

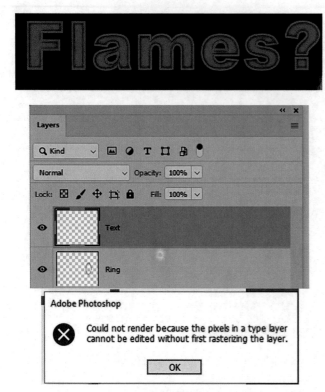

Figure 8-155. *While the path is selected, make sure that you select your blank layer first before you try to use the Flame Filter. If the type layer is still selected, you will get a warning message*

Now go to Filter➤Render ➤ Flame

You will get a warning message. Long paths over 3000 pixels will often render slower, so sometimes it is best to have one path for each letter, depending on the effect you are trying to achieve. In this case, click OK. Refer to Figure 8-156.

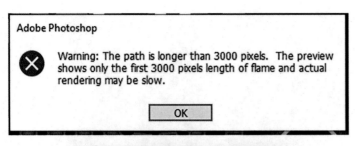

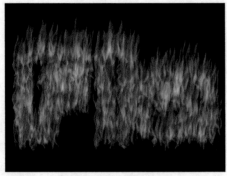

Figure 8-156. *For paths longer than 3000 pixels, you will get a warning message that the flame may take longer to render, but click OK anyway*

Enter the dialog box again. In this case, I only altered my Basic tab and left the Advanced tab with the same settings as the earlier flames. Set Length to 111, Width to 39, Angle to 7, and Internal to 44. Refer to Figure 8-157.

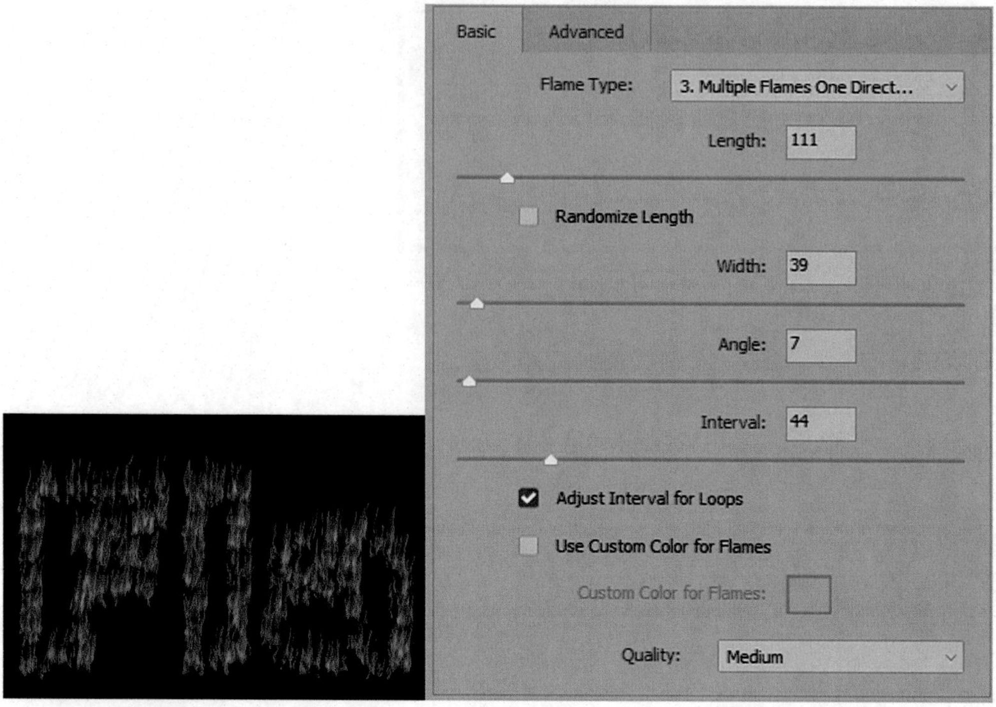

Figure 8-157. *Due to the length of the word, only part of it will render in the preview, but this allows you to set your settings in the Basic or Advanced tabs*

In the preview, you may not see the whole word, only a portion. This is the case for most larger or complex paths where only part of the path will preview. Once you make your settings, click OK and give Photoshop a few moments to render the flame letters. Refer to Figure 8-158.

Figure 8-158. *The flames are applied to the created text path*

Deselect the Flame Text in the Paths panel to view your work. Refer to Figure 8-159.

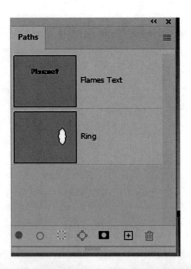

Figure 8-159. *Deselect your path so that you can see how the flame letters appear without the path blocking them*

■ **Tip** Afterwards, if you need to scale or transform the flame down or slightly up in size, make sure to convert a copy of this layer to a smart object layer. Refer to Chapter 4, as well as Chapters 6 and 7, for additional warp ideas that you could apply to this text.

File ➤ Save your example at this point. You can view an example of mine in flame_jump_final.psd.

Picture Frame

Picture Frame is a useful render filter to use when you need to create a custom frame for one of your projects. For this filter you do not need to create a path to have detail added around a square or rectangle frame or a background or normal layer. Just make sure to set your page size so that you get the frame size that you need. Later, you can also scale the layer if you turn it into a smart object.

File ➤ Open the project frame_example_start.psd. Make an Image ➤ Duplicate for practice. Refer to Figure 8-160.

Figure 8-160. *An image of a rose that you can apply the Frame filter to*

Select the blank layer called Frame and now go to Filter ➤ Render ➤ Picture Frame. Refer to Figure 8-161.

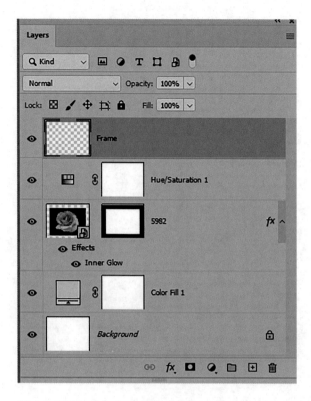

Figure 8-161. *Select your blank layer so that you can apply the Picture Frame filter*

Let's take a tour of the Frame dialog box. Refer to Figure 8-162.

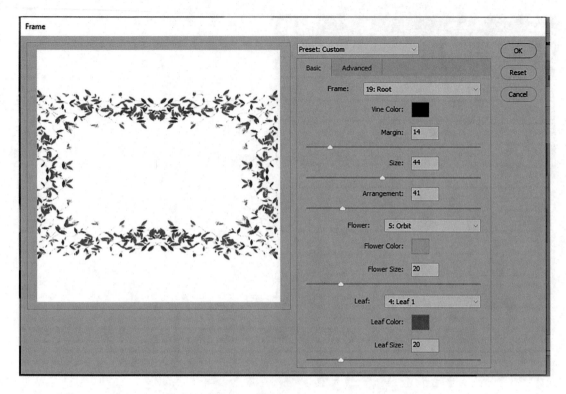

Figure 8-162. *Frame filter dialog box and basic tab settings*

The Frame filter in the basics tab has 47 frames you can choose from the dropdown menu. Depending on the frame you choose, some options will be grayed out and not available. I set it to Number 19: Root. Other options in the basic tab include

- Vine color or basic frame color. I set to R: 64 G: 84 B:35.

- Margin (1-100). How far the frame is away from the edge of the canvas. I set to 14.

- Size (1-100). Thickness of frame. I set it to 44.

- Arrangement (1-200). Shadows and highlights on frame or the way the vine flower and leaf elements appear on frame. I set to 41.

- Flower None and 22 options. I set to 5: Orbit. Flower Color (R: 145 G: 200 B:255) and Flower Size (1-100): I set to 20.

- Leaf None and 23 options. I set to 4: Leaf 1, Leaf Color (R: 57 G: 172 B:45), Leaf Size (1-100): I set to 20. Refer to Figure 8-162.

The Advanced tab, depending on the options chosen in the Basic tab, allows you to set the following:

- Number of Lines (1-30). In this case, it is disabled and only works for frame options 36-47.

- Thickness (1-200) sets frame thickness. I set to 5.

- Angle (0-360) twists the frame and, depending upon frame type and the angle chosen, you can achieve a more rounded or unusual frame. I choose an angle of 10.

- Fade (0-100) alters the opacity. I set to 0 to keep the pattern solid.

- Invert the shapes, lines, or shadows when enabled. In this example, it is disabled. Refer to Figure 8-163.

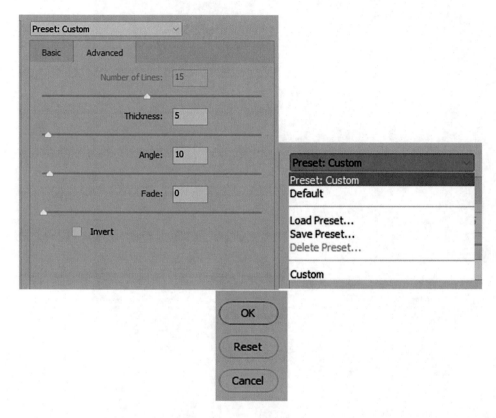

Figure 8-163. *Frame filter dialog box and Advanced tab settings. You can also reset the preset to default and use the same preset options as the Flame filter. Press OK or Cancel to exit*

As you make alterations, the preset of the frame becomes custom. And you have the options of loading or saving these presets for other users as an .xml file, or resetting to the default, or clicking the Reset button while working in the dialog box. Refer to Figure 8-163.

Once you have built the frame you want, you can click OK or press Cancel to exit the dialog box. Upon clicking OK, the frame is rendered on the layer. Refer to Figure 8-164.

Figure 8-164. *The Frame filter is applied to the layer*

For an additional feature, you could add a layer style Drop Shadow to the design to make it stand out more. Refer to Figure 8-165.

Figure 8-165. *Add a layer style effect of Drop Shadow to enhance the Frame layer*

File ➤ Save your example at this point. You can view an example of mine named `frame_example_final.psd`.

■ **Note** If you need rounded frames with brush strokes or even patterns on an open path, I recommend using Illustrator to create a custom path and border and then copying it into Photoshop as a smart object. After reading this book, if you would like to know more about pattern creation in Illustrator, check out Volume 2.

Tree

The final filter I will mention in the Render filter area is Tree. It is great filter if you need to add trees, shrubs, and wreaths to bare patches of your landscape or decor. Refer to Figure 8-166.

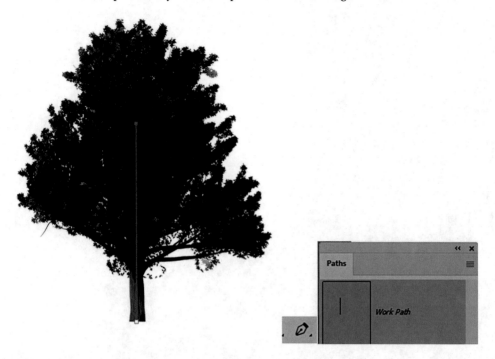

Figure 8-166. *A tree created with the Tree filter and a work path in the paths panel to control the shape of the tree*

As with the Flame filter, it is best to start with a path if you want to create a warped or straight-looking tree. You can use the Pen tool to do that. Tip: Click point 1 at the base and then Shift+Click the next point for the top. Note that while a straight vertical tree can be created without an open path, the path acts a guide to how tall or what shape the tree should be. Make sure to create your path from bottom to top or the tree may be upside down.

Project: Wreath

File ➤ Open `tree_wreath_example_start.psd`. Make an Image ➤ Duplicate for practice.

Now make sure, in the Layers panel, to select the layer named wreath and then, in the Paths panel, select the closed path called Circle. To review the path creation, see the flame project in this chapter. Keep the visibility of the group folders of `Pine Cones` and `Berries` and `Bow` hidden for now. Refer to Figure 8-167.

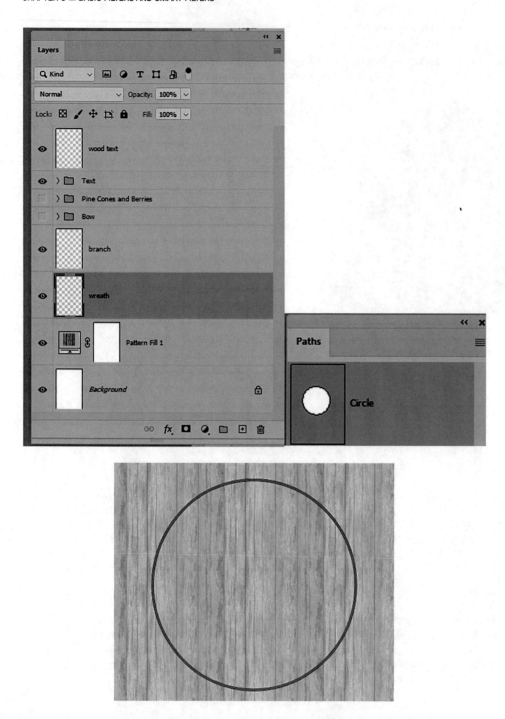

Figure 8-167. *The Layers panel with the wreath layer selected and a path in the Paths panel*

Select the created circle path that was created using the Ellipse tool.
Go to Filter ➤ Render ➤ Tree. Let's take a tour. Refer to Figure 8-168.

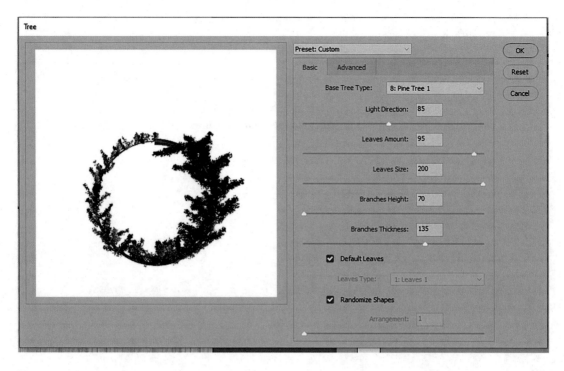

Figure 8-168. *Tree dialog box and Basic tab options*

In the Basic tab, there are 34 base tree types that you can choose from. Depending on the tree you choose, this will affect the other options. I chose 8: Pine Tree 1 for my wreath. You can then alter the other options in the Basic tab. They include the following:

- Light Direction (0-180). I set mine to 85.

- Leaves Amount (0-100). I set mine to 95.

- Leaves Size (0-200). I set to 200.

- Branches Height (70-300). I set to 70.

- Branches Thickness (0-200). I set to 135.

- Default Leaves, when disabled, lets you choose 16 different leaf types and can give a bushier appearance. I left this checkbox enabled.

- Randomize Shapes, when disabled, lets you set the arrangement. I kept this checkbox enabled.

- Arrangement (1-100). Currently disabled. Refer to Figure 8-168.

The Advanced tab lets you adjust the angle of the tree to be in perspective with the background. Refer to Figure 8-169. This includes the following:

- Camera Tilt (0-24) can be used to alter the direction and spread the branches apart.

- Use Custom Color for Leaves, when enabled, lets you set custom colors from the system's Color Picker.

- Use Custom Color for Branches, when enabled, lets you set custom colors from the system's Colors Picker.

- Flat Shading – Leaves

- Enhance Contrast - Leaves

- Flat Shading - Branches

- Leaves Rotation Lock means they do not rotate with the camera tilt.

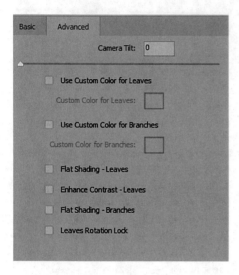

Figure 8-169. *Tree dialog box and Advanced tab options*

I left these settings at 0 and all checkboxes disabled.

As you make alterations, the preset of the tree becomes custom. And you have the options of loading or saving these presets for other users as an .xml file, or resetting to the default settings, or using the Reset button. Refer to Figure 8-170.

Figure 8-170. *Tree dialog box and Preset options, which you can use to reset the filter, and the same preset options as the Flame filter, and you can click OK or Cancel to exit*

Once you have built the tree you want, you can click OK or click Cancel to exit the dialog box. Upon clicking OK, the tree wreath is rendered on a layer based on the path's shape. Then deselect the path in the Paths panel so that you can view it better. Refer to Figure 8-171 and Figure 8-172.

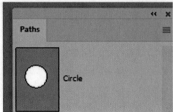

Figure 8-171. *The tree is applied to the selected path and then you can deselect the path to view the layer*

Figure 8-172. *Warped tree without path*

Like the Flame and Frame examples, it is best to render your tree on a normal blank layer as you can then use your Move tool to move it around. In this case, the wreath is not very full and needs more branches. Refer to Figure 8-172.

Select your wreath Layer and drag it twice over the Create a new layer button. Refer to Figure 8-173.

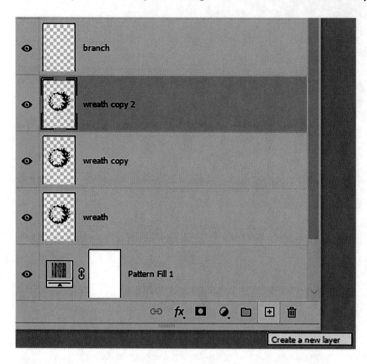

Figure 8-173. *Create copies of the wreath layer so that you can create a fuller wreath*

Select the layer named wreath copy and go to Edit ➤ Transform ➤ Flip Horizontal and then Edit ➤ Transform Flip Vertical. Refer to Figure 8-174.

Figure 8-174. *Rotate the wreath copy layer*

Then use the Move tool to move the wreath copy over the wreath layer so they appear on top of one another. Refer to Figure 8-175.

Figure 8-175. *Move the wreath copy layer into place with the Move tool*

Now select the layer named wreath copy 2 and Edit ➤ Transform ➤ Rotate 90 ° clockwise and use the Move tool to move over the other wreaths' layers. Refer to Figure 8-176.

Figure 8-176. *Rotate the wreath copy 2 layer*

If you feel the branches are full on one side but not on the other, add a few more branches to the top or where you think you need them.

Select the branch layer and the branch open path in the Paths panel, which was created with the Pen tool. Refer to Figure 8-177.

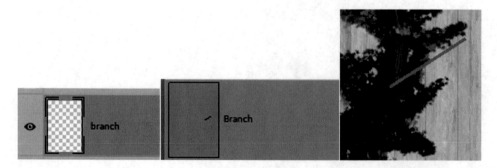

Figure 8-177. *On the blank layer with the branch path selected, use it to create new branches*

Then, while you have the same Tree Filter setting, select Filter ➤ Tree (Alt/Option+Ctrl/CMD+F). Refer to Figure 8-178.

Figure 8-178. *Render part of a tree with the recently used filter options*

This uses the exact same filter setting without having to enter the dialog box again. Deselect the branch in the Paths panel. Then make a copy of the layer (drag over the Create new layer button) and move your new branch to a new location with the Move tool. Refer to Figure 8-179.

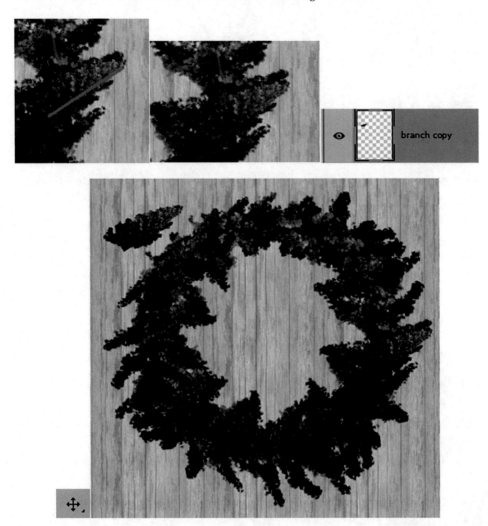

Figure 8-179. *Move and create multiple branches to fill in the gaps*

Use Edit ➤ Transform ➤ Rotate and then, using your bounding box handles as in Chapter 4, rotate and add it to a new location on the upper left to make the wreath more even and full. Click the check in the Options panel to commit. Then repeat the steps for another two or more branches until it is fuller on the top. You can also flip or scale the branches as well using Edit ➤ Free Transform and move those layers behind the other parts of the wreath. Refer to Figure 8-180.

Figure 8-180. *Use your Free Transform options to rotate or scale branches and commit the change using the Options panel*

Here is how my layers order appears so far. I have added about five branches. Refer to Figure 8-181.

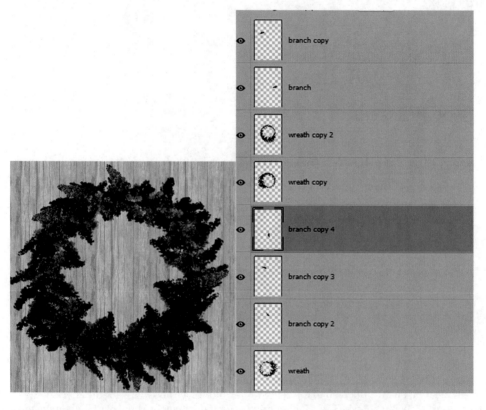

Figure 8-181. *Drag the copies of your completed branches up or down on in the Layers panel to arrange them on the wreath*

■ **Tip** Likewise, for your own projects, as with the flames, you can use your Path Selection tool to move the path and then render in the same or a different location. Or use your Direct Selection tool to alter the path as you create new branches.

In this project, I also added some images in the group folder for `Pine Cones and Berries`. You could add, copy, or clone these from your own images as the tree filter does not come with these extra items. Make the folder visible to see the layer. Refer to Figure 8-182.

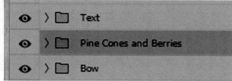

Figure 8-182. Add your own decorations to the wreath like pine cones, berries, and a bow

Lastly, make the Bow group folder visible and you can see how this adds interest and completes the wreath. Note that part of the bow is using a Perspective Warp as part of the distortion, which you can review on your own and refer to in Chapter 7.

Tree Type

In addition, just like the Flame filter, the Tree filter can even be used on large type. However, if you plan to do this with the type, in this case you need to have each letter as a separate path and not as multiple paths, as you did with the flame. Each letter needs its own work path. Refer to the Paths panel and select the blank layer in the Layers panel called wood text. Refer to Figure 8-183.

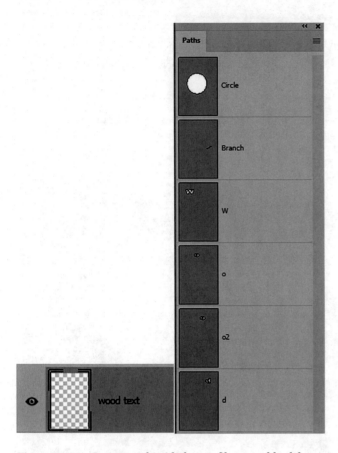

Figure 8-183. *Create words with the tree filter on a blank layer and path added to the Paths panel*

In this case I have already created the paths. I did this earlier when I selected my Magic Wand tool and disabled the Sample All Layers checkbox in the Options panel so that I would not select other backgrounds by mistake, and then I selected the type layer Wood found in the Text group folder. Refer to Figure 8-184.

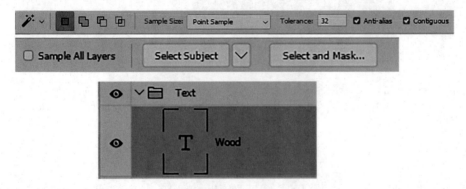

Figure 8-184. *Use your type layer and Magic Wand tool to create a type selection*

To create paths quickly, I clicked on one letter at a time with the Magic Wand tool to create a selection, like you did in Chapter 5 with the text, and then in the Paths panel I chose the Make work path from selection icon. Refer to Figure 8-185.

Figure 8-185. *Add your selection to the Paths panel as a work path*

This created a path from the selection. Refer to Figure 8-186.

Figure 8-186. *A work path of the letter is created*

And then, as shown earlier with the Flame filter, I double-clicked the path named W and clicked OK in the dialog box to save it. Refer to Figure 8-187.

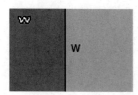

Figure 8-187. *Rename the work path to save it*

Then, with the Magic Wand tool, I clicked on the next letter, o, and repeated the path creation steps until all the letters had separate paths. I named my second o as o2 so that I could keep track of it. And I created a path for the d letter as well. Refer to Figure 8-188.

Figure 8-188. *Create a work path for each of the letters in the word Wood in the Paths panel*

■ **Tip** Because the trees have so much detail, generally for my tree letter paths I like to use a large font that I can easily read, like Arial Black or Helvetica Bold, and keep the word fairly short.

Then I create a new blank layer renamed wood text and deselect the type layer and any active selection. Use Select ➤ Deselect.

In this project example, select the W path and select the wood text layer. Refer to Figure 8-189.

Figure 8-189. *Select the W path while on the blank layer so that you can use the Tree filter*

Choose Filter ➤ Render Tree. Do not alter the Advanced tab but just edit in the Basic tab: Light Direction: 85, Change the Leaves Amount to 26, Leaves Size: 200, Branches Height to 185, and Branches Thickness to 0. Leave the Default Leaves and Random Shapes check boxes enabled. Refer to Figure 8-190.

Figure 8-190. *Tree dialog box and Basic tab settings*

And click OK. And view the result. Refer to Figure 8-191.

Figure 8-191. *Branches are now growing out of the w*

This causes the letter to appear as if branches are growing out of the wood. Now select the o path from the Paths panel and on the wood text layer, go to Filter ➤ Tree to repeat the same settings. Refer to Figure 8-192.

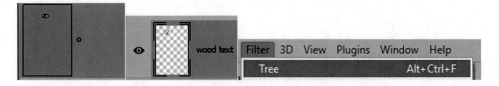

Figure 8-192. *Now select the o path and on the same alter apply the Filter ➤ Tree settings again*

Then select the o2 path. Repeat the Filter ➤ Tree steps and do the same for the d path and then deselect this path in the Paths panel to see the result. Refer to Figure 8-193.

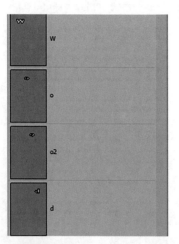

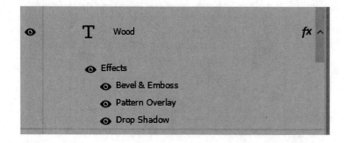

Figure 8-193. *Select the next path and apply the Tree filter again until each letter has branches and then deselect the paths in the Paths panel to see the word*

The text in this case had a few layer styles applied to it so that the branches looked more natural growing out of it. Refer to Figure 8-194.

Figure 8-194. *Adding layer styles to your text can make the text appear more tree-like*

File ➤ Save your document at this point. You can view the files so far in `tree_wreath_example_final.psd`.

■ **Tip** For your own projects, if you need to scale or transform the tree down or slightly up in size, make sure to save a copy of that layer or selected layers as smart object layer(s) and refer to Chapter 4 as well as Chapters 6 and 7 for additional warp ideas.

Other Render Filters

The second section of render filters does not apply to the topic of discussion in this book. Clouds, Difference Clouds, and Fibers do not distort the image, only cover it with a random cloud or fiber pattern that is dependent on your Tools panel foreground and background colors. Lens flare adds a lighting flare to the image using settings in its dialog box for Brightness (10-300%) and one of the four Lens Type options. Refer to Figure 8-195.

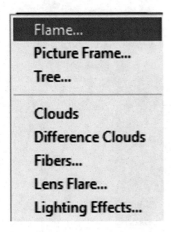

Figure 8-195. *Render filters*

■ **Warning** Lighting Effects is being removed from Photoshop due to association with 3D features, which are being moved to the Substance Collection. Using this filter in the current Photoshop version may cause errors or a crash. You can still use it in versions of Photoshop 22.5 and older. However, after you have read this book, you can explore 3D options with basic lighting in Illustrator in Volume 2.

Sharpen Filters

While useful for making an image less blurry, the Sharpen filters are not relevant to this topic and are more for image touch ups and do not create warps and distorts. The five options included here are Sharpen, Sharpen Edges, Sharpen More, Smart Sharpen, and Unsharp Mask. Refer to Figure 8-196.

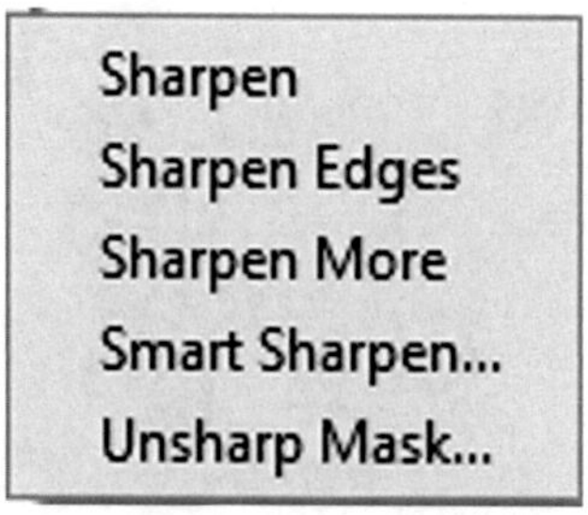

Sharpen
Sharpen Edges
Sharpen More
Smart Sharpen...
Unsharp Mask...

Figure 8-196. Sharpen filters

■ **Note**   If you are trying to correct blurry images, I prefer using Smart Sharpen and Unsharp Mask, in which you can alter and preview the settings in either the dialog box or workspace. The other Sharpen filters do not have dialog boxes.

Stylize Filters (Extrude and Oil Paint)

Stylize filters can create a variety of color and paint-like effects. Under Stylize are a few useful filters for distorting:

- **Diffuse**: Blurs and moves pixels around, creating a softened yet grainy quality mode of either Normal, Darken Only, Lighten Only, or Anisotropic

- **Emboss**: Creates an embossed relief, based on the angle (-180, 0, 180), pixel height (1-100) and amount (1-500%)

- **Extrude**: Makes shapes out of the image into either blocks or pyramids based on size and depth. See the Extrude selection for more details.

- **Find Edges (no dialog box)**: Creates an inverse effect of emboss

- **Oil Paint**: An oil painting bush effect, which can also emulate embroidery thread-like effects. See the Oil Paint section for more details.

- **Solarize (no dialog box)**: A negative film effect

- **Tiles**: Like the filter gallery patchwork, allows you to set tile number, maximum offset tiles (1-99%), and fill in empty areas based on either background color, foreground color, inverse image, or unaltered image. This creates a broken block effect.

- **Trace Contour**: Creates a colorful edge along the boundaries of brightness in the image, based on level (0-255) and edge settings of lower or upper

- **Wind**: A motion blur effect with settings like Wind, Blast, or Stagger and a direction from the right or the left of the image. Refer to Figure 8-197.

Figure 8-197. *Stylize filters*

Let's look at two of my favorites, Extrude and Oil Paint.

Extrude

The Extrude filter extrudes the pattern in either a type of blocks or pyramids and is similar to Texture ➤ Patchwork in the Filter Gallery. Set Pixel Size (2-255) and Depth (1-255) at Random or Level-Based, and then set Solid Front Faces (for Block only) or Mask Incomplete Blocks. Refer to Figure 8-198.

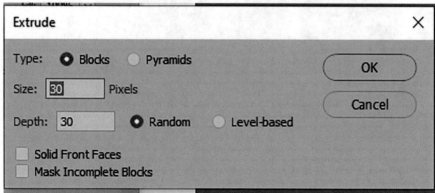

Figure 8-198. On a sample image, use the Extrude Filter dialog box and its settings

I used an Image ➤ Duplicate of `marbles_start.psd` and worked in the smart object layer. Click OK.
Because this dialog box has no preview options, working on a smart object layer is ideal so that you can enter and exit the dialog box and adjust for the best extrude. Refer to Figure 8-199.

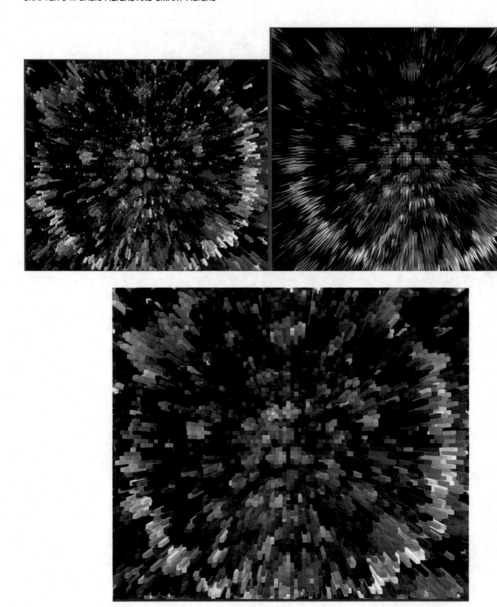

Figure 8-199. *Samples of using the Extrude filter to alter the image on a smart object layer*

Oil Paint

The Oil Paint filter can be used to create a paint texture that appears like oil paint or embroidery thread. I am going to show you how to turn a landscape photo into a painting.

File ➤ Open `oilpainting_start.psd`. Make an Image ➤ Duplicate of the file if you want to practice. It's a photo of a nice day at the Sand Cliffs somewhere on the West Coast of the USA. Refer to Figure 8-200.

Figure 8-200. *Sand cliffs by the beach*

In the Layers panel, select the smart object layer and then go to Filter ➤ Stylize ➤ Oil Paint.

Make sure that Preview is enabled, and you can zoom in or out of areas to see a close-up of how the filter affects certain areas. Refer to Figure 8-201.

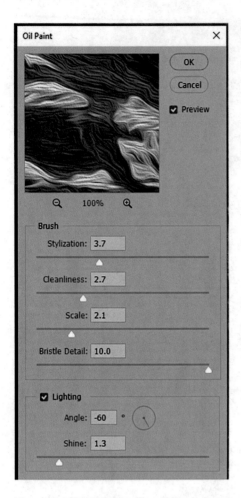

Figure 8-201. *Oil Paint filter dialog box options and preview*

The options are the following:

- **Brush options**:

  Stylization (0.1-10): Stroke smoothness style, (I set to 3.7)
  Cleanliness (0.0-10): Stroke length and purity, (set to 2.7)
  Scale (0.1-10): Thickness or width of the paint-like effect (set to 2.1)
  Bristle Detail (0.0-10): Indentation of the hairs on the brush from soft to strong
  groove marks (set to 10)

- Lighting:

  Angle(-180, 0, 180): Alters lighting angle incidence and how highlights would position
  onto the painted surface, but not the brushstroke angle
  Shine (0.0-10): The brightness of light source and how it bounces or reflects off the
  painted surface.

  I set the angle to -60 and the shine to 1.3.
Click OK when you have completed your settings. Refer to Figure 8-202.

Figure 8-202. *Finished image with Oil Filter applied*

Updates about the filter can be found here: `https://helpx.adobe.com/photoshop/using/oil-paint-filter.html`.

■ **Tip** You can use the same Oil Paint filter on a logo. Based on similar settings, oil paint can resemble embroidery threads on cloth when applied to an Illustrator smart object layer.

To make it appear even more paint-like and abstract, I then added one more filter from the Filter ➤ Filter Gallery of Artistic ➤ Fresco with a Brush Size: 2, Brush Detail: 8, and Texture: 1. Click OK to commit the filter. Refer to Figure 8-203.

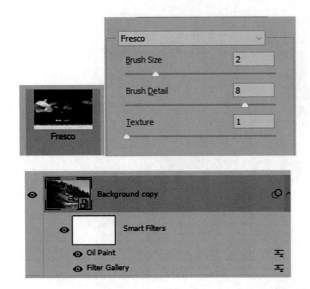

Figure 8-203. Add a filter from the Filter Gallery to the Oil Paint filter on the smart object layer

This gives the oil paint bolder strokes and appears more paint-like to me. File ➤ Save your project. You can refer to my file, `oilpainting_final.psd`. Refer to Figure 8-204.

Figure 8-204. Finished image with Oil Filter and Filter Gallery Fresco applied

Video and Other Filters (Maximum, Minimum)

Most of the filters under video (De-Interlace and NTSC Color) and Other (Custom and HSB/HSL) are not relevant to this book except for the Offset filter, which has already been mentioned in Chapter 3 and in this chapter's Filter Gallery section for Pattern and Texture creation. Offset can be used on smart object layers. However, I will just mention that Other ➤ High Pass is similar to Emboss but adds an overall gray tone. Set the radius to 0.1-1000 pixels. Refer to Figure 8-205.

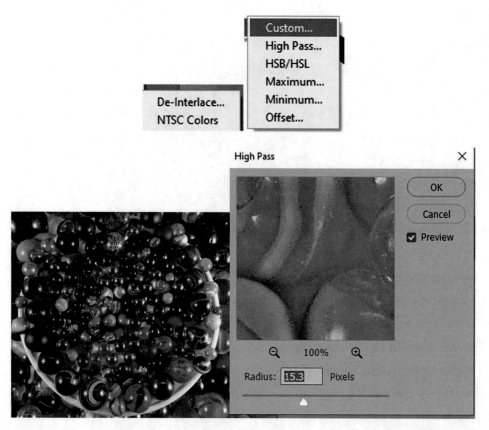

Figure 8-205. *Video and Other Filters, the High Pass dialog box used on sample image and preview*

You can also use filters Maximum with Radius (0.2-500 px) and Minimum with Radius (0.2-500 px) filters to persevere squareness or roundness to create some additional unusual blurs when the radius in pixels is adjusted. A squareness or roundness setting can affect the radius range. And with these filters you can zoom in for a closer, more detailed look. I used an Image ➤ Duplicate of the marbles_start.psd file to test these filters on the smart object layer. Refer to Figure 8-205 and Figure 8-206.

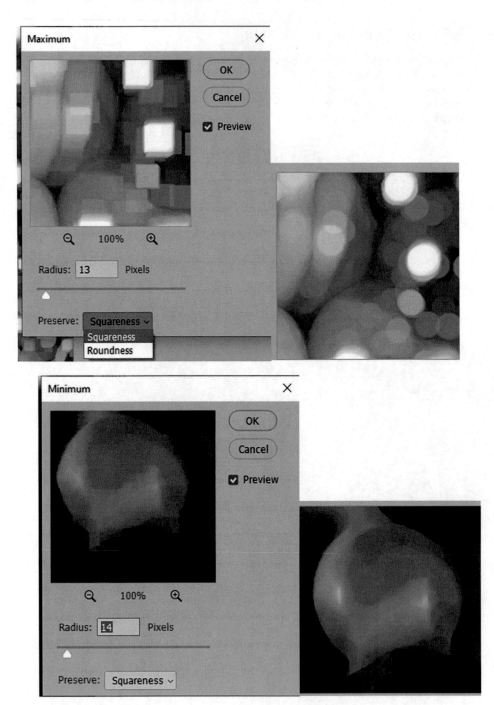

Figure 8-206. *Dialog boxes for Maximum and Minimum filters and preview*

Combining Smart Filters and Using Masks

Remember, as you combine your smart filters on your smart object layer, you can edit your layer mask, vector mask, and smart filter mask to change or paint away areas of the distortion. Refer to Figure 8-207.

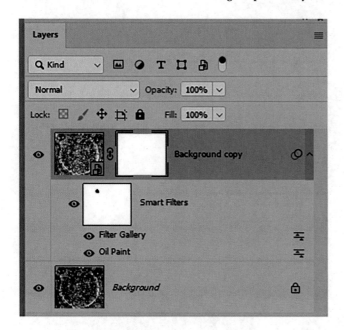

Figure 8-207. *Use your masks layer, vector, or filter when you want to hide parts of the image or filter*

In the Layers panel, some smart filters will combine better with others. Filter order is important to consider as well, and you can drag them on top or below another smart filter as you did in the Filter Gallery. Refer to Figure 8-208.

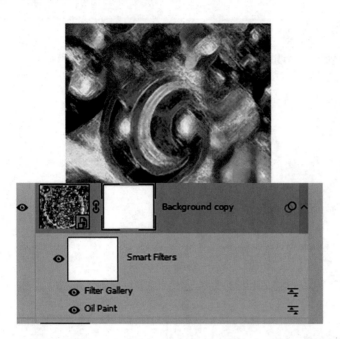

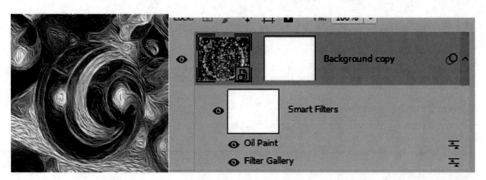

Figure 8-208. *Drag filters above or below others when you want to see alternative results*

If you are finding that a filter is not what you want, you can drag it over to the trash icon or right-click and choose Delete Smart Filter. Refer to Figure 8-209.

Figure 8-209. *Delete smart filters that you do not want*

Also consider that if the filter mask is not working for all layers, you may need to make duplicates of the smart object layers and then use separate smart filters and masks. Refer to Figure 8-210.

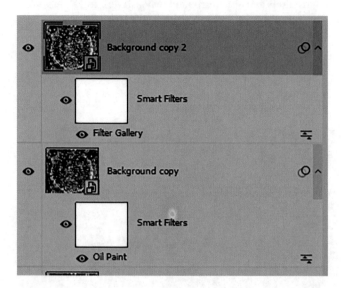

Figure 8-210. *Use a smart filter on separate layers for different results to compare or alter*

You can also duplicate a smart filter for another smart object layer by Alt/Option dragging it to the other smart object. If you do not hold down the Alt/Option key, the smart filter will only be moved to the new layer. Refer to Figure 8-211.

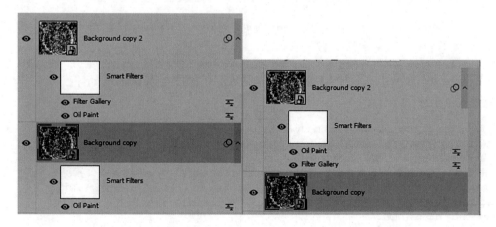

Figure 8-211. *Copy or move a smart filter from one smart object to another*

To clear all smart filters from a Layer, Choose Layer ➤ Smart Filter ➤ Clear Smart Filters.

Smart Filters for Shapes and Type Layers

Remember, as mentioned in Chapters 6 and 7, smart filters can also be applied to type layers and shape layers if they are first converted to a smart object using your Layers menu. This way the type or shape remains editable and you can apply additional layer styles as well as filter effects to the layer and then double-click the smart object if you need to edit the text or shape at some point inside the .psb file and then save your changes and return to the .psd file. Refer to Figure 8-212.

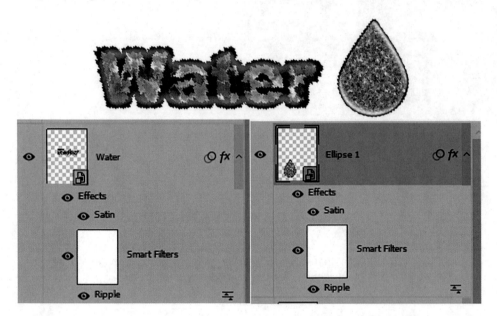

Figure 8-212. *Apply smart filters to your text or shapes after you have converted the layers to smart object layers*

Project: Create a Simple GIF Animation Using Filter Distortions, The Swirling Tree Painting

As a final project for this chapter, I'll show you briefly how you can take some images that you have distorted with your filters and apply that knowledge to a GIF animation.

I will not be going into every detail of the Timeline panel and the Save for Web dialog box, only the basic steps. However, if you would like to learn more about these topics, you can check out my book *Graphics and Multimedia for the Web with Adobe Creative Cloud* as well as the following links: https://helpx.adobe.com/photoshop/how-to/make-animated-gif.html and https://helpx.adobe.com/photoshop/using/creating-frame-animations.html.

To create a GIF animation requires planning and preparatory work, so before creating an animation you need to decide what you want your animation to do. In my case, I wanted to animate the Distort ➤ Twirl filter in some creative way so I decided to spin the branches on the tree and create a swirl of bright red leaves.

File ➤ Open the file animation_tree_highres.psd. This file is complete, so I will describe how I used filters to create the parts of the file.

For this file, I created a new document that is 8.5 inches height and 11 inches width and of landscape orientation. The other settings I kept the same as in Chapter 1 and I kept the resolution at 300 ppi. I usually build my animation in a high resolution first and then, when I have all the pieces, I create a copy with a lower resolution of 72 ppi for the GIF animation. Refer to Figure 8-213.

Figure 8-213. *Creating a GIF animation using filters*

To this high resolution file I added a background image. In order to copy it, I chose Select ➤ All and then Edit ➤ Copy and returned to the new document, `animation_tree_highres.psd`, and Edit ➤ Pasted it onto a new layer in the document. Then I converted that layer into a smart object layer using my Layers menu and renamed it Landscape. Refer to Figure 8-214.

Figure 8-214. *Start with a background and then turn it into a smart object layer*

However, after doing that, I realized that the sky was not very exciting so I double-clicked the layer to enter the .psb file and used the Edit ➤ Sky Replacement command. You can review how to do that in Chapter 7. This added a nicer looking sky. Refer to Figure 8-215.

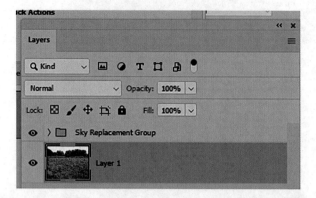

Figure 8-215. *Inside the smart object (.psb) I altered with Edit ➤ Sky replacement*

I then File ➤ Saved the .psb file, closed it, and then saved my file as .psd so that I could continue to add more layers. The layer Landscape is the background of my animation and it will not change or move. Refer to Figure 8-216.

Figure 8-216. *Select the smart object layer*

Now, because this is an animation that I wanted to make look painting-like, I went to Filter ➤ Filter Gallery and applied Palette Knife from the Artistic folder with Stroke Size: 25, Stroke Detail: 3, and Softness: 0. Then I clicked OK to exit the dialog box and committed the change. Refer to Figure 8-217.

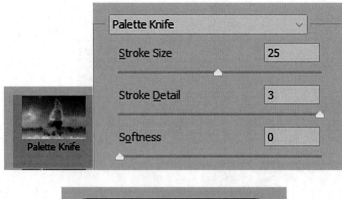

Figure 8-217. *Add a filter from the Filter Gallery and click OK to commit*

This added a more abstract feeling to the landscape. Refer to Figure 8-218.

Figure 8-218. *The filter applied to the smart object in the Layers panel*

Then, above that layer, I applied an adjustment layer of Levels to darken the landscape slightly and give a more golden tone. I altered the mid-tone range slider, from 1.00 to 0.75, in the Properties panel. Refer to Figure 8-219.

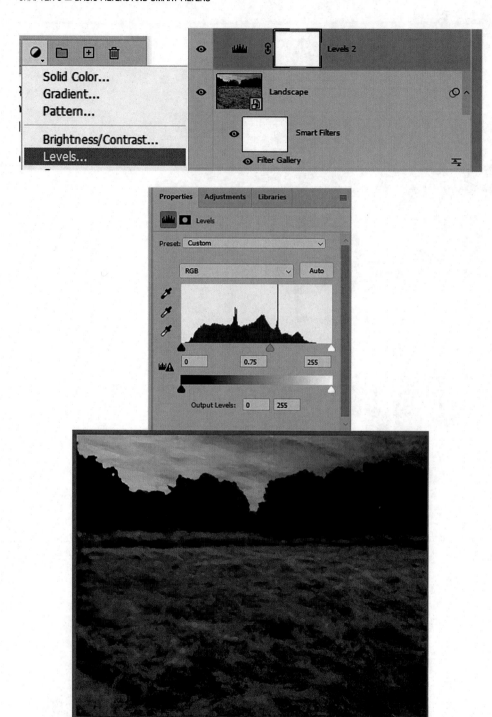

Figure 8-219. *Add a layer adjustment above the smart object Layer of Levels, as seen in the Properties Panel*

Now I wanted to add a tree to my image. As mentioned earlier, to create a tree of a certain height, you should first create a blank layer. Then with the Pen tool, you set to Path mode in the Options panel. I clicked out a straight path (click point 1 at the base and then Shift+Click the next point for the top). Refer to Figure 8-220.

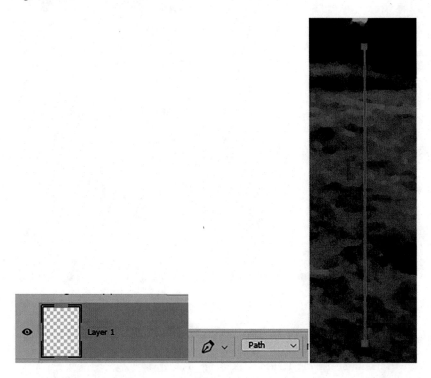

Figure 8-220. *Blank layer created and selected, and path created using the Pen tool in Path mode*

I then saved the work path I created by double-clicking the name in the Paths panel and renaming it Tree. Refer to Figure 8-221.

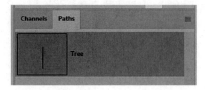

Figure 8-221. *Work path in the Paths panel saved and renamed as Tree*

Then, on the selected blank layer, I went to Filter ➤ Render ➤ Tree. Refer to Figure 8-222.

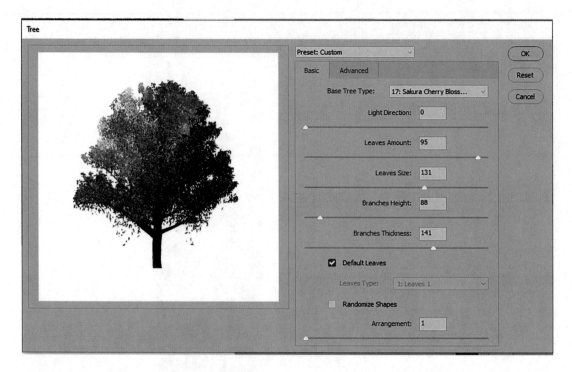

Figure 8-222. *Tree filter with the Basic tab settings*

I only altered the Basic tab as follows: Base Tree Type: 17: Sakura Cherry Blossom, Light Direction: 0, Leaves Amount: 95, Leaves Size: 131, Branches Height: 88, Branches Thickness :141. Default Leaves enabled, Random Shapes disabled, and Arrangement:1. Then I clicked OK. Refer to Figure 8-222.

Then I deselected the tree path for the moment by clicking in a blank area in the Paths panel. Refer to Figure 8-221.

This created a nice tree. However, if I used the tree with the Distort ➤ Twirl filter it would also distort the tree trunk and parts of the branches, which I don't want. I made a copy of this layer and named the original Full Tree and then I made a copy and converted it into a smart object layer just in case I should need to scale it later and keep it as a backup. And I turned off the visibility for the Layer 1 copy. Refer to Figure 8-224.

Figure 8-223. *Tree layers created and renamed and then a copy turned into a smart object layer*

To split the branches from the trees, I created two more new blank layers and named them Branches and Leaves. Refer to Figure 8-224.

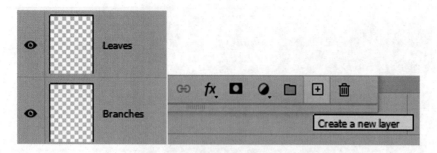

Figure 8-224. *New layers created using the Layers panel: Leaves and Branches*

I selected the tree path again, in my Paths panel, and selected the Branches layer and went back to Filter ➤ Render ➤ Tree. Refer to Figure 8-225.

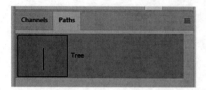

Figure 8-225. *Select the tree path in the Paths panel*

This time the only setting I altered in the Basic tab was that I reduced the number of Leaves Amount from 95 to 0. Then I clicked OK to exit the dialog box. This created a tree with no leaves. Refer to Figure 8-226.

Figure 8-226. *Tree filter dialog box. A tree with no leaves is created when we reduce the Leaves Amount to 0*

I selected the Leaves layer while the tree path was still selected, and again went back to Filter ➤ Render ➤ Tree. I returned the Leaves Amount to 95 and then selected the Branch Thickness and set this from 141 down to 0 and clicked OK. Refer to Figure 8-227.

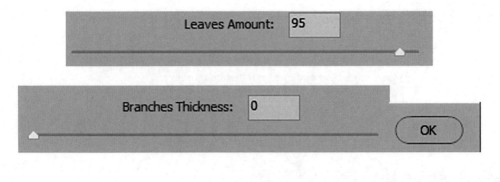

Figure 8-227. *Tree filter dialog box. A tree with only leaves is created when we add the Leaves Amount and reduce the Branches Thickness to 0*

This created a tree with no branches. I rearranged these layers, as you can see in Figure 8-228.

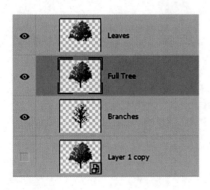

Figure 8-228. *Reorder the layers for the animation*

I then deselected my tree path in the Paths panel.

Next, I made a copy of the Leaves layer (drag over the Create new layer icon) and converted this layer into a smart object layer using my Layers menu. Refer to Figure 8-229.

Figure 8-229. *Create a copy of your Leaves layer and convert it to a smart object*

I then went to Filter ➤ Distort ➤ Twirl. I set the angle to – 99° to rotate counterclockwise and clicked OK. Refer to Figure 8-230.

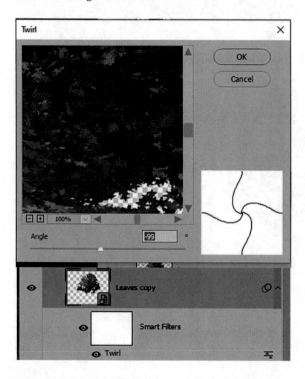

Figure 8-230. *Twirl dialog box and distort options*

At this point, I could keep on making more smart object layers and altering the rotation. However, this would increase the file size, so what I did was make a copy of the smart object layer each time I made an angle change, and then selected the layer copy and right-clicked on the layer and from the pop-up menu chose Rasterize Layer. Refer to Figure 8-231.

Figure 8-231. *Make a copy of your smart object layer and rasterize it*

This created a normal pixelated layer that had the filter applied. I don't intend to scale the leaves so this is OK. Then I renamed the layer (double-click the name) with the earlier twirl setting I used. Refer to Figure 8-232.

Figure 8-232. *Rename the layer to keep track of your settings*

I repeated these steps with the smart object layer Leaves Copy by first double-clicking the smart filter name in the layer and then, one at a time, changing the setting and clicking OK.

Then next angles that I used were -199°, -299°, -399°, -499°, -599°, -699°, -799°, -899°, and -999° (which is the highest setting). Each layer that I copied and rasterized with the new settings created a step-by-step or frame-by-frame animation. And you can see the order that I used for the layers here. Refer to Figure 8-233.

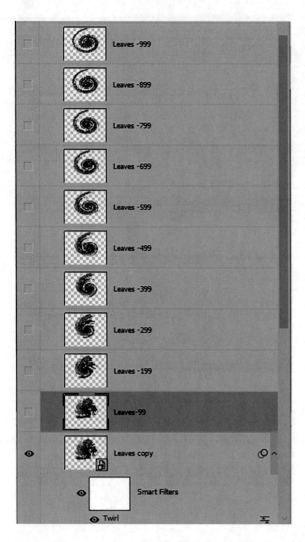

Figure 8-233. *Layer order in the Layers panel of the Twirl*

Some layers I kept hidden for now. I turned off the eye visibility.

To keep the layers aligned I selected Leaves Copy and Shift+Clicked on layer Leaves -999. With the Move tool, using the Options panel, I clicked once on the button Align Horizontal Centers and then on the button Align Vertical Centers. Refer to Figure 8-234.

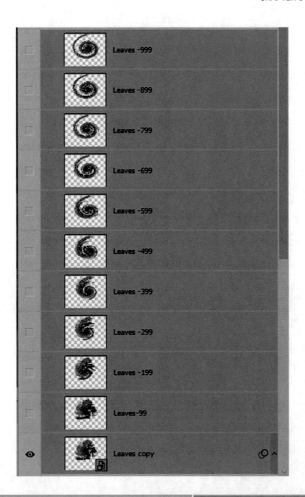

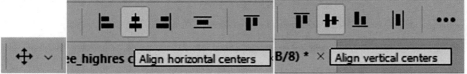

Figure 8-234. *Use the Move tool and its align options to align the layers*

This ensures all the leave twists are centered on one point. I made sure to select Ctrl/CMD+Click my other tree layers to select them all and put them into a group folder. I renamed the folder trees to keep them organized. Refer to Figure 8-235.

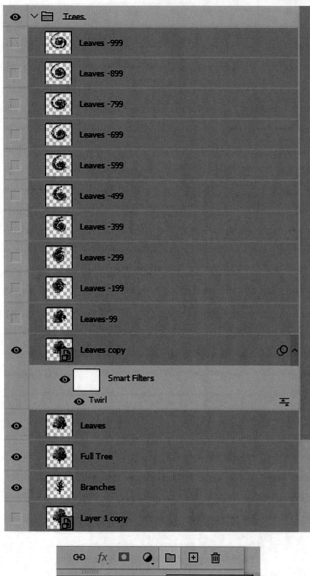

Figure 8-235. *Create a new froup folder to keep your your tree layer organized*

I collapsed that folder for now.

After creating the tree, I felt it was a bit dull and I wanted it to be red to match the background better, so above my Trees group folder I created a new adjustment layer of Hue/Saturation. In the Properties panel, I set Hue: 0, Saturation: 49, Lightness: 0, and enabled the Colorize checkbox. I set the adjustment layer to a blending mode of Overlay. Refer to Figure 8-236.

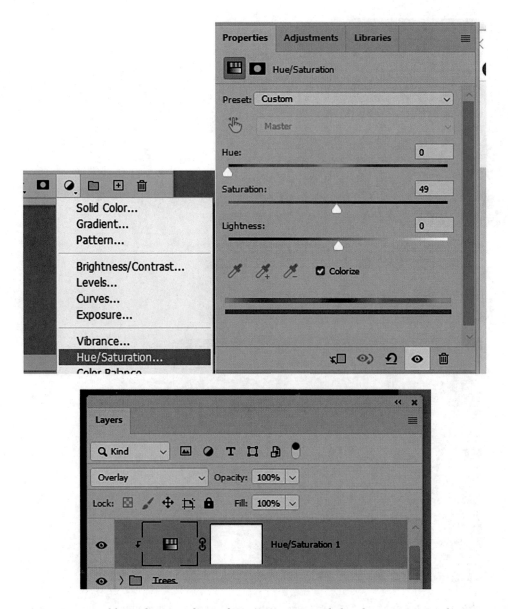

Figure 8-236. *Add an adjustment layer of Hue/Saturation and alter the settings using the Properties panel*

However, this causes the whole image to become red. To correct this, while the adjustment layer is selected, I choose Layer ➤ Create Clipping Mask (Alt/Option+Ctrl/CMD+G) and this links the adjustment layer with the group folder of Trees, making only the tree parts red. Refer to Figure 8-237.

Figure 8-237. *Create a clipping path to isolate the adjustment layer to the Trees layer only*

To complete the design, I then added a few blank layers, which I painted with my Brush tool and Clone Stamp Tools to add some shadow and cover the base of the trunk so that it would blend into the ground. Refer to my layers: Base (Blending Mode: Subtract) and Shadow (Blending Mode: Multiply and Opacity: 35%). Refer to Figure 8-238.

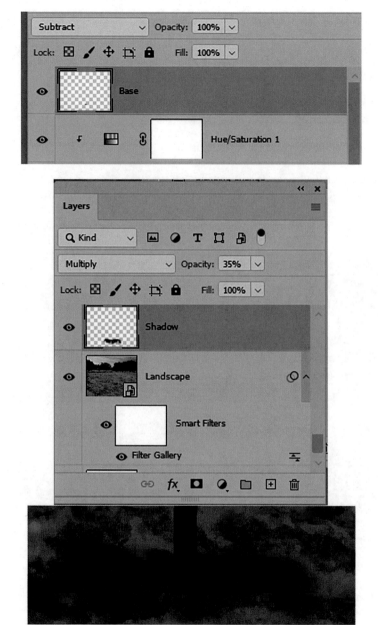

Figure 8-238. *Add a blank layer that can be pained and or cloned on and adjust layer blending modes and opacity for shadows*

I have now created all the parts I needed for the animation. I File ➤ Saved the document and then made an Image ➤ Duplicate and clicked OK. Refer to Figure 8-239.

Duplicate Image ✕

Duplicate: animation_tree_highres.psd | OK

As: `animation_tree_highres copy` | Cancel

☐ Duplicate Merged Layers Only

Figure 8-239. *Create an Image ➤ Duplicate of the files to create the animation*

I then went to Image ➤ Image Size and set the Resoution of the file to 72 Pixles/Inch and made sure to enable the Resample Bicubic (smooth gradients) checkbox and click OK to exit the Image Size dialog box. Refer to Figure 8-240.

Figure 8-240. *Image Size dialog box to lower the resolution of the file*

I then selected my Landscape layer, right-clicked on it, and and chose from the pop-up menu Rasterize Layer to apply the filter as well to keep the file size small for the animation. Refer to Figure 8-241.

Figure 8-241. *Rasterize the smart object layer to apply the filter and lower the file size*

Then I File ➤ Saved the document as a .psd file. You can see this example in my file `animation_tree_lowres.psd`, which you can open to see the next steps that I did to create the animation.

Create GIF Animation with the Timeline Panel

Go to Window ➤ Timeline to open the Timeline panel. In this case, I created the timeline already for you to view, with a total of 30 frames. Refer to Figure 8-242.

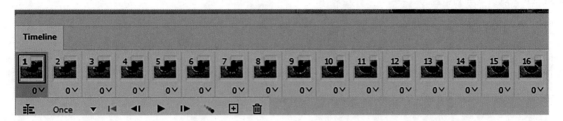

Figure 8-242. *Timeline panel with frames*

I will briefly explain how this was done.

When the Timeline panel was first opened, I clicked the button Create Frame Animation. Refer to Figure 8-243.

Figure 8-243. *Timeline panel before frames are added*

This created my first frame. I can alter what appears on the first frame by what is currently visible in the Layers panel. In this case some of the layers visibility eyes are turned off. Refer to Figure 8-244.

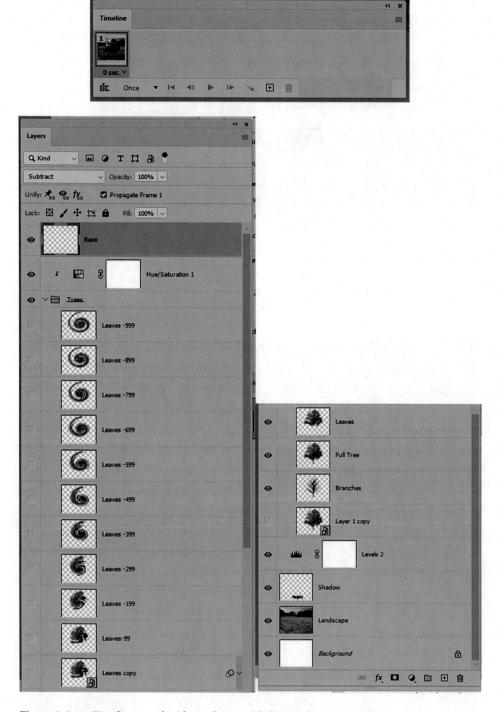

Figure 8-244. *Timeline panel with one frame added. Some layers in the Layers panel are visible*

Next in the Timeline panel, to create Frame 2, I clicked on the Duplicates selected frames button. Refer to Figure 8-245.

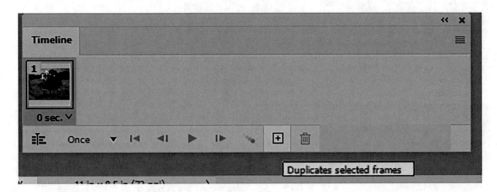

Figure 8-245. *Duplicating the selected Frame 1*

This created Frame 2. With this frame selected, I changed the visibility for some of the layers to show and then hide other layers. In this case, I made visible the smart object layer Leaves copy. Refer to Figure 8-246.

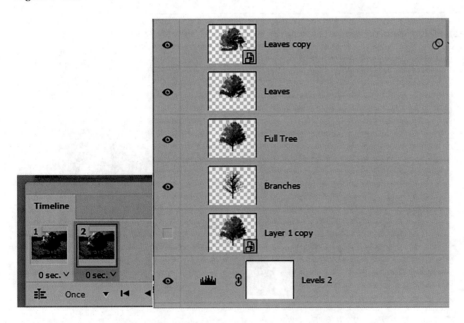

Figure 8-246. *Frame 2 is created and a new layer is made visible*

I then added Frame 3 to the timeline and followed the same process. You can see what layers were turned on and off as you click on each frame up to Frame 30 in the Timeline panel. Refer to Figure 8-247.

Figure 8-247. Frame 3 is created and another layer is made visible in the Layers panel

---

■ **Tip**　For your own project, if you need to delete a frame, use the trash can icon in the timeline panel when the frame is selected.

To create the transparent opacity blend effect that you can see for frames 18-24 and then 24-30 with the tree, I had to create two separate tweens. Tweens are created using the Timeline panel to help you blend one effect into the other. In this case, when I created Frame 18, I wanted the twirl to fade to a state where only the branches were showing. So I created frame 19 with all the leaves layers turned off. Refer to Figure 8-248 and Figure 8-249.

Figure 8-248. Frames are created but a transition needs to happen between the two

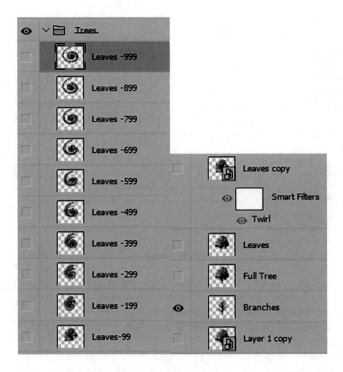

Figure 8-249. *Layers panel currently at Frame 19, later frame 24*

I selected 18 and Shift-selected 19 and then in the timeline panel clicked the button Tweens Animation Frames. Refer to Figure 8-250.

Figure 8-250. *Create tween animations from frames*

This brings up the Tween dialog box. Refer to Figure 8-251.

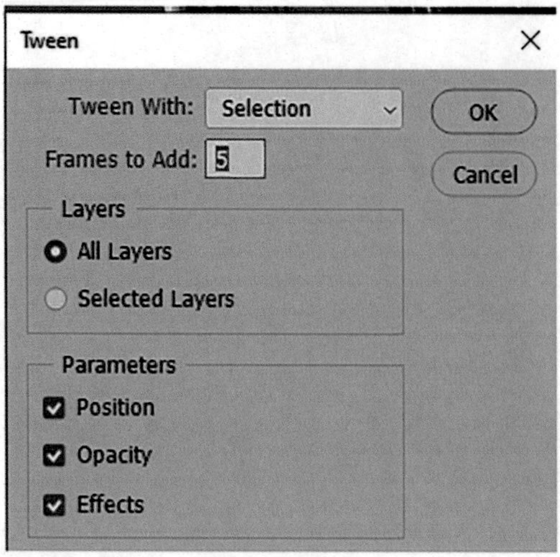

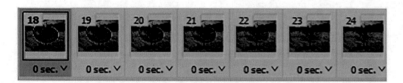

Figure 8-251. *Tween dialog box options*

I made a tween with the Selection (Frames 18 and 19) Frames to Add 5 with the All Layers option. And in this case, I enabled all the Parameters of Position, Opacity, and Effects, and clicked OK to exit the dialog box.

This created 5 tweens or transitionary frames, making frame 19 now frame 24. Refer to Figure 8-252.

Figure 8-252. *Five tween frames are added between frame 18 and 24*

To create Fames 24-30, I selected frame 1 again to make a copy and clicked the Duplicates Selected Frames button. This created a copy frame. Refer to Figure 8-253.

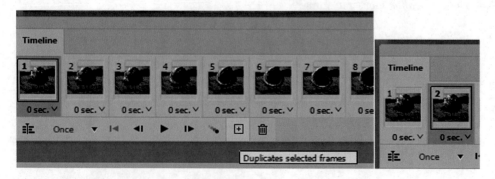

Figure 8-253. *Make a duplicated of Frame 1, now Frame 2*

I dragged it to the end of the timeline making it frame 25. Refer to Figure 8-254.

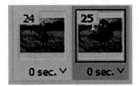

Figure 8-254. *Drag the frame to the end of the timeline*

Then I selected frame 24 and Shift+Click-Selected frame 25 and again clicked Tween Animation Frames. Refer to Figure 8-255.

Figure 8-255. *With frames 24 and 25, selected you can create another tween*

I used the same setting as I did for the first tween in the Tween dialog box and clicked OK, and then I had 30 frames. The tree animation now ends as it has begun. Refer to Figure 8-251 and Figure 8-256.

Figure 8-256. *A tween is added between Frames 24 and 30*

To preview how the animation plays, you can use your play controls at the bottom of the Timeline panel and preview the duration. Press the right pointing solid triangle. In my case, I just want it to play once but you may want your project to play forever or a set number of times (Other). From the dropdown menu, choose an option. Refer to Figure 8-257.

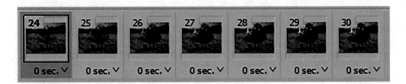

Figure 8-257. *Set the duration of the GIF animation play in the Timeline panel*

Click the square icon in the Play settings to stop the preview. Refer to Figure 8-258.

Figure 8-258. *Preview the animation using the Timeline panel*

Lastly, to export your .psd animation file as a .gif, go to File ➤ Export ➤ Save for Web (Legacy). Refer to Figure 8-259.

■ **Note** File ➤ Export ➤ Export As can, as of the current version, only export single GIF frames so you still need to use the Save for Web (Legacy) if you want to create GIF animations. However, this may change in future versions of the Photoshop application. Refer to Figure 8-259.

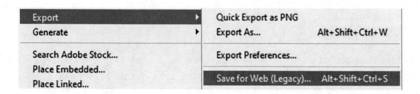

Figure 8-259. *Use the File ➤ Export ➤ Save for Web (Legacy) to save your GIF animation*

In the Save for Web dialog box, I set the preview to 2-up to view the original and the GIF files setting you will use on the right. Refer to Figure 8-260.

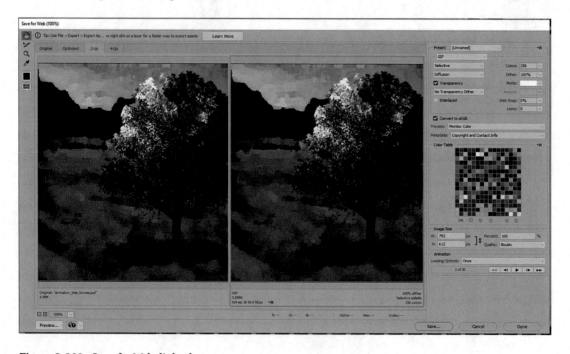

Figure 8-260. *Save for Web dialog box*

■ **Note**   For more details in this area, refer to my book that I mentioned earlier. Here I will just let you know the settings I used. You can alter the settings if you want; however, some settings may degrade the quality of the animation so make sure to compare the original with the GIF file you are optimizing.

Refer to the panel on the right:

- Preset: Is [Unnamed] as it is Custom. I selected the GIF format from the dropdown menu for the file type as it is the only option capable in this list for animation.

- Color reduction algorithm: Selective and Colors are 256 at the highest level.

- Dither algorithm: Diffusion, Dither: 100%

- Transparency is enabled. This is useful when creating transparent GIFs. Matte Swatch is white if transparency is present. Refer to Figure 8-261.

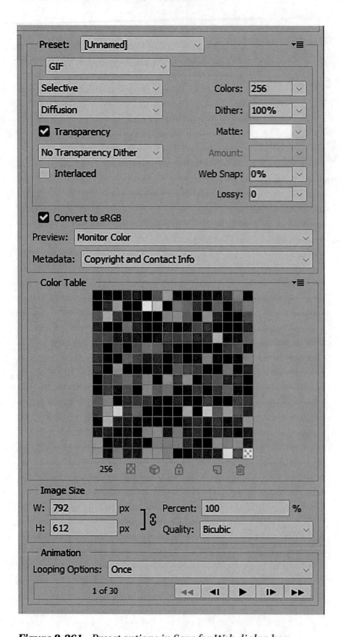

Figure 8-261. *Preset options in Save for Web dialog box*

- No Transparency Dither Algorithm: No Transparency Dither as there is currently no transparency and the amount is disabled. Refer to Figure 8-261.

- Interlaced check box is disabled and Web Snap for color is set to 0% and Lossy compression is set to 0.

- Leave the Convert to sRGB options enabled to the default of Preview: Monitor Color and Metadata: Copyright and Contact Info.

- Leave the Color Table as it is as well as the default setting.

- Leave Image size for the current Width (W: 792 px), Height (H: 612 px), Percentage: 100%, and Quality: Bicubic. However, for your own projects, you may want to make smaller copies of your animation so you can adjust this as required.

- Set the Animation Looping Options to Once as I did in the Timeline panel or choose another option. You can preview the animation again from here as well with the Play buttons.

When done, click the Save button. The Done button will only save settings and return to Photoshop but not create the GIF animation. Refer to Figure 8-262.

Figure 8-262. *Click Save in the Save for Web dialog box*

Upon clicking Save, find a location to save the GIF animation, name the file, and make sure in the Save Optimized As dialog box to set Format: Images Only and leave the default settings as is. Then click Save to save the GIF animation. Refer to Figure 8-263.

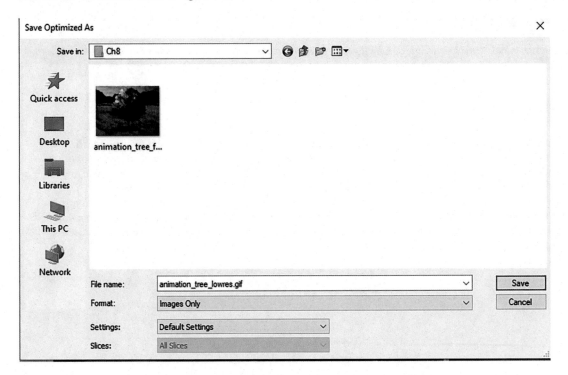

Figure 8-263. *Enter the Save Optimized As dialog box, set the options, and save your file*

You can view my file, animation_tree_final.gif, in your browser. Then click Done in the Save for Web dialog box to exit and return to your Photoshop file. Refer to Figure 8-264.

Figure 8-264. *Click Done to exit the Save for Web dialog box*

In your own projects, if you have made changes to your .psd animation, make sure to File ➤ Save the document to save the settings for the timeline panel.

You can close any open projects at this point as we have completed the filter projects.

Advanced Tip: While not relevant to this chapter, if you are working with smart objects from a file from a client who may have been working with stacked photos or video frames and some parts of the image are not appearing with the filter or on the smart object itself as you work with the file, familiarize yourself with the advanced menu feature Layer ➤ Smart Objects ➤ Stack Mode. Go to https://helpx.adobe.com/photoshop/using/image-stacks.html.

In my examples, all my smart object layers are always automatically created with the default settings of Stack Mode ➤ None. However, a client may have adjusted this setting by mistake, and you may need to set it back to None as you work on the file. Refer to Figure 8-265.

Figure 8-265. *Check your Stack Mode if you are experiencing image issues with client's smart objects in a file*

Summary

In this chapter, you looked at a number of basic filters and smart filter options that are available in Photoshop. The Filter Gallery has many filters that can be used to create unique distorts as well as others outside the gallery that create a distort such as Spherize, Twirl, and Wave, which can be edited at any time. The Filter Gallery also lets you reuse custom textures that were originally patterns in Chapter 3.

Some of the most unusual filters for warping lettering or shapes are the render filters of Flame and Tree when converted to a path. Likewise, you can later combine some filters to create a GIF animation to show how the warp and distort happens. In the next chapter, you will look at advanced filters that are for correction and distortion.

CHAPTER 9

■ ■ ■

Advanced Filters and Working with Smart Filters Part 1

Chapter goal: While there are many filters in Photoshop, not all can be considered true warps and distorts; some are more alterations of color, as you saw in Chapter 8. This chapter, like the previous chapter, will focus on select filters that either distort or correct distortion in an image; however, this time we will explore various advanced filters.

Advanced filters are used for correcting distorts in Photoshop. These included Adaptive Wide Angle Camera Raw Filter and Lens Correction. For warping and distorting, we will look at Liquify, and in Chapter 10, we will look at the Vanishing Point filter and two of the latest Neural Filters.

■ **Note**   You can find the projects for this chapter in the Chapter 9 folder.

Advanced Filters

Advanced filters often have an entire workspace area with tools and options panels specifically devoted to one filter. You saw some workspaces earlier in Chapter 8 when we looked at the Filter Gallery and the Blur Gallery, but these were devoted to multiple filters that were part of a grouped collection. Most of these advanced filters can be used on smart object layers as well. For this section, refer to the upper area of the Filter menu. Refer to Figure 9-1.

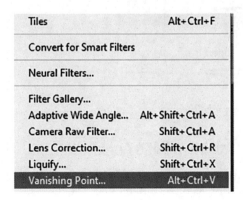

Tiles	Alt+Ctrl+F
Convert for Smart Filters	
Neural Filters...	
Filter Gallery...	
Adaptive Wide Angle...	Alt+Shift+Ctrl+A
Camera Raw Filter...	Shift+Ctrl+A
Lens Correction...	Shift+Ctrl+R
Liquify...	Shift+Ctrl+X
Vanishing Point...	Alt+Ctrl+V

Figure 9-1. *Advanced filters in the Filter menu*

© Jennifer Harder 2023
J. Harder, *Perspective Warps and Distorts with Adobe Tools: Volume 1*,
https://doi.org/10.1007/978-1-4842-8710-1_9

Adaptive Wide Angle (Correcting Distortion of Structures)

Adaptive Wide Angle is a filter that can be used for correcting lens distortion in an image, as you saw earlier with the Perspective Crop tool in Chapter 2 and Perspective Warp in Chapter 7. This filter is useful when we want to correct issues with a wide angle or fisheye lens that cause the slight curve of a structure within the image to appear to be pinched inward or bloated outward. This could include what is known as the pincushion or barrel effect. Refer to Figure 9-2.

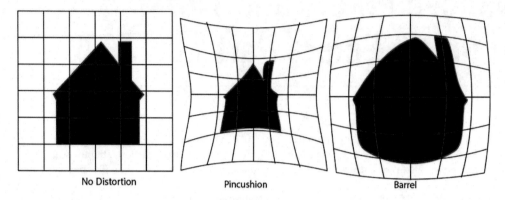

Figure 9-2. *An image without distortion, pincushion distortion, and barrel distortion*

So that you can return anytime to edit your image distortion, make sure that you turn your image layer or a copy of it into a smart object first, using your Layers panel menu. Refer to Figure 9-3.

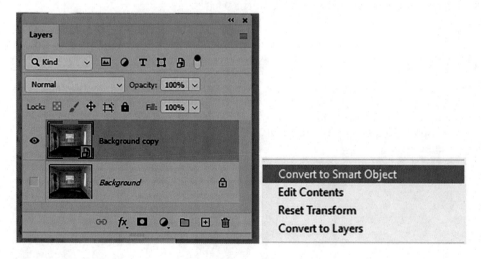

Figure 9-3. *Make sure your image is converted to a smart object layer before your use the filters*

Project: Straightening Room Dimensions with Adaptive Wide Angle

In this project, we are going to use a model of a room that I created and wall papered for a dollhouse. This was easy for me to photograph with my smart phone, without the distractions of furniture, and I could control the lighting. However, you can use what you learn here for your own photos of your house renos or if you are taking pictures in an indoor environment. Refer to Figure 9-4.

Figure 9-4. *A room with noticeable distortions*

File ➤ Open IMG_0868_room_1_start.psd. Make an Image ➤ Duplicate for practice. In this example, I have a smart object layer and a normal background layer so that you can review certain settings and easily compare the before and after. In this case, I have turned off the visibility of the background layer so that I can easily see what alterations are happening to my smart object layer. Refer to Figure 9-3.

Besides a slight keystone distortion that affects perspective, the room is a bit tilted to one side, which we need to correct.

Now Choose Filter ➤ Adaptive Wide Angle (Alt/Option+Shift+Ctrl/CMD+A).

Let's take a tour of the workspace. Refer to Figure 9-5.

Figure 9-5. *Adaptive Wide Angle filter workspace*

In this workspace, you can see that it has some tools on the left. Some of these tools may already be familiar to you, as seen in the Tools panel. As you hover over the tool, Photoshop puts an informational message across the top of the workspace to guide you on what the tool is for. Refer to Figure 9-6.

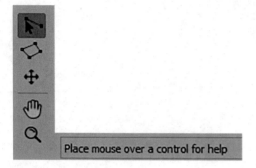

Figure 9-6. *Adaptive Wide Angle filter tools/control and, upon mouse hover, informational help*

Adaptive Wide Angle Tools (From Top to Bottom)

Constraint tool (C): Allows you to straighten the sides of a wall and you can add or edit a constraint by clicking the image or by dragging and clicking in one point and then clicking an endpoint. This creates a line. Refer to Figure 9-6 and Figure 9-7.

Figure 9-7. *Drawing a Constraint tool on the image and the selected constrain line*

You can click and then hold down the Shift key and click the next point to add a horizontal/vertical constraint. Refer to Figure 9-8.

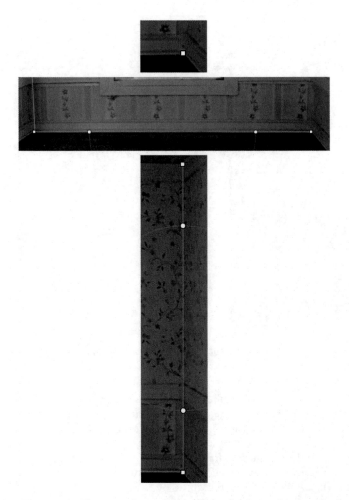

Figure 9-8. *The start of a constraint line, a horizontal constraint (yellow) and vertical constraint (magenta)*

Alt/Option+Click to delete a selected constraint. The cursor will change to a scissor and delete upon the click. Or while constraint is selected, press the Backspace/Delete key. Refer to Figure 9-9.

Figure 9-9. *Add Alt/Option. The mouse pointer changes to an arrow and scissor if the selected constraint can be deleted, then click*

You can use this tool to rotate, scale, or drag from the center point outward to correct a bulge on a fisheye lens. Refer to Figure 9-8 and Figure 9-10.

Figure 9-10. *Use one of the angle guides to rotate and its end point to scale the constraint*

If not done correctly, you may get the following warning message. Refer to Figure 9-11.

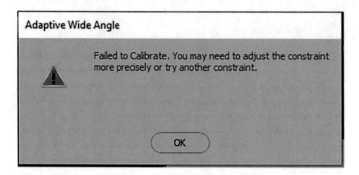

Figure 9-11. *Adaptive Wide Angle alert message that the constraint failed to calibrate and you need to adjust the constraint more precisely or try another constraint. Click OK*

In this example, I clicked and dragged to add constraints along the wall, floor, and ceiling to the straighten lines and edges in the key parts of an image. On straight edges, I clicked and held down the Shift Key to keep the constraints vertical or horizontal while dragging and then released the mouse. Refer to Figure 9-12.

But in other cases, after I created the line to straighten the door frame, I then rotated using the circle end points to make the lines level, one at a time. And in the case of the floor, you can drag the edge of the constraint to scale it further if the image's edge is still skewed. Refer to Figure 9-12.

Figure 9-12. *Adding constraints to the room*

The loop appears while dragging, so that I can see the point I am dragging closer up if I need to edit where an end point rests. Refer to Figure 9-13.

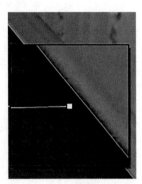

Figure 9-13. *Use the loop to view the constraint und point close up*

The filter will detect the curvature and straighten the contour of that part of the object, often pulling away and dragging inward part of the outer edge in the process of correcting the distort within. Refer to Figure 9-14.

Figure 9-14. *Adjusting the constraints to straighten the room causes its border to alter and leave some gaps*

■ **Note** A faster way to correct some constraint lines is to, when the line is selected, right-click on a constraint line if you want to choose an orientation from the menu. Refer to Figure 9-15.

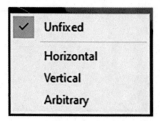

Figure 9-15. *Use the pop-up menu to can set the type of constraint you want*

Choose whether to straighten vertically or horizontally for a specific constraint. The color of the line of the constraint will change: Unfixed (default is cyan), Horizontal (yellow), Vertical (magenta), and Arbitrary or Fixed orientation (green).

You may need to drag out multiple constraints especially for images without a lens profile or when correcting unusual distortions. Refer to Figure 9-14.

Polygon Constraint tool (Y): This can help you straighten a wall or window in a room. Add points by clicking out four or more perspective points, as you did with the Perspective Warp tool in Chapter 7. You could go around a wall or, in this case, a window. Click the initial starting point to end or close, or double-click to close gap. Refer to Figure 9-16.

Figure 9-16. *The Polygon Constraint tool can be used to square off some areas*

If the points are invalid, the line will turn from cyan to red. Refer to Figure 9-17.

Figure 9-17. *Invalid constraints appear red*

You can then edit a constraint by clicking the polygon constraint and dragging an endpoint. Alt/Option+Click on a selected constraint to delete or press the Backspace/Delete key.

By creating this kind of geometric constraint, you can adjust the image around part of the distorted image.

However, just using this polygon constraint tool solely on walls, while it may square some areas of the room, will not entirely straighten the room, so I find it is better to use the Constraint Tool for sides of walls and set to Horizonal or vertical, as seen earlier. Refer to Figure 9-14 and Figure 9-18.

Figure 9-18. *Polygon Constraints don't appear to correct the room's angle*

Move tool (M): Drag to move the content in the canvas. This will allow you to drag the image if you see any unwanted corner gaps. You can use this with your scale slider on the right of the workspace. Refer to Figure 9-19.

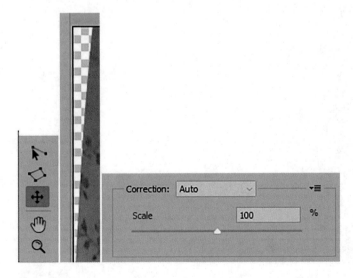

Figure 9-19. *Use the Move tool when you want to move the image around the preview. You can also access the Hand and Zoom tools here*

Hand tool (H): Drag to move the image in the window without shifting the image or constraints. Or hold down the spacebar if working with another tool. Refer to Figure 9-19.

Zoom tool (Z): Click or drag over the area you want to zoom in, or to zoom out by holding Alt/Option. Likewise, you can still use Ctrl/CMD++ and Ctrl/CMD+- if you want to zoom around in your image. Or use your navigation area at the bottom left of the panel. Refer to Figure 9-19 and Figure 9-20.

Figure 9-20. Lower left navigation area to zoom in or out instead of using the Zoom tool

---

■ **Note** Use Ctrl/CMD+Z when you need to undo the last step when editing a constraint.

Now look to the right of the workspace preview. Use your mouse to hover over other buttons and sliders so that you are guided with information in the top area of the workspace as to what each option will do or what it is for. In this case, I hovered over the Correction dropdown menu while in Auto settings. Refer to Figure 9-21.

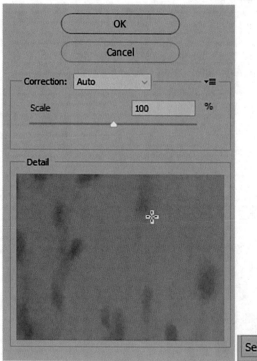

Figure 9-21. Adaptive Wide Angle filter options and info as you hover over an option

Here are some of the options you may encounter:

- OK: Commit changes and return to Photoshop.

- Cancel: Close the workspace without making any changes or reset dialog while holding Alt/Option.

- Correction: Select a Projection Model of either Fisheye, Perspective, Auto, or Full Spherical. Refer to Figure 9-22.

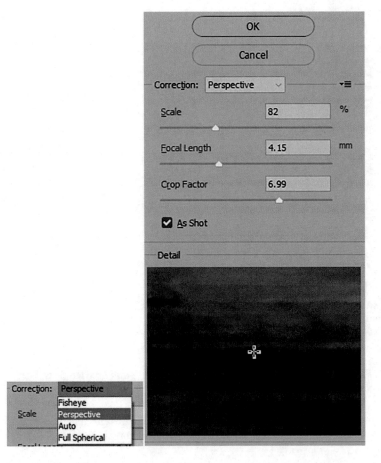

Figure 9-22. *Adaptive Wide Angle Filter Correction Options for Perspective*

Fisheye and Perspective can easily be used on any smart object layer. Fisheye corrects the extreme curves caused by a fisheye lens even before you add constraints. However, the Constraint tool can be used together with it to make additional adjustments. In this instance, for this image, it is not ideal unless you manually want to adjust the focal length. Refer to Figure 9-23.

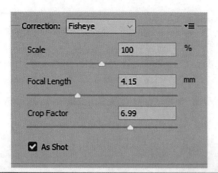

Figure 9-23. *Adaptive Wide Angle Filter Correction Options for Fisheye with settings and how it affects the room and constraint tools*

Perspective is used to correct the angle of view and camera tilts when dealing with lines that converge. It works well with the Constraint and Polygon Constraint tools. I find it to be an ideal correction option. Refer to Figure 9-24.

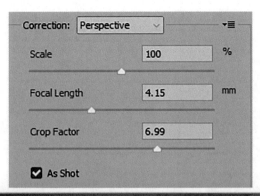

Figure 9-24. *Adaptive Wide Angle Filter Correction Options for Perspective with settings and how it affects the room and constraint tools*

The following settings for these two corrections included Scale, Focal Length, Crop Factor, and As Shot, which I will describe shortly. Refer to Figure 9-24.

However, while working on your own project's smart object layer, when you select the next Correction option: Auto, you may get the following warning message: "No matching lens profile found." Click OK to exit the message and return to the previously selected option. Refer to Figure 9-25.

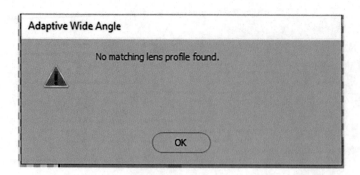

Figure 9-25. *If your image has no lens profile or model available, you will get an alert message when you try to select the correction to Auto*

In this project, when you entered the Adaptive Wide Angle workspace, Photoshop automatically applied this correction as Auto. This is because, whether working on a normal or smart object layer, the initial image from your smart phone needs to include lens model information (metadata) which, when detected, will appear at the bottom of this workspace. Refer to Figure 9-26.

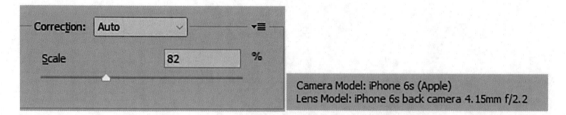

Figure 9-26. *Adaptive Wide Angle Filter Correction Options for Auto because you have a lens model available*

For example, if you download and open an image from the iPhone 6s, you will have access to correction settings of Auto and Scale, because the lens model of the iPhone 6s back camera is 4.15 mm f/2.2. If your camera model and lens is recognized by the filter, an auto lens correction can be applied. However, you can still use Fisheye or Perspective if you need access to additional settings.

While most digital cameras will record the camera model for the image, not all smart phones or digital cameras record the lens model profiles, so in that case just use either Fisheye or Perspective options and adjust your constraints manually. In my case, Perspective worked best as an alternative.

The next Correction option: Full Spherical, depending on the size of your image when selected, will give the following warning message. Refer to Figure 9-27.

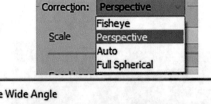

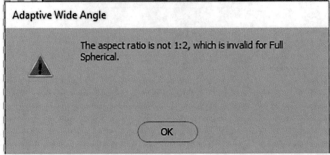

Figure 9-27. *When you try to select Full Spherical, if your aspect ratio, is not correct you will see this alert message. Click OK to exit*

"The aspect ratio is not 1:2, which is invalid for Full Spherical." Click OK to exit and return to the previously selected Correction Options Example: Auto or Perspective.

In this case, your image needs to be a 360-degree panorama or image with this width and height ratio. In addition, for you to use this filter option, it will not work on a smart object layer unless it has been cropped as a normal layer first to the correct size, before converting to a smart object layer. Like Auto Correction, the image must have a lens profile. I will point out how to do that here, although it is not part of the current project.

Cropping an Image for Full Spherical

To crop an image so that you can use the Full Spherical option, make sure to work on a duplicate image file with a normal layer or background layer. Refer to Figure 9-28.

Figure 9-28. *Work on a background or normal layer when you want to alter the aspect ratio*

With your Crop tool Options panel, first set Ratio to 2:1 for width and height and click the check to commit the crop (not 1:2, as it says in the alert box). The image should be wider (2) than its height (1). Refer to Figure 9-29.

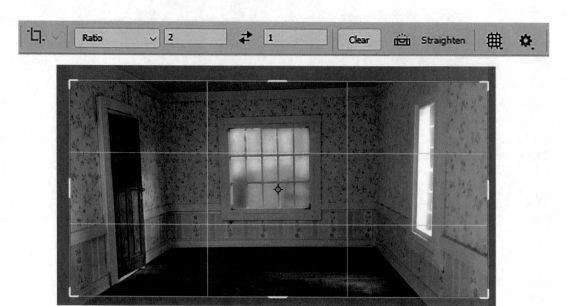

Figure 9-29. Use the Crop tool and its Options panel with a ratio option of 2:1 to crop to the correct size

Exit the Crop options by clicking the check in the Options panel. At this point, you could then convert this layer into a smart object using your Layers panel menu or leave as a normal layer or background layer. Refer to Figure 9-30.

Figure 9-30. Convert a copy of your layer to a smart object before you enter the Adaptive Wide Angle filter again

When you enter the Adaptive Wide Angle filter again, you will be presented with the Auto option and then you can choose Full Spherical from the list and use the scale option 50%-150%. Refer to Figure 9-31.

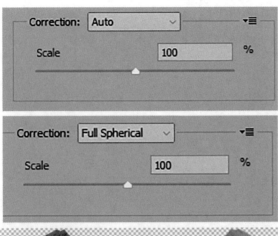

Figure 9-31. *Change your Correction setting from Auto to Full Spherical*

This creates a unique distortion, which may be useful for projects.

■ **Tip** If you have created a photomerge panorama using File ➤ Automate ➤ Photomerge, the Adaptive Wide Angle filter has an additional correction option called Panorama, which is similar to Auto. After this setting is applied, it allows you to scale the image. You can also switch to Full Spherical as well as long as the panorama is cropped to the correct ratio of 2:1. For more information on how to work with Photomerge, visit https:// helpx.adobe.com/photoshop/using/create-panoramic-images-photomerge.html.

■ **Tip 2** When working with Panoramas manually with single layers, Edit ➤ Auto Align Layers and Edit ➤ Auto Blend Layers can also be useful commands. Go to https://helpx.adobe.com/photoshop/using/ combine-images-auto-blend-layers.html.

Adaptive Wide Angle Options Continued

Returning back to the project, let's continue to review the options on the right in the correction of Perspective. Refer to Figure 9-32.

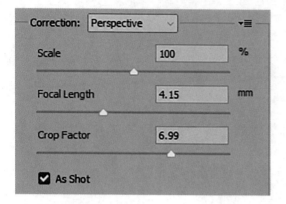

Figure 9-32. *Adaptive Wide Angle Settings for Correction Perspective*

Next to the Correction menu is another dropdown menu that allows you to manage preferences or load or save constraints. Constraints are loaded and saved as a .wac format. Refer to Figure 9-33.

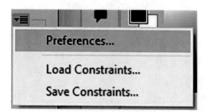

Figure 9-33. *Set your Adaptive Wide Angle preferences and load and save constraints*

Preferences include Constraint Colors of

- Unfixed Orientation (cyan), Horizontal (yellow), Vertical (magenta), Fixed Orientation (green), Invalid (red)

- Mesh Color (green). The colors can be changed by clicking them and using the Color Picker.

- Floating Loupe check box can be enabled for, Show/hide loupe when dragging and Loupe Size set slider: (100-300). Refer to Figure 9-34.

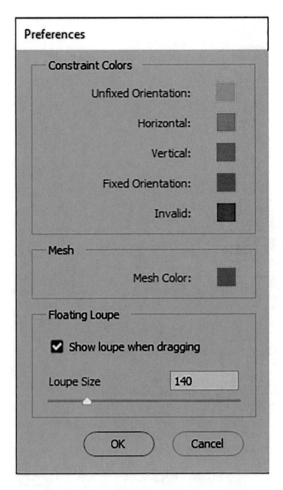

Figure 9-34. *Set your Adaptive Wide Angle preferences for Constraint Colors, Mesh Color, and Floating Loupe options*

Below the Correction options dropdown menu are the following sliders, depending on what correction is used:

- **Scale slider**: Scale image after correction (50-150%). Scales the image down to see the edge of the distortion or enlarge to trim or crop. As noted, as you correct the distortion, some of the areas around the border will that have missing information due to the added constraints. This slider is the only option available for Auto, Full Spherical, and Panorama. Refer to Figure 9-35.

Figure 9-35. Adaptive Wide Angle setting of Scale for all Correction options and how it affects the room

- **Focal Length slider**: To specify focal length (approximately 0.39-11.59mm or higher). Pinches some areas of an image when the length is lowered or squares the image when raised. If lens information is known, this value is automatically populated. In my case, it was 4.15mm. However, I can use the slider to override manually. Note that these numbers can vary based on the type of camera used to capture the image. Refer to Figure 9-36.

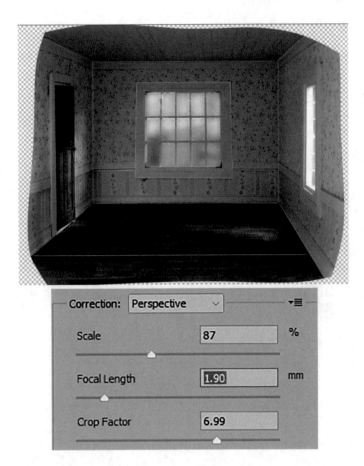

Figure 9-36. *Adaptive Wide Angle settings of Scale, Focal Length, and Crop Factor for Perspective and how it affects the room*

- **Crop Factor slider**: To specify the crop factor (0.10-10). When crop is lowered, it decreases the area to be cropped down to an elliptical area with multiple pointed edges for Fisheye and Perspective. Depending on which numbers for scale and focal length are set, crop factor is more of a bloated rounded shape. Refer to Figure 9-37.

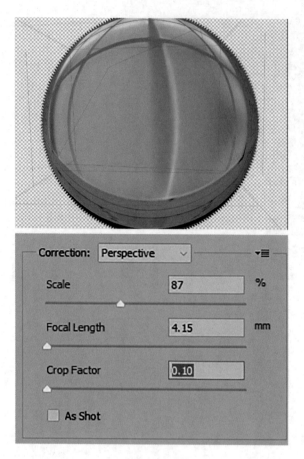

Figure 9-37. *Adaptive Wide Angle settings of Scale, Focal Length, and Crop Factor for Perspective and how it affects the room, causing it to appear spherical*

■ **Note** Further distortion can be added when you drag the center rotation points of the selected Constraint tool to compensate for the curved distortion. Likewise, you can use this Crop Factor slider to raise the crop factor and along with the Scale slider make your image more rectangular and remove some blank areas. Refer to Figure 9-38.

Figure 9-38. *Adaptive Wide Angle settings of Scale, Focal Length, and Crop Factor for Perspective and how it affects the room, causing it to appear more square*

- **As Shot check box**: When enabled, applies the focal length and crop factor from the metadata or lens profile. You will not have access to this option if there is no lens profile. Refer to Figure 9-39.

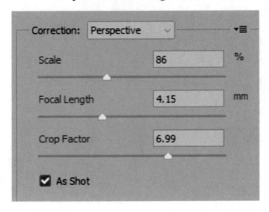

Figure 9-39. *Adaptive Wide Angle settings of Scale, Focal Length, Crop Factor, and As Shot, for Perspective*

829

- **Detail**: Preview of the loupe detail as you move your mouse about the screen. Refer to Figure 9-40.

Figure 9-40. *Use the Detail area of the Adaptive Wide Angle workspace to see an area close up*

As noted earlier, on the bottom of the workspace are the zoom area buttons, camera model, and lens model (metadata embedded in the photo), if this information is known, from the image file. You can locate it under File ➤ File Info ➤ Camera Data when you return to the Photoshop workspace. Refer to Figure 9-41.

Figure 9-41. *Look in the lower left of the Adaptive Wide Angle workspace to find out the camera model and lens model*

Finally, the following check boxes show additional options when checked:

- **Preview checkbox**: Disable to show original or enable to see the corrected Image. Refer to Figure 9-42.

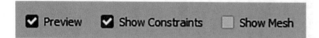

Figure 9-42. *Check boxes in the lower area of the Adaptive Wide Angle filter for Preview, Show Constraints, and Show Mesh*

- **Show Constraints**: Show/hide constraints while working on the image. Refer to Figure 9-42 and Figure 9-43.

Figure 9-43. *Show and hide the constraints in the preview*

- **Show Mesh**: Show/hide mesh. In this case, the mesh or grid is green as set in the earlier Preference. Refer to Figure 9-42 and Figure 9-44.

Figure 9-44. *Show the mesh in the preview*

After you have added your constraints and made additional adjustments, you can click OK. I left it at a Correction of Auto but did add constraints, as mentioned earlier. Refer to Figure 9-45.

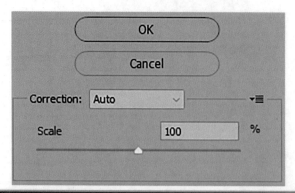

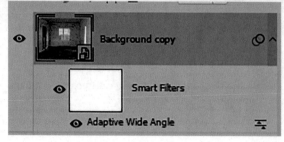

Figure 9-45. *Using Auto Correction and Constraint tools to Straighten the room and then exiting the workspace and looking at the smart filter in the Layers panel*

If you notice that there are some blank areas that are left in the image, as with the Perspective Warp tool of Chapter 7, you could try any one of the various Content-Aware options that I mentioned for filling those blank areas on a blank layer above the smart object layer. Alternatively, you could later use your Clone Stamp or Eraser tool to blend areas into the image. And you can use the Free Transform Tools from Chapter 4. See those chapter if you need more detail. Also, you can use Blend mode options for this filter.

You can review my final file, `IMG_0868_room_1_final.psd`.

Camera Raw Filter (Optics and Geometry)

The Camera Raw Filter workspace is generally used for color correction. Some people prefer to use it on a single layer in Photoshop or a single photo in Bridge (under File ➤ Open in Camera Raw). Refer to Figure 9-46.

Figure 9-46. Both Adobe Photoshop and Bridge apps can use Camera Raw

Rather than use adjustment layers, in some situations the color correction can be more accurate and easier to control in Camera Raw, especially when you need to adjust or remove chromatic aberration and vignetting after you have photographed an image or created a panorama of several images. Refer to Figure 9-47.

Figure 9-47. The Camera Raw filter corrects chromatic aberration (upper before/after) and vignetting (lower before/after)

However, like the Adaptive Wide Angle filter, it also has distortion correcting features that you should be aware of. While the focus of this book is not color correcting, I will go into more detail about two of these workspaces tabs, Optics and Geometry, as well as some of the Tool panels. Also, while my focus is on Photoshop, I will show some basic differences to the interface in Bridge, which will appear as black rather than the gray interface in Photoshop.

Project: Working with Camera Raw to Straighten Room Dimensions

File ➤ Open IMG_0886_room_2_start.psd and make an Image ➤ Duplicate of the image for practice. Select the smart filter layer in the Layers panel. Refer to Figure 9-48.

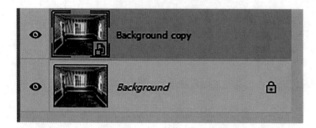

Figure 9-48. *Select your smart object layer before you enter the Camera Raw filter*

Go to Filter ➤ Camera Raw Filter (Shift+Ctrl/CMD+A). The current version I am using is 15.0, but every few months Adobe updates the settings. Refer to Figure 9-49.

Figure 9-49. *The Camera Raw filter workspace*

Some more complex areas of this workspace will give you helpful information as you hover over the options. Refer to Figure 9-50.

Figure 9-50. Pop-up info box explaining what Tone Curve is

Also, Photoshop Camera Raw and Bridge Camera have a few key differences in their workspace, which I will point out as we take a quick tour of the workspace.

Upon entering the workspace, you will find the image preview area. In the lower left area are the zoom navigation tools. Refer to Figure 9-51.

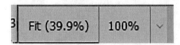

Figure 9-51. Camera Raw navigation area for zooming in and out of an image

On the lower right are various view settings. You can cycle between before and after views (Q) of either single view or a split of before and after, either across the top/bottom or left/right.

The other button is to toggle default settings (\) and is active after changes have been made to the image to see a before and after. Refer to Figure 9-52.

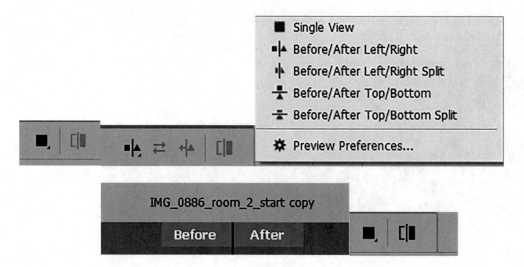

Figure 9-52. Camera Raw viewing options when previewing before and after work

Holding down the views cycle button allows you to access the Preview Preferences. Refer to Figure 9-53.

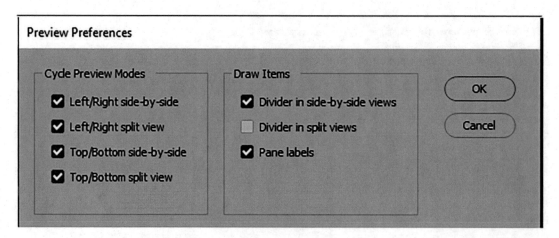

Figure 9-53. Camera Raw Preview Preferences dialog box

On the upper right is the Camera Raw preferences gear icon (Ctrl/CMD+K). Below that is the histogram with its shadow (U) and highlight clipping warnings (O). When clicking on a black or white arrow on the Preview, you can view these areas of concern on screen, in red. Refer to Figure 9-54.

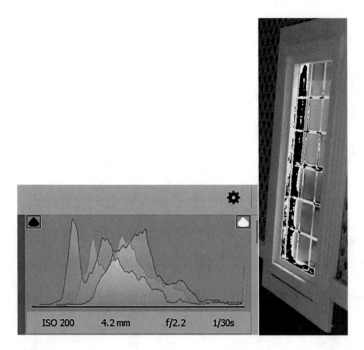

Figure 9-54. *Camera Raw Histogram with warning selected for highlight areas*

Click the arrow again to turn this warning off and continue to look at the lower tabs. If any camera information is preset, it will show below the histogram. Example: ISO 200, 4.2mm f/2.2 1/30s.

The next section below is a series of tabs found within the Edit panel. Most of these I will only describe briefly as they do not relate to this chapter on distortion and are for color correction. Refer to Figure 9-55.

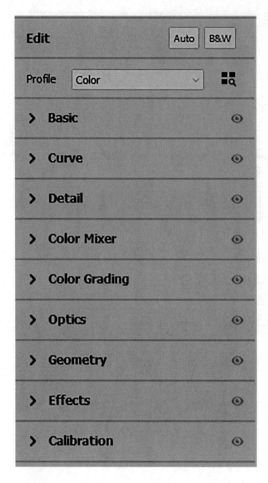

Figure 9-55. Camera Raw filter Edit panel and its tabs. Arrows indicate that it contains additional options

Edit Panel

Edit allows you to choose auto color or black and white (B&W) settings. Auto Color can be adjusted further from the Profile dropdown menu of Color, Monochrome, or Browse for a profile. Refer to Figure 9-56.

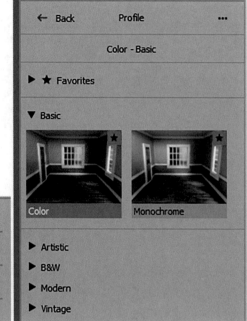

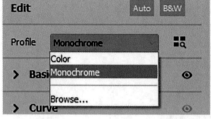

Figure 9-56. *Camera Raw filter Edit panel and its profile options*

Browse or the Browse Profiles button on the right brings up alternate profiles not listed here. They are found under the arrow tabs of Favorites, Basic, Artistic, B&W, Modern, and Vintage. Under the right ellipse button, you have the option of managing and adding other profiles to the list, imported in .zip folders. Refer to Figure 9-56 and Figure 9-57.

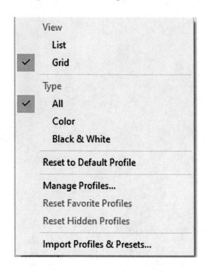

Figure 9-57. *Camera Raw filter Edit panel and additional profile options*

To return to the other tabs, click the back arrow on the left. Refer to Figure 9-56.

Basic Tab

This tab has many slider settings that allow you to control the basic white balance of the image, such as Temperature, Tint, and Exposure. You can also use the White Balance Tool (I) eyedropper to select color areas more accurately. Refer to Figure 9-58.

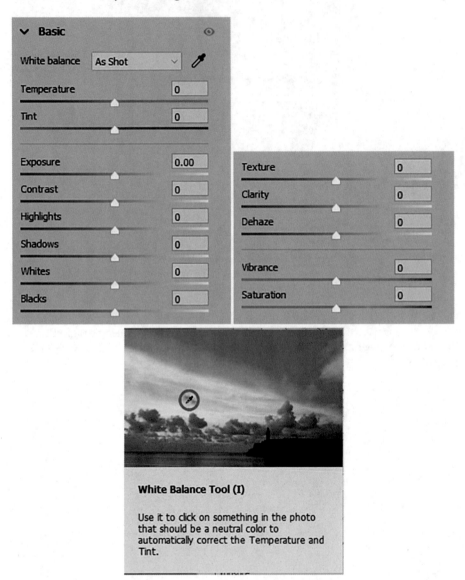

Figure 9-58. *Camera Raw filter Edit panel: Basic tab options and info box on White Balance Tool*

■ **Note**   Once a change is made for any tab (for example, the White balance changes from As Shot to Custom), the visibility eye icon will be enabled. Click it if you need to see the before and after. Refer to Figure 9-59.

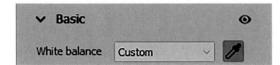

Figure 9-59. *The Basic tab is active with a visibility eye when a change has been made*

Curve Tab

Tone curve, like the adjustment layer of Curves, gives you greater range over the tonal range and contrast of the photo. There are several adjust settings for your RGB Channels, and they target specific areas of the curve with additional tool settings. You can manually adjust points of the curve, as well as sliders to adjust Highlights, Lights, Darks, and Shadows. Refer to Figure 9-60.

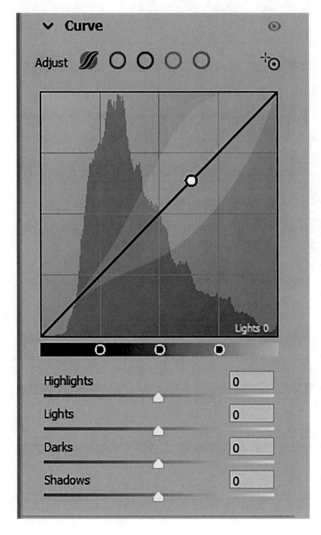

Figure 9-60. *Curve tab and its options*

Detail Tab

The sliders in this area are for Sharpening, Noise Reduction, and Color Noise Reduction. They are like the Sharpen and Noise filters we talked about briefly in Chapter 8 and are more for adjusting blurry or grainy Images. Under their arrow tab are more advanced sub-sliders for adjusting Detail, Radius, Masking, Contrast, and Smoothness. They are enabled once you move one of the primary sliders. Zooming into the image often helps to make adjustments with these controls. Refer to Figure 9-61.

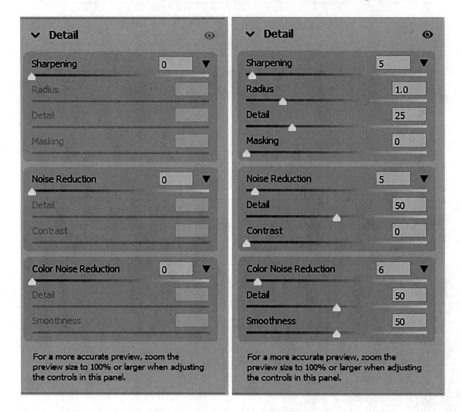

Figure 9-61. *Detail tab and its options with sliders altered*

Color Mixer Tab

Color Mixer often gives you control over the individual colors in your photos. This is similar to the adjustment layer of Selective Color. The Adjust dropdown menu settings allows you to control HSL (Hue Saturation Luminance) sliders or by individual colors represented by icons. Next to the menu when HSL is selected, there is also a Hue Targeted Adjustment tool (Ctrl/CMD+Alt/Option+Shift+H) that lets you target the colors more accurately on the preview image as your drag your mouse back and forth. Refer to Figure 9-62.

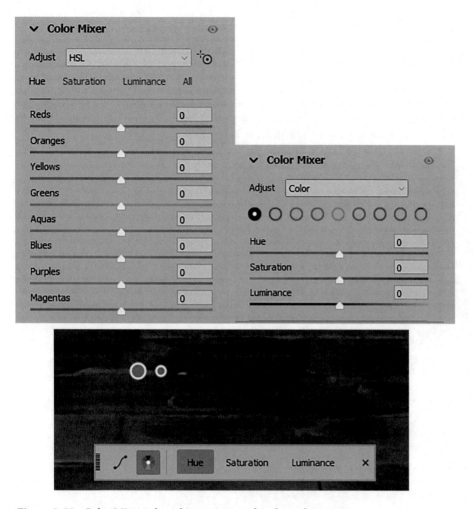

Figure 9-62. *Color Mixer tab and its options and tools on the preview*

■ **Note** This tab will change to B&W Mixer if only grayscale colors are present, or the Edit Profile of Monochrome is detected and has instead a Grayscale Mixed Targeted adjustment tool (Ctrl/CMD+Alt/ Option+Shift+G).

Color Grading Tab

Color Grading is a more advanced color correcting area that allows you to stylize your photo by adding color tints to the shadows, midtones, and the highlight hues. Having a knowledge of color theory and complimentary or opposite colors on the color wheel can assist you in this area. For example, you can try cooler blues in the shadows and warm yellows in the highlights to improve the overall tint to the image, and this is similar to the adjustment layer of Photo Filter, but it has more options. After making 3-way, Single: Highlights, Midtones, and Shadows or global adjustments to the Hue, Saturation, and Luminance values, you can then alter the blending and balance sliders of the hues. Refer to Figure 9-63.

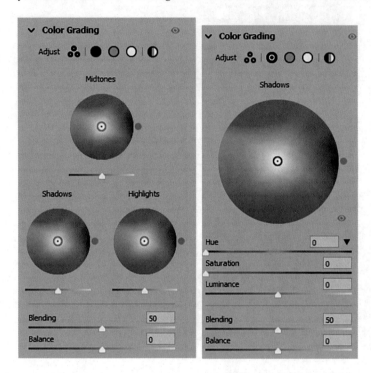

Figure 9-63. *Color Grading tab and its options*

Optics Tab

The Optics tab allows you to manually alter the Distortion Slider (-100,0,100) for basic fisheye and barrel issues. Refer to Figure 9-64.

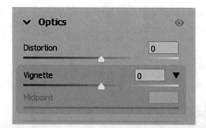

Figure 9-64. *Optics tab and its options and how the room alters if you move the distortion slider to the left then the right*

Set the Vignette slider (-100, 0, 100) and Midpoint slider (0-100) to correct lens vignettes, when there are lighter or darker areas around the boundary of the image. Refer to Figure 9-65.

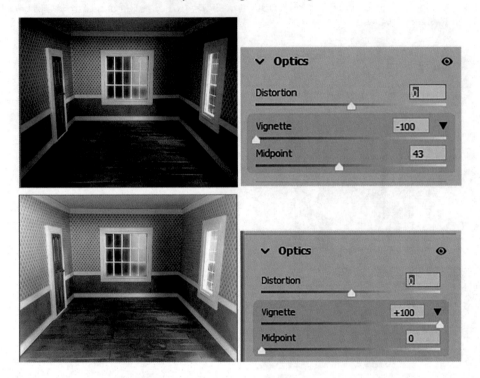

Figure 9-65. *Optics tab and its options and how the room alters if you move the Vignette slider to the left, then the right, and adjust the Midpoint slider*

■ **Note** If you are working with Bridge Optics instead, you will have two tabs. The Manual tab is the one we just talked about. However, in Bridge, the Profile tab allows you to make distortion and vignette corrections based on your image's lens profile when that setting is enabled. Refer to Figure 9-66.

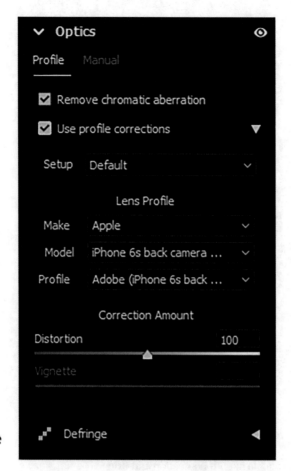

Figure 9-66. *Optics tab in Profile options for Bridge not available in Photoshop*

I mentioned Profile and how it appears and is used in the Adaptive Wide Angle filter. However, to use these same Profile options in Photoshop, make sure you have applied your Filter ➤ Lens correction filter first to your smart object. We have not looked at that filter yet but will in the next section.

Below the Vignette slider is the Defringe option, which allows you to adjust the control of the sample fringe color areas further and is also known as chromatic aberration in certain situations. Sometimes you will see an extra-colored edge on images that have a lot of glare. With so much light, the lens can fail to focus all colors to the same point, and the fringe will often appear in a red/purple or green edge. Use these sliders after you have clicked on a fringe area with your Sample Fringe Eyedropper. Then use the sliders to adjust the color until it is white or gray. Refer to Figure 9-67.

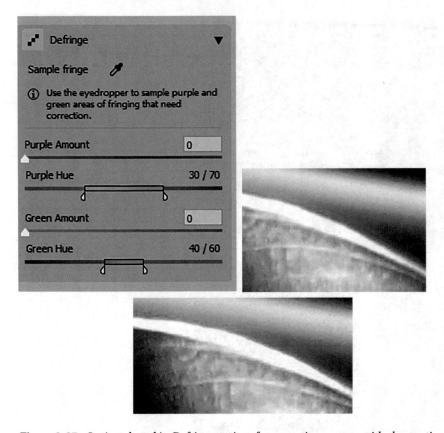

Figure 9-67. *Optics tab and its Defringe options for correcting an area with chromatic aberration*

These Defringe options are available in both Photoshop and Bridge.

Geometry Tab

This slider has additional image distort correction options for perspective correction. Refer to Figure 9-68.

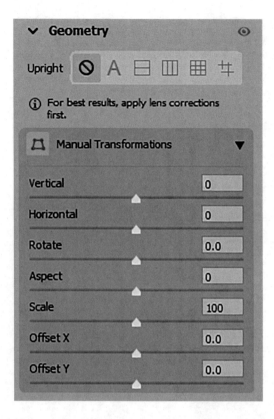

Figure 9-68. *Geometry tab and its options*

They include for Upright:

- **Off**: No distortion correction. Default of disabled. Refer to Figure 9-69.

- **Auto**: Apply balanced perspective corrections to correct vertical and horizontal convergence. This can correct our example's perspective quickly and crop the image at the same time. Refer to Figure 9-69.

Figure 9-69. *Geometry tab Upright: Auto and how it affects the room*

- **Level**: Apply only one level of perspective correction to ensure that the image is level. This option corrects some distortion but leaves the room with a bit of keystone effects as though you are looking downwards. Refer to Figure 9-70.

Figure 9-70. *Geometry tab Upright: Level and how it affects the room*

- **Vertical**: Applies level and vertical perspective corrections. This option corrects the distortion of the room, but you still may notice a slight horizontal distortion on the floor. Refer to Figure 9-71.

Figure 9-71. *Geometry tab Upright: Vertical and how it affects the room*

- **Full**: Applies level, horizontal and vertical perspective corrections. This option is closest to Auto and stretches the image a bit more. Refer to Figure 9-72.

Figure 9-72. *Geometry tab Upright: Full and how it affects the room*

- **Guided**: Draws or drags out two or more guides to customize perspective corrections when this option is enabled. Refer to Figure 9-73.

851

Figure 9-73. *Geometry tab Upright: Guided and how it affects the room when guides are added*

As you draw the guides, the images adjust to the distort, similar to the Adaptive Wide Angle filter you looked at earlier.

When you draw two or more lines parallel to each other with the Transform tool (Shift +T) enabled, this will make the image perfectly horizontal or vertical. Refer to Figure 9-74.

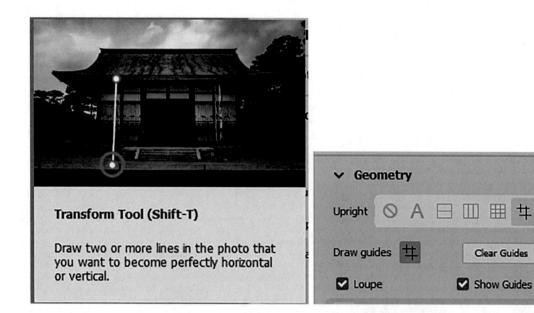

Figure 9-74. *Geometry tab Transform tool info box and Draw Guides setting enabled*

You can have up to four guides. In this case, you can see two vertical (magenta stripe) and two horizontal (green stripe) guides. Refer to Figure 9-75.

Figure 9-75. *Two sets of guides are added to straighten the room vertically (magenta) and horizontally (green)*

Watch out, however, for invalid guide configuration. Using the Options in the Geometry tab, you can turn off and on the show guides preview or enable and use the loupe for more close-up viewing.

Press the Backspace/Delete key to delete a selected guide or click the Clear guides button to remove all the guides.

Some of the transformation sliders will reset themselves when another option is selected again from the Upright list. Refer to Figure 9-74.

■ **Note** For best results with the Geometry tab, it is recommended to use the Lens Correction filter first, which we will see in the next section. Refer to Figure 9-76.

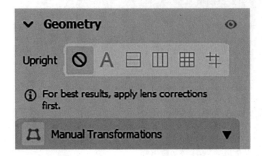

Figure 9-76. *In Photoshop, the Camera Raw filter Edit panel: Geometry tab recommends you apply a lens correction first*

■ This section, below the Upright options in Photoshop, is slightly different than Bridge. In the Photoshop version, you rely on your Lens Correction filter, while in Bridge you work with the Profile settings for the lens found in the earlier Optics Profile tab. In Bridge, because you are only working with one layer, you can also use the Constrain crop check box (see Crop tool). Refer to Figure 9-77.

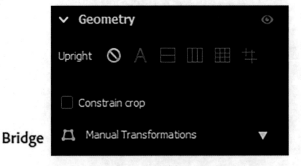

Figure 9-77. *In Bridge, the Geometry tab has an additional constrain crop option*

■ This crop option is not available in Photoshop as you do not want to crop all layers in Photoshop while in this filter.

- In addition, if your Upright options are not accurate enough or you want to create an intentional distortion, you can set Manual Transformations using the sliders for correcting Vertical (-100, 0, +100), Horizontal (-100, 0, +100) to correct key stoning, Rotate(-10, 0, +10), Aspect (-100, 0, +100) similar to wide angle lens, Scale (50-150), Offset X(-100, 0, +100) and Offset Y (-100, 0, +100). Refer to Figure 9-78.

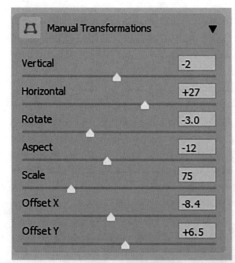

Figure 9-78. *Geometry tab Manual Transformations option sliders*

As you drag the slider, the grid appears in the preview and displays the changes.

Effects Tab

This tab allows you to adjust the sliders for grain and vignetting. When these sliders are moved further, the sub-option sliders and a dropdown menu become active so that you can further refine the settings of these primary sliders. Refer to Figure 9-79.

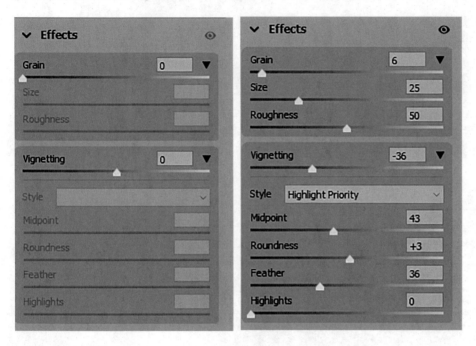

Figure 9-79. *Effects tab and its options for Grain and Vignetting*

Calibration Tab

This tab has different process versions in the dropdown menu for accurate calibration with sliders of the Shadows Tint, and Red, Green and Blue Primary Hue and Saturation. Refer to Figure 9-80.

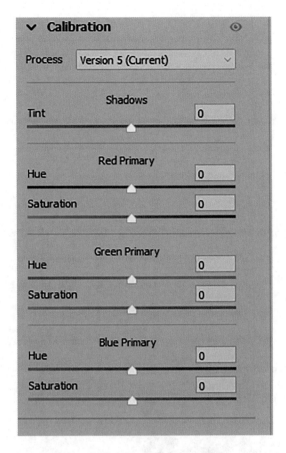

Figure 9-80. *Calibration tab and its options*

Other Camera Raw Tool Panels for Photoshop and Bridge

Lastly, I will just point out the basic tools in this area, running down the far-right side. Note that if you want to toggle to Full Screen mode while working, press this button or the (F) key.

The currently highlighted button that we just discussed is the Edit Panel (E). Refer to Figure 9-81.

Figure 9-81. *Additional panels and options*

Crop and Rotate Tool (C)

This panel is not found in the Camera Raw version of Photoshop for Layers. This tool is only found in the Bridge version of Camera Raw. It is assumed that after you work on the layer, you would do your cropping and rotating for the layer outside of Camera Raw so as not to disrupt other layers while working in this workspace. Refer to Figure 9-82.

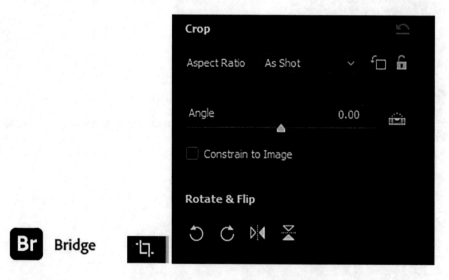

Figure 9-82. *Bridge Camera Raw filter Crop panel: Crop and Rotate & Flip options*

Healing (B)

Healing is Similar to the Clone Stamp Tool, you can use it to touch up your image by painting over the area you want to remove or click to remove a spot. Refer to Figure 9-83.

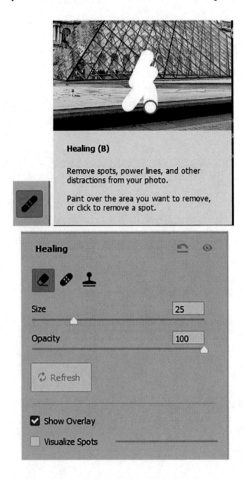

Figure 9-83. *Camera Raw Filter Healing Panel: with an Info Box on how to use the Content-Aware remove, heal and clone options*

This panel has three options of Content-Aware Removal, Heal, and Clone. Refer to Figure 9-84.

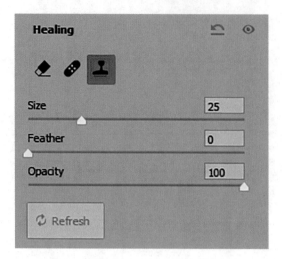

Figure 9-84. *Camera Raw Filter Healing Panel: Options*

For example, with the Clone option (Figure 9-84), you can then choose a clone location for your brush that you can drag and move around after you paint. You can alter the size, feather, and opacity of your clone stamp. Or press the / key on your keyboard or Refresh button to update and sample a new area or spot with different content.

The area with the clone stamp is your selection, while the other area with the arrow is the designated sampling area, both can be moved. Refer to Figure 9-85.

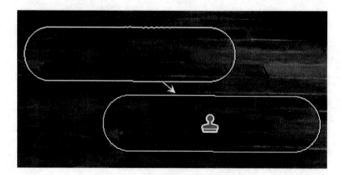

Figure 9-85. *Camera Raw Filter Healing Panel: using brush setting to clone on the preview*

■ **Note** While on smart object layers, the cloned area is applied; it is internal and not on the smart filter as part of the adjustment. Refer to Figure 9-86.

Figure 9-86. *This heal or clone does not appear on the smart filter mask; it's only within the Camera Raw filter, so you can edit it only within the smart filter*

Likewise, you can switch the selection to the Heal option and instead use the Heal sliders. You can adjust the size, feather, and opacity. Brush size can also be decreased or increased by using the left bracket [or right bracket] on your keyboard. To remove a sample area and selection, hold down the Alt/Option key to select and click to remove when the scissor pointer appears, or while selected, press the Backspace/Delete key. Refer to Figure 9-87.

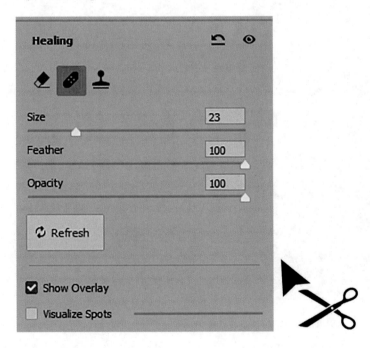

Figure 9-87. *Camera Raw Filter Healing Panel: with its options for the brush and you can use the Alt/Option key to change the mouse pointer to an arrow and scissor to click on a selected heal in the preview to delete it*

Or to remove all selections, click the reset heal button in the upper right next to the Visibility eye. (Figure 9-87).

Ctrl/CMD +Click to create a circular spot. Ctrl/CMD +Alt/Option +Click to drag and scale the selection and sample area at the same time. Later, you can drag on either boundary area edge to scale or inside it to move further. Refer to Figure 9-88.

Figure 9-88. Click to add a heal to the preview area

Click then hold down the Shift key to drag in a straight vertical or horizontal line to create a larger heal or clone area and then adjust the selection and sources afterwards. Refer to Figure 9-89.

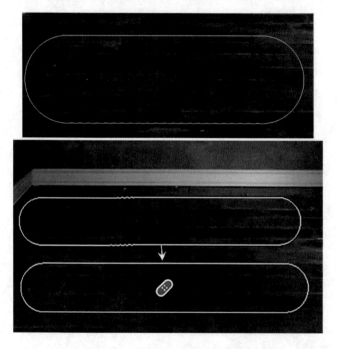

Figure 9-89. Hold down the shift key as you drag to heal or clone a larger area

Content-Aware Remove eraser is a new feature that will allow you to adjust the size and opacity of the brush head. Ctrl/CMD+drag on photo to select a custom source for removal of blemishes or unwanted items in an image. Refer to link for more details:

https://helpx.adobe.com/camera-raw/using/whats-new/2023.html#content-aware-remove

As well, you can enable and adjust spot visualization threshold slider, which as an overlay, allows you identify potential spots and imperfections as you move the slider left or right. Refer to Figure 9-90.

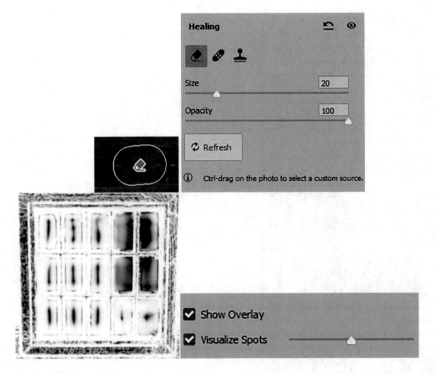

Figure 9-90. *Camera Raw Filter Healing Panel: options for Content Aware remove and visualize spots and overlay and how to visualize spots previews*

Above that visualize spots slider is the Show Overlay checkbox which can Enable or disable the view of the Healing Adjustment overlay boundaries to better visualize the selection with the clone or heal. Refer to Figure 9-91.

Figure 9-91. *Show Overlay Preview on and off of a heal*

■ **Note**   The Healing tool samples will update with the Geometry Tab if altered.

Masking Tool (M)

This panel Offers a variety of masking options like the Quick Mask (Q) or Select and Mask a selection, including selecting People. Refer to Figure 9-92.

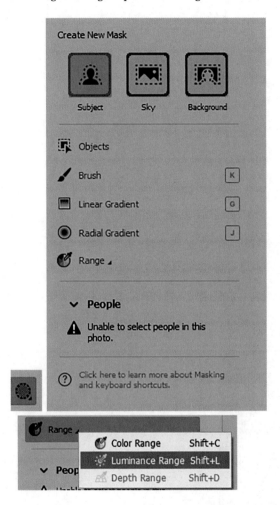

Figure 9-92. Camera Raw Filter Masking Tool Panel: and its options

In my book, Accurate Layer Selections Using Photoshop's Selection Tools, I talk about Select Subject and Select Sky for Illustrations. However, similar and more complex options can be applied to the Camera Raw Filter as well. For more assistance with this area, Photoshop includes a visual tour of selection mask options when you hover over each option. Then you can click on an Icon and either enter the Tool or gain more information from the (?) icon. Refer to Figure 9-93.

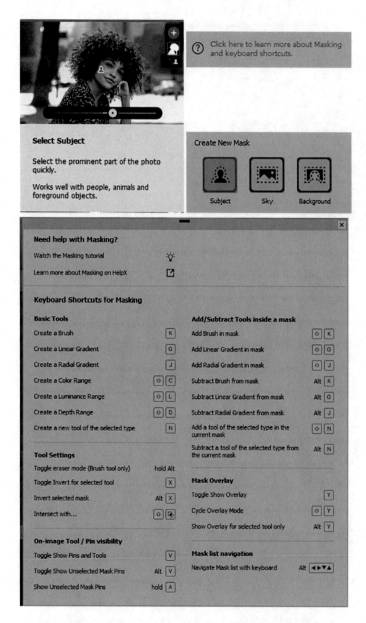

Figure 9-93. Camera Raw Filter Masking Tool Panel has info boxes as well as masking helps with key commands

Creating a mask is useful when you want to edit or color correct specific parts of an image such as the main subject, the sky, a structure, a background, etc. You can Create a new mask based on selecting the Subject, Select Sky icon or create your own custom mask using Objects, Brush (K), Linear Gradient (G), Radial Gradient (J), Color Range (Shift+C), Luminance Range (Shift +L) or Depth Range (Shift+D). Refer to Figure 9-94 and Figure 9-95.

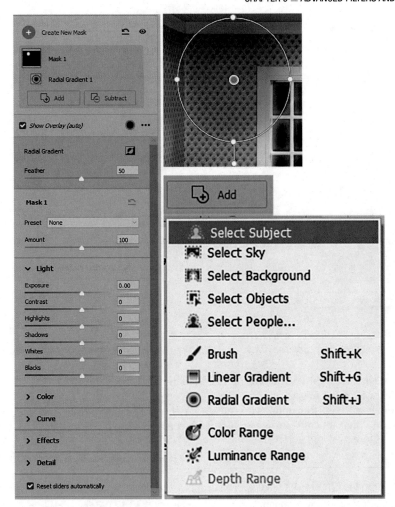

Figure 9-94. *Camera Raw Filter Masking Tool Panel: when a mask type is chosen more options are then available to edit the mask*

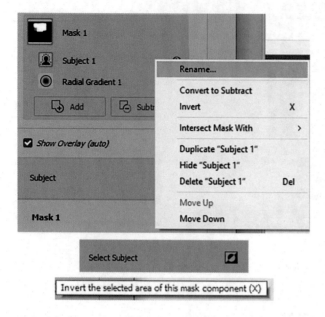

Figure 9-95. *Camera Raw Filter Masking Tool Panel: when a mask type is added and chosen more options are then available to edit the mask including inverting the mask*

Once a mask is created it can be inverted, you can add or subtract from the mask using the same selection options as well as intersect with other masks.

Each new mask you create comes with sub-tool options that offer a variety of settings so you can adjust the new mask selection and then use sliders for color correction for that selected area such as light, color, curve, effects, and details. Refer to Figure 9-94 and Figure 9-95.

■ **Note**   This mask does not appear on the Smart Filter once applied as it is a selection only applied within Camera Raw. For more details and instructions on this updated area, visit: `https://helpx.adobe.com/camera-raw/using/masking.html`.

Some Mask features, like depth range, may not be available if you do not have supported lens profiles for your images. Refer to Figure 9-92.

Red Eye (Shift-E)

This tool can also be found in the Tools panel, and while not relevant to this book, I will point out that it does offer more options than the Tools panel Red Eye tool, in that you can manually or auto adjust pupil size and darkening for human by dragging a selection area, but also make adjustments for pet eye size and catchlight. Refer to Figure 9-96.

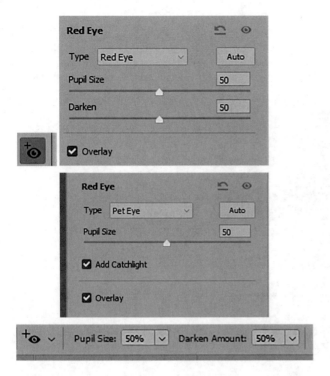

Figure 9-96. *Camera Raw Filter Red Eye Panel: you can use this panel to alter red eye or pet eye and is more advanced than the Red Eye Tool in the Photoshop Tools panel*

Most pets gave golden eyes, but some have red so you may need to test both ways to see which works best. In this case, pet eye worked for both. You can also scale each red eye selection while in Camera Raw. Refer to Figure 9-97.

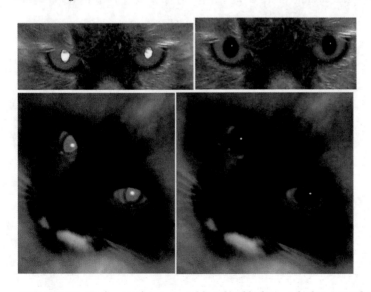

Figure 9-97. *Cat's or pet's eyes in gold and red before and after using the Camera Raw Red Eye panel and then adjusting the selections*

Snapshots (Shift+S)

This tool panel is only found in the Bridge version of Camera Raw and not in the Photoshop version for layers. You can use it to capture all the edits on your photo up to the moment you create a snapshot and easily compare and save different edits of the same photo without creating duplicates. Refer to Figure 9-98.

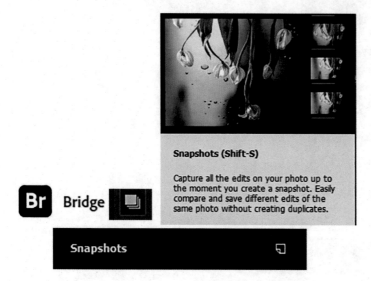

Figure 9-98. *The Camera Raw filter Snapshots panel is only available in Bridge, not Photoshop*

Presets (Shift-P):

This tool panel area lets you look at more beta and default presets, which allow you to create your own tonal looks that you can add to and save. You can select and preview them in the Preview area of the workspace. Refer to Figure 9-99.

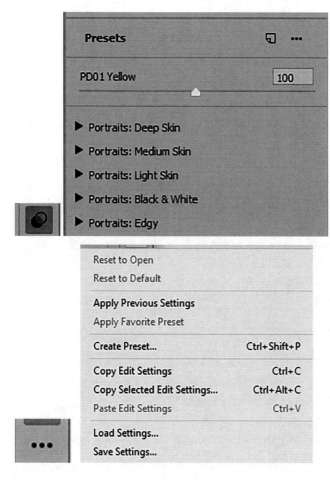

Figure 9-99. *Camera Raw filter Presets panel and more image settings*

The ellipse area allows for additional image setting options of loading and saving settings as .xmp files. Refer to Figure 9-99.

Additional tools in the lower right are

- **Zoom tool (Z)**: Use to zoom in or out and double-click to fit in view. Refer to Figure 9-100.

Figure 9-100. *Camera Raw filter tools*

- **Hand tool (H):** To move around a close-up of the images without moving geometry guides by mistake. Use the Spacebar key if you are using other tools. Refer to Figure 9-100.

- **Toggler Sampler Overlay (S):** Color sampler settings. Options appear in the area above the preview area. Refer to Figure 9-100 and Figure 9-101.

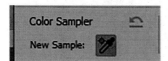

Figure 9-101. *Camera Raw filter options for the Toggler Sampler Overlay tool*

- **Toggle Grid Overlay (Ctrl/CMD+Shift+G):** Shows or hides the grid overlay. Options appear in the area above the preview area for Grid Size and Grid Opacity. Refer to Figure 9-100 and Figure 9-102.

Figure 9-102. *Camera Raw filter options for the Toggle Grid Overlay*

■ **Note** Bridge also allows for you to view multiple images at one time as a film strip, in the lower areas below the Preview. However, this option is not available in Photoshop since we are working with single layers.

Hold down the Alt/Option key and your Cancel button will change to a Reset button if you need to reset changes and click. Refer to Figure 9-103.

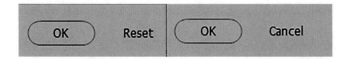

Figure 9-103. *Hold down the Alt/Option key when you want to reset all changes and click the button*

Click OK to confirm your settings or Cancel and then, if you have made changes, click Yes to dismiss the changes in order to exit the workspace without saving your changes.

In my case, I clicked the OK button and this message did not appear. Refer to Figure 9-104.

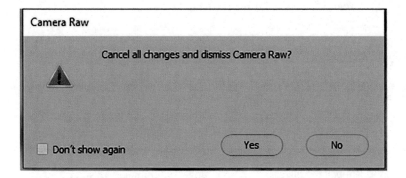

Figure 9-104. *Camera Raw alert message if you click the Cancel button and don't commit your changes. Click Yes to exit*

■ **Note** In the case of Bridge, use the Convert and Save image button in the upper right of the workspace. Refer to Figure 9-105.

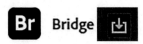

Figure 9-105. *Bridge icon and its Convert and Save button*

For additional information on color correction in Camera Raw, visit these links: https://helpx.adobe.com/camera-raw/using/introduction-camera-raw.html and https://helpx.adobe.com/camera-raw/using/whats-new.html.

You can look at my file, IMG_0886_room_2_final.psd, to review the settings I used to straighten the room and double-click on the smart object filter Camera Raw. Refer to Figure 9-106.

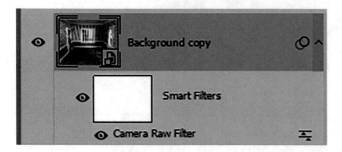

Figure 9-106. *Double-click to enter the Camera Raw filter any time to make changes*

■ **Note** Like Adaptive Wide Angle, you can also access blending modes for the layer by double-clicking the icon beside the filter name.

Lens Correction

Before using Camera Raw filter in Photoshop, if the distort is extreme, convert your image to a smart object Layer first and then you can use the Lens Correction filter on your image. You can correct distortions such as key stoning, color fringes, and vignettes. Doing so after applying the Camera Raw affects the Optics and Geometry tabs in the Camera Raw filter so you may need to enter it again to make adjustments. Make sure that your image remains in RGB color mode for this filter to work or continue to work with your copy of the file IMG_0886_room_2_start.psd. But turn off the Camera Raw filter visibility for the moment. Refer to Figure 9-107.

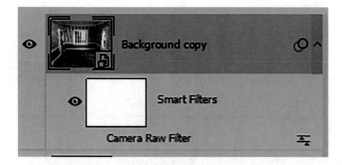

Figure 9-107. *Use your smart object layer if you want to add Lens Correction while the Camera Raw filter visibility is hidden*

While the smart object layer is selected, go to Filter ➤ Lens Correction (Shift+Ctrl/CMD+R).

Let's take a tour of the workspace. Refer to Figure 9-108.

Figure 9-108. *Lens Correction filter workspace*

On the left are a few tools you can hover over with the mouse to get further information on how they are used. Refer to Figure 9-109.

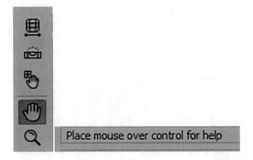

Figure 9-109. *Lens Correction filter tools and help when you hover over them with the mouse*

Lens Correction Tools

- **Remove Distortion tool (D)**: Drag outwards from or inwards to the center to correct distortion. This will cause the image to bulge or pinch. Refer to Figure 9-110.

Figure 9-110. *Remove Distortion tool and how it affects the appearance of the room*

Hold down the Alt/Option key and click the Cancel/Reset button to reset. Refer to Figure 9-111.

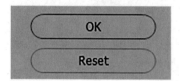

Figure 9-111. *Hold down the Alt/Option key when you want to access the Reset button*

Check your before and after by enabling or disabling the Preview check box (P) at the bottom of the panel. Refer to Figure 9-112.

Figure 9-112. *Lens Correction filter lower navigation area with camera info, preview, and grid options*

- **Straighten Tool (A)**: Draw a line to straighten the image to a new horizontal or vertical access. Refer to Figure 9-113.

Figure 9-113. *Straighten tool and how it affects the appearance of the room*

Hold down the Alt/Option key and click the Cancel/Reset button to reset. Refer to Figure 9-111.

- **Move Grid tool (M):** Drag to move the alignment grid. The grid adjustment can be found on the lower area of the workspace next to the camera profile info and Preview check box. Use Show Grid to show the grid when enabled and adjust the color using the Color Picker and adjust the Grid Size (8-256). Refer to Figure 9-114.

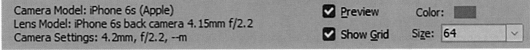

Figure 9-114. *Move Grid tool and how it affects the appearance of the room and grid options in the lower area of the Lens Correction workspace*

- **Hand Tool (H):** Drag or move the image in the window when zoomed in to an area. Or hold down the spacebar key if working with another tool. Refer to Figure 9-11.

- **Zoom Tool (Z):** Click or drag over the area you want to enlarge. Press Alt/Option to zoom out. You can also adjust your zoom area in the lower left of the panel by clicking on the plus or minus keys or from the dropdown. Refer to Figure 9-112 and Figure 9-115.

Figure 9-115. *Hand and Zoom tools*

In my case, I did not use any of the tools; however, I am going to make sure that I have the correct settings in the Auto Correction tab.

Auto Correction Tab

On the right are the various lens correction settings that you can use. Refer to Figure 9-116.

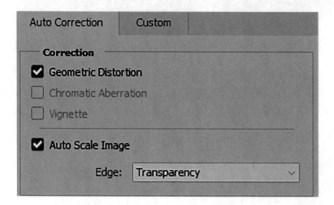

Figure 9-116. *Lens Correction filter Auto Correction tab and its options*

- **Geometric Distortion check box**: Enables automatic geometric distortion correction. I have this enabled.

- **Chromatic Aberration check box**: Enables automatic chromatic aberration correction. In this case, there was none and it is disabled, but you can reset this in the Camera Raw filter manually if required.

- **Vignette check box**: Enables automatic vignette correction. In this case, there was none and it is disabled, but you can reset this in the Camera Raw filter manually if required.

- **Auto Scale Image check box**: Enables automatic scaling when correcting distortions and unintentional scale while adjusting perspective and angle. This crops the transparent gap edge when enabled. Refer to Figure 9-116 and Figure 9-117.

Figure 9-117. *Auto Correction tab, Auto Scale Image option when disabled and enabled for image*

- **Edge**: Specifies edge treatment for correction images. From the dropdown menu, choose one of the options: Edge extension, Transparency, Black Color, White Color. This is apparent only when the Auto Scale Image check box is disabled. Refer to Figure 9-118.

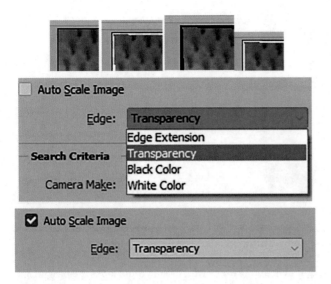

Figure 9-118. *Auto Scale Image option disabled and then edge options from dropdown menu as they appear in the image, and then Auto Scale image enabled to crop edge*

In my case, I left the Edge at the Transparency setting and kept Auto Scale Image enabled.

- **Search Criteria Menu**: When set to Match Image Sensor Size or Prefer Raw Profiles, this can alter how the distortion is corrected. In my case, I set it to Match Image Sensor Size and because my image had a profile, the Camera Make filled itself in automatically. See the camera model profile on the lower left of the workspace. Refer to Figure 9-119.

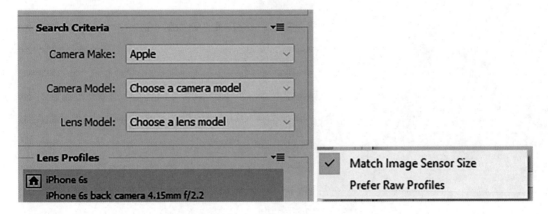

Figure 9-119. *Lens Correction filter Search Criteria and menu options*

Then I can choose the camera model by looking at my profile or another one. I chose iPhone 6s. Refer to Figure 9-120.

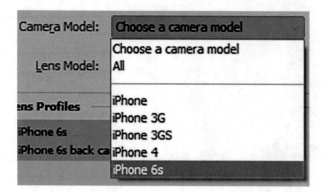

Figure 9-120. Search criteria for camera model

Lastly, I can set my Lens Model from the dropdown. This gradually eliminates various lens models in the lens profile box. I can keep the lens model not filled to a specific one at the default of All and then have many options to choose from and can click through them and preview which one I think looks the best for this image. Refer to Figure 9-121.

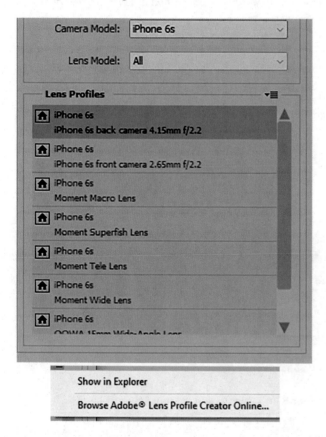

Figure 9-121. Searching for camera model, lens model, and lens profile

- **Lens Profiles**: You can view optional lens profiles under this menu such as Show in Explorer (to see the lens profiles in the Explorer window on your computer) or Browse Adobe Lens Profile Creator Online to see addition lens profile options if available. Refer to Figure 9-121.

■ **Note** If you cannot access Adobe Lens Profile Creator, refer to this link: `https://helpx.adobe.com/camera-raw/digital-negative.html#Adobe_Lens_Profile_Creator`.

Custom Tab

Click the Custom tab to adjust your settings further. This is a good area to use if you have an older camera that does not have a lens profile and the Auto Correction tab is grayed out. You can use it with your images with profiles as well. Many of these settings are similar to the ones found in the Camera Raw filter that you reviewed under the Optics and Geometry tabs. Refer to Figure 9-122.

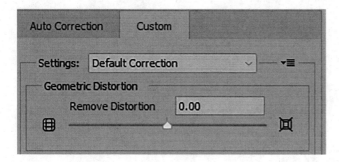

Figure 9-122. Lens Correction filter Custom tab and its options

- **Settings**: Use Lens Default, Previous Correction (Last used setting), Custom, Default Correction, or saved settings. From the Settings menu to the right you can Load, Save, Delete settings, Set Lens Default, and Delete Lens Default. These settings are in an .lcs file format. Refer to Figure 9-123.

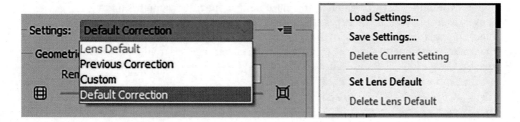

Figure 9-123. Lens Correction filter Custom tab and its options for settings

- **Geometric Distortion**: Remove distortion slider: Move left to fix a pincushion distortion (-100 to 0) or right to fix a barrel distortion (0 to +100). Refer to Figure 9-124.

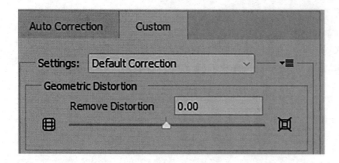

Figure 9-124. *Lens Correction filter Custom tab and its options for correcting geometric distortion*

- **Chromatic Aberration**: Fix Red/Cyan Fringe slider, Fix Green/Magenta Fringe slider, and Fix Blue/Yellow Fringe slider. Use the sliders to correct specific color fringes around edge details within the image. The default for each slider is 0 but you can move the sliders left (-100) or right (+100). Use your Zoom tool to make sure the changes are occurring. Refer to Figure 9-125.

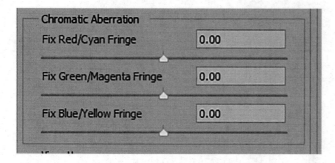

Figure 9-125. *Custom tab and its options for correcting chromatic aberrations*

- **Vignette**: Amount (darken, lighten from -100, 0, +100) adjusts the vignette's under- or over- exposure around the edges of the image. Midpoint modifies the midpoint to affect the spread and restriction of the vignette correction (0 to +100). Alternatively, you can use the vignette sliders to create an artistic effect if you are trying to give your image a vintage look. Refer to Figure 9-126.

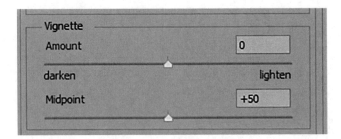

Figure 9-126. *Lens Correction filter Custom tab and its options for correcting a vignette*

- **Transform**: Vertical Perspective modifies the vertical perspective at the top or bottom of the image to make the image's vertical lines parallel (-100, 0, +100).

  Horizontal Perspective modifies the horizontal perspective at the left or right side of the image to make the horizontal lines parallel (-100, 0, +100).

  Angle set the angle of rotation for the image and you can use the Straighten tool to set this to 0-360° or alter with the dial or enter in the text box.

  Scale scales the image after correction (50-150%). This does not affect the document size, but rather crops the image to avoid blank areas while you are altering other options. Refer to Figure 9-127.

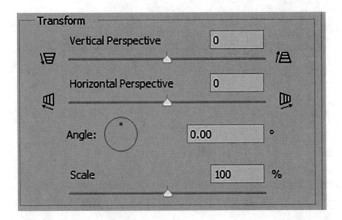

Figure 9-127. *Lens Correction filter Custom tab and its options for making image transformations*

You may need to return to your auto correction tab and adjust further to correct settings.

In this case, I left the settings in the Custom area at default. But for your project, you may want to alter the sliders.

■ **Tip** Use the File ➤ Automate ➤ Lens Correction dialog box when you have multiple photos in a batch that need lens correction.

Then, in the upper right, click OK to save changes or cancel to exit. Refer to Figure 9-128.

Figure 9-128. *Click OK to commit your Lens Correction settings*

I clicked OK and this applied the Lens Correction above the Camera Raw filter. Refer to Figure 9-129.

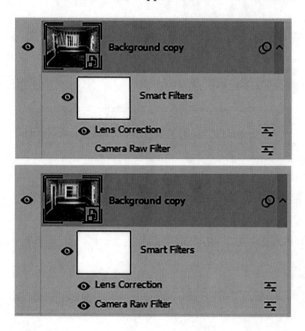

Figure 9-129. *Turn the Camera Raw filter visibility back on to compare your work so far*

I then click to enable the visibility eye for the Camera Raw filter. To preview the current results and see if an adjustment needs to be made, I can double-click the Camera Raw filter and adjust the Geometry settings tab in the Filters workspace. Refer to Figure 9-130.

Figure 9-130. *The room is now straighter with both filters applied to the smart object layer*

You can look at my file IMG_0886_room_2_final.psd to review settings that I used to straighten the room and double-click either the smart object filters, Lens Correction filter, or Camera Raw filter.

Likewise, as mentioned with the Adaptive Wide Angle Lens, if there is any stretching or distortion or gaps after you have applied your Camera Raw filter and Lens Correction filter, you can always add back to image's blank areas on a new layer, as you did with the Perspective Warp tool of Chapter 7. You could try any one of the various Content-Aware options that I mentioned in that chapter. Later, you can fill in the blanks using the Clone Stamp and Eraser tools to blend areas in the distorted image.

For additional lens and noise reduction options, you can visit https://helpx.adobe.com/photoshop/using/correcting-image-distortion-noise.html.

Liquify Filter

If you want to really warp and distort part of an image like the Smudge tool in Chapter 2 or the Puppet Warp tool in Chapter 6, then the Liquify filter might be just what you are looking for. It also might be considered a correction tool, depending on your project. While this tool is generally associated with the other touch-up tools for doing cosmetic adjustments on models, there is no reason why you cannot use it on other types of photographs as well or even on images of your pets. As you saw earlier with other advanced filters, for your projects, working with a smart object layer so that you can return and edit any time by double-clicking the smart filter name, is the best solution.

Project: Liquify (Minerals)

In this first example, we will start practicing with the Liquify filter on a copper rock and a piece of shiny metal copper. I want to see the copper pool and flow over the rock so I think this filter will give me at least the starting point for that effect.

File ➤ Open IMG_2619_copper_melt_start.psd. Make an Image ➤ Duplicate if you want to practice with this file and select the smart object layer named Copper Rock. Refer to Figure 9-131.

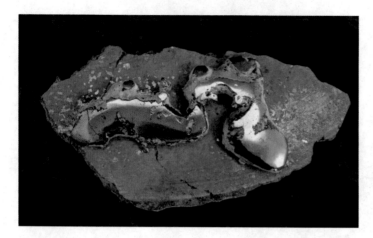

Figure 9-131. *Copper rock samples on a stone background*

To start, go to Filter ➤ Liquify (Shift+Ctrl/CMD+X). Let's explore the workspace. Refer to Figure 9-132.

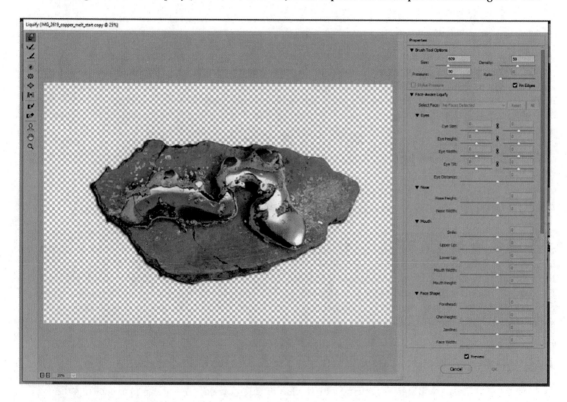

Figure 9-132. *The Liquify Filter workspace*

On the left side are a few tools for working on the Preview image, some of which you may already be familiar with. After you have finished this book, if you are interested in similar tools found in the Illustrator, make sure to check out Volume 2. Refer to Figure 9-133.

Figure 9-133. Liquify Filter tools

Liquify Tools

- **Forward Warp Tool (W):** Similar to a Brush or Smudge tool, drag with the tool left, right, up, or down to create a warp-like smudge based on the drag direction. See Brush tool options in the Properties panel on the right for tool options. Refer to Figure 9-134.

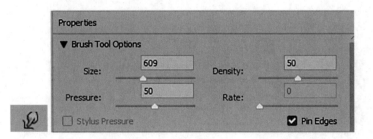

Figure 9-134. Forward Warp tool and its Brush Tool Options properties

You can adjust the brush's Circumference Size (1-15000, for size of selected brush currently in use), the Density Brush edge strength (0-100, used for feathering), the Pressure distortion strength (1-100, used as you drag the brush), Rate for stationary brush (0-100, controls flow rate when mouse button is held down in one location and is disabled for this brush and for other stationary brushes), Stylus pressure (if available when using a stylus, is affected by the brush pressure), Pin edges check box (to lock image's edges and prevent missing information in the corners when the brush is passed over). Refer to Figure 9-134.

Like other mentioned Brush tools, you can Click and then Shift+Click to move in a straight line. Use the left ([) and right (]) bracket keys on the keyboard to decrease or increase the brush size quickly. The smaller the brush, the less noticeable the distortion.

In this case, I will use a Large Brush of Size: 609, Density: 50, and Pressure: 50. I might occasionally lower and raise its size in order to make the liquid and rock appear like it is melting and flowing over the edge of the copper rock. Refer to Figure 9-135.

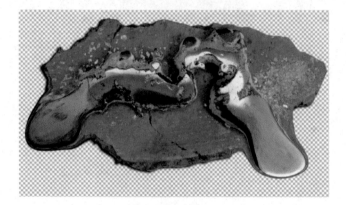

Figure 9-135. *Liquify Filter with Forward Warp tool applied to the copper melt ends*

Do not worry at this point if your rock below the copper melts as well, as you can clean that up later using the smart filter mask or even a layer mask after you exit the Liquify filter. So, the results do not have to be perfect because you are getting the feel of how the tool operates.

- **Reconstruct tool (R):** Acts much like an eraser or History Brush tool, as seen in Chapter 2. It restores areas altered by the Forward Warp tool or other brush tools, which we will look at next.

  Like the Forward Warp tool, you can find additional settings in the Properties Brush Tool Options and the rate setting is available. Use your left and right bracket keys to decrease or increase the brush size quickly. Refer to Figure 9-136.

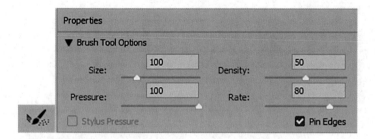

Figure 9-136. *Reconstruct tool and its Brush Tool Options properties*

■ **Tips**   Click and then Shift +Click to move in a straight line. Add the Alt/Option key while dragging to turn it into the Smooth tool instead.

Further options for this brush can be found in the lower area of the Properties panel; see the section on brush reconstruct options later in this section.

In this example, I'll try using a smaller brush of Size: 100, Density: 50, Pressure: 100, Rate: 80, and try painting back a few areas near the rock edge as it flows over so that it is not quite so melted. You can use Ctrl/CMD+Z if you need to undo a reconstruct step. Likewise, you can return to your previous brush or any other brush we will be discussing, to adjust the melting effect as you work. Refer to Figure 9-137.

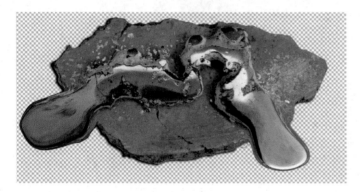

Figure 9-137. *Reconstruct Tool applied to copper melt ends*

- **Smooth tool (E)**: Like the Reconstruct tool, it can be used to smooth out the ripple areas altered by the Forward Warp tool or other brush tools, which we will look at next. Like the Forward Warp tool, you can find additional settings in the Properties Brush Tool Options and the rate setting is available. Refer to Figure 9-138.

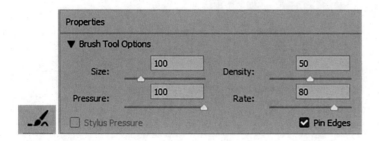

Figure 9-138. *Smooth tool and its Brush Tool Options properties*

■ **Tip**   Use your left and right bracket keys to decrease or increase the brush size quickly.

In this case, I will use the same setting as I did with the earlier Reconstruct Tool Brush and will smooth out any uneven edges around the melt on the left or right side. Here is a before and after of the left melt, as my right melt appeared OK. But every project will be different. Use Ctrl/CMD+Z when you need to go back a step. Refer to Figure 9-139.

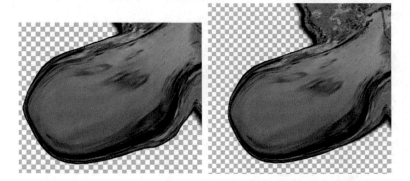

Figure 9-139. *Smooth tool applied to edge of copper melt before and after*

- **Twirl Clockwise tool (C)**: Gradually, with your set brush size, twirl in an area clockwise. The longer you hold down the mouse, the more that area will bend and twirl. Like the Forward Warp tool, you can find additional settings in the Properties Brush Tool Options. Refer to Figure 9-140.

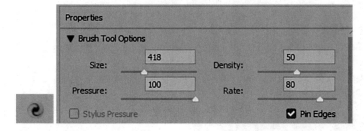

Figure 9-140. *Twirl Clockwise tool and its Brush Tool Options properties*

■ **Tips**   If you want to twirl counterclockwise, add the Alt/Option key as you hold the mouse down. Add the Shift key for a more aggressive clockwise twirl or Alt/Option+Shift for the aggressive twirl to be counterclockwise.

Use your left and right bracket keys to decrease or increase the brush size quickly.

In this example, test your twirl on another area of the stone. Use Size: 418, Density: 50, Pressure: 100, and Rate: 80. Hold down the mouse key with or without the Alt/Option key on your keyboard and then release the mouse to see the effect. Afterwards, using your Reconstruct tool or Ctrl/CMD +Z, undo the twirl painting back to the original construction. Refer to Figure 9-141.

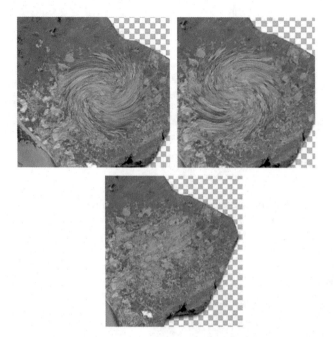

Figure 9-141. *Twirl Clockwise tool applied, then Alt/Option key added, and then the Reconstruct tool used to erase the twirl*

- **Pucker tool (S)**: Creates an area of pucker based on your brush size, gradually pulling the area inside the brush inward the longer you hold the mouse down. Like the Forward Warp tool, you can find additional settings in the Properties Brush Tool Options; however, the Pressure setting is not available. Refer to Figure 9-142.

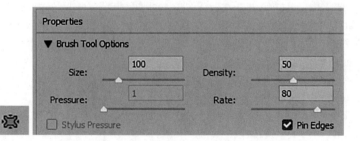

Figure 9-142. *Pucker tool and its Brush Tool Options properties*

■ **Tips** Adding the Alt/Option key causes the tool to change to the Bloat tool. Add the Shift key for a more aggressive pucker or Alt/Option+Shift for a more aggressive bloat. Like other brushes, you can Click and then Shift+Click or Alt/Option+Shift+Click if you want the pucker or bloat to follow a straight line. Use your left and right bracket keys to decrease or increase the brush size quickly.

Try using the Pucker tool of Size: 100, Density: 50, and Rate 80 on one of the shiny copper spots and notice how it disappears slightly or shrinks as you hold down the mouse key. Use Ctrl/CMD+Z if you want to undo this step or use the Reconstruct tool. Refer to Figure 9-143.

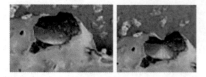

Figure 9-143. *Pucker applied to one of the copper spots before and after*

- **Bloat tool (B)**: Creates an area of bloat based on your brush size, gradually pushing the area inside the brush outward the longer you hold the mouse down. Like the Forward Warp tool, you can find additional settings in the Properties Brush Tool Options; however, the Pressure setting is not available. Refer to Figure 9-144.

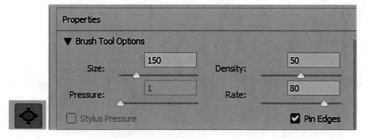

Figure 9-144. *Bloat tool and its Brush Tool Options properties*

■ **Tips** Adding the Alt/Option key causes the tool to change to the Pucker tool. Add the Shift key for a more aggressive bloat or Alt/Option+Shift for a more aggressive pucker. Like other brushes, you can Click and then Shift+Click or Alt/Option+Shift+Click if you want the bloat or pucker to follow a straight line. Use your left and right bracket keys to decrease or increase the brush size quickly.

Try using the Bloat tool of Size: 150, Density: 50, and Rate: 80 on one of the shiny copper spots and notice how the area grows and expands as you hold down the mouse key. Click around the area, holding the mouse key down for a greater area of expansion. Use Ctrl/CMD+Z if you want to undo this step or use the Reconstruct tool. Refer to Figure 9-145.

Figure 9-145. *Bloat applied to one of the copper spots before and after*

- **Push Left tool (O)**: like the Forward Warp tool, it pushes the pixels in the brush left or right by dragging and moving the brush up or down, depending on how you drag over the image. As with the Forward Warp tool, you can find additional settings in the Properties Brush Tool Options; however, the Rate setting is not available. Refer to Figure 9-146.

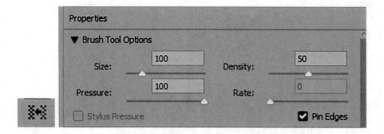

Figure 9-146. *Push Left tool and its Brush Tool Options properties*

■ **Tips** Adding the Alt/Option key causes the tool to change to the Push Right tool, while dragging and moving up or down and shifting the pixels. Add the Shift key for a more aggressive left push or Alt/Option+Shift for a more aggressive right push. Like other brushes, you can Click and then Shift+Click or Alt/Option+Shift+Click if you want the push to follow a straight line. Use your left and right bracket keys to decrease or increase the brush size quickly.

Try using this tool to modify your melted areas, redirecting areas of the flow. Use Size: 100, Density: 50, and Pressure: 100. Use Ctrl/CMD+Z if you want to undo this step or use the Reconstruct tool. Refer to Figure 9-147.

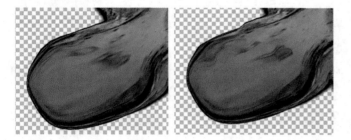

Figure 9-147. *Push Left tool used to smooth out the melt and modify it*

- **Freeze Mask tool (F)**: Use this tool to prevent areas from being affected by the other brush liquify tools while you create distorts. This includes the Reconstruct tool. Like the Forward Warp tool, you can find additional settings in the Properties Brush Tool Options; however, the Rate setting is not available. Refer to Figure 9-148.

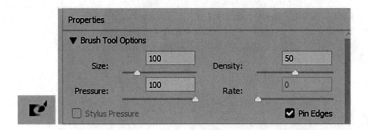

Figure 9-148. *Freeze Mask tool and its Brush Tool Options properties*

It paints a red mask, depending on your brush size. We'll look at the mask option and details in the Properties panel later in this section. Now, if you paint in those areas with another tool, they will not be affected by the warp because that area is locked or frozen as it would be if you were using a mask or selection. Refer to Figure 9-149.

■ **Tips**   As you paint, you can add the Alt/Option key and it will switch to the Thaw Mask tool, allowing you to erase the Freeze Mask.

Like other brushes, you can Click and then Shift+Click or Alt/Option+Shift+Click if you want the Freeze Mask tool or Thaw to follow a straight line.

Use your left and right bracket keys to decrease or increase the brush size quickly.

Here you can see how I added a Freeze Mask of Size: 100, Density: 50, and Pressure: 100, so that if I paint with other brush tools afterwards, this area is not affected by that brush. Refer to Figure 9-149.

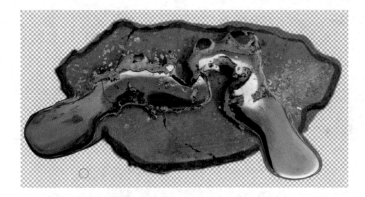

Figure 9-149. *Freeze Mask painted around the edge of the copper rock to prevent distortion from other tools*

- **Thaw Mask tool (D)**: Use this tool when you want to erase the red mask that you created with the Freeze Mask tool and to restore areas affected by the other brush liquify tools while you create distorts. We'll look at the mask options and details in the Properties panel later in this section. As with the Forward Warp tool, you can find additional settings in the Properties Brush Tool Options; however, the Rate setting is not available. Refer to Figure 9-150.

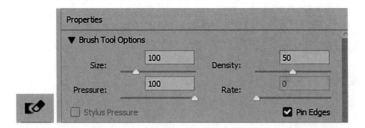

Figure 9-150. *Thaw Mask tool and its Brush Tool Options properties*

■ **Tips** As you paint, you can add the Alt/Option key and it will switch to the Freeze Mask tool, allowing you to add a Freeze mask. Like other brushes, you can Click and then Shift+Click or Alt/Option+Shift+Click if you want the Thaw Mask tool or Freeze to follow a straight line. Use your left [and right] bracket keys to decrease or increase the brush size quickly.

In this example, I used the Thaw Mask tool to erase the Freeze Mask at Size: 100, Density: 50 Pressure: 100, so now all edges of the rock can be distorted. Refer to Figure 9-151.

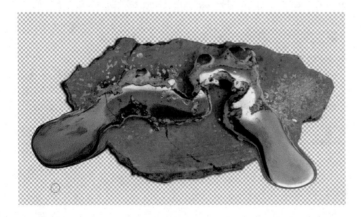

Figure 9-151. *Use the Thaw Mask tool to erase the Freeze Mask tool*

- **Face tool (A):** If you are working with human faces, this tool may be helpful to you. However, pet faces may not be detected, and as this copper stone example contains no faces, you will get a warning message when you click on this button. Click OK and click on another tool to exit. Refer to Figure 9-152.

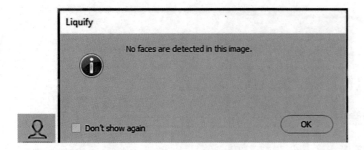

Figure 9-152. *Face tool will not operate and will show an info message if no face is present. Click OK*

Later, after we have finished this copper project, we will explore Faces further, along with the Face-aware liquify options in the Properties panel.

- **Hand Tool (H)**: Move around the image while zoomed in or hold down the spacebar if working with another tool. Refer to Figure 9-153

Figure 9-153. *Liquify filter Hand tool, Zoom tool, and zoom in and zoom out navigation*

- **Zoom Tool (Z)**: Zoom in or Alt/Option zoom to zoom out, or use the navigation buttons, or use the dropdown menu in the lower left.

■ **Note** For additional reconstruct settings, refer to the Properties Panel Brush reconstruct options mentioned at the end of the section on the Liquify filter.

At this point, continue to work on your melted effect with the various brush tools that you have learned so far. Once you are happy with the effect (it does not have to be exactly the same as mine), click the OK button to commit and exit the dialog box. Refer to Figure 9-154.

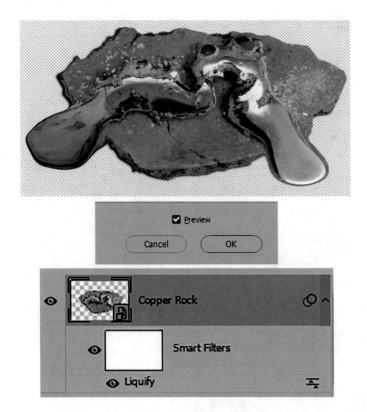

Figure 9-154. *When finished with your Liquify filter, click OK to exit and view the smart object filter in the Layers panel*

Now, at this point, to further restore some of the original edges around the rock so that it does not appear melted, select your smart filters mask and, with your Eraser tool, hide areas so that it appears that only the copper and not the rock is melting. You can vary the size and hardness of the eraser. I used a General Brush of either Soft Round or Hard Round, using the Options panel as required to conceal parts of the Liquify melt. Refer to Figure 9-155.

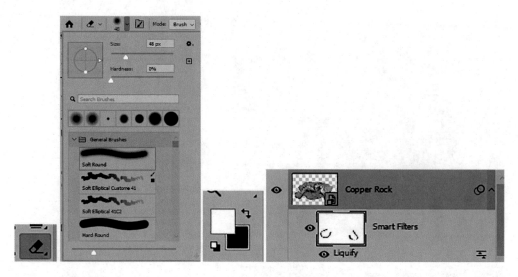

Figure 9-155. *Use your Eraser tool brush options and Tools panel default colors to paint on the smart filter layer to clean up edges*

Remember to press D to reset your brush; use your X key to switch between revealing and concealing the Liquify Filter areas. Here is how it looks so far. Refer to Figure 9-155 and Figure 9-156.

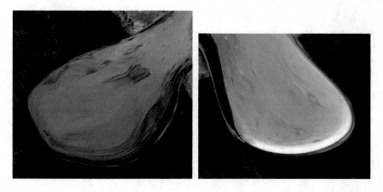

Figure 9-156. *Erasing on the smart filter restored some edges around the rock where the copper melts over*

■ **Note** You should usually edit the mask as a last step, because if you decided to make further modifications at this point to the warp or liquify after exiting the Liquify filter, the mask will not update and so you will need to manually modify the smart filters mask. Refer to Figure 9-155.

Afterwards I added blank layers for additional blends and shadows to make the melt look more realistic. Using a layer blending mode like Overlay, and painting with a white brush in a new layer and lowering the opacity to 67%, can add back some highlights on the Copper Blend layer. The Shadow layer was painted with black and blended with Multiply.

You could use the Clone Stamp and Smudge tools (refer to Chapter 2) on a blank layer, and this will further enhance the Liquify effect. Remember to set in the Options panel for the Clone Stamp that you want to Sample Current & Below; for the Smudge tool Options panel, make sure that Sample All Layers is enabled so that you can acquire details from the smart object. Refer to Layer Clone Stamp and Smudge Tool. Refer to Figure 9-157.

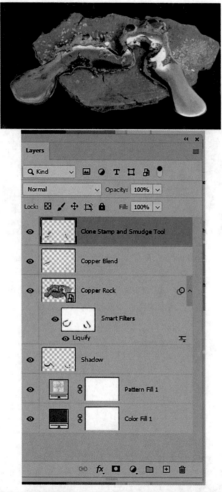

Figure 9-157. *Use additional layers with blending modes and tools like Clone Stamp and Smudge with their options to make the copper melt appear more realistic*

■ **Tip** Use your Eraser tool if you need to remove part of the clone or smudge.

You can view those layers in my file, IMG_2619_copper_melt_final.psd.

Project 2: Liquify (Human Faces)

To continue exploring the Liquify panel, File ➤ Open womens_heads_start.psd.

I took a picture of these female mannequins and realized they would not feel upset if I altered their facial features for this book. Face aware works best with faces facing the camera. Again, select the smart object layer and then go to Filter ➤ Liquify. Refer to Figure 9-158.

Figure 9-158. *Mannequin model heads are great for working in the Liquify filter on a smart object layer*

Now we will be looking at the next section of the Properties panel. This time, select the Face tool (A). Refer to Figure 9-159.

Figure 9-159. *Liquify filter Face tool*

Properties Panel

On the right hand side, we have already looked at the Properties panel Brush Tool Options, which are similar for most brush tools regarding size, density, pressure, and rate. We could use these tools on the mannequins' faces to alter them, but there is another way to do this. Refer to Figure 9-160.

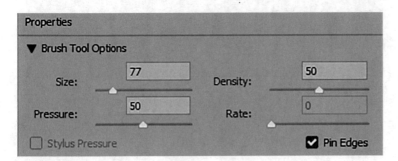

Figure 9-160. *Liquify filter Brush Tool Options*

Let's look at an option below the Brush tool area, called Face-Aware Liquify. Use whatever setting you want as you test these options.

Properties for Face-Aware Liquify

Face-Aware Liquify (Eyes, Nose, Mouth, Face Shape): As mentioned earlier, these properties work with the Face tool when selected. However, if there is no face to detect, as with landscapes, minerals, or pets, then these setting are unavailable, and you receive a warning, and this area is disabled. Refer to Figure 9-161.

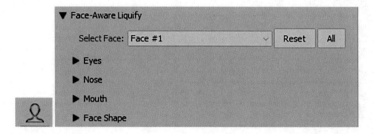

Figure 9-161. *Liquify filter Face-Aware Liquify options*

However, if you have a human figure and a face that can be detected, then you can use Liquify to more accurately modify the following areas. Select a detected face dropdown and use the buttons to Reset a current face or All faces, once they are altered, if you need to reset any alterations you make. Refer to Figure 9-162.

Figure 9-162. *Face-Aware Liquify options for Select Face*

In this project, choose a specific face as there is more than one. I will work with Face #1 on the right in this example, but you can switch to Face #2 at any time. A type of guide or grid will appear for each component of the face in Preview. Use the open arrow for each option as you work on a specific area of the face and hover over text box names if you need more details. Refer to Figure 9-163.

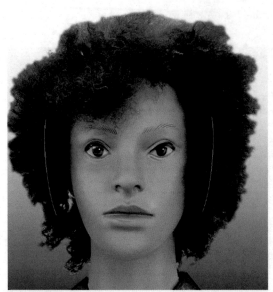

Figure 9-163. Face-Aware Liquify options for eyes and guides on model

---

■ **Note**   If you cannot see the face guides, make sure that Show Face Overlay is enabled in the View options, which we will look at in more detail later. Refer to Figure 9-164.

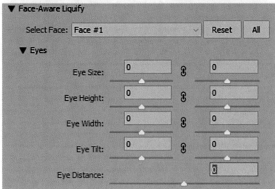

Figure 9-164. Make sure that Show Face Overlay is enabled

- **Eyes:** Adjust with the sliders to set the left and right eye for Eye Size, Eye Height, Eye Width, Eye Tilt, and Eye Distance between both eyes. Refer to Figure 9-165.

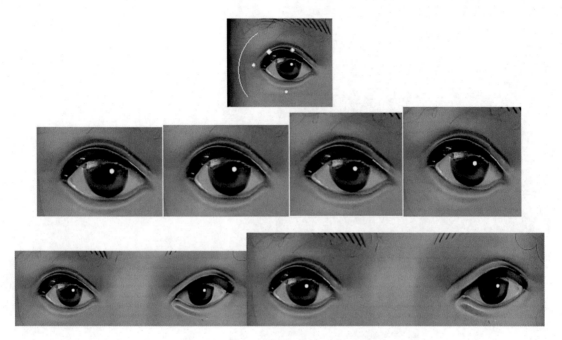

Figure 9-165. *Use the overlay guides or sliders to adjust the eye's size, height, width, tilt, and distance (before and after)*

For example, the setting for eyes range from -100 (eye smaller) to 0 (normal) to +100 (eye enlarged) and you can either use your slider or the guides on the Preview to make the adjustments while dragging inwards or outwards. Refer to Figure 9-166.

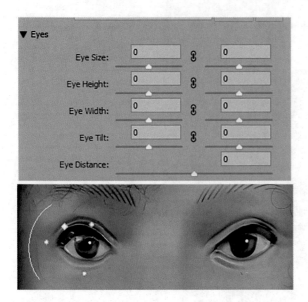

Figure 9-166. *Adjusting each eye with different settings*

Use the link icon for each one of the settings to make changes to the right and left eye together with the same settings, rather than independently if unlinked. Refer to Figure 9-167.

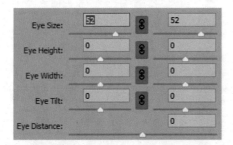

Figure 9-167. *Adjust both eyes at the same time when the link is enabled*

- **Nose**: Adjust with the sliders to set the Nose Height (-100,0, +100) and Nose Width (-100,0+,100). Guides on the Preview are also available to move the nose up or down or enlarge or shrink the nose. Refer to Figure 9-168.

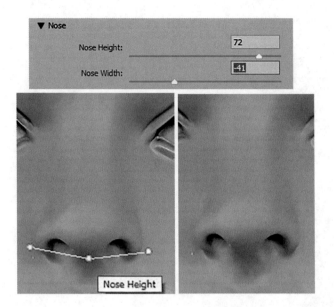

Figure 9-168. *Use the slider or overlay guide to adjust settings for nose height and width*

- **Mouth:** Adjust with the sliders to set the Smile, Upper Lip, Lower Lip, Mouth Width, and Mouth Height. The range for each slider is -100, 0, +100. Guides on the Preview are also available to move around areas of the mouth. Sad or happy lips can be created when you move the smile slider left or right. Refer to Figure 9-169.

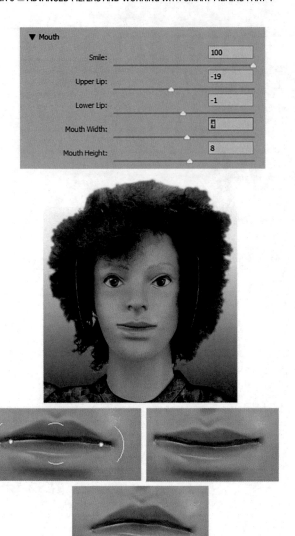

Figure 9-169. *Use the sliders or overlay guides to adjust the smile, upper lip, lower lip and mouth width and height*

- **Face Shape:** Adjust with the sliders to set the Forehead, Chin Height, Jawline, and Face Width. The range for each slider is -100, 0, +100. Guides on the Preview are also available to move around areas of the face. Refer to Figure 9-170.

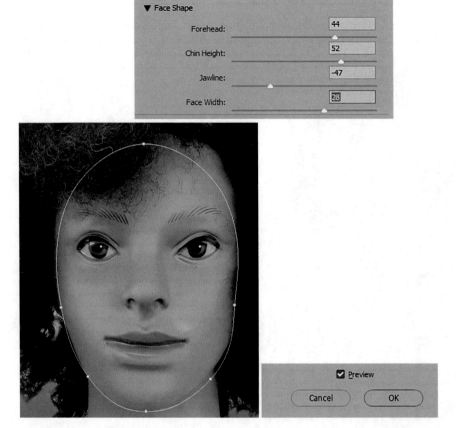

Figure 9-170. *Use the sliders or overlay guides to adjust the face shape for forehead, chin height, jawline, and face width, and click OK to exit when done*

Once you have adjusted the face to your liking, click OK to exit the dialog box and look at the result.

Keep in mind, however, that when working with distortions on the face, it requires practice and patience if you want to make the effect look natural rather than distorted or clown-like. That is why it is good to work on a smart object layer. Refer to Figure 9-171.

Figure 9-171. *A smart filter in the Layers panel stores the settings so that you can return to them any time*

If you don't get it right the first time, you can always try again later when you double-click on the Liquify filter name in the Layers panel.

Double-click to enter the Liquify filter again and continue to look at the Properties Panel. Look at Face #2 on the left and make similar adjustments if you want. Refer to Figure 9-172.

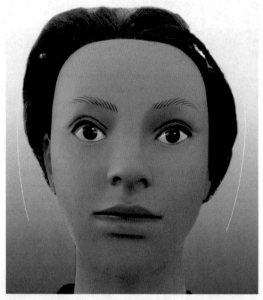

Figure 9-172. *Select the second face if you want to alter it as well*

Parts of the face like ears, if present, would require you to use the other Liquify Brush tools manually to alter them, such as one the brushes mentioned earlier. Use your Freeze Mask Brush to halt certain distorts prior to working on the face. Refer to Figure 9-173.

Figure 9-173. *Use the Freeze Mask when you want to alter areas like ears so that you do not disrupt the hair while working with another brush*

■ **Tip** For those who want to make additional cosmetic changes, after you have used the Liquify filter, make sure to use your other Healing Brushes, Clone Stamp, Smudge, Blur, and Eraser tools (always on a blank layer) to soften the effect and cover up any additional unwanted artifacts or blemishes. Refer to Figure 9-174.

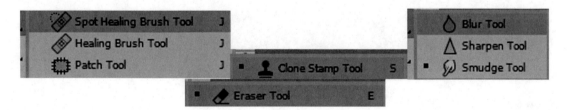

Figure 9-174. *Upon leaving the Liquify tool, you can use anyone of these tools to make further cosmetic changes to your model on a blank layer*

Let's look at the final properties in the Liquify filter in reference to the current image.

Properties for Load Mesh Options and View Options

To see the current mesh, you need to enable the Show Mesh check box. The current mesh is altered when you are in the Liquify preview, with various brushes dragged over it, causing the grid of the mesh to change and bend. Refer to Figure 9-175.

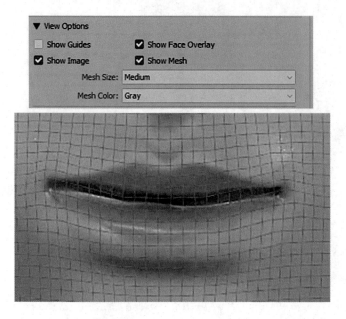

***Figure 9-175.** Liquify filter View options with Show mesh enabled in Preview*

When the show mesh is enabled in the View Options tab, you also have the option to change options using the dropdown menus, such as the mesh size (Small, Medium, or Large) and mesh color (Red, Yellow, Green, Blue, Cyan, Magenta, or Gray) if it makes it easier to preview.

To load a mesh that someone created, return to the Load Mesh options and click the Load Mesh button and locate the mesh file (.msh). Or load the last mesh used previously, by choosing Load Last Mesh. This will reset the mesh. Refer to Figure 9-176.

***Figure 9-176.** Load Mesh Options*

Clicking on the Save Mesh button will allow you to save the mesh you created as a .msh file if you need to use it for other projects that require similar alterations. With smart object layers, the mesh is saved and embedded in the file so you do not have to load it again. Refer to Figure 9-176.

■ **Note** According to Adobe, loaded meshes from other projects that are not the same size as current image are scaled to fit.

In the View options you can also enable the Show Guides check box, if you set guides earlier in the Photoshop file prior to entering the Liquify workspace. They are useful when you need to line up areas. Refer to Figure 9-177.

Figure 9-177. *Liquify Filter View options*

The Show Image check box turns on or off the image preview. As noted earlier, Show Face Overlay allows you to see the preview of the Face Liquify options when you work with the Face tool.

Properties For Freeze Mask Options and View Options

As noted earlier, you can create custom masks to prevent distortion, but you can also alter the mask further with a selection or saved channel selection created prior to entering the Liquify filter. These can then be further adjusted with the properties of the Mask options. Refer to Figure 9-178.

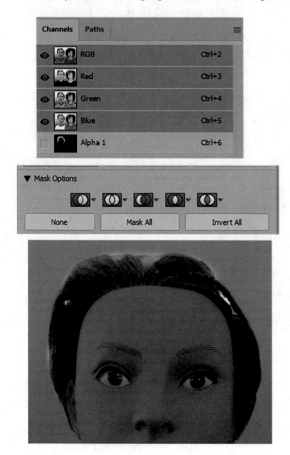

Figure 9-178. *Mask options using a selection stored externally in the Channels panel*

Whether or not you have a current Freeze Mask present, the following mask option icons are available: Replace Selection, Add to Selection, Subtract from Selection, Intersect with Selection, and Invert Selection. The selection can be either a selection that you created before you entered the Liquify filter, or a transparency, a layer mask, or an alpha channel (Alpha 1) found in the Channels Panel. You can choose a mask option from the dropdown menu for each section option. Refer to Figure 9-179.

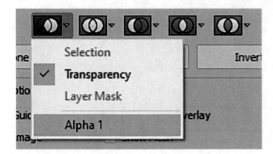

Figure 9-179. *Selecting the Alpha 1 selection stored in the Channels panel*

Multiple selections, transparencies, layer masks, and channel selections can be used in combination, depending on the order they are chosen to create a better Thaw and Freeze mask. Likewise, if you have a mask present already, you can delete it by pressing None. To mask the whole area, click Mask All. To invert the mask, click the Invert All button. Freeze Masks are not stored in the Liquify filter upon exiting, so creating a mask prior to entering the filter is a good idea if the mask will be complex and will be used again. Refer to Figure 9-180.

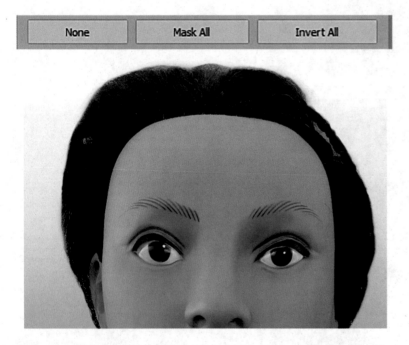

Figure 9-180. *Mask Options. Choose Invert All for the current mask*

In the View options menu, to see the mask clearly, make sure to enable the Show Mask check box. If you do not want the default red mask color, you can choose another color from the Mask Color dropdown menu, like you did with the mesh. Refer to Figure 9-181.

Figure 9-181. *View Options for Show Mask when enabled*

For a more through discussion on masks, selections, and channel creation outside the Liquify filter, make sure to check out my book *Accurate Layer Selections Using Photoshop's Selection Tools*.

You can see the selection I used and stored in the channels panel in my file named `womens_heads_final.psd`. See the alpha 1 channel. This was useful so that I could adjust the Face #2 hair with the Forward Warp tool. Refer to Figure 9-182.

Figure 9-182. *Adjust the woman's hair using the Forward Warp tool*

Additional View Options

Besides the View options already mentioned as they relate to the preview image, mesh, and mask, you can also enable the Show Backdrop check box.

Use this in your own projects to compare or preview the Liquify layer with all layers outside the Liquify filter or blend with a specific layer or background. The Mode can be set to In Front, Behind, or Blend. The Opacity slider value ranges from 0-100%. Refer to Figure 9-183.

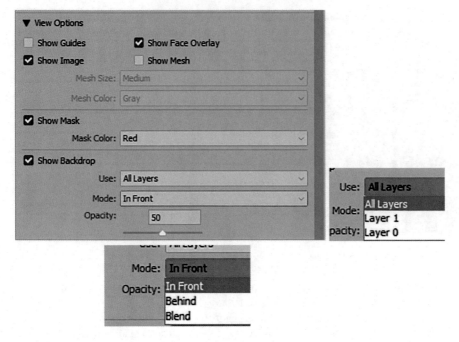

Figure 9-183. *View options for Show Backdrop*

■ **Note** This Show Backdrop check box does not alter the Liquify filter in any way. However, I recommend that before you leave the filter and click OK, you uncheck it so that seeing faces or other items overlaying the preview does not confuse you. Refer to Figure 9-184.

Figure 9-184. *Disable Show Backdrop before you exit the Liquify filter so that you are not confused by the odd preview when you enter the filter again*

Brush Reconstruct Options

For the Reconstruct tool, further options include the reconstruct button to revert the reconstruction by a set amount (0-100, the default is 100) or Restore All to reset the image back to its original state as well as in frozen areas. Refer to Figure 9-185.

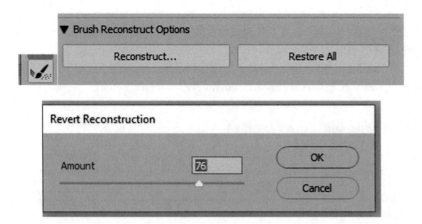

Figure 9-185. *Brush Reconstruct Options for the Reconstruct tool and Revert Reconstruct dialog box*

Turn the Preview check box on and off when you want to see the before and after. Refer to Figure 9-186.

Figure 9-186. *Use the Preview check box to see the before after and click OK to exit the dialog box*

Once done, click OK or Cancel to exit. Refer to Figure 9-187.

Figure 9-187. *The model's faces have been altered and the Liquify filter has been applied to the smart object Layer in the Layers panel*

■ **Remember** As you saw with the copper example, you can also use your smart filter mask to hide any area and with the Brush or Eraser tool to blend in any area to reveal parts of the original thumbnail.

For some additional related face distort, make sure to check out the Neural filter options in Chapter 10.

Tips: Working with Pet's Faces with the Liquify Filter

Most of what you learned in these two Liquify projects you can apply to animal faces as well. However, as mentioned earlier, Liquify cannot detect pet faces. So, you must rely on the other Liquify brush tools to alter the animal's face.

Using Freeze Mask tool is useful if you want to avoid distorting certain parts of the face around hair or eyes. For example, in this case, I used the Bloat tool to enlarge the eyes, but with the Freeze mask applied to the fur areas around the eyes, they were not disturbed. Refer to Figure 9-188.

Figure 9-188. *Appling a Freeze mask to the cat's face before I use the Bloat tool on the eyes so as not to disturb the fur*

■ **Tip** If working with a Shape layer or Type layer that you want to Liquify, make sure that is it is converted to a smart object layer first before you apply the filter, as you saw in earlier projects. Refer to Figure 9-189.

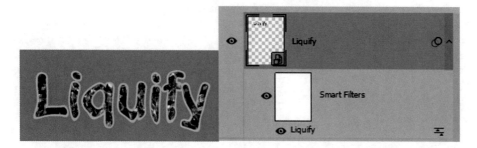

Figure 9-189. *Use the Liquify filter on text when its inside a smart object layer*

Summary

In this chapter, you looked at several of the advanced filters and workspaces. Some are for lens correction, like Adaptive Wide Angle and Camera Raw, and others, like the Liquify filter, are for warping and distorting.

In the next chapter, you will look at more advanced filters, some of which can be used with smart objects layers and in combination with other smart filters on a single layer.

CHAPTER 10

■ ■ ■

Advanced Filters and Working with Smart Filters Part 2

Chapter Goal: In this chapter we will continue to explore various advanced filters found in the Filter menu. For warping and distorting, we will look at Vanishing Point and how it compares to Perspective Warp. We'll also look at two of the latest Neural Filters. Later I will mention how you can acquire additional filters.

■ **Note**   You can find the projects for this chapter in the Chapter 10 folder.

Advanced Filters

As mentioned in Chapter 9, advanced filters often have an entire workspace area with tools and options panels specifically devoted to one filter. You saw some workspaces earlier in Chapter 8 when we looked at the Filter Gallery and the Blur Gallery, but they were devoted to multiple filters that were part of a grouped collection. Most of these advanced filters can be used on smart object layers as well. For this section, refer to the upper area of the Filter menu. Refer to Figure 10-1.

Tiles	Alt+Ctrl+F
Convert for Smart Filters	
Neural Filters...	
Filter Gallery...	
Adaptive Wide Angle...	Alt+Shift+Ctrl+A
Camera Raw Filter...	Shift+Ctrl+A
Lens Correction...	Shift+Ctrl+R
Liquify...	Shift+Ctrl+X
Vanishing Point...	Alt+Ctrl+V

***Figure 10-1.** Advanced filters in the Filter menu*

© Jennifer Harder 2023
J. Harder, *Perspective Warps and Distorts with Adobe Tools: Volume 1*,
https://doi.org/10.1007/978-1-4842-8710-1_10

Vanishing Point

The Vanishing Point filter is very similar to the Perspective Warp tool in Chapter 7 but does have some important differences that I will point out. This filter does not work with smart object layers. However, you can have smart object layers within the file. In this case, we will be working with several normal layers, as I will be demonstrating in this section of the Chapter.

For this project, you can use your own files or you can follow along with me and use the files in the projects folder.

Project 1: Using the Vanishing Point Filter to Alter a Road Area and Place Graffiti Graphics on a Fence

File ➤ Open vanishing_point_paint_stamp_start.psd. Like the other projects we've worked in so far, it is in RGB Mode so that I can use this filter.

Make an Image ➤ Duplicate the file if you don't want to save over the original. Click OK. Refer to Figure 10-2.

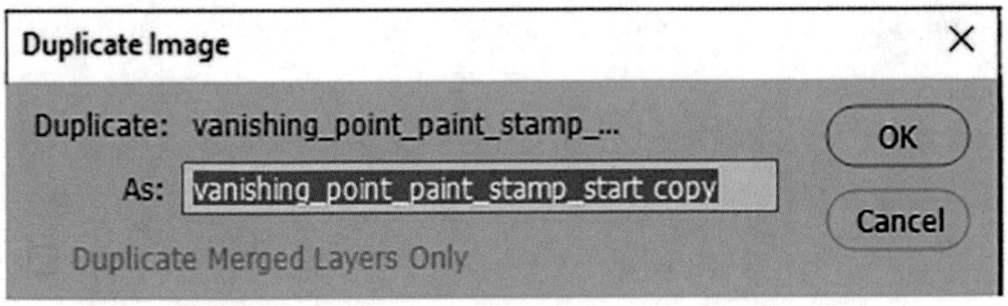

Figure 10-2. Duplicate Image dialog box

In this example, we are going to draw some graffiti on a fence, add another fence post, and remove signage from the pavement. Refer to Figure 10-3.

Figure 10-3. A road with a long fence moving into the distance on the left

■ **Note**   I do not condone destroying or altering other people's property. You should only be painting your artwork or murals on other people's walls or fences after you have received permission from the owner or business. However, in the virtual world of Photoshop, you can be as artistic as you want, and nobody will be upset.

The Vanishing Point filter is probably one of the most complex filters to master in Photoshop, and to a beginner or intermediate student of the program it can appear a bit confusing. However, I am going to show you some simple ways that you can use this filter if you have a concept image design that requires artwork or signage to be added to a wall digitally before you add it to a wall in reality.

Adding artwork to a wall that you are looking at directly at it is easy. But if you are given a picture by a client where the wall, building, or ground are at an angle or certain perspective, it's quite a challenge.

Remember, perspective is the art of drawing solid objects on a two-dimensional surface so as to give the right impression of their height, width, depth, and position in relation to each other when viewed from a particular point.

In Chapter 4, we figured that out manually by just using Edit ➤ Transform ➤ Perspective or Warp, solely using the bounding box handles on a layer in the Layers panel. But that is not always the best solution. We found a better way in Chapter 7 using Edit ➤ Perspective Warp, which gave better results and could be stored as a smart object layer. To become a Photoshop artist, your eyes need to be trained to recognize the correct perspective.

■ **Note**   We will review Perspective Warp in the third part of this project.

Thankfully, Photoshop makes it very easy to learn with the Vanishing Point tool. And you can create perspective in a less destructive way when you follow the filter's rules.

■ **Note**   If you are using your own background images in this project, you may need to Edit ➤ Transform ➤ Rotate or even use the Filter ➤ Adaptive Wide Lens and use guides if you need make the scene level before you proceed, as this could affect how the filter interprets the perspective planes. In my images that you are using, I have already adjusted for that.

For this filter, as well as the others, I am working with a file format .psd which, as you have seen, can have multiple layers. This is best because you will be working over more than one photo layer to create the vanishing point perspective.

For the first part of this project, make sure to add a blank layer on top of your background layer, as this will be used for painting on so as not to destroy the original below. Click the Create a new layer button on the Layers panel. You don't have to rename it. Just leave it as the default of Layer 1. Refer to Figure 10-4.

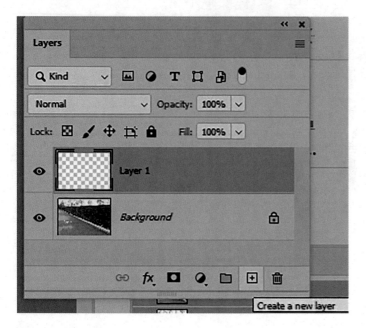

Figure 10-4. *Always work on a blank layer in your Layers panel when using the Vanishing Point filter*

Go to Filter ➤ Vanishing Point filter (Alt/Option+Ctrl/CMD+V). The workspace will open, and you will be presented with some tools on the left-hand side and options for each tool will appear above the preview image.

Before we begin, I will just give a brief overview of what each of the tools is used for and then we will use most of them throughout the three projects. Some of these tools may already be familiar to you and they operate similarly outside of this workspace. Refer to Figure 10-5.

Figure 10-5. *The Vanishing Point filter workspace*

As well, I will be mentioning some keyboard shortcuts throughout the project that should be used within the filter.

Vanishing Point Workspace

First, look at the tools on the left-hand side and the Options area. Refer to Figure 10-6.

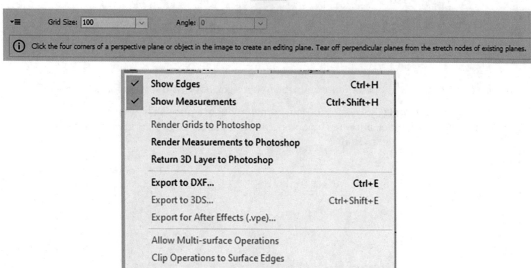

Figure 10-6. *Vanishing Point filter Tool Options panel and menu for settings and commands*

■ **Note** From the drop-down menu of Settings and Commands for the Vanishing Point, we will not be looking at any 3D files (DFX, 3DS, After Effects (.vpe)). Also, we will not look at render measurements for import or export to 3D programs using this filter because that is an advanced topic that is not relevant to this chapter. If you need information from Adobe on this topic and how 3D in new versions is moving to the Substance Collection, refer to this link: `https://helpx.adobe.com/photoshop/using/vanishing-point.html`

(see in link "Work in Vanishing Point Export measurements, textures, and 3D information").

However, make sure that Show Edges and Show Measurements are checked in this menu. Refer to Figure 10-6.

Vanishing Point Tools and Options

On the left, the tools in this dialog box are the following:

- **Edit Plane tool (V):** Selects, edits, moves, and resize planes. First, a plane must be drawn using the Create Plane tool before you can use this tool to move the plane. It is very much like a combination of the Move tool and Path Selection tool outside of this dialog box. Here you can set the Grid Size of the plane (1-1000) as well as the Angle (0-360) of additional planes when added. Refer to Figure 10-7.

Figure 10-7. *Edit Plane tool and its Options panel*

Whenever I click a tool, its options appear on the upper right along with some informational tips.

- **Create Plane tool (C):** Defines the four corner nodes of a plane in blue when placement is correct, but when incorrect it appears as yellow with a grid or red with no grid. Refer to Figure 10-8.

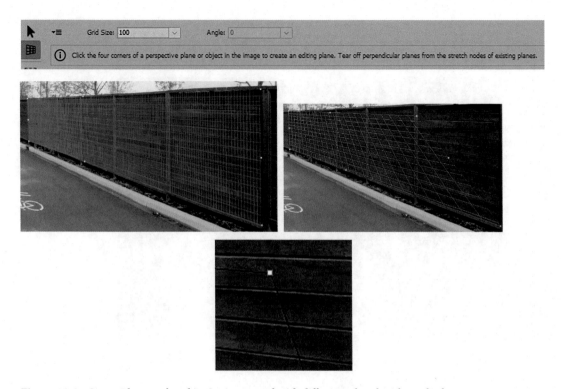

Figure 10-8. Create Plane tool and its Options panel with different colored grids on the fence

You can then adjust the size and shape of the plane with the Edit Plane tool, and it allows you to tear off a new plane that extends off the original at a different angle with Ctrl/CMD+Drag on one side in the center. Refer to Figure 10-9.

Figure 10-9. *Tear off additional planes with the Edit Plane tool*

You can have more than one plane while working in the Vanishing Point filter and they are saved in the document should you want to return after you have closed the application. In the Options area, you can adjust the grid size and angle of the tear off plane with the Edit Plane tool. Refer to Figure 10-10.

Figure 10-10. *The Edit Plane tool can adjust the angle for the tear off plane*

■ **Tip** To delete a grid plane while selected, press the Backspace/Delete key on your keyboard. If you can't see the edge of your plane, make sure that Show Edges is checked in the Settings and Commands drop-down menu. Refer to Figure 10-11.

Figure 10-11. *Menu option settings*

- **Marquee tool (M)**: Makes square or rectangular selections that can be filled and allow you to move or clone selections. Refer to Figure 10-12.

Figure 10-12. *Marquee tool and its Options panel*

For the Move Mode dropdown menu, to use Destination and then Source, the Info panel says that you can Click+Drag in a plane to select an area on that plane or create a marquee selection.

When you create a marquee, the Move mode of Destination will allow you to move the selection, but not copy underlying image. Refer to Figure 10-13.

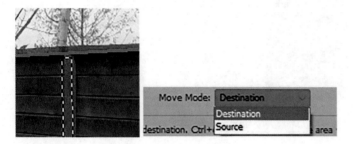

Figure 10-13. *Alter the Move mode of the selection marquee*

Once the selection is in in place, you can Alt/Option+Drag the selection to copy the area to a new destination.

This is the same as creating a copy of the active selection using the key commands of Copy (Ctrl/CMD+C) and Paste (Ctrl/CMD+V) and then drag and move floating selection. Refer to Figure 10-14.

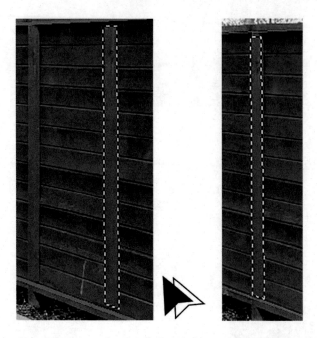

Figure 10-14. *Make a copy of you selection and move it to a new destination*

Another option is to Ctrl/CMD+Drag within a selection to fill the area with the source image. This is the same as, once your selection is created with the Marquee tool, setting your Move mode to Source and then dragging within the floating selection. Refer to Figure 10-15.

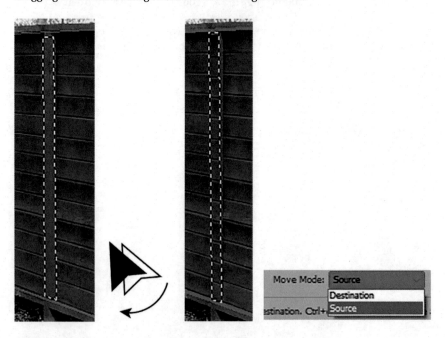

Figure 10-15. *Clone the area within your selection from a new source*

A selection can span more than one plane. All selections can be scaled, rotated, or transformed while using the Transform tool, which we will look at shortly.

■ **Note** Adobe mentions that items from one Vanishing Point dialog box can be copied to another while opening, then closing, and opening the other document and pasting again into the vanishing point preview.

The other options for the Marquee tool include Feather (0-50), which will blur the selection and set the feather to the edge.

Opacity (0-100) will affect what is obscured below the selection and effect the opacity of the copy. Refer to Figure 10-16.

Figure 10-16. *Marquee tool and its Options panel settings for Feather and Opacity*

Heal is a blend mode in which you can choose to blend or not blend moved pixels into the surrounding pixels, based on the option selected after choosing a Move mode of Source on a copied selection. You can then set a heal for the copy of Off for no blend, Luminance to affect lighting, and On to affect color, lighting, and shading. Refer to Figure 10-17.

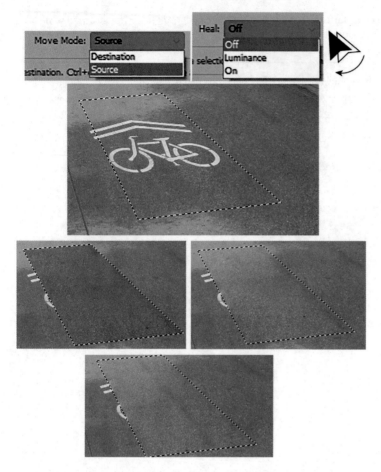

Figure 10-17. Marquee tool and its options panel settings for Move mode with the Heal options of Off, Luminance, and On

The Heal options apply to the Brush tool and Stamp tool as well.
Ctrl/CMD+D will deselect a selection.

- **Stamp tool (S)**: Paints with a sample of the image. Unfortunately, unlike the Clone Stamp tools, outside of the dialog box, it can`t clone elements from another image externally, only the current image inside the preview area. Refer to Figure 10-18.

Figure 10-18. Stamp tool and its Options panel

Alt/Option+Click in a plane to set the source point for the clone. Once point is set, Click or Click+Drag as you would to paint or clone. Refer to Figure 10-19.

Figure 10-19. *Using the Stamp tool on the ground plane to clone over the bike logo*

Shift+Click to extend the stroke to the last click. To make a better blend, you can change the brush's Diameter (1-500), Hardness (0-100), Opacity (0-100), and Heal options (Off, Luminance, On) as you paint. Check Aligned to keep the brush source in sync with the destination. Refer to Figure 10-18.

■ **Note**　The plane outline turns green when using this tool. Refer to Figure 10-19.

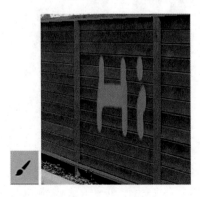

Figure 10-20. *Use the Brush tool to paint within a plane*

- **Brush tool (B)**: Paints a selected brush color on a plane using Click or Click+Drag as you would with any paint brush. Shift+Click to extend the stroke to the last click. Ctrl/CMD+Click in another plane to paint there instead. You can even paint outside the plane. Refer to Figure 10-20.

Like the Stamp tool, there are options for the brush's Diameter, Hardness, and Opacity. Select Heal to change from Off to Luminance or On to adapt the paint to shadow or texture as you paint. By default, it is Off. Refer to Figure 10-21.

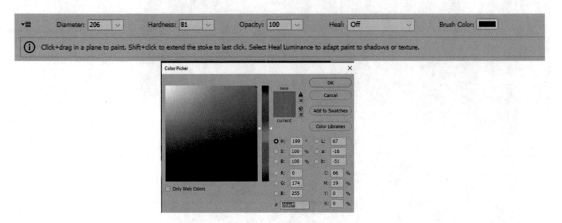

Figure 10-21. *Brush tool and its options panel and the Color Picker dialog box*

You can change the brush color by clicking on the swatch and entering the Color Picker. Click OK to exit once you have selected a new color.

■ **Note**   Once out of filter's workspace, you can continue to do color adjustments with the layer's blending modes, which we will look at later in this project.

- **Transform tool (T)**: Scales, rotates, and flips the current floating marquee section by moving the bounding box handles. Its behavior is like the free transform command on a rectangular selection, as we saw in Chapter 4. Refer to Figure 10-22.

Figure 10-22. *Use the Transform tool to scale and rotate a selection*

In the Transform options area, checking Flip is a horizonal transformation and checking Flop is vertical transformation. You can enable one or both check boxes. Refer to Figure 10-23.

Figure 10-23. *Transform tool and its options panel with settings used on a selection for flip and flop*

- **Eyedropper tool (I)**: Click to select a color for the Brush tool for painting from the preview image. Click the color swatch to open the Color Picker and choose a color. Refer to Figure 10-24.

Figure 10-24. *Eyedropper tool and its Options panel*

- **Measure tool (R)**: Click two points to measure an angle and a distance or length (1-999). Edit the distance to set the scale for measurement. If you can't see the measurements, make sure Show Measurements in the dropdown menu of Commands and Settings is enabled. You can enable Link Measurement to Grid to link the measurement units with the grid size. Refer to Figure 10-25.

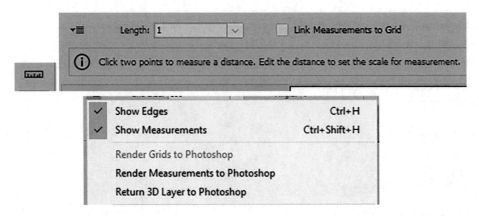

Figure 10-25. *Measure tool and its Options panel with additional menu options*

This tool is useful if you need to record or render the measurements of a room in Photoshop or for 3D purposes but is not relevant to this book.

- **Hand tool (H)**: Move the image in the Preview window via Click+Drag with the mouse. Holding down the spacebar key while using another tool will change the cursor to the Hand tool. This tool allows you to move about the Preview image without disturbing the planes. Refer to Figure 10-26.

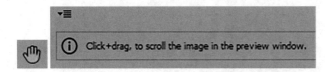

Figure 10-26. *Hand tool and Options panel info*

- **Zoom tool (Z)**: Magnifies the image in Preview. Click to zoom in and Alt/Option-Click to zoom out. Click+Drag will allow you to zoom in on an area. Ctrl/CMD++Ctrl/CMD+- and Ctrl/CMD+0 to zoom in and out will also work. Or just use the Navigation area at the bottom of the screen. Refer to Figure 10-27.

Figure 10-27. *Zoom tool and Options panel info with zoom navigation in the lower left of the workspace*

■ **Note**   If you would like to review a few more keyboard shortcuts, go to `https://helpx.adobe.com/photoshop/using/default-keyboard-shortcuts.html#keys_for_vanishing_point`.

When you are done in this area, you can click Cancel to exit without making changes or OK to confirm changes. Refer to Figure 10-28.

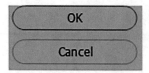

Figure 10-28.   *Click OK or Cancel to exit the workspace*

However, for now, let`s stay in dialog box for this image and use some of the tools.

Creating and Editing Planes with Vanishing Point Tools

First, using the Create Plane tool, click out a gridded plane for the fence. It has four points that you may need to adjust with the handles. If you need to move the entire plane, you can use the Edit Plane tool. Refer to Figure 10-29.

Figure 10-29.   *Create a plane for the fence using the Create Plane tool*

Once you create a rectangular plane, you can continue to use the Create Plane tool or Edit Plane tool to scale, move, and reshape the handle nodes to your perspective plane. Refer to Figure 10-30.

936

Figure 10-30. *Edit your plane using the Edit Plane tool*

■ **Note**   Zooming in or out with the Zoom tool may also help you when working with the plane. The filter will guide you as the grid plane changes color. As mentioned, when it is blue, the perspective is normal or valid. However, you still need to make sure that the grid lines up with your wall or ground to get an accurate perspective. If the nodes are placed incorrectly, the bounding box and grid will turn either red or yellow. This means you need to move the nodes around until they are blue.

Now create a second plane so that you can work on the ground as well. If you have more than one plane, make sure that they are not overlapping. Use the Create Plane tool again to click out the four node points you want. Remember to use your Edit Plane tool if you need to scale a side, like near the road or curb. Refer to Figure 10-31.

Figure 10-31. *Create another plane on the ground using the Create Plane tool*

■ **Remember**   For your own projects, you can tear or pull off additional planes by first selecting a plane with the Edit Plane tool and then selecting side and center handles and Ctrl/CMD+Drag away. You can then Shift+Click to select both planes or use the Edit Plane tool and continue to adjust it. This is good if you are working with a continuous surface, and this keeps them related to one another. The angles of these plane can be adjusted together. Refer to Figure 10-32.

Figure 10-32. *You can tear off a second plane using the Edit Plane tool with Ctrl/CMD+Drag when the mouse pointer changes to an arrow with a plane grid*

To delete the selected the plane, click on it with the Edit Plane tool and then click with the Backspace/ Delete key on the keyboard. Or you can Ctrl/CMD+Z to undo these steps and then use the Edit Plane tool to reselect the nodes and readjust the plane.

Now let's use the Paint Brush tool on the fence. Make sure to select that grid with your Edit Plane tool. Refer to Figure 10-33.

Figure 10-33. *Use your Edit Plane tool to select the plane you want to edit*

Select the Brush tool and choose a Diameter of 150, Hardness of 81, Opacity of 100%, Heal at Off, and a red paint color using the Color Picker, and then click OK in the Color Picker. Or use whatever settings you want. You can view my settings here. Refer to Figure 10-34.

Figure 10-34. *Use the Brush tool and its Options panel to set your settings and then paint on the Preview*

I can paint with any brush color and the graffiti design will appear in perspective.
Write the word Hello! You can adjust the brush sizes and switch colors at any time. Refer to Figure 10-35.

Figure 10-35. *Painting in perspective on the fence with red and cyan paint*

As you can see, the brush does have its limitations as it can only be round. In the second half of Project 2, I will show you a way to add improved graffiti artwork to this wall. To undo basic painting mistakes, use the keyboard shortcut Ctrl/CMD+Z because there is no Eraser tool option with this filter. Just another good reason to work on a blank layer!

Now click on the second plane on the road with the Edit Plane tool. This time, use the Stamp tool to remove the bike logo that is currently on the road. Refer to Figure 10-36.

Figure 10-36. *Select the ground plane with the Edit Plane tool*

The options for the Stamp tool are Diameter: 310, Hardness: 50, Opacity: 100, Heal: Off, and check the Aligned option. Refer to Figure 10-37.

Figure 10-37. *Use the Stamp tool and its Options panel to set your settings before you start to clone*

Alt/Option+Click an area of the pavement so that you have a clone source and then you can stamp over the bike signage to cover it. Refer to Figure 10-38.

Figure 10-38. *Set a clone source and then begin to paint*

Choose another clone source area if required (Alt/Option+Click) and adjust the settings like Stamp tool diameter so that the area is covered in a realistic way. And click again. Refer to Figure 10-39.

Figure 10-39. *Cover the bike logo so that you can no longer see it on the ground*

You can also use Ctrl/CMD+Z to undo steps. As mentioned, you can use this Clone Stamp tool outside of the Vanishing Point workspace, but the perspective might not be as accurate.

Lastly, select the fence plane again with the Edit Plane tool. Refer to Figure 10-40.

Figure 10-40. *Select the fence plane with the Edit Plane tool*

You can clone items by first using the Marquee tool and making a selection around the fence post near the foreground to create a selection. Then Ctrl/CMD+C to copy and Ctrl/CMD+V to paste to create a floating selection. Then use the mouse to move the copy. Refer to Figure 10-41.

Figure 10-41. *Use the Marquee tool to create a rectangular marquee and make a copy of the fence board that you can drag to a new location further to the right*

These selections can be used in multi-surface operations where a tear off plane might extend onto the curb.

Ctrl/CMD+D to deselect the selection area, and the new post is in place. Refer to Figure 10-42.

Figure 10-42. *Deselect the marquee selection and then the new board is in place*

Afterwards, you might want to use the Stamp tool again to clean the selection up and make the fence boards blend in. Either way, if you are working on top of a blank layer, you are not destroying the background layer below.

■ **Note** The graphic will be clipped off near the selection and plane surface edges. So, in your own project, if you wanted the lower half of the post, you would have to adjust the plane before doing a copy/paste.

Here is the result of my work so far. Refer to Figure 10-43.

Figure 10-43. Once you are finished editing in the Vanishing Point filter, you can click OK to exit

I'll click OK to exit and commit the changes I made. Notice that they are on the previously blank Layer 1, and I did not destroy the image below. I can turn the layer eye visibility off and on in the Layers panel to compare. I can also copy items off that layer, like the graffiti. Refer to Figure 10-44.

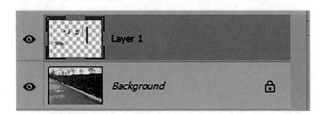

Figure 10-44. The edits created in the Vanishing Point filter are now on Layer 1

To do that, use the Rectangular Marquee tool (M) and drag a selection around the words. Refer to Figure 10-45.

Figure 10-45. *Use your Rectangular Marquee tool in Photoshop when you want to copy and paste a selection outside of the Vanishing Point filter to another layer*

From the menu, Edit ➤ Cut and then Edit ➤ Paste Special ➤ Paste in Place. In the Layers Panel, this creates Layer 2. Then apply a blending mode of Darken to the layer, so that it blends into the fence and appears more realistic as paint on a wooden fence. Refer to Figure 10-46.

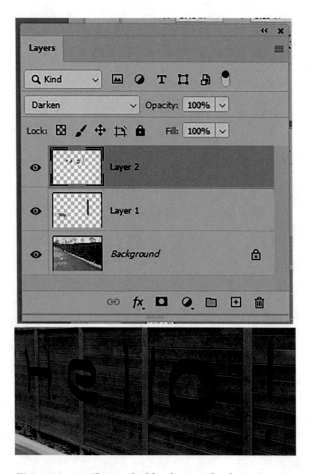

Figure 10-46. *Change the blending mode of your Layer 2 to Darken so that the letters blend in with the wood*

If you zoom in with the Zoom tool, you can see some of the wood showing through. Layer blending modes like Multiply, Darker Color, or Lighten are all good to use, but you can try any one of the options in this dropdown menu. Refer to Chapter 2 for more details.

It's important to experiment, and the blending mode you use depends on your project and what you are trying to blend.

Finally, you can use your Eraser tool or add a layer mask to Layer 1 and paint on the mask if you need to clean up your artwork further near the fence post, in a non-destructive way. Refer to Figure 10-47.

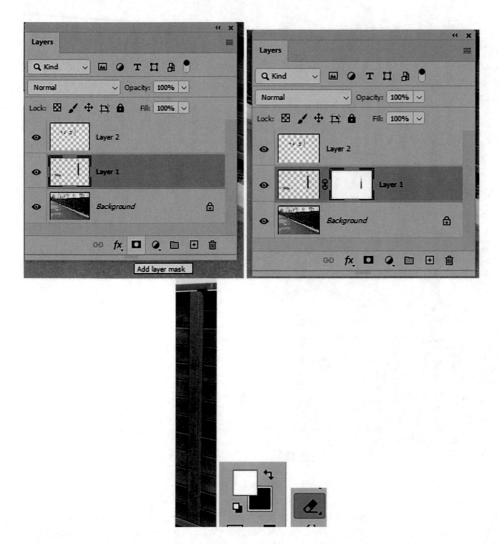

Figure 10-47. *Use a layer mask when you want to edit your fence board using the default colors (D) in the Tools panel and the Eraser tool on the mask*

As you can see, the Vanishing Point Stamp tool did a pretty good job on the road. However, the Brush tool graffiti still looks amateurish. This is because we are learning the basics of the Vanishing Point tools. Refer to Figure 10-48.

Figure 10-48. *How my artwork currently appears on the fence and the covered bike logo on the ground*

So set this part of the project aside for now. You'll return to it once you understand how to add better graphics to the Vanishing Point filter, which you will see in the second part of the project. File ➤ Save your work as a .psd file. You can see my file, vanishing_point_paint_stamp_final.psd.

Project 2: Adding Graphics to Walls, Roads, and Fences

Now we will look at how signage or artwork can appear in perspective on the wall using the same Vanishing Point filter. File ➤ Open vanishing_point_image_start.psd and make an Image ➤ Duplicate for practice. To avoid repetition, some of the work has already been done for you in this file and I have corrected the main image distortion using the Adaptive Wide Angle filter. Refer to Figure 10-49.

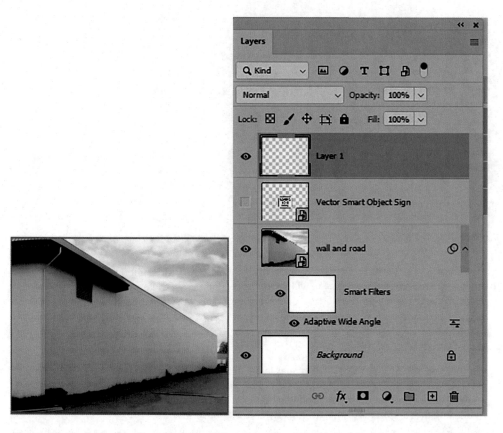

Figure 10-49. *A blank wall and road leading to a loading zone and a blank layer selected in the Layers panel*

I have layer named wall and road and some signage in a layer called Vector Smart Object Sign that I created in Adobe Illustrator. The original file is found in the project folder named signage.ai.

When I copied the file from Illustrator directly to Photoshop, I pasted it as a smart object so that I could use it elsewhere in this project later. Refer to Figure 10-50.

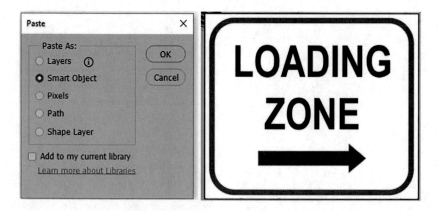

Figure 10-50. *This layer for the sign was pasted from Illustrator into Photoshop as a smart object*

However, if we want to use this artwork in the Vanishing Point filter workspace, we must select the layer and right-click and choose Rasterize Layer.

Do this to a copy (drag the layer over to the Create new layer icon) so as not to destroy the original. Refer to Figure 10-51.

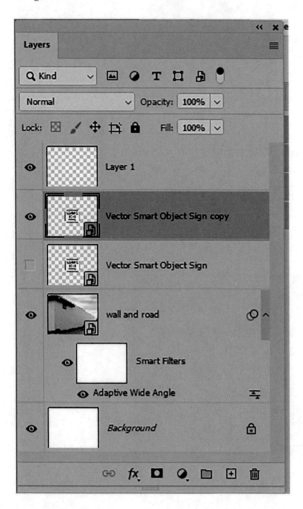

Figure 10-51. *Make a copy of your smart object layer*

Turn the visibility eye off on original smart object layer to hide it.

Right-click the copy layer and choose Rasterize Layer from pop-up menu. Refer to Figure 10-52.

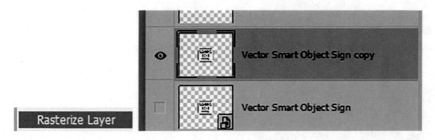

Figure 10-52. *Rasterize the copy of your smart object layer*

■ **Note** Type and shape layers must also be rasterized (rasterize type) if your intent is to use them in the Vanishing Point filter workspace.

We'll look at an example of type later when we return to the graffiti on the fence in this project.

To copy the signage so you can add it in perspective to the Vanishing Point filter, select the whole layer, so Select ➤ All (Ctrl/CMD+A) and then Edit ➤ Copy (Ctrl/CMD+C). Refer to Figure 10-53.

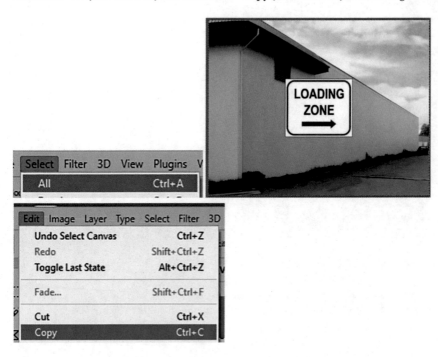

Figure 10-53. *Select the whole layer for the sign and then copy to the computer's clipboard*

■ **Note**   Choosing to select using Ctrl/CMD when you click the layer's thumbnail icon and then Ctrl/CMD+C won't work and the shape will not copy. So always use Select ➤ All before you Edit ➤ Copy.

Turn off the visibility on the rasterized layer Vector Smart Object Sign copy and then select the blank Layer 1. Refer to Figure 10-54.

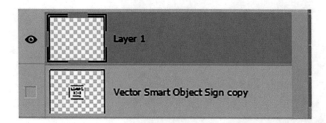

Figure 10-54. *Make sure you are on your blank layer and that your graphic sign layer is turned off*

■ **Remember**   For your own projects, before you enter the Vanishing point filter again, make sure that you always work on a new blank layer so as not to destroy the original, because there is no eraser in the Vanishing Point filter. You do not want to destroy your layer containing the signage if you make a mistake.

Go to Filter ➤ Vanishing Point.
In this case, I have already drawn out two planes with the Create Plane tool and saved them in the file. Refer to Figure 10-55.

Figure 10-55. *Vanishing Point filter: Use the planes that were created earlier for you with the Edit Plane tool*

For your own projects, you would have to draw them out yourself. You can review how we did that in Project 1. Remember to draw out your first plane the wall with your Create Plane tool. Click to create the four points. You may need to adjust if the plane is not blue. I created a plane for the road as well, but you do not need this now.

Now on your keyboard, press Ctrl/CMD+V. This will paste the artwork as a floating selection outside of any plane. Refer to Figure 10-56.

Figure 10-56. *Paste the loading zone graphic into the Vanishing Point filter as a floating selection*

Do not deselect it. Right away, drag it into the grid plane, in this case on the wall. It will come in quite large and appear to be chopped off. Refer to Figure 10-57.

Figure 10-57. *Drag onto the wall plane*

Use the Transform tool to scale and move the shape to the location where you want it to be placed. Refer to Figure 10-58.

Figure 10-58. *Use the Transform tool to scale the loading zone sign*

Use the handles for scaling. Holding down the Alt/Option Key while dragging on the handles will make the sign smaller. Refer to Figure 10-58.

Scaling is important if the graphic comes in larger than the plane area and you don't want areas of the design to be missing.

Holding down the Shift key while dragging will also allow the scale to be more proportionate with the wall. However, scale to the size you think is correct.

Once done, click away from the selection outside the plane with your Edit Plane tool and then Ctrl/ CMD+D to deselect the selection and commit the perspective on that layer. Refer to Figure 10-59.

Figure 10-59. *Deselect the sign while using the Edit Plane tool*

Then click OK to exit the filter's workspace. Refer to Figure 10-60.

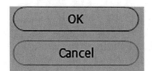

Figure 10-60. *Click OK to confirm changes and exit the Vanishing Point filter workspace*

The signage is now on Layer 1 and is separate from the background. Refer to Figure 10-61.

Figure 10-61. *The graphic now appears on Layer 1*

Select ➤ Deselect (Ctrl/CMD+D) if your layer still has the full marching ants selection on. Afterwards you can apply blending mode of Darker Color to Layer 1. Refer to Figure 10-62.

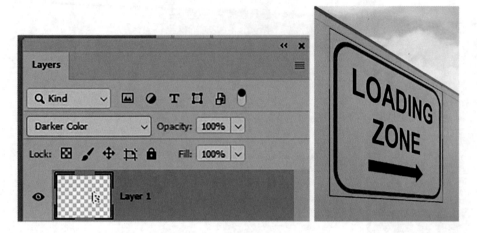

Figure 10-62. *Change the Blending Mode of Layer 1 to Darker Color*

■ **Tip** As in a previous project, using a layer mask you can as erase with the Eraser tool any areas you don't want visible.

Now File ➤ Save your work as a .psd. You can refer to my file vanishing_point_image_final.psd at this point.

Adding More Graphics to the Road and Wall

Open the file in the projects folder called vanishing_point_image_final_2.psd. As you can see, I added a few more graphics to my file on separate layers in group folders. One is an arrow on the road and another is a gear logo on the wall.

I will explain how these graphics were added to the wall and ground by repeating the steps I did with the other sign. Refer to Figure 10-63.

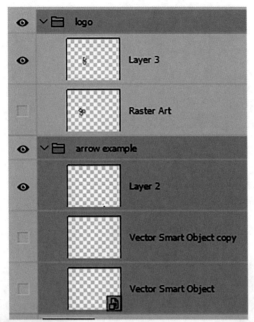

Figure 10-63. *You can add graphics to other blank layers for the wall and road*

First, I will explain how that was done here with the arrow and then the gear logo.

In this case, in the Layers panel in the group folder Arrow example, I selected the smart object layer Vector Smart Object and created a copy of the layer by dragging it over the Create a new layer icon. Then I turned that layer into a rasterized layer by right-clicking on it and choosing Rasterize Layer. Refer to Figure 10-64.

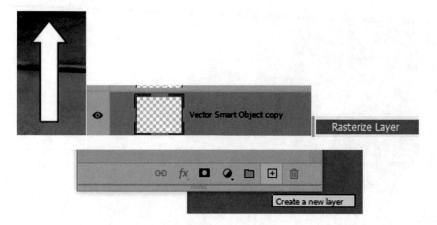

Figure 10-64. *Rasterize the graphic of the arrow first if you want to use it for the road*

I chose Select ➤ All and Edit Copy (Ctrl/CMD+C) to copy the specific layer and then I turned off the rasterized layer and selected the blank Layer 2. Refer to Figure 10-65.

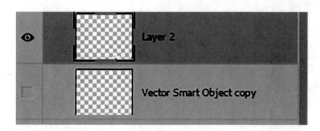

Figure 10-65. *Select a blank layer before you enter the Vanishing Point filter*

I entered the Vanishing Point filter and pasted (Ctrl/CMD+V) the graphic in and immediately dragged it to the lower plane. You can see how I laid it out on the plane. Refer to Figure 10-66.

Figure 10-66. *Paste as a floating selection and then drag onto the road plane to start scaling the arrow*

I then repeated the same steps I did with the loading zone signage, now with the arrow. While in the Vanishing Point filter you may need to scale and rotate the graphic using the Transform tool so it matches your plane. Refer to Figure 10-67.

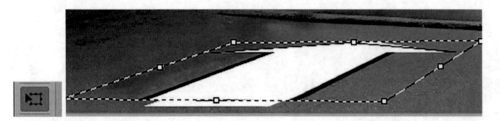

Figure 10-67. *Use the Transform Tool to scale and rotate the arrow*

After clicking outside the plane with the Edit Plane tool and deselecting (Ctrl/CMD+D), click OK to exit the workspace. Refer to Figure 10-68.

Figure 10-68. *Select the Edit Plane tool and deselect the arrow before clicking OK to exit the Vanishing Point workspace*

In the case of the gear logo in the logo group folder, I repeated the same steps with the layer named Raster Art after a Select ➤ All and Edit Copy (Ctrl/CMD+C). Then I turned off the visibility of that layer and selected Layer 3. Refer to Figure 10-69.

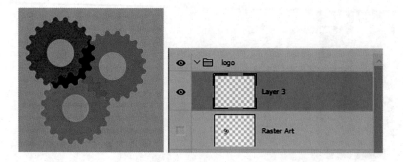

Figure 10-69. *Add another logo to the wall on a blank layer*

Then I used Filter ➤ Vanishing Point and pasted (Ctrl/CMD+V), creating the floating selection. Refer to Figure 10-70.

Figure 10-70. *Paste the logo into the Vanishing Point filter as a floating selection and drag it onto the wall plane*

I used the current wall plane to create the perspective and scaled using the Transform tool. I clicked outside the plane with the Edit Plane tool and deselected with Ctrl/CMD+D and clicked OK to exit the workspace. Refer to Figure 10-71.

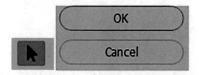

Figure 10-71. *Select the Edit Plane tool and deselect the logo before clicking OK to exit the Vanishing Point workspace*

Made sure to Select ➤ Deselect (Ctrl/CMD+D) any active selection.

Then I used the Move tool to move the gear on the layer farther left on the wall to a new location. Refer to Figure 10-72.

Figure 10-72. *In Photoshop, use the Move tool to move the logo to a new location*

I applied different blending modes to those layers. I used Lighten on the arrow (Layer 2) with an opacity of 66%. Refer to Figure 10-73.

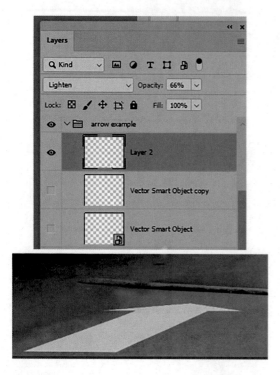

Figure 10-73. *Alter the layer blending mode and opacity in the layers panel to blend the arrow into the road*

I used a blending mode of Multiply on the gear logo (Layer 3), leaving the opacity at 100%. Refer to Figure 10-74.

Figure 10-74. *Alter the layer blending mode in the Layers panel to blend the gear into the road*

Now you can see some of the road or wall through the graphics. There are many possibilities when it comes to using the Vanishing Point filter. These same ideas can be applied to interior walls and floors of buildings as well.

Finishing Project 1: Adding Graffiti to the Fence

Now that you have seen these ideas, let's return to Project 1 to add some improved graffiti artwork.

I have supplied you with some in the projects folder. Look at the file brush_text_art.psd and the layer named brush design. Refer to Figure 10-75.

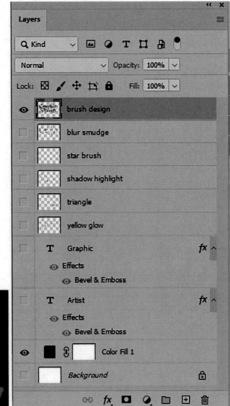

Figure 10-75. *Creating graffiti and the layers used in the Layers panel*

This layer is a composite of various brush stokes, smudging, selections, and the font Matura MT Script Capitals - Regular.

With layer blending modes such as Dissolve and styles like Bevel & Emboss, you can make the letters appear more graffiti-like. Because logo creation is not the topic of this project, take time afterwards to look at the file and review the layers, which have their visibility currently turned off.

They were then made into a composite without merging all layers using Ctrl/CMD+Shift+Alt/Option+E, which combines all visible layers into a new layer on top of the other layers. Refer to Figure 10-75.

■ **Note**   In this case, I did not use Merge Visible or Flatten Image from the Layers panel menu. Refer to Figure 10-76.

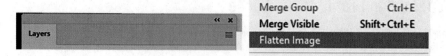

Figure 10-76. *Do not use these options from the menu to flatten your graphic*

If you don't want certain layers to combine, turn them off before using this key command. Then Edit ➤ Copy the selected layer and Edit ➤ Paste it into the file vanishing_point_paint_stamp_final.psd.

Do this copy/paste for your own Project 1 file if you want to follow along.

After I did this, I made an Image ➤ Duplicate of that file and saved the file and renamed it as vanishing_point_paint_stamp_final_2.psd. You can open this file in the project folder if you want to follow and review what I did.

For the layer named brush design, I created a new blank layer above called Layer 3. Refer to Figure 10-77.

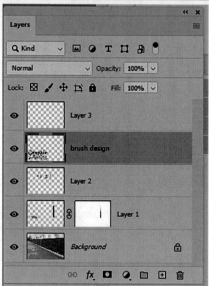

Figure 10-77. *The copied artwork in the new file*

As we did in the earlier in Project 2, you can treat this brush design layer like the raster sign graphics.

I renamed my Layer 2, calling it Old Hello Art, and turned off the layer visibility as we don't need it anymore. Refer to Figure 10-78.

964

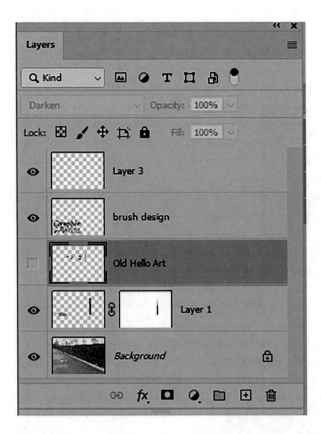

Figure 10-78. *Turn off the old version of the artwork as you don't need it*

To review, select the layer **brush design**. In the Layers panel, choose Select ➤ All and then Edit ➤ Copy and then turn off the brush design layer visibility as the graphic is now on the clip board. Refer to Figure 10-79.

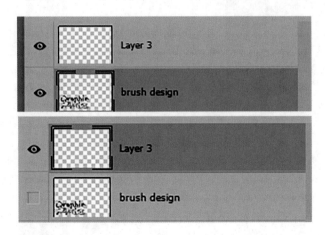

Figure 10-79. *Select ➤ All of your brush design layer and copy it. Then turn off the visibility and select the new blank Layer 3*

Make sure you have a blank Layer 3 selected.

Go to Filter ➤ Vanishing Point and then Ctrl/CMD+V to paste to create the floating selection. Refer to Figure 10-80.

Figure 10-80. *Paste into the Vanishing Point filter as a floating selection*

The graphic appears in the upper left. Drag the graphic into the wall plane. Refer to Figure 10-81.

Figure 10-81. *Drag into the wall plane*

To fit the area of the wall, you can use your Transform tool to move and scale the graffiti further. Refer to Figure 10-82.

Figure 10-82. *Use the Transform tool to scale the graffiti*

Then deselect outside the plane using the Edit Plane tool and Ctrl/CMD+D to deselect. Refer to Figure 10-83.

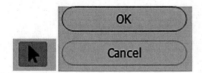

Figure 10-83. *Select the Edit Plane tool and deselect the artwork before clicking OK to exit the Vanishing Point workspace*

If you are happy with the results, click OK to exit. Refer to Figure 10-84.

Figure 10-84. *The artwork appears on Layer 3 now in perspective*

Select ➤ Deselect to remove the selection marching ants. As you can see, Layer 3 now contains the graphic.

Now look at my layer final artwork, which is turned off. Turn on and off the Layer 3 visibility so you can compare. Refer to Figure 10-85.

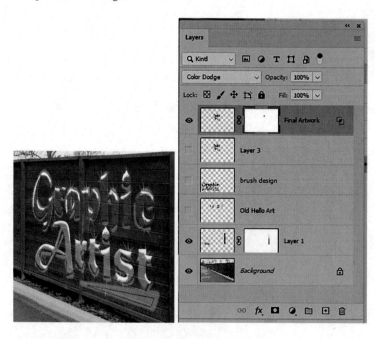

Figure 10-85. *Add a blending mode to the layer*

I used layer blending modes Color Dodge so that it appears blended into the wood. Double-click the layer style blending mode to see the Blending Options. Alter the Underlying Layer sliders on the shadow from 0/80. You saw how blending options could be used on text in Chapter 5. Refer to Figure 10-86.

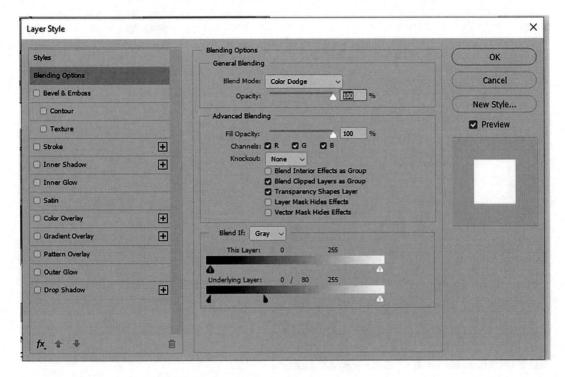

Figure 10-86. *Add a layer style blending option to the logo*

Click Cancel to exit the Layer Style Dialog box.

For your own artwork, you can right-click on the layer named `final artwork`. From the pop-up menu, choose Copy Layer style and then select your new layer and right-click. From the menu, choose Paste Layer Style. Refer to Figure 10-87.

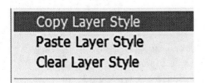

Figure 10-87. *Copy and paste a layer style from my layer to yours*

This applies the style to your layer. You can then turn off the final artwork layer. In your project, you can turn on your Layer 3 so that you can compare.

Then File ➤ Save your file as a .psd and you have completed Project 1. Refer to my file `vanishing_point_paint_stamp_final_2.psd` if you need to compare you work to mine.

Project 3: Perspective Warps in Three Points. Do We Use the Perspective Warp or the Vanishing Point Filter?

To finish off the discussion of the Vanishing Point tool, we need to answer a final question: which should we use, the Perspective Warp or the Vanishing Point filter, when it comes to complex perspectives? So far, in both cases we have dealt with two planes of coverage. But in the case of a cube where we have three planes, which filter will do a better job? Refer to Figure 10-88.

Figure 10-88. *How do you add perspective to a cube?*

There is no easy answer to this question. You need to first decide on your intention when you work with the cube. Do you want to distort the actual cube or just cover it with a pattern or distorted object?

Cube Perspective Distortion

Let's consider distortion of the actual cube first.

In Chapter 7, you saw how to use Perspective Warp on a smart object layer to straighten a wall. You may want to review that chapter and some of the options in the workspace. In that case, when we used Edit ➤ Perspective Warp initially on the wall, we created two quad shape planes in Layout mode. Refer to Figure 10-89.

Figure 10-89. *Straightening the wall with Perspective Warp in Chapter 7*

However, in the case of a cube, you need to create three planes and connect and drag them together using the cube as your guide on how to lay them out. Then, when you switch to Warp mode, as you did with the wall, you can easily move the sides of the cube to manipulate them. In this case, the cube is separate from the background so that the background does not distort along with the cube. Refer to Figure 10-90.

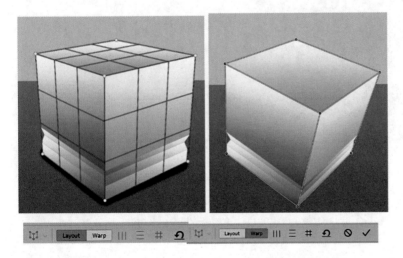

Figure 10-90. *Adding planes in Layout mode and then altering in warp mode with Perspective Warp in the Options panel*

You commit your settings and can edit your cube at any time because Perspective Warp was added as a smart filter. Refer to Figure 10-91.

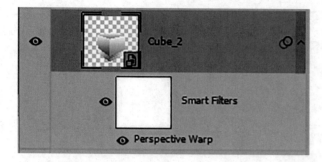

Figure 10-91. Using a smart object allows you to alter the Perspective Warp at any time

Can this manipulation be done with the Vanishing Point Filter? No, as we saw, the Vanishing Point filter is good for covering areas with perspective but there is no way you can distort the actual structure so as to alter its current perspective. In this situation, the Perspective Warp is best for the manipulation of the cube.

Now let's look at the second situation: pattern coverage of the cube in perspective.

Cube Perspective Coverage Distortion (Perspective Warp)

In some situations, you may want to cover the cube with a pattern. You saw how to do this with the cherry blossom pattern on two sides of a box using the Perspective Warp in Chapter 7. Refer to Figure 10-92.

Figure 10-92. Adding a wrapping graphic in Chapter 7 using Perspective Warp on a box

But now we are trying to cover three sides. In the case of the cube, when you want to cover three sides, you need to consider how the box would lay flat or wrap around the top. When you build a pattern for Perspective Warp, I think using an L-shaped pattern is best, with the white area having no pattern and being transparent. Refer to Figure 10-93.

Figure 10-93. *Make an L-shaped graphic in Illustrator if you want to wrap around a cube*

I created this square box pattern in Illustrator, making sure the edge has some similar repeats, and then I copied it into Photoshop as a smart object layer. Click OK. Refer to Figure 10-94.

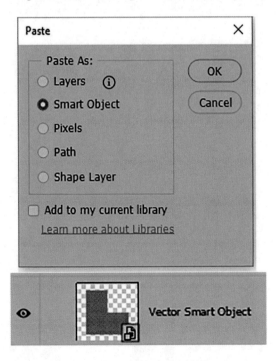

Figure 10-94. *Paste your graphic as a smart object into Photoshop*

To this layer I applied an Edit ➤ Perspective Warp. In Layout mode I created and connected three quad planes to match the L shape. I also lowered the layer's opacity to 49%. Refer to Figure 10-95.

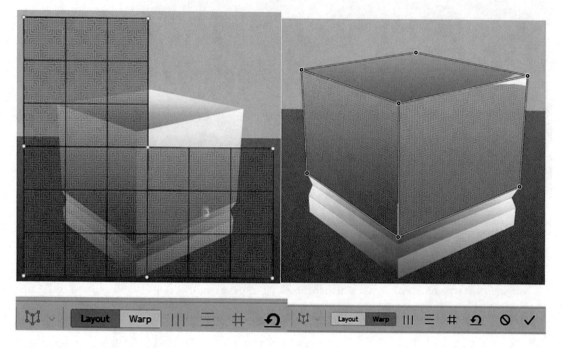

Figure 10-95. *Use Perspective Warp in Layout mode to make three planes and then manually warp using Warp mode in the Options panel*

Then in Warp mode I dragged the points on the quad plans so that they conformed to the shape of the box. You may notice that where the top corner and right corner touch, there is a slight distortion. However, this is just part of Preview; when you click the check in the Options panel to commit, the pattern wraps around the box and joins quite well. Refer to Figure 10-96.

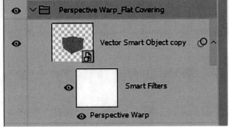

Figure 10-96. The pattern warps around the cube seamlessly if warped correctly

Cube Perspective Coverage Distortion (Vanishing Point Filter)

When working with the Vanishing Point filter to cover three side or planes at once, you need to do things slightly differently. In this case, for my pattern, I worked with a single rasterized square, as the Vanishing Point filter does not know how to manipulate the earlier L-shaped pattern. I copied (Ctrl/CMD+C) a single patterned square out of Illustrator and pasted (Ctrl/CMD+V) it as a Pixels layer. Click OK. This layer is now a normal and rasterized. Refer to Figure 10-97.

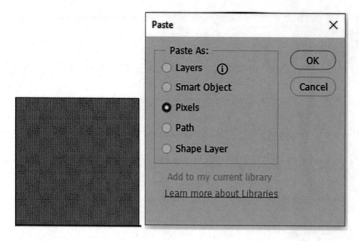

Figure 10-97. *Use only a square of the graphic from Illustrator and Paste As Pixels for the Vanishing Point filter*

As in the earlier Vanishing Point projects, after Select ➤ All of the entire pattern and Edit ➤ Copy, I turned off the pattern layer's visibly and selected a blank layer that I created. Refer to Figure 10-98.

Figure 10-98. *Select ➤ All of the layer Rasterized Pattern and Edit ➤ Copy to clipboard and then select the blank layer and turn off the visibility for the pattern layer*

I then entered the Filter ➤ Vanishing Point Filter and created the following planes with the Create Plane tool and Edit Plane tools. With the Create Plane Tool, I first created the Left Plane and then Ctrl/CMD+Dragged on the top center handle with the Create Plane tool to create a tear or pull off plane, Then, on that top plane I Ctrl/CMD+Dragged with the Create Plane tool on the right side center handle and dragged downward to create the third plane so that they joined together. I then used the Edit Plane tool to alter the planes as close as the cube shape as possible. Refer to Figure 10-99.

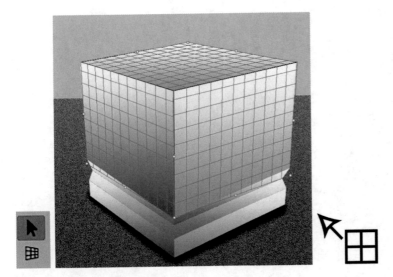

Figure 10-99. *Create and edit planes in the Vanishing Point filter first on the left and then create two tear-off planes on the top and then the right using those tools*

Then I used Ctrl/CMD+V to paste my pattern in as a floating selection. And right away I dragged it over the three planes. Refer to Figure 10-100.

Figure 10-100. *Paste your selection and then drag the floating selection over the three planes*

I then used the Vanishing Point filter's Transform tool to scale the pattern, being aware of edge coverage. Refer to Figure 10-101.

Figure 10-101. *Use the Transform tool to drag the edges of the selection so that it covers the box*

This can be tricky because you need to move around the inside of the planes to balance the graphic areas out. When done, I clicked the OK button to exit the workspace. Refer to Figure 10-102.

Figure 10-102. *Click OK to exit the Vanishing Point filter*

The distorted pattern appeared on the previously blank layer. You may need to clean up the edge with a layer mask if the perspective is a bit off the edge of the cube. Refer to Figure 10-103.

Figure 10-103. *The graphic appears on the layer and I added a layer mask to remove any extra graphic from the bottom of the box*

My conclusion with three-sided pattern coverage is, while it is possible to do so with the Vanishing Point filter, I prefer using the Edit ➤ Perspective Warp because

1. It is fast and straightforward to use.

2. It works on smart object layers along with multiple filters, and either it or the smart object can be altered at any time without having to recopy the artwork on a new layer each time.

This is not to say that the Vanishing Point filter is not useful, as we saw in the previous two projects, but with specific warps it does have some limitations that the Perspective Warp can overcome.

If you want to see examples of the options mentioned here, you can refer to my file cube_background_persepective_warp.psd. I have put the examples in three group folders in the Layers panel so that you can review and compare what I have done. You can also review my file box_cover.ai if you need to see the pattern I used in this example. Refer to Figure 10-104.

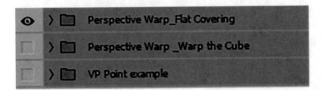

Figure 10-104. *You can look in these group folders in the file if you want to explore further the options discussed here*

Enhancing the Perspective Warp: Flat Surface Warp and Warps That Melt and Appear 3D-Like

So far, what we have seen was OK for flat surfaces with no additional external distortions. However, here are a few final advanced tips that you can use to make your Edit ➤ Perspective Warp appear more melted and 3D-like.

To see how this can be accomplished on a face, look at my file cube_background_persepective_warp_melt.psd. Refer to Figure 10-105.

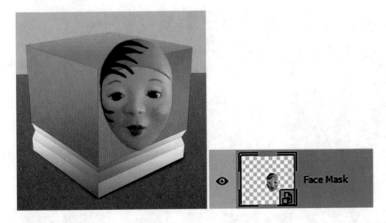

Figure 10-105. *A mask can be molded over a box if it is a smart object layer*

Using the smart object filters such as Perspective Warp from Chapter 7 on a smart object layer of a Face mask, I added and joined two quad planes in Layout mode. Then, in Warp mode, I bent the planes over the box shape on the right and committed this warp. Refer to Figure 10-106.

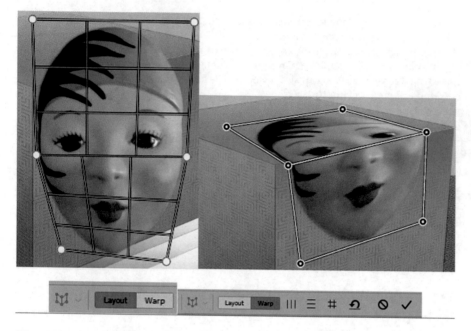

Figure 10-106. *Use the Perspective Warp to create two planes in Layout mode and bend in Warp mode in the Options panel*

Then I added the Edit ➤ Puppet Warp filter, as seen in Chapter 6, to add multiple pins and pull the face further into a distortion and make it a bit puffier. Then I committed the warp. Refer to Figure 10-107.

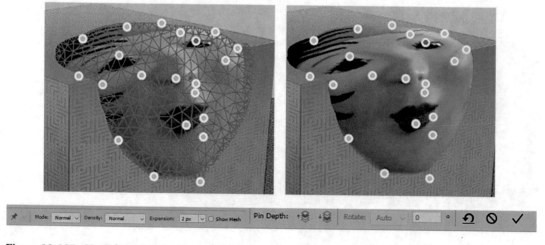

Figure 10-107. *Use Edit ➤ Puppet Warp and its Options panel when you want to stretch the face to look melted*

Lastly, I modified it further with the Filter ➤ Liquify filter and its various brush tools, such as the Forward Warp tool to make it appear more melted and clicked OK. Refer to Figure 10-108.

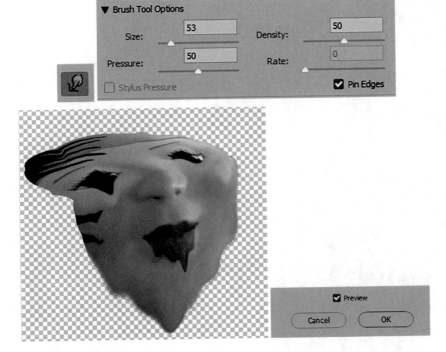

Figure 10-108. Use the Liquify filter for a really meted look using the Forward Warp tool and its brush tool options

I then added a layer style Drop Shadow. Refer to Figure 10-109.

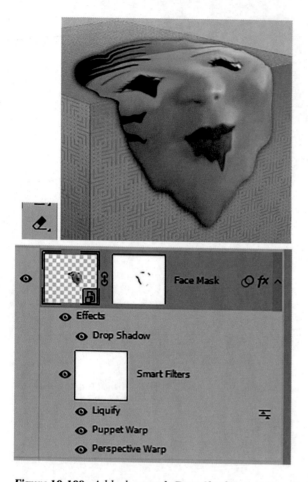

Figure 10-109. *Add a layer style Drop Shadow to add a shadow to the mask*

I then added a layer mask which I painted on with my Eraser tool to hide any unwanted areas around the edges of the melted mask. Refer to Figure 10-109.

I then added other layers with blending modes that I either painted on or added as a gradient fill to create additional shadows. Refer to Figure 10-110.

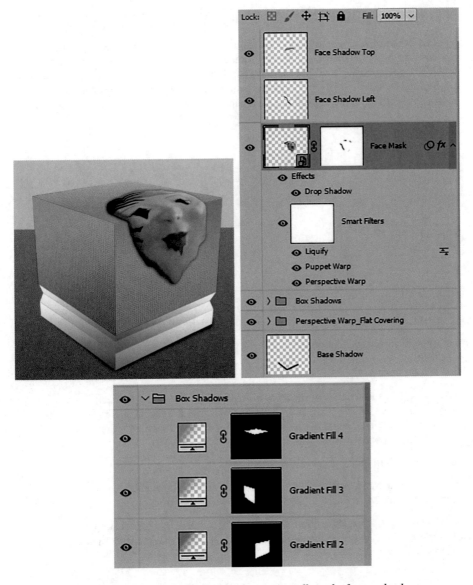

Figure 10-110. *Add layers to add further shadows manually to the face and cube*

This is a good example of how multiple filters on a smart object layer can be used to distort and warp an object to appear like it is melting yet still retain a 3D-like appearance using the shadows found in the original photo.

Neural Filters Workspace (Smart Portrait, Landscape Mixer)

Some of the most recent and exciting filters to be added to Photoshop are the ever-changing and improved Neural Filters. You can preview them and then decide if you want to add them to your collection if you download them from the cloud. I will talk about Smart Portrait and Landscape Mixer. However, new ones are being added every few months so make sure to check this area regularly for new distort options.

Go to Filter ➤ Neural Filters to enter the workspace. To the left you will find a few common tools. Refer to Figure 10-111.

Figure 10-111. *Neural Filter tools*

Here I will list them, and you can see their options in the Options panel above:

- The left-pointing arrow in the Options panel allows you to exit the Neural Filter workspace without saving changes. This is the same as clicking the Cancel button in the Neural Filter panel.

- **Add to selection (B) (add to current mask):** This tool allows you to add to a created mask. Like most brushes, you can set the size, hardness, spacing, angle, and roundness of the brush for the mask as well as size based on Pen Pressure or Stylus wheel and Tolerance, currently set to Off.

- Next is the Opacity (1-100%).

- Next is the Show/Hide Mask Overlay check box and beside this you can set the mask color by clicking on the swatch and using the Color Picker dialog box.

- Lastly, additional mask/selection adjustment options of Invert, Clear, Select Subject (most prominent objects in the image), Select Sky, and Reset the mask to the original state. Refer to Figure 10-112.

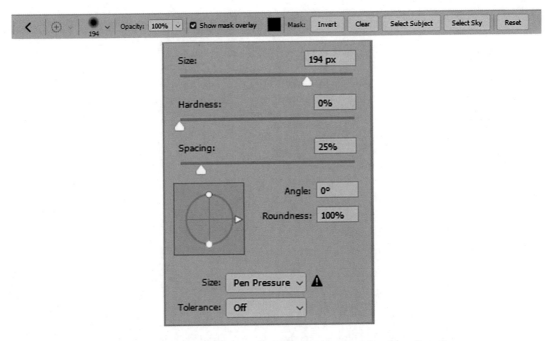

Figure 10-112. *Neural Filter's Add to selection tool with its Options panel and brush options*

- **Subtract from selection (E) (subtract from current mask):** This tool is basically like the Eraser tool for the mask and has all the same settings as the Add to Selection tool, except now you are erasing the mask. Refer to Figure 10-113.

Figure 10-113. *Neural Filter Subtract from selection tool with its Options panel*

- **Hand tool (H):** Allows you to move about an image when zoomed without disturbing the graphics or the painted mask. The options panel allow you several zoom presets of Scroll All Windows, 100%, Fit Screen, and Full Screen. Refer to Figure 10-114.

Figure 10-114. *Neural Filter Hand tool with its Options panel*

- **Zoom tool (Z):** Same as the Zoom tool in the Tools panel with the same options; it allows you to zoom in or out of an image. Other options include Resize Widows to Fit, Zoom All Windows, Scrubby Zoom, and the same three buttons found in the Hand tool of 100%, Fit Screen, and Fill Screen. Refer to Figure 10-115.

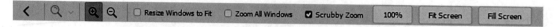

Figure 10-115. *Neural Filter Zoom tool with its Options panel*

Next, on the right, is the Neural Filters panel, which contains various filters in the All Filters tab that are or are not installed on your machine, but you may want to try as part of your subscription. They should be able to access your graphics processor (GPU). Refer to Figure 10-116.

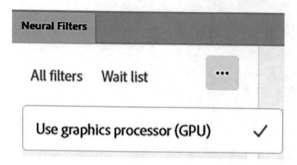

Figure 10-116. *Neural Filters panel with GPU enabled*

Currently in my panel, one Neural filter is already downloaded called Color Transfer in the Beta area, which I can click on the toggle to activate or deactivate if not using. Refer to Figure 10-117.

Figure 10-117. *Neural Filters panel with Filter options and the Color Transfer filter enabled*

This is how you can enable or disable all Neural filters that are available to you.

Next, I will talk about two filters in this panel that I think may be of interest for causing distorts or changes in photos. With any filters that you have never used, before you download them from the cloud, make sure to read their description first and then test one at a time.

■ **Note**   If you notice that before you download a filter, that the name of the filter is grayed out but not the download button in the Options area, this means you can still download the filter. But when you work with that filter, make sure that your image contains that component which the filter is meant to do. For example, if Smart Portrait, which we'll look at next, cannot detect a portrait, it is greyed out. However, when I have a portrait image open, the name is no longer grayed out and the filter is active. Refer to Figure 10-118.

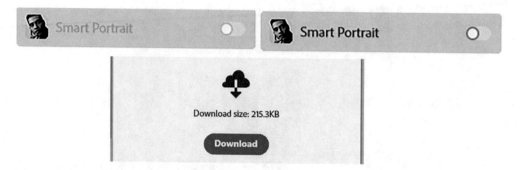

Figure 10-118. *Download filters but check first to see why the filter is disabled in the Neural Filters panel.*

Smart Portrait (Featured)

While Liquify may be good for some facial feature adjustments, a new filter that you may want to try is Smart Portrait. This filter has additional content-aware features that allow you to modify faces in advanced ways the Liquify filter cannot manage. It creatively adjusts portraits by generating new features like expressions, facial age, lighting, pose, and hair. Refer to Figure 10-119.

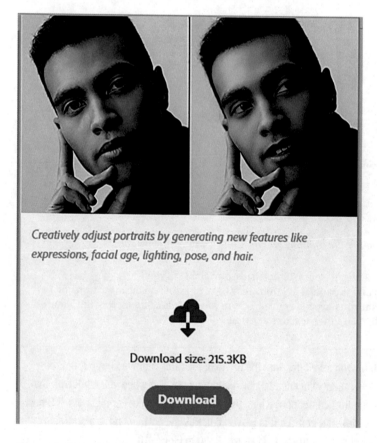

Figure 10-119. *Download the Smart Portrait filter so that you can use it*

If you do not have this filter active on your system already, you need to download it by clicking the Download button. Currently it is in the Portraits Section of the Neural filters while in past versions you would find it under Beta. For this example, you need to have a human face or faces present in the file for it to work.

At this point, I clicked Cancel to exit the Neural Filter workspace to locate my project file. Refer to Figure 10-120.

Figure 10-120. *Click Cancel to exit the Neural Filters workspace so that you can locate your file*

In this case, open file we used earlier called womens_heads_start.psd and make an Image ➤ Duplicate for practice. Then select the smart object layer and returned to the Filter ➤ Neural Filters workspace. Refer to Figure 10-121.

Figure 10-121. *Test the Neural Filter Smart Portrait on our models*

In the Neural Filter panel, activate the filter in the list and then view the options to the right of the list. Refer to Figure 10-122.

Figure 10-122. *In the Neural Filters panel, activate the filter and then select a head that you want to test the filter on*

Now you can start to work with the sliders and use data that is generated in the cloud. The cloud has facial data that it has collected and, using that data, can interpret and generate new information for the face. Refer to Figure 10-122.

A selected face has been chosen but you can use the dropdown list to select the other face. Also, the check box for Auto balance combinations is enabled. Refer to Figure 10-122.

The following sections and sliders are available:

- **Featured**: Happiness, Facial age, Hair thickness, Eye direction. The slider range for each is -50, 0, 50. Refer to Figure 10-123.

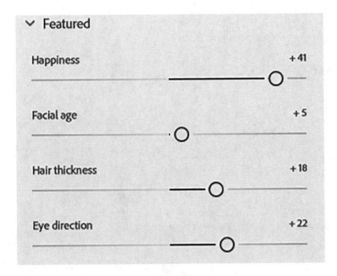

Figure 10-123. *Smart Portrait Featured options*

- **Expressions**: Surprise and Anger. The slider range for each is -50, 0, 50. Refer to Figure 10-124.

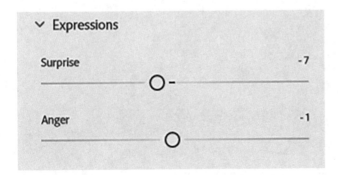

Figure 10-124. *Smart Portrait Expression options*

- **Global**: Head direction, Fix head alignment, Light direction. Fix head alignment is only active if you have altered Head direction. The slider range for each is -50, 0, 50. Refer to Figure 10-125.

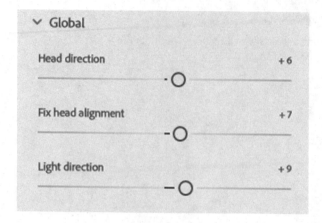

Figure 10-125. *Smart Portrait Global options*

- **Settings**: Retain unique details runs from 0-100. The default is 90. Mask feathering runs from 0-100; the default is 10 if a mask is present. Refer to Figure 10-126.

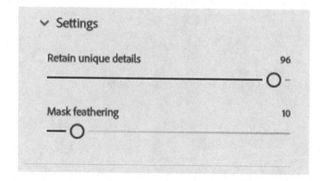

Figure 10-126. *Smart Portrait Settings options*

Use the upper arrow to reset changes or parameters. Refer to Figure 10-127.

Figure 10-127. *Reset the Smart Portrait filter if you made a mistake*

To experiment, take some time to move the sliders to see how the face or faces change, becoming happy, angry, or the addition of teeth, which is something the Liquify filter could not generate when you wanted the model to smile. Every face will be different, so create what you think is interesting and then switch to the other head and try different or similar facial expressions. Refer to Figure 10-128.

Figure 10-128. *Alter the expression on the second face as well*

■ **Note** The Cloud may take a moment to process as you alter the expressions.

To me, this is kind of spooky. As an idea, you could use this on an old family photo. Suddenly an ancestor could be doing things that we don't have original photos for. Did they really make a facial expression like that? You'll never really know. I think it will be interesting to see how this filter will improve over time. Things that I hope that will be added in the future are the ability to open and close eyes, eye color alterations, nose and ear adjustments, more teeth options, and being able to modify animal faces like cats and dogs. Perhaps the upcoming wait listed filter called Portrait Generator will do much of that?

In the Neural Filters panel, in the lower area, you can now choose from the icons to either Show original (this is a before and after preview) and a layer preview of either Show all Layers (Default) or Show selected layer. Refer to Figure 10-129.

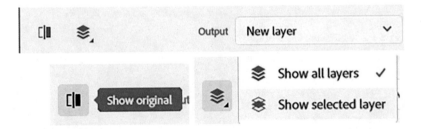

Figure 10-129. *View options for Neural filters*

The Output options are Current layer, New layer, New layer masked, Smart Filter, and New document. Current Layer is only available if you are working on a normal layer and not a smart object layer. Refer to Figure 10-130.

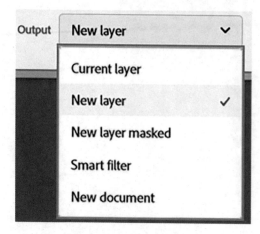

Figure 10-130. *Output options for your Neural Filters*

In this case, because we are working with a smart object layer, choose smart filter from the list in case you want to edit the file another day.

Then click OK to commit and exit the workspace. Refer to Figure 10-131 and Figure 10-132.

Figure 10-131. *Choose the Output option of Smart filter and click OK to exit*

Figure 10-132. *The filter is applied to your smart object layer*

■ **Note**   If you notice any alteration to the women's heads, such as around the neck, that you don't like, you can use the Smart Filter mask to erase or blend in those areas with the Eraser tool. However, as mentioned with the Liquify tool, only do the mask change as the last step, as you may decide to double-click and enter the Neural Filters a few times, but this will not update the Smart Filter mask. Refer to Figure 10-133.

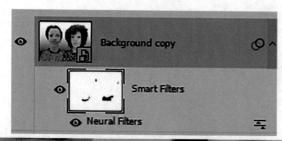

Figure 10-133. *Use an Eraser tool to blend and alter areas on your Smart Filters mask around the neck area*

This filter also comes with Blend Mode options.

File ➤ Save your document as a .psd file. You can view my file `womens_heads_final_smart_portrait.psd`.

Landscape Mixer (Beta)

If you liked the Edit ➤ Sky replacement in Chapter 7, then maybe the Landscape Mixer might be what you are looking for. This Filter ➤ Neural Filters is found in the All Filters ➤ Creative folder. Make sure to download it first before you use it to magically transform a landscape by mixing another image or changing the attributes like time of day and season. To work with this filter, make sure you have an image of a landscape open so that you can see this file with the name not grayed out. Refer to Figure 10-134.

Figure 10-134. Download the Neural Filter Landscape Mixer

Once you have downloaded the filter, click Cancel to exit and locate the landscape you want to work with. File ➤ Open IMG_3030_landscape_mixer_start.psd and then make an Image ➤ Duplicate. While it is to me a beautiful image, it was a rather rainy day and I think Landscape Mixer can improve the image.

Make sure that you have the smart object layer selected, then enter the Neural Filter again and activate the Landscape Mixer using the toggle. Refer to Figure 10-135.

Figure 10-135. Using a smart object layer, activate the Landscape Mixer filter in the Neural Filter workspace

Then you can apply a preset image to your image or choose your own custom image to combine. Refer to Figure 10-136.

Figure 10-136. *Use a preset or custom image to alter your landscape*

In this project, I will just experiment with the Presets tab. Try any one of the following. I tried the winter image and then on the second row, I set the Strength to 100 and Winter to 100, and then tried various settings with the middle sunrise image. Refer to Figure 10-137 and Figure 10-138.

Figure 10-137. *These are the presets I used on the same photo*

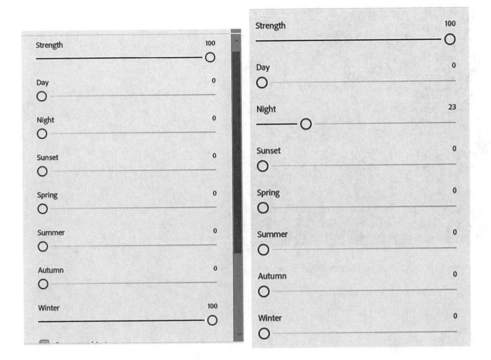

Figure 10-138. *Landscape Mixer Filter options*

Wow! You would never know it was the same photo. In many ways, this reminds me of experiments I did with the Color Lookup adjustment layer and LUTs. However, this is more complex in the fact that part of the landscape and not just colors are being blended together.

You can then use the sliders for Strength, Day, Night, Sunset, Spring, Summer, Autumn, and winter. The range for these sliders is 0-100. Refer to Figure 10-138.

In this case, I left the Strength at 100 but moved the Night Slider to 23. This created an almost twilight, fairy land kind of effect. Refer to Figure 10-139 and Figure 10-140.

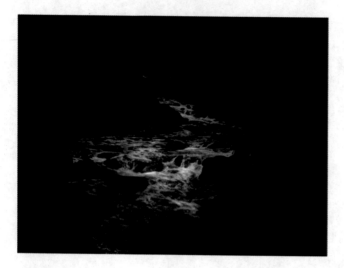

Figure 10-139. *Adding more night to the sunset scene is quite magical*

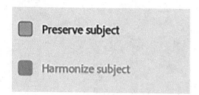

Figure 10-140. *Additional Landscape Mixer filter options*

The checkboxes Preserve Subject and Harmonize Subject are currently disabled. Refer to Figure 10-140.
Use the Reset parameters button in the upper right of the filter if you need to reset to the original state.
Refer to Figure 10-141.

Figure 10-141. *Reset the Landscape mixer filter*

Take some time to experiment. When you find a Landscape Mixer that you like, save as a smart filter.
Refer to Figure 10-142.

Figure 10-142. *Output the setting as a smart filter and click OK to commit*

Then click OK to commit and exit the workspace. Then File ➤ Save your document as a .psd file. You can see my alterations in IMG_3030_landscape_mixer_final.psd. Refer to Figure 10-143.

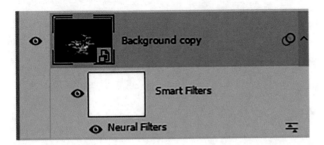

Figure 10-143. *The smart filter now appears in the Layers panel*

■ **Note** Due to the fact that this filter is in Beta, some settings and sliders may have altered depending on what version of the filter you are using, so your results may look slightly different than mine and you may have to adjust additional sliders. Filters without the beta label are more stable, so once this filter reaches that status, the colors and settings should be more accurate.

If you are interested in how color lookup relates to alterations in the look of an image's color, make sure to check out this link: https://helpx.adobe.com/photoshop/how-to/edit-photo-color-lookup-adjustment.html.

Other Neural Filter Options

As you have time, make sure to explore some of the other filters that you may want to use for image correction, such as Skin Smoothing, Colorize, Style Transfer, Depth Blur, or even Makeup Transfer. Refer to Figure 10-144.

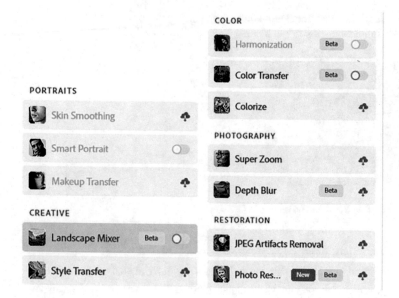

Figure 10-144. *On your own, take time to look at other Neural Filters in the various sections*

As possible new filters become available, you can view them in the wait list tab and tell Photoshop if you are interested in them. In this version, Portrait Generator and Shadow Regenerator sound interesting to me. Refer to Figure 10-145.

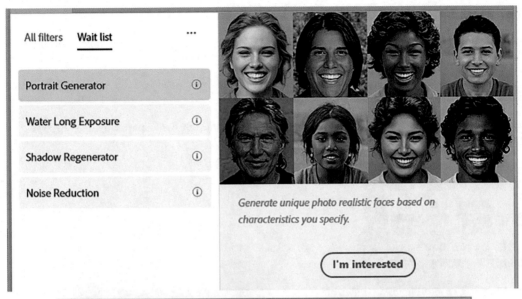

Figure 10-145. *The wait list mentions neural filters that will be added at some point to the collection*

For more information on filters and the new Neural filters, refer to these links:
https://helpx.adobe.com/photoshop/using/filter-effects-reference.html
https://helpx.adobe.com/photoshop/using/neural-filters-list-and-faq.html
https://helpx.adobe.com/photoshop/using/neural-filters.html
https://helpx.adobe.com/photoshop/using/neural-filters-feedback.html

Acquiring Additional Filters via Creative Cloud

Besides Neural Filters, you can acquire additional Photoshop filters online. Just make sure that they match with your current version of Photoshop and update them if they no longer work in newer versions.

Third-Party Plugins

However, the best way to look for compatible filters is to choose from your Photoshop. Plugins ➤ Browse Plugins. Refer to Figure 10-146.

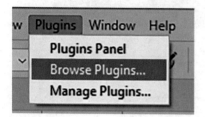

Figure 10-146. *Use your Photoshop menu to browse for plugins*

This brings up your Creative Cloud desktop application. Refer to Figure 10-147.

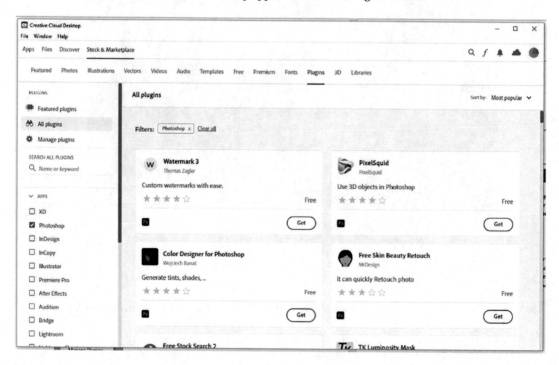

Figure 10-147. *Creative Cloud desktop can help you locate other filters*

From the Creative Cloud desktop, Stock & Marketplace Plugins Tab, select Photoshop and type in the word filters and press Enter/Return to refine your search. Refer to Figure 10-148.

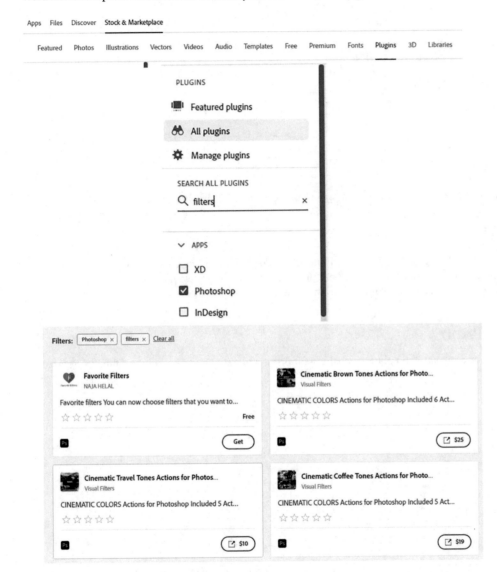

Figure 10-148. *Stock and Marketplace under the Plugins tab is a good place to find more filters*

Click on the Name of the Plugin if you want to look at Pricing and Version compatibility. You can find Pattern generators like Cloth Texture Generator this way as well. Refer to Figure 10-149.

Figure 10-149. Click on the Plugin name when you want to find out more about a filter or Plugin

Summary

In this chapter, you looked at more advanced filters and workspaces. You saw how to combine filters from this chapter and past chapters. You also saw that Photoshop has some new Neural Filters that are content-aware and can assist you in altering your images in unique and unexpected ways.

Saving for Print

As with any of your projects, if you plan to use them for print, make sure to make a copy of the file. Refer to Figure 10-150.

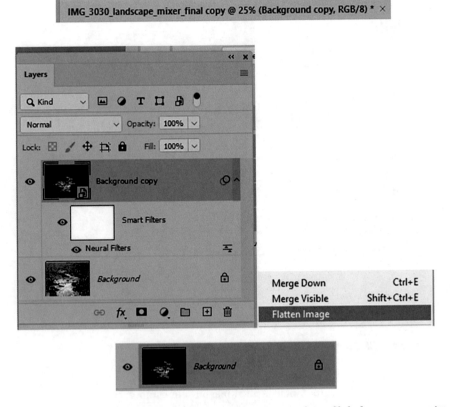

Figure 10-150. *Use the Layers panel menu to flatten a copy of your file before you convert it to CMYK Color mode*

Then flatten the layers using your Layers panel menu (Flatten Image) before converting to CMYK color mode. Use Image ➤ Mode ➤ CMYK Color 8 Bits/Channel and click OK to the message. Refer to Figure 10-151.

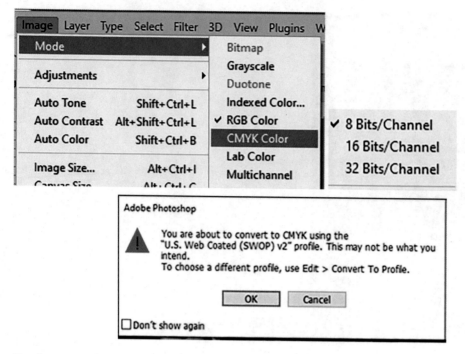

Figure 10-151. *Before converting to CMYK mode, you may see a warning message. Click OK to convert to that profile*

Then you can File ➤ Save the file you plan to Print in a .tiff format on your computer and print on your home printer. Refer to Figure 10-152.

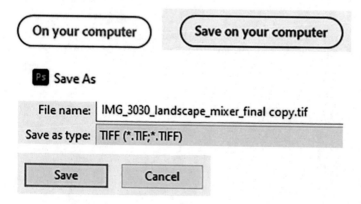

Figure 10-152. *Save your file as a .tiff before you print it on your home printer*

I keep my TIFF option settings at the default of Image Compression None and Pixel Order: Interleaved (RGBRGB). Byte Order could be IBM PC or Macintosh, depending on what computer or printer you are using. Click OK. Refer to Figure 10-153.

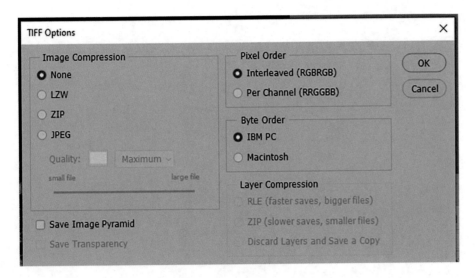

Figure 10-153. *Tiff Options dialog box save settings*

I hope that you enjoyed working with the Photoshop projects in this volume of the book and that you saw how you can use Illustrator files as well to enhance your work in Photoshop.

Further Suggested Reading

Wow, after reading this book, you can now successfully create your own warps and distorts in Photoshop. So, what is the next step you should take?

If you are interested in focusing on Adobe Illustrator, get a copy of Volume 2, where I will be looking at how similar warps and distorts can be applied using Illustrator tools and effects. I'll also offer information about other Adobe applications that you can use to enhance your next project further.

Index

■ M

■ N

■ Q

■ R

■ W, X, Y

■ Z